Borkowski's Textbook on Roman Law

To all students of Roman law at the University of Bristol for making
the teaching of the subject a delightful experience.

Andrew Borkowski

Borkowski's

Textbook on

Roman Law

Fifth Edition

Paul du Plessis
PhD

OXFORD
UNIVERSITY PRESS

OXFORD
UNIVERSITY PRESS

Great Clarendon Street, Oxford, OX2 6DP,
United Kingdom

Oxford University Press is a department of the University of Oxford.
It furthers the University's objective of excellence in research, scholarship,
and education by publishing worldwide. Oxford is a registered trade mark of
Oxford University Press in the UK and in certain other countries

Second Edition 1997
Third Edition 2005
Fourth Edition 2010

Impression: 4

Published in the United States of America by Oxford University Press
198 Madison Avenue, New York, NY 10016, United States of America

British Library Cataloguing in Publication Data
Data available

Library of Congress Control Number: 2014957918

ISBN 978–0–19–873622–6

Printed in Great Britain by
Bell and Bain Ltd, Glasgow

CONTENTS

PART V   **Roman Law and the Modern World**

11   Roman law and the European *ius commune* 365

PREFACE TO THE FIFTH EDITION

For the latest edition of this popular textbook, I have limited my amendments to certain areas of the existing text, largely on advice from external reviewers of the fourth edition. Additional references to primary sources and to secondary literature (books and articles) have been integrated into the text to act as a guide for further inquiry. Although I have been restricted in this selection to books and articles published in English, this should not be seen as a limitation of this textbook as I have taken account of current scholarly views in Italian, German, and French on the topics covered in this textbook. By giving prominence to books and articles published in English, I have attempted to demonstrate the immense, yet often neglected, contribution that scholars from the English-speaking world have made to the study of Roman law. As in the previous editions, I have not attempted to cite every contribution on the topic. Rather, I have limited the reading to a few important works that may act as a guide to further research. Although in its current state, this book falls somewhere between an elementary textbook and a manual (in the Italian style), I hope that it will be of use to many students (whether undergraduate or postgraduate) of Roman law.

In summary, the major developments for this edition are as follows:

- The text has been refined and updated to reflect current scholarly opinions.
- References to important new research have been included to enable students and course lecturers to follow the most recent developments in the field.
- The accompanying website has been comprehensively reworked to ensure greater interaction between the text and the online material.

Paul du Plessis
November 2014

PREFACE TO THE FIRST EDITION

I feel passionately about Roman law. I have taught the subject for many years and have found it to be a richly rewarding experience, at least in the intellectual sense. Roman law provides an invaluable introduction to the understanding of legal concepts and a passport to the appreciation of Continental legal systems. But even if Roman law did not have these 'uses', it would be eminently worthy of study for its own sake. For it is the product of the genius for good order and organized common sense of a remarkable ancient civilization, and it constitutes a legacy that has had profound influence in subsequent ages.

This book is written for students. It is intended as a first book of Roman law for use at undergraduate level and it reflects, I trust, certain beliefs which I hold strongly about the teaching of the subject:

(a) *Historical context.* Roman law cannot be understood without some appreciation of Roman political and constitutional history (social and economic too). Unfortunately, many students who study Roman law for the first time lack a sufficient knowledge of Roman history. I have therefore begun the book with a fairly extensive account of the history of Rome, with special emphasis on political and constitutional developments.

(b) *The use of Latin.* In my experience, the majority of students of Roman law are not familiar these days with Latin. To be confronted by textbooks in which Latin words and phrases are used in profusion can be very discouraging for those without a command of Latin. I have therefore attempted to keep the use of Latin words to a minimum wherever possible, and have included translations whenever appropriate.

(c) *Modern relevance.* An appreciation of the influence of Roman law on subsequent legal systems is important. I have endeavoured, therefore, to emphasize the ways in which the content and historical evolution of modern systems (particularly English law) have been affected by Roman law. The book ends with a chapter specifically devoted to this aim.

(d) *Illustrative extracts.* I believe that the subject can best be taught by illustrating the rules and concepts of Roman law with extracts from original sources. The extracts used in this book are shown in bold font. They are taken from Justinian's *Digest*, by far the richest and most important source of Roman law. These extracts serve several purposes: some are quoted as authority for a particular rule; some are used to illustrate a rule; some are meant to indicate controversial issues; and some are aimed mainly to entertain and thus to make the subject even more memorable. Occasionally, the extracts combine several or all of these functions.

The book covers the basic content of Roman civil law. The criminal law is not dealt with, a few sporadic references apart. I have attempted to give as detailed a treatment as appropriate of the civil law, given the confines within which the book had to be written.

As there are many areas of Roman law which are the subject of controversy and speculation, or about which little is known for certain, a textbook on the subject is bound to reflect this state of affairs. Hence, words and phrases such as 'possibly' or 'probably' or 'it seems that' or 'the most plausible view is that' are conspicuous by their presence.

To some extent Roman law was Roman men's law: substantial parts of it were decidedly male-orientated and described in masculine terms. Consequently, it is difficult to write about Roman law exclusively in gender-neutral terms—and it would be a distortion of the subject to do so. A further complication is that occasionally it is not clear from the Roman texts whether males and females are being differentiated when rules of law are described. As a *general* guideline, references in this book to the masculine pronoun or to males (e.g. 'patron', 'freedman', 'master') include females except where the contrary is stated or clearly implied from the context. I have generally avoided referring to secondary sources. This was partly for reasons of space, partly because the choice of such sources can best be left to the recommendation of individual teachers. There is included, however, a short bibliography of works likely to be useful to the student.

I would like to thank all at Blackstone Press (as it then was) for making this book possible. Their enthusiasm, encouragement, editorial assistance, and preparation of the index were invaluable. The University of Pennsylvania Press was kind enough to allow me to use extracts from the *Digest of Justinian* (edited by Alan Watson). For copyright reasons the North American spelling of certain words has been retained. I have occasionally shortened some of the extracts; the relevant omissions are indicated by ellipses.

My grateful thanks are owed to a number of colleagues at the University of Bristol for their assistance in various guises. In particular, Thomas Wiedemann, Reader in the History of the Roman Empire, made many useful suggestions concerning chapters 1 and 4. Patricia Hammond not only processed the manuscript with superb efficiency but also improved it in several respects through her interest in and understanding of ancient Rome.

My family, particularly my wife, Margaret, proved a tower of strength at all times, and helped me to find a reasonably sane balance between the demands of family life, writing the book, playing competitive chess, and lecturing on Italian opera.

The law is stated as at 14 November AD 565.

Andrew Borkowski
Faculty of Law University of Bristol
The Ides of March 1994

ACKNOWLEDGEMENTS

I wish to thank the reviewers of the fourth edition of *Borkowski's Textbook on Roman Law*, whose detailed comments have greatly aided me in revising the text. Needless to say, I take full responsibility for those errors that remain. This book would not have been possible without the existence of a set of 'course handouts' which have formed the basis of the civil law course at Edinburgh University since time immemorial.

The University of Pennsylvania Press has kindly granted me permission to use extracts from Watson, A. (1998), *The Digest of Justinian*, translation edited by Alan Watson (Philadelphia, PA: University of Pennsylvania Press). Originally published in 1985 by the University of Pennsylvania Press Copyright © 1985 University of Pennsylvania Press. Revised English-language edition copyright © 1998 University of Pennsylvania Press. Owing to copyright restrictions, the North American spelling of certain words in these citations has been retained.

DATES

For further detail and an interactive timeline, consult the Online Resource Centre.

MONARCHY 753–510 BC

BC

c.753	Foundation of Rome
578–34	(?) Servius Tullius: *comitia centuriata*
510	Expulsion of Tarquinius Superbus

REPUBLIC 509–27 BC

494	First Secession of the plebeians
451–50	The Twelve Tables
367	*Leges Liciniae Sextae*
	Institution of the praetorship
326	*Lex Poetelia*
295	Defeat of Samnites at Sentinum
287	*Lex Hortensia*
(?)	*Lex Aquilia*
264–41	First Punic War
242	Institution of peregrine praetor
241	Annexation of Sicily
218–201	Second Punic War
c.150 (?)	*Lex Aebutia*
133, 123–2	Tribunates of Tiberius and Gaius Gracchus
91–89	The Social War
67	(?) *Actio Publiciana*
44	Assassination of Julius Caesar
31	Octavian defeats Antony at Actium

EMPIRE: THE PRINCIPATE 27 BC–AD 284

27	Octavian becomes Augustus
18–17	*Lex Julia de maritandis*
	Lex Julia de adulteriis

AD

4	*Lex Aelia Sentia*
9	*Lex Papia Poppaea*
14	Death of Augustus
41–54	Reign of Claudius
52	*S. C. Claudianum*
117–38	Reign of Hadrian
c.130	*S. C. Tertullianum*
c.135	*Edictum Perpetuum*
c.160	*Institutes* of Gaius

161–80	Reign of Marcus Aurelius
212	*Constitutio Antoniniana*
223	Ulpian murdered
270–5	Reign of Aurelian

EMPIRE: THE DOMINATE (FROM AD 284)

284–305	Reign of Diocletian
c.295	*Codex Hermogenianus*
306–37	Reign of Constantine I
313	Edict of Milan
379–95	Reign of Theodosius I
395	Division of the Empire
408–50	Reign of Theodosius II
410	Sack of Rome by Visigoths
426	Law of Citations
438	*Codex Theodosianus*
476	End of the Western Empire
506	*Lex Romana Visigothorum*
527	Justinian becomes Emperor of the East
533	*Institutes*
	Digest
534	*New Code*
565	Death of Justinian

AFTER JUSTINIAN

c.890	*Basilica*
c.1055–1130	Irnerius
c.1184–1263	Accursius
1314–57	Bartolus
1495	*Reichskammergericht*
1532	Court of Session
1583–1645	Grotius
1681	Stair's *Institutions of the Law of Scotland*
1756	Bavarian Civil Code
1804	French Civil Code
1900	German Civil Code

ABBREVIATIONS

C.	*Codex Iustinianus*
Const.	*Constitutio*
C. Th.	*Codex Theodosianus*
D.	*Digesta*
Inst.	*Institutiones* (Institutes of Justinian)
Inst. Gai.	*Institutiones Gai* (Institutes of Gaius)
pr.	*prooemium* (preface)
S. C.	*Senatus Consultum*

Journals cited

AG	Archivio Giuridico 'Filippo Serafini' (Bologna, Pisa, since 1921 Modena →)
AJ	Acta Juridica (Cape Town 1958 →)
American Historical Review	The American Historical Review (New York 1895 →)
Anglo-Am. LR	The Anglo-American Law Review (Chichester 1972 →)
ANRW	Aufstieg und Niedergang der römischen Welt: Geschichte und Kultur Roms im Spiegel der neueren Forschung (Berlin 1972 →)
Arctos	Arctos: Acta philologica fennica (Helsinki 1930 →)
Athenaeum	Athenaeum: Studi periodici di letteratura e storia dell'antichità (Pavia 1913 →)
BIDR	Bullettino dell'Istituto di diritto romano (Rome, since 1942 Milan →) [Volume 42 (1934) = volume 1 of the New Series (Vittorio Scialoja)]
Cambridge LJ	The Cambridge Law Journal (Cambridge 1921 →)
CQ	The Classical Quarterly (London 1907 →) [New Series London 1951 →]
Edinburgh LR	The Edinburgh Law Review (Edinburgh 1996 →)
Historia	Historia: Zeitschrift für Alte Geschichte (Baden-Baden 1950 →)
ICLQ	International and Comparative Law Quarterly (London 1952 →)
IJ (N.S.)	Irish Jurist (New Series) (vol. 1 = Dublin 1966 →)
Index	Index: Quaderni camerti di studi romanistici (Naples 1970 →)
IVRA	IVRA: Rivista internazionale di diritto romano e antico (Naples 1950 →)
JLH	The Journal of Legal History (London 1980 →)
JRS	Journal of Roman Studies (London 1911 →)
Juridical Review	The Juridical Review (Edinburgh 1889 →)

Klio	Klio: Beiträge zur alten Geschichte (Leipzig 1906 →)
Labeo	Labeo: rassegna di diritto romano (Naples 1955 →)
Latomus	Latomus: revue d'études latines (Brussels 1965 →)
Legal Studies	Legal Studies: The Journal of the Society of Public Teachers of Law (London 1981 →)
LHR	Law and History Review (Ithaca, NY 1983 →)
LQR	The Law Quarterly Review (London 1885 →)
Michigan LR	Michigan Law Review (Ann Arbor, MI 1902 →)
Northern Ireland LQ	Northern Ireland Legal Quarterly (Belfast 1936 →)
Oxford Journal LS	The Oxford Journal of Legal Studies (Oxford 1981 →)
Phoenix	Phoenix: Journal of the Ontario Classical Association [1946–spring 1947; of the Classical Association of Canada, autumn 1947 → (Toronto)]
RIDA	Revue internationale des droits de l'antiquité (First series Brussels from 1948, presently RIDA (3) (third series) from 1954 →)
Roman legal tradition	Roman legal tradition (Kansas/Aberdeen 2002 →)
Scripta Classica Israelica	Scripta Classica Israelica: Yearbook of the Israel Society for the Promotion of Classical Studies (Jerusalem 1974 →)
SDHI	Studia et documenta historiae et iuris (Rome 1935 →)
THRHR	THRHR: Tydskrif vir Hedendaagse Romeins-Hollandse Reg = Journal for Contemporary Roman-Dutch law (Durban 1959 →)
TR	Tijdschrift voor Rechtsgeschiedenis = Revue d'histoire du droit (Haarlem 1918 →) (Since 1951 Groningen)
Tulane LR	Tulane Law Review (formerly the Southern Law Review 1916–1918 (vols 1–3), continued as the Tulane Law Review (vol. 4) = New Orleans 1929 →)
University of Missouri LR	The University of Missouri at Kansas City Law Review (Kansas City, MO 1964 →)
ZEP	Zeitschrift für europäisches Privatrecht (Munich 1993 →)
ZPE	Zeitschrift für Papyrologie und Epigraphik (Bonn 1967 →)
ZSS (rA)	Zeitschrift der Savigny-Stiftung für Rechtsgeschichte, romanistische Abteilung (Weimar 1880 →)

GUIDE TO THE ONLINE RESOURCE CENTRE

The Online Resource Centre is designed to be used in conjunction with the text and aims to provide students and teachers of the subject with additional resources to be used either in formal or in informal teaching. The website can be accessed at: www.oxfordtextbooks.co.uk/orc/borkowski5e/

The website contains the following resources:

- A comprehensive timeline intended to supplement the list of dates featured in the introduction to the textbook. It may also be used as a schematic guide to chapter 1 (Introduction: Rome—a historical sketch). The timeline provides a chronological overview of the development of Roman private law in its political and historical context.

- Short biographies of key figures. These should be used in conjunction with the timeline to supplement the discussion of the jurists in chapter 2 (The sources of Roman law).

- A glossary of Latin terms used in the textbook.

- A guide to locating original Latin versions of the texts cited in translation.

- Guidance on finding Roman law texts and associated literature.

- Tips regarding textual analysis to guide the reader in interpreting the texts.

- Multiple-choice questions covering each chapter of the textbook. These are interactive and, once completed, provide the correct answer to each question and a reference to the relevant part of the textbook.

- Annotated web links. There is much information about Roman law and European legal history on the World Wide Web, but the quality and accuracy of the information is often questionable. These annotated web links are designed to act as a guide for further enquiry. They include sites specifically devoted to Roman Law, online library catalogues, and databases on Roman law (books and articles) as well as other sites of interest.

1

Introduction: Rome—a historical sketch

The history of Rome is traditionally divided into three main periods based on the dominant constitutional structure in Roman society during these three periods. These are the Monarchy (eighth century BC–510 BC), Republic (509–27 BC), and Empire (27 BC–AD 565).

1.1 Monarchy

1.1.1 The origins of Rome

The origins of Rome are obscure. It is impossible to be certain of the chief events, let alone the details. Legends abound; facts do not. The archaeological evidence is rather slight and the literary sources cannot be relied on with confidence. The earliest detailed accounts of Rome's origins date from the third century BC—a long time after the events that they purport to describe (see Tellegen-Couperus, *Short History*, s. 1.1; Mousourakis, *Legal History*, 3–18). Later writers such as Cato the Elder and Livy were able to do little more than to expand on the earlier unreliable accounts.

The founding of Rome has traditionally been dated as 753 BC, although other dates (ranging some 50 years either side) have been suggested. The founders, according to tradition, were Romulus and Remus, supposedly the descendants of the legendary Trojan hero, Aeneas. He was said to have escaped with a band of survivors following the defeat of Troy by the Greeks in the Trojan War. Driven by storms onto the north African coast, Aeneas resided for a while at the court of Dido, the Queen of Carthage. The heart-rending tale of her eventual abandonment by Aeneas has provided artistic stimulus for writers, poets, and composers down the ages. On reaching the west coast of Italy, Aeneas and his descendants reputedly established settlements in the vicinity of the Tiber at Lavinium and Alba Longa (Castelgandolfo). Archaeological evidence tends to confirm aspects of the Aeneas legend, particularly the establishment of these settlements long before the founding of Rome, though modern scholarly opinion favours the Etruscans as the true founders of Rome (see Tellegen-Couperus, *Short History*, s. 1.2). Literary evidence suggests that the Romans believed that their origins were traceable to Aeneas.

1.1.2 The kings

There are said to have been seven kings of Rome from Romulus to Tarquinius Superbus. Given that the aggregate period of their rule was almost 250 years, one must regard a total of seven kings with a little scepticism. An average reign of 35 years seems rather lengthy for that era. During this period, Rome acquired some of her most important institutions, particularly in the sphere of government. Under Romulus a consultative body of elders and eminent citizens was established—the Senate. Their descendants, known as 'patricians', were to play a significant role in the affairs of Rome, especially in the early years of her existence. The Senate became identified with the fortunes of Rome. Further, Romulus divided Roman citizens into three 'tribes', each consisting of 10 *curiae* (administrative and political units possessing voting powers) that formed a primitive assembly, the *comitia curiata*. Its primary function was to confirm the King in office and to vest authority in him: there was no hereditary right of succession.

Numa Pompilius, elected King when Romulus died, reputedly organized the religious life of Rome. The ritualistic taking of vows to the gods, in order to placate their spirits and to seek their favours, became a central feature of daily life, both at a public and private level. The *paterfamilias*, the head of the Roman household, was entrusted with the performance of daily acts of family worship—one of his most important duties.

Numa's successors pursued a limited policy of territorial expansion, but it was during the reigns of the last three kings, Tarquinius Priscus, Servius Tullius, and Tarquinius Superbus, that Rome began to achieve an important status among its Latin neighbours—a sign of things to come.

1.1.3 Etruscan influence

The two Tarquins—and possibly Servius Tullius—were Etruscans, a flourishing and sophisticated civilization situated in Etruria to the north and northwest of Rome. They were a well-organized and energetic people—warriors, craftsmen, builders, and city dwellers. And they were outward looking and expansionist. It was hardly surprising that in the seventh century BC, possibly earlier, an Etruscan migration occurred, leading to a peaceful fusion between the immigrants and the native Roman population. The Etruscans came predominantly from the southern cities of Etruria such as Veii. Rome provided a convenient point for crossing the Tiber and was thus regarded by the Etruscans as vital to their control of Latium and Campania, the area between Rome and the Bay of Naples. The Etruscan kings undertook an ambitious programme of public works and buildings, providing Rome with paved streets, temples, shrines, city walls, and a drainage system. Rome was transformed into a city.

There were administrative and political achievements too. In the middle years of the sixth century BC, Servius Tullius established the *comitia centuriata*, an assembly in which the citizen body was divided into centuries along military lines. This was a far-sighted attempt to ensure that the newly reorganized Roman army had some say in the affairs of the State. Servius had radically altered the composition of the army by opening its ranks to all citizens wealthy enough to equip themselves. The assembly had important functions, including the appointment of high-ranking officers for the army. Consequently, this assembly had a crucial role in the affairs of Rome.

A policy of gradual territorial expansion is discernible in the activities of the Etruscan kings. Rome, acting in league with its powerful Etruscan neighbours, soon proved to be the dominant force in the area, adept at furthering her interests through a mixture of high-handed diplomacy and well-timed military conquest. A ring of neighbouring towns was colonized in order to provide a protective shield for Rome. They included Alba Longa, Rome's ancestral city. And it is probable that the first steps were taken at this time to establish a port at Ostia, where the Tiber meets the sea. By 510 BC, Roman territory covered an area of some 300–400 square miles, considerably larger than any Latin community.

1.1.4 The events of 510 BC

Aggressive tactics by the Etruscan kings might have paid dividends in Rome's relations with its neighbours, but such a policy ran obvious risks if pursued internally. An elective monarchy needs the constant support of the people. Tarquinius Superbus somehow lost it; a surprise, perhaps, because in many ways he had proved even more energetic and successful than his predecessors. However, his apparently tyrannical ways precipitated an aristocratic revolt against him. The accusation that one of his sons had allegedly raped Lucretia, the wife of a Roman noble, was used by later Roman poets and historians to justify the revolt. The fact that it led to the abolition of the monarchy, and not just to the expulsion of the particular incumbent of the office, does suggest that the Romans had wearied of rule by kings. The expulsion of Tarquinius Superbus was one of several incidents at that time which demonstrated that Etruscan domination of parts of Italy was diminishing. Superbus attempted to regain Rome but was unsuccessful, as were several other Etruscan leaders.

1.2 Republic

The Republic is generally regarded as having lasted from 509 BC to 27 BC, when Octavian (taking the name Augustus) became the *de facto* Emperor of the Roman world. A historical sketch can do no more than highlight a few of the momentous events and trends in these five centuries in which Rome became a power of immense size and influence.

1.2.1 Constitutional and political developments

1.2.1.1 The magistrates

A hierarchy of magistrates was established during the early centuries of the Republic. The chief magistrates were:

(a) Consuls. The abolition of the monarchy did not result in a totally new constitutional framework, but it did lead, according to some scholars, to the transference of kingly power to two supreme magistrates, the consuls. This power pertained in theory to all aspects of government. The traditional symbol of consular authority consisted of the *fasces*—bundles of sticks—carried by the consuls' lictors (personal attendants); hence the derivation of 'fascist'. As their very name implies, the consuls were supposed to *consult* each other and to govern in tandem. They could veto each other's proposals, a principle that was intended to prevent tyranny but which, if abused, was a potential recipe for inaction and disaster. Since they were the commanders of the army, the consuls were appointed by the *comitia centuriata*, although ratification by the Senate was necessary. The appointment lasted for a year, as was the case with most magistrates. Although ultimate power lay with the consuls, there was provision in the Republican constitution for one-man rule in times of national crisis. Either consul could nominate the appointment (for a maximum of six months) of a *dictator* with supreme power, subject to the Senate's ratification. Such appointments occurred rarely.

For a period of some 80 years or so in the early Republic prior to 367 BC, army officers (called military tribunes) possessing consular power could be elected—and frequently were—in place of consuls on the authority of the Senate. Normally, six such tribunes were elected. This procedure was probably necessitated by the almost continuous wars in which Rome was engaged at the time.

(b) Praetors. This magistracy was created in 367 BC with the aim of reducing the legal jurisdiction of the consuls. The praetors, appointed by the *comitia centuriata*, became the chief administrators of the Roman legal system, somewhat akin to modern ministers of justice. Their jurisdiction was originally exercised over Roman citizens within Rome—hence they came to be known as the urban praetors. Their contribution to the development of Roman civil law was immense, as later chapters will reveal. (See Brennan, *Praetorship* I, chs. 2 and 3.)

(c) Quaestors. They were the counterparts of the praetors in financial matters, assisting the consuls in the fiscal administration of Rome. They were elected by the *comitia tributa* and until 421 BC had to be patrician. But they had other duties—e.g. helping the consuls in the administration of criminal jurisdiction. In the later Empire, the quaestors became the principal law officers of the State, following the decline in the importance of the praetors.

(d) Censors. The first censors were appointed in 443 BC by the *comitia centuriata* to relieve the consuls of their duty of compiling a census, in which the Roman people were classified by wealth, tribal background, and military ranking. Initially, censors had to be of patrician origin, but by the middle of the fourth century BC, this position was opened to the plebeians. The census was vital in determining the eligibility to vote, to serve in the legions, and liability to taxation. In compiling their census, the censors had the power to place a *nota* ('a mark of disgrace') against the name of any person who was suspected of misconduct. Serious consequences could result (see 4.4.2.5). The possession of this power naturally gave the censors considerable authority and influence. It was best to avoid displeasing the censors. The census was compiled every four or five years, the task taking about 18 months—an exception to the practice of appointing magistrates for a year. Moreover, the censors acquired the function of appointing members of the Senate. This was in theory a highly important function, although in practice it came to be limited to the power to exclude from the Senate. And the censors had fiscal duties, too: they had responsibility for the collection of revenue for the treasury, and for spending it on contracts involving the State.

(e) Tribunes. The tribunes were magistrates (first created in *c.*494 BC, allegedly as a result of the class struggle between the plebeians and patricians) who were elected to represent the plebeian body of the people, i.e. citizens other than patricians. They themselves had to be plebeians. Important powers were vested in the tribunes: they presided over the *concilium plebis*—the plebeian legislative assembly; they were members of the Senate and had the power to convene it; and they had the right to veto the acts of other magistrates, thus enabling the tribunes to protect individuals against the arbitrary exercise of power. From 449 BC, the tribunes became 'inviolable'—anyone who attacked the tribunes or hindered them in their duties would be outlawed by the *concilium plebis*. All this made the tribunes a potential threat to the authority of the Senate, a threat that was to materialize at times in the often anarchic conditions of the late Republic.

(f) Aediles. Their primary function was to exercise 'care' over the city and its inhabitants—e.g. ensuring an adequate supply of water and corn; maintaining public roads and buildings; controlling trade; and arranging public games. At first the aediles (normally two in number) were plebeian assistants of the tribunes. But in 367 BC, two extra aediles were created, known as 'curule' as a mark of their originally patrician status.

1.2.1.2 Class warfare: the struggle of the orders

Many of the early constitutional and political developments in the history of the Republic were engendered by friction between the orders—the patricians and the plebeians.

(a) Plebeian discontent. The main political grievance of the plebeians was that the magistracy was entirely in the hands of the patricians in the earliest years of the Republic. Moreover, there was considerable anxiety about the exercise of consular power, and uncertainty about its extent. Another important cause of friction was the status of the plebeian assembly—its resolutions (*plebiscita*) were not considered to be binding on the whole people. Moreover, there were economic causes for plebeian discontent—the Draconian law of debt, for example. A man who was unable to pay his debts, often a plebeian, could be seized by his creditor and sold as a slave, or even executed (see 3.2.3.1). And the plebeians complained that they were prevented from acquiring rights in land belonging to the State (*ager publicus*).

(b) Concessions. In the course of this struggle, the general trend was towards a gradual improvement in the position of the plebeians. It was brought about by concessions that were forced mainly by the threat of secession. The plebeians would simply leave the city (or threaten to do so) and encamp in the surrounding hills until the patricians agreed to their demands. The city would grind to a halt. And there were occasional threats to establish a rival city. The potential consequences were so serious that the plebeian demands were usually conceded promptly.

The earliest important concession was to allow all Roman citizens the right of appeal to the people against a sentence of death imposed by a magistrate. In 494 BC, the plebeians were allowed magistrates of their own—the tribunes—with power to protect the plebeians and veto the acts of other magistrates. In 451–450 BC the plebeians secured the publication of the Twelve Tables, Rome's first 'code of law', as a response to the complaint that the consuls were administering the law in an arbitrary fashion. A clear statement of the law was essential, and the Twelve Tables largely provided it. The struggle of the orders was thus directly responsible for this vital development in the evolution of Roman law. Soon after the publication of the Twelve Tables, the plebeians obtained the important concession that *plebiscita* should bind all Roman citizens, and not just plebeians, although patrician ratification was necessary. One of the earliest *plebiscita* removed the ban on intermarriage between the orders, a rule which had caused some friction. And in 421 BC, plebeians became eligible for the office of quaestor.

A particularly violent period of discord led to crucial developments in 367 BC. Two new magistracies (the praetors and the curule aediles) were created; and new laws were enacted, the *leges Liciniae Sextiae*, which constituted a landmark in the struggle of the orders. This legislation provided *inter alia* that one of the consuls had to be a plebeian; that there should be a restriction on the maximum amount of public land that a citizen could hold; and that the colleges of priests should be opened to plebeians—a most significant development because the executive government of Rome often turned on the priestly interpretation of the oracles. Moreover, the military tribunate was abolished. The enslavement or execution of debtors for non-payment of debts was eventually ended by the *lex Poetelia* of 326 BC.

In 287 BC came the final chapter in the struggle of the orders—the *lex Hortensia*. This law removed the need for patrician ratification of *plebiscita*. More than two centuries of conflict came to an end. Henceforth, the plebeian assembly was to prove to be the most politically powerful and important of the Republican legislative assemblies.

1.2.2 Territorial expansion

1.2.2.1 Within Italy

The defeat of the Etruscans in 505 BC by the Latin League ensured that the fledgling Roman Republic would be free of Etruscan hegemony. Rome herself eventually fought the Latin States and managed to defeat them at Lake Regillus in *c.*496 BC. A treaty followed that established peace and an alliance between the combatants. Significantly, Rome agreed to extend some of the rights of Roman citizenship to her neighbours, including the rights of intermarriage and participation in the Roman legal process. And she offered citizenship to those who settled in Rome. Such treatment of her neighbours proved crucial in enabling Rome to foster a feeling of shared identity and a common destiny. She even incorporated, on several occasions, the deity of a defeated enemy. Former enemies of Rome tended to become her allies and to look to her for leadership. Progress through partnership was the dominant theme of Rome's steady territorial advance in the early years of her existence as a republic. There were setbacks, of course: fierce wars were fought against the Sabines, the Aequi, and the Volsci. A bitter struggle against the powerful city of Veii, only a few miles north of the Tiber, threatened Rome's existence. Again, she emerged victorious, successfully capturing Veii in 396 BC. Barely had Rome recovered before she had to face, in *c.* 386 BC, marauding tribes from Gaul, some of which had settled in northern Italy. Rome's allies failed to come to her aid. She suffered a heavy defeat, and the city itself was sacked.

Somehow Rome survived. Soon her armies were on the march again, extending her borders and her sphere of influence. Three wars were fought against the Samnites (from the Apennines east of Rome). They had become the dominant power in several areas once held by the Etruscans. Rome suffered a crushing defeat at the Caudine Forks in 321 BC but eventually emerged triumphant following the victory at Sentinum in 295 BC. Roman hegemony was established over much of the mainland of central Italy, helped especially by the policy of founding colonies of settlers in new areas and building impressive roads radiating from Rome. A network of alliances was carefully maintained. Historians have tended to deny that Rome's expansion at this time was the result of some conscious policy or grand design. It was more a case of reaching *ad hoc* solutions to problems as they arose: 'The whole approach was empirical, working from precedent to precedent according to each individual case, the relationship with every community in turn being considered on its own merits' (Grant, M., *History of Rome* (1996), 55). A similar approach—but in a different context—would be evident in a later age in the problematic litera-ture of the classical jurists (see 2.3.4.3). But, although some of the conflicts that befell Rome were essentially defensive in origin, the planting of colonies all over Italy makes the thesis that there was no policy of expansion difficult to justify. Certainly, the ending of the internal struggle of the orders enabled Rome to direct her energies outwards.

There were bound to be considerable dangers in extending Roman power throughout Italy. To the north, beyond Etruria, lay Cisalpine Gaul ('Gaul this side of the Alps'). Occasional aggression by its tribes against Roman interests necessi-tated action. After another Gallic invasion was repulsed in 225 BC, Rome decided to pacify the area. Mediolanum (Milan) was captured by a Roman army in 222 BC, and there followed the establishment of several colonies in the Po Valley. A large part of Cisalpine Gaul was annexed.

Potentially greater problems lay in the south, where Greek and Carthaginian influence was strong. As Rome expanded southwards, some of the cities that had been originally founded by the Greeks welcomed alliance with her. Others did not, fearing that Rome was attempting a unification of Italy under her yoke. One such reluctant entrant to the Roman orbit was the thriving maritime city of Tarentum—it asked for aid from Pyrrhus, the King of Epirus (in Greece). He gave it, but at some cost. The Roman armies, although initially defeated, inflicted such heavy losses on Pyrrhus that his position became precarious—the 'Pyrrhic vic-tory'—forcing him to abandon Tarentum, which eventually surrendered to the Romans in 272 BC. Rome was now the mistress of Italy, sustaining her hegemony through the foundation of more colonies, and by the maintenance of generally good relations with her allies throughout Italy.

However, the loyalty of Rome's allies was strained to breaking point in the last century of the Republic over the issue of citizenship. Rome, once so magnanimous in her grants of citizenship (or its attendant privileges) to her neighbours, gradually became decidedly less generous. Roman citizenship had become highly prized and jealously guarded; so, when it was refused even to the staunchest of allies, it is hardly surprising that their resentment became acute. In 91 BC, Rome's Italian allies rebelled. Although the revolt was crushed two years later, the Social War resulted in a political triumph for the 'defeated' allies—Rome conferred its citizenship throughout Italy. Henceforth, Rome and Italy were synonymous.

1.2.2.2 **Beyond Italy**

(a) Carthage. The capture of Tarentum brought Rome within the sphere of influ-ence of the Carthaginians, a proud trading people who had become masters of the western Mediterranean. Relations between Rome and Carthage had been good since the earliest days of the Republic (secured by various treaties), but deteriorated sharply once Rome established control over the ports of southern Italy. This was Rome's first contact with a mighty foreign empire that had arisen after the fall of the Macedonian Empire of Alexander the Great. Control of Sicily was the ostensible issue that eventually drove the two powers to war. The first Punic War (264–241 BC) was one of the most bitterly fought in Rome's history, both sides sustaining terrible losses. Rome emerged victorious: the Carthaginians were forced to abandon Sicily. In 238 BC, Rome annexed Sardinia and Corsica. The newly acquired territories became provinces that were directly ruled from Rome. They were not granted any substantial degree of autonomy—both a departure from previous practice and a model for the future. Here we have the beginnings of Rome's overseas Empire, a new epoch in her history.

Despite the losses resulting from the first Punic War, Carthage remained the chief power in the western Mediterranean. Control of Spain proved to be the catalyst for further hostilities—the second Punic War (218–201 BC). The early stages of this cataclysmic conflict saw Rome brought to her knees by Hannibal's armies as they swept their way through Italy following an epic crossing of the Alps. After a terrible defeat at Cannae in 216 BC, Rome seemed certain to fall to the invaders; but her allies in central Italy held firm in their allegiance. The Romans refused to fight another open battle, or to negotiate peace. Within sight of Rome, Hannibal turned aside, lacking the means to sustain a potentially long siege. This proved to be the turning point of the war. From then it was a tale of virtually unbroken Roman success: Hannibal was confined to the role of a marauder; his brother was killed trying to reinforce him; and Rome found a great general, Scipio Africanus, who ended Carthaginian power in Spain and attacked Carthage herself. Hannibal was forced to retreat from Italy in order to defend his homeland. At Zama in 202 BC, Scipio won the decisive battle that broke Carthage and resulted in her having to cede her powerful fleet and Spain. Rome triumphed, but she had been stretched to the limit.

The acquisition of territory by conquest inevitably brings problems. Despite the severe losses sustained in defeating Hannibal, Rome was soon engaged in seemingly incessant warfare as she strove to protect her gains and her allies, especially in Spain and Africa. One can certainly detect in this era an unyielding resolve to retain what had been bloodily acquired. Carthage was again defeated in 146 BC, this time in a mercifully short war that broke her power forever. Rome ruled supreme in the western Mediterranean.

(b) The eastern Mediterranean. The death of Alexander the Great in 323 BC was followed by the collapse and fragmentation of his once mighty Empire. Rome's interests enmeshed her in a complex series of diplomatic manoeuvres in the area. She made and broke alliances, played off one State against another, and generally engaged in promoting her interests in a manner that any skilled practitioner in *realpolitik* would applaud. Philip V of Macedonia was confronted by Rome at the request of one of her Greek allies, and defeated in 197 BC. Macedonia and Greece were added in 146 BC to the burgeoning total of Roman provinces.

In Asia Minor, Rome was at first content to foster a loose confederation of allies that acknowledged her supremacy. However, such diplomacy did not always bring the peace and stability that Rome craved: Mithridates VI, King of Pontus, proved a particularly troublesome fellow. In 88 BC, he overran a large part of Asia Minor and then invaded Greece, where he was greeted as a liberator rather than as a tyrannical aggressor—much to Rome's consternation. Several expeditions against him failed. He was not finally defeated until 66 BC, when he fell victim to the brilliant generalship of Pompey, who restored order throughout the area, as well as further increasing Rome's territory and income. Syria was annexed; and Jerusalem was captured in 63 BC.

(c) The Gauls. Cisalpine Gaul continued to be a prickly thorn in Rome's side. Effective control over the area was a Roman dream rather than reality. There were frequent uprisings by the Gallic tribes settled there, and incursions by marauding Gauls from over the other side of the Alps. In any case, Rome needed to protect the land route to Spain. Roman armies started to venture further north beyond the mountains, and were generally successful. The conquest and annexation of southern Gaul in the late second century BC led to the creation of a new province—Gallia Narbonensis. But in 105 BC, the Roman army was heavily defeated at Arausio (Orange) by Germanic tribes advancing westwards. They occupied the province for several years before being crushed by the Roman general, Marius.

Roman control of Gaul remained confined to the south for the next 50 years until Julius Caesar (made governor of Gaul in 59 BC) defeated a succession of Gallic tribes in a protracted campaign lasting some 10 years. Caesar's victory at Alesia in 52 BC against the formidable Gallic leader Vercingetorix proved to be the decisive engagement. This campaign greatly extended the size of the province. Across the sea lay the mysterious land of Britain. Twice Caesar invaded it, mainly to protect his northern frontier and to claim the glory of having extended Roman power beyond the seas.

1.2.3 The collapse of the Republic

The Republican constitution was inherently flawed. In particular, the concept of joint magistracy, coupled with the magisterial right of veto, was potentially fraught with problems (Mousourakis, *Legal History*, 39–48). So, too, was the vesting of military, executive, and even judicial powers in magistrates who could easily transpire to be rivals. Fortunately for Rome, the control exercised by the Senate, and the good sense of most of her office-holders, prevented serious problems for much of the time. The position of the Senate was paradoxical. It enjoyed, throughout much of the Republic, a pre-eminent position in terms of prestige and moral authority. It was *the* consultative and advisory body of government. The convention became established that magistrates had to consult the Senate on all-important matters. Moreover, it exercised a large measure of control over the State's finances and foreign relations—the Senate authorized and ratified treaties and alliances with other powers (see further Jolowicz and Nicholas, *Historical Introduction*, 30–45). On the other hand, the Senate lacked the right to make law. But woe betide the magistrate or the general who disregarded the Senate's advice. Of course, the authority and prestige of the Senate depended on the way that it discharged its functions. Until the late Republic, the leadership that the Senate provided was generally of a high order. Its astute handling of the various crises during the desperate years of Hannibal's invasion earned it a formidable reputation for years to come as a repository of political, legal, and military experience. For a century-and-a-half after the end of the struggle of the orders, the internal political situation of Rome was relatively stable. But with hindsight, we can see that if anyone successfully challenged the authority of the Senate, the Republican constitution would be in the greatest jeopardy.

1.2.3.1 **The Gracchi brothers**

Things started to go seriously wrong in the period of the Gracchi brothers. Tiberius Gracchus, tribune in 133 BC, tried to deal with the plight of the peasant farmers who had been dispossessed of their smallholdings while engaged on military service. The farmer-soldier often found on his return that his smallholding had been absorbed into a larger estate. Tiberius' agrarian reforms imposed limits on the amount of public land that could be held by any individual. The land recovered from overlarge estates was to be distributed to the dispossessed. These proposals threatened the interests of wealthy landowners, many of whom were members of the Senate. So, Tiberius took the radical step of putting his plans to the plebeian assembly for enactment without first consulting the Senate. His enemies regarded his behaviour as arrogant and autocratic and murdered him.

A similar fate befell Tiberius' brother, Gaius, tribune in two successive years, 123–122 BC. His reform programme was far more radical and wide-ranging than that of Tiberius. Hardly any aspect of the government of Rome was left untouched by him. One particular measure earned Gaius great unpopularity with the Senate—he excluded senators from hearing cases of provincial mismanagement. This action was seen as a serious diminution of the powers of the Senate. Moreover, Gaius ignored the Senate and took his proposals straight to the plebeian assembly, which he dominated through his oratory and the force of his personality. He seems not to have learned the lessons of his brother's demise and he, too, was struck down.

The Gracchi brothers had exposed fundamental flaws in the Republican constitution. A man with ideas, courage, and a charismatic personality could appeal directly to the people as its 'protector', thus reducing the Senate to the role of an impotent bystander. The only reason that the Gracchi had failed was that at the critical moment, they had lacked an army. But the army, as a key player in the internal politics of Rome, was about to take the field.

1.2.3.2 **Armies and generals**

The heavy defeat suffered at Arausio in 105 BC hastened the reorganization of the Roman army into a fully professional, volunteer force dependent for its pay and conditions of service on individual commanders. A popular general had a dangerous weapon in his hands, capable of crushing any resistance, including that of the Senate. The remaining years of the Republic were plagued by crises, disorder, and civil war, often precipitated by the abuse of power by military strongmen—something that the Republican constitution was meant to prevent. The chief figures in this unhappy phase of Roman political history were:

(a) Marius. A highly successful general who achieved distinction in campaigns against Jugurtha in Numidia (Africa) and against the Germanic tribes in Cisalpine Gaul. His victories ended a series of reverses that had thrown doubt on Roman military supremacy, and which had brought the Senate much criticism. Marius proved adept at exploiting the hostility felt towards the senatorial class, thus further weakening the Senate's waning authority. Greatly popular with the army, he managed to be elected consul six times between 107 and 100 BC. This was unprecedented and (legally) highly dubious. Marius was quite capable of using the army to sweep away political opposition. In 100 BC, senatorial resistance to Marius' reforms quickly evaporated at the sight of his soldiers marching on the Senate—a black day for the Republic. Blacker days were to follow.

(b) Sulla. He succeeded Marius as the strongman of Rome. Sulla was a redoubtable general, distinguishing himself in the Social War and against the formidable Mithridates. Sulla was not averse to using his army against fellow Romans in the pursuit of personal ambition. Twice his legions marched on Rome and ruthlessly crushed senatorial opposition from his rivals for power. But Sulla was much more than a ruthless soldier. He was responsible for a considerable amount of reform—legal, constitutional, and administrative. He reformed the criminal process by establishing a system of jury courts to try particular categories of crime. He considerably restricted the powers of tribunes, thereby ensuring that the Senate recovered some of its lost authority and prestige. Further, Sulla doubled the size of the Senate (from 300 to 600) by introducing many of his supporters from the equestrians, an order which formed a very important power bloc, largely consisting of the wealthiest citizens of Rome other than those of patrician stock. They were termed the *equites* ('horsemen' or 'knights') because in early Rome they constituted the bulk of the cavalry.

(c) Pompey. Following Sulla's death, Pompey eventually established himself as the most powerful man in Rome. He was a superb general, perhaps the finest of all Republican commanders. In 67 BC, Pompey was entrusted with unprecedented powers of command, which he used to great effect to crush the threat of piracy in the Mediterranean before embarking on a most successful campaign in the east. On his triumphant return, Pompey tried to obtain ratification for his reorganization of the Roman provinces in the east, but he met unexpected political opposition. It was overcome with the aid of Julius Caesar, a patrician who had acquired great prestige and influence during Pompey's absence. Renewed opposition from sections of the nobility led Pompey to make an informal alliance in 60 BC with Caesar and Crassus ('the First Triumvirate'). Caesar then secured for himself the governorship of Gaul, where he displayed impressive qualities as a general and empire builder. Crassus was less fortunate, leading his army to a terrible defeat at Carrhae in 53 BC by a much smaller Parthian army. An unprecedented barrage from mounted archers destroyed the Roman legions and the victors executed Crassus.

A rift eventually developed between Pompey and Caesar, partly the result of Pompey's irritation that memories of his past military deeds were being eclipsed by the news of Caesar's Gallic exploits. The untimely death of Caesar's daughter, whom Pompey had married to cement the political alliance, led to a further weakening of the ties between the two men. In 52 BC, Pompey was elected as sole consul after a period of anarchy during which factional discord had resulted in the murder of candidates for high office and the burning down of the Senate. Pompey restored order but made the rift between himself and the absent Caesar seem irrevocable by passing laws openly aimed at Caesar. Such actions did Pompey little credit—a pity, since for much of his distinguished career he had acted with a measure of integrity unusual for the age.

(d) Julius Caesar. Returning to Italy after his long absence in Gaul, Caesar crossed the river Rubicon with his army in 49 BC, ignoring a decree that he was to resume the status of a private citizen on his return. The crossing of the Rubicon was perceived as a culmination of the deteriorating relations between Pompey and Caesar—a virtual declaration of civil war. The prospect of the two ablest Roman generals of the time in open conflict, of Roman armies slaughtering one another, was what the Republicans most feared. The critical weakness of the Republican constitution, the vesting of military and executive authority in potential rivals, had become tragically evident.

In the hostilities that followed, Julius Caesar emerged totally triumphant. Pompey fled to Egypt and was murdered there in 48 BC. Caesar became the undisputed master of the Roman world. He had himself appointed *dictator* for life. The title was not a hollow one, for Caesar was the complete autocrat. However, he showed remarkable clemency (for that time) towards those who had formerly opposed him. Such magnanimity enabled him to restore good order after the bitter civil war of the previous years—a considerable achievement. And he instituted an ambitious programme of reform that demonstrated his understanding of some of the administrative and economic problems that beset the Roman world at that time. His astonishing energy, multifarious talents, and consuming interest in a diverse range of matters mark him out as one of the outstanding figures in world history. Had he lived longer, who knows what more he might have achieved? But he was destined to rule Rome for no more than four years. Caesar became hated by elements of the senatorial aristocracy for his autocratic ways and disregard of the Republican constitution, and in 44 BC, he was assassinated.

(e) Octavian (later Augustus). He stands at the crossroads of Roman history—the last of the great figures of the Republic, but the first Emperor. He was related to Caesar, and was named by him as his heir. Although aged only 18 when Caesar was murdered, Octavian's connections immediately marked him out as a potential leader of the Caesarian party, and as a rival to Mark Antony (who had been Caesar's closest colleague). So, the last few years of the Republic witnessed intermittent feuding between Antony and Octavian. For a while, they formed an alliance with Lepidus, another of Caesar's lieutenants—a new triumvirate. Its object was to take revenge on those Republicans implicated in Caesar's murder. They succeeded, and their revenge was terrible. In 43 BC, a large number of senators were butchered, including that redoubtable orator, statesman, and man of letters, Cicero. A year later, the forces of Brutus and Cassius, Caesar's murderers, were defeated at Philippi. The Republican cause was effectively finished.

For a few years there was a measure of harmony between the rulers of the Roman world. Antony, still the senior partner in the triumvirate, married Octavian's sister. But Antony's obsession with pursuing war in the east against the Parthians, one of Caesar's unfinished projects, led him to Egypt, and to the arms of her scheming queen, Cleopatra. The whole world knows about their romance. It has inspired some great works of art. Life with Cleopatra seems to have made Antony forget his wife, his duties, his very homeland. It may be that he was planning to establish an empire of the East as a rival to Rome. With hindsight, we can see that Octavian and Antony were on a collision course even more inevitable than that between Pompey and Caesar. Rome was again plunged into civil war. The naval battle at Actium in 31 BC proved to be a significant victory for Octavian. Antony and Cleopatra committed suicide soon after, and Octavian annexed Egypt. His triumph was complete—he was now the master of the Roman world. He was to remain master for the next 45 years.

1.3 **Empire**

It has to be stressed at the outset that 'Empire' takes on an additional connotation from 27 BC. Until Octavian's emergence as master of Rome, 'Empire' has only one meaning, i.e. the extent of Rome's territorial possessions. In this sense, the Roman Empire began with the annexation of Sicily in 241 BC—or much earlier, if expansion within the Italian mainland is taken as the starting point. But from 27 BC, the word has also a constitutional meaning, referring to the form of government that evolved in Rome during Octavian's reign and thereafter—an autocratic State where ultimate power resided not with elected representatives but with one man, the Emperor.

1.3.1 **Augustus and the principate**

By 31 BC, Octavian was already a proven commander and statesman of considerable experience. He understood well the lessons to be learned from the mistakes of the past. So he moved tentatively in seeking to establish his power, eschewing the type of precipitate action that had brought down Caesar. Gradually, he acquired dictatorial powers but wisely avoided calling himself *rex* or *dictator*, titles which had hateful associations. He used his powers astutely, always careful to act constitutionally, or at least to give that impression (see Mousourakis, *Legal History*, 88–99).

1.3.1.1 **Constitutional developments**

The constitutional settlement that emerged during the course of Octavian's long rule was a novel mix—a restoration of the traditional forms of Republican government, but under the aegis of a *princeps*, i.e. first citizen. This was one of the many titles that Octavian acquired from a grateful nation. Other titles included *pater patriae* ('father of the nation') and *augustus*, a title conferred on Octavian by the Senate in 27 BC in recognition of the powers vested in him, and to signify the Janus-like nature of his position—as a harbinger of good things to come, yet associated with the glories of the past. Henceforth, Octavian called himself Augustus. A month of the year was named after him.

There were other titles of significance. As chief pontiff, Augustus stood at the head of the religious life of the State. He instituted an ambitious programme for the building of new temples and shrines. His personal mission to regenerate Rome, and to revive the glories of the past, led him to encourage her to adopt a more moral and godly existence than she had experienced of late. As *caesar* and *divi filius* ('son of the divine one'), Augustus stressed his close links with the deified Julius Caesar—a vital ingredient in securing his power base, and in giving the appearance of some continuity with the past. He took care to diminish the fears of his potential enemies of a return to the terrible days (as they saw it) when Caesar ruled Rome. He even offered high office to his political opponents. Augustus took the title of *imperator*, but this signified that he was the commander of the army, and not that he was 'Emperor' in any formal sense. In addition to these titles and honours, Augustus held the consulship until 23 BC and was then elected tribune for life. Moreover, he was granted special rights, (e.g. the governorship of provinces, the right to select senators) that, in combination with his other powers, eventually made him the most powerful man in Rome's history since the monarchical period.

The traditional dating of the Empire from 27 BC reflects that it was in that year that Augustus and the Senate agreed on the substantial reorganization of the government of Rome that historians later designated as imperial. Rome was to be governed by the *princeps* and the Senate acting in partnership. Also, Augustus was granted a number of provinces (including Egypt and Gaul) that were ruled by governors considered to be his delegates rather than those of the Senate. The other provinces remained in the control of the Senate. This division of the Empire into imperial and senatorial provinces was a major innovation of the time. In the provinces Augustus even encouraged the notion that he was of divine status:

The different forms which the worship of Augustus took in Rome, Italy and the provinces illustrate the different aspects of his rule—he is Princeps to the Senate, Imperator to army and people, King and God to the subject peoples of the Empire—and recapitulate the sources of his personal power in relation to towns, provinces and kings. The sum of power and prestige was tremendous. (Syme, R., *The Roman Revolution* (1939), 475.)

1.3.1.2 The Augustan age

Rarely has a man used absolute power in such a sagacious and constructive manner, and with such impressive results. Rome was transformed to such an extent that 'the Augustan age' has become a favourite phrase of historians to describe this remarkable period of her history. Of special interest to lawyers was Augustus' attempt to change Roman society through the medium of legislation, i.e. 'social engineering' (see, e.g. 5.2.4.3). Augustus brought to Rome the internal peace, stability, sound administration, and good government for which she craved. Further, the Augustan age was famous for a flowering of the arts unparalleled in Rome's history, especially in the field of literature. Poets and historians were inspired by the momentous events of the period. Often the themes of their work were distinctly nostalgic, portraying a yearning for the distant past. Virgil's *Aeneid* is perhaps the finest manifestation of this rich period of artistic creativity, much encouraged by Augustus.

Augustus extended his firm government throughout the Roman provinces, reorganizing their administration, and tackling the corruption that was allegedly rife at the time. As regards territorial expansion, it was a time mainly of consolidation, especially at the western and eastern borders of the Empire. In central Europe, however, the Roman armies advanced towards the Danube and across the Rhine, but suffered a disastrous defeat in AD 9 at the hands of the Germans. The news of this catastrophe deeply affected the ailing Emperor. The defeat proved significant, for it marked—as it transpired—the end of Roman expansion into Germany. It was the first serious setback in Augustus' remarkably long career. By the time he died in AD 14, Augustus had been continuously at the forefront of affairs (since Julius Caesar's murder) for 58 years, and the sole ruler of Rome for the last 45.

1.3.2 The first and second centuries AD

1.3.2.1 Constitutional developments

In this period, despite some notorious Emperors, Rome reached the zenith of her power and prestige. The constitutional 'system' that had evolved under Augustus was resilient enough to withstand the presence at the helm of the affairs of Rome of the occasional monster or halfwit as Emperor. The Republican constitutional framework remained basically intact. The Senate, the assemblies of the people, and the magistrates continued for a while performing their traditional roles, but with the Emperor pre-eminent as the *princeps*. However, the importance of the Republican institutions gradually waned. For example, the assemblies came to be regarded as little more than conveyor belts for the Emperor's proposals. By AD 100, they were ceasing to have an independent existence. A similar pattern can be discerned in the position of the Senate. It simply became a mouthpiece of the Emperor, a passive and subservient tool of the imperial will. Moreover, the Republican magistracies gradually lost much of their traditional importance, or disappeared altogether.

1.3.2.2 The role of the army

Every Emperor needed the unswerving support of the army. If he neglected interest in the army, or failed to reward it properly, or showed himself incompetent as a commander-in-chief, he was unlikely to reign for long. Armies made and unmade Emperors; and sometimes murdered them. It became customary for Emperors to nominate their successors, but the nominee would need the army's support to succeed. In AD 41, there occurred an ominous event—the murder of the Emperor by some of his own troops, the praetorian guard. The victim was the deranged Caligula. The troops then chose Claudius as his successor, a man who seemed ill-fitted to be Emperor. Perhaps the army hoped that it would be able to rule through a puppet. In the event, Claudius proved to be one of the ablest of the early Emperors.

Strictly, there was no such thing as 'the army'. There were normally several armies at any one time, dispersed over various parts of the Empire. Grave complications arose when the armies did not agree on the choice of successor—anarchy, civil war even. Take, for example, the death of Nero in AD 68. The succession to the imperial throne had proceeded fairly smoothly after the death of Augustus, apart from the murder of Caligula. It had passed in turn to Tiberius, Caligula, Claudius, and Nero, all descendants of Augustus' family. But Nero lost the support of the army, which, on his suicide, decided to choose his successor. However, the main army groups could not agree, and so they put forward their own nominees. This resulted in civil war—in little over a year Rome had four different Emperors! The eventual victor, Vespasian, was the first of a new dynasty—the Flavians. The army had ended the rule of one dynasty and replaced it with another, not for the last time.

1.3.2.3 A golden age

The civil war of AD 68–9 proved to be a watershed in the fortunes of imperial Rome. For much of the next century and a half, Rome was ruled by three dynasties (the Flavians, Antonines, and Severans) that served Rome well for the most part. During this period, the Emperors were mostly talented and successful rulers—Vespasian, Trajan, Hadrian, Antoninus Pius, Marcus Aurelius, and Septimius Severus, all soldier-statesmen of great ability, even a distinguished philosopher amongst them. Marcus Aurelius's *Meditations*—written mostly while on campaign—were a collection of private musings inspired by Stoic and Platonic philosophy. They emphasize the need to live in harmony with nature, and are predominantly introspective in character, concerned with knowledge of the self. The period can justifiably be described as a golden one in Rome's history. It was a time of comparative peace and prosperity, despite occasional revolts and setbacks. Britain was largely conquered, and the fierce Dacian wars resulted in greater control of the Danube valley.

1.3.2.4 **Romanization**

This period witnessed a process of 'Romanization' (a controversial term in modern scholarship) whereby the inhabitants of the Empire were educated in Roman ways, dressed in Roman clothes, and encouraged to adopt the life of city or town dwellers. A vast amount of building was done in the provinces. New cities were created and old ones rebuilt on the Roman model.

An important consequence of Romanization was the narrowing of the gulf between Rome and her provinces. Rome still remained the capital, and Italy the focal point of the Empire, but other cities and regions were growing in importance—an inevitable development, given the massive size of the territory under Roman rule. Their inhabitants were playing an increasingly major part in Rome's affairs. The Roman army began to be dominated (numerically, at least) by recruits from the provinces. The governing class of Rome ceased to be exclusively 'Roman', and came increasingly to be filled from the ranks of provincials. Several of the outstanding lawyers of this golden age were men of provincial origin, including Julian (Africa) and Ulpian (Syria). Even the imperial throne ceased to be the preserve of men from traditional Roman origins. But then descent from pure Roman stock was no longer the most important attribute demanded of an Emperor. What had come to matter most was the ability to earn the respect and loyalty of the Roman army. Trajan and Hadrian were both of Spanish origin; Antoninus Pius was from Gaul; while Septimius Severus hailed from near Carthage. How Dido, Hannibal, and others from Carthage's proud past would have rejoiced at the news that someone of Punic stock ruled Rome!

1.3.3 **The third century AD: the Empire under strain**

The murder of Alexander Severus in AD 235 can be regarded as another milestone in Rome's imperial history. The Severan dynasty had brought Rome over 40 years of generally stable and wise government. In contrast, the 50 years after Alexander's murder was a period of almost continuous anarchy during which the Roman Empire came close to disintegration.

1.3.3.1 **Rome on the defensive**

The reason for the murder of Alexander Severus was the familiar one of an Emperor losing the confidence of his soldiers at a time of military crisis. Rome was being forced on the defensive as virtually all parts of her huge Empire came under attack: it had become too large for a single Emperor to organize and defend against determined enemies. The most sustained pressure came from the east, where the resurgent Parthians invaded Roman provinces at will, inflicting a series of heavy defeats. And there was serious trouble on the Rhine and Danube frontiers from new tribal coalitions—in AD 271 Rome was forced to abandon Dacia to the Goths. There was even the occasional audacious foray by Germanic tribes into Italy, a precursor of things to come. However, although Rome's military situation was serious, the Roman army was still a superb fighting machine. It continued to inflict defeats on most of its enemies, but not as regularly as before.

1.3.3.2 **A plethora of Emperors**

The confusion and anarchy of these years can best be illustrated by reference to the imperial succession. From AD 235 to 284 there were 18 Emperors, and scores of rival candidates. The life expectancy of Emperors fell dramatically. Some were deposed, some were murdered, some were captured or killed in battle. Few died in their beds. Emperors had, indeed, become the puppets of the generals. An army in some distant corner of the Empire would proclaim its general as Emperor, only to find that the same process was being repeated elsewhere by other armies with their own candidates.

But even in this troubled and anarchic period there were outstanding successes and Emperors, especially Aurelian (AD 270–5). He proved to be the finest Roman commander of the period, consistently defeating foreign enemies all over the Empire and recovering much territory in the East. And he found time to build a massive defensive wall around Rome, the substantial remains of which you may still see.

1.3.3.3 **Economic problems**

There was also a marked change in the economic position of the Roman Empire. The relative prosperity of the second century gave way to a grave economic crisis. The army had to be greatly increased in size to meet defensive commitments. The effect on agricultural output was serious, food shortages becoming commonplace. Moreover, the army had to be properly equipped and paid if the Emperor wished to remain in favour with his troops. Consequently, army pay was increased dramatically in the third century AD. Who paid for all this? The taxpayer: under a system that was becoming increasingly corrupt and incompetent. It was also a period of high inflation, the result partly of the occasional debasing of the currency in order to increase army pay. Many of Rome's economic problems at this time stemmed from her increasing military expenditure.

1.3.4 **Diocletian, Constantine, and the fourth century AD**

Diocletian and Constantine, who transformed the State and checked the remorseless pressure on the borders of the Empire from Rome's enemies, ended 50 years of anarchy and disintegration. Her military recovery was emphatic. The achievements of the two men gave Rome a fresh start, similar in some ways to the age of Augustus (see Mousourakis, *Legal History*, 135–56).

1.3.4.1 **Diocletian**

He became Emperor in AD 284 in the (by now) 'traditional' manner—elevation to the imperial throne by the army. He set about reforming the ailing Roman Empire with great vigour, realizing that it was too large for one man to rule effectively. Delegation of imperial power was essential. So he divided the Empire into East and West, putting an old friend, Maximian, in charge of the West while Diocletian took charge of the East, a sign of its increasing importance. Each then adopted a junior partner to be their heir apparent. Thus was born the 'Tetrarchy', the rule of the four Emperors, each having his own particular sphere of responsibility, but under the ultimate control of Diocletian.

To increase the authority of the Emperor, Diocletian actively promoted a more exalted concept of royalty. He identified closely with the traditional gods of Rome and surrounded himself with an elaborate court full of pomp and ceremonial. He was no longer *princeps*, the first citizen, because he had to be *above* the citizen body—after all, almost anyone could be a citizen. The Emperor was now *dominus*, i.e. 'lord' of his people. Accordingly, Diocletian's reign is often described as the beginning of the Dominate (in contrast to the Principate that Augustus had inaugurated). It was important also to weaken the political influence of the army. This was achieved by removing from commanders their executive powers in civil administration. The army was confined to an exclusively military role.

Diocletian reformed virtually every level of government. The provinces were divided into smaller units, each with its own army of administrators. The civil service grew much larger, much of its effort directed at administering the labyrinthine tax system. *Decuriones* (town councillors) were given the unenviable task of collecting taxes, and were made personally responsible for any shortfall. Not surprisingly, the position was not eagerly sought thereafter. And there were some important economic reforms. The State adopted a more interventionist role in protecting essential economic interests: farm labourers and smallholders were tied to the land; arms factories were taken into State control; and the currency was reformed in a vain attempt to check inflation. An edict was passed in AD 301 that fixed an upper limit on goods and wages. This was unprecedented legislation. Various consumables were listed with their maximum prices; e.g. 4 *denarii* for a measure of Gallic beer, but 2 for Egyptian beer; 250 *denarii* for a fattened pheasant, but 125 for a wild pheasant. The maximum daily wage for a sewer cleaner was 25 *denarii*; 50 for a carpenter, 75 for a teacher of arithmetic, and so forth. Severe punishment was prescribed for breaking the edict, but it failed to check inflation, one of the few failures in an exceptional reign. Diocletian suddenly decided to abdicate in AD 305, spending his remaining days in a decidedly less stressful manner—growing cabbages.

1.3.4.2 Constantine

The excellent teamwork demonstrated during the Tetrarchy under Diocletian was unfortunately not maintained immediately after his abdication. Eventually, Constantine emerged as Emperor of the West, following his victory in AD 312 against his chief rival, and in AD 324 became the sole ruler of the whole Empire after defeating the Emperor of the East. The renewed civil war of these years suggests that Diocletian's reforms were little more than an interruption in a prolonged period of anarchy, but Constantine shared much of his power with his sons, and it was by them that he was succeeded. Diocletian's system thus survived, albeit in a revised form. Constantine wisely adhered to many of Diocletian's policies, continuing the restructuring of the Empire. Foreign invaders were repulsed, Constantine proving himself to be a formidable commander-in-chief. But his reign was truly remarkable in two particular respects: the conversion of Rome to Christianity, and the building of Constantinople as the capital of the Eastern Empire.

(a) Conversion to Christianity. The appeal of Christianity to the poor and underprivileged gave it a potentially revolutionary flavour, as did the ready acceptance by its followers of martyrdom. Failure to understand the Christian message, as well as its frequent misinterpretation, contributed to the terrible persecution inflicted on early Christians by some Emperors. The persecution under Diocletian, more systematic than in the past, provided a catalyst for change. Christians were to be found by now in all walks of life; some were even members of the imperial court. The wives of Diocletian and Constantine were thought to have been Christians, or to have had Christian sympathies.

It is not clear when Constantine's conversion to Christianity occurred, but he ascribed the victory in AD 312 to divine intervention. Soon after, Constantine initiated the process that led to Rome's conversion. The Edict of Milan in AD 313 formally ended the persecution of the Christians and proclaimed the religious neutrality of the State. But, as the Emperor declared himself to be a Christian, the example of his own personal beliefs, coupled with his programme of building Christian churches all over the Empire and donating much land to them, effectively transformed Rome into a Christian State by the time of his death. In AD 325, he summoned the Council of Nicaea to attempt a formulation of a common creed for all Christians.

(b) Constantinople. When Constantine became sole ruler of the whole Empire, he decided (as an act of thanksgiving) to establish a capital for the Eastern Empire. This was the inevitable culmination of the eastward shift of the centre of gravity of the Empire that had begun to manifest itself in the second century AD. The site chosen was the ancient city of Byzantium overlooking the Bosphorus. A magnificent new city was built, replete with Christian churches, and named Constantinople after its founder. The virtually impregnable position of the site made it an ideal choice as a capital.

1.3.4.3 **After Constantine**

On his death in AD 337, Constantine was succeeded by his three sons, who ruled for a while as joint Emperors. Eventually, they began to quarrel, and this bout of infighting was to set the tone for much of the rest of the century, a period generally of tension and some confusion. Power-sharing between Emperors rarely worked smoothly for long—it seemed to be a recipe for constant friction. There was an attempt even to reverse Rome's espousal of Christianity, but the attempt was short-lived. Revolts occurred frequently in various parts of the Empire, and serious incursions on its borders. Roman armies were beginning to suffer some terrible defeats again.

However, Theodosius I, Emperor of the East in AD 379, and sole ruler of the entire Empire for a short while before his death in AD 395, reversed the run of defeats, proving himself to be a strong ruler at a critical time. He was to be the last ruler of a united Roman Empire before the West collapsed. Significantly, Theodosius established Mediolanum as his western base—further evidence of Rome's diminishing importance as a focal point of the Empire. Indeed, in the fifth century, Ravenna replaced Rome as the official seat of imperial government in the West.

It was during the reign of Theodosius I that the power of the Church became very evident. The Emperor was forced to do public penance for his alleged authorization of a massacre of citizens at Thessalonica in AD 390. This was a significant moment in the developing relations between Church and State. The possibility that one day the Christian Church would humble a distinguished Roman Emperor would have been treated as a joke only 80 years earlier. Bishop Ambrose of Milan, the man who insisted on the Emperor doing penance, thus demonstrated that the Church could play a vital role in the secular affairs of the State. Indeed, he acted as an unofficial magistrate during his bishopric, and came to be seen as the protector of the people against the worst excesses of civil government.

His two young sons, Arcadius and Honorius, neither of them possessing their father's sterling qualities, succeeded Theodosius in AD 395. The Empire was entrusted to Stilicho, an able general of barbarian descent, related to Theodosius by marriage. Within a few years the Empire had witnessed its Emperor prostrate before the Bishop of Milan, and someone of barbarian stock in supreme control. How the world had changed!

The death of Theodosius led to a division of the Empire into East and West. Now that two children ruled the Empire there was a need to reorganize its government. Under the new arrangement, each was to be regarded as sovereign within his Empire, and as equal to the other. Diocletian's system of joint rule under the aegis of a supreme ruler was abandoned. From now, the history of the Roman Empire was essentially the story of two Empires, not one, although the division was somewhat less formal than was once supposed.

1.3.5 The Western Empire: collapse and oblivion

Much ink has been spilt down the ages describing and explaining the collapse of the Western Empire. Here is just a little more. It is a tortuous story, and can be told only in the briefest detail.

1.3.5.1 Rome falls

Constant incursions into Roman territory forced Rome to make alliances (never very secure) with various invaders. Emperors resorted to making friends with former bitter enemies, or even to buying their way out of trouble when all else failed. The policy was doomed. Within 80 years of the death of Theodosius, the Western Empire had been overrun. Britain, one of the remotest provinces, was abandoned at an early stage. Arthur, if he existed at all, was probably a Romano-British chief trying to stem the westward advance across Britain of heathen invaders.

Now, the loss of a Chester or a Gloucester could have been coped with, but when the Visigoths captured Rome in AD 410, the Empire was clearly in a terminal state. Attila and his Huns, the fiercest of the barbarian invaders, invaded Italy in AD 452 and threatened Rome, but were eventually persuaded to depart. A few years later, the Vandals, who were aided by dissension among her senatorial factions, sacked Rome. But the story was not one of total defeat and collapse. The West could still produce able soldier-statesmen (if not Emperors) capable of at least holding together what remained of the Empire. Stilicho had been such a man; another, even more successful, was Aetius—he managed to delay the relentless onslaught of Attila. Tragically for Rome, success against the invaders did not receive its due reward. Both Stilicho and Aetius were murdered with the connivance of their respective Emperors. In AD 476 came the final indignity. A barbarian leader, Odoacer, deposed the last Emperor of the West, Romulus Augustus. Apart from a relatively short period in the sixth century, Italy was henceforth to be ruled by Germanic chiefs, sometimes in exemplary fashion, as under Theodoric (Odoacer's successor). Many of these rulers were admirers of Rome and her traditions, and preserved much of what they found.

1.3.5.2 The causes of collapse

Why did the Western Empire collapse? This is one of the most intriguing questions in world history. The single most important factor was that the Empire was subjected from the early years of the third century to continuous attacks from fierce and determined enemies—a tidal wave of peoples on the move, pressing against Rome's frontiers. Such an irresistible force could not have been successfully contained for long. And how did Rome resist? She still fielded huge armies, if anything larger than those in the past, but these armies were composed mainly of troops of doubtful loyalty—Germanic allies and mercenaries. The army that fought the barbarian invaders was itself largely a barbarian force. Changing sides was not uncommon. Much of this army lacked patriotic fervour: it cared mostly about who was to pay it, and how much, but very little about notions such as defence of the 'homeland'. In any case, the army's homeland was no longer Rome. This 'barbarization' of the army, itself made necessary by a pronounced shortage of citizen recruits, was the crucial military weakness of the era.

But was the Western Empire worth defending? It was riven with dissension and disunity. Emperors faced frequent crises, often precipitated by their own ineptitude and by the ambitions of rivals and usurpers. Successful generals seemed to pay the ultimate price for their achievements—assassinated on the orders of the Emperor. The ruling classes alienated the rest of the population by their alarming complacency in these difficult times, and by their failure to contribute more to the affairs of Rome, and to her coffers, than their wealth and power warranted. The gulf between the rich and the poor; between the rulers and the ruled; between the bureaucrat and the peasant smallholder; was too great to permit any reasonable degree of harmony. Moreover, there was racial conflict between Rome and her neighbouring allies, i.e. those Germanic tribes that she was forced to allow into Italy, and there was discord among the tribes themselves. In addition, the advent of Christianity precipitated considerable religious disunity. First, it was Christian against pagan; then, Christian against Christian. Heresies abounded, necessitating a painful search for a common creed. There was disagreement whether doing good works or devoting one's life to prayer and meditation best served the Christian ideal. Many took the latter course, and the Empire lost their talents. Furthermore, a lack of harmony was apparent even in relations between the two Empires. They were very unalike in any case, possessing different cultures and speaking different languages, but one could have expected perhaps greater cooperation between them than actually occurred in the fifth century. A fuller account of the extent of the disunity affecting the Western Empire can be found in Michael Grant's *The Fall of The Roman Empire* (1990).

There were grave economic problems. A shortage of manpower contributed to a decline in agricultural produce—cities faced serious famine at times in this era. High levels of taxation were imposed, largely because of the need to maintain huge armies and to bribe enemies. Life for many Romans had, indeed, become unbearably grim in this land of decaying cities, roaming barbarians, pillaging armies, corrupt bureaucrats, high taxes, and severe food shortages—a land plagued by complacency; lacking in patriotism; torn asunder by disunity at every level; the traditional Roman virtues seemingly dead and buried. Is it any surprise that the wealthy landowner may have wondered whether life under the rule of the enemy might in some ways be preferable?

Were we to adopt the attractive 'what if?' approach to explaining historical phenomena, stressing the importance of the 'human' factor at the expense of underlying causes, we would probably find a different scenario emerging. What if in AD 395, just one of the sons of Theodosius had possessed his father's qualities?

What if Aetius had not been murdered? Could he not have held the remnants of the Western Empire together? What if the East had given the West more help in the fifth century? And so on. Still, one is left with the distinct impression that the problems confronting the West were of such a magnitude that its fall was inevitable. Disunity in the face of sustained and overwhelming attack spelled certain disaster sooner or later. The only surprise was that the Western Empire did not crumble earlier—its longevity is perhaps the more interesting historical question, not its demise.

1.3.6 The Eastern Empire: dazzling achievements

The Eastern Empire was fortunate in having a capital that was a formidable stronghold. The Emperors of the East were able to rule for centuries from Constantinople, secure from external attack. The city was considered virtually impregnable by reason of its heavy fortifications and its commanding defensive position, largely surrounded by water. The building of the massive Theodosian walls in the fifth century (still visible) added to the city's redoubtable defences.

1.3.6.1 The survival of the Empire

Despite the occasional internal crisis, or external threat from Persians, Goths, and Vandals, the fifth century was predominantly a time of peace, prosperity, and tolerably good government in the Byzantine Empire, under a succession of able Emperors—Theodosius II, Marcian, and Leo I. However, the East was not immune from some of the problems that the West experienced. Religious disunity, for example, was perhaps even more acute than in the West. Why then did the Byzantine Empire survive while that in the West fell? One reason was that the East had a sounder social and economic structure. The gulf between the classes, and between rich and poor, was less pronounced than in the West. Besides, there was less poverty—the East was far wealthier, possessing some rich provinces.

Taxation was high, but there was a greater ability and willingness to pay. The wealthy contributed much more to the State than their counterparts in the West. The East seemed to have an abundance of much that the West lacked, including manpower. And it was internally more stable: it had fewer insurrections, fewer usurpers and claimants to the imperial throne, and fewer enemies resident within its borders.

None of this might have saved the East if it had been attacked with the same degree of sustained aggression that befell the West. Certainly, the Eastern Empire was engaged in some bitter fighting, and its armies suffered the occasional crushing defeat, particularly against the Vandals. But such reverses were relatively light compared to the hammer blows that rained on the West. In any case, the geographical position of the Western Empire made it more susceptible to invasion. Once invaders crossed the Rhine or the Danube, the West was very difficult to defend. The Eastern Empire provided a far greater challenge for invaders; and its great capital was unassailable.

1.3.6.2 Justinian

The achievements of Justinian's long reign (AD 527–65) mark him out as the greatest of the Byzantine Emperors. He carried out a massive building programme. Old cities such as Carthage and Antioch were rebuilt on a lavish scale. Magnificent churches and public buildings appeared all over the Empire. The building of the cathedral of St. Sophia in Constantinople was one of the wonders of the age. This vast edifice was built at huge cost on an unprecedented scale by the finest architects of the day, using materials from all over the Empire. Justinian certainly spent lavishly. Perhaps he did empty the imperial coffers and left the Empire poorer than he found it; but he enriched it in so many ways. In any case, he was not a reckless spender—his spending had a greater purpose. He dreamed, as Augustus had done, of a return to the past, and of a revival of the greatness of Rome. He regarded this as his God-given mission. Magnificent buildings were only a part of his dream. A united Empire, free of discord and disunity, free of Germanic tribes and other invaders—that constituted his mission.

Dreams became reality in many respects. His great generals, Belisarius and Narses, defeated a variety of foes. The Vandals and Ostrogoths were crushed beyond recovery. The regularity of imperial victories recalled distant memories of Rome at her zenith. It seemed like old times with Roman armies crushing numerically superior forces. For a while, the Italian mainland and much of the Mediterranean was clear of hostile forces. The Emperor of the East had recovered an important part of the former Western Empire, something that had eluded Justinian's predecessors. In the East, the Persians, potentially the most dangerous foe, were kept largely at bay through a series of truces and inconclusive wars. But the recovery was short-lived. Soon after Justinian's death, Italy (those parts of northern Italy which had been recaptured during his reign) was again reverting to the rule of barbarian tribes.

Another aim that obsessed Justinian was doctrinal unity. Repeatedly, he summoned councils of Christian churchmen in an attempt to end their differences. Success proved elusive. Even Justinian's wife, Theodora, was strictly a heretic, a committed Monophysite (belief that there is only one nature—the divine—in Jesus Christ). If anything, doctrinal rifts deepened as the result of his well-meant efforts. Nor was Justinian particularly successful in his administrative reforms. He made strenuous efforts to eliminate corruption—long a major disease in the Byzantine Empire—but achieved little of permanence. More effective was his contribution to the needs of industry and commerce, especially his success in establishing new trade routes.

Justinian's most important achievement was his codification of Roman law. It can safely be said that this monumental work has had a lasting and significant influence on subsequent civilizations. There are few countries in the modern world that have been unaffected by Justinian's codification. He attempted to summarize the Roman law of the past, at the same time updating it and propounding it as a model for the future. The codification constitutes one of our great legacies from the ancient world.

As can be imagined, Justinian was a man of restless energy as well as boundless ambition. However, a large measure of credit for his achievements belongs to the remarkable Theodora. A sensational past as an actress and courtesan did not prevent her marriage to Justinian, a union regarded as scandalous by the Byzantine nobility. She proved to be a rock by her husband's side. In AD 532, a serious insurrection—the Nika riots—nearly ended Justinian's reign. He appears to have lost his nerve at the height of the crisis, and was all for fleeing from Constantinople. It was apparently Theodora who saved the day, persuading her husband to stay and, it seems, to give the order for a ruthless suppression of the revolt. Without Theodora's nerves of steel, it is very doubtful whether Roman law would have become the foundation of the legal systems of many countries of today.

 Please consult the Online Resource Centre for revision guidance on this chapter.

FURTHER READING

Those with a keen interest may wish to consult Goodman, M. (1997), *The Roman World 44 BC–AD 180*, London: Routledge; Sidwell, K. and Jones, P. (1997), *The World of Rome*, Cambridge: Cambridge University Press; Boardman, J., Griffin, J., and Murray, O. (eds.) (2001), *The Oxford History of the Roman World*, Oxford: Oxford University Press. The chapters collected in Maas, M. (ed.) (2005), *The Cambridge Companion to the Age of Justinian*, Cambridge: Cambridge University Press, also provide a fascinating insight into the reign of Justinian.

PART I

The Roman Legal System

2

The sources of Roman law

It is difficult to provide a comprehensive and finite list of the sources of Roman law, since the Roman jurists never defined the term 'source of law' and different sources were emphasized at certain periods in the history of the Roman legal system to reflect their prominence as instruments of legal reform. There are three statements in which the sources of Roman law are listed, seemingly without any specific order. The earliest is by Cicero (*Topica* 5.28) in the first century BC. The second is a comment by the second-century jurist Gaius in his Institutes (Inst.Gai.1.1.–7.). The latter was adopted and amended in Justinian's Institutes of the sixth century AD (Inst.1.2.). All three list legislation (laws and plebiscites), resolutions of the Senate, and edicts of the magistrates as sources of law. Apart from these, Cicero also mentions equity, custom, and decided cases in his list of sources. This has puzzled modern scholars, since some of these 'sources' are not included in the statements by Gaius and the drafters of Justinian's Institutes. In an attempt to explain this inconsistency Robinson (*Sources*, 25–9) has shown that Cicero's account of the sources of Roman law had a rhetorical purpose as weapons in the arsenal of the Roman advocate, whereas the two later comments by Gaius and the drafters of Justinian's Institutes merely listed the sources of both the *ius civile* and the *ius gentium*. Gaius added imperial enactments to his list since the legislative activities of the Emperor were fast becoming a prominent source of law during the second century. The Institutes of Justinian adopted Gaius' list of sources and restored custom as a source of law. Robinson has demonstrated (*Sources*, 29), however, that custom had a different meaning by the sixth century AD. Cicero understood 'custom' as ancestral tradition (*mos maiorum*) in the context of the *ius civile*, while the term custom in the Institutes of Justinian referred to local and regional variations on the law of the Roman Empire.

For a good recent account, see Ibbetson, D., 'Sources of Law from the Republic to the Dominate', in *Cambridge Companion*, 25–44.

2.1 Sources of law in the archaic period

Many of the characteristic institutions of Rome (such as the Senate and the *comitia centuriata*) had emerged during the Monarchy and had survived the expulsion of the Kings in 510 BC, so had early Roman law. But what kind of law was it? Our evidence for this period is inevitably scanty, but it appears that the law was essentially a mixture of custom embellished by royal decree, see Mousourakis, *Legal History*, 19–30.

2.1.1 **Custom**

Custom was *ius non scriptum*—law that was 'not written down'. It consisted of those practices so firmly established as to have acquired obligatory force. The recognition of custom, however, was hardly an exact science. Roman jurists were later to debate whether custom could be properly termed 'law', or whether it was only indirectly binding, i.e. needing formal recognition through juristic interpretation or some other agency.

But there is no doubt that Roman law was almost entirely customary in origin. Many of the most important and long-lasting customs in the realm of civil law were concerned with the family—its creation, structure, and operation. For example, custom regulated the formation of marriage, the rights and duties of family members, and the position of the *paterfamilias* (the head of the household). And some of the basic notions and procedures in Roman property law originated in custom, e.g. the formal mode of conveyance, *mancipatio* (see 7.1.1). Later, when law became subject to authoritative interpretation by the pontiffs and jurists, and tended to be written down, custom virtually ceased to be a formal source of law: 'Custom was important in early times before the *Twelve Tables* and was recognized in the codification of Justinian, but in between it scarcely existed, thanks to the role of the jurists' (Watson, *Spirit of Roman Law*, 60). Nevertheless, custom continued to influence the law, albeit as an indirect source, particularly in the later Eastern Empire (see 2.4.3.2).

2.1.2 **Royal decrees**

The decrees of the Kings (*leges regiae*) had direct binding force as law but doubt exists about the manner and extent of this form of primitive legislation. It seems that decrees were made periodically throughout the regal period, sometimes in substantial numbers, as in the reigns of Romulus and Servius Tullius. However, they were probably no more than a gloss on the main, custom-based body of the law. How were these decrees made? Let Pomponius, a jurist and legal historian of the second century AD, be our guide:

Pomponius, *Manual, sole book*: ... The fact is that at the outset of our civitas, the citizen body decided to conduct its affairs without fixed statute law or determinate legal rights; everything was governed by the kings under their own hand. When the *civitas* subsequently grew to a reasonable size, then Romulus himself, according to the tradition, divided the citizen body into thirty parts, and called them curiae on the ground that he improved his curatorship of the commonwealth through the advice of these parts. And accordingly, he himself enacted for the people a number of statutes passed by advice of the *curiae*...his successor kings legislated likewise. All these statutes have survived written down in the book by Sextus Papirius, who was a contemporary of Superbus...(D.1.2.2.1–2.)

(*Civitas*: State.)

Pomponius, writing some 900 years after the reign of Romulus, is hardly a reliable guide, but is the best that we have. His account has been doubted. The Papirian compilation was possibly drawn up by another Papirius (Gaius), the first Chief Pontiff. It may even have been a much later compilation. On the possibility of the actual existence of the *leges regiae*, see Watson, A., 'Roman Private Law and the *Leges Regiae*' (1972) 62 JRS, 100–5, where the author argues, contrary to mainstream scholarly opinion, that the idea of legislation existing in the time of the

Kings is not implausible even though it cannot be proven; see also Watson, *Twelve Tables*, 3–8.

The reputed royal decrees had a predominantly religious character, the appeasement of the gods being clearly discernible as the motivating factor behind many of the commands (see Tellegen-Couperus, *Short History*, s. 3.2). For example, no funeral rites were to be performed for a man struck by lightning—it was presumed that Jupiter, the chief god, had killed him. The decrees were mainly prescriptive or condemnatory. The prescriptive laws prescribed 'correct' behaviour. For example, Numa is alleged to have decreed that no one should sprinkle wine on a funeral pyre. The condemnatory laws, on the other hand, laid down severe penalties for various wrongs. These penalties sometimes consisted of self-help or private redress against the wrongdoer, e.g. retaliation (*talio*) was allowed in some circumstances as satisfaction for certain types of personal injury. The most serious wrongs were punished by more public forms of sanction, including ritual execution. One such offence, *parricidium* (killing one's ascendants), was regarded as a heinous crime and was punished in a horrific manner:

Modestinus, *Encyclopaedia, book 12*: **According to the custom of our ancestors, the punishment instituted for parricide was as follows: A parricide is flogged with blood-colored rods, then sewn up in a sack with a dog, a dunghill cock, a viper, and a monkey; then the sack is thrown into the depths of the sea.** (D.48.9.9pr.)

Whom should we 'credit' with the invention of this imaginative form of execution? It is not clear whether 'our ancestors' refers to Rome's earliest days or some later period.

For a very good account of the *leges regiae*, see Cornell, T., *The Beginnings of Rome: Italy and Rome from the Bronze Age to the Punic Wars (c. 1000–264 B.C.)* (1995).

2.2 Sources of law in the Republic

The chief sources of law in Republican Rome were legislation, the edicts of the magistrates, and latterly the *interpretatio* of those learned in the law (see Mousourakis, *Legal History*, 27–30, 49–64).

2.2.1 Legislation

The expulsion of the Kings and the formation of a Republican constitution resulted in some confusion as to what was binding law:

Pomponius, *Manual, sole book*:...**the Roman people set about working with vague ideas of right and with customs of a sort rather than with legislation...**(D.1.2.2.3.)

The extent of the legal powers of the consuls became a particularly sensitive issue in this period of uncertainty, and was one of the major grievances of the plebeians in the struggle of the orders (see generally 1.2.1.2). The power of the tribunes to intercede on behalf of plebeians was another source of confusion. The patricians were eventually forced to agree to the demands of the plebeians for publication of the law. The result was the enactment of the Twelve Tables in 451–450 BC, the first important landmark in Roman legal history. This enactment has been regarded as a concession extracted by the plebeians during the struggle of the orders (see Livy, *Ab Urbe Condita*, 3.31–59). 'The compilation of the XII Tables was an episode in the struggle of the orders, and constituted a victory for the plebs' (Jolowicz and Nicholas, *Historical Introduction*, 14). However, Livy's account has been doubted in *Roman Statutes*: 'Nor need any historian feel obliged to accept the traditional account of the first college as legislating in response to plebeian and popular pressure. The Twelve Tables may as readily be the result of self-regulation by a patrician elite' (II, 560).

2.2.1.1 The Twelve Tables

Pomponius, *Manual, sole book*: . . . **it was decided that there be appointed, on the authority of the people, a commission of ten men by whom were to be studied the laws of the Greek city states and by whom their own city was to be endowed with laws. They wrote out the laws in full on ivory tablets and put the tablets together in front of the *rostra*, to make the laws all the more open to inspection. They were given during that year sovereign right in the *civitas*, to enable them to correct the laws . . . They themselves discovered a deficiency in that first batch of laws, and accordingly, they added two tablets to the original set. It was from this addition that the laws of the *Twelve Tables* got their name.** (D.1.2.2.4.)

(*Rostra*: platforms used by speakers in the Forum Romanum, Rome's commercial, political, and legal centre.)

The main thrust of Pomponius' account can be accepted, even if parts of it are questionable, especially the reference to the study of Greek models. On the other hand, this is not the only reference to possible Greek influence on the Twelve Tables. Livy also mentions that the commissioners visited Greece to study the laws of the great Athenian legislator, Solon. However, modern scholarly opinion on the matter is more cautious. It is improbable that the commission would have made a potentially perilous voyage to Greece; more likely that 'the Greek city states' mentioned referred to cities in southern Italy. But there is little in the Twelve Tables that can be clearly identified as Greek, although some provisions—e.g. those concerning behaviour at funerals—appear very similar to Athenian legislation (see *Roman Statutes*, 560). (See, however, the interesting alternative theory proposed by Westbrook, R., 'The Nature and Origins of the Twelve Tables' (1988) 105 ZSS (rA), 74–121 on the Twelve Tables and its resemblance to legal codes of the Ancient Near East.) The constitution was suspended for a while and supreme executive power was vested in the commission. The provisions of the Twelve Tables were eventually enacted by the *comitia centuriata* and given publicity. The original tablets were said to have been destroyed when the Gauls sacked Rome in *c.* 386 BC; so our knowledge of the Twelve Tables is based on references by later writers. The style of the provisions appears to have been clear and simple, as one would expect given the demands for an intelligible publication of the law. The basic format involved the use of the conditional imperatives, e.g. 'If someone does so and so, let him be . . .'.

The Twelve Tables can be broadly described as Rome's first code of law, although the provisions fell short of the comprehensive restatement of the law that a modern codification normally entails. It is likely that in some areas of the law, only the main rules were stated, or those which needed clarification. Procedure was dealt with rather skimpily and acquisition of property received little mention. This may have been a deliberate ploy to limit the amount of expertise that the plebeians could acquire in the law: 'The *Twelve Tables* were prepared by patricians as the law they were willing to share with plebeians, in response to the latter's demand for equal rights of liberty' (Watson, *Spirit of Roman Law*, 38). Overall, the Twelve Tables were probably based on the existing customary law of Rome, but with some royal decrees and a few innovations added. The content can be broadly classified as consisting of public and private law, the latter greatly predominant.

(a) Public law. The Tables contained some provisions of a religious or constitutional character. Table X, entitled 'Of sacred law', prescribed detailed rules on burials and funerals: e.g. bodies are not to be buried or burned within the city; not more than 10 flautists can be hired to play at a funeral; and women mourners must refrain from mutilating themselves or displaying excessive grief. Table IX contained vital constitutional provisions: e.g. legislation inflicting capital punishment can be passed only by the *comitia centuriata*; no one can be ordered to be executed except after a trial; there is a right of appeal against a death sentence.

(b) Private law. The Twelve Tables contained provisions relating to procedure as well as substantive law. The first three tables were devoted to procedure. Table I deals with the question of summoning a defendant before a magistrate, i.e. starting a case: if the defendant refuses to go to court, force may be used to ensure his appearance; but if he is ill or aged, the plaintiff must provide a means of transportation. Table II specifies the amounts that must be deposited in court by the parties before the commencement of certain types of action. Table III deals with the enforcement of judgments: a debtor is allowed 30 days after judgment to pay the debt; if he fails, he may be seized by the creditor and brought before the court; if the debt is still unpaid, he may be detained by the creditor with severe consequences (see 3.2.3.1). The importance of procedure is evidenced by its placement at the beginning of the Twelve Tables. However, the *amount* of procedure included was modest compared to that found in other early codes of law. There is some useful detail on how to begin proceedings and how to enforce judgment, but little else. Most citizens, however well versed in the procedures stated in the Twelve Tables, would have lacked sufficient knowledge and expertise to pursue an action successfully.

A major part of the Twelve Tables was concerned with substantive private law. For example, Table IV contained the fundamental principle of Roman family law: a *paterfamilias* has absolute power over his children. Table VII, concerned with land, laid down some rules of practical importance, especially for neighbours, e.g. action can be taken in respect of overhanging branches from a neighbouring tree. Table VIII penalized the commission of various wrongs, e.g. theft; pasturing cattle on another man's land; charging excessive rates of interest; setting fire to houses. Table XI prohibited marriage between a patrician and plebeian, a highly controversial measure that was repealed within a few years. (For a reconstruction of the text and a comprehensive survey of recent literature on the Twelve Tables, see *Roman Statutes* II, 555–721.)

The Romans considered the Twelve Tables as the foundation of their civil law. The reverence felt in later ages for the code was reflected in Cicero's story—even allowing for a modicum of exaggeration—that in his time, children could recite parts of the Tables. (However, it seems to have had ceremonial rather than legal authority by the time of the late Republic; see Watson, *Law Making*, 111–22.) The literature of the Roman jurists was full of references to the Twelve Tables, and this is reflected in parts of Justinian's codification, the *Digest* especially. The Twelve Tables have helped to shape Western jurisprudence.

2.2.1.2 **The assemblies**

After the enactment of the Twelve Tables, legislation did not constitute the dominant force in substantive law reform during the Republic. The Roman assemblies rarely enacted laws that conflicted with the Twelve Tables. Until the late Republic, there were only a handful of statutory changes. The most important, as regards private law, was the *lex Aquilia c.*287 BC, which reformed the law on wrongful damage to property (see generally 10.2). Statutes dealing with constitutional and administrative reform, such as the *leges Liciniae Sextiae* and the *lex Hortensia* were more frequent (see 1.2.1.2).

The *comitia centuriata* was the most important of the assemblies. It elected high-ranking magistrates and was organized as the Roman people (or later their representatives) in military array. It enacted the Twelve Tables. The *comitia curiata* was the oldest assembly but had a minor role in legislation, its main function being formally to confer powers on superior magistrates. The *comitia tributa*, an assembly based on a geographical division of the populace into 'tribes', handled routine legislation and elected lesser magistrates. The *concilium plebis*, the plebeian assembly, became the dominant assembly long before the end of the Republic, both in terms of political clout and legislative reform: 'Though the legislative competence of all the assemblies was equal, the *concilium plebis* became the usual organ for the passing of laws in the later Republic as its presidents, the tribunes, had more time for, and interest in, legislation than the consuls, who were frequently engaged in military duties' (Jolowicz and Nicholas, *Historical Introduction*, 26).

A plebiscite (*plebiscitum*) is what the plebeians laid down in response to a proposal from a plebeian magistrate, like a tribune...But once the *Lex Hortensia* had been passed [c.287 BC], plebiscites came to have as much validity as statutes. (Inst.1.2.4.) (cf. 1.2.1.2.)

Although the assemblies differed in their functions, they had certain features in common. Each was sovereign within its own particular jurisdiction, and met only when summoned by the presiding magistrate. The assemblies could not initiate legislation—they met to vote on proposals drawn up in a draft bill that normally would have been debated in the Senate. It was the task of the assembly to accept or reject the bill, but not to debate or amend it. Each citizen of age voted orally and publicly within his particular group in the assembly. A simple majority of votes within a group carried the vote of that group. The possibilities of bribery and corruption in such circumstances necessitated the introduction of a secret ballot in the late Republic. Although the procedure was ostensibly democratic, in practice some votes counted for more than others. In the *comitia centuriata*, for example, the centuries voted in order of rank, beginning with the highest: thus, those voting first tended to have an influence on the later voters. Women could not appear in the assemblies and thus could not vote. On the organization, voting procedures, and purpose of the Republican assemblies see Lintott, *Constitution*, 40–64.

2.2.1.3 **The Senate**

Although the Senate was the pre-eminent body in Republican Rome, it did not possess legislative power. It acted as an advisory council, exercising influence and control over the leading men of the State, who would invariably be among its members. The Senate's directives, *senatus consulta*, carried great persuasive weight, but were not legally binding unless they had been incorporated into a resolution of an assembly or an edict of the magistrates. A magistrate who wished to put a proposal before one of the assemblies of the people would normally have to obtain the Senate's approval. Indeed, the Senate was often the prime mover in the initiation of legal reform although it could not meet until convened by the appropriate magistrate. Its 'advice' would be conveyed by a magistrate to the appropriate assembly: *senatus consulta* were thus a vital (if indirect) source of Republican legislation. Additionally, the Senate had the power to declare laws invalid for want of form and could even suspend the operation of valid laws in emergencies. On the organization and authority of the Senate in the Republic see Lintott, *Constitution*, 65–93.

2.2.2 **Edicts of the magistrates**

High-ranking magistrates had the *ius edicendi*, the right to issue edicts, i.e. legally binding statements of intent within their appropriate sphere of jurisdiction. The edicts of the praetors can be fairly said to have revolutionized Roman civil law in the late Republic, forming a body of law later described as the *ius honorarium*—'the law laid down by magistrates' (cf. D.1.2.2.10.). The significance of the *ius honorarium* in the history of Roman law was immense. This body of law constituted a gloss or a supplement to the main body of civil law, the *ius civile*, in a manner comparable to the relationship between equity and the English common law. The *ius honorarium* infused Roman law with new vigour and a fresh direction, transforming an introverted, parochial body of law into an outward-looking, cosmopolitan system. This process helped to give Roman law widespread appeal, making it relatively easy to assimilate in later ages. Lintott, *Constitution*, 94–146, provides a comprehensive account of the functions and powers of the various magistrates during the time of the Republic.

2.2.2.1 *Praetor urbanus* and *praetor peregrinus*

Pomponius, *Manual, sole book*: **And when the consuls were being called away to the wars with neighboring peoples, and there was no one in the *civitas* empowered to attend to legal business in the city, what was done was that a praetor also was created, called the urban praetor on the ground that he exercised jurisdiction within the city. [28] Some years thereafter that single praetor became insufficient, because a great crowd of foreigners had come into the *civitas* as well, and so another praetor was established, who got the name peregrine praetor, because he mainly exercised jurisdiction as between foreigners (*peregrini*).** (D.1.2.2.27–8.)

We have already seen that the office of urban praetor was created in 367 BC to conduct the administration of justice. Later, the influx of foreigners into Rome led to the creation in *c*.242 BC of the peregrine praetor. He came to exercise jurisdiction over cases in which at least one of the parties was a foreigner, although it is probable that initially the jurisdiction was confined to disputes between foreigners. And Rome's territorial growth necessitated the creation of praetors for the provinces. Two praetorships were introduced for Sicily and Sardinia in 227 BC and another two positions were created for the two Spanish provinces in 198 BC (see Brennan, *Praetorship* I, chs. 6 and 7). The number of praetors was later increased (the Sullan reform created eight positions) but the urban and peregrine praetors were the only ones with full jurisdiction over the civil law.

How was the *ius honorarium* developed? The praetors did not necessarily regard themselves as creating a supplementary body of law, but that is what in effect they did. The crucial factors that made this possible were their role in litigation and their right to issue edicts.

2.2.2.2 Litigation

The urban praetor inherited a system of procedure enforced by the *legis actiones*, 'the actions-at-law'. It was a highly formal system and claims had to be fitted into a limited number of set forms of action (see 3.2). The praetor would have to decide whether to grant the plaintiff an action, and what form of trial was appropriate. Despite his position, the praetor had scant opportunity to influence the development of the law because he was strictly bound to follow the *ius civile*, where applicable. However, the influx of foreigners into Rome in the third century BC brought about a fundamental change. They could not participate in the procedure by *legis actiones* since it was confined to citizens. So a new procedure was developed by the peregrine praetor for the benefit of foreigners—the formulary system. It was much more flexible than the *legis actiones*: the issues between the parties were stated in writing—the *formula*—and did not have to be accommodated within rigid forms of action. The peregrine praetor thus acquired considerable discretion in influencing the law that was applicable to disputes involving foreigners. (See Brennan, *Praetorship* I, 130–5.)

The irony was that whereas foreigners enjoyed the advantages of the formulary system, citizens were presumably restricted to the ancient actions-at-law. But not for long: the urban praetor found himself under pressure to adopt the new procedures, with the result that the procedure applicable to disputes involving foreigners were generally absorbed into the *ius civile*. Consequently, the formulary system gradually ousted that of the *legis actiones*, which became largely obsolete well before the end of the Republic.

2.2.2.3 Issuing edicts

Pomponius, *Manual, sole book*:...in order to let the citizens know and allow for the jurisdiction which each magistrate would be exercising over any given matter, they took to publishing edicts. These edicts, in the case of the praetors, constituted the *jus honorarium* (honorary law): 'honorary' is the term used, because the law in question had come from the high honor of praetorian office. (D.1.2.2.10.)

Edicts were issued on wooden boards (*alba*) displayed in the Forum at the beginning of the praetors' tenure of office. They consisted of a mixture of directives and proposals concerning the performance of the magistrates' functions, e.g. 'I will grant an action if...' or 'I will allow possession of the goods if...'. The praetor could allow new remedies or new defences, but the greater part of his edict normally consisted of measures adopted from that of the previous praetor. In this way, a stock body of rules was carried over from year to year, thus contributing to the evolution of the *ius honorarium*. Since the praetors at times lacked legal expertise, they tended to consult those learned in the law. Edicts thus proved to be an ideal vehicle for law reform.

The peregrine praetor issued an edict similar to that of the urban praetor, but normally far shorter. Although the content of their respective edicts necessarily differed at first, by the end of the Republic there was considerable assimilation between them. Edicts were also regularly issued by the aediles and by provincial governors. The latter had considerable discretion in administering the law to take account of local circumstances, but the main thrust of their edicts was to provide the local inhabitants with the same legal remedies that applied in Rome.

Once an edict had been published, the praetor was expected to act in conformity with it, though initially there appears to have been no legal sanction except for public opinion to compel him to do so. In 67 BC, a *lex Cornelia* was passed (precipitated partly by the irregular behaviour of Verres) which required magistrates to act in a manner consistent with their own edicts.

2.2.2.4 *Ius civile* and *ius honorarium*

Papinian, a jurist of the late classical period (see 2.3.4.4), described the *ius honorarium* (which he identified with praetorian law) as:

Papinian, *Definitions, book 2*:…**that which in the public interest the praetors have introduced in aid or supplementation or correction of the *jus civile*.** (D.1.1.7.1.)

The praetor would 'aid' the civil law by granting more convenient and effective remedies for the enforcement of civil law claims. 'Supplementation' occurred when the praetor granted a remedy in circumstances for which the civil law did not cater. For example, the somewhat narrow provisions of the *lex Aquilia* (concerning wrongful damage to property) were significantly extended by the grant of supplementary remedies (see 10.2.5). 'Correction' of the *ius civile* occurred less frequently—a praetor would have to exercise the greatest caution in such a case. But he did have the overriding power to act in the interests of the Roman people (when he saw fit to do so) and thus to act in contradiction of the civil law. For example, the praetor could allow an inheritance to be taken by a claimant in preference to the rightful heir under the civil law (see generally 8.3.2).

In the early years after the creation of the office, the urban praetor had little room for manoeuvre: aiding the civil law was the limit of his intervention because of the formalism of the *legis actiones*. Later, the praetors became more radical, particularly after the *lex Aebutia* c.150 BC formally recognized the applicability of the formulary system to disputes between citizens: 'the history of the praetorian edict reveals itself as a progress from *adjective* to *substantive* law' (see Kelly, J. M., 'The Growth-Pattern of the Praetor's Edict' (1966) 1 IJ, 341–55). Indeed, by the late Republic, the praetors had become the leading reformers within the Roman legal system. Among the important praetorian innovations of that period were the introduction of remedies for robbery, fraud and duress, more effective protection of proprietary interests, and the recognition of informal agreements. More radical still was the development of an alternative form of succession to property on death. The fact that the praetors were able to 'correct' the civil law in such important matters demonstrates the extent of their indirect lawmaking powers in the late Republic.

2.2.3 *Interpretatio*

Interpretatio was the elucidation of existing rules of law. It was not initially a direct source of law—the 'interpreter' could not create new law. But the process of *interpretatio* inevitably led to a gloss being put on enacted law through a process of implication and extension by analogy. The skeletal bones of the law thus acquired some flesh. Who were the interpreters of the law?

Pomponius, *Manual, sole book*: **In relation to all these statutes, however, knowledge of their authoritative interpretation and conduct of the actions-at-law belonged to the College of Priests, one of whom was appointed each year to preside over the private citizens.** (D.1.2.2.6.)

Given the connection between religion and the civil law in early Rome, the pontiffs were the most obvious interpreters of the law. Their advice on the meaning and applicability of the law constituted *interpretatio*. At times, it could be very creative: a rule of the Twelve Tables that a father who sold his son three times thereby lost power over him became through *interpretatio* the basis of the institution of emancipation not only of sons, but of daughters and grandchildren as well (see 5.1.2.4; Jolowicz and Nicholas, *Historical Introduction*, 88 ff.). The enactment of the Twelve Tables and the vesting of their interpretation with the pontiffs were developments of huge long-term significance: 'The major characteristics that shaped Roman law forever flowed from these circumstances' (Watson, *Spirit of Roman Law*, 37). The characteristics that Watson particularly attributes to pontifical *interpretatio* were 'the importance subsequently attached... to the giving of legal opinions, and the acceptance by the State of the individual's important role in lawmaking' (*Spirit of Roman Law*, 39).

The Twelve Tables, while containing some detail on litigation procedure (see 2.2.1.1), did not describe the operation of the system in much depth. This allowed the pontiffs to exercise influence over civil litigation for a considerable period thereafter. However, their monopoly was eventually broken:

Pomponius, *Manual, sole book*: **Thereafter, when Appius Claudius had written out these actions-at-law and brought them back into a common form, his clerk Gnaeus Flavius... pirated the book and passed it over to the people at large.** (D.1.2.2.7.)

A nice story; some of it may even be true. The Appius Claudius mentioned above was known to have been censor in 312 BC. His collection of actions-at-law was made public in the closing years of that century, and was later known as the *ius Flavianum*. Its significance was that the pontiffs were no longer necessarily the *only* interpreters of the law. A tradition evolved whereby eminent individuals, learned in law, gave legal opinions (*responsa*) in public. They came to be known as 'jurists'.

The first jurist to give legal advice in public, it seems, was Tiberius Coruncanius:

Pomponius, *Manual, sole book*: ...**tradition has it that of all those who mastered this knowledge, none earlier than Tiberius Coruncanius made a public profession of it. The others up to his time either thought it right to keep the civil law unknown or made it their practice only to give private consultations rather than offering themselves to people wishing to learn.** (D.1.2.2.35.)

Coruncanius is known to have been Chief Pontiff in *c.* 253 BC, the first plebeian to achieve that office. Pontifical influence was therefore not yet at an end, but the number of jurists outside the college of pontiffs was gradually increasing.

The jurists of the second half of the Republic can hardly be described as a class, still less as a profession, but they did have some features in common. They tended to be rich men from aristocratic families, bent on a political career. The gratuitous sharing of their legal expertise for the public good earned them considerable gratitude, respect, and a step on the political ladder: see generally Bauman, R., *Lawyers in Roman Republican Politics* (1983). In the late Republic, jurists increasingly specialized in the law on a full-time basis. The number of jurists grew, partly as the result of the manifold legal disputes arising in the disturbed conditions of that time. It is very likely that the pronounced increase in the citizen population following the Social War, and the expansion in commercial activity were also contributory factors. See Frier, B. W., *The Rise of the Roman Jurists* (1985) (see, however, Alan Watson's criticism of this work in 'The Birth of the Legal Profession' (1987) 85 Michigan LR, 1071–82). There is evidence that some of the jurists in the later Republic came from humble backgrounds, and that they were happy to receive payment for their services. A profession was emerging.

2.2.3.1 The work of the jurists

What sort of work was done by the jurists of the late Republic? The giving of advice was their most important function, because of its potential effect on the whole Roman legal system. Consider the variety of persons that might approach the jurist for advice: judges—normally they would be distinguished citizens but lacked legal expertise; praetors—the administration of litigation and the drafting of edicts would invariably be done with the help of jurists; magistrates and provincial governors—they would need advice on the performance of their duties; advocates—most were skilled orators but unskilled in the law; members of Senate; prospective litigants; and ordinary citizens. The advice that the jurists gave was not binding—it did not create a precedent—but the accumulation of *responsa* helped to elucidate the law, to give it shape, and to fill in the gaps.

Apart from advising, the jurists were engaged in cautelary jurisprudence—they drafted formal written documents such as wills; coached people in the uttering of the set words that were required in some legal ceremonies and transactions; and prepared prospective litigants and advocates in the presentation of their cases. The less eminent jurists probably did some formal teaching. The leading jurists taught by example: a young man, intending a legal or political career, would attach himself to a leading jurist and assist him in his work. In this way, the most eminent jurists attracted a following of adherents, with the result that a tradition of loyalty and continuity was fostered:

When I had assumed the *toga virilis*, I was taken by my father to Scaevola [consul 117 BC] with the intention that, so far as I was able and he would permit, I would never leave the old man's side. So I committed to memory many points skillfully expounded by him and also many of his brief and well-expressed opinions....After his death I took myself to Scaevola the pontiff [consul 95 BC]. (Cicero, *De Amicitia*, 1.1.)

What else did the jurist do in his busy day? He wrote. The literature of the jurists was varied: collections of forms and *responsa*; commentaries on the Twelve Tables or on individual statutes; general treatises on the civil law; and monographs, i.e. detailed exposition of specific legal topics. See Watson, A., 'Limits of Juristic Decision in the Later Roman Republic', ANRW I, 2 (Berlin 1972), 215–25. The Republican jurists established a tradition of legal writing, a development of fundamental importance in the history of Roman law. Juristic literature converted Roman law into a science—a body of rules that was analysed in writing, thus providing a rich source of material for further study and comment. (On the use of writing in Roman law generally, see Meyer, E.A., 'Writing in Roman Legal Contexts', in *Cambridge Companion*, 85–96.) But these jurists were not purely academics, spending their lives secreted behind books. Many of them achieved distinction in other fields of endeavour, whether as statesmen, governors, high-ranking magistrates or distinguished generals. And, although advocacy was not regarded as a normal pursuit for the jurist, the occasional individual achieved distinction in both professions.

The extent of Greek influence on the work of the Republican jurists is controversial. Schulz takes the view in *History of Roman Legal Science* (1946) that the influence was extensive: indeed, he describes the later Republic as the 'Hellenistic' period of Roman jurisprudence. On the other hand, Watson, in *Spirit of Roman Law*, considers that the influence was minimal as regards the borrowing of rules (hence, 'Hellenistic period' is a misnomer in his view), while accepting that other aspects of Roman life—literature, philosophy, rhetoric, and architecture—were affected. Kunkel, *An Introduction to Roman Legal and Constitutional History* (1966) takes a middle view, arguing that there was some, though not extensive, Greek influence on Roman jurisprudence: e.g. the employment of dialectical methods of reasoning; the trend towards a more systematic arrangement of materials; and the evident exponential growth of juristic literature (ascribed to Greek literary traditions).

2.2.3.2 Some outstanding jurists

Consult the timeline on the Online Resource Centre for dates.

Among the leading jurists of the later Republic were the following:

(a) Sextus Aelius. Consul in 198 BC; the author of the earliest important juristic work—a commentary on the Twelve Tables and the actions-at-law. He was probably the author of the *ius Aelianum*, an updating of the *ius Flavianum* (see 2.2.3). His interest in the actions-at-law suggests that they had not yet been superseded by the formulary system at the time when he wrote.

(b) Quintus Mucius Scaevola. Tribune in 106 BC, praetor in 98, consul in 95, governor of Asia in 94, and Chief Pontiff in 89. He came from a distinguished family—'the greatest politico-legal family in Roman history' (Bauman, R., *Lawyers in Roman Republican Politics* (1983), 422). Scaevola was one of the last in the long line of pontiffs to influence the development of Roman law. He appeared as advocate in some famous trials, notably the *causa Curiana* (concerning the interpretation of a will). His most important achievement as a jurist was his treatise on the *ius civile*. This was a trail-blazing work—the first comprehensive treatment of the civil law; the first to attempt a classification and detailed analysis of the law; and an inspiration and model for later writers. Scaevola's talents and influence made him a dangerous enemy—he was murdered in 82 BC.

(c) Aquilius Gallus. Praetor in 66 BC. He was responsible for some of the important praetorian innovations of the period, the edict on fraud, for example. He seemed to earn widespread respect and popularity, a rare phenomenon in those troubled times. Declining the very highest honours, he preferred to devote himself to writing and teaching.

(d) Servius Sulpicius Rufus. Praetor in 65 BC, consul in 51; a pupil of Aquilius Gallus, he initially earned a reputation as a distinguished advocate. He became the most eminent of all Republican jurists, apart from Scaevola, a meeting with whom appears to have inspired Servius. Pomponius relates how Servius:

Pomponius, *Manual, sole book*:...once sought out Quintus Mucius to consult him about the business of a client of his. When Servius failed to understand Quintus's opinion on the law, he questioned Quintus again; again an opinion was given, and again not understood; then he was severely reproached by Quintus. For, indeed, he told him that it was disgraceful for a patrician of noble family who regularly appeared as advocate in courts to be ignorant of the law on which his cases turned. Stung by this near insult, Servius applied himself to learning the civil law...(D.1.2.2.43.)

He applied himself well. He became a prolific author, his works including *Ad Brutum* (the first commentary on the praetorian edict) and the *Notata Mucii*, a correction of some of Scaevola's analyses of the civil law. Several distinguished jurists, among them Ofilius and Alfenus, regarded Servius as their 'teacher'. See, furthermore, Stein, P. G., 'The Place of Servius Sulpicius Rufus in the Development of Roman Legal Science', in *Festschrift Wieacker*, 175–84.

2.3 Sources of law in the Empire

2.3.1 An overview

The period of the Empire before the accession of Justinian can be divided into two halves. In the classical period, corresponding broadly to the first two-and-a-half centuries AD, some of the earlier sources of law (particularly the legislative assemblies and the praetorian edicts) gradually lost their importance, whilst other sources, e.g. juristic *interpretatio* and imperial decrees, became very prominent. It was at this time that Roman law achieved its highest level of development, due mainly to the work of the jurists. The second half of the period has traditionally been presented as a period of some decline, when imperial decrees became virtually the sole source of law. The classical period was the period when Rome reached its peak as a political force, whilst her decline and fall in later centuries was reflected in the state of legal development in the three centuries prior to Justinian. See Mousourakis, *Legal History*, 100–25, 157–69.

2.3.2 Legislation

By far the most important source of legislation in the Empire was to prove the imperial decree. In the early years of the period, the Republican assemblies and the Senate were still responsible for some important law reforms.

2.3.2.1 Republican assemblies

Augustus was anxious to preserve elements of the Republican constitution. Since the assemblies represented (in theory) the sovereign will of the people, Augustus was astute enough to make considerable use of them in effecting the extensive changes that he desired. The assemblies had been rather inactive as regards law reform in the late Republic. Their revival under Augustus could thus be seen as a return to the good old days of stability and wise government unknown to Rome for over a hundred years. A series of enactments was passed that had a substantial effect on the operation of the civil law, especially regarding slavery, matrimonial law, and the law of inheritance. This did not last long. The assemblies simply implemented the wishes of the Emperor. When Emperors found it more convenient to use other forms of legislation, the assemblies became obsolete as legislative organs. The last significant enactment affecting private law was probably the *lex Junia Velleia c.* AD 28 (see 8.7.1.1), while the *lex de imperio Vespasiani* AD 70—granting certain powers to Vespasian—was the last important comitial enactment. See *Roman Statutes* I, 549 ff. (where it is convincingly argued that this was a *lex* and not a *senatus consultum*, as sometimes supposed).

2.3.2.2 **The Senate**

Although the Senate had a pronounced influence on legislation in the Republic, it had no direct lawmaking powers. However, in the early Empire, the Senate increasingly came to be regarded as the primary organ of legislation in place of the Republican assemblies. The close association between the Emperor and Senate—he was its leading member—resulted in its resolutions, *senatus consulta*, being regarded as very persuasive. The Senate came to be identified with the imperial will, putting into legislative effect the policy of the Emperor. And it began to exercise very strict control over magistrates, depriving them of a large measure of their former discretionary powers.

When did *senatus consulta* become legally binding? In the first century AD, the Senate passed a number of measures that had the force of law (enforceable through praetorian remedies). These *senatus consulta* can be described as *ius novum*, a new form of law—senatorial directions that magistrates were bound to observe and which were given the force of law through the exercise of their *imperium*. An important early example was the *S. C. Silanianum* AD 10:

Ulpian, *Edict, book 50*: **As no home can be safe except if slaves are compelled to guard their masters both from members of the household and from outsiders at the risk of their own lives, *senatus consulta* have been introduced concerning the questioning on public authority of the household slaves of those who have been killed.** (D.29.5.1pr.)

The aim of this law was to punish slaves who failed to protect their masters from attack. All slaves living in the household of a master who was murdered in his own house were liable to be put to death after questioning and torture (see Harries, J., 'The Senatus Consultum Silanianum: Court Decisions and Judicial Severity in the Early Roman Empire', in *New Frontiers*, 51–70). Not surprisingly, this law sometimes provoked riots, as on the occasion in Nero's reign when some 400 slaves belonging to a murdered consul were put to death. Another example of an early *senatus consultum* was the *S. C. Claudianum* AD 52, which was concerned with cohabitation between female citizens and male slaves (see 4.3.3.2). It seems that *ius novum* included many *senatus consulta* concerned primarily with the routine administration of the State, intended to implement the many facets of imperial policy. See A. Schiller, *Roman Law* (1978), ch. 10.

It was probably in the reign of Hadrian that *senatus consulta* acquired direct binding force without the need for praetorian intervention. The *S. C. Tertullianum c.* AD 130, an amendment of the law of intestacy (see 8.3.3.1), appears to have been the first *senatus consultum* to have had direct binding force. But the Senate had by this time become a tool of the imperial will, automatically confirming the Emperor's proposals. Its importance as a legislative organ gradually waned, even if Emperors still went through the motions of seeking the Senate's ratification of their proposals. By *c.* AD 200, the Senate had to all intents and purposes ceased to make law.

2.3.2.3 **The Emperor**

Ulpian, *Institutes, book 1*: **A decision given by the Emperor has the force of a statute. This is because the populace commits to him and into him its own entire authority and power...** (D.1.4.1pr.)

This statement by the late classical jurist, Ulpian, is something of an *ex post facto* rationalization. In his time, it was certainly not doubted that the Emperor could make law. But Augustus and his successors had not claimed to possess such a general power. Nor is it clear by what means 'the populace' committed to the Emperor its 'entire authority'. It seems that during the second century, the jurists came to regard the Emperor as having the powers of an independent legislator: a convention emerged that he could make law, as Ulpian's statement confirms (albeit for specious reasons) (cf. Inst.Gai.1.5. and Inst.1.2.6.).

Imperial lawmaking was of overwhelming importance in the later Empire. Legislation became the exclusive preserve of the Emperor. And once the jurists ceased to influence the law, Roman law was reformed by imperial decree alone. Modern scholarship recognizes four main forms of imperial decree: *edicta, decreta, mandata*, and *rescripta*, but there is some debate about the inclusion of *mandata* in this list, see Tellegen-Couperus, *Short History*, s. 9.2.3.

2.3.2.4 *Edicta*

The Emperor, in common with high-ranking magistrates, had the power to issue edicts. But whereas magistrates' powers were limited by their specific jurisdiction, the Emperor could make edicts about an unlimited range of matters. However, it became the practice from Augustus onwards for the Emperor to consult his advisers before issuing an edict. A number of advisory bodies emerged in the early Empire, but the one with greatest influence on legislation was the judicial council. Originally, it was an informal body, assisting the Emperor when he acted as a judge in cases brought before him. It later became permanent, advising the Emperor on the general development of the law. Hadrian was largely responsible for making the judicial council, staffed by leading jurists, an indispensable institution of the imperial government. One can assume that the edicts issued in the Emperor's name were the result of a consultative process with his jurists.

There was some doubt in the early Empire as to the longevity of imperial edicts. In theory, since edicts of magistrates had force only during their term of office, those of the Emperor lapsed on his death. But by the late classical period, no one doubted that imperial edicts remained valid until repealed.

The scope of imperial edicts was very wide, affecting every area of law. One of the best known was Augustus's edict justifying the torture of slaves in exceptional circumstances:

Paul, *Adulterers, book 2*: **I do not think that interrogations under torture ought to be requested in every case and person; but when capital or more serious crimes cannot be explored and investigated in any other way than by the torturing of slaves, then I think that those [interrogations] are the most effective means of seeking out the truth and I hold that they should be conducted.** (D.48.18.8pr.)

Other famous imperial edicts included the *constitutio Antoniniana* AD 212, extending citizenship throughout the Empire; the Edict on Prices AD 301, imposing a maximum on certain prices and wages; and the Edict of Milan AD 313, ending the persecution of Christianity.

2.3.2.5 *Decreta*

Emperors had extensive judicial powers. They could decide cases on appeal or at first instance. The extent to which Emperors exercised their powers varied enormously. Some took an obsessive interest in judicial proceedings—Augustus reputedly heard cases well into the night on occasion. The Emperor was normally guided by advisers from his council, even if he had some expertise in the law, as had, e.g., Nerva (AD 96–8). He was concerned to apply existing law but had considerable discretion in its *interpretatio*. He could presumably devise new principles and could even overrule existing law, although his council would normally advise caution against any radical departure from the *ius civile*.

Decisions by judges usually affected only the actual parties in the case—the decisions were not regarded as precedents of general applicability. But imperial *decreta* were different. They were reported and filed in the imperial archives. And because they were made by the Emperor they came to be regarded as authoritative. Jurists made collections of such decisions. As a result of these factors, *decreta* acquired the status of binding precedents by the late classical period.

2.3.2.6 *Mandata*

These were instructions from the Emperor, acting on the advice of his council, to subordinate officials concerning the performance of their duties. Provincial governors and proconsuls, in particular, were the recipients of a steady stream of such orders. Among the most memorable was the following:

Ulpian, *Duties of Proconsul, book 1*: **A proconsul is not absolutely obliged to decline gifts, but he should aim for a mean, neither sulkily holding completely back nor greedily going beyond a reasonable level for gifts. On this subject the Deified Severus and the present Emperor Antoninus have most delicately given guidelines in a letter, whose words are as follows: 'So far as concerns presents, attend to what we say: there is an old proverb "neither everything nor every time nor from every person". For certainly, it is unmannerly to accept from no one, but to take from everyone is utterly contemptible and to take everything offered is sheer greed'.** (D.1.16.6.3.)

Mandata usually consisted of detailed administrative instructions—hardly the stuff of exciting legal development. It could be argued that this was not law at all, especially as *mandata* were often an abbreviated version of imperial edicts or other forms of legislation. But not all *mandata* were tedious administrative orders. Consider, for example, the following dramatic exhortation:

Paul, *Sabinus, book 13*: **The governor of a province has authority only over the people of his own province....Sometimes he has power even in relation to non-residents, if they have taken direct part in criminal activity. For it is to be found in the imperial warrants of appointment that he who has charge of the province shall attend to cleansing the province of evil men; and no distinction is drawn as to where they may come from.** (D.1.18.3.)

It was the practice for *mandata* to be dispatched with the new governor of a province. In the case of Pliny the Younger, appointed governor of Bithynia by Trajan (AD 98–117), the *mandata* clearly were not precise enough since an exchange of letters was necessary concerning the interpretation of the instructions. It was Trajan who was responsible for the famous mandate that allowed soldiers to make informal wills (see 8.4.2.6).

2.3.2.7 *Rescripta*

These were written replies from the Emperor to questions or petitions addressed to him. It was rescripts that provided perhaps the richest source of imperial legislation. There were two kinds of rescript: *epistulae* (letters) and *subscriptiones* (notes attached to an existing document). The former were replies to queries from officials or public bodies about their rights and duties. They were handled by a special office 'of letters' (*ab epistulis*) staffed by jurists. The reply was in the form of a letter signed by the Emperor:

Ulpian, *Duties of Prefect of the City, sole book*: **The Emperors Severus and Antoninus issued rescripts to Junius Rufinus, prefect of the city guard, in the following terms: 'You can also order to be beaten with sticks or flogged those flat-dwellers who have kept their house-fires carelessly.' (D.1.15.4.)**

(cf. the wording of the written reply given by the Emperor Antoninus Pius to Aelius Marcianus in Inst.1.8.2.)

Subscriptiones were answers to queries from private citizens. The queries had to be presented in the form of a petition (*libellus*) (rather than a letter) since private citizens were not normally permitted to write to the Emperor. The query was dealt with by the bureau of petitions (*a libellis*), which would attach its answer to the petition. The whole document was then signed by the Emperor. An answer to a legal query effectively rendered unnecessary the further pursuance of the matter in court. As the office of petitions was usually staffed by the leading jurists of the day, the issuing of *subscriptiones* became an ideal medium for the interpretation and development of the law. For example, the secretaryship of the office appears to have been held in turn by Papinian and Ulpian. See Honoré, A. M., *Ulpian* (1982).

2.3.3 Edicts of the magistrates

In the early years of the Empire, praetors continued to be elected, to issue edicts, and to control the pre-trial stages of litigation. However, as in the case of the Republican assemblies, the importance of the praetors gradually waned during the first century AD. The prestige of the office suffered on account of the further increases in their number, and because the praetorship came to be seen largely as a reward for loyalty to the Emperor. Moreover, as the domination of the Emperor over the State increased, the importance of its magistrates declined. The praetors lost their influence on legal development, especially after Hadrian commissioned his leading jurist, Julian, to draft a revision and consolidation of the praetorian edicts. The publication of Julian's consolidation, the *Edictum Perpetuum*, in *c.* AD 135 was probably not originally intended to end *all* development of the *ius honorarium*. Indeed, praetors continued to issue the edict at the beginning of their year of office; but they no longer had any opportunity to be innovative. Consequently, the *Edictum Perpetuum* came to be regarded as the final version of the praetorian edict as regards structure and content, although there was still a need to interpret it.

2.3.4 The classical jurists

It was the jurists of the classical period who gave Roman law its distinctive colour, and who enabled it to have such great influence on later civilizations. However, their work was essentially a continuation of that of the Republican jurists. The main change was in relation to *how* jurists worked rather than *what* they did. They were increasingly employed by the State, first on an *ad hoc* basis, then regularly—especially from Hadrian's reign onwards. This trend is emphasized by Kunkel in *Roman Legal and Constitutional History* (1966), ch. 7. He distinguishes between three stages within the classical period—early, mid-classical (AD 96–180), and late—during which the collective character of the jurists changes from that of essentially private individuals to one of very close connection with the Emperor. To some extent, the jurists became glorified civil servants and bureaucrats; but not wholly, for many of them resembled their Republican predecessors in holding some of the important bureaucratic offices of State. Their work consisted mainly of advising, teaching, and writing.

2.3.4.1 Advising

Undoubtedly, the most important advice was that given to the Emperors in the jurists' capacity as members of the imperial councils. 'Advice' must be understood in a broad sense—it included the drafting of imperial decrees. Moreover, the practice of giving *responsa* to judges, magistrates, private citizens, and litigants continued, especially in the early classical period. But there was an interesting development in the reign of Augustus:

Pomponius, *Manual, sole book*: ...**before the time of Augustus the right of stating opinions at large was not granted by Emperors, but the practice was that opinions were given by people who had confidence in their own studies. Nor did they always issue opinions under seal, but most commonly wrote themselves to the judges, or gave the testimony of a direct answer to those who consulted them. It was the deified Augustus who, in order to enhance the authority of the law, first established that opinions might be given under his authority.** (D.1.2.2.49.)

Pomponius describes here the *ius respondendi*, the right that was conferred on some jurists to give *responsa* sanctioned by the Emperor. Long before the reign of Augustus, the problem of conflicting opinions had arisen. Augustus attempted to make some *responsa* more authoritative than others. A written reply given under seal to a judge by a jurist with the *ius respondendi* was to be regarded as highly persuasive, if not strictly binding. There was probably a political motivation behind this development: by conferring what was seen as a favour, Augustus was more likely to earn the loyalty of the type of men whose support was vital to him. It can be presumed that most of the leading jurists of the early classical period were granted the *ius respondendi*, although there is little concrete evidence of the identity of the actual recipients.

The later history of the *ius respondendi* is unclear. It would appear that by Hadrian's reign, the problem of authority had arisen again. Gaius, a jurist writing not long after Hadrian's death, states that *responsa* are the opinions of men permitted to lay down the law. If the opinions are unanimous, they have binding force; but if they are not, the judge can choose which to follow (Inst.Gai.1.7.). He attributes this rule to a rescript of Hadrian. It would appear that the rescript was emphasizing that *responsa* were binding only if given by jurists with the *ius respondendi*, and provided that the opinion was unanimously held by such jurists. Hadrian was probably planning to abandon the practice of granting the *ius respondendi*. Little is heard about the practice after his reign. (See Bauman, *Lawyers and Politics*, ch. 9.)

2.3.4.2 Teaching

Legal education in the era of the classical jurists broadly followed the traditions established by the Republican jurists. There were perhaps more jurists willing to give formal lectures and classes, but teaching remained generally informal, aspirants learning juristic skills by attaching themselves to eminent jurists. The loyalty and allegiance that this system encouraged led to the emergence of differing schools of legal thought. This development originated in the reign of Augustus, and involved the two leading jurists of the time, Labeo and Capito:

Pomponius, *Manual, sole book*: **These two men set up for the first time rival sects, so to say. For Ateius Capito persevered with the line which had been handed down to him, whereas Labeo...set out to make a great many innovations....And so when Ateius Capito was succeeded by Massarius (read Massurius) Sabinus and Labeo by Nerva, these two increased the above-mentioned range of disagreements.** (D.1.2.2.47.–8.)

The rivalry between Labeo and Capito appears to have been both political and jurisprudential. Labeo, a staunch Republican, dared to refuse the consulship from Augustus. Capito, on the other hand, was a fervent supporter of Augustus. As regards legal issues, the above text suggests that Labeo was a progressive, Capito a conservative. Certainly, in Labeo's case, the mantle of progressive innovator was apt since he was responsible for some interesting and important contributions to Roman law, e.g. the doctrine of unjust enrichment (see 9.9.2). The differences between Labeo and Capito were accentuated by their followers. It was probably for that reason that the two schools came to be named, not after their original founders, but after two zealous disciples, Proculus and Sabinus—hence the Proculians (adherents of Labeo) and the Sabinians (followers of Capito). Some scholars have attempted to trace the origins of these schools to the days of Scaevola and Servius, but there is insufficient evidence to justify such speculation.

Hadrian had little time for conflicts and disputes between his leading jurists. So, the tradition of rivalry faded in his reign; but legal disputes did not, and jurists continued to propose conflicting solutions, even if they no longer acknowledged allegiance to any particular school.

There were many disagreements between the schools, often presented in the form of set disputations. It is likely that all the leading jurists before Hadrian regarded themselves as members of one or other of these schools. But it must not be imagined that every jurist blindly followed the position adopted by his school. What were the differences between the Proculians and Sabinians? First, it is clear that whatever had been the political differences between Labeo and Capito, political allegiance was not a major distinguishing factor between the schools. We find Republican sympathizers in both camps in the early years of the Empire. But *personal* allegiance was an important factor, ties of friendship and family (as well as teacher and student) playing a part in encouraging support for one school rather than another. Other differences may be detected, although none can satisfactorily account for the conflicting opinions in *all* the known disputes. Proculians tended to favour reasoned decisions based on principle, whereas Sabinians were more pragmatic in their approach, generally trying to find the most practical and fair solution on the merits of each particular case:

The Sabinians countered the Proculian emphasis on logic by stressing the importance of custom and practice. It was more important to them that the law should conform to the facts of life, both in the physical and in the social sense, than that it should be rational. Where the Proculians appealed to the *ratio*, the logic, of the civil law, the Sabinians justified a rule by reference to the nature of things, *natura rerum*. (Stein, *Character and Influence*, 45.)

Stein considers that the differences between the two schools were to some extent a reflection of the grammarian controversy between the analogists—who believed that language was orderly and governed by general rules—and the anomalists—who viewed language as the product of usage and practice.

A striking example of the difference in approach between the schools was the controversy concerning the age at which males reached puberty, and thereby potentially acquired legal capacity. For the Sabinians, the question turned on the physical development of the individual child: in cases of doubt, a physical examination might be necessary. The Proculians, on the other hand, favouring an objective rule applicable to all, regarded the attainment of the age of 14 years as the criterion (their rule prevailed). Several other disputes will be considered in later chapters. On the law schools, see Viton, P. A., 'On the Affiliations of the Severan Jurists' (1980) 46 SDHI, 507–11; and the interesting, yet controversial argument by Tellegen, J. W., 'Gaius Cassius and the Schola Cassiana in Pliny's Letter' vii, 24,8 (1988) 105 ZSS (rA), 263–311, that the 'schools' were sections of the Senate specializing in current legal problems whose leaders were given the *ius respondendi*. (See also the criticism raised against Tellegen's argument by Van den Bergh, G. C. J. J., 'Seeing Roman Law as History?' (1989) 106 ZSS (rA), 573–4; and see also, comprehensively, Bauman, *Lawyers and Politics*, chs. 1, 2, 8, and 9.)

2.3.4.3 Writing

The classical jurists continued the literary traditions of their Republican predecessors, but the literature of the classical age was more varied and certainly more voluminous. The character of classical legal writing was primarily casuistic, i.e. involving extensive discussion of cases, both actual and hypothetical. There was little abstract reasoning, philosophical inquiry, or historical content. Neither did the jurists reveal in their writings any particular bent for law reform, although many of them were involved in the drafting of imperial decrees. Nor did they appear interested in moral, political, social, or economic issues, or even procedural questions. Watson, in *Spirit of Roman Law*, considers that the absence of such factors in juristic literature demonstrates legal isolationism: 'Roman jurists argue as if they lived in a vacuum, remote from economic, social, religious, and political considerations' (66). So what was it that informed juristic literature? It was the jurists' concern with interpreting and expounding the law, 'striving for clarity of legal concepts' (Watson, *Spirit of Roman Law*, 40). (For criticisms of this view, see Tellegen-Couperus, O. E. and Tellegen, J. W. '*Artes Urbanae*: Roman Law and Rhetoric', in *New Frontiers*, 31–50.) In achieving a high degree of conceptualization, the jurists employed techniques of reasoning which have proved fundamental to the development of Western jurisprudence: 'The Roman legal tradition was characterized not so much by its substantive rules as by its intellectual methodology. Between about 100 BC and AD 250 the Roman jurists developed techniques of analogical and deductive reasoning which produced a jurisprudence of enormous refinement and sophistication' (*Roman Law Tradition* (1994), 1).

The main categories of classical juristic literature were:

(a) Problematic literature. This is a description for a group of works that focused on the discussion of difficult legal questions, problems, and cases. It is the problematic literature that can be most obviously described as casuistic and, therefore, as particularly characteristic of juristic output. The most substantial collections of problems are to be found in works entitled *Digesta*—e.g. that of Julian (in 90 books). Smaller collections, consisting mainly of opinions given by jurists in matters specifically referred to them, were entitled *Responsa, Quaestiones*, or *Disputationes*.

(b) Commentaries. Large-scale commentaries on the *ius civile* and the edicts of the praetors constituted a highly important category of writing, often comprising the most substantial works of the leading jurists. For example, Pomponius' commentary on the Edict consisted of 150 books (but the 'books' of that period were akin to modern chapters). Ulpian's *Ad edictum* and *Ad Sabinum* were heavily excerpted by Justinian's *Digest* commissioners (see 2.5.3.1).

(c) Monographs. These specialized treatments of a particular statute or legal topic continued to be written in the classical period. Hadrian's bureaucratic reforms led to an increase in the number of monographs concerned with the performance of public duties by magistrates and other officials.

(d) Textbooks. The increased emphasis on legal education in the early Empire resulted in the publication of works intended specifically for the use of students, a notion uncommon in the Republican era. The *Institutes* of Gaius, written *c.* AD 160, was the best-known textbook from the classical age, if not necessarily the first.

(e) Notes and epitomes. These were comments by jurists on extracts from published works of other jurists, a category of literature that did occasionally provoke controversy. It was the most suitable form of writing when criticism was the main object of the author. For this reason, notes and epitomes were the least reliable of the juristic works.

(f) Practitioner materials. This was a group of works intended primarily for legal practitioners but of use also to students, e.g. collections of basic rules and procedures, brief summaries of rules, and principles. They were called (variously) *Regulae, Definitiones, Sententiae*. See generally on juristic literature, Schulz, *History of Roman Legal Science* (1946) and Schiller, *Roman Law* (1978).

2.3.4.4 Some outstanding jurists

Consult the timeline on the Online Resource Centre for dates.

(a) Labeo:

Pomponius, *Manual, sole book*: **Labeo declined to accept office when Augustus made him an offer of the consulship. . . . Instead, he applied himself with the greatest firmness to his studies, and he used to divide up whole years on the principle that he spent six months at Rome with his students, and for six months he retired from the city and concentrated on writing books.** (D.1.2.2.47.)

Labeo was a prolific writer, the author of a diverse range of works, including commentaries on the Twelve Tables and the praetorian edicts. His opinions and works were seminal in the development of the Proculian school, and his innovatory thinking enriched the development of Roman law. Labeo was probably the first jurist to stress the importance of *analogy* in legal reasoning; this became a major characteristic of the Proculian school. He was a distinguished scholar, undoubtedly the outstanding jurist of the period of transition from Republic to Empire.

(b) Sabinus. In contrast to most jurists, he had an unprivileged background, never held high office, and was supported by his students:

Pomponius, *Manual, sole book*: **. . . to Sabinus the concession was granted by Tiberius Caesar that he might give opinions to the people at large. He was admitted to the equestrian rank when already of mature years and almost fifty. He never had substantial means, but for the most part was supported by his pupils.** (D.1.2.2.50.)

Such was his reputation, that the Sabinians were named after him. He is known for certain to have received the *ius respondendi*. His chief contribution as an author was his commentary on the *ius civile* in three books—not many when compared to the efforts of some jurists. It appears to have been little more than an outline summary of the law; but it was treated as a work of the front rank, inspiring major commentaries on the civil law by later jurists such as Paul and Ulpian.

(c) Julian. He was possibly the most distinguished of all Roman jurists. An inscription found in Tunisia (from where he originated) lists the numerous offices that he held, including that of quaestor, tribune, praetor, consul, and governor of Germany, Spain, and Africa. These honours were achieved over a long career, serving a succession of distinguished Emperors—Hadrian, Antoninus Pius, and Marcus Aurelius—during Rome's greatest years. Under Hadrian, he was given the task of consolidating the Edict (see 2.3.3), which suggests that he was pre-eminent among his contemporaries. The Tunisian inscription speaks of the doubling of his salary as quaestor on account of his 'extraordinary legal knowledge'.

Julian became head of the Sabinians—indeed, the last head. The era of rivalry between the schools appears to have ended in his time. The suggestion that this was the result of Julian's pre-eminence amongst his contemporaries is unconvincing since it underestimates the importance of Celsus, the last head of the Proculians. Celsus was an eminent teacher and prolific writer, perhaps not quite Julian's equal but, nevertheless, a distinguished jurist. Julian's published works were numerous and of the highest quality. His style was a model of clarity and elegance. His greatest work, his *Digesta*, was regarded as an exemplary casebook, a catalyst for some of the important work of the late classical jurists.

(d) Pomponius. He took a particular interest in Roman legal history, his works—especially the *Enchiridion*, an elementary account of legal history—being the source of much of the historical material to be found in Justinian's codification. Moreover, Pomponius wrote important commentaries on Scaevola and Sabinus, and an extensive treatment of the praetorian Edict. A contemporary of Julian, he confined his activities mainly to writing and teaching, and appears not to have held high office in the imperial government.

(e) Gaius. Similar in several respects to Pomponius (a contemporary), Gaius was a jurist of the Sabinian school, a teacher, and writer who did not hold high office. He was not well-known in his day, but acquired posthumous fame through his most important work, his *Institutes*. This textbook for students came to be regarded as a model exposition of the law. Its simplicity and lucidity ensured it lasting influence in the post-classical era and beyond. Justinian based his own *Institutes*, an important part of his codification, on Gaius' work. Gaius propounded a tripartite division of the law into 'persons', 'things', and 'actions', a classification which was to prove seminal in Western jurisprudence, see Kelley, D. R., 'Gaius Noster: Substructures of Western Social Thought' (1979) 84 American Historical Review, 619–48.

As the focus in his *Institutes* was on exposition and summarization rather than on casuistic analysis, the work may seem to lie outside the mainstream of classical juristic literature; but this was a factor that partly accounted for the work's later popularity. It is the only juristic work of the classical period to have survived substantially intact—a fifth-century manuscript (thought to be authentic and virtually complete) was discovered in Verona in 1816. Gaius wrote several other important works, including valuable commentaries on the *ius civile* and on the provincial Edict. *Res Cottidianae* ('Everyday matters')—traditionally attributed to Gaius—was another elementary work to have acquired considerable posthumous popularity.

Gaius' career remains something of a mystery. Hard facts are scarce, speculation plentiful. He appears to have lived or travelled outside Rome for a substantial part of his career. But his firm adherence to the Sabinian school throws doubt on the possibility that he was simply a jurist rooted in the provinces. He may have started his juristic career in Rome but then carried on his work in the eastern provinces. See generally Honoré, A. M., *Gaius* (1962).

(f) Papinian. His *Quaestiones* (37 books) and *Responsa* (19 books) were two of the outstanding examples of problematic literature. Papinian earned a formidable reputation and attained the highest office, becoming *praefectus praetorii*, chief of the praetorian guard (the Emperor's closest adviser), in AD 203, having previously been the head of the office of petitions. He visited Britain in AD 208, experiencing the delights of York in the company of Paul, Ulpian, and the Emperor Septimius Severus. The accession of Caracalla proved to be fatal for Papinian: the jurist's alleged refusal to condone the murder by Caracalla of the Emperor's brother cost Papinian his life in AD 212.

(g) Paul. A somewhat enigmatic character about whom little is known for certain. Early in his career, he appears to have been engaged in teaching and advocacy. Later, he acted as assistant to Papinian and held high office. He was a prolific author, his work demonstrating a critical intellect and a considerable range in terms of subject-matter and category of writing: elementary works for students and practitioners, several monographs, problematic works, notes and epitomes, collections of decisions, and large-scale commentaries on the *ius civile* and the Edict. His *Sententiae* was used extensively in the *lex Romana Visigothorum* (see 2.4.3.3). His reputation and influence in the post-classical era was immense. Only Ulpian is more extensively quoted in Justinian's *Digest*.

(h) Ulpian. His career illustrates the increasingly prominent role being played in the affairs of Rome during the course of the Empire by men from the provinces. Ulpian was a Syrian, probably born in Tyre. His writings were voluminous and are extensively quoted in Justinian's *Digest*, one-third of which consists of passages from Ulpian. He may perhaps have lacked the critical insight of Paul but his writings were considered to be models of clarity, simplicity, and reliability. Ulpian gained a reputation as a scholar, possessing an unrivalled knowledge of juristic literature and displaying an interest (unusual for a jurist) in philosophical issues. For Ulpian, law was the highest form of philosophy: it was concerned with notions of right and wrong and consisted of rational rules free of prejudice: see generally Honoré, A. M., *Ulpian* (1982). Ulpian's writing dates mainly from AD 213–17 and appears to have been intended as a single-handed codification of the law. Honoré controversially argues that Ulpian probably felt that there was a need for a comprehensive exposition of the law for the peoples of the Empire following the general grant of citizenship in AD 212 by the *constitutio Antoniniana* (which he may have personally drafted). The chief works were *Ad edictum* and *Ad Sabinum*, as fine as any written in that genre.

Ulpian held several offices in the imperial government. He was probably the head of the office of petitions in the early years of the third century. Later, he became chief of the Praetorian Guard under Alexander Severus but showed a lack of adroitness in his tenure of the office, incurring the enmity of his own guards—they murdered him, probably in AD 223, allegedly in the presence of the Emperor.

(i) Modestinus. Definitely not in the class of that formidable late classical trio, Papinian, Paul, and Ulpian; Modestinus is, nevertheless, important as perhaps the last distinguished jurist of the classical period. Ulpian refers to him as his 'pupil':

Ulpian, *Edict, book* 37: **If someone drove off my male ass and set him loose among his own mares to impregnate them, he will not be guilty of theft unless he has a theftuous intent; I gave this reply to my pupil, Herennius Modestinus, who consulted me from Dalmatia concerning horses to which a man was alleged to have submitted his mares for the same purpose, that he would be liable for theft if he had guilty intent...** (D.47.2.52.20.)

Modestinus held only minor office in government, but allegedly gained influence at the imperial court. As a writer, he eschewed the large-scale commentary, concentrating instead on student handbooks, practice manuals, and monographs.

2.4 The post-classical era

The three centuries between the end of the classical period and the enactment of Justinian's codification can be viewed as a period of decline in the history of Roman law. There was a great deal of legislation, necessitated by the vast changes occurring in the later Empire. For example, the conversion of Rome to Christianity resulted in a mass of new laws that defined the powers of the Church. Legislation by the Emperor became the sole source of law, and the importance of the jurists waned. The intellectual spirit of the classical period was largely missing. The decline was more pronounced in the West, probably due to its increasing political fragility and eventual disintegration. In the East, the decline was partly arrested through the development of flourishing law schools that paved the way for Justinian's epic work. See Mousourakis, *Legal History*, 157–69.

2.4.1 Whither the jurists?

Perhaps the most dramatic change in the character of post-classical legal development was the absence in that period (as far as we know) of outstanding jurists. No totally convincing explanation has been offered to account for this. Perhaps it was because legal science of the classical period could not be sustained indefinitely. After all, the juristic literature of the classical period was of enormous variety and volume. The law had been analysed in great detail, some subjects many times over. After such an outpouring of legal literature, what was there left to be done? Who could follow a Paul or an Ulpian? Why should anyone attempt to do so? Or, perhaps the answer should be sought in the political instability of the period: the increasing weakness of the Empire from the third century onwards made juristic activity less likely. How could anyone write legal texts when the Empire was crumbling all around? But political instability is not necessarily a cause of intellectual aridity—witness the last century of the Republic, when there was no shortage of distinguished jurists. Or, perhaps we must attribute it to Rome's conversion to Christianity, which resulted in many men of high intellectual calibre devoting themselves to serve the Church. That deprived the State of the type of talented individuals who might have become jurists in former times. This explanation, however, fails to account for the absence of eminent jurists in the period between the death of Modestinus (AD 244) and Rome's conversion.

A more satisfactory explanation may be that Diocletian's bureaucratic reforms required anonymity among the draftsmen of his legislation—everything had to appear to emanate from the Emperor. The transition of the Roman Empire from Principate to Dominate meant that juristic activity lost its individuality. But this theory, too, fails to explain the absence of outstanding jurists in the generation *before* Diocletian. In any case, even under Diocletian, a talented individual could make his name, e.g. Hermogenianus. He was the author of a collection of imperial decrees, the *Codex Hermogenianus*, some of which he may have personally drafted. Honoré identifies him (*Emperors and Lawyers*, 1981) as secretary of the office of petitions for a while under Diocletian, and considers his rescripts to have been of the highest quality: they constitute 'a legal education in themselves' (119). His work was of sufficient importance to be quoted in Justinian's *Digest*.

Not all juristic activity in the later Empire was confined to drafting imperial decrees. There was a post-classical literature of sorts; but it was anonymous and lacking in originality. The most important examples, *Collatio legum Mosaicarum et Romanarum* and the *Fragmenta Vaticana*, date probably from the early fourth century, and consist of summaries from classical works and imperial legislation. Even the most competent summary runs the risk of distorting the original to some extent. In the confusion caused by post-classical summaries, Gaius' *Institutes* understandably came to be regarded as a model exposition of classical law. The work hardly needed summarizing.

The problems resulting from the distortion of classical writings necessitated the establishing of an authoritative canon of such works, and rules to deal with conflicting texts. Constantine, for example, prohibited the use of the notes of Paul and Ulpian on Papinian. In AD 426, the Law of Citations was enacted, by which five jurists were singled out as having primary authority in disputed cases: Gaius, Papinian, Paul, Ulpian, and Modestinus. Quotations by these jurists of other jurists' works were to be considered authoritative. If there was a conflict of opinion among the authoritative texts, the majority view was to prevail. In the event of there being no majority, the judge had a discretion to decide the case as he pleased unless Papinian had expressed a view, in which case it had to be followed. This somewhat mechanical rule had the merit of practical expediency. Nevertheless, the counting of heads (rather than the assessment of the merits of opinions) may be seen as a regrettable basis for a rule that was intended to resolve conflicting authorities. The rule has been criticized as being symptomatic of the alleged intellectual fatigue of the age.

2.4.2 Post-classical legislation

The amount of legislation increased in the later Empire, especially in the East. This was hardly surprising, in view of the manifold problems of that era. The forms of imperial legislation were broadly the same as in the classical period, although there was perhaps a greater variety of *rescripta*. Imperial decrees became increasingly verbose, full of rhetorical flourishes glorifying the achievements of the Emperor. The large number of decrees issued, not all carefully drafted, created confusion and conflicts. Some attempts to resolve the problem were not particularly effective. For example, Constantine decreed that rescripts 'contrary to the law' were invalid—an ambiguous provision which seemed to ignore that rescripts themselves were 'law', and that later law normally repealed earlier law (see C.Th.1.2.2.). At the end of the fourth century, it was decreed that rescripts were not to be regarded as authoritative except for the case for which they were issued (see C.Th.1.2.11.). Theodosius II amended that rule by making rescripts *generally* authoritative if they were expressed to be of general application (cf. Justinian's decree in C.1.14.12pr.).

The informal division of the Empire that resulted from Diocletian's reforms created a problem over the validity of imperial decrees. Were decrees issued by an Emperor binding on other Emperors? The early practice was for imperial decrees to be issued in the name of all the Emperors: they were thus regarded as valid throughout all parts of the Empire. But the rule eventually proved to be inconvenient. In AD 439, Theodosius II enacted that decrees should not be applicable in the territory of another Emperor without his consent.

The post-classical era witnessed a number of compilations of imperial decrees. The *Codex Gregorianus c.* AD 291 contained all the extant decrees issued in the previous 100 years. The *Codex Hermogenianus c.* AD 295 consisted of decrees made in the years immediately before its publication. Both compilations were 'unofficial' in that they were not issued in the name of a specific Emperor (possibly Diocletian). Nevertheless, it is inconceivable that they could have been issued without imperial approval. But easily the most important compilation of the later Empire was the Theodosian Code AD 438, which consisted of all the imperial legislation (then in force) enacted since the reign of Constantine. The material was contained in 16 volumes, each divided into titles within which the decrees were listed in chronological order. This scheme was not original: it had been used in the compilations under Diocletian, which themselves had followed the arrangement of material in some of the works of the classical period. The Theodosian Code reflected the tensions and problems of the age, especially in relation to taxation and ecclesiastical issues. Historians regard it as a prime source of evidence for the tumultuous events of the period. Apart from the Twelve Tables and Justinian's codification, the Theodosian Code was the most important code in Roman legal history. Indeed, it proved a model to some extent for Justinian's own codification. Theodosius II also planned a compilation of juristic literature, but the plan was not implemented. See Harries, J., 'Roman Law Codes and the Roman Legal Tradition' in *Beyond Dogmatics*, 125–38.

2.4.3 Legal development

The practice and development of Roman law in the post-classical era was particularly influenced by the Roman Empire's conversion to Christianity, by Eastern customs, the barbarian invasions, and the work of the law schools.

2.4.3.1 Christianity

The conversion to Christianity had some impact on the content and character of the law. A complex ecclesiastical law was developed in an attempt to define the relationship between Church and State. The status of the clergy and church functionaries had to be clarified. New offences were created that were intended to protect ecclesiastical property and those working in the service of the Church. Further, parts of the civil law were affected by the conversion, especially the law of persons. For example, causeless divorce was subjected to strict sanctions (see 5.2.4.4). But the introduction of Christianity did not lead to the abolition of divorce or slavery, although the legal position of slaves was improved under Justinian (see 4.3.4.1).

2.4.3.2 Eastern influence

The gradual shift eastwards of the fulcrum of the Roman Empire had important consequences for legal development. Constantine and his successors were sympathetic to Eastern customs and ideas, with the result that Roman law acquired a Byzantine hue in the late Empire. The law of persons was considerably influenced by Greek practices. For example, the custom whereby the bridegroom made a substantial gift to his bride on marriage was given recognition by late imperial legislation (see 5.2.5.5). The converse practice (recognized in early Roman law) by which the husband was given a dowry by the wife or her family was also affected by Greek custom: legislation reduced his rights in the dowry. The significance of custom as an indirect source of law in the late Empire was reflected in Justinian's codification:

Julian, *Digest, book 84*: **Age-encrusted custom is not undeservedly cherished as having almost statutory force....For given that statutes themselves are binding upon us for no other reason than that they have been accepted by the judgment of the populace, certainly it is fitting that what the populace has approved without any writing shall be binding upon everyone.** (D.1.3.32.1.)

Although this passage is attributed to Julian, the attribution is suspect, given what we know about the centralizing tendencies of his time. It is doubtful whether Julian would have described custom as having 'almost statutory force'. The authors of the text were most probably the compilers of Justinian's *Digest*, reflecting the revived importance of custom following its relative demise as a source of law after the Twelve Tables.

2.4.3.3 Barbarian codes

The collapse of the Western Empire resulted in large parts of it coming under the control of victorious barbarian kings, some of whom issued codes of law for the conquered territories. These codes were intended primarily for Roman citizens. The most important example was the *lex Romana Visigothorum*, promulgated in AD 506 by the Visigoth chief, Alaric II. It consisted of a mixture of legislation (mainly from the Theodosian Code) and abridged extracts from classical jurists, especially Gaius and Paul—a debased form of Roman law, but of enduring influence. It remained in use in parts of the former Western Empire until the early medieval period. The *lex Romana Burgundiorum* (early sixth century) was intended for Roman citizens living in the area that now broadly constitutes eastern France. It was a collection of legal rules, systematically arranged into titles and based on mainly classical sources. The *Edictum Theodorici* dates from roughly the same period, and was most probably the work of the Ostrogoth chief, Theodoric. Unlike the other codes mentioned above, the *Edictum Theodorici* applied to barbarians as well as Romans, and was primarily intended to aid the interpretation of existing law.

'Vulgarization' is the term which has sometimes been used to describe the influence of Christianity, Eastern custom, and the barbarian codes on Roman law in the post-classical era—not an especially illuminating term since it is capable of different meanings. In its most derogatory sense, vulgarization refers to the debasement of Roman law that the barbarian codes particularly can be said to represent. Or, vulgarization can be taken (in a more technical sense) to refer to the overt departure from the classical norms of legal development. The term can also encompass the inevitable divergence between the law practised in remote parts of the Empire and that applied in and around Rome and Constantinople. Further, vulgarization can be interpreted as the way in which the *practice* of Roman law allegedly became crude and unscientific in the later Empire.

2.4.3.4 Law schools

The temptation to portray the whole of the post-classical era as one of decline and intellectual fatigue must be resisted. In the East, there was a substantial revival of legal learning in the fifth century, under Theodosius II especially, the work principally of the law schools at Beirut and Constantinople. There were other schools—Rome, Alexandria, Athens—but Beirut and Constantinople achieved by far the greatest eminence. The basic method of instruction was by lectures, involving detailed consideration of classical texts. This concerted return to the original texts heralded a renaissance in the science of law, and fostered the intellectual climate necessary for Justinian's great works of the sixth century.

2.5 Justinian's codification

We have already seen that Justinian's codification of Roman law was not the only achievement of that remarkable reign. But it was by far the most durable success, making possible the Reception of Roman law in medieval Europe and (thereafter) in many other parts of the world. The codification process was begun in AD 528, just a few months after Justinian succeeded to the imperial throne. This seems to be a remarkably short period before the commencement of a major project, but Justinian had been the effective ruler of the Eastern Empire during much of his predecessor's short reign, and it is likely that he planned the codification before becoming Emperor. The confused state of the law was a source of great concern for Justinian. The Theodosian Code was not designed to be a comprehensive restatement of the law and the decline in legal science precipitated by the law of citations, combined with the existence of a host of new imperial legislation, made it difficult to ascertain the law on any given matter. His chief minister for much of the codification project was Tribonian, the holder of several important offices, including that of consul and quaestor, and a man of great learning who was familiar with the works of the classical jurists. Justinian had the highest regard for Tribonian's abilities, and was prepared to overlook, according to the Greek writer Procopius (to a large extent), the latter's involvement in corrupt practices, his allegedly pagan leanings, and his marked unpopularity with sections of the Constantine nobility. The main stages of the codification comprised the *Codex vetus*, the Fifty Decisions, the *Digest*, the *Institutes*, the New Code, and the *Novellae*. See Mousourakis, *Legal History*, 179–91. It should be stressed that the *Codex vetus* and the Fifty Decisions do not form part of the eventual *Corpus Iuris Civilis*. They were merely preparatory in purpose.

For a good recent account, see Kaiser, W., 'Justinian and the *Corpus Iuris Civilis*', in *Cambridge Companion*, 119–48.

2.5.1 The *Codex vetus*

In the *Constitutio Deo auctore*, the imperial decree which authorized the compilation of the *Digest*, Justinian explains the first stage of the codification:

> [W]e have found the whole extent of our laws which has come down from the foundation of the city of Rome...to be so confused that it extends to an inordinate length and is beyond the comprehension of any human nature. It has been our primary endeavor to make a beginning with the most revered Emperors of earlier times, to free their *constitutiones* (enactments) from faults and set them out in a clear fashion, so that they might be collected together in one *Codex*, and that they might afford to all mankind the ready protection of their own integrity, purged of all unnecessary repetition and most harmful disagreement. (C. *Deo auctore*, 1.)

This first stage consisted of a compilation of all extant imperial legislation. Justinian, by way of an imperial pronouncement (*Constitutio Haec*), created a commission of ten men to collect all imperial enactments still in force. It was an updating exercise, a revision particularly of the Theodosian Code and the codes of Diocletian's reign. The compilation was carried out by a commission under John of Cappadocia, one of Justinian's leading ministers. It included Tribonian and Theophilus, professor at the Constantinople law school. The commission had wide powers to eliminate obsolete and confusing material. The work took little over a year and was published in AD 529. The code superseded all previous imperial legislation—the Theodosian Code and all others were thereby repealed. No copy of this code has survived and its content is only known from an extant index page. The description *vetus* ('old') was appended later to distinguish the code from the New Code AD 534. The drafting of the New Code was necessitated by the growing mass of imperial legislation produced by Justinian after the enactment of the first code.

2.5.2 The Fifty Decisions

In AD 530, Justinian issued a series of decrees that abolished obsolete rules and resolved a number of controversial points of law found in juristic literature. These decrees were published (probably in the same year) in the form of a separate collection—the Fifty Decisions of which no copy has survived.

The publication of the Fifty Decisions and the *Codex vetus* would have done much to eliminate the confusion in the law that plagued the practitioners of the time. It is possible that this was the limit of Justinian's original scheme, and that it was Tribonian who persuaded him to embark on the much more daunting task of summarizing the literature of the jurists. After all, Tribonian was a distinguished scholar, the possessor of an outstanding library, and a man who in some ways resembled the great jurists of the past. On the other hand, everything that we know of Justinian suggests that he was a man of huge ambition who was unlikely to have been satisfied by a relatively modest tampering with the law. He was well aware that Theodosius II had planned, but failed to achieve, a compilation of classical juristic literature a century or so earlier. A desire to outdo his illustrious predecessor was no doubt a strong motivating factor for Justinian. Honoré concludes that the credit for the *Digest* conception must be shared between Justinian and Tribonian. See Honoré, A. M., *Tribonian* (1978), 141.

2.5.3 The *Digest*

The *Digest* (or *Pandects*) was the centrepiece of Justinian's work, a legal encyclopaedia that is regarded as by far the most important source of Roman law. It has survived intact in a manuscript made not long after the *Digest*'s compilation—the so-called Florentine text. The *Digest* was the culmination of the rebirth of legal learning that was evident in the law schools of the Eastern Empire in the fifth century. It consists of an anthology of juristic literature, mainly of the late classical period, updated for contemporary use by Justinian's compilers. It has provided a fecund source of material, a treasure house of riches for use in subsequent ages. Few works from the ancient world have had such a profound influence on modern civilization. Justinian intended the *Digest* to be a model for his empire, but he failed in his aim. The *Digest* was too large, too complex, too ill-arranged, ever to succeed; but it did contain a huge mass of material that was found to be invaluable in later ages. Justinian thus achieved a great deal, although not in the way that he had envisaged.

2.5.3.1 The compilation of the *Digest*

The *Constitutio Deo auctore*, enacted in December AD 530, and the *Constitutio Tanta* (December 533) reveal much about the compilation of the *Digest*, or at least what Justinian chooses to tell us. Tribonian was put in charge and instructed to find suitable assistants:

> [W]e commanded you to select as colleagues in your task those whom you thought fit, both from the most eloquent professors and from the most able of the robed men of the highest lawcourt. These men have now been brought together, introduced into the palace...and we have entrusted to them the execution of the entire task, on the understanding that the whole enterprise will be carried out under your own most vigilant supervision. (C. *Deo auctore*, 3.)

The chosen commissioners comprised a mixture of leading academics, practitioners, and government ministers—a total of 17 (including Tribonian). There were four professors from the law schools: Dorotheus and Anatolius from Beirut; Theophilus and Cratinus from Constantinople. What was the task of the commission?

> We therefore command you to read and work upon the books dealing with Roman law, written by those learned men of old to whom the most revered Emperors gave authority to compose and interpret the laws, so that the whole substance may be extracted from them, all repetition and discrepancy being as far as possible removed, and out of them one single work may be compiled, which will suffice in place of them all. (C. *Deo auctore*, 4.)

This was a most ambitious task, especially the elimination of 'repetition and discrepancy', an aim which was not attained. There are many examples of repetition and inconsistencies to be found in the *Digest* (as will be seen later), despite the following proud claim:

> As for any contradiction occurring in this book, none such has found a place for itself, and none will be discovered by anyone who reflects acutely upon the modes of diversity. (C. *Tanta*, 15.)

One should applaud the ambition of the compilers, but the most acute reflection down the centuries has failed to reconcile some of the conflicting passages in the *Digest*.

A large number of juristic works from various periods were read and excerpted—as many as were available and thought worthy of use. Some of the works were supplied by Tribonian himself:

> Of the ancient learning, that most excellent man Tribonian has supplied us with a very large quantity of books, many of which were unknown even to the most learned men themselves. All these were read through, and whatever was most valuable was extracted and found its way into our excellent composition. (C. *Tanta*, 17.)

We are informed that approximately 2,000 books were read and excerpted. This was an exaggeration: the evidence suggests between 1,500 and 1,600. An index of authors and works was issued with the *Digest*; it indicates that excerpts were taken from the works of 38 different jurists, but many more are quoted in turn by those writers. The compilation necessitated the repeal of the Law of Citations (see 2.4.1), since all jurists who were quoted in the *Digest* were to be regarded as of equal authority. However, the works of the jurists who were specifically named in the Law of Citations form the bulk of the *Digest*, especially Ulpian, Paul, and Gaius, who between them account for over half the excerpts. The overall arrangement of the contents followed the traditional scheme to be found in the major classical commentaries. On the imperial decree which set this project in motion, see Pugsley, D., 'The Constitution ad senatum of 22 July 530' 1995 (42) RIDA, 289–329 (reprinted in Pugsley, D. (2000) *Justinian's Digest and the Compilers*, 100–42.)

2.5.3.2 Interpolations

Justinian intended the *Digest* not only to be a summary of the literature of the jurists, but also to provide the practitioners of his own time with a workable text. In trying to achieve the latter aim, Justinian's commission was given the power to amend juristic writing in some circumstances:

> All we have done is to provide that if in their legal rulings there seemed to be anything superfluous or imperfect or unsuitable, it should be amplified or curtailed to the requisite extent and be reduced to the most correct form. (C. *Tanta*, 10.)

That the power was used extensively cannot be doubted, despite the fact that the amendments, known as interpolations, are not obvious. The compilers attributed excerpts to named jurists but did not acknowledge interpolations. So a jurist may be quoted as saying something that he did not write. Then interpolations can be detected in various ways. For example, comparison of surviving classical or Byzantine texts with those quoted in the *Digest* may reveal interpolations; so may the lack of coherence or logic in a quoted passage, although it is dangerous to assume that classical jurists were incapable of such lapses. Another fruitful way of detecting interpolations has been to compare the style, construction, and vocabulary of passages in the *Digest* with what is known about the use of Latin in the classical era, and about the style of a particular jurist. The *Digest* was compiled in Latin by commissioners whose first tongue was probably Greek (although Latin was the official language of the courts). And the Latin of the time was not identical to that of Paul and Ulpian. But there are dangers in the linguistic approach: it cannot be assumed that classical jurists never lapsed into sloppy, unidiomatic language. Interpolations can also be detected by the presence of legal terminology not known to have been used until late law.

Modern scholarship has pointed to the existence of numerous interpolations, but it is not always clear who was responsible for them. The assumption that they were necessarily made by Justinian's commission should be resisted. Some interpolations could have been made earlier, possibly by the academics of the law schools of the East. Justinian's commission may well have been using some texts that had already been interpolated. In the early twentieth century, the search for interpolations by Romanists became an obsession. Certainly, interpolations do matter if attention is focused solely on classical law, because then it is important to discover its true content (for which the *Digest* is scarcely a reliable indicator). But it would be shortsighted to focus exclusively on classical law. Classical law is not Roman law, or at least not the whole of it. Interpolations should not be viewed in a derogatory sense, as if they indicated some impurity or debasement of the law, but rather as necessary amendments for the provision of a working code. The heyday of interpolation criticism has now given way to a more balanced (and cautious) approach to the identification of interpolations. While it is universally accepted that interpolations exist in the *Corpus Iuris Civilis*, scholars now generally assume, given the scope of the mandate given to the drafting commission and the speed with which the compilation was completed, that the classical 'core' of most texts must have remained intact and that the majority of changes were purely cosmetic. On the current state of interpolation criticism in Romanist scholarship, see Johnston, D., 'Justinian's Digest: The Interpretation of Interpolation' (1989) 9 Oxford Journal LS, 149–66; Watson, A., 'Prolegomena to Establishing Pre-Justinianic Texts' (1994) 62 TR, 113–25 where the author argues, using the instructions given by Justinian to the compilers, to what extent the substance of the law set out in Justinian's *Digest* and *Code* were altered, and Lokin, J. H. A., 'The End of an Epoch: Epilegomena to a Century of Interpolation Criticism', in *Collatio Iuris Romani* I, 261–73. See also Robinson, *Sources*, 105–13.

2.5.3.3 Preventing distortion

Justinian's regard of the *Digest* as a model for the future can be seen from his attempts to ban any commentaries on the work:

No skilled lawyers are to presume in the future to supply commentaries thereon and confuse with their own verbosity the brevity of the aforesaid work, in the way that was done in former times, when by the conflicting opinions of expositors the whole of the law was virtually thrown into confusion. (C. *Deo auctore*, 12.)

However, he allowed translations to be made, and explanatory notes on difficult passages. How were difficulties to be resolved?

But if ... anything should appear doubtful, this is to be referred by judges to the very summit of the Empire and made clear by the imperial authority, to which alone it is granted both to create laws and to interpret them. (C. *Tanta*, 21.)

It is likely that the rules laid down by Justinian to prevent confusion applied to other parts of the codification, not just to the *Digest*. Despite his best efforts, it seems that commentaries were beginning to appear even before the end of his reign.

2.5.3.4 **The speed of compilation**

The *Digest* was completed in three years rather than the 10 years originally envisaged. Given that most of the commissioners probably did not work full-time on the *Digest* (because of their other activities), the time taken for its compilation does seem remarkably short. The compilers not only had to read and excerpt books but also had to amend the texts where necessary. It is quite conceivable that an earlier digest could have been compiled at one of the law schools before Justinian's accession, perhaps by one or more of the professors who served on the commission (the Peters-theory of the Pre-Digest). Could that have been an unstated reason for their appointment? The work would then have been already mostly done. Such speculation is attractive, but lacking in hard facts. No copies of an earlier digest are known to have survived. Would the commission have suppressed such a work and lied about their achievements? Hardly—it would have been difficult to maintain a conspiracy of falsehood for long. In any case, Tribonian may have been involved in some dubious practices, but he was hardly a burner of books; nor were the professors from the law schools. A more convincing explanation may be that the books that allegedly were read by the compilers were actually *not* read. The commission contained the finest legal brains of the Empire. These men would already be familiar with the texts that they were excerpting, particularly Tribonian and the academics on the commission. But the weakness in this explanation is that we are specifically told by Justinian that many books were read which had been previously unknown to the commissioners, apart from Tribonian (see C. *Tanta*, 17, earlier). Honoré considers—principally in *Tribonian*, ch. 5—that three years was quite feasible given the high degree of organization evident in Tribonian's commission, and the fact that the books read were on average only about 10,000 words in length.

Another plausible explanation is the effect of the Nika riots AD 532, which nearly ended Justinian's reign (see 1.3.6.2). Traditionally, the two leading political factions in Constantinople, the Blues and the Greens, expressed their rivalry through chariot races at the Hippodrome, each party cheering on its representatives. Great discontent with Justinian's government, especially because of the imposition of a stricter tax regime on the wealthy, led to the Blues and Greens for once uniting in rebellion against the Emperor. The riots probably acted as a catalyst for the speedy completion of the work. They demonstrated to Justinian the insecurity of his tenure of the imperial throne, and the need for him to achieve a notable success as quickly as possible: 'Justinian gave instructions for it to be completed as a matter of top priority. The publication of the final text would be a major event in itself, but it would also be an occasion for a substantial public-relations exercise' (Pugsley, *Justinian's Digest and the Compilers*, 2). The fact that some of the work was done rather sloppily, especially the final editing, tends to support this explanation. On the other hand, Justinian had already urged speed, well before the Nika riots, when instructing Tribonian to accomplish the task as quickly as possible. Ironically, one of the causes of the riots had been the alleged maladministration of justice due to Tribonian's devotion of his time to the work on the *Digest*. Honoré regards the riots as having only a slight impact on the work of the commission (*Tribonian*, 56), but it is hard to accept that this near-fatal jolt to Justinian's reign had an insignificant effect on its progress. See also Pugsley, D., 'Twin Texts and the Compilers' Working methods,' 1997 (3) Orbis Iuris Romani, 40–56, reprinted in Pugsley, D. (2000), *Justinian's Digest and the Compilers*, 143–60.

2.5.3.5 **Arrangement of material**

Justinian does not tell us everything about the compilation of the *Digest*. Modern scholarship has filled in much that is missing. In particular, the work of Bluhme, a German scholar of the early nineteenth century, has demonstrated that the arrangement of material within each title (i.e. major section) of the *Digest* is not as haphazard as would appear at first sight. The material divides broadly into three groups (or 'masses') of works, each group probably compiled by a subcommittee of Tribonian's commission. The three subcommittees were: *(a)* the Sabinian, concerned with commentaries on the *ius civile* produced by Paul, Ulpian, and other classical jurists that were arranged according to the system introduced by Sabinus; *(b)* the Edictal, concerned with works on the *ius honorarium* and more specifically on the praetorian edict; and *(c)* the Papinian, concerned with problematic literature, the genre in which Papinian excelled. In the editorial stage, the excerpts within each title were arranged in the order Sabinian, Edictal, Papinian. Moreover, Bluhme identified a smaller group, the Appendix mass, consisting of miscellaneous works that he claimed did not readily fit into the three main masses. Excerpts from the Appendix mass are normally found placed last within each title. Bluhme suggested that the works in the Appendix probably came to the notice of the commission late in the day, and that the excerpting was done by the Papinian committee as it appears to have had the lightest workload. The outlines of Bluhme's theory have been widely accepted. The probability that the work was divided between three subcommittees helps to explain the speed of the compilation. However, the part of the theory pertaining to the Appendix has been criticized. It is rather unlikely that the commission discovered books late in the day that it had not known about previously.

The 11 practitioners on the commission were probably co-opted onto the subcommittees only when the need arose. The other six commissioners were probably divided into three groups of two and were assigned to a particular subcommittee. Tribonian had overall responsibility for the compilation, which appears to have been actively supervised by Justinian. Professor Honoré regards the work of the commission as meticulously planned, the emphasis on careful delegation of key tasks (he likens it to a modern law commission). He has proposed that the committees worked in parallel on the list of books assigned to each, the Sabinian and Edictal committees reading and excerpting seven books per week, the Papinian five. Each committee had two senior commissioners (a chairman and a junior member) and within each committee 'the excerpting was divided between the two commissioners, each assisted by a team of barristers when necessary' (*Tribonian*, 142). The excerpting took some 18 months to complete, whereupon 'the assembled excerpts, classified by titles and committees, were united in the form of a first draft of the *Digest*' (Honoré, *Tribonian*, 142). This first draft took about eight months to complete, followed by final editing before enactment in December 533. Honoré regards Tribonian's chairmanship of the *Digest* commission as: 'one of the most brilliant feats of organisation in the history of civil administration' (*Tribonian*, 186). Osler, D. J. doubts Professor Honoré's assertion that each subcommittee divided the work of reading and excerpting equally between its two senior commissioners: see (1985) 102 ZSS (rA), 129–84 where the author argues that the numerical basis of Honoré's theory on the work of the commissioners is without foundation. Moreover, Pugsley (*Justinian's Digest and the Compilers*) questions whether the degree of planning and organization was as pronounced as Honoré claims, and suggests that the Papinian committee started late because it did not exist when work on the *Digest* commenced: it was established only when a trial run revealed that a third committee was required (17–39). See most recently Honoré, 'Late Arrivals—The Appendix in Justinian's Digest Reconsidered', in *Mapping the Law*, 497–512.

2.5.4 The *Institutes*

Justinian reorganized legal education, decreeing that students should receive formal tuition for the first three years, followed by two years of private study. The *Digest* was intended to provide the core of the new programme. Realizing that the *Digest* was likely to prove rather daunting for beginners, Justinian instructed Dorotheus and Theophilus (under the supervision of Tribonian) to prepare an introductory textbook:

So after the completion of the fifty books of the Digest or Pandects, in which all the ancient law is collected (a work we completed through that same exalted person Tribonian and other illustrious and capable men), we ordered the *Institutes* to be divided into these four books, and to provide the first elements of the whole science of law. In them there is a brief exposition of the law which used to be in force and then that which, obscured by disuse, has been clarified by Imperial reform. They have been compiled from all the books of Institutes written by the classical lawyers, and especially from the works of our Gaius, both his Institutes and his Daily Matters, and many other commentaries. (*Prooemium* to the *Institutes*, §§ 4–6.)

They were to draw on the elementary works of the classical period, especially the *Institutes* of Gaius. The compilers divided the material into four books, as Gaius had done, but divided the work into titles (unlike Gaius). The *Institutes* were promulgated on the same day as the *Digest* and received the force of law, an unusual distinction for a student textbook. See Van Warmelo, P., 'The Institutes of Justinian as Students' Manual', in *Studies in Justinian's Institutes*, 164–80.

2.5.5 The New Code and *Novellae*

The flurry of legislative activity that occurred after the enactment of the *Codex vetus* soon necessitated a revision of the earlier code. The work was carried out by Tribonian, aided by a small commission, and was promulgated in AD 534. The New Code superseded all previous codes. It was designed to incorporate imperial constitutions produced after the enactment of the first Code as well as to remove unnecessary repetitions and obsolete matters. The New Code consisted of 12 books subdivided into titles covering specific topics. Individual imperial pronouncements are arranged in chronological order within these titles.

Justinian's reign lasted for over 30 years after the promulgation of the New Code. He continued to legislate frequently, introducing important reforms in the law relating to the family and inheritance (see, e.g. 8.3.4). These changes were effected by a series of individual decrees, the *novellae constitutiones* ('the new decrees'). The *novellae* are best regarded as constituting part of the codification, although this is not a view held universally.

Justinian's codification (sometimes referred to as the *Corpus Iuris Civilis*) was partly intended to reduce the law to manageable proportions, and to make it more easily available:

We saw it was necessary, therefore, that we should make manifest the same system of law to all men, so that they might perceive how greatly they have been relieved from a state of confusion and uncertainty.... In the future may they have laws that are straightforward as well as brief, and easily available to all, and also such that it is easy to possess the books containing them, so that men may not need to obtain with a great expenditure of wealth volumes containing a large quantity of redundant laws, but the means of procuring them for a trifling sum may be given to both rich and poor and great learning be available at a very small cost. (C. *Tanta*, 13.)

The reality was that parts of the codification were too complex. Even practitioners struggled with the *Digest*, so that it was scarcely being used in the courts at the time of Justinian's death.

Justinian did much more than *just* codify the law. His reforms of the substantive law and of legal education were manifold and far-reaching. Hardly an area of the law was left untouched by him. Simply as a law reformer he stands supreme among Roman Emperors, with the possible exception of Augustus.

 online resource centre   Please consult the Online Resource Centre for revision guidance on this chapter.

FURTHER READING

On Roman society and the state of the law in the time of the Twelve Tables, see Watson, A. (1975), *Rome of the Twelve Tables: Persons and Property*, Princeton: Princeton University Press.

On the Roman Emperor and his judicial functions, see Millar, F. (1977), *The Emperor in the Roman World (31 BC–AD 337)*, London: Duckworth.

On the jurists of the Empire, see Syme, R., 'Fiction about Roman Jurists' (1980) 97 ZSS (rA), 78–104, in which the author refutes various inaccuracies about the lives of Roman jurists.

On the Theodosian Code, see Harries, J. and Wood, I. (1993), *The Theodosian Code: Studies in the Imperial Law of Late Antiquity*, London: Duckworth; Honoré, A. M. (1998), *Law in the Crisis of Empire, 379–455 AD*, Oxford: Clarendon Press; and Matthews, J. F. (2000), *Laying Down the Law: A Study of the Theodosian Code*, New Haven/London: Yale University Press.

On Justinian's project, see Honoré, T. (2010), *Justinian's Digest: Character and Compilation*, Oxford: Oxford University Press.

3

....

Roman litigation

3.1 **The perils of litigation**

'Who is the good man?', asks Horace, the Roman poet (*Epistles*, I, xvi, 40). He tells us that the attributes of the 'good man' include serving as a witness, acting as a guarantor, and settling cases as a judge (cf. Bablitz, *Actors and Audience*, ch. 4). This may seem an unpoetic reply to the tantalizing question posed, but Horace wanted to emphasize the sense of duty and responsibility that was expected of the Roman citizen. To have shied away from such involvement in the legal process, without a compelling reason, would have been considered to be distinctly bad form. But when it came to appearing as a *litigant*, the Roman citizen would normally blanch at the prospect. Of course, there were occasions when a citizen found it difficult to avoid going to court—e.g. when it was necessary to protect his honour and reputation. But sensitivity over one's good name could act as an inhibiting factor. Anyone whose reputation might suffer by exposure in the courts would be reluctant to sue. Litigation should be avoided like the plague, Cicero advised, even when the law was on your side. Litigation was regarded by many as undignified and not to be seriously considered by the man of good sense and restraint.

3.1.1 **The Roman advocate**

The danger of losing your reputation was but one of the perils involved in litigation. Another was the sheer abuse that you would suffer from your opponent's advocate. Roman advocates (a profession which emerged during the mid-Republic) generally lacked the jurists' expertise in the finer points of the law, but were skilled in oratory—Cicero, for example. Many of them, especially those of the late Republic, were trained in the Greek rhetorical method of oratory, which the advocate could use in both stages of the trial (see Cicero, *De Oratore* I., 166 ff.) to blacken the name of his client's opponent. See Tellegen, *Short History*, 58–9. Imagine yourself in court confronted by a Cicero in full cry: you would have to put up with a great deal of ritual abuse (*vituperatio*) about your looks, habits, breeding, and so forth. For example, in *Pro Quinctio* (a partnership dispute) Cicero likened his client's opponent to a clown, and alleged that he was ill-bred and a dabbler in fraudulent practices, *inter alia*. It is probable, however, that such abuse was less intimidating than might be supposed. The very fact that it was *ritual* abuse robbed it of some of its sting (see further, Kelly, *Civil Judicature*, ch. 4; Bablitz, *Actors and Audience*, ch. 6).

3.1.2 **The procedural system**

The system of procedure, or lack of a system, constituted a major disincentive to involvement in litigation, especially in Republican Rome, since the State's involvement in civil procedure was minimal (in both the *legis actio* and formulary procedure). This was because of the notion that litigation was essentially 'a private arbitration established under the approval of the State, as a substitute for self-help, the business of the State officials being only to see that this arbitration is conducted in proper form' (Buckland and McNair, *Roman Law and Common Law*, 400). For example, (apart from the *cognitio* procedure) the plaintiff was solely responsible for ensuring the presence of the defendant in court. That could prove a difficult or impossible task. Further, even if the plaintiff got his defendant into court and succeeded in winning his case, the State took a minor role in the enforcement of the judgment. Moreover, between summons and judgment, there were several procedural stages that were characterized by a high degree of formalism, when the slightest mistake could be fatal to the success of the action.

For a comprehensive recent account, see Metzger, E., 'Litigation', in *Cambridge Companion*, 272–98.

3.1.3 **Economic factors**

There was an economic disincentive inherent in early procedure—the requirement in certain types of action that the parties should deposit a sum of money as a wager on the outcome of the case (see the *legis actio sacramento* at 3.2.2.1). This constituted a major hurdle for some prospective litigants, especially during the currency shortages that regularly affected the Republic in its early days. Although the winner recovered the deposit, the risk of losing it—as well as the case—was undoubtedly an inhibiting factor. On the other hand, the actual cost of litigation was not prohibitive, at least until the later Empire. Republican advocates frequently did not take fees: they came from predominantly wealthy, aristocratic backgrounds, and pursued their advocacy partly out of a sense of duty to fellow citizens, partly as a hopeful step on the road to achieving political distinction, and partly as a way of earning favours. A formal prohibition against taking fees was introduced in 204 BC, but was eventually ended under Claudius when a maximum fee was fixed. See Crook, *Law and Life of Rome*, 90 ff., cf. Bablitz, *Actors and Audience*, chs. 3 and 6.

3.1.4 **Corruption**

It is hard to conceive that a legal system has ever existed (or could exist) that was totally free of corruption. Roman law was certainly not such a system. Severe penalties were imposed on corrupt judges in early law and thereafter, which suggests that the problem of corruption was a constant factor in Roman legal history. Some praetors were known to bend the rules occasionally to suit themselves and their friends. Some were accused of legacy hunting, i.e. doing favours for wealthy litigants in the expectation of a legacy in the litigant's will. These were important factors in the loss of prestige that the praetorship experienced in the transitional era from Republic to Empire. See Bablitz, *Actors and Audience*, ch. 4.

Roman literature contains much sarcastic comment about corrupt practices in the law. A common allegation was that the successful litigant was the one who could afford to bribe the judge. Even allowing for some degree of artistic licence, the literary evidence does suggest that corruption was rife, particularly in the late Republic. Corruption could take a variety of forms: e.g. bribing the praetor, the judge, the jurors, or even the opponent's advocate and witnesses; or influencing the outcome of a case through the exercise of social, political, or economic power, or through the desire to please and earn a favour. The advantages possessed by the wealthy and powerful over their weaker brethren were reflected in the course of litigation. Cases where the defendant was clearly the 'stronger' man in terms of wealth, power, or influence were rare. The weak generally did not sue the strong (see Kelly, *Roman Litigation*, 61, and see generally Chapter 2).

3.1.5 Shaming

Another factor which had an important bearing on litigation was the practice, found particularly in early Rome, of ritual shaming (*flagitatio*). If a man was suspected of dishonourable conduct, he might be subjected to concerted shaming, intended to cause him the maximum public embarrassment. Often it took the form of rude songs and vociferous abuse by a mob congregated outside the home of the 'offender'. Imagine yourself to be an ambitious politician subjected to this kind of treatment. Would you really want it known in the best circles that all this *flagitatio* was going on night after night outside your villa? Most probably you would desist from the conduct that was giving offence, in order to spare yourself further embarrassment. For example, having initially failed to respond to your opponent's summons to court, you would be more persuaded to put in an appearance. On the other hand, as a plaintiff, you would consider abandoning an action if it was likely to provoke public abuse of yourself or your family (see 10.4).

3.1.6 Settlement

The overall effect of the factors outlined above was to create a distinct pressure on parties to settle their disputes rather than go to court. The importance of this practice was demonstrated by the development of specific contractual remedies for the enforcement of settlements (see 9.7.2). Judges would normally encourage the parties not to proceed to judgment. For a large part of Rome's legal history, the typical judge in a civil case was a distinguished layman, frequently a senator, who would worry at having to decide between two powerful men in case he incurred the wrath of the loser. How delighted the judge was when they settled! He might even be viewed as a 'good man' for negotiating a settlement.

3.1.7 Defying the perils

Despite the various perils associated with litigation, people did go to court; but it is not clear with what frequency. However, Kelly, *Civil Judicature*, ch. 4, provides an invaluable insight into the *type* of cases which featured in civil litigation by analysing references in Justinian's *Digest to responsa* and *rescripta* (regarded as reliable indicators of litigation in practice). This shows that cases concerned with the law of inheritance were easily the most frequent, followed by contract and family law. On the other hand, personal injuries (delict) seemed a comparatively rare cause of litigation—the converse of the position in modern English law. The predominance of inheritance cases is perhaps not surprising, given the apparent interest of Romans in will-making and inheritance. But the conclusions must be regarded as tentative—as Kelly readily admits—since it may be, for example, that what attracted juristic attention (and that of the *Digest's* compilers) was not necessarily representative of actual litigation.

3.2 Early procedure: the *legis actiones*

Pomponius, *Manual, sole book*: **Then about the same time actions-at-law whereby people could litigate among themselves were composed out of these statutes [the laws of the** *Twelve Tables*]. **To prevent the citizenry from initiating litigation any old how, the lawmakers' will was that the actions-at-law be in fixed and solemn terms. This branch of law has the name** *legis actiones,* **that is, statutory actions-at-law. And so these three branches of law came into being at almost the same time: once the statute law of the** *Twelve Tables* **was passed, the** *jus civile* **started to emerge from them, and** *legis actiones* **were put together from the same source.** (D.1.2.2.6.)

Pomponius' account of the formulation of the *legis actiones*, the five early forms of action in Roman law, masks the antiquity of some of the actions. They did not all emerge as a result of the Twelve Tables. At least two of the actions predated the Twelve Tables; another dated most probably from the later Republic, see Kelly, *Roman Litigation*, 81–4, and Watson, A., 'The Law of Actions and the Development of Substantive Law in the Early Roman Republic' (1973) 89 LQR, 387–92 (a controversial article about the relationship between substance and procedure in archaic Roman law). All the *legis actiones* were characterized by strict formalism and were only available to Roman citizens. The actions-at-law were the foundation of early civil procedure. The operation of that procedure comprised three main stages—summons, trial, and execution. See Mousourakis, *Legal History*, 31–8.

3.2.1 Summons

The plaintiff was responsible for getting the defendant into court. This was done by oral summons (*in ius vocatio*)—a request with stated reasons that the defendant should go to court with the plaintiff. Because civil litigation was regarded as essentially private arbitration, the theory was that proceedings were not possible without the consent of the parties—a conspicuous feature of Roman civil process. Nevertheless, the defendant was expected to comply, unless he could find someone to guarantee that he would appear in court when required. Failure by the defendant to follow the plaintiff to court or to find a guarantor (*vindex*) allowed the plaintiff to call witnesses and then to drag the defendant to court by force. If the defendant was sick, or infirm through age, transportation had to be arranged. Some restrictions were placed on when a summons could be made. For example, a person engaged in harvesting crops or producing wine could not be compelled to go to court at certain times. If the defendant could not be got to court, proceedings could not continue; however, he was regarded as *indefensus* ('undefended'), a status that entitled the plaintiff to seize his property on the authorization of the praetor.

Where was the action to be brought? The general principle was that the action had to be brought in the forum of the defendant. It is not clear, however, how rigidly this principle was applied: it could obviously cause considerable inconvenience, even to both parties in some circumstances. It seems that the parties were therefore allowed to agree a different forum, but this may not have been possible until classical law (see Crook, *Law and Life of Rome*, 75 and 96).

3.2.2 **Trial**

For the greater part of Roman legal history, the trial stage in civil proceedings was divided into two—a preliminary hearing, followed by a full trial.

3.2.2.1 **Preliminary hearing**

A hearing took place before a magistrate (the praetor after 367 BC) in order to settle the issues between the parties (who had to be present) and to appoint a judge. Proceedings began with a formal exchange of the set words appropriate to the particular course of action. A party could lose his claim through the slightest mistake at this stage. This seemingly excessive formalism is typical of legal systems in their early stages of development, e.g. the English system of writs in the medieval period displayed similar traits. The set form of words that had to be uttered by the parties constituted the actions-at-law of the trial stage. There were three such actions: *sacramentum, postulatio*, and *condictio*.

(a) *Sacramentum* (*Legis actio sacramento*). This was the standard action-at-law in the early Republic. Gaius described it as the 'general' way of starting a case, to be used when no other way was prescribed by statute (Inst.Gai.4.13.). It is probable that *sacramentum* signified the oath made to the gods by the parties when asserting the justice of their claims, and that originally the trial consisted of the exchange of oaths, the issue being decided by ordeal or supernatural invocation, not by a judge.

The procedure in *sacramentum* required the parties to make formal oaths and to deposit a sum of money as a wager on the outcome. The usual requirement was for 50 *asses* (units of early Roman currency) to be staked, but 500 if the matter at issue was worth 1,000 or more. The successful party recovered the deposit, but the loser's was forfeited to the State. The reasons for requiring a deposit from the parties probably lay in the religious origins of *sacramentum*—the deposit was an offering to the gods—rather than in any deliberate attempt to oppress the poorer members of the community. Despite its drawbacks, the requirement of a deposit had the practical consequence of inhibiting frivolous litigation. The sum of 500 *asses* was substantial, and 50 was not a trifling amount.

The procedure in *sacramentum* depended on whether the action was *in rem* or *in personam*. An action *in rem* was an assertion of ownership in a thing, whereas an action *in personam* lay for the enforcement of an obligation owed to the plaintiff by a particular person. Where the action was *in rem*, the disputed thing was normally brought before the magistrate—if it was land, a symbolic sod of earth sufficed. The parties made their respective claims, touched the property with a ceremonial rod (the *festuca/vindicta*), and challenged each other to the wager described earlier. The magistrate then awarded temporary possession to one of the litigants (usually the party in actual possession) until the trial before the judge. This party had to give security (usually a third party known as a *praes* who was willing to pledge his land (*praedium*) as security) that the property would be returned if the case were eventually lost. If the action was *in personam* the procedure was much simpler since title to property was not in issue. The parties made formal assertions, the plaintiff claiming the existence of an obligation, the defendant either conceding or denying it; and they challenged each other to a wager. Whatever the form of *sacramentum*, the rule became established that an interval of 30 days had to elapse before a judge was appointed. This allowed the parties an opportunity to settle.

(b) *Iudicis arbitrive postulatio* (*Legis actio per iudicis arbitrive postulationem*) ('The complaint before the judge or arbiter'). This procedure, introduced after *sacramentum*, was intended as a more convenient form of action for certain types of case (only available for actions *in personam*). It was available when specifically allowed by statute, and then only as an alternative to *sacramentum*, the choice of procedure lying (most probably) with the plaintiff. *Postulatio* was used mainly for claims arising from *stipulatio* (a type of formal contract) and for disputes concerning the division of inheritances and common property. The procedure required the plaintiff to make his claim and to state the grounds for the action, the defendant conceding or denying the claim. This was much simpler than *sacramentum*, no formal oaths, wagers or security being required. With no possibility of forfeiture, *postulatio* was a less risky procedure for the litigants. And it was relatively speedy—a judge was normally appointed forthwith rather than after the lapse of a month.

(c) *Condictio* (*Legis actio per condictionem*). The origins of this procedure are to be found in statutes of the third century BC, thus somewhat later than the previous two actions-at-law. (See St. Tomulescu, C., 'Origin of the Legis Actio per Condictionem' (1969) 4 IJ, 180–6 where the author argues that this action-at-law was created in the third century BC when the position of the plebeian debtor had become stronger than that of the patrician creditor.) The introduction of *condictio* at that time reflected the growing importance of the consensual contracts (such as sale and hire) and the need for a more convenient procedure than *sacramentum*. The interchange of claims and assertions was much less formal than in *sacramentum*, formal oaths not being required. If the defendant denied the claim, the plaintiff gave notice (the *condictio*) that the defendant should appear in 30 days for the appointment of a judge. The action lay for the recovery of a specific thing or specific sum of money. The denial of a claim for a sum of money necessitated an exchange of promises, whereby the successful party was additionally entitled to one-third of the disputed sum, i.e. a plaintiff would recover one and one-third times the sum claimed; a winning defendant would receive one third of the plaintiff's claim.

3.2.2.2 Joinder of issue

Whatever the form of procedure used in the preliminary stage, the critical moment was reached when issue was joined (*litis contestatio*). This occurred on the completion of the parties' assertions, i.e. on the formulation of the issues between them. As seen already, there could not be *litis contestatio* unless both parties submitted to the process: litigation could be pursued only though the consent of the parties. The effect of joinder was to 'consume' the plaintiff's right of action: it could not be brought again on the same facts. But joinder gave the plaintiff a new right—that a trial should be held by a judge, the defendant to be 'condemned', i.e. found liable, if he lost. If the case did not proceed to judgment, however, the plaintiff could not raise the same issues again.

3.2.2.3 **Appointment of judges**

The final stage of the preliminary hearing required the appointment of a judge. Who were the judges, and how were they appointed? Many cases were decided by a single lay judge, the *iudex* or *arbiter*. The terms may have been synonymous but it is more likely that there was a distinction, the *arbiter* tending to hear cases involving a considerable use of discretion, e.g. the division of common property. Several *arbitri* might be appointed in important cases. Or a case could go before the *centumviri* ('the hundred men'), a court usually consisting of some 30 members chosen from a panel that originally contained about 100 representatives of the ancient tribes of Rome (but which later nearly doubled in size). Their jurisdiction lay primarily over inheritance cases, especially those involving large estates. The importance of such cases made the *centumviri* court a prestigious forum. Although the most famous cases brought before the court dated from the late Republic, its origins probably lay much earlier. Another possible forum was the court of the *decemviri* ('the ten men'), minor magistrates of whom little is known other than that they originally heard claims to personal freedom, and that they presided over the *centumviri* court from the time of Augustus (see Tellegen-Couperus, *Short History*, s. 6.4.3). And cases could be heard by *recuperatores* ('recoverers'), a speedy tribunal of lay jurors appointed by a magistrate, which exercised jurisdiction mainly over crime but also over some civil cases, particularly those involving delicts, e.g. robbery and insulting behaviour (see Frier, *Roman Jurists*, 197–268 and Bablitz, *Actors and Audience*, ch. 2).

Judges were normally chosen from an official list (the *album iudicum*) consisting of senators authorized to judge cases. In the late Republic, members of the equestrian order and other classes were included. The judge was appointed by the magistrate involved in the preliminary hearing, following consultation with the parties. If the parties agreed, the magistrate normally followed their choice; if they disagreed, he imposed his choice or settled the matter by drawing lots (see Birks, P., 'New Light on the Roman Legal System: The Appointment of Judges' (1988) 47 Cambridge LJ, 36–60, where the author argues, using the information brought to light by the *Lex Irnitana*, that the practice for the appointment of judges explained in this Spanish municipal charter reflects the practice in Rome during the first century AD). The latter procedure lacked sophistication, but it had its points. A magistrate, faced by two powerful disputants, would be anxious to avoid upsetting either of them by having to make a personal decision.

3.2.2.4 **Full trial**

The trial before the judge was remarkably informal compared to the strict formality of the preliminary hearing. According to the Twelve Tables, the judge was to hear the case in a public place. The trial was often held in the open air. The Forum Romanum was frequently chosen. The parties normally had to be present, but in exceptional cases, (e.g. sickness) could appoint a representative (*procurator*) to take their place. It was presumably through a wider recognition of this practice that the profession of the advocate (*orator*) was born.

The trial proceeded by means of alternate speeches from the advocates, the judge acting as an umpire. There were very few rules of evidence to guide him. Written and oral testimony was allowed, the latter being preferred due to its immediacy. Witnesses were generally not compellable, but refusal to appear as a witness could bring social opprobrium and the status of *intestabilis* (see 4.4.2.6).

The burden of proof was regarded as being on the plaintiff. The hearing was supposed to finish at sunset but occasionally would last into the night. Adjournments were not uncommon, the presence of the parties for the resumption of the case being secured by a *vadimonium*, a formal promise originally made by sureties for the parties (later, the parties themselves made the promise). It seems that the *vadimonium* procedure was used for all adjournments, at whatever stage of proceedings they arose. The judge was often assisted by a body of advisers, consisting mainly of men learned in the law. The judgment—*sententia*, strictly an 'opinion'— was delivered orally in the presence of the parties or their representatives. If the case had been brought as a *sacramentum*, the judgment declared that the oath of one of the parties was 'just'. There was no system of appeals. If the judge was unable to reach a decision, the case was remitted to the original magistrate for the appointment of another judge.

The division of proceedings into preliminary hearing and full trial remained a cardinal feature of Roman civil litigation until well into the Empire. Why the division? The answer lies in the notion of civil litigation as a form of private arbitration where judgment must be the preserve of the layman, the State's role being to police the preliminary stage only:

[F]rom the outset, the Romans regarded the deciding of a dispute not as the function of one who bore authority in the State, but as a task for persons from whom the parties could anticipate an impartial decision. It is the function of authority to supervise the institution and continuation of the action, to issue directions and orders for the course of the proceedings and to prevent their failure; but it is not the magistrate's task to decide the case. Giving judgment is not an act of *will* like the commands and orders which constitute the everyday activity of the magistrate. It is a decision from *knowledge* on the rights of a given dispute, an opinion which the Romans call *sententia*'. (See Kaser, M., 'The Changing Face of Roman Jurisdiction' (1967) 2 IJ, 129–43 at 132.)

3.2.3 **Execution**

In modern legal systems, we take for granted that judgments will be effectively enforced ('executed') with the full authority and backing of the State. But for much of Rome's history, the State took only an indirect role in the execution of judgments. It authorized the successful plaintiff to pressurize the defendant into complying with the judgment—a form of regulated self-help, the onus being firmly on the plaintiff to obtain satisfaction.

The method of execution depended on whether the action had been *in rem* or *in personam*. If *in rem*, there was no problem if the party who had been granted temporary possession of the disputed property won the case. The question of execution did not arise: the successful party simply kept the property that he already possessed. But if he lost, he had to surrender it. What if he refused to comply? The person entitled to the property could enforce the security that had been promised when the temporary possession was originally granted. If the security was unforthcoming or insufficient, further proceedings could be brought to assess the compensation payable for the loser's failure to satisfy the judgment. When the amount had been assessed, execution of the judgment proceeded along the lines of a case *in personam* (see 3.2.3.1 and 3.2.3.2). This convoluted procedure was necessary because of the absence in the early Roman legal system of an effective State sanction for failure to comply with a court decision.

Two actions-at-law were possible for the execution of judgments *in personam: manus iniectio* ('the laying on of the hand') and *pignoris capio* ('the taking of a pledge').

3.2.3.1 *Manus iniectio*

This was the standard form of execution in early law, and remained in use (albeit in modified form) at least until the mid-Empire. It consisted of the authorized physical seizure of the judgment debtor, i.e. the party failing to comply with the judgment. Under the Twelve Tables, an interval of 30 days was allowed for the payment of the debt from the pronouncement of the judgment. If the debt was not paid within that period, the judgment creditor was entitled to seize and take the debtor before a magistrate. The debtor was released only if he paid the debt or if a *vindex* intervened to take his place. The function of the *vindex* was to protect the debtor from private imprisonment by the creditor by disputing the formal validity of the original judgment. Such intervention was risky since he became liable for double if he failed to contest the debt successfully. The original judgment could not be opposed on its merits; only its validity could be questioned. It seems that intervention by the *vindex*, even if unsuccessful, freed the debtor.

If the debtor failed to pay and a *vindex* did not come forward, the magistrate would authorize the creditor to imprison the debtor for 60 days. During that time, the creditor had to display the prisoner on three consecutive market days in the hope that someone would pay the debt. If no one did so within the 60 days, the debtor could be sold into foreign slavery or be put to death. There was little economic purpose in executing a debtor except where the body could be sold, as was sometimes done. This may explain the macabre rule (of the Twelve Tables) which permitted the dismemberment of a debtor's body by joint creditors—aptly named in this instance. Alternatively, and more plausibly, the dismembering of the creditor's body and its distribution between the creditors exerted a form of religious pressure on the family to pay the debt for fear of being haunted, since the soul of the deceased creditor could not rest without a proper Roman funeral, see MacCormack, G., 'Partes Secanto' (1968) 36 TR, 509–18.

These harsh rules were radically altered by the *lex Poetelia* 326 BC, which took away the creditor's rights to sell the debtor into slavery or to kill him, see MacCormack, G., 'The Lex Poetilia' (1973) 19 Labeo, 306–17. Instead, the creditor could keep the debtor for as long beyond the 60 days' limit as it took for the latter to work off the debt. Since the value of labour could be calculated quite easily, there was little problem (in theory) in assessing when the debtor was to be released. Reforms continued to be made in the later Republic. The debtor was given the personal right to impugn the validity of a judgment (but not the merits) when hauled before the magistrate on the lapse of the 30 days' period. However, if the debtor failed to contest the judgment successfully, he was liable for double the debt.

3.2.3.2 *Pignoris capio*

This ancient action-at-law, predating the Twelve Tables, was similar to the English remedy of distraint. The person trying to enforce the performance of an obligation was allowed, in limited circumstances, to seize the property of the other party in order to pressurize him into performing the obligation. *Pignoris capio* means 'the taking of a pledge'—the pledge was the property that was seized as security for the performance of the obligation. What could the distrainor do with the property seized? Very little. His hope was that the other party would perform his obligation, in which case the property would be returned. It is not clear what the position was if the obligation was not satisfied. The distrainor probably could retain the seized property, but could not sell or dispose of it.

The circumstances in which distraint was allowed were a mixture of statutory and customary rules. For example, the Twelve Tables allowed seizure against a buyer of an animal for religious sacrifice who had failed to pay the price; and a soldier had a customary right of seizure against his paymaster for unpaid wages. The common link in such cases appears to have been that the State's interests were involved in the enforcement of the obligations incurred.

3.3 **The formulary system**

The faults in the *legis actiones* system—its excessive formality, archaic nature, and limited effectiveness—made it unsuitable in the long term for a rapidly expanding, economically vibrant Rome. The system fell largely into disuse in the late Republic and was formally abolished by Augustus in 17 BC, by which time the formulary procedure had long become established. The history of the formulary system began with the creation of the peregrine praetor in 242 BC (see 2.2.2.1), necessitated mainly by the influx of foreigners into Rome at that time. Since the actions-at-law were confined to Roman citizens, the peregrine praetor developed a special procedure for cases involving foreigners, many of whom were traders. The largely commercial disputes in which they were involved required a more speedy and informal procedure than was possible under the actions-at-law system. This was achieved through the use of *formulae*—standardized written pleadings which contained both the action on which the claim was based and the defence(s) raised against it. Before long, citizens were presumably demanding that the formulary system be introduced for disputes among themselves (see Birks, P., 'From Legis Actio to Formula' (1969) 4 IJ, 356–67). The urban praetor duly obliged, and the new practice was formally recognized by the *lex Aebutia c.*150 BC. It is generally believed that the statute confirmed what had been the practice for some time. See also Mousourakis, *Legal History*, 65–82.

3.3.1 **Summons**

The old system of oral summons continued, but with some modifications. The plaintiff summoned the defendant to appear before the praetor, giving notice of the claim (often done by showing the defendant a draft *formula*):

Ulpian, *Edict, book 4*: **Where anyone wishes to bring an action, he should give notice; for it seems most fair that one who is about to bring an action should give notice so that the defendant accordingly may know whether he ought to admit the claim or contest it further and so that if he thinks it should be contested, he may come prepared for the suit, knowing the action by which he is sued.** (D.2.13.1pr.)

The defendant had several options. He could go immediately before the praetor; or he could provide a *vindex* as a guarantor of his future appearance; or—the most favoured option—he could make a promise (*vadimonium*) to appear on a particular day, in which case he would promise to provide security and to pay a penalty for failure to appear at the agreed time in the proximity of the court. (See Metzger, E., 'The Current View of the Extra-Judicial Vadimonium' (2000) 117 ZSS (rA), 133–78 for a critical examination of the scholarly views on this subject as well as Metzger, *Litigation*, chs. 5–7; see also Cloud, D., 'Some Thoughts on Vadimonium' (2002) 119 ZSS (rA), 143–76 for a discussion on the later history of this legal institution.) Breach of *vadimonium* resulted not only in loss of the security but also in liability to pay the penalty and the possible loss of the case.

Sanctions were imposed on an *indefensus*—a defendant—who tried to avoid being summoned, (e.g. by hiding) or who refused to obey the summons or to provide a *vindex*. For example, the praetor could allow the plaintiff the possession of the defendant's estate, with a possible right of sale. The right to seize a reluctant defendant and drag him to court still survived but was probably used only as a last resort. See Metzger, E., 'Absent Parties and Bloody-Minded Judges' in *Mapping the Law*, 455–73.

3.3.2 Trial

As before, trial procedure was divided into two distinct stages—the preliminary hearing and the full trial. As a system of appeals gradually emerged, the jurisdiction of local courts in the Roman Empire became restricted in terms of the financial value of the claim and nature of the action (e.g. where it involved *infamia*) brought before the court (see ch. 84 of the *Lex Irnitana*) (but see now Metzger, E., 'Agree to Disagree: Local Jurisdiction in the *Lex Irnitana*', in *Judge and Jurist*, 207–26). These restrictions were imposed by various pieces of legislation. Where a matter, which exceeded these statutory limits, was brought before a local magistrate, the preliminary proceedings were interrupted and the plaintiff was required to make a formal promise (a judicial *vadimonium*) to appear in the court that had jurisdiction over the matter (see Rodger, A. J., 'Vadimonium to Rome (and Elsewhere)' (1997) 114 ZSS (rA), 160–96). The plaintiff would have to appear before the court of the provincial governor or that of the praetor in Rome, but not both consecutively (see Johnston, D., 'Vadimonium, the Lex Irnitana, and The Edictal Commentaries', in *Quaestiones Iuris*, 111–23).

3.3.2.1 Preliminary hearing

The plaintiff presented a draft *formula* containing the essentials of his claim, and asked for the action to be allowed on that basis. The defendant could suggest amendments—e.g. in order to plead a specific defence. The praetor could make any changes that he thought were desirable. He would wish to be satisfied that the draft *formula* was one of the standard ones allowed. If it was not, the praetor would normally disallow the action. Occasionally, he might be tempted to allow a new *formula*, but he had to exercise his discretion carefully in case he was accused of departing from the published Edict. This effectively constituted 'new law' (see 2.2.2.4). Any departure would be obvious since the *formulae* and the Edict were displayed in the Forum Romanum. Indeed, taking the defendant there was one method of giving notice of the ground of action:

Ulpian, *Edict, book 4*: **Labeo says that a person also gives notice if he brings his adversary to the tablets proclaiming the edict and points out the action which he is about to dictate or declares the one which he intends to use.** (D.2.13.1.1.)

A praetorian edict introduced a rule concerning discovery: the plaintiff had to produce any documents on which he intended to rely at the subsequent trial (but the defendant was not subject to a similar duty). Another change was that the requirement of a deposit of a substantial sum of money as a wager was abandoned. In effect, litigation became free rather than being subject to financial penalty—a fundamental departure from the norms of the past.

3.3.2.2 The *formula*

What was in the *formula*? It was a document containing the total 'programme' of litigation—all the questions of law and fact—and it was made up of a number of possible clauses, some essential, others not (depending on the circumstances):

(a) *Nominatio*: the appointment of the judge. The procedure for selecting a judge was similar to the previous system, the plaintiff suggesting names from the official list until the defendant agreed, failing which the praetor would make the choice himself. A *nominatio* was essential in a *formula*.

(b) *Intentio*: the plaintiff's statement of claim. This was the very heart of the *formula*, whereby the plaintiff stated the cause of action, alleging either an existing civil law right or the presence of such facts as justified the allowing of his claim. The *intentio* too was essential (cf. Inst.Gai.4.41.).

(c) *Condemnatio*: the clause that directed the judge to make a decision by 'condemning' or 'absolving' the defendant (cf. Inst.Gai.4.43.). The *condemnatio* was expressed in money terms, the amount being stated if the plaintiff was seeking a liquidated (specific) sum; otherwise, the amount was left to the discretion of the judge (especially where the *condemnatio* contained the clause *ex fide bona*). But a *taxatio* could be inserted—a clause limiting the amount that the judge could award. In an action for the recovery of property, a direction was invariably added to the *condemnatio*, instructing the judge to condemn the defendant only on failure to restore the disputed thing. The defendant, if he failed to restore, would have to pay the value of the property as assessed by the plaintiff on oath. This procedure was necessary because the judge, being a layman whose function was to give an 'opinion', strictly could not order the defendant to do anything—there was no equivalent in the *ius civile* to specific performance. Where the object of the action was not to condemn the defendant but to seek a declaration of rights, an *adiudicatio* (rather than a *condemnatio*) was put in the *formula*, directing the judge to give to a party 'as much as should be adjudged to him'. However, an *adiudicatio* could also be used to assign rights—rather than just to declare them—as in the action for division of common property (see 7.2.8).

(d) *Demonstratio*: a clause stating the facts from which the claim arose (cf. Inst. Gai.4.40.). It was used only in actions *in personam* for unliquidated damages, i.e. where the judge had a discretion as to the amount awarded. In such cases a clause *demonstrating* the facts on which the claim was based was obviously essential.

(e) *Exceptio*: if a defendant wished to raise a specific defence, he would do so in a special clause, the *exceptio*, that would defeat the plaintiff if it was upheld. A simple denial of the facts did not require an *exceptio*. If the plaintiff wished to counter the *exceptio*, he could insert a *replicatio*—a set of facts which (if proved) defeated the alleged defence. It was not possible, however, to plead a *replicatio* that alleged fraud against a defendant if he was relying on a plea of fraud against the plaintiff:

Ulpian, *Edict, book 76*: **Marcellus says that a replication of fraud is not allowed against a defense of fraud. Labeo is also of the same opinion; for he says that it is inequitable that mutual wickedness, in fact, should serve as a reward to the plaintiff, but serve as a penalty against him who is being sued, since it is far more equitable that the plaintiff recover nothing from an act which was performed with perfidy.** (D.44.4.4.13.)

Exceptio and *replicatio* were not necessarily the end of the saga. The defendant could plead a reply, if he had one, to the *replicatio*; the plaintiff could plead a reply in turn, and so forth. These defences and counter-defences were placed in sequence in the *formula*. Whichever was the last (in the sequence) to be proved on the facts 'won' the case.

(f) *Praescriptio*: a clause placed, if necessary, after the nomination of the judge. Its chief function was to limit the cause of action as narrowly as was desirable in the circumstances. This benefited the plaintiff since he thereby ensured that the proceedings did not consume the whole of his action. Suppose, for example, that the defendant had contracted to make payments to the plaintiff in instalments, and had failed to make the first payment. The plaintiff would insert a *praescriptio* into the *formula*, limiting the action to the unpaid instalment; otherwise, he might not be able to sue for later breaches of the contract. This had to be done to avoid the effect of *litis contestatio*, which effectively 'consumed' the previous cause of action (see 3.3.2.4).

3.3.2.3 **Typical** *formulae*

(a) 'Let Titius be judge. If it appears that the property which is disputed belongs to Aulus Agerius at civil law, and it be not restored to him in accordance with the judge's decision, you, judge, condemn Numerius Negidius to Aulus Agerius for so much of his property as the thing will be worth; if it does not appear, absolve him.'

This was the basic *formula* used in a *vindicatio*, the standard remedy for resolving disputes over the ownership of property. Aulus (plaintiff) and Numerius (defendant) were the stock names used in examples of *formulae*. There is no *demonstratio* in this *formula* since the action is *in rem*. The clause beginning 'If it appears' is the *intentio*.

(b) 'Let Titius be judge. If it appears that Numerius Negidius should pay Aulus Agerius 100 *denarii* [silver coins], then, if there is no agreement between Aulus Agerius and Numerius Negidius that the sum should not be sued for, or if there has been any fraud on the part of Numerius Negidius, you, judge, condemn Numerius Negidius to Aulus Agerius for 100 *denarii*; otherwise absolve him.'

Here we have an action *in personam* to enforce an obligation to pay a liquidated sum. The defendant has pleaded a defence (*exceptio*) that there was an agreement that the sum would not be sued for. There is a *replicatio* by the plaintiff based on the alleged fraud of the defendant. There is no need for a *demonstratio* in this formula since the action is for a liquidated sum.

(c) 'Let Titius be judge. Whereas Aulus Agerius sold to Numerius Negidius the slave who is the object of this action, which sale is the matter involved in this case, whatever on that account the defendant ought in good faith to pay to or do for the plaintiff, that thing the judge is to condemn Numerius Negidius to pay to Aulus Agerius; if it does not appear, absolve him.'

This is the *formula* that would typically be used in action on the contract of sale. Since the action is for unliquidated damages, a *demonstratio* is required, consisting of the opening clauses, i.e. 'Whereas...case'.

3.3.2.4 **Acceptance of the *formula***

On the appointment of the judge and the insertion of his name in the *nominatio*, the defendant would formally 'accept' the *formula*. The acceptance terminated the preliminary hearing and brought joinder of issue, the effects of which were much as they had been under the actions-at-law system, i.e. the original cause of action was consumed.

3.3.2.5 **Representation**

Another important departure from the previous system was that representation of parties became generally possible. If either party wished to proceed through a representative (*procurator*), the name of the latter had to be substituted in the *formula* (for that of the principal) *before* joinder of issue. Thus, the representative became the actual party in the action, the judge directed to give judgment for or against him. Originally, the legal consequences of having a representative differed according to whether he had been appointed formally or informally. But, by the late classical period, such differences had disappeared. The principal came to be regarded as fully bound by the representative, but was entitled to enforce the judgment obtained by the latter. The function of the representative was thus rather different from that of the modern lawyer (but similar to that of the medieval attorney), see Buckland and McNair, *Roman Law and Common Law*, 407–8; Bablitz, *Actors and Audience*, chs. 6–7.

3.3.2.6 **Taking oaths**

The dispute could sometimes be decided entirely at the preliminary hearing, obviating the need for a full trial before the judge—e.g. when the plaintiff withdrew his case or where the defendant admitted liability. Or the matter might be decided (in the praetor's presence) through the use of oaths. The plaintiff could challenge the defendant to take an oath. If the defendant accepted and took the oath, swearing to the justice of his case, he won; if he refused, he lost. There was a third possibility—the defendant could tender the oath to the plaintiff, who won if he took the oath, but otherwise lost (he could not offer the oath back). The procedure may seem absurd to modern readers but the taking of a formal oath to the gods was a matter of the utmost solemnity for most Romans. Even the worst rogue would hesitate to perjure himself in such circumstances and the penalties for perjury were severe. However, the procedure could only be used in limited circumstances—in cases involving claims to a specific thing or specific sum of money—although it is possible that the category of actions was widened later. It seems that the oath-taking procedure continued to be used during the Empire. A title of the *Digest* is devoted to oaths, and Gaius is quoted as stating that oath taking is an important means of expediting litigation (D.12.2.1.).

3.3.2.7 **Full trial**

There was little change from the procedure under the former system. The trial took place on a day fixed by the praetor and was normally held in public (Bablitz, *Actors and Audience*, chs. 1, 2, and 5). The existence of the written *formula* shortened the oral exchanges. Rules of evidence still hardly existed, although it was recognized that any assertion should be proved by the person making it. Witnesses were not yet generally compellable. Oral evidence was still preferred, but written evidence was being increasingly used. The judges relied on the advice of jurists in reaching a decision (Bablitz, *Actors and Audience*, ch. 4). Although the *formula* directed a judge to condemn or absolve the defendant, it seems that a judge could declare that he was unable to reach a decision, in which case another judge would have to be appointed. There was still no *system* of appeals, although some of the early Emperors heard the occasional appeal by way of granting a favour.

3.3.2.8 **Limitation of actions**

As a general rule, there was no limitation period on *ius civile* actions. They were 'perpetual', i.e. they did not have to be brought within a fixed period of time from the date when the action arose. The same was largely true of those praetorian actions that were compensatory in nature; but those that were penal normally had to be brought within a year. For the purposes of this rule, a 'year' was more than a calendar year, since days on which litigation was not possible were excluded from the calculation. Other limitation periods were possible, e.g. six months for the *actio redhibitoria* for the rescission of a contract of sale.

3.3.3 **Execution**

The judgment debtor still had to be taken before a magistrate after the lapse of 30 days from the court's judgment. However, the creditor had to pursue an *actio iudicati*, 'an action on the judgment', under which the debtor was given a last chance to satisfy the judgment before any further execution procedures were invoked. The debtor could contest the validity of the judgment, in which case he had to provide personal security, and was liable to double damages if his claim failed. It was at the next stage of the execution process that two important changes were introduced under the formulary system—sale of assets, and surrender of the estate.

3.3.3.1 *Bonorum venditio* (**'Sale of the assets'**)

If the debtor had not satisfied or successfully contested the judgment, the creditor was authorized to take him away to private custody to work off the debt, as before. But, in addition, the creditor was allowed *bonorum venditio*, a praetorian remedy that was introduced in the late Republic. This entitled the creditor to seize the property of the debtor with a view to sale. If the debtor had worthwhile assets, the creditor would often waive his right of imprisoning the debtor.

How did *bonorum venditio* operate? The creditor requested the praetor to grant *missio in possessionem* ('a sending into possession'), an order that authorized taking possession of the debtor's property. Once the order was granted, the creditor could seize the whole of the property. He had to advertise the seizure so as to allow other creditors to make their claims. After a lapse of 30 days, the creditors met to appoint a manager to conduct the sale. He normally prepared an inventory of the property, a list of the debts, and organized a public auction—a process that has served as a model for bankruptcy procedure in modern legal systems. The estate of the debtor was sold to the bidder who offered the highest dividend (i.e. percentage of the debt) to the creditors. The debtor remained fully liable for any unpaid part of the debt. This was a deliberately harsh process, the threat of which was intended to force payment from the debtor. If he failed to pay he would probably suffer *infamia*, i.e. legal disgrace (see 4.4.2.5), lose all his property, and incur the social stigma of bankruptcy. Not surprisingly, there were restrictions on the use of the auction procedure. For example, it could not be ordered against a *pupillus* (a ward in guardianship) or someone away on public service. And it was not normally granted against persons of high rank, for whom a less embarrassing procedure was provided, which did not involve *infamia*, or the sale of the *whole* of the estate—only what was required to pay the debts.

3.3.3.2 *Cessio bonorum* ('Surrender of the estate')

This was a procedure, introduced in Augustus' reign, whereby a judgment debtor voluntarily surrendered his property to the creditors. The property was sold off, but the debtor would not be subjected to legal disgrace or to possible imprisonment by the creditors. Surrender was not available as of right: it applied only where the praetor was satisfied that the debtor had genuine assets and that the bankruptcy was the result of misfortune. See Pakter, W., 'The Mystery of Cessio Bonorum', in *Ommagio à Peter Stein*, 323–42.

3.3.4 **Praetorian remedies**

The jurisdiction of the praetor in civil litigation under the formulary system was complemented by a number of legal powers that were available to him through his possession of *imperium*. These powers were of great practical importance, often enabling a praetor to dispose of an issue without the need for a trial.

3.3.4.1 *Restitutio in integrum* (rescission)

This was an order nullifying a transaction and restoring the parties to their original position, i.e. 'a return to the beginning'. When could such an order be granted?

Ulpian, *Edict, book 11*:…**the praetor helps men on many occasions who have made a mistake or been cheated, whether they have incurred loss through duress or cunning or their youth or absence or through change of status or justifiable mistake.** (D.4.1.1.)

The order normally had to be sought within one year of the transaction (four years under Justinian). The person seeking it had to show that he had suffered some proprietary loss or that he had incurred a future commitment as the result of the transaction. And he had to show 'cause', i.e. grounds such as those specified above.

3.3.4.2 *Missio in possessionem* (distraint)

This was an order authorizing the seizure of property. It could be used to seize the whole of an estate, as in the case of a judgment debtor (see earlier), or only a part of the assets. The order generally entitled the recipient to take possession of the property. Sometimes, however, *missio* authorized little more than the right to enter property and to hold it temporarily in order to pressurize a person to do or to abstain from doing something. Such orders were of considerable practical importance in the effective operation of the Roman legal system.

3.3.4.3 **Praetorian stipulations**

These were formal promises that were made by parties as the result of praetorian intervention, either in the course of litigation ('judicial' stipulations) or outside it.

An example of the latter was where an owner of property in a dangerous condition promised security to indemnify his neighbour against damage. In such a case, refusal to make the stipulation could result in an order for distraint being granted to the neighbour. Another stipulation that was relatively common in practice was the promise, demanded of certain guardians, to give security for the safety of the property of their ward (see 5.4.1.3).

3.3.4.4 Interdicts

These were perhaps the most important of the praetorian remedies. They were orders, normally issued after a complaint by an aggrieved person, instructing a person to do or refrain from doing something (comparable in some ways to injunctions in English law). Sometimes, an interdict was obtained without full investigation by the praetor of the merits of a case. In such a case, the summary finding of the praetor might prompt the aggrieved party to go to trial before a judge. In this way, the granting of the interdict resulted in a bypassing of the usual preliminary hearing: the interdictal proceedings *were* the preliminary hearing, as emphasized by Buckland and McNair, *Roman Law and Common Law*—'The interdict is essentially the initiation of a piece of litigation' (422). And, sometimes, there were no further proceedings at all, if the interdict was not contested, in which case the praetor would have effectively resolved the dispute himself.

Interdicts were classified in various ways, e.g., as possessory and non-possessory. The latter category (much used in practice) included interdicts protecting public rights in the use of roads and highways:

Pomponius, *Sabinus, book 30*: **It is open to anyone to claim for public use what belongs to the use of all, such as public roads and public ways. Therefore, interdicts are available to safeguard these at anyone's demand.** (D.43.7.1.)

The possessory interdicts were very important in the development of the law of property, offering effective protection in various ways of a person's right to possession (see 6.5.5.1). And interdicts were central to the development of the *ius honorarium*. The speedy, summary justice dispensed through their widespread use was invaluable to the operation of the Roman legal system in the later Republic and the Empire.

3.4 **The *cognitio* procedure**

The formulary system remained the operative system of civil procedure well into the Empire. It was not formally abolished until AD 342, although it had become obsolete before then. Still, the system had served Rome well for several centuries. To some extent, the formulary system had reflected the Republican constitution: the separation of proceedings before the praetor and the judge was not untypical of the division of power and authority in the Republican constitution. The changes emanating from the transition to Empire were bound to have serious consequences for the legal system. Imperial autocracy was not conducive to the survival of the lay judge. The magistrate, the delegate of the Emperor, became even more the cornerstone of the system of civil procedure—there was little room for the amateur layman.

3.4.1 **The development of** *cognitio*

The beginnings of *cognitio* ('an investigation') are traditionally ascribed to the reign of Augustus. It began as a procedure created by order of the Emperor under Imperial law. The distinctive feature of *cognitio*, the adjudication of the *whole* case by a magistrate (at this point a salaried bureaucrat), was present in certain aspects of the formulary procedure, notably in the praetorian use of interdicts. The opportunity for magistrates to dispose of the whole case was extended by Augustus. He gave jurisdiction to the consuls to enforce trusts (*fideicommissa*): previously trusts had not been legally binding (see 8.9.2.1). Claudius created a new praetorship specially to deal with trusts, and vested the supervision of guardians in the consuls. Other new magistracies were created, (e.g. the city and praetorian prefects) vested with important legal powers. Moreover, the Emperors contributed to the development of *cognitio* by occasionally hearing cases themselves. When they did so, they were acting outside the normal system of civil procedure under the formulary system, i.e. they were acting 'extraordinarily' (as were the magistrates mentioned earlier). Hence, the *cognitio* procedure came to be described as *extraordinaria* in recognition that it was 'unusual'. The name persisted even when *cognitio* became the standard procedure. However, the most important factor in the development of *cognitio* was the growing practice whereby provincial governors decided cases themselves, a development that made good sense in areas where the selection of suitable judges could prove troublesome. It is likely that this practice was followed from the outset in the imperial provinces, see Kaser, M., 'The Changing Face of Roman Jurisdiction' (1967) 2 IJ, 129–43. Diocletian's decree of AD 294, directing governors to adjudicate cases themselves, confirmed what had become a widespread practice.

The eventual formal abolition of the formulary system reflected the profound change which had emerged in the previous centuries. Virtually all aspects of civil procedure were now firmly in the hands of the State, and subject to increasingly detailed regulation, as has tended to occur in modern legal systems. Since the *cognitio* procedure evolved over a period of some 500 years, its operation can best be considered in its developed form in the later Empire. See Mousourakis, *Legal History*, 126–34, 170–8.

3.4.2 **Summons**

Proceedings began with the plaintiff lodging a written statement of claim (*libellus conventionis*) with the magistrate, who sent a copy (normally delivered by a court official) to the defendant ordering him to enter a defence and to appear in court on a fixed date. (The *formula* in its classical form did not exist in the *cognitio* procedure.) Gone were the days of plaintiffs dragging reluctant defendants to court. The defendant had to undertake to appear in court and had to provide security for his appearance. Failure to do so could result in his arrest by the official. If the defendant disregarded the summons, he committed the offence of *contumacia* ('obstinacy'). The trial could then take place in his absence, normally after three summonses, and judgment could be awarded by default. This was impossible under the earlier systems of procedure since a trial could not take place without the defendant's consent.

3.4.3 **Trial**

The old system, comprising a preliminary hearing and full trial, was abandoned. The case now consisted of a *cognitio*—an investigation by the magistrate, who conducted the whole trial and made the decision himself. The use of courthouses became increasingly frequent as a venue for trials. The parties took an oath at the beginning of the trial that they would tell the truth. Joinder of issue occurred at this stage, but with less serious consequences than before, e.g. it no longer consumed the plaintiff's action. Only the judgment could now have the effect of barring the bringing of a fresh case based on the same facts.

The magistrate had complete control over the conduct of the case, especially over questions of evidence. Witnesses could now be compelled to attend by the magistrate's order, the *subpoena*, and were subject to thorough interrogation. The inquisitorial character of the *cognitio* trial procedure became one of the most distinctive features of late Roman civil process. Documentary evidence was by now regarded as of crucial importance: indeed, a rule was introduced that a document could not be defeated by oral testimony alone. The judgment was delivered in writing, read out in court in the presence of the parties (each of whom received a copy). As the procedure was no longer governed by a *formula*, the magistrate had a wider discretion in reaching a decision than the judge under the formulary system. He did not have to 'condemn' or 'absolve', or to frame the judgment in money terms.

3.4.4 **Execution**

The 30-days rule for the satisfaction of judgments was no longer strictly followed—the period could be adjusted according to circumstances. Justinian eventually fixed the period at four months. What happened if the judgment was not satisfied? There was a fundamental change in the procedure for enforcement since the State was now in control through its delegate, the magistrate. He had a discretion as to how the judgment should be enforced. The usual procedure under the developed *cognitio* system involved the seizure of the debtor's property by court bailiffs. If the judgment was for a sum of money, the property seized was sold at auction to raise the required amount, further seizures being made if necessary. The plaintiff could accept property in lieu of a sum of money, thus avoiding the need for an auction. Personal imprisonment of the debtor by the creditor had become obsolete, although imprisonment was occasionally ordered by a magistrate, the debtor being confined in a public prison. Execution against property was very much the preferred option.

3.4.5 **Appeals**

A systematic appeals procedure was developed under the *cognitio* system—the first in Roman legal history. The bureaucratic tendency of the age contributed to the emergence of a hierarchy of courts, which made an appeals system possible. In the capitals of the Empire, appeals were heard by the courts of the city prefect and the chief of the praetorian guard (the praetorian prefect). In the provinces, governors often appointed subordinates to hear cases at first instance; the governor would hear appeals. Appeals could then be taken through the hierarchy of the urban system, if necessary. Emperors still heard appeals occasionally but their jurisdiction was more clearly delineated than before. The possibility of multiple appeals through the extensive hierarchy of courts resulted in the imposition of curbs in the late Empire, e.g. Justinian ruled that a decision could not be appealed more than twice. Appeal procedure was intended to achieve a speedy final determination of the issue, but could have a discouraging effect on an intending appellant since notice of appeal had to be lodged within a few days of the previous decision, and because a failed appeal attracted penalties.

Apart from hearing appeals, Emperors were sometimes asked to give written rulings in cases where the magistrate was unsure of what decision to make. The answer of the Emperor normally constituted the final judgment in the case. Further, anyone could petition the Emperor for a ruling in a matter that had not yet gone to court, if the petitioner feared that he would not be dealt with justly. The ruling would guide the court that subsequently tried the issue.

By the late Empire, the Romans had developed a civil procedure that in many respects was to provide a model for later legal systems. But the *cognitio* system had drawbacks. A mass of rules, the result of bureaucratic over-regulation, clogged the system, and delays became acute. Theodosius II decreed that there should be a general limitation period of 30 years for actions that had previously been unlimited, i.e. perpetual. This was a step in the right direction, but a tiny step. Justinian was forced to rule that no case was to continue for more than three years after joinder of issue. Moreover, the introduction of an official fee system meant that litigation became much more expensive than before. Litigants now had to pay for every official act by an officer of the court. Not surprisingly, those officers amassed fortunes, as their counterparts did in the pre-Victorian Chancery. Nevertheless, the *cognitio* system can be regarded as a notable product of the Roman genius for structure and order. And its drawbacks—expense, delay, and bureaucracy—were features which modern lawyers will readily recognize in their own system.

 online resource centre Please consult the Online Resource Centre for revision guidance on this chapter.

FURTHER READING

On Roman civil procedure, see the dated, yet indispensable, Greenidge, A. H. J. (1901), *The Legal Procedure of Cicero's Time*, Oxford: Clarendon Press; and Kelly, J. M. (1966), *Roman Litigation*, Oxford: Clarendon Press, for a comprehensive survey of the Roman law of procedure. These works should be read in conjunction with more recent contributions by Rodger, A., 'The Lex Irnitana and Procedure in the Civil Courts' (1991) 81 JRS, 74–90 (on the jurisdiction of local magistrates and the civil procedure in municipal courts in light of ch. 90 of the *Lex Irnitana*), and Metzger, E. (1997), *A New Outline of the Roman Civil Trial*, Oxford: Clarendon Press. Turpin, W., 'Formula, Cognitio and Proceedings Extra Ordinem' (1999) 46 RIDA 3, 499–574, presents an interesting argument on the three phases of the transformation of Roman civil procedure from the *formula* to the *cognitio extra ordinem*. For the use of documents in Roman courts, see Meyer, E. A. (2004), *Legitimacy and Law in the Roman World*, Cambridge: Cambridge University Press, chs. 8 and 9. For an interesting, if controversial account of Cicero's influence on the development of Roman law, see Harries, J. (2006), *Cicero and the Jurists—From Citizens' Law to the Lawful State*, London: Duckworth.

On the physical location of Roman courts, see De Angelis, F. (2010), *Spaces of Justice in the Roman World*, Leiden/Boston: Brill (Columbia Studies in the Classical Tradition, volume 35).

On the Roman advocate, see Kennedy, G. A. (1972), *The Art of Rhetoric in the Roman World 300 B.C.–300 A.D.*, Princeton: Princeton University Press; and Crook, J. A. (1995), *Legal Advocacy in the Roman World*, London: Duckworth, on the rhetorical aspects of Roman advocacy. A recent study by Powell, J. (ed.) (2004), *Cicero the Advocate*, Oxford: Oxford University Press, also contains excellent contributions on Roman advocacy in the context of Cicero's works.

On the development of Roman legal practice in late Antiquity, see Humfress, C., (2007), *Orthodoxy and the Courts in Late Antiquity*, Oxford: Oxford University Press.

On the Roman influences on the development of the legal profession in the middle ages, see Brundage, J. A. (2008), *The Medieval Origins of the Legal Profession*, Chicago: University of Chicago Press.

PART II

The Law of Persons

4

Status, slavery, and citizenship

Status lay at the heart of the law of persons. Rome developed into a highly strati-fied society in which the different gradations of status were reflected in a myriad of detailed rules. So the law of persons describes the various categories and degrees of status in Roman law, and how status could be acquired or lost. Issues such as slavery and citizenship are fundamental, but the bulk of the law is concerned with the family. However, before considering the rules on status, something must be said about the related question of legal personality.

4.1 Legal personality

Who or what was a 'person' in Roman law? To a modern lawyer, a legal person comprises an entity that is capable of legal relationships, i.e. of being the subject of legal rights and duties. Human persons clearly come within this category. But legal persons can include non-human entities, e.g. a corporation has a legal per-sonality which is separate from its individual members. For the Roman jurists, 'persons' essentially meant human beings, but there were instances in the Empire where non-human entities were recognized as acquiring rights and duties. In some respects, these entities were *treated* as legal persons, although they were not *described* as such. The most important examples were *collegia, municipia*, churches, charities, and the State. See generally, Duff, P. W. (1938), *Personality in Roman Private Law*, Cambridge: Cambridge University Press.

4.1.1 *Collegia*

These were mainly private associations or societies, often formed as trade guilds or burial clubs, and dedicated to a particular god. Their numbers flourished in the Republic, with potentially dangerous consequences in the disturbed conditions of the last century BC. Consequently, Julius Caesar reduced the number of *collegia* drastically, and Augustus banned the creation of new *collegia* without the authority of the Senate and the Emperor. Restrictions were later imposed on the frequency of meetings and on the number of *collegia* that an individual could join:

Marcian, *Institutes, book 3*: **It is not permitted to belong to more than one *collegium*...and if someone belong to more than one, it is provided by rescript that he must choose the one to which he wishes to adhere and receive from the association which he leaves the share of the common fund which is due to him.** (D.47.22.1.2.)

It is unclear how much legal personality such associations possessed. It seems that they could be allowed to hold property, to benefit from legal obligations and to appear as parties in legal proceedings. Marcus Aurelius allowed *collegia* to set slaves free and to receive legacies, whilst Justinian ruled that *collegia* could be appointed as heirs in a will.

4.1.2 *Municipia*

Municipia ('municipalities') comprised the different types of local community to be found in the Roman Empire. They possessed varying degrees of corporate character, depending on how much had been granted to them on their incorporation within the Empire. The community acted through its representatives, but it was regarded as having a legal personality distinct from them and its inhabitants. Communities could thus own property, could be beneficiaries under trusts, could receive legacies, and in the late Empire could even be appointed as testamentary heirs.

4.1.3 Churches and charities

After the conversion to Christianity, Constantine ruled that gifts and legacies could be left to the Church generally or to individual churches. In the latter case, the property was regarded as owned by the members of the church of the deceased, not as individuals but as a body. The local bishop or his delegates administered the property. Moreover, it seems that churches could be appointed as testamentary heirs.

Gifts to charities were not unknown before the adoption of Christianity, but proliferated thereafter. Often, such gifts were made to a particular church or bishop to administer on behalf of the charity. Where a charitable gift was made without reference to a church, the bishop or the church of the donor's locality administered it unless that was contrary to the donor's wishes. Even then the bishop had a supervisory power, following a decree by Justinian.

4.1.4 The State

In the Republic, the Roman people were regarded as owning certain types of property that was not capable of private ownership, e.g. provincial land, the seashore (see generally 6.1.2). Magistrates could act for the people in relation to such property (including gifts made to certain deities) but only as representatives—the property in theory belonged to the people as a body:

Gaius, *Institutes, book 2*: **Those things which are subject to human right are either public or private. Public things are considered to be nobody's property for they belong corporately to the whole community.** (D.1.8.1pr.)

In the Empire, the importance of the concept of the Roman people as an entity waned somewhat when the full extent of the Emperor's position became apparent. The imperial treasury (*fiscus*), which contained the Emperor's purse, acquired a distinct legal personality. It could appear through its officers as a party in litigation and could acquire property in a variety of ways, e.g. through the confiscation of inheritances. Who owned the property acquired by the *fiscus*? It appears that in the early Empire, the Emperor was regarded as the owner, jointly with the Roman people. Later, the property was regarded (in theory at least) as belonging to the State rather than the

Emperor because strictly it could not be disposed by him in his *private* capacity, but had to pass to his successor (see further, Schulz, F., *Classical Roman Law* (1951), 86–102).

For a good recent account, see Lewis, A.D.E., 'Slavery, Family and Status', in *Cambridge Companion*, 151–74.

4.2 Status

There were three constituent elements of status in the Roman law of persons—*libertas*, *civitas*, and *familia*. The person of full status was the one who possessed all three elements: he had *libertas* (freedom) in that he was not a slave; he had *civitas* (citizenship) in that he was a citizen of Rome, not a foreigner; and he had *familia* ('family') in that he belonged to a Roman household (usually as its head). Loss of any or all of these elements resulted in *capitis deminutio* ('a loss of status'), the gravity of which depended on the circumstances:

Paul, *Sabinus, book 2*: **There are three kinds of change of civil status: the greatest, the middle, and the least. For there are three things which we have: freedom, citizenship and family. Therefore, when we lose all three . . . the change of civil status is the greatest. But when we lose citizenship and retain freedom, the change of status is the middle. When both freedom and citizenship are retained and only family is changed, it is plain that the change of civil status is the least.** (D.4.5.11.)

The 'greatest' loss of status (*maxima*) occurred when a person lost his liberty, because it necessarily involved the loss of citizenship and family rights as well. This resulted, for example, when a citizen was enslaved. The 'middle' change of status (*media*) comprised the loss of citizenship, but not freedom. It occurred mostly where a person was ordered to be deported for some misdemeanour. Loss of citizenship normally carried with it loss of family. The 'least' change of status (*minima*) was occasioned by loss of family alone—in practice the most frequent type of change. For example, if a child was emancipated, i.e. freed from the legal power of the head of the household, the child's legal status altered from subjection to independence. The child lost rights of inheritance on intestacy as a result of this change—to that extent there was a 'loss' of family rights. On the other hand, the child gained legal independence, which could be an advantage in certain circumstances. Such a loss of status was not necessarily detrimental—more a *change* of status than a loss.

The three elements of status—freedom, citizenship, and family rights—must now be considered in detail. They constitute the law of persons.

4.3 Freedom and the law of slavery

(Inst.Gai.1.9.–10., Inst.1.4., D.1.5.)

4.3.1 Basic notions

Gaius, *Institutes, book 1*: **Certainly, the great divide in the law of persons is this: all men are either free men or slaves.** (D.1.5.3.) (cf. Inst.Gai.1.9.)

Gaius states in this passage the primary classification in the law of persons: people either have freedom or they are slaves. But what is freedom?

Florentinus, *Institutes, book 9*: **Freedom is one's natural power of doing what one pleases, save insofar as it is ruled out either by coercion or by law.** (D.1.5.4pr.) (cf. Inst.1.3.1.; D.50.17.106.)

This definition recognized that freedom is a 'natural' condition—there is a presumption that men are free. This is reassuring but somewhat hollow in view of the great importance of slavery as a social, economic, and legal institution in the Roman world. Definitions (in the modern sense) were not one of the strengths of juristic literature, as is clear from the above attempt. Watson, in *Spirit of Roman Law*, considers that the jurists were generally wary of definitions; this contributed to a 'central indefiniteness' at the heart of Roman law (ch. 12). But then, concepts such as freedom are notoriously difficult to define satisfactorily. Of more practical importance was the definition of slavery:

Florentinus, *Institutes, book 9*: **Slavery is an institution of the *ius gentium*, whereby someone is against nature made subject to the ownership of another.** (D.1.5.4.1.)

Florentinus is using here the phrase *ius gentium* ('the law of nations') to describe the basic 'common' laws to be found in most States in contrast to the special laws of particular States. However, the phrase was sometimes used (not always consistently) in a secondary sense to signify the part of Roman law that applied to citizens and foreigners alike, in contrast to the *ius civile*. Since slavery was widely practised in ancient civilizations, its attribution to the *ius gentium* (in its primary sense) is understandable. As for slavery being 'against nature', that is consistent with the definition of freedom—if freedom is natural, slavery must be unnatural. The description of a slave as an object of 'ownership' is very significant: in many ways, slaves were regarded as property rather than as human beings. They could be acquired, owned, and disposed. However, slaves were a special type of property, *res mancipi* (see 6.1.5), which in theory necessitated that their transfer should be effected by formal methods of conveyancing. Furthermore, their humanity was recognized to some extent in the law, however tenaciously the Romans might have tried to adhere at times to the notion that a slave was simply a 'thing'.

According to the above definition, a slave was in the ownership of 'another'. This was broadly true. Slaves were mostly owned by individual masters (or mistresses)—but not always. For example, public slaves (*servi publici*) worked for the Roman civil service, and were not considered to be owned by anyone except perhaps the State. The definition omits to mention that slaves were without rights, as a general rule, although that is clearly implied—things generally do not have rights. The rightlessness of slaves has often been seen as the essential feature of the Roman law of slavery. Nevertheless, there were circumstances in which slaves had certain privileges or the power to alter legal relationships, e.g. a slave could make contracts on behalf of his master in some circumstances, and public slaves could marry and make wills.

4.3.2 The slave in Roman society

Before examining the details of the law of slavery, it is important to appreciate the role of the slave in Roman society. The overall treatment of slaves varied from period to period. In early Rome, it seems that slaves were generally treated well, possibly because they were relatively few in number. Their treatment deteriorated when Rome's overseas expansion began in the third century BC. Wars of conquest fought abroad resulted in the enslavement of large numbers of foreigners. Slaves became cheap and disposable, conditions in rural areas being particularly bad. A serious revolt led by a slave, Spartacus, occurred in 73 BC and took two bloody years to suppress. Thereafter, legislation was occasionally passed to protect slaves against brutal treatment (see 4.3.4.1). Although there were some harsh times, there was probably never a general *policy* of brutality towards slaves. Moreover, slaves could always hope to improve their status through manumission, the legal release of a person from slavery. Manumission was widely practised at certain periods of Rome's history: slavery was used to some extent as a mechanism to integrate outsiders into Roman society (see Wiedemann, T., *Greek and Roman Slavery* (1981), 69 ff.). In fact, the Roman treatment of slaves was relatively humane among ancient civilizations. In some respects, it was less brutal than the treatment of slaves prior to the American civil war.

Slaves played a vital role in Roman society and the economy. Many performed menial tasks and 'dirty' jobs, but a slave with talent could go far, especially in the cities. Such slaves were valued assets, capable of making fortunes for their masters. They were to be found in many walks of life—as business managers, entrepreneurs, accountants, physicians, doctors, actors, and actresses: 'The slave is regarded by many historians as the determining factor in the economic, social and intellectual life of antiquity. There is scarcely a title of the *Digest* in which he does not figure' (Crook, *Law and Life of Rome*, 55).

The talented slave would usually be rewarded by his master with money and gifts that the slave could use and enjoy, even though he could not legally own the property. Such slaves, if cared for by a kindly master, were sometimes the envy of those citizens who were free, but poor. The treatment of slaves therefore often depended on how useful they could be to their masters. Social standing played a part as well—an important citizen, bent on impressing his peers, would probably not wish it to be known that he was mistreating his slaves. Nor would he wish to be seen carried in his litter or served at his dinner party by bruised, emaciated, and unkempt slaves in rags.

4.3.3 Enslavement

Enslavement could arise mainly through the sale of children, through punishment, by capture, or by birth. (cf. Inst.Gai.1.51., Inst.1.3.4.)

4.3.3.1 Sale of children

In early law, the *paterfamilias* had the right to sell children into slavery. This power fell into disuse during the Republic and was eventually banned. However, it was revived in the later Empire in limited circumstances: newly born children could be sold into slavery by their parents on the grounds of poverty. But a right of redemption was reserved to the parents should their circumstances improve. When redeemed, the child regained its original status.

4.3.3.2 Punishment

Enslavement could be imposed as a punishment in a variety of circumstances:

(a) Crime. Under the Twelve Tables a thief who was caught stealing became the slave of his intended victim. If the thief was already a slave he would normally be executed, at least in early law. Moreover, enslavement could result from conviction for certain crimes—where the sentence involved working in the mines or fighting wild beasts. Such convicts were described as penal slaves (*servi poenae*) and were regarded as the most degraded category of slaves. The category included persons who had been sentenced to death and were awaiting execution. Penal slaves were regarded as ownerless and incapable of being manumitted. A pardon was their only realistic hope of survival (see Burdon, J., 'Slavery as a Punishment in Roman Criminal Law', in *Slavery and Unfree Labour*, 68–85, where the author demonstrates in which cases and to which class of offenders this form of punishment applied).

(b) Evasion of duty. Those who evaded being listed in the census, and thus escaped liability to be taxed or to serve in the legions, could be enslaved by the State. Debtors who failed to pay their debts could be sold into slavery in early Rome, as the result of *manus iniectio* (see 3.2.3.1).

(c) Ingratitude. A freedman (i.e. an ex-slave) who showed ingratitude to his patron (the former master) could be punished in a variety of ways, including re-enslavement in exceptional circumstances. A decree of the late classical period provided:

Modestinus, *Manumissions, sole book*: **Where it is proved that a patron has been violently attacked by his freedman or badly beaten or abandoned while suffering from the effects of poverty or illness, he must first be placed in his patron's power again and forced to serve him as master. If he does not take this warning, he should be sold on the authority of the consul or governor and the price given to the patron.** (D.25.3.6.1.)

The possibility of re-enslavement for ingratitude first arose in the early Empire when certain Emperors began to re-enslave freedmen in exceptional cases. It seems, however, that there was never a *general* rule allowing re-enslavement for ingratitude.

(d) *S. C. Claudianum* AD 52. This legislation ostensibly discouraged a female citizen from cohabiting with another person's male slave. If she persisted, following the owner's formal warnings, she could be enslaved by the owner in some circumstances, but not without a magistrate's decree.

(e) Selling oneself. What happened if a freeman tried to sell himself into slavery? Such a sale was invalid, *prima facie*: a free person could not in theory be the object of a contract of sale. However, attempts to sell oneself were punished—enslavement was imposed to try to deter such behaviour. Paradoxically, the very thing that the freeman could not do in law, the law did for him. But why should a free person even contemplate selling himself into slavery? In some circumstances, slavery might be considered preferable to freedom—e.g. where the slave managed the affairs of a powerful and kindly master. Or the object might simply be fraud: the freeman, pretending to be a slave, would arrange for an accomplice to sell him to an unsuspecting customer. After the sale, the freeman would establish his freedom and share the purchase price with the accomplice. Hence, the need was felt for the sanction of real enslavement to deter such practices. Hadrian allowed the freeman the possibility of escaping slavery by repayment of the full price to the buyer.

(f) Straying *dediticii* ('the capitulated'). Originally, *dediticii* were persons from communities that had taken up arms against Rome and then surrendered. Later, under the *lex Aelia Sentia* AD 4, ex-slaves of degraded character were added to the category. *Dediticii* were free but could never attain citizenship—they were excluded from the general grant of citizenship in AD 212—and had to live at least 100 miles from Rome. But if they returned within the forbidden limits, they were liable to be re-enslaved. Justinian abolished this class.

4.3.3.3 Capture

This mode of enslavement resulted mainly from the capture in war of foreign prisoners. It also occurred where a foreigner was arrested on Roman territory in times of peace, not having a lawful justification for his presence there. Capture in war became the main source of slaves in the late Republic, campaigns such as those of Julius Caesar in Gaul resulting in the enslavement of large numbers of foreigners. In theory, these captives belonged to the Roman people as a whole, but it became the practice for successful generals to hold the captives as booty with a view to their eventual sale. Most enemy prisoners probably became slaves in private hands.

What was the position if a Roman citizen was captured by the enemy? The captive was regarded as a slave of the enemy. He therefore suffered *capitis deminutio maxima*—the 'greatest' change of status—involving the loss of freedom, citizenship and family, and thus the cessation of all legal relationships affecting him. He lost all the legal powers that he previously might have possessed. He was no longer an owner of property, or a party to contract; and his will was void. Even his marriage was terminated automatically. The law seems to have been impossibly brutal in this instance, but may be viewed as a recognition of the reality of the situation—the chances of a captive returning were not high. In any case, such rules were motivated partly by the need to deter Roman soldiers from being captured. Better to die fighting than to fall into the hands of the enemy. However, the rules were relaxed in due course. Legislation under Sulla provided:

Julian, *Digest, book 42*: **By the *lex Cornelia* the wills of those who have died while in the power of the enemy are confirmed with the same effect as if those who had made them had not fallen into the power of the enemy, and, in the same way, their inheritance belongs to whoever is entitled.** (D.28.1.12.)

This provision operated on the fiction that the captive had died at the moment of capture, i.e. while still free. As for the rules on marriage, Justinian provided that marriage did not terminate on capture if the captive was known to be alive. If the captive's fate was not known, the marriage ended but the wife could not remarry for five years. These various rules (and relaxations) applied equally to Romans captured abroad in times of peace.

But what were the legal consequences if the captive returned to Roman territory, having escaped or been released? In theory, he remained a slave unless he was entitled to *postliminium* ('the benefit of re-entering the borders'):

Pomponius, *Quintus Mucius, book 37*: **The right of *postliminium* applies both in war and peace. In war, when those who are our enemies have captured someone on our side and have taken him into their own lines; for if during the same war he returns he has *postliminium*, that is, all his rights are restored to him just as if he had not been captured by the enemy. Before he is taken into the enemy lines, he remains a citizen. He is regarded as having returned from the time when he passes into the hands of our allies or begins to be within our own lines.** (D.49.15.5pr.–1.)

For the ex-captive to be entitled to the benefits of *postliminium*, it had to be shown that the capture had occurred in honourable circumstances and that the return to Rome (or to her allies) had been made at the first reasonable opportunity. Whether the return *had* to be 'during the same war' (as stated above) is unclear. Strict insistence on such a rule would have severely limited the operation of *postliminium*. The effect of *postliminium* was to restore the ex-captive to his previous legal status as far as possible. His former rights over property were restored, where feasible; and his marriage could be revived, but only if the wife consented and had not remarried in the meantime. And *potestas*, the legal power over descendants (see generally 5.1.2), was restored to the ex-captive if he had been a *paterfamilias*. Similarly, if he had been in the power of a *paterfamilias*, he became subject to that power again (cf. D.49.15.).

4.3.3.4 **Birth**

The basic rule (of the *ius gentium*) was that a child took the status that its mother had at the time of the child's birth (see D.1.5.5.1.–2.). Slavery through birth thus occurred if the child's mother was a slave when the child was born, the status of the father being irrelevant. A child born to a male citizen and a female slave would be a slave, owned by the mother's master. (Ownership of the children of slaves, subject to a usufruct, created a unique problem, see Birks, P., 'An Unacceptable Face of Human Property', in *New Perspectives*, 61–73.) If the parents were a female citizen and a male slave, the child was born a citizen. However, a number of exceptions to the basic rule emerged in the course of time. For example, the *S. C. Claudianum* AD 52 provided that if a female citizen cohabited with another's male slave, despite the owner's objection, any issue resulting from the union belonged to the slave's owner, who could claim the mother as well. One of the purposes of this provision may have been to enable the Emperor to have control over the children of public slaves, thus preserving a hereditary imperial service. See Crook, *Law and Life of Rome*, 62–3. Hadrian decreed that the owner could claim either the mother and child together or neither—an attempt to avoid the separation of mother and child. Justinian repealed the *senatus consultum*. Another important exception was introduced by a rescript under Hadrian: a child born to a slave mother was free if the mother had been free at the time of conception or at any time between conception and birth.

4.3.4 **The legal position of the slave**

Slaves lacked rights, but their legal position constituted a complex area of the law, as is evidenced by the considerable amount of space devoted in juristic literature to legal issues affecting slaves. Slaves were human 'things' (the objects of rights) without legal personality owned by their masters as *res mancipi*. The jurists did not question the existence of the institution—most were slave-owners themselves. Nor were they much concerned in their writings with the reform of the law of slavery, although some would have drafted the occasional imperial decree that improved the legal position of slaves.

4.3.4.1 **Maltreatment**

It cannot be denied that the financial value of the slave would have influenced the master's treatment of it. Although uneducated slaves were inexpensive and readily expendable, they were of limited use (mainly as manual labourers). Educated slaves, on the other hand, were expensive commodities that would have been properly 'maintained' by their masters to preserve their investment. In early law a master could do what he liked with his slave, over whom he had the (theoretically) unrestricted power of life and death (see Inst.Gai.1.52.). However, brutal treatment of slaves could result in disapproval from the censors, resulting in legal disgrace. Whether such factors acted as an effective deterrent against brutality is doubtful—slaves had no access to censors, who, in any case, were not continuously in office. See Watson, A., *Roman Slave Law* (1987), 115 ff. Some protection against maltreatment was eventually achieved through legislation. In 81 BC, the unjustified killing of another's slave was made a crime. A *lex Petronia* of the first century AD penalized masters who forced their slaves to fight wild beasts in the arena without the consent of a magistrate. Claudius issued an edict of considerable practical importance under which a slave who had been abandoned because of old age or sickness obtained freedom and the status of Junian Latin (see 4.4.3.1). Domitian AD 81–96 prohibited the castration of male slaves and took measures to discourage the trade in eunuchs. Nevertheless, the castration of slaves remained a problem, necessitating the imposition of strong sanctions, as evidenced by a rescript from Hadrian's reign:

Ulpian, *Duties of Proconsul, book 7*: ...**for no one should castrate another, freeman or slave, willing or unwilling, nor should anyone voluntarily offer himself for castration. Should anyone act in defiance of my edict, the doctor performing the operation shall suffer a capital penalty, as shall anyone who voluntarily offered himself for surgery.** (D.48.8.4.2.)

Hadrian enacted several other measures aimed at protecting slaves, the most important of which forbade masters from killing their slaves without the consent of a magistrate. Antoninus Pius decreed that the unjustified killing of slaves by their masters constituted criminal homicide (cf. Inst.Gai.1.53.; Inst.1.8.2.). And he provided slaves with some means of protecting themselves—a rescript, issued to a magistrate who had learned of the brutal behaviour of a certain master, stated:

Ulpian, *Duties of Proconsul, book 8*: **The power of masters over their slaves certainly ought not to be infringed and there must be no derogation from any man's legal rights. But it is in the interest of masters that those who make just complaint be not denied relief against brutality or starvation or intolerable wrongdoing. Therefore, judicially examine those who have fled the household of Julius Sabinus to take refuge at the statue and if you find it proven that they have been treated more harshly than is fair or have been subjected to infamous wrongdoing, then issue an order for their sale subject to the condition that they shall not come back under the power of their present master.** (D.1.6.2.)

For the first time, a slave could *initiate* a process that might lead to an improvement in his treatment. He could provoke an inquiry by clinging to a statue of the Emperor or seeking sanctuary in a temple. Under Constantine it was made an offence to kill a slave, even with cause, if the manner employed was deemed excessively cruel (cf. C.Th.9.12.2.). But the conversion to Christianity did not lead to any substantial short-term improvement in the conditions of slavery, let alone its abolition. In AD 428, however, it was decreed that any slave forced into prostitution by her master was automatically freed. The long line of legislative enactments culminated in Justinian's decree that the maximum power of a master over his slave was reasonable chastisement. The amelioration of the slave's position as regards maltreatment had progressed a long way.

4.3.4.2 Property—the *peculium*

(D.15.1., D.49.17., D.33.8., C.7.23.)

A slave could not own property: he *was* property. Anything that he acquired, from whatever source—earnings, gifts, legacies—belonged to the master:

Gaius, *Institutes, book 2*: **Anything which our slaves receive by delivery and anything which they acquire, whether on a stipulation or any other ground, is acquired by us; for a person in the power of another can hold nothing for himself.** (D.41.1.10.1.)

However, masters often allowed their slaves a *peculium*—property for the slave's use and enjoyment:

Pomponius, *Sabinus, book 7*: **It follows that it is what the slave holds with the master's consent which constitutes the *peculium*, not what the slave holds without his master's knowledge; otherwise, a thing which the slave had filched from his master would form part of the *peculium*, and that is not the law.** (D.15.1.4.2.)

The *peculium* could take many forms besides a sum of money. 'It was very often a commercial establishment, an industrial shop or factory, or some separate piece of property…derived from the word *pecus*, which means cattle, the *peculium* in the earlier agricultural stage of Roman history must have consisted of a flock of sheep or other domestic animals. It could even consist of other slaves, who had *peculia* of their own…', Johnston, *Roman Law in Context*, 31–2. It is important to appreciate that a *peculium* was not a static fund, but could grow and diminish according to the slave's business acumen. The size of the *peculium* was only determined upon condemnation if a creditor sued the *paterfamilias* on the basis of a debt incurred by the slave using his *peculium*.

It was granted by a master to his slave (or by a father to his son in power) for the latter's utilization, development, and enlargement through labour, transaction, and manipulation. This is often termed 'free administration' of the *peculium* (Kirschenbaum, A., *Sons, Slaves and Freedmen in Roman Commerce* (1987), 33–4; see also Cha, Y.-G., 'The Function of Peculium in Roman Slavery during the First Two Centuries A.D.', in *Forms of Control*, 433–6.)

Allowing a slave to hold property provided an incentive for the slave to work hard, and it would do a master's reputation no harm for it to be known that he owned slaves who held a sizeable *peculium*. A talented slave could easily amass a small fortune, especially if he was employed by his master in commerce and allowed to use the *peculium* for business purposes. Strictly, the slave had no rights in the *peculium*: the master was its absolute owner. However, so ingrained was the custom of allowing slaves a *peculium* that they were generally regarded as virtual owners. Indeed, a slave was often allowed to buy his freedom with his *peculium*. And when slaves were freed in their master's will, it was common for them to receive the *peculium* by way of a legacy. For a survey of the complexities relating to the *peculium*, see the texts collected in Frier and McGinn, *Casebook*, 265–90. For a good recent account, see Aubert, J.J., '*Dumtaxat de peculio*: What's in a Peculium, or Establishing the Extent of the Principal's Liability', in *New Frontiers*, 192–206.

4.3.4.3 Contracts

Slaves generally could not make contracts for themselves, but they could for their masters. However, in the latter case, the master was not bound by the contract (although he could enforce it). These rules proved inconvenient when Roman commerce started to expand. The usefulness of a slave in business dealings was clearly limited if agreements made by him could not be enforced against the master. The praetors made a crucial intervention in the late Republic by allowing actions against the master in certain circumstances. These actions, collectively known as the *actiones adiecticiae qualitatis* (see 9.3.3.4), were available against the owner (as well as the *paterfamilias* or employer of a son in power) whose slaves (or sons in power) had incurred debts while acting as business agents.

Although agreements made by slaves for themselves were not legally enforceable by them, they were recognized as creating a 'natural obligation', which in exceptional circumstances could have legal consequences on the slave's manumission (see 9.1.2.1).

4.3.4.4 Legal proceedings and noxal surrender

Although slaves lacked legal personality, and thus had no standing before the courts, there were occasions when the processes of law involved the participation of slaves. They certainly could not be parties to a civil action, but they were personally liable for any *crimes* that they committed. Moreover, they could be compelled to act as witnesses (but not against their own masters) in criminal and civil proceedings, and were examinable under torture, when necessary (see 2.3.2.4). If a slave was the victim of a delict (civil wrong), it was his master who would sue. If a slave committed a delict, the master was liable—the slave could not be sued. The master had a choice whether to pay for the damage or to surrender the slave to the victim (although in early law it seems that the master's primary duty was to surrender the slave). Under Justinian, but probably not before, a slave who had been surrendered and who had worked off the damage was presumably entitled to freedom (see Inst.4.8.5.). The option of surrendering a slave, known as noxal surrender (because it was the *noxa*—'the mischief'—that was surrendered), dated back to the early Republic.

How did noxal liability operate if there was a change of master after the commission of the delict? The general rule was that liability followed the wrongdoer—whoever was the master at the time when the victim took proceedings was liable:

Ulpian, *Edict, book 3*: **A noxal action is not granted against me unless the slave is in my hands, and if he is in my hands, even though he was not at the time when he committed the delict, I am liable**... (D.9.4.7pr.)

This is the reason why the seller of a slave had to reveal to the purchaser that the slave was still subject to noxal liability. However, a master could evade liability by manumitting his slave before joinder of issue in the proceedings brought by the plaintiff. In such cases, the general rule was that an ex-slave was personally liable for delicts committed before his manumission unless the victim had already obtained compensation from the master.

4.3.4.5 Personal relationships

Slaves could not be parties to a lawful marriage (except for public slaves). However, sexual union between slaves of the opposite sex was legally recognized for some purposes. For example, suppose that a child was born to a union between two slaves, and all the parties were later manumitted. It was accepted that the child could not enter into a marriage with a parent because of the blood tie, even though the relationship resulted from the servile state. Moreover, evidence suggests that—in large households particularly—slaves often did cohabit in stable relationships as though husband and wife. See Gardner, *Women in Roman Law*, 213 ff.

4.3.5 Release from slavery

(Inst.Gai.1.23.–5., Inst.1.6., D.40.1.)

As already seen, a slave could gain freedom in a variety of circumstances, e.g., if his master abandoned him. Moreover, just as slavery could be imposed as a form of punishment, so the status could be removed from persons as a reward for services to the State. The release from slavery in such circumstances was normally accompanied by the conferment of citizenship. Various services were rewarded, particularly the denouncing of criminals or those who evaded military service or the payment of tax.

However, by far the most important form of release from slavery was manumission, the process whereby a master freed his slave (see Inst.1.5pr.) (see Daube, D., 'Two Early Patterns of Manumission', in *Daube Collected Studies* I, 165–91). Formal manumission resulted in the slave becoming free and a citizen. The grant of citizenship to manumitted slaves—a liberal rule within an illiberal institution—was certainly one of the most civilized features of Roman law compared with other slaveholding societies, and was seen by Rome's enemies as one of the reasons for her strength. There were several recognized modes of formal manumission: *vindicta* ('by the rod'), by census, by will, and by declaration in church (see Gardner and Wiedemann, *Roman Household*, 145–51). (On documentary proof of manumission, see Gardner and Wiedemann, *Roman Household*, 163–4.)

4.3.5.1 *Manumissio vindicta*

(D.40.2.)

The master, his slave, and a third party, the *adsertor libertatis* ('the assertor of freedom'), appeared before a high-ranking magistrate, normally the praetor. The *adsertor* often was a lictor, the magistrate's assistant. The *adsertor* claimed the slave to be free, touching him with a ceremonial rod. The master ceded the slave by remaining silent and touching him in turn with the rod. The ceremony was similar to that used to recover a property through *sacramentum* (see 3.2.2.1). The magistrate's consent was necessary; if it was given, the slave was unconditionally freed forthwith. Within the formal process a certain amount of informality was possible, as suggested by a passage from Ulpian:

Ulpian, *Edict*, book 5: **When I was at a villa with a praetor, I raised no objection to a manumission before him, although no lictor was present.** (D.40.2.8.)

Manumissio vindicta was still to be found in Justinian's reign, although by then much of the ceremonial procedure had become obsolete.

4.3.5.2 Manumission by census

(D.40.3.)

If a slave was enrolled on the census with the master's approval, he was formally manumitted. The consent of the censors was necessary; they could refuse if they regarded the proposed manumission as undesirable in some way. Much would depend on who the master was. The manumission probably occurred when the slave's name was enrolled, although it is possible that the date on which the census became operative was the critical moment. This form of manumission became obsolete when the practice of taking a census died out in the early Empire.

4.3.5.3 Manumission by will

(D.40.4.)

This was the most common form of manumission. Freedom could be granted in a will, either as a direct legacy to the slave, or by way of a trust imposed on the heir, or a legatee to manumit him. The words granting freedom had to be express and phrased in the imperative, e.g. 'Let my slave Balbus be free.' In later law, this rule was partly relaxed, implied manumission being allowed by Justinian, e.g. 'Let my slave Balbus be my heir.' Previously, such a phrase may have been insufficient to manumit Balbus as it did not contain an express grant of freedom, although some jurists thought the contrary. The slave had to be clearly identified but this rule was generally interpreted in a liberal manner. Small mistakes in naming the slave, such as misspelling his name, could be ignored. Indeed, a name did not have to be stated as long as the slave could be clearly identified:

Gaius, *Common Matters or Golden Words, book 1*: **Slaves ordered to be free are thought to be expressly designated, if they have been unambiguously identified by their craft, office, or in some other way, for example, 'my steward', 'my butler', 'my cook', 'the son of my slave Pamphilius'.** (D.40.4.24.)

Testators could impose conditions when freeing slaves—a regular occurrence, if the considerable amount of juristic discussion of conditional manumission is a reliable guide. Slaves who were freed conditionally (*statuliberi*) were in a limbo-like position. They remained slaves until the condition was satisfied but their position was preferable to that of ordinary slaves. For example, they could not normally be subjected to torture when giving evidence in legal proceedings. The testator's heir became the owner of *statuliberi* on the testator's death, including any children born to a female slave before the satisfaction of the condition. However, the heir's right of ownership was temporary, and he (or anyone else) could not lawfully obstruct the satisfaction of the condition:

Ulpian, *Sabinus, book 27*: . . . **if Arethusa was given freedom subject to the condition of her bearing three children and the heir was responsible for her not giving birth, for example, by the administration of a contraceptive, she would be free at once; for what is the point of waiting? So, too, if the heir had procured an abortion; for she might have born triplets.** (D.40.7.3.16.)

Conditions that were illegal or immoral were ignored, as were impossible conditions, i.e. those impossible in the nature of things (e.g. 'if Balbus flies to the sun'). Such conditions were simply struck out—the slave was freed unconditionally.

When did testamentary manumission take effect? The general rule was that the slave was freed from the moment when the heir entered upon the inheritance, i.e. when he did anything that was characteristic of an heir. The general rule did not apply to *statuliberi*, who normally were freed when the relevant conditions applicable to their release were satisfied. Where freedom was granted through the imposition of a trust, the slave was not freed until the trust was carried out. An heir who accepted an inheritance had to carry out any trusts imposed upon him, at least from Augustus onwards.

4.3.5.4 **Manumission in church**

This form of manumission was introduced by Constantine. It consisted of a formal declaration of a slave's freedom by the master before a bishop and the assembled congregation, often made during important church festivals. It seems that the master's written confirmation was necessary.

4.3.5.5 **Informal manumission**

This occurred when a master did not follow the recognized modes of formal manumission, but, nevertheless, showed a clear intention that the slave should be regarded as free. The relevant intent could be demonstrated *per epistulam* (by letter) or *inter amicos* (between friends). In the former case, the master freed the slave by writing appropriate words in a letter to him, freedom arising from the time when the slave was appraised of the fact. The freeing of slaves *inter amicos* originally required a declaration of freedom by the master in the presence of his family or friends, e.g. at a dinner party. In later law, it is possible that any witnessed act which showed the master intentionally treating his slave as an equal was sufficient.

What was the position of a slave manumitted informally? Before the reforms of Augustus (see 4.3.5.6), the manumission was regarded as legally void: the slave remained a slave. But he was recognized as having *de facto* freedom, protected by the praetor should the master attempt to exercise his full rights. It seems that the master could not maltreat the slave or force him to work; but any acquisitions by the slave belonged to the master.

4.3.5.6 **The manumission reforms of Augustus**

The reign of Augustus witnessed major reforms in the law of manumission, a series of enactments that transformed the law from its previous unsatisfactory state. He was concerned to restrict large-scale, reckless manumissions, fearing both the potential consequences for public order and, perhaps, the possibility of the citizen body being swamped by large numbers of foreigners (but that had already occurred). Also, he wished to protect the interests of the creditors and heirs of slave-owners—manumission of slaves had been an effective method of reducing assets. At the same time, Augustus wished to encourage an expansion of the citizen body, particularly so as to provide recruits for the army, see Atkinson, K. M. T., 'The Purpose of the Manumission Laws of Augustus' (1966) 1 IJ, 356–74. To some extent, these were contradictory aims; but he certainly achieved an increase in the citizen population—it rose by almost a quarter in his reign.

The main reforms were as follows:

(a) *Lex Fufia Caninia* 2 BC. (Inst.Gai.1.42.–6., Inst.1.7., C.7.3.) This enactment restricted the number of slaves that could be manumitted by will. The maximum that could be freed was 100, the permitted quota varying in proportion to the number of slaves owned by the deceased. One of the reasons for this reform may have been to prevent the number of mourners at funerals being swollen by large numbers of grateful freedmen—a potential threat to order in disturbed times. The restrictions were not universally popular; it appears that testators tried various stratagems to evade them. It proved necessary to curb the evasions. If too many slaves were named in the will, the first named (within the permitted number) were freed; and if the testator put the names in a circle, so that no clear order was

ascertainable, none of the slaves were freed. The *lex Fufia* did not apply to manumission other than by will.

(b) *Lex Junia (Norbana).* This enactment is of uncertain date. It is possible that it
was enacted in AD 19 but the most plausible view, given that the *lex Aelia Sentia*
(see (c)) appears to refer to Junian Latins, is that the *lex Junia* must have preceded
AD 4. In any case, the reform brought about by the *lex Junia* is the kind of measure that Augustus is likely to have engineered. The statute tackled the problem of
the uncertain status of informally manumitted slaves by creating a new status for
them, that of Junian Latin, whereby the slave acquired freedom, but not citizenship (see 4.4.3.1). (See Sirks, A. J. B., 'Informal Manumission and the Lex Iunia'
(1981) 28 RIDA 3, 247–76, where the author argues that Junian Latinity was merely
a grade of dependence within the system of slavery and patronage; see also by
the same author, 'The Lex Iunia and the Effects of Informal Manumission and
Iteration' (1983) 30 RIDA 3, 211–92.)

(c) *Lex Aelia Sentia* AD 4. (Inst.Gai.1.36.–41., 47.) This enactment contained several important provisions:

(i) It established a council (both in Rome and in the provinces) to investigate
manumissions.

(ii) Any manumission was deemed void if the master was under 20 years of age
unless he obtained permission from the council on showing good cause. What
constituted good cause? Paul provides some examples:

Paul, *Lex Aelia Sentia, book 1*: **Past events can provide several grounds for manumission;
thus, the slave may have aided the master in battle, protected him against brigands, healed
him in sickness, uncovered a plot. And it is a long business, should we wish to make a
list, since many services can occur for which it is honorable to grant freedom by a formal
decision**...(D.40.2.15.1.)

(iii) A slave aged under 30 years could not be manumitted except for good cause,
and with the permission of the council. A manumission in breach of this rule
resulted in the slave becoming a Junian Latin.

(iv) Certain slaves with criminal records were prohibited from becoming citizens
on manumission. They were given the status of *dediticii* (see 4.3.3.2).

(v) Manumissions made to defraud creditors were deemed void. A manumission
made by an insolvent master fell within the rule, irrespective of the master's
intention:

Gaius, *Common Matters or Golden Things, book 1*: **It is deemed that a man manumits to the
detriment of creditors if he is insolvent at the time of the manumission or would become
insolvent after the grants of freedom; for men often hope that their assets are greater than
they actually are.** (D.40.9.10.)

4.3.5.7 Justinian's reforms

Justinian considerably simplified the law of manumission. The status of Junian
Latins and *dediticii* was abolished. Citizenship was acquired on informal as well as
formal manumission. As regards informal manumission, the old methods (*per epistulam* and *inter amicos*) continued to be used but needed to be evidenced by a document attested by five witnesses. In testamentary manumission, the restrictions

on numbers were abolished—the *lex Fufia* was repealed. *Manumissio vindicta* still required an appearance before a magistrate, but with less formality. Manumission in church continued as before. The rule that slaves normally had to be aged at least 30 years was abolished. Masters still had to be at least 20 years old, as a general rule, but 17 sufficed for a manumission by will (later reduced to 14). (See generally Gardner and Wiedemann, *Roman Household*, 159–62.)

4.4 Citizens and non-citizens

We now turn to a consideration of the legal position of free persons. They can be divided into two broad categories—citizens and non-citizens.

4.4.1 Roman citizenship

(Inst.Gai.1.11., Inst.1.4.)

4.4.1.1 Basic rights and duties

The Roman male citizen of full legal capacity had a number of rights by virtue of his status. The chief constitutional rights were the right to appeal against a death sentence, to vote in the assemblies, and to stand for public office. Women had the right of appeal but could not vote or stand for public office. Of greater interest to us were the citizen's private law rights—*commercium*, *testamenti factio*, and *conubium*. As a general rule, these rights were possessed by both men and women, although there were some important limitations in the case of the latter (see 4.4.2.2).

(a) *Commercium* was the right (of overriding importance) to participate in the processes and transactions of the *ius civile*, including the right to make formal contracts and conveyances, and to seek legal remedies in the courts. Essentially, it was the bundle of private law rights to which a citizen was generally entitled other than *testamenti factio* and *conubium*.

(b) *Testamenti factio* was the right to participate in the making of a valid will, whether as testator or witness, and the capacity to be made a beneficiary. It can be viewed as an adjunct of *commercium* but was often treated as a separate right, and one of considerable importance (given the significance of will-making in Roman society).

(c) *Conubium* was the right to enter a civil law marriage. Since such a marriage potentially created *potestas*, i.e. the legal power of a *paterfamilias* over his children, it can be appreciated that *conubium* was regarded as a most important right.

Citizenship carried with it some duties. Military service in the legions was compulsory at certain times in Rome's history. Since citizens fought in the legions—considered the elite troops—whereas non-citizens made up the auxiliary forces, service with the legions was viewed by some as a privilege rather than as a duty. When the Roman army or the Emperor was on the move, it was the duty of citizens of the relevant area to provide appropriate accommodation and sustenance, a potentially onerous burden. Some cities preferred to pay large sums to avoid the army being quartered on them for the winter. Moreover, citizens were responsible for the upkeep of roads in their communities and for the provision of transport animals for the State's postal service. Also, they owed a duty to act as guardians, judges, and jurors, when requested to do so, and were specifically subjected to the payment of certain taxes, notably the very unpopular 5 per cent inheritance tax introduced by Augustus. Although some of these duties were burdensome, the legal position of a Roman citizen, compared with that of a non-citizen, was generally advantageous. It helps to explain why citizenship was generally prized so highly, and even fought over at times.

4.4.1.2 Becoming a citizen

How was citizenship acquired? Citizenship was based predominantly on a principle of personality rather than territoriality, status depending on birth (the status of the parents) or some kind of grant. See Crook, *Law and Life of Rome*, 38 ff., cf. Inst. Gai.1.26.–35.

(a) Birth. The basic *ius gentium* rule applied under which the child normally took the status of the mother (see 4.3.3.4). Thus, a child was born a Roman citizen if its mother had been a citizen at the time of its birth. However, this rule did not apply in the case of a Roman civil law marriage (*iustum matrimonium*): the child took the status that its father had at the time of the child's conception. As such marriages were generally confined to citizens, any resulting children were normally born as citizens. But it was possible for non-citizens to be parties to a *iustum matrimonium* if they had *conubium*, in which case the child would not be born a citizen if the father had been a non-citizen when the child was conceived.

The operation of these rules could create anomalies. Suppose that a female citizen, married to a non-citizen without *conubium*, gave birth to a child. The *ius gentium* rule applied since the marriage was not a *iustum matrimonium*. Consequently, the child was a citizen—it took its mother's status. Had the father had *conubium*, the other facts being identical, the child would not have been a citizen because it would have taken the father's status. To end this absurdity, a *lex Minicia* (passed probably in the late Republic) provided that if a female citizen married a non-citizen without *conubium*, the child did not acquire citizenship.

(b) Manumission. As we have seen, formal manumission conferred citizenship; so did informal manumission under Justinian.

(c) Grant. Citizenship was granted by the State in various circumstances—e.g. to individuals as a reward for special services to Rome, to veterans on their retirement from the auxiliary forces of the army, and to magistrates and town councillors from non-citizen communities. Occasionally, a whole community or people received a grant of citizenship. This occurred with some frequency in the early Empire, with the result that the citizen body expanded greatly. The most important grant of all was the *constitutio Antoniniana* AD 212, the decree which extended citizenship to all the peoples of the Roman Empire. It applied to all free people other than *dediticii*. However, it did not abolish the different categories of non-citizens for the future, i.e. it applied only to existing persons. The enactment appears to have been a magnanimous gesture, but was probably prompted by the need to increase revenue through taxation: the more citizens there were, the greater the tax revenues. Also, it is likely that the decree was intended to foster a greater bond between the inhabitants of the Empire at a time when its borders were beginning to be seriously threatened.

4.4.1.3 **Proof of citizenship**

This was a considerable problem at certain times in Roman history. The possession of three names (e.g. Marcus Tullius Cicero) was regarded as a distinctive, if not invariable, characteristic of the Roman citizen. However, the clearest proof was provided by the census, which supposedly contained a list of all citizens. The political upheavals of the late Republic, and the increasing tendency to make block grants of citizenship to communities, resulted in the census becoming less reliable. Consequently, in the *lex Aelia Sentia* Augustus introduced a system of birth registration for citizens. And a register was established to record citizens created by individual grant.

4.4.2 **Categories of citizens**

A wide disparity in legal status was possible within the citizen body because of the privileges or disabilities that were applicable to particular groups of citizens or individuals. For example, special privileges (mainly in the realm of public rather than private law) were granted to the senatorial and equestrian orders in the early Empire, such as eligibility for posts in imperial administration. However, it was disabilities that most affected status, and to which we must now turn.

4.4.2.1 **Persons** *alieni iuris*

The most important classification of citizens was into those who were *sui iuris* and those who were *alieni iuris*. The former were 'of their own law', i.e. legally independent: they were not in the *potestas* of a *paterfamilias*. But *alieni iuris* persons were subject to *potestas*—they were 'of another's law'. The distinction was fundamental in Roman family law, and will be considered in detail in Chapter 5.

4.4.2.2 **Women**

Papinian, *Questions, book 31*: **There are many points in our law in which the condition of females is inferior to that of males.** (D.1.5.9.)

Disarming honesty from Papinian—and, yet, the position of women in Roman law and society was favourable compared with other ancient societies (some modern ones too). For example, Roman wives achieved a degree of legal emancipation that would have been the envy of married women in many European legal systems prior to the late-nineteenth century. Still, comparisons aside, Papinian was right—the Roman woman was legally disadvantaged in many ways compared to her male counterpart, owing to her lack of *potestas*, see Gardner, *Roman Citizen*, 85–108. She lacked, for example, certain constitutional rights, such as the right to hold office and to vote in the assemblies. As regards private law rights, women suffered various disabilities. The *sui iuris* woman of full age was required to have a guardian; the man was not. She could not act as a guardian; the man could. There were restrictions on her *testamenti factio* and if she entered a *manus* marriage (see 5.2.3.1) she was unable to own property, as a general rule, or to make contracts. The full extent of the Roman woman's legal disabilities will become evident in later chapters (see generally, Gardner, *Women in Roman Law*). cf. Inst. Gai.1.108–10 as well as the texts collected in Frier and McGinn, *Casebook*, 450–70. For a good survey of the sources, see also Evans Grubbs, J., *Women and the Law in the Roman Empire*.

4.4.2.3 **Freedmen**

(Inst.Gai.1.12., Inst.1.5., D.38.1.–3., C.6.7., and 10.58.)

Another basic classification of citizens was into the freeborn (*ingenui*) and the freed (*libertini*), i.e. those who had been freed from slavery. Freedmen (the term comprises freedwomen) and their issue were subjected to a number of legal disabilities, both in public and private law. They could not stand for the Senate or for public office, and were unable in early law to marry freeborn citizens. Augustus ended the ban on such marriages but prohibited freedmen from marrying members of the senatorial order. As regards private law, although freedmen were released from slavery by manumission, they did not become totally independent of their patron (the ex-master). The relationship between patron (or patroness) and freedman was one of the most interesting and arcane areas of Roman civil law. It will be considered first; then the question of how freedmen could change their status.

(a) Patron and freedman. A freedman owed certain duties to the patron:

(i) Services (*operae*). Provided that the manumission had been voluntary, the freedman had to perform services for his master (see Gardner and Wiedemann, *Roman Household*, 152–8). In a sense, these services constituted part of the 'price' of manumission. Which services could be claimed? First, they must have been agreed at the time of the manumission:

Modestinus, *Rules, book 1*: **Where no services have been imposed, a slave who has been manumitted cannot be compelled to perform services which he has not promised, even if he has performed them of his own free will at some time or another.** (D.38.1.31.)

The services had to be specified with sufficient certainty. Often, the agreement would specify how many days of work were involved in the performance of the services. Only reasonable services could be compelled, whatever the agreement:

Callistratus, *Monitory Edict, book 3*: **Only those services are understood to have been imposed that can be performed without endangering reputation or life. For if a prostitute has been manumitted, she should not perform the same services for her patron, although she still earns her living by prostitution; nor should a gladiator offer such services after manumission, because they cannot be performed without endangering life.** (D.38.1.38pr.)

Services that were illegal, immoral, or impossible would not be regarded as reasonable; nor could the freedman be compelled to do anything that was detrimental to his status. The services had to be appropriate to the abilities of the freedman and his circumstances.

Performance of services would normally be free and could benefit the patron's friends:

Julian, *Minicius, book 1*: **If a freedman practices the profession of a ballet dancer, it is true that he should provide his services free, not only for his patron himself but also for the latter's friends' entertainments; just as it is true that a freedman too who practices medicine will attend, if his patron wishes it, the latter's friends without payment. For the patron, in order to use his freedman's services, is not obliged to be forever giving entertainment or being ill.** (D.38.1.27.)

Unless otherwise specified, the freedman had to perform the services at the patron's home; however, the time spent on the journey normally counted as part of the service, i.e. the patron 'lost' the travelling time. The patron had to feed the freedman when the latter was performing services, or give him the opportunity to obtain food. Services were not compellable if the freedman was ill; or if he had either two children (of any age) or one child aged at least 5 years; or if he had opted to pay a money settlement in place of the services. Further, a patron lost his right to the services of a freedwoman if she attained the age of 50; or if he married her or if she lived with him as his concubine (see 5.2.6.2).

(ii) Gifts (*munera*). The freedman would be expected to make gifts to the patron or his family on certain specified occasions, e.g. the marriage of the patron's children. (Freedmen were expected to contribute to the dowry.) Such gifts were compellable only if they had been agreed at the time of manumission.

(iii) Respect (*obsequium*). The relationship between patron and freedman was broadly comparable to that of parent and child. Indeed, Title 15 of Book 37 of the *Digest* is entitled 'The obedience to be offered to parents and patrons'. The freedman normally took the patron's name and owed a duty to behave respectfully to the patron and to his immediate family. So he could not instigate criminal proceedings against the patron or be a witness in such case. Nor could he bring any civil action that involved discredit to the patron: other actions required a magistrate's consent. If the freedman was sued by the patron, no defence could be pleaded which discredited the latter. The freedman had to give financial assistance, as far as he reasonably could, if his patron fell on bad times. And competing in business could be considered disrespectful if such trade harmed the patron (comparable with modern restraint of trade cases):

Scaevola, *Replies, book 2*: **Can the freedman of a clothing merchant engage in the same business in the same community and the same area without the permission of his patron? [Scaevola] has given it as his opinion that there is no rule to prevent him, if his patron will not suffer as a result.** (D.38.1.45.)

Serious breach of the duty of the freedman to show respect could exceptionally result in his re-enslavement for ingratitude (see 4.3.3.2).

(iv) Property (*bona*). Under the Twelve Tables the patron had a right to succeed to a freedman's estate if the latter died intestate and without leaving heirs. Later, the patron was able to take half of his freedman's property left by will (see Inst. Gai.3.41.); but Justinian allowed this only if the freedman was not survived by children. This was the basic position as regards the inheritance of freedmen's property. There was much complex detail in this area of the law, which lies outside the confines of this book.

The patron, too, had certain duties. For example, he had to show his freedman some respect; he could not treat him as a slave. Thus, the freedman could not be compelled to live in the patron's household, although many did so of their own accord. And if the freedman was in need, the patron had to offer him assistance, otherwise he could lose his rights as patron.

(b) Change of status. It became possible in the early Empire for the status of the freedman (but probably not the freedwoman) to be changed to that of a freeborn citizen through the following devices:

(i) *Restitutio natalium* ('the restoration of birthrights'). The Emperor could declare the freedman to be henceforth a freeborn citizen, the patron's consent normally being required since the patron–freedman relationship would be terminated:

Marcian, *Institutes, book 1*: . . . **this man is treated in regard to his entire legal status as if he had been born free, nor can his patron enter on the succession. For this very reason the**

Emperors are generally reluctant to restore anyone to his birthrights without the patron's consent. (D.40.11.2.)

'Restore anyone to his birthrights' implies that the declaration could be made only in respect of freedmen who had actually been freeborn. However, *restitutio natalium* was often granted on a fictional basis, i.e. even though the freedman had not been freeborn.

(ii) *Ius annuli aurei* ('the grant of a gold ring'). This was a mark of equestrian status, given by the Emperor to a freedman to make the latter freeborn, thus enabling him to stand for public office. Unlike the case of *restitutio natalium*, the grant did not terminate the relationship between freedman and patron: the latter retained rights of inheritance (but could not insist on services). Justinian gave all freedmen the *ius annuli aurei*, their relationship with the patron being unaffected unless he expressly waived them. The practical effect of this grant was that the legal and practical disabilities associated with freedmen status disappeared.

Freedmen constituted a crucial part of Roman society and took an important role in Rome's economic development. Many freedmen possessed the sort of talents that were essential to Rome's economic well-being and prosperity. By the end of the Republic, they constituted a sizeable part of the citizen body, and found themselves much envied and disliked by various classes in Roman society, especially by the senatorial class (who tended to view freedmen as *nouveaux riches*). See Crook in *Law and Life of Rome*, who describes freedmen as 'the nearest thing Rome ever had to a middle class' (50). See also Gardner, *Roman Citizen*, 7–51.

4.4.2.4 **Bondsmen**

In some situations a person, though theoretically free, was subjected to civil bondage (*mancipium*), a semi-servile status in which his rights as a free man were in effect suspended. This occurred, for example, in the formal process required in emancipation (see 5.1.2.4), when the state of bondage was only very temporary. A more permanent form of bondage resulted when a *paterfamilias* sold a child into slavery within the city of Rome or gave up a child (who had committed a delict) through noxal surrender (see further 5.1.2.1). Although the bondsman remained free, his legal position was similar in some respects to that of slavery as regards his relationship with the person into whose power he had been transferred. For example, any property acquired by the bondsman during civil bondage belonged to his 'master'. But the latter did not have the power of life and death over the bondsman, and had to treat him with the respect owed to a free man. Sale of children into civil bondage became obsolete by the classical period, but noxal surrender of sons survived until Justinian. cf. Inst.Gai.1.138.–41.

4.4.2.5 *Infames*

These were citizens who were subjected to various legal disabilities on account of their disreputable conduct—they were in legal disgrace (*infamia*). The concept of *infamia* had its beginnings in the activities of the censors, who, in drawing up the census, could mark the name of a citizen involved in misconduct. The praetors, too, contributed to the development of *infamia*, through their edicts and control of civil litigation. They could blacklist persons for undesirable activities and thus prevent them from acting as advocates or as a *procurator* in litigation, or from being represented (see 3.3.2.5). And they could decree that condemnation in certain actions carried with it *infamia*. Although the censorial system faded in the early Empire, praetorian *infamia*, embellished occasionally by legislation, remained an important feature of Roman civil law. Indeed, the category of *infames* was to be found in Justinian's law—it was never abolished. cf. C.10.59.

What sort of conduct incurred *infamia*? Consider the following selection of disreputable activities:

Julian, *Edict, book 1*: **The praetor's words are: 'The following incur *infamia*: one who has been discharged from the army in disgrace...one who has appeared on the stage to act or recite; one who has kept a brothel; one who in criminal proceedings has been judged guilty of vexatious litigation or collusion in anything; one who has been condemned in his own name for theft, robbery with violence, insult, fraud, trickery or compromised in such a case...'** (D.3.2.1.)

This list is far from exhaustive, but gives some insight into the variety of conduct considered to be sufficiently disreputable to incur *infamia*. The low regard in which acting was held is evident from the text. However, appearing on stage did not result in *infamia*, it seems, unless it was done for reward. *Infamia* could be imposed for breach of certain contracts, particularly those involving trust or good faith, e.g. partnership or deposit. And *infamia* resulted where a person simultaneously entered into agreements for betrothal or marriage with different persons, or was in breach of the rules concerning the mourning of deceased husbands, e.g. anyone who married a widow before the end of the customary period of mourning (the widow, too, was liable). But it was different if it was the wife who had died:

Paul, *Edict, book 5*: **Husbands do not have to mourn for their wives.** (D.3.2.9.)

What were the consequences of *infamia*? Social disgrace was certainly involved, and legal disabilities: e.g. *infames* could not hold offices or positions of honour, could not vote (at least in early law), or bring criminal accusations, or appear as advocates, or act as representatives (or be represented) in litigation, as we have seen. And *infames* would often be *intestabiles* as well (4.4.2.6). The true impact of *infamia* as a legal penalty can only be fully understood in the context of Roman society where commerce and social progression was based on family and status connections. These ties were effectively severed when a person was branded infamous, which is why infamy is often described as social (and for that matter also economic) 'death'. See Greenidge, A. H. J., *Infamia: Its Place in Roman Public and Private Law* (1894), and more recently Gardner, *Roman Citizen*, 110–54, on the nature of *infamia* as a legal measure.

4.4.2.6 *Intestabiles*

Under the Twelve Tables, persons who were involved in discreditable conduct could not act as witnesses, either in litigation or in formal transactions (such as the making of wills or the conveyance of property). Moreover, it is probable that *intestabiles* could not make wills or formal conveyances, although the rule was not beyond doubt. According to Gaius:

Gaius, *Provincial Edict, book 22*: **When a person is declared by a statute to be *intestabilis*, the effect is that he is not acceptable as a witness and furthermore, in the view of some, that witnesses cannot act for him either.** (D.28.1.26.)

But Ulpian was less tentative, although it is not clear whether he was stating a general rule or simply the position as regards defamatory conduct:

Ulpian, *Sabinus, book 1*: **If someone has been found guilty of writing defamatory verses, it is expressly laid down by** *senatus consultum* **that he be** *intestabilis*, **and, therefore, he will be able neither to make a will nor to be used as a witness to a will.** (D.28.1.18.1.)

There was a close correlation between *intestabiles* and *infames*—persons subject to *infamia* were usually classed as *intestabiles* as well. But it was possible to be one without the other.

4.4.2.7 *Humiliores*

In the early Empire a distinction developed, compounded later by Caracalla's grant of citizenship in AD 212, between persons of low social status (*humiliores*) and those from the 'respectable' upper classes (*honestiores*), the latter consisting chiefly of the senatorial and equestrian orders. The distinction was predominantly of importance in terms of social status, but there were some legal consequences, especially concerning the criminal process. The *honestiores* were exempt from certain types of punishment reserved for the *humiliores*—flogging, condemnation to the mines, casting to the beasts, and crucifixion, for example.

4.4.2.8 *Coloni Adscriptii*

This was a class of agricultural serfs that arose during the Empire. Originally, *coloni* were undifferentiated from ordinary citizens; but in the late Empire, their status suffered and became the subject of considerable legislation, which made their position in relation to their landlord very onerous, similar to medieval villeinage. They were tied to the land: they committed an offence if they left without their landlord's consent, and could be reclaimed by him. Nor could they sell or assign their interest without his consent. Suing the landlord was not possible apart from exceptional cases. On the other hand, the landlord could not dispossess *coloni* from their land; nor could he raise the rent, which normally consisted of part of the agricultural produce resulting from the tenant's labour.

4.4.3 **Non-citizens**

There were two main classes of free persons who were not citizens: Latins and peregrines, i.e. foreigners. Within that classification there were further subdivisions.

4.4.3.1 **Latins**

(a) *Latini prisci* (the 'ancient' Latins). These were the inhabitants in the early Republic of communities neighbouring Rome and allied with her in the Latin League (see 1.2.2.1). They had most of the important rights of Roman citizenship, including *commercium, conubium, testamenti factio*, and the right to vote in the Roman assemblies. The status disappeared following the dissolution of the Latin League in 338 BC, after which *Latini prisci* were given full citizenship.

(b) Colonial Latins. They were the inhabitants of the colonies that had been established at strategic points in Italy (and beyond) during the centuries of Roman expansion. These colonies possessed Latin rights whereby they enjoyed a degree of legal independence and self-government. The status disappeared in Italy following the general grant of citizenship after the Social War. However, colonies continued to be founded abroad in the early Empire. The status of colonial Latin therefore continued to be granted until Caracalla's grant of citizenship in AD 212, see Fear, A. T., 'Cives Latini, Servi Publici and the Lex Irnitana' (1990) 37 RIDA 3, 149–66.

The status of colonial Latins was inferior to that of the *Latini prisci*, but still worth having. They had *commercium* and could vote in the assemblies; but they lacked *conubium*, had a restricted *testamenti factio*, and could not hold public office in Rome. However, special opportunities were created for them to become full citizens: local magistrates and town councillors (*decuriones*) were given citizenship, mainly to encourage persons to stand for these potentially onerous offices.

(c) Junian Latins. This status was specially created by the *lex Junia (Norbana)* for informally manumitted slaves and survived until its abolition by Justinian (see Inst.Gai.1.22.). Junian Latinity could occur in various ways—informal manumission under the *lex Junia*; defective formal manumission, e.g. if a slave aged under 30 was manumitted in breach of the *lex Aelia Sentia* (see 4.3.5.6); reward from the State; or abandonment of a sick or aged slave. The list is not exhaustive—new ways of creating Junian Latinity continued to be found in the later Empire.

What was the legal position of a Junian Latin? He could marry, but his marriage could not be a Roman civil law marriage as he lacked *conubium* (apart from exceptional cases). Junian Latins had *commercium*, but only a very limited *testamenti factio*, restricted to the capacity to witness wills. They could not make wills or benefit under them except under a trust. They owed the usual duties that were owed by freedmen towards their patrons. And when a Junian Latin died, he was somewhat perversely regarded as dying as a slave, with the result that all his property reverted to his patron or the patron's heirs, even if the Junian Latin was survived by his own children—a harsh rule, indeed, and one that encouraged Justinian to abolish the status.

A number of methods of acquiring citizenship were made available to Junian Latins. The chief ones were:

(i) *Iteratio* ('repetition'). If a defective manumission had occurred, the Junian Latin could acquire citizenship by repetition of the manumission procedure without defect.

(ii) *Anniculi probatio* ('proof of a one-year-old'). Under the *lex Aelia Sentia*, a Junian Latin who had been incorrectly freed from slavery, while under 30 years of age, could acquire citizenship by proving to a magistrate that, *inter alia*, he had married a citizen or a Latin (colonial or Junian) before seven witnesses and that a child, born of the marriage, had attained one year of age. The Junian Latin acquired citizenship not only for himself but also for his wife (if not a citizen) and the child. If the husband died before making use of the process, the widow was given the right to use it to acquire citizenship for herself and the child. In AD 72 *anniculi probatio* was made available to all Junian Latins.

(iii) *Erroris causae probatio* ('proof of a mistaken ground'). This occurred where a party was seeking *anniculi probatio* (see (ii)) but was mistaken as to the status of their spouse, i.e. the latter proved to be a foreigner, and not a citizen, or Latin. On proof of the error, citizenship would be granted provided the other conditions of *anniculi probatio* were satisfied. The application could fail if the error had been due to gross negligence. There were other forms of *erroris causae probatio* (see 5.2.2.3). The provision of such procedures (and their apparently frequent use) to rectify mistakes as to status was symptomatic of a society that, in its developed form, was highly stratified, racially very mixed, and dynamic in the manner whereby status could rapidly change.

Apart from these procedures, Junian Latins could acquire citizenship through a variety of specific enactments (applying to colonial Latins too) that were aimed as inducements to perform valuable services for the State. For example, the *lex Visellia* AD 25 gave citizenship to those who had spent six years as *vigiles* ('watchmen'). Their main duty was to fight fires—a dangerous occupation in Rome at the best of times, but particularly in the reign of Nero. See Robinson, O. F., *Ancient Rome: City Planning and Administration*, 2nd edn. (1994), 106 ff. Moreover, citizenship was offered by Nero to any Latin who built a house in Rome, spending a specified minimum amount of money on its construction. The building of substantial houses was encouraged to fill the void created by the great fire of AD 64 in Nero's reign.

4.4.3.2 **Peregrini (foreigners)**

Peregrines were free persons who were neither citizens nor Latins, but subject to a municipal law of their own. They lacked the rights, both in public and private law, that went with Roman citizenship; but *commercium* or *conubium* (or both) were occasionally granted to such communities or individuals as a reward for meritorious service to Rome. Nevertheless, the vast majority of peregrines were without such rights. This meant that they were outside the *ius civile* but were not totally excluded from the Roman legal system because the rules of the *ius gentium* (see 4.3.1) applied to them. For example, peregrines were able to acquire ownership over property through the *ius gentium* modes of acquisition (see generally 7.2). They were able to take part in Roman commercial life since some of the important contracts were of the *ius gentium*, and thus open to all. Indeed, the influence of foreigners was of fundamental importance in the evolution of the Roman law of contract in the later Republic. As regards legal procedure, foreigners came to be integrated into the legal system through the peregrine praetor and the development of the formulary system. Virtually all peregrines living within the Empire became citizens on the grant of citizenship in AD 212.

And for a good recent account of the complexities surrounding the application of Roman law in the provinces, see Richardson, J., 'Roman Law in the Provinces', in *Cambridge Companion*, 45–58 as well as Humfress, C., 'Law's Empire: Roman Universalism and Legal Practice', in *New Frontiers*, 73–101.

 online resource centre   Please consult the Online Resource Centre for revision guidance on this chapter.

FURTHER READING

The literature on Roman slavery is immense, see Watson, A., 'Morality, Slavery and the Jurists in the Later Roman Republic' (1968) 42 Tulane LR, 289–303, on the moral attitude of the later Republican jurists to slavery.

On the interaction between slaves and citizens in the workforce, see Garnsey, P. (ed.) (1980), *Non-Slave Labour in the Greco-Roman World*, Cambridge: Philological Society (Suppl. vol. 6), chs. 6–9.

On manumission, see Wiedemann, T., 'The Regularity of Manumission at Rome' (1985) 35 CQ, 162–75, where the author investigates whether Roman slaves could almost always count on being freed during the course of their lives. See furthermore, Watson, A., 'Slavery and the Development of Roman Private Law' (1987) 29 BIDR, 105–18, on *peculium* and manumission.

On freedmen, see Treggiari, S. (1969), *Roman Freedmen during the Late Republic*, Oxford: Clarendon Press; Weaver, P. R. C. (1972), *Familia Caesaris—A Social Study of the Emperor's Freedmen and Slaves*, New York: Cambridge University Press. See also Garnsey, P., 'Independent Freedmen and the Economy of Roman Italy under the Principate' (1981) 63 Klio, 359–71, where the author examines the phenomenon of the successful freedman in the context of the economy and society of Italy in the period of the Principate. Gardner, J. F., 'The Adoption of Roman Freedmen' (1989) 43 Phoenix, 236–57, explores the extent of this practice as well as its social and political implications. Weaver, P. R. C., 'Children of Freedmen (and Freedwomen)', in *Marriage, Divorce and Children*, 166–90, demonstrates the problems arising from the legal status of children of former slaves. See also recently Mouritsen, H. (2011), *The Freedman in the Roman World*, Cambridge: Cambridge University Press. On patronage and friendship, see the texts collected in Gardner and Wiedemann, *Roman Household*, 166–83.

5

The Roman family

5.1 The *paterfamilias* and his household

(Inst.Gai.1.48., Inst.1.8., D.1.6.)

5.1.1 Basic notions

Roman family law was based on the fundamental concept that each family had a *paterfamilias*—the head of the household. He was the eldest living male ancestor of a specific family. He had in his power (*potestas*) all *descendants* traced through the male line (and also exercised forms of control over other members of the household). The *paterfamilias* was *sui iuris*, i.e. legally independent—he could not be in anyone else's power:

Ulpian, *Institutes, book 1*: **Heads of households are those who are in their own power (*potestas*), whether they are over or under the age of puberty** ... (D.1.6.4.)

It seems absurd that the head of a household could be under the age of puberty, but this was the logical consequence of the rules. A child became *sui iuris* on the father's death, assuming that the father had been the *paterfamilias*. If the child was male, he himself became a *paterfamilias*, whatever his age, although if he was under puberty, he would have to have a guardian. The Roman household could consist in some circumstances of only one person:

Ulpian, *Edict, book 46*: **Someone is called the head of the household if he holds sway in a house, and he is rightly called by this name even if he does not have a son ... we can even call a *pupillus* a head of a household. And when the head of the household dies, all the individuals who were subjected to him begin to hold their own households for as individuals they enter into the category of heads of households.** (D.50.16.195.2.)

(*Pupillus:* a ward below the age of puberty.)

The above text needs qualification. It was not strictly accurate to say that *all* the individuals previously subject to the *paterfamilias* would themselves take that status on his death. Suppose that Balbus, a *paterfamilias*, dies leaving two sons, each with children of his own. While Balbus is alive his sons and grandchildren will all be in his power. When he dies, his sons will each become *paterfamilias* with power over their respective children, i.e. the grandchildren will remain in power, but now that of their father rather than their grandfather.

Everyone who was in the power of a *paterfamilias* was related to him and to one another. This form of relationship was known as *agnatio*. The agnates remained in this relationship even if the *paterfamilias* died. Thus, the test of *agnatio* was subjection to a common *potestas*, whether actual or hypothetical, i.e. all those who were in the power of a *paterfamilias*, or would have been if he had been alive, were agnatically related. Another way of describing the agnatic relationship is to define agnates as those tracing their descent through males to a common male ancestor. Most agnates were blood relations (i.e. cognates) but there were some exceptional cases. For example, a child adopted from another family became the agnate of his adoptive family. Conversely, a child given in adoption, or emancipated, lost his agnatic ties with his natural family.

The agnatic system dated from Rome's earliest days and remained important as the basis of family legal relationships for much of Rome's history. Being an agnate had vital consequences in the law, especially as regards rights of inheritance and guardianship. It was important to know to whom one was agnatically related. In later law, the importance of cognatic relationships was increasingly recognized, hardly surprising given the artificiality of the agnatic relationship. For a useful overview of the complexities surrounding agnatic relationships, see the texts collected in Frier and McGinn, *Casebook*, 16–17.

5.1.2 *Potestas*

Gaius, *Institutes, book 1*: **Also in our *potestas* are our children whom we have begotten in lawful wedlock. The right over our children is peculiar to Roman citizens.** (D.1.6.3.)

Gaius is not quite accurate here. The concept that the family was in the power of the eldest male ancestor was not unusual in ancient societies. What was 'peculiar' was the rigid, structured manner in which Roman law embraced this concept, see Gardner, *Roman Citizen*, 52–84. As a general rule, *all* legitimate descendants (as well as wives *in manu*) were in the power of the *paterfamilias*, whatever their age. The child's public standing in the world was irrelevant: a father may have had very distinguished children, and yet they were in his *potestas*. There were some exceptions, e.g. a *paterfamilias* did not have power over a daughter who had become a Vestal virgin (priestess in the cult of Vesta, Rome's goddess of the hearth). Vestal virgins were legally independent although subject to the discipline of the chief pontiff. If a Vestal retired after the compulsory 30 years' service, she would return to the *potestas* of her *paterfamilias* or, if he was dead, she would require a guardian: see Gardner, *Women in Roman Law*, 22 ff. It deserves mention that the powers of the *paterfamilias* over his children did not extend to public affairs:

Pomponius, *Quintus Mucius, book 16*: **A *filiusfamilias* is held to have the same position as a *paterfamilias* in public matters, so he can, for example, hold magisterial office or be appointed as tutor.** (D.1.6.9.)

We must now consider the various powers that were comprised in *potestas*.

5.1.2.1 Rights over the person

(a) Exposure. The *paterfamilias* had the right in early law to expose newborn infants if he wished to reject them. Exposure entailed abandoning them to their fate. This could result in the infant's death but often it would be left at a place where it was likely to be picked up by strangers. Such a child would normally be reared as a slave although in theory it remained free. Some restrictions were later placed on the right to expose children. Eventually, exposure was totally prohibited in AD 374:

Everyone should nourish his own offspring. If anyone meditates exposing them, he will be liable to the penalty laid down for this. (CJ.8.51.2pr.) [a response of the Emperors Valentinian, Valens and Gratian to one Probus]

(b) Power of life and death. Even if a child was accepted by the *paterfamilias*, it was subject to a general power over life and death, similar to that of a master over his slave, see Yaron, R., 'Vitae Necisque Potestas' (1958) 30 TR, 243–51. On the early history of this power and its similarity to forms of control in other legal systems of the ancient world, see also Westbrook, R., 'Vitae Necisque Potestas' (1999) 48 Historia, 203–23. The Twelve Tables described the power as absolute—it included the right to flog, to imprison, or to put children to death, however distinguished their rank. However, instances of children being killed by virtue of these powers were infrequent—the causeless killing of one's children would result most probably in *infamia*. When death was imposed, it was usually as a form of punishment for serious misconduct. For example, unchastity in daughters was considered as particularly reprehensible. The *lex Julia de adulteriis c.* 18 BC allowed a father to kill his married daughter if she was found committing adultery in his house or that of her husband. However, it seems that the daughter could not be killed unless her seducer was killed as well: if only one of them was killed, the *paterfamilias* would be open to a charge of homicide.

The power over life and death was gradually curtailed. Killing a child, even with cause, came to incur serious consequences:

Marcian, *Institutes, book 14*: **It is said that when a certain man had killed in the course of a hunt his son, who had been committing adultery with his stepmother, the deified Hadrian deported him to an island [because he acted] more [like] a brigand in killing him than as [one] with a father's right; for paternal power ought to depend on compassion, not cruelty.** (D.48.9.5.)

In addition to the imposition of such *ad hoc* sanctions, a more general rule was introduced later in the second century AD:

Ulpian, *Adulterers, book 1*: **A father cannot kill his son without giving him a hearing but must accuse him before the prefect or the provincial governor.** (D.48.8.2.)

Under Constantine, the killing of a child was declared to be the equivalent of the heinous crime of parricide; this provision effectively ended the power over life and death. By the time of Justinian, the right of the *paterfamilias* was no more than the power to inflict reasonable chastisement, the same rule that was applied in the master–slave relationship. For a summary of cases, see Frier and McGinn, *Casebook*, 193–210.

(c) Sale, surrender, and recovery. In early law the *paterfamilias* could sell children into slavery, a power that became obsolete during the Republic but which was revived by Constantine as an aid to impoverished parents. And there was a right in early law to place or sell children into civil bondage (see 4.4.2.4). For example, children who had committed delicts could be noxally surrendered to the victim. They did not revert back into the power of the *paterfamilias* on working off the damages, but became *sui iuris* (on release by the victim of the delict). Noxal surrender of daughters became obsolete in the Republic, but continued for sons until its abolition by Justinian.

The impression that children were to some extent treated as *belonging* to the *paterfamilias* is strengthened by the fact that he had available to him the standard proprietary remedies of an owner. Thus, if a child was kidnapped, it was regarded as 'stolen', which enabled the *paterfamilias* to recover it through a *vindicatio* and to sue for damages under the action for theft (see 10.3.1.3). Further, the praetors allowed an interdict to compel the production of a child-in-power (if unlawfully held). Proof that the child was subject to the legal power of the claimant would lead to the grant of a further interdict, authorizing the removal of the child and its restoration to lawful *potestas*. This became the normal method in the Empire for the recovery of kidnapped children.

(d) Marriage and divorce. The *paterfamilias* had important rights concerning the marriage of his child. Originally, he could compel his child to marry, but this power became generally obsolete during the Republic (although Augustus compelled his daughter Julia to marry his stepson Tiberius). However, the *paterfamilias* retained the right to refuse consent to marry:

Paul, *Edict, book 35*: **Marriage cannot take place unless everyone involved consents, that is, those who are being united and those in whose power they are.** (D.23.2.2.)

Augustus allowed consent to be dispensed with if it was refused without good cause, but it is not clear whether the dispensation was made available to sons as well as daughters. It is possible that sons could not obtain a dispensation until Justinian's time. The marriage of a son (who one day would himself be a *paterfamilias*) had potentially more serious legal consequences than that of a daughter. An absolute veto over a son's marriage, but not that of a daughter, would be understandable within the context of Roman society. However, the better view is that Augustus's dispensation provision did apply to sons since it refers to the wrongful prevention of *children* from marrying (D.23.2.19.). There were other circumstances, apart from unreasonable refusal, in which dispensation from consent could be sought, e.g. where the *paterfamilias* was insane; or where he was absent, his whereabouts unknown (Justinian insisted that the absence must have been of at least three years' duration).

A *paterfamilias* had the power also to compel his child to terminate a marriage through divorce (see 5.2.4). If the *paterfamilias* was a grandfather he was entitled to the children of his son's marriage on the divorce of the son, i.e. there was no change of *potestas*. If the husband was *sui iuris*, and therefore a *paterfamilias*, he retained *potestas* over the children of the marriage on his divorce. As a general rule, the wife had no rights to the custody of the child. However, in practice, children often continued to live with their mother after her divorce, particularly where the father was involved in affairs of State.

5.1.2.2 Rights over property
Children originally could not own property; anything that they acquired belonged absolutely to their *paterfamilias*:

Anything received by children in our *potestas* or our slaves...is acquired for us, because a person in *potestas* can have nothing of his own.... (Inst.Gai.2.87.)

However, as in the case of slaves, children were often allowed to keep and enjoy a certain amount of property as *peculium*. Its extent depended on their age and circumstances. The *peculium* of a child-in-power of mature years, from a wealthy family, could obviously be of considerable size. cf. Frier and McGinn, *Casebook*, 240–50, 265–91.

In the Empire, there were a number of reforms that improved the position of sons-in-power. Augustus, aiming to encourage recruitment to the army, allowed sons legal rights in property acquired during military service (*peculium castrense*):

Pomponius, *Rules from Marcellus's Notes, sole book*: **It is agreed that nothing is owed to fathers from the military property of their sons.** [Macer, *Military Law, book* 2[11]]: **The *peculium castrense* is that which is given by parents or blood relations to a man engaged in military service, or that which a son-in-power has himself acquired in the army, and which he would not have acquired had he not served.** (D.49.17.10–11.)

Military property came to comprise a wide category of things, including gifts on entering service, military pay, captured booty and enemy personnel, and legacies from army colleagues. What could the son-in-power do with this property? He could dispose of it *inter vivos* or by will, although before Hadrian the son had to make the will while on military service (see Inst.2.12pr.).

Constantine considerably extended the category of property in which a son could have rights. First, he included earnings acquired in State service (*peculium quasi castrense*). The son's position in respect of such acquisitions was similar to that applicable to military property, the main difference being that they could not be disposed by will until Justinian's reign. Further, Constantine provided that gifts or legacies acquired by sons and daughters on their mother's death (*peculium adventitium*) should be regarded as a separate fund that the *paterfamilias* did not own but could use, retaining any resulting profits. In practice, this meant that he was entitled to the income from the fund, but not to the capital. On the other hand, the child could not dispose of the property while the *paterfamilias* was alive. If the child was emancipated, the *paterfamilias* could retain one-third of the property absolutely, the child taking the remainder; but Justinian altered this rule, allowing the *paterfamilias* to use half the property (and retain the profits) but not to retain any of the capital. By Justinian's reign, the category of *peculium adventitium* had been widened so considerably that it included virtually all property acquired by the child other than *peculium castrense* or *quasi castrense*. Thus, in its final form, Roman law allowed significant proprietary interests to children-in-power (see Daube, D., 'Actions between Paterfamilias and Filiusfamilias with Peculium Castrense', in *Studi Albertario* I, 433–74 on whether a *paterfamilias* could sue a *filiusfamilias* with a *peculium castrense* on the basis of contract, delict, or a right *in rem* in classical Roman law). See Johnston, D., 'Suing the *Paterfamilias*: Theory and Practice', in *Beyond Dogmatics*, 173–84.

5.1.2.3 Contracts

A child-in-power could make contracts for itself on reaching the age of puberty. Benefits under the contract passed to the *paterfamilias*, but not liabilities. Although a son was in theory bound by the contract—daughters probably were not until the late Empire—the other party could not enforce it until the son became *sui iuris*. And even then the contract was enforceable only to the extent of the son's assets. Frankly, contracting with children-in-power was not an attractive proposition. A party would be more willing to contract with a son-in-power if the latter had *peculium castrense* or *quasi castrense*, since in these cases the son was treated as owning assets out of which his obligations could be satisfied.

What was the position where the child was allowed a *peculium* by the *paterfamilias* or made contracts with his authorization? In such a case, the *paterfamilias* was liable under the same actions that the praetors allowed against masters to enforce contracts made by slaves (cf. Frier and McGinn, *Casebook*, 251–64). Moreover, a *paterfamilias* was normally bound by non-contractual acts that he had authorized. For example, if he allowed his son to manumit slaves, the manumission was *prima facie* valid, according to Paul:

Paul, *Questions, book 12*: A father wrote to his son in the knowledge that he was at Rome, permitting him to free by *vindicta* anyone of his choice among the slaves in his actual service; thereafter the son manumitted Stichus before the praetor; I ask if he thus made him free. I replied: Why should we not think that the father is allowed to permit his son to manumit one of the slaves in his service? In fact, it was only the choice that he allowed to the son, but it is he himself who manumits. (D.40.2.22.)

5.1.2.4 **Emancipation**

(Inst.Gai.1.124.–6., Inst.1.12., D.1.7., C.8.48.)

This was the formal release of a child-in-power from *potestas* by the *paterfamilias*. The child became *sui iuris*: the agnatic ties between the child and its natural family were broken. Originally, the child lost the right to inherit on the intestacy of the *paterfamilias*, but the praetors allowed emancipated children a claim (see 8.3.2.1). As for *peculium*, the child would retain it on emancipation if there were an entitlement to it, e.g. *peculium castrense*; otherwise, the *paterfamilias* could retain it since he was its legal owner. However, in practice, a child would often be allowed to keep the *peculium* as a means of financial assistance on becoming independent. Unless the *peculium* was expressly taken away, there was a virtual presumption that the child could keep it.

What if the emancipated child had children of his own? Were they automatically emancipated?

Gaius, *Institutes, book 1*: A man who has in his *potestas* a son and through him a grandson has a free choice as to releasing the son from his power while retaining the grandson or *vice versa* as to keeping the son in power while manumitting the grandson or as to making them both *sui juris*. (D.1.7.28.)

Emancipation could be used as a sensible family arrangement where a child was of mature years and in need of legal independence. Such an emancipation would be amicable: the child would be provided with a sizeable *peculium*, if possible, and would be made an heir or legatee in the will of the *paterfamilias*, thus rendering unimportant the loss of the right to succeed on intestacy. However, emancipation could be a disaster for the child when used as a punishment. Becoming legally independent was scant recompense for being thrown out on to the streets without any *peculium* by an angry *paterfamilias*. Emancipation could thus be a hostile act, the threat of it used by the *paterfamilias* to control unruly children. Of course, the *paterfamilias* had to be careful in case his actions incurred *infamia*. Under Justinian (possibly earlier) the consent of the child became necessary for a valid emancipation. As a general rule, the *paterfamilias* lost his rights over the child when it was emancipated. However, Constantine allowed the recall of a child into *potestas* for gross ingratitude; and any property given to the child on emancipation would have to be returned. If the child was below puberty when emancipated, the *paterfamilias* became the child's guardian (see 5.4.1.1).

How was emancipation effected? Imaginative use was made of the rule of the Twelve Tables that three sales of a son into bondage by a *paterfamilias* freed the son from *potestas* (one sale sufficed for a daughter or grandchild). (See in general

Stoop, B. C., 'The Sins of their Fathers: Si Pater Filium Ter Venum Duit' (1995) 42
RIDA 3, 331–92, for a particularly gruesome hypothesis concerning the origin of
this practice.) A convoluted process was used whereby the son was sold three times
to a 'purchaser' (acting in collusion), who manumitted the son after the first two
sales. Emancipation by imperial rescript was made possible in the late Empire if the
child was absent. Under Justinian, the standard process for emancipation required
an appropriate declaration by the *paterfamilias* and the son before a magistrate. See
Frier and McGinn, *Casebook*, 315–19.

5.1.2.5 **Miscellaneous rights**

The *paterfamilias* had a number of rights which cannot easily be classified under
the headings dealt with so far. For example, he had the important right to appoint
guardians for his children should he die before they attained puberty (see 5.4.1.1).
Moreover, the *paterfamilias* was regarded as the representative of his family for litigation purposes—actions were brought or defended by him on behalf of his family,
as a general rule. If a delict was committed against his child, it was the *paterfamilias*
who normally took action, although there were some exceptional cases where the
child could sue personally, e.g. for personal insults.

It is evident from the above outline of the rights of the *paterfamilias* that the
extent of his *potestas* was all embracing, at least in theory. To what degree the
theoretical position obtained in practice is, however, not clear. For example, it is
difficult to see how the Roman economy could have thrived if the *paterfamilias* was
the only male with legal rights. It may well be that the rules on *potestas* were not
strictly applied, and were confined to the Roman upper classes. See Crook, J. A.,
'Patria Potestas' (1967) 17 CQ, 113–22, and Daube, *Roman Law*, 76 ff.

5.1.2.6 **Illegitimacy and legitimation**

Ulpian, *Sabinus, book 27*: **This is a law of nature: that a child born without lawful wedlock
belongs to his mother unless a special statute provides otherwise.** (D.1.5.24.)

There could be no *potestas* over an illegitimate child. It followed that a *paterfamilias*
had no right (in theory at least) to expose a newborn illegitimate child, nor did
he have any other of the rights associated with *potestas*. The illegitimate child
was thus in a more favourable position (*sui iuris*) than the legitimate one in some
respects—a curious consequence of the rigid rules of *potestas*. Nor could an illegitimate child be agnatically related to anyone since such a relationship depended
on subjection to a common *potestas*. The child 'belonged' to the mother, but in a
practical rather than a legal sense since a mother could not have *potestas* over anyone. Nevertheless, their relationship had legal consequences: the child took the
mother's status, was recognized as her blood relation, acquired the right to succeed
on her intestacy (and vice versa), and could not sue her.

The general test of legitimacy was whether the child had been conceived within
a lawful marriage. Certain presumptions and inferences were applied: e.g. a child
was presumed to be legitimate if born within 10 months of the death of the mother's husband, or if born as early as the seventh month of a marriage:

Paul, *Replies, book 19*: **That a child can be born fully formed in the seventh month is now a
received view due to the authority of that most learned man Hippocrates. Accordingly, it is
credible that a child born in the seventh month of a lawful marriage is a lawful son of the
marriage.** (D.1.5.12.)

Conception within marriage normally led to an inference that the child was legitimate, but everything depended on the circumstances, as the following passage by Ulpian vividly illustrates:

Ulpian, *Sabinus, book 9*: But if we suppose that a husband has been away for a spell, let us say, ten years, and has on his return found a year old boy in his house, we agree with Julian's opinion that this child is not the son of the husband. Julian, on the other hand, says that we should not listen to someone who has stayed constantly with his wife but who refuses to recognize her child as his own. But on this my opinion, which Scaevola also holds, is that a child born in a man's house even with full knowledge of the neighbors is not that man's son if it is proved that the husband for some time has not slept with his wife... (D.1.6.6.)

Legitimation of illegitimate children was generally not possible until the reign of Constantine. However, the adoption of an illegitimate son by his father by *adrogatio* (see 5.3.1.2) had the effect of making him a *filiusfamilias*. Constantine's reforms, and those of subsequent Emperors, were applicable only to the children of concubines. Concubinage was a settled union, normally involving cohabitation but falling short of marriage because of the absence of the necessary marital intent (see further 5.2.6.2). Constantine decreed that children of such a union would be legitimated if their parents married, the decree applying only to existing children. Several conditions had to be satisfied: e.g. the child had to consent since legitimation would result in a change of status, i.e. the child would become *alieni iuris*; the father must have no legitimate children; and the mother must be freeborn. Legitimation by subsequent marriage was later extended to future births within concubinage; but more conditions were added—the parties must have been capable of marrying each other at the time the child was conceived (i.e. children born in adultery were excluded) and a written marriage settlement had to be drawn up. However, the requirements that the mother should be freeborn and that the father must not have legitimate children were dropped.

Justinian introduced another form of legitimation—by imperial rescript. It applied where marriage to the concubine was impossible for some reason, or undesirable because of her 'unworthiness'. The father could apply to the Emperor (by petition or will) for the legitimation of the child, provided that the father was without legitimate issue. Additionally, children born in concubinage could be legitimated by *oblatio curiae* ('an offering to a municipal council'), an imaginative method introduced in the late Empire in an attempt to encourage persons to become municipal councillors (*decuriones*), an office normally to be avoided like the plague. Legitimation occurred if a man (without legitimate children) gave his son sufficient property to qualify the son to become a *decurio* or if the father married off his daughter to one. Such children acquired rights on their father's intestacy, but did not come under his *potestas*. It was not true legitimation, until Justinian decreed that *potestas* did result in such a case. Further, he allowed *oblatio curiae* even if the father had legitimate children.

5.2 Marriage and divorce

(Inst.Gai.1.108.–15b., Inst.1.10., D.23.2.)

Marriage, or matrimony, is a joining together of a man and a woman, implying a united lifestyle. (Inst.1.9.1.)

Modestinus, *Rules, book 1*: **Marriage is the union of a man and a woman, a partnership for the whole life involving divine as well as human law.** (D.23.2.1.)

The word *matrimonium*—the normal word for marriage—is partly derived from *mater* (mother). The emphasis on motherhood suggests that the Romans regarded marriage (at least on some level) as an institution that resulted in the birth of legitimate children. See Treggiari, S., *Roman Marriage* (1991), 5 ff. Marriage in Roman law was not a sacrament (a medieval canonist notion), but purely a social fact with certain legal consequences.

Although there were times, notably the late Republic, when the evidence points to a certain moral laxity and a casual approach to personal relationships, marriage was, nevertheless, regarded for much of Rome's history as a solemn union with important consequences. It was the prime way by which *potestas* could be acquired. The seriousness with which marriage was treated is demonstrated by the profusion of rules laying down various bars and impediments. These rules suggest that the Romans had a highly developed sense of what constituted a desirable and lawful marriage. See Evans Grubbs, *Women*, 81–2.

5.2.1 Betrothal

(D.23.1.)

Betrothals were common in Roman society at all periods, especially among the wealthier classes. The betrothal ceremony would often be conducted by the respective fathers. The presence of the happy couple was not necessary:

Ulpian, *Edict, book 6*: **When betrothals are being contracted, it does not matter much whether this is done by the parties themselves (in person, by sending a messenger, or by letter) or by someone else. The conditions in the marriage contract are nearly always settled by intermediaries.** (D.23.1.18.)

The betrothal ceremony was usually a solemn affair, especially in early times, involving the exchange by the fathers of promises of marriage on behalf of their children. But solemnity was not obligatory: senators are said to have sometimes betrothed their children during the conviviality of a dinner party. In early Rome, a *paterfamilias* could insist on betrothing his child to whom he wished, but by the late Republic the consent of the parties was required. However, one cannot imagine that the wishes of a *paterfamilias* would often be thwarted (cf. D.23.1.12.).

At what age could children be betrothed?

Modestinus, *Distinctions, book 4*: **There is no fixed age for the parties in betrothal as there is in the case of marriage. So betrothal can take place at a very early age, provided that what is being done is understood by both parties, that is, as long as they are not under seven years of age.** (D.23.1.14.)

The betrothal of young children to one another in their absence was not peculiar to Roman society. It occurred frequently in the past—e.g. in the dynastic marriages of European sovereigns—and still occurs in some societies of today.

In early law, it seems that betrothal promises were actionable if broken (because the ceremony was similar to the undertaking of a *stipulatio*), but by the late Republic they could no longer be sued on, even where a penalty had been agreed for breach. After the conversion to Christianity, betrothal again came to be regarded as of great importance, the law attaching to it some of the consequences of marriage (e.g. infidelity by a betrothed woman was regarded as adultery). Moreover, the practice developed of exchanging tokens of good faith on betrothal. These tokens could be quite valuable. They were forfeited on breach of promise, Justinian allowing double forfeiture (i.e. the token was forfeited plus its equivalent value).

It must be stressed that despite its social and legal importance, betrothal was never a formal requirement of a valid marriage. Nevertheless, it served as important evidence of *affectio maritalis*, the intention to marry, which *was* a vital constituent of marriage. See Frier and McGinn, *Casebook*, 65–71 as well as Evans Grubbs, *Women*, 88.

5.2.2 Formal requirements of marriage

A Roman civil law marriage (*matrimonium iustum*) had to satisfy various requirements: the parties had to be of the required age; they had to consent; they had to have *conubium*; and the marriage had to be free of bars and impediments. See Frier and McGinn, *Casebook*, 27–40.

5.2.2.1 Age

The basic rule was that marriage was not legally possible until the attainment of puberty. In early law, a physical examination of the parties was involved, but eventually the ages were fixed as 12 for females, 14 for males:

Roman citizens can marry each other when they are legally united, males having reached puberty and females having become marriageable...(Inst.1.10pr.)

The ancients judged puberty in males not by age, but also by the development of their bodies. But we, from a desire to conform to the purity of the present times, have thought it proper that what seemed indecent even to the ancients, that is, the inspection of the body, should be thought equally so in the case of males...(Inst.1.22pr.)

The schools had disputed the issue, the Sabinians favouring a physical examination, the Proculians typically preferring a fixed rule. The latter view prevailed.

Women tended to marry at a relatively young age. Men tended to marry at a higher age; that fact, coupled with their greater susceptibility to dying in war or civil disturbance, meant that widowhood was a frequent occurrence. Cicero's daughter was apparently betrothed at 12, married at 16, and widowed at 22, not an unusual scenario. The sensational Agrippina, Claudius' last wife, was first married at 12. The general tendency to marry at a young age must be viewed in the context of the average life span of Roman citizens—probably below 30 years of age in the early Empire. See Gardner, *Women in Roman Law*, 38 ff. The fixing of puberty as the age at which marriage was possible was a recognition that marriage was regarded as a means of procreating children and acquiring *potestas*.

The view of marriage as a means of increasing the birth rate was one particularly emphasized by Augustus. He imposed a duty to marry on men aged between 25 and 60, and on women between 20 and 50. Sanctions were enacted against those in breach of their duty (see 8.4.1.4). See also Evans Grubbs, *Women*, 88.

5.2.2.2 Consent

Consent to marriage has to be distinguished from consent to betrothal, e.g. a party could consent to a betrothal, but might then refuse to marry. The consent of the parties to marry was normally necessary because they had to have *affectio maritalis*, the intention to enter marriage. Consent could be proved in a variety of ways, particularly by evidence that the couple had undergone the ceremonial customs traditional in Roman marriages. For example, it was normal for the couple to exchange vows in the bride's home, normally in the presence of an *auspex*, a formal witness to a wedding (originally someone adept at reading omens from studying the flight of birds). There then followed a procession to the bridegroom's home, during which the guests often indulged in pranks and *risqué* humour—not unlike the case at some weddings of today. The *deductio in domum* ('leading into the home') was a legally significant moment:

> Pomponius, *Sabinus, book 4*: **It is settled that a woman can be married by a man in his absence, either by letter or by messenger, if she is led to his house. But where she is absent, she cannot be married by letter or by messenger because she must be led to her husband's house, not her own, since the former is, as it were, the domicile of the marriage.** (D.23.2.5.)

The parties had to have the capacity to consent at the time of the marriage— supervening insanity did not invalidate it. If either party was in *potestas*, the consent of the *paterfamilias* was required (see 5.1.2.1). In addition, the bridegroom's father had to consent if the latter was not a *paterfamilias*. If the parties were *sui iuris*, the bridegroom did not require anyone's consent, but the bride might need permission from her guardian (see 5.4.2.2). See Frier and McGinn, *Casebook*, 41–53 as well as Evans Grubbs, *Women*, 89–91.

5.2.2.3 *Conubium*

A Roman civil law marriage required that both parties should have *conubium*, the *ius civile* right to enter such a union. Roman citizens had *conubium*, but non-citizens did not (unless it was specially granted). So, a marriage where one or both of the parties lacked *conubium* could not be a *ius civile* marriage, but was, nevertheless, recognized as a valid marriage, governed by the *ius gentium*. Since both were valid, did it matter whether a marriage was a *ius civile* or *ius gentium* union? Most certainly— the legal consequences were quite different. In a *ius gentium* marriage, the children took the status of their mother rather than their father; they were *sui iuris* since *potestas* did not arise in such a marriage; there was no agnatic relationship; and the wife could not be under the legal control (*manus*) of her husband (see 5.2.3.1) (cf. Inst.Gai.1.78.).

What if the parties were mistaken as to their status? If one of the parties, mistakenly thought to be a citizen, lacked citizenship (and therefore *conubium*), the marriage could not be regarded as a Roman civil law marriage. However, legislation in the early Empire allowed *erroris causae probatio* (see 4.4.3.1) in such cases, whereby the non-citizen was entitled to citizenship on proof that a child had been born to the marriage. This converted the marriage from a *ius gentium* union to a *ius civile* one. The same consequence resulted if a citizen, mistakenly thought not to be a citizen, married a spouse without *conubium*: proof that a child had been born to the marriage converted the union into a civil law marriage. See Frier and McGinn, *Casebook*, 31–3.

5.2.2.4 **Prohibited marriages**

The parties to a civil law marriage had to be free of the many bars and prohibitions imposed by the law in its attempt to prevent undesirable marriages. This was a highly detailed area of Roman family law, and can be considered only in outline.

As a general rule, a marriage in breach of these rules was void, and was often punishable, e.g. through the imposition of *infamia*. For a good survey of the texts, see Evans Grubbs, *Women*, ch. 3.

(a) Status and occupation. Under the Twelve Tables a marriage between a patrician and plebeian was banned, a rule repealed within a few years of its enactment. Marriage between the freeborn and freed persons was originally not possible, although this ban fell into disuse during the Republic. Augustus allowed such marriages except for members of the senatorial order. The marriage of a patron and his freedwoman was not prohibited (in later law) but such unions could incur social disapproval (See McGinn, *Prostitution*, ch. 3). Consequently, the relationship between them would often be one of concubinage rather than marriage. A marriage between a patroness and her freedman was thought to be very bad form. Such marriages were banned in the late classical period except in the following case:

Ulpian, *Sabinus, book 34*: **If a patroness is so degraded that marriage at least with her own freedman is honorable, it should not be prohibited by the judge who is investigating the matter.** (D.23.2.13.)

In an attempt to tighten military discipline, Augustus banned soldiers from marrying while on military service. And the marriage of a soldier was considered ended if he entered the army as a married man, any children becoming illegitimate. This resulted in recruits divorcing their wives, since the children of divorced parents remained legitimate. These rules proved very unpopular and contributed to a pronounced increase in concubinage during the early Empire. The ban was lifted in AD 197 by Septimius Severus in an effort to retain the support of the army.

A person could not legally be a party to two marriages at the same time—the Romans regarded marriage as a monogamous union. Bigamy incurred *infamia*, and occasionally could have extreme consequences, as Messalina discovered when she attempted to marry her lover while still married to Claudius. A widow could not marry within 10 months (extended in the Empire to one year) of the death of her husband. A guardian could not marry his ward, nor could the guardian's son. A conflict of interests could well arise in such a case, if the rule were otherwise, as also where a high-ranking officer in provincial government attempted to marry a woman from the province—the marriage was void.

(b) Religious factors. Vestal virgins obviously could not marry—indeed, if they lost their virginity, they were subject to the death penalty. However, once they retired from office they became eligible for marriage. Rome's conversion to Christianity led to a number of restrictions on religious grounds—those who became monks or entered the priesthood could not marry; and marriage between Christians and Jews was prohibited.

(c) Moral grounds. Augustus prohibited the senatorial order from marrying not only freed persons, as we have seen, but also a variety of people engaged in activities considered to be morally dubious, such as prostitutes, procurers, actors, and actresses:

Modestinus, *Formation of Marriage, sole book*: **As far as marriages are concerned, it is always necessary to consider not just what is lawful but also what is decent. [1] If the daughter, granddaughter, or great-granddaughter of a senator marries a freedman, or someone** who was an actor, or whose father or mother were actors, the marriage will be void. (D.23.2.42pr.–1.)

Justinian eventually abolished this rule, having been granted dispensation by his predecessor to marry that *grande dame* of the stage, Theodora. Augustus banned an adulterous wife from marrying her lover after divorce. Justinian limited the ban to the lifetime of the innocent party.

(d) Consanguinity. Marriages were prohibited between persons related by blood. The basic rule was that lineal ascendants and descendants could not marry, e.g. parent and child; grandparent and grandchild. As regards collaterals, the rule emerged by the late Republic that collaterals could not marry if at least one of them was only one degree removed from the common ancestor. Thus, brother and sister could not marry; nor could uncle and niece, nor aunt and nephew. Cousins could marry, even first cousins (both are two degrees removed from the common ancestor). Claudius altered the rules to enable him to marry his niece, Agrippina: he allowed a man to marry his brother's daughter, but not that of his sister. Claudius's decree was repealed in AD 342:

If anyone should be so abominable as to believe that the daughter of his brother or sister should be made his wife, or should fly to her embrace not as her paternal or maternal uncle, he will be liable to a penalty of capital punishment. (C.Th.3.12.1.)

It is not clear how strictly the rules on consanguinity were applied throughout the Empire. It seems that regional variations did occur, with confusing consequences after the general grant of citizenship in AD 212—old practices may have continued in ignorance of the general rules. In AD 295, a decree condemned those who 'rushed into illicit unions in the promiscuous manner of farm animals or wild beasts, driven by execrable lust, with no regard for decency or righteousness' (quoted in Gardner, *Women in Roman Law*, 36).

(e) Affinity. One could not marry an ascendant or descendant of one's former spouse, e.g. a man could not marry his former mother-in-law. Nor could one marry the former spouse of an ascendant or descendant, e.g. a former stepmother or stepdaughter. Marriage to a brother/sister-in-law was possible until prohibited after Rome's conversion to Christianity.

(f) Adoption. When persons were adopted they became for all legal purposes members of the family of the adoptive parents. Hence, there could be no marriage between an adopted child and the adoptive parent, even if the child was later emancipated. As regards persons related collaterally through adoption, Gaius states:

Gaius, *Provincial Edict, book 11*: When the relationship of brother and sister arises because of adoption it is an impediment to marriage while the adoption lasts. So I will be able to marry a girl whom my father adopted and then emancipated. Similarly, if she is kept in power and I am emancipated, we can be married. (D.23.2.17pr.)

Compare Frier and McGinn, *Casebook*, 34–8.

5.2.3 Types of marriage

Roman civil law marriage was of two types: *manus* marriage, in which the wife was in 'the hands' of her husband, i.e. in his legal control; or 'free' marriage, where she was not subject to that control.

5.2.3.1 *Manus* marriage

(a) Form. *Manus* marriage was very common in early law but gradually diminished in importance and frequency during the Republic (see Looper-Friedman, S. E., 'The Decline of Manus-Marriage in Rome', (1987) 55 TR, 281–96, on the reasons for the decline). See Frier and McGinn, *Casebook*, 89–95.

A *manus* marriage could be created in the following ways (see Inst.Gai.1.110.):

(i) *Coemptio* ('purchase'): a form of bride purchase, effected through a formal conveyance *per aes et libram* in the presence of witnesses. The husband 'bought' the bride in a manner similar to that used for the purchase of certain types of property, the bride 'selling' herself with the permission of her *paterfamilias or* if she was *sui iuris* with the permission of her guardian.

(ii) *Confarreatio* ('sharing of bread'): a religious ceremony before witnesses and the chief pontiff, requiring, *inter alia*, the eating of special bread by the couple. It was reserved for marriages of patricians and members of the college of priests. Its significance lay in the fact that it provided a means of entry to the highest echelons of the priesthood: only children of a marriage by *confarreatio* were eligible for such elevated office.

(iii) *Usus*: if a man and woman cohabited for a year with *affectio maritalis*, i.e. regarding themselves as man and wife, a *manus* marriage was created even though the parties had not undergone any form of wedding ceremony. The required marital intention would normally be presumed from the fact of cohabitation. However, *manus* would not arise (according to the Twelve Tables) if the woman absented herself for three nights in each year—probably three consecutive nights. There was a marriage in these circumstances but it was a free marriage, not with *manus*.

(b) Legal consequences. In *manus* marriage, the husband (or his *paterfamilias* if alive) exercised a power and control over the wife comparable to the *potestas* of a father over his child. Indeed, the wife was regarded as her husband's daughter in certain respects, e.g. under the intestacy law (see 8.3.1.1). She could not own property except for very personal belongings. Property owned by her before marriage automatically passed to the husband or *paterfamilias*, subject to the rules on dowry (see 5.2.5.1), as did anything that she acquired during marriage. She could not make binding contracts without her husband's permission, and generally was not able to participate in litigation and the processes of law. Moreover, entry into *manus* marriage severed her former agnatic ties: she exchanged one family for another and left the power of her *paterfamilias*. When the *paterfamilias* of her husband died, the wife came under the *potestas* of her husband (if he became *paterfamilias*) and remained under his *manus* by virtue of their marriage. A wife could be released from *manus* by a similar procedure to that used for the emancipation of a daughter (Inst.Gai.1.137.). There were, however, important differences between the position of the wife in a *manus* marriage and a child in *potestas*. The husband did not have the power of life and death over his wife; nor could he sell her into slavery, or surrender her noxally, or give her in adoption. She attained the position of wife *in manu* in the household.

5.2.3.2 Free marriage

This type of marriage, the norm from the late Republic onwards, was 'free' mainly in the sense that the wife was legally independent—the husband did not hold legal power over her. See Frier and McGinn, *Casebook*, 96–103.

(a) Form. A free marriage was created by the cohabitation of the parties, provided that they regarded themselves as man and wife. As soon as such cohabitation began, i.e. with the necessary intent, the marriage came into existence. For Ulpian, the intention of the parties seems to have been more important than the fact of cohabitation:

Ulpian, *Sabinus, book 35*: . . . **for it is consent, not sleeping together, which makes a marriage.** (D.35.1.15.)

This is somewhat misleading if interpreted to mean that everything depended on the intention of the parties. Most probably, it was cohabitation which was the crucial element, and from which the necessary marital intention could be presumed. Besides, the parties would often have undergone the ceremonies customary in Roman weddings, which served as evidence of the required intent. The betrothal or the giving of a dowry—both customary, if not strictly necessary, would provide further evidence. It could be, however, that there was no betrothal, no dowry, no wedding ceremony, but simply cohabitation with the necessary intent. Such a union was a perfectly valid marriage. The ease with which free marriage could be created may suggest a rather casual approach by the Romans to marriage as a legal institution, but this is belied, as we have seen, by their great concern to prevent undesirable marriages.

(b) Legal consequences. The wife did not exchange families—she remained an agnate of her original family. If she had a *paterfamilias*, she remained in his power. If she was *sui iuris*, she continued under the guardianship of her tutor (see generally 5.4.2) but otherwise was legally independent: her property remained her own and she could keep whatever she acquired during the marriage. The wife could make contracts and could generally participate in the legal process. Indeed, one senator's wife, Gaia Afrania, earned some notoriety as a vexatious litigant. She probably was the 'shameless woman' who, according to Ulpian (D.31.1.5.), annoyed a magistrate, thus provoking a praetorian edict prohibiting women from acting as representatives in litigation. See Gardner, *Women in Roman Law*, 262–3 as well as Evans Grubbs, *Women*, 60–70.

Since the husband in a free marriage did not acquire his wife's property, he might be tempted to persuade her to make gifts to him. The possibility that wives could be tricked out of their property resulted in a ban on *inter vivos* gifts between husbands and wives:

Ulpian, *Sabinus, book 32*: **As a matter of custom, we hold that gifts between husband and wife are not valid. This rule is upheld to prevent people from impoverishing themselves through mutual affection by means of gifts which are not reasonable, but beyond their means.** (D.24.1.1.1.)

It is not clear when the ban on gifts was introduced—Ulpian's reference to the ban as 'a matter of custom' is not very illuminating—but most probably it was imposed in the late Republic, see Cherry, D., 'Gifts Between Husband and Wife: The Social Origins of Roman Law', in *Speculum Iuris*, 34–45. By then free marriage was prevalent, and the problem of the tricked wife had surfaced. There were some exceptions to the general rule, e.g. inexpensive anniversary presents were allowed, as were gifts that did not enrich the donee:

Ulpian, *Sabinus, book 31*: **If a husband gives his wife money to buy perfumes and she pays the money to his creditor and then buys perfumes with her own money—she will not be held to have been enriched by this.** (D.24.1.7.1.)

Important financial protection for wives was provided in the early Empire when women were prohibited from standing as guarantors for their husbands or taking over their debts. On the property of the spouses, see the texts collected in Frier and McGinn, *Casebook*, 122–39 as well as Evans Grubbs, *Women*, 98–101.

5.2.4 Divorce

Divorce was normally effected by the act of one or both of the parties to the marriage. It was, like marriage, concluded through a private process and it was not judicially controlled. A marriage could also end in divorce at the insistence of the *paterfamilias* of the husband or wife, even where the marriage was a happy one (but the *paterfamilias* ran the risk of *infamia* if he behaved unreasonably). In the Empire the power was restricted, but never abolished—it could be exercised if grave cause was shown.

Divorce by the parties differed according to whether the marriage was free or with *manus*. For a good survey of the texts, see Evans Grubbs, *Women*, ch. 4.

5.2.4.1 Divorce in *manus* marriage

In early Rome, when *manus* marriage was prevalent, divorce appears to have been a rare phenomenon. It seems that if a husband wished to divorce his wife, he would normally consult their respective families, who might try to reconcile the parties or at least to supervise the divorce arrangements. The first attested divorce—*c.*306 BC—concerned a senator said to be expelled from the Senate for divorcing his wife without proper consultation. See Treggiari, S., *Roman Marriage* (1991), 442. If the husband divorced his wife without good cause, he ran the risk of incurring *infamia*. Evidence of what constituted good grounds is scanty, but they apparently included poisoning of children, theft of keys, and the imbibing of wine—conduct thought to be unbecoming in the responsible wife of the early Republic. It is not clear whether a wife could divorce her husband in a *manus* marriage. In early law she probably could not initiate a divorce; but in the early Empire, it seems that she could end the marriage unilaterally by *repudium* (see 5.2.4.2).

The procedure required to terminate a *manus* marriage was largely a variation of the ceremonies required to create the marriage, since the wife had to be transferred back to the authority of her (remaining) family. For example, a ceremonial resale of the wife terminated marriage by *coemptio* (and probably by *usus*, too). By the end of the Republic, the forms of divorce in *manus* marriage had become virtually obsolete, so that such marriages came to be terminated in the same way as free marriages. See Frier and McGinn, *Casebook*, 94–5.

5.2.4.2 Divorce in free marriage

No grounds were necessary to end a free marriage but a causeless divorce could incur the wrath of the censor, as in the case of a *manus* marriage. As regards form, terminating a free marriage was basically as informal as the manner in which it was created:

Paul, *Edict, book 35*: **A true divorce does not take place unless an intention to remain apart permanently is present. So things said or done in anger are not effective until the parties show by their persistence that they are an indication of their considered opinion. So where repudiation takes place in anger and the wife returns shortly afterward, she is not held to have divorced her husband. (D.24.2.3.)**

In essence, all that was required was that at least one of the parties should have ceased to have the intention to be married (see Frier and McGinn, *Casebook*, 156–69). The parties could divorce by mutual consent (*divortium*) or unilaterally (*repudium*). The former method required that the parties should intentionally cease living together, whereupon it could be presumed that they had both lost the necessary marital intent. *Repudium* occurred where only one spouse wished to end the marriage—it was normal to notify the other party by letter or messenger:

A woman in the *manus* of her husband can, if she has sent him a notice of repudiation, compel him to release her [by *emancipatio*] just as if she had never been his wife. (Inst. Gai.1.137a.)

Augustus required the presence of seven witnesses for the sending of a notification of *repudium* (see D.24.2.9.), but it is not clear whether this rule applied generally or only where a husband repudiated his wife on the grounds of her adultery. Although the sending of the notification terminated a marriage, the consequences could be unexpected and unwelcome, especially for the third party. Consider what happened to this playboy:

Papinian, *Adultery, book 2*: **The deified Hadrian relegated a man for three years where he had led someone else's wife to his house while she was on a journey, and she sent a notice of repudiation to her husband from there.** (D.24.2.8.)

Relegation involved banishment and possible loss of citizenship and civil rights—a fate best avoided.

In AD 48 Messalina, Claudius' third wife, went through a ceremony of marriage with her lover, Silius. She was considered to have committed bigamy and was executed. Mere cessation of *affectio maritalis* was insufficient: in practice, there had to be some visible evidence of it, such as sending a note. But then, was not going through a very public wedding with Silius sufficient evidence? It seems not: the divorce logically must precede the subsequent marriage—thus, it is difficult to maintain that the same act, the wedding, can simultaneously create a new marriage and extinguish the previous union. See Treggiari, S., *Roman Marriage* (1991), 457–8.

5.2.4.3 The *lex Julia de adulteriis*

(D.48.5., C.9.9.)

The alleged decline in moral standards (at least among the Roman upper classes), coupled with the prevalence of free marriage and the ease with which divorce could be obtained, apparently caused a sharp increase in the divorce rate in the late Republic. Augustus tackled the problem in typically direct fashion. His *lex Julia de adulteriis c.* 18 BC was a remarkable piece of 'social engineering', designed to improve moral standards by making adultery by a *wife* a criminal offence—triable by special adultery courts—with serious consequences. The wife was banned from remarrying her lover after divorce; she suffered a diminution of her rights in property—half her dowry entitlement and confiscation of a third of her separate property—and she could lose her citizenship and be relegated to an island. A husband who knew of his wife's adultery was placed under a duty to prosecute his wife. A conviction led to the termination of the marriage. If he failed to act within the required time, he was guilty of the crime of *lenocinium*, i.e. acting like a pimp, which was punished in a similar way to adultery. Any act by the husband, which could be regarded as encouraging or condoning his wife's adultery, amounted to *lenocinium*:

Ulpian, *Adulteries, book 4*: The statute has punished the *lenocinium* of a husband who after catching his wife in adultery has kept her and let the adulterer go; for he ought to have avenged himself on the man and also vented his rage on his wife, who has violated their marriage. (D.48.5.30pr.)

The wife had to be prosecuted by the husband within 60 days of the event. Her *paterfamilias* could prosecute her within that period but the husband had precedence. If neither took action, anyone had the right to prosecute within the next four months, i.e. up to six months from the event.

What of the lover? He was subject to prosecution and penal consequences— forfeiture of half of his property and possible relegation; or sentencing to hard labour, (e.g. in the mines) if he was of lowly status. He could be killed in certain circumstances (see 5.1.2.1) by the *paterfamilias* of the woman. The husband, too, had a right to kill the lover if he caught him committing adultery with the wife in the husband's home, provided that the lover was of inferior status, e.g. an actor or dancer. Or the husband could detain the lover (of whatever status) for up to 20 hours 'for the purpose of testifying to the matter' (D.48.5.26pr.). The wife's *paterfamilias* probably had the same right. But the husband had no right to kill an adulterous wife (although in practice husbands who did so were often not convicted). Persons outside the triangle of husband, wife, and lover could be punished under the *lex Julia de adulteriis*. It would be *lenocinium* for anyone to aid the commission of adultery—e.g. by acting as a go-between or allowing premises to be used by the lovers.

The enormous scope of Augustus's law can be further appreciated from the fact that it applied to adultery in *all* marriages, not just Roman civil law marriages. As can be imagined, the *lex Julia de adulteriis* had a sensational impact on Roman society. The satirists had a field day. The element of compulsion, whereby a husband was forced to divorce his wife, was ridiculed as not being conducive to the stability of family life that Augustus was apparently seeking. The Emperor was castigated for having apparently conflicting aims. See further Nörr, D., 'The Matrimonial Legislation of Augustus: An Early Instance of Social Engineering' (1981) 16 IJ, 350–64. Nevertheless, Augustus's legislation remained the cornerstone of Rome's matrimonial law for centuries—if somewhat erratically enforced—although 'there is little evidence that Augustus changed opinions or standards of behaviour in his own time' (Treggiari, S., *Roman Marriage* (1991), 292). On this law, see extensively McGinn, *Prostitution*, chs. 5 and 6. See also Evans Grubbs, *Women*, 83–7.

5.2.4.4 Later developments

The Christian Emperors frowned on divorce but did not abolish it. The tendency was to penalize causeless divorce harshly through bans on remarriage, loss of property rights, and deportation. For example, Constantine punished *repudium* by a husband unless his wife was proved to have committed undesirable acts such as adultery or homicide (see C.Th.3.16.1.). Moreover, it seems that Constantine made adultery by a wife a capital offence. Justinian abolished divorce by mutual consent, apart from exceptional cases, but the ban was lifted after his death. And some attempt was made in the late Empire to make divorce procedure less informal: in *repudium* it became compulsory to send a formal divorce petition as notification of the ending of the marriage. For a survey of cases and examples, see Evans Grubbs, *Women*, ch. 4.

It is important to appreciate that throughout the whole history of Roman divorce law it was never *essential* to have a ground for divorce. Causeless divorces were valid, but attracted penal consequences. For example, under Justinian the penalties were: for a wife—loss of dowry and compulsory entry into a nunnery; for a husband—loss of a third of his estate and compulsory entry into a monastery. Justifiable grounds for divorce under Justinian included adultery by the wife, cohabitation by the husband with a concubine, entering the religious life, and plotting against the Emperor. On this topic, see extensively Evans Grubbs, J., *Law and Family in Late Antiquity—The Emperor Constantine's Marriage Legislation* (1995).

5.2.5 Dowry (*dos*)

(D.23.3–5, D.24.3, D.25.1.)

5.2.5.1 The expectation of a dowry

Dowry was a crucial element in property relations between spouses throughout Roman legal history. The dowry consisted of property (or some other contribution) given to the husband by the wife or her *paterfamilias* or others (like the clients of her *paterfamilias*) on her behalf (see Saller, R. P., 'Roman Dowry and the Devolution of Property in the Principate' (1984) 34 CQ, 195–205 for an interesting discussion of the use of the dowry to ensure the continuation of senatorial family lines during the Principate). It was normally given on marriage, but could be given before or after it. Although a husband was not strictly under a legal duty to maintain his wife, or vice versa, in practice he would feel a moral and social obligation to do so. The dowry would help him—it was regarded as the wife's contribution to the running of the matrimonial home. The giving of dowry by a wife constituted the major exception to the rule invalidating gifts between spouses. See Frier and McGinn, *Casebook*, 72–86. There is a natural affinity between any discussion of the dowry and discussions of broader elements of the law of property. These should therefore be taken into account when studying this area of law. Since the dowry was intimately connected to marriage and divorce in Roman law, we prefer to treat it here.

On a *manus* marriage, the husband acquired the wife's property if she was *sui iuris* (see 5.2.3.1). Originally, it seems that such property was not regarded as dowry, but by the late Republic it was. If the wife was not *sui iuris*, then her *paterfamilias* would be expected to provide a dowry. The position was similar in a free marriage: either the wife or her *paterfamilias* would be expected to provide dowry. The husband did not have a *right* to a dowry unless it had been specifically promised; but he certainly had an *expectation* of a dowry since it became an invariable practice to give one, at least among the Roman propertied classes. The search for wives with handsome dowries by ambitious young men was a familiar scenario for Roman satirists. It seems that a decree of the late classical period imposed a legal duty on the bride's *paterfamilias* to provide a dowry: he could be forced by a magistrate to do so (D.23.2.19.).

5.2.5.2 Rights in the dowry

Who owned the dowry? The general position in early law was that the husband became the absolute owner of the dowry. He could do what he liked with it, and did not have to return it, or any part of it, on the termination of the marriage. So it became the practice for the donor to insist on a formal promise by the husband to return the dowry when the marriage ended, or to dispose of it in the agreed manner (see Gardner, J. F., 'The Recovery of Dowry in Roman Law' (1985) 35 CQ, 449–53 whose article builds on the article by Saller (cited earlier)). See Frier and McGinn, *Casebook*, 140–53 as well as Evans Grubbs, *Women*, 91–101.

Such a dowry was known as *dos receptitia* ('a returnable dowry'), the husband's promise enforceable by the *actio ex stipulatu*, one of the standard contractual remedies. From this practice emerged the concept that the husband was not entitled to the capital, but was entitled to the fruits (i.e. the profits or income) of the dowry:

Ulpian, *Sabinus, book 31*: **Equity demands that the profits on a dowry shall belong to the husband; since he bears the burdens of marriage, it is only fair that he receives the profits.** (D.23.3.7pr.)

An alternative practice was for the dowry to be valued (*dos aestimata*), the husband promising to pay the agreed valuation on the termination of the marriage. The advantage to the husband, compared with *dos receptitia*, was that he could do as he wished with the property. He did not have to return the capital; his only duty was to pay the valuation. However, he did take the risk of deterioration or damage to the property.

Eventually, the praetors introduced the *actio rei uxoriae* ('the action for the wife's property') in an attempt to protect wives, particularly as regards dowries that were not valued or returnable. It is likely that the introduction of this remedy was a response to a notorious divorce in *c.*230 BC when Spurius Carvilius Maximus Ruga divorced his wife because she was allegedly sterile. Under the action the divorced wife could recover whatever the judge thought was a fair share of the dowry, subject to allowing the husband to make reasonable deductions. The action was extended to cases where the husband predeceased the wife. The effect of these developments was that the husband's position by the end of the Republic was in many respects little better than a form of temporary stewardship. Indeed, the husband came to be regarded as owing a duty of care in respect of the dowry—consider the following text concerning one of the most famous of all Romans, Gaius Gracchus (see 1.2.3.1):

Javolenus, *From the Posthumous Works of Labeo, book 6*: **According to Servius, a husband is responsible for fraud and negligence in connection with all the property in the dowry apart from money. This is also the view of Publius Mucius; for he stated it in the case of Licinnia, the wife of Gracchus, whose dotal property had perished during the insurrection in which Gracchus was killed, saying that the property should be restored to Licinnia since Gracchus was to blame for the insurrection.** (D.24.3.66pr.)

What degree of negligence was required to make the husband liable for losses? Paul states:

Paul, *Sabinus, book 7*: **In matters relating to the dowry, the husband…must exercise the same diligence as he shows in his own affairs.** (D.23.3.17pr.)

This was a subjective standard of care—how had that husband behaved in the past? The 'diligence' expected of a husband may have been different in the early classical period, when the duty of care that was required was probably that of the *bonus paterfamilias* (the prudent head of the household)—normally this was a higher standard of care (but not necessarily), and an objective one.

5.2.5.3 **Reforms of Augustus**

Augustus introduced important reforms, the general trend of which was to improve the position of the wife. The husband was banned from selling dotal immovables (dowry consisting of land) without the consent of the wife if they comprised Italic land, i.e. land south of the river Po (in the Lombard Plain). In addition, mortgages created on such land (even with the wife's consent) were invalidated. Further, Augustus established detailed rules (some originally introduced previously) concerning the return of the dowry on termination of marriage (see Frier and McGinn, *Casebook*, 170–87). The rules applied particularly to dowry other than *dos receptitia* or *aestimata* (which continued to be governed by the original agreement between the parties) and depended on whether the marriage ended through divorce or death:

(a) Divorce. The wife (or her *paterfamilias*, if alive) could recover dowry by the *actio rei uxoriae* as before, but Augustus formalized the position regarding deductions and the recovery of expenses. The husband generally had to care for the dowry at his own expense; but he could claim for 'necessary' expenses, i.e. those that arose out of necessity:

Ulpian, *Sabinus, book 36*: . . . if a husband rebuilds a house which was falling into ruin but was useful to his wife, or if he replants an olive orchard where trees have blown down . . . [Paul, *Sabinus, book 7* [2]] or spends money on curing slaves, [Ulpian, *Sabinus, book 36* [3]]: or plants vines or looks after trees or nurseries for the good of the land, he will be held to have incurred necessary expenses. (D.25.1.1.3.; D.25.1.2.; D.25.1.3.)

The husband could deduct the value of gifts made by him to the wife *de facto* (such gifts being legally invalid under the general rule prohibiting gifts between spouses). And the husband could deduct the value of property wrongfully appropriated by the wife; alternatively, he had the *actio rerum amotarum* ('the action for things removed') for the recovery of such property (D.25.2.). Further, the husband could retain a sixth of the dowry if the wife was guilty of serious misconduct, or an eighth for lesser behaviour. If the wife (or her *paterfamilias*) was responsible for the ending of the marriage in divorce, the husband could retain, in addition to the other deductions, one-sixth of the dowry per child to a maximum of half the dowry. The person 'responsible' for ending a marriage was the one who ended it without good reason or caused its breakdown, but not necessarily the one who initiated the divorce:

Papinian, *Adulterers, sole book*: I have married a woman charged with adultery; I have divorced her as soon as she was convicted. Am I regarded as having provided the grounds for the divorce? The reply was: Since, in accordance with the *lex Julia*, you are forbidden to keep a wife of this kind, it is clear that you are not to be regarded as having provided the grounds for the divorce. For this reason then, the question of right shall be treated as though the divorce had been brought about because of the fault of the woman. (D.48.5.12.13.)

How soon after the divorce did the husband have to return the dowry? The basic rule was that dotal property or its value had to be returned immediately except for fungibles, i.e. property consumed through use (such as money or corn), which could be returned in no more than three annual instalments. But if the husband was to blame for the divorce, the whole dowry had to be returned immediately, and it seems that he could claim no deduction.

(b) Death. When the wife predeceased the husband, the basic rule was that he retained the dowry but had to return any part that had been donated by the wife's *paterfamilias* or other donor (if alive). The duty to restore was subject to the husband's rights to deduct for expenses, gifts, and misappropriated property, as on divorce. And the husband could retain one-fifth of the returnable dowry in respect of every child of the family. If the husband predeceased the wife, she (or her *paterfamilias*) could recover the dowry from the husband's heirs, who could make the usual deductions for expenses, gifts, and misappropriated property.

Following Augustus' reforms, the position of the wife as regards dowry was reasonably secure. The husband's rights were similar to those of a usufructuary (see generally 6.3.4.1), i.e. he was entitled to use the property and take its fruits, but with a duty to restore the capital intact. And if he was insolvent, the wife was given priority over all unsecured creditors.

5.2.5.4 Reforms of Justinian

Further improvements to the wife's position were enacted later, especially by Justinian. He prohibited the alienation of dotal immovables even with the wife's consent. Moreover, the wife was given the right to bring proceedings during the marriage: she no longer had to wait for its termination. For example, she was allowed to recover the dowry if her interests in it were threatened. The *actio rei uxoriae* was abolished—the standard remedy for recovery of the dowry became the *actio ex stipulatu*, which could now be brought even though the parties had not made an agreement about the disposal of the dowry. Justinian held that there was an *implied* agreement in such a case that disposal would be determined by the standard provisions of the law. The husband's rights to automatic deductions were abolished, but he was allowed to bring a claim for expenses. If the wife predeceased the husband, the dowry went to her heirs, not to the husband. Dowry had to be returned within one year unless it consisted of land, in which case return had to be immediate. Further, the wife was allowed a tacit hypothec (implied mortgage) over the husband's property to secure her interests, thus giving her priority over *all* creditors of the husband, whether secured or unsecured.

The improving position of the wife as regards dowry, from the late Republic onwards, helped to secure some measure of financial protection for the wife, especially on divorce. This was a major development in the gradual improvement of the legal position of women in Roman law.

5.2.5.5 *Donatio propter nuptias* ('Gift on account of marriage')
(D.24.1.)

This was the converse of dowry—a gift by the bridegroom to his wife before the marriage. The property belonged to the wife but would normally be managed by the husband during marriage. The usual purpose of such gifts was to ensure provision for the wife in the event of the husband predeceasing her. In the East, there was considerable legislation in the late Empire that elevated *donatio* from a customary practice into an important legal institution subject to many of the rules applicable to dowry. A transfer of property was originally necessary, but later a *promise* of a *donatio* became actionable. The gift had to be made before the commencement of the marriage so as to evade the rule banning gifts between spouses. But Justinian enacted that a gift made during the marriage could be a valid *donatio*. Moreover, he specified that the value of the *donatio* had to be equal to the dowry; and he applied rules similar to those of dowry to the matter of the alienability of the property and its ultimate disposition.

5.2.6 Relationships outside marriage

Some relationships outside marriage could have legal consequences. The most important cases were *stuprum* and concubinage. For a good survey of the texts, see Evans Grubbs, *Women*, ch. 3.

5.2.6.1 *Stuprum*

A sexual union outside marriage between free persons was termed *stuprum*. The term comprised relations between unmarried persons, and adulterous unions. In the Republic there were occasional trials (but no regularized procedure) in which *stuprum* was alleged—usually against adulteresses. Condemnation normally involved exile or fines. However, there were instances where a father put his daughter to death for her *stuprum*. Her 'misbehaviour' was seen as ruining the chances of a respectable marriage. A child born in *stuprum* was regarded as illegitimate.

Although Augustus was apparently not averse to *stuprum* in his own personal life, he legislated against such behaviour and established special courts to deal with alleged cases. The legislation (the *Lex Julia* on adultery) was aimed at stamping out immorality (as it was perceived) and ensuring that Roman women remained eligible for marriage. This may explain why intercourse with a prostitute was not considered to be *stuprum* (she was not a suitable prospective wife), whereas intercourse between betrothed couples did constitute the offence.

5.2.6.2 Concubinage

(D.25.7.)

In some ways, concubinage resembled marriage. It was regarded (according to certain modern scholars) as a monogamous union—a man could not have two concubines (at the same time) or a wife and a concubine (though see D.25.7.3.1.). It seems that a partner could prosecute an unfaithful concubine but such proceedings were infrequent. Concubinage usually involved a union between a man and woman inferior to him in status, e.g. a patron and his freedwoman. Emperors were occasionally known to take concubines, e.g. Vespasian and Marcus Aurelius. The children of concubines were regarded as illegitimate until the Christian Empire, when legitimation by subsequent marriage was introduced (see 5.1.2.6). Gifts between a concubine and her partner were valid since the ban on gifts applied only to married couples.

Concubinage strictly amounted to *stuprum*, and thus could be prosecuted. This could occur especially where the partners were of equal legal status—the view was taken (at least by Augustus) that they should be married and not living in concubinage. To avoid prosecution for *stuprum* it was usually desirable that the concubine should be of lowly status:

Marcian, *Institutes, book 12*: **Another person's freedwoman can be kept as a concubine as well as a freeborn woman, especially where she is of low birth or has been a prostitute. But if a man would rather have a freeborn woman with respectable background as his concubine, he will not be allowed to do this unless he clearly states the position in front of witnesses. (D.25.7.3pr.)**

The spread of concubinage, particularly following Augustus's ban on marriage by soldiers, helped to make the institution more acceptable. However, the Christian Emperors made various attempts to discourage concubinage but failed to eradicate it.

5.3 Adoption

(Inst.Gai.1.97.–107., Inst.1.11., D.1.7., C.8.47.)

By the late Republic, the Romans had an established adoption law *in situ*, mainly because adoption was regarded as an important method for acquiring *potestas*, creating heirs, and perpetuating families in danger of extinction. 'A well-known feature of the social history of Rome is the infertility of the governing class, its failure to rear enough children to maintain its numbers . . . the characteristic remedy for a family in danger of dying out was adoption, and that was the primary purpose of the institution' (Crook, *Law and Life of Rome*, 111). Roman adoption was thus very different from that in modern Western society, where it is often seen primarily as a legal process for the benefit of children in need of a stable home.

5.3.1 Forms of adoption

There were two forms of adoption in Roman law: *adrogatio*, the adoption of a *sui iuris* person; and *adoptio*, the adoption of someone *alieni iuris*. However, before considering each form separately, it is useful to summarize their common features. See Frier and McGinn, *Casebook*, 304–14.

5.3.1.1 Similarities between *adrogatio* and *adoptio*

(a) Until late law the adopter acquired *potestas* over the adopted person in both forms of adoption.

(b) Until late law the adopted person changed families, i.e. became for all legal purposes a member of the family of the adopter, and ceased to be a member of his previous family.

(c) Under the principle that 'adoption imitates nature' it was established that the adopter must be at least 18 years older than the adopted person:

Modestinus, *Distinctions, book 1*: **Not only when someone is adopting but also when he is adrogating, he must be older than the person he is making his son. What is more, he must be of complete puberty, that is, he must be eighteen years older than the person in question.** (D.1.7.40.1.)

The requirement of 'complete puberty' ensured that the adopter was mature enough to be a father. It is likely that the age-difference rule was a post-classical development (D.1.7.40.1. is probably an interpolation).

(d) As a general rule—certainly of late law if not earlier—the adopter had to be physically capable of marriage, though there seems to have been an exception in the case of eunuchs. This rule too followed from the principle that 'adoption imitates nature'.

(e) Women could not adopt since they could not have *potestas*. But Diocletian allowed an exception: women whose children had died could adopt (by *adoptio*) as a consolation for their loss. *Potestas* could not ensue in such a case, but the adopted child did acquire rights of intestate succession in its adoptive mother's estate.

(f) As regards public rank and status, adoption had the effect of raising the status of the adopted person, but not lowering it:

Paul, *Replies, book 1*: **A person's rank is not lowered by adoption, but it is raised. Thus, even on adoption by a plebeian a senator remains a senator**...(D.1.7.35.)

(g) The adoptive relationship created a bar to marriage in certain cases (see 5.2.2.4).

(h) Adoption involved a transfer of obligations:

Paul, *Lex Julia et Papia, book 3*: **There are transferred to an adoptive father any legal burdens incumbent on the person given in adoption.** (D.1.7.45.)

The delictual obligations of the adopted person bound the adopter, who would have the choice of payment of damages or noxal surrender. Contractual obligations, however, did not generally bind the adopter since they were usually extinguished by the adoption. So, the praetors sometimes allowed contractual remedies to the innocent party (under the contract) on the fiction that the adopted person was *sui iuris*.

5.3.1.2 *Adrogatio*

This was originally the adoption of a *sui iuris* male, i.e. of a *paterfamilias*. Thus, adrogation involved the termination of a Roman family—one *paterfamilias* adopted another. The usual purpose of adrogation was to preserve a family that was in danger of extinction through lack of heirs, a device occasionally employed by Emperors. The general rule was established that adrogation was possible only if the adopter was childless, unlikely to have children, and at least 60 years of age; and he could normally adopt only one person.

Since adrogation involved the extinction of a Roman family, it is not surprising that the formal requirements were strict. Adrogation took place before the *comitia curiata*, presided over by the chief pontiff, who investigated the desirability of the proposed adrogation. If satisfied, he would ask the parties and the assembly in turn whether they consented to the adoption. The term *adrogatio* was derived from this question and answer procedure:

Gaius, *Institutes, book 1*: **This species of adoption is called *adrogatio* because, on the one hand, the adopter is rogated, that is, asked, if he wishes the person he is about to adopt to be his own lawful son, and, on the other, the adoptee is rogated if he will allow that to happen.** (D.1.7.2pr.)

Since boys under the age of puberty and women could not appear before the *comitia calata* (the term used for the *comitia curiata* when it dealt with wills), they could not originally be adrogated. However, adrogation of boys under the age of puberty became possible under Antoninus Pius subject to strict conditions; and Diocletian allowed women to be adrogated, although it is unlikely that this occurred often. Moreover, Diocletian changed the adrogation process. An inquiry was still necessary, but the adrogation was effected by imperial rescript (see Thomas, J. A. C., 'Some Notes on Adrogatio per Rescriptum Principis' (1967) 14 RIDA 3, 413–27, for the use of this form of adrogation during the reign of Diocletian. The article also contains interesting information about adrogation by and of women).

The effect of adrogation was that the adopted person passed into the adopter's *potestas* for all legal purposes. The adopter thus acquired the adoptee's property, legal rights, and family (apart from a wife in a free marriage):

Modestinus, *Distinctions, book 1*: **On the adrogation of a head of the household, those children who were in his power become grandchildren to the adrogator and come into his power at the same moment as does their father.** (D.1.7.40pr.)

The adopted person acquired something too—the right to succeed on his adoptive father's intestacy. In practice, an intestacy was unlikely after an adrogation: as the whole purpose of such an adoption was to perpetuate a family through the creation of an heir, the probability was that the adopter would make a will appointing the adoptee as his heir. If the latter was illegitimate, the *adrogatio* had the effect of making him the legitimate son of the adopter until the late Empire (when this method of legitimation was prohibited). A derivative form of *adrogatio* could also occur by way of a will, the so-called comitial will, where a *sui iuris* person assumed the position of the son and heir at the moment of the testator's death. It was generally known as adrogation in contemplation of death.

5.3.1.3 *Adoptio*

This was the adoption of *alieni iuris* persons, involving their removal from the power of the previous *paterfamilias*, and the creation of *potestas* and new agnatic ties within the adoptive family. The procedure used in early law for *adoptio* was similar to that in emancipation (see 5.1.2.4)—mock sales and resales between the *paterfamilias* and the adoptive father, utilizing the Twelve Tables rule that the son was freed from his father's power on the third sale. Only one sale was required for the *adoptio* of a daughter or remoter issue. This procedure gradually became obsolete in the Empire. It became the practice for the parties to appear before a magistrate with a written assertion that the sales had taken place (even though they had not).

Did the adoptee have to consent to the adoption? Not in early law, it seems; but the rule later emerged that an *adoptio* could not occur if the adopted person *objected* (there need not be any evidence of positive consent, however). In *adoptio*, it was possible to adopt a person as a *grandchild*, whether or not the adopter had any children:

Paul, *Views, book 2*: **One can adopt somebody as a grandson even though one has no son.** (D.1.7.37pr.)

However, since 'adoption imitates nature', it is probable that a person could not be adopted as a grandchild unless the adopter was old enough to be a grandparent—it seems there had to be a gap of two generations between them in age.

The legal consequences of *adoptio* were that the adoptee became a member of the adoptive family and acquired rights of intestate succession to his adoptive father. But he lost rights in his natural father's intestacy unless he was emancipated by the adopter, in which case the adoptee reacquired intestacy rights to his natural father (under the praetorian law of succession). A major difference from *adrogatio* was that in *adoptio* only the adopted person (and not his family) passed into the *potestas* of the adopter. But any children of the adopted person conceived after the adoption entered the power of the adopter.

5.3.2 Justinian's reforms

Adoption was one of the few areas of the law of persons that was not altered significantly by Augustus. Justinian, however, did make major changes. The most important were:

(a) In *adrogatio* the adopter no longer had absolute rights to the property of the adopted person, but was given rights similar to that of a usufructuary—the right to enjoy the property and take its fruits.

(b) Justinian simplified the procedure in *adoptio*. All that was required was for the three parties to make the appropriate declarations before a magistrate, recorded in the court archives.

(c) Justinian altered the legal effects of *adoptio* if the adopter was not a natural ascendant of the adopted person: the latter did not pass into the *potestas* of the adopter, and remained a member of his natural family—there was no exchange of families. But he acquired rights in the estate of the adopter (should the latter die intestate), thus giving the adoptee rights in the intestate estate of both his natural and adoptive father, a useful measure of protection against capricious emancipation. Such adoption was termed *adoptio minus plena*, i.e. 'less than full adoption'. Where the *adoptio* was by a natural ascendant, the legal consequences were as before, i.e. it was a 'full' adoption (*adoptio plena*).

5.4 Guardianship

(Inst.Gai.1.142.–200., Inst.1.13.–22., D.26.–27., chiefly C.5.28., 5.33., 5.42.)

Various categories of *sui iuris* persons were regarded as needing legal protection—children under the age of puberty, women, minors, spendthrifts, and the insane—a sizeable part of the population, which helps to explain the high incidence of guardianship in Roman society, see Gardner, *Roman Citizen*, 155–78. See Frier and McGinn, *Casebook*, 425–47.

5.4.1 Guardianship of children below puberty

Paul, *Edict, book 38*: **Tutelage is, as Servius defines it, force and power granted and allowed by the civil law over a free person, for the protection of one who, on account of his age, is unable to protect himself of his own accord.** (D.26.1.1pr.)

This definition can serve as a convenient starting-point, even if it is not strictly accurate. It cannot be said that the main purpose of guardianship (technically a *tutor* who exercised *tutela*—tutelage) was to protect children; rather, it was to protect their *property* for the benefit of those with rights of intestate succession in it. This was particularly evident in early law, and still important in the late Republic (when Servius was writing), although by then guardianship was increasingly seen as being in the interests of the child. Every Roman child that was *sui iuris* and *impubes* (below the age of puberty) had to have a guardian (*tutor*). The main reason for the frequent occurrence of this form of guardianship was the death of the child's *paterfamilias*, usually his father.

5.4.1.1 Types of guardianship

There were four forms of this category of guardianship (*tutela*): testamentary, statutory, fiduciary, and magisterial.

(a) Testamentary guardianship (*tutela testamentaria*):

Gaius, *Provincial Edict, book 12*: **By the *Law of the Twelve Tables*, parents are permitted to appoint by will tutors to their children, whether of the feminine or masculine gender, provided that they are in power.** (D.26.2.1pr.)

The right under the Twelve Tables to appoint a guardian by will was of considerable practical significance—testamentary guardianship was the most common form of *tutela impuberum*. The appointment had to be made in formal terms, e.g. 'Let Balbus be tutor', although in late law any form of appointment sufficed provided that it was sufficiently clear. At all times it was necessary to identify the guardian and the ward (*pupillus*).

(b) Statutory guardianship (*tutela legitima*). If there was no testamentary guardian, the guardianship vested under the Twelve Tables in the nearest agnate. If the nearest was a woman, the guardianship passed to the nearest *male* agnate. What if several agnates were equally entitled?

Gaius, *Provincial Edict, book 12*: **If there are several agnates, the most closely related obtains the tutelage, and if there are several in the same degree, they all obtain the tutelage.** (D.26.4.9.)

Why did the nearest agnates have the primary right? Because they would be entitled to succeed on the intestacy of the child. Since the child could not make a will (while an *impubes*), the agnates had an obvious interest in the protection of the child's property. In the absence of male agnates, the guardianship originally vested in the *gens*—the child's 'clan', i.e. a group of families linked by a common name—but the *gens* gradually became obsolete (as an institution) during the Republic.

There were two other forms of statutory guardianship. Under the Twelve Tables a patron had inheritance rights on the intestacy of his freedman. Consequently, a master who freed a slave under the age of puberty became the statutory guardian of the freedman. If the patron died, his children became the guardians of the freedman (since they acquired the right of inheritance). The third form of statutory guardianship occurred where an *impubes* was emancipated: the former *paterfamilias* became the child's guardian (again because of the acquisition of rights of inheritance on intestacy).

(c) Fiduciary guardianship (*tutela fiduciaria*). This form of guardianship was associated with emancipation. If a *paterfamilias* emancipated an *impubes* and then died before the latter had attained puberty, the male children of the deceased were entrusted with the guardianship of the ward. There were other forms of fiduciary guardianship, but the one described was the only one to survive Justinian. It is not clear why fiduciary guardianship was separately classified—there was no compelling reason for making a distinction between fiduciary and statutory guardianship, and the former in any case seems to have occurred rarely.

(d) Magisterial guardianship (*tutela dativa*). If there was no testamentary, statutory, or fiduciary guardian, magistrates were given the power to appoint a guardian under the *lex Atilia c.*210 [?] BC. Hence, this form of guardianship was called *dativa* ('appointed') or *decretalis* ('decreed'). It is unclear what happened before 210 BC if a child lacked a guardian. Schulz suggests that it may be that 'numerous minors were actually without guardians' (*Classical Roman Law* (1951), 167). Under the *lex Atilia*, the appointment could be made in Rome by the urban praetor and the tribunes; a similar power was granted in the late Republic to provincial governors for appointments in the provinces. In the Empire, a special praetor dealing with guardianship was created and given jurisdiction over appointments, as were city prefects. In the provinces, local magistrates acquired jurisdiction over the appointment of guardians where the property of the *impubes* was not of substantial value.

How did the matter come before the magistrate? Anyone with an interest in the child, including a creditor, could apply for an appointment to be made, and might suggest a particular individual. The magistrate could make the appointment if satisfied with the proposed appointee. In some instances persons had a duty to apply—mothers, for example, and freedmen in respect of their deceased patron's child:

Modestinus, *Exemptions, book 1*: . . . **there are those, on the other hand, who are obliged to request tutors, such as a mother and freedmen; for of these the former are fined and the latter are even punished if they do not request lawful guardians.** (D.26.6.2.1.)

Apart from guardianship under the *lex Atilia*, magistrates could be involved in other ways in the appointment of guardians. For example, a praetor could appoint a temporary guardian to act for an *impubes* in litigation between the child and its normal guardian. And the praetor had a general supervisory jurisdiction over the appointment of testamentary guardians, including the power to reject the appointee:

Tryphoninus, *Disputations, book 14*: . . . **the praetor follows what is advantageous to the *pupilli* and not what is written in the will or codicil.** (D.26.3.10.)

The involvement of the State in the appointment of guardians, following the *lex Atilia*, was instrumental in the gradual change in the nature of Roman guardianship during the course of the Republic. The magistrate could scrutinize the proposed appointment, require security for good management from the guardian, and supervise the performance of the guardian's duties. Such factors eventually made the interests of the child the prevalent concern in guardianship. Guardianship came to be seen more as a public duty.

5.4.1.2 Capacity to act as guardian

The basic requirement was that a guardian had to be a male citizen and must have attained puberty. Women could not be guardians, as a general rule, but in the late Empire a widow was allowed to apply for the guardianship of her children (or grandchildren). She had to promise not to remarry; if she broke the promise, the guardianship ended. A guardian did not have to be *sui iuris*: a son-in-power could be appointed, it being normal for his *paterfamilias* to act as guarantor.

Not everyone who was a male citizen of the age of puberty was eligible to be a guardian. A number of grounds for disqualification were established in the course of time, as well as excuses that the eligible could claim in order to be released from guardianship:

(a) Disqualification. Anyone who was deaf or dumb was disqualified. The insane were not disqualified but were regarded as temporarily incapacitated: a *curator* would act on their behalf (see 5.4.3.1). Persons engaged in certain occupations were disqualified, e.g. ambassadors, bishops, monks, soldiers. Justinian banned creditors or debtors of the ward, and anyone under 25.

(b) Excuses. Those who wished to avoid guardianship could plead a variety of excuses. Since it had become a potentially onerous public office by the late Republic, one can appreciate why an extensive law on excuses emerged—the topic became the subject of important monographs by jurists such as Modestinus, and merited a long title in Justinian's *Digest*.

Who could be excused? In early law, a testamentary guardian had the right to refuse the office, but in the early Empire the right was limited to refusal on set grounds (see later). Similarly, magisterial guardians could refuse only on set grounds. The position regarding statutory and fiduciary guardians is unclear. It seems that they had to *accept*, but could not be forced to *act* as guardians. This unsatisfactory position lasted until the Empire, when they *could* be compelled to act.

Where a person was relying on an excuse, he had to plead it within certain time limits, time running from the moment when he learned that he had been appointed. The rules on time limits demonstrated the Roman penchant for detail and orderly administration:

Modestinus, *Excuses, book 4*: **Someone living in the same city where he is appointed or within a hundred miles of it must excuse himself within fifty days; after this time, his plea will not be accepted, and he will have to undertake the administration....Someone who is abroad more than a hundred miles from the city will have a day allowed for every twenty miles, starting from the time he finds out (for the magistrates must inform him either in person or at his house) and besides this another thirty days for the preparation and presentation of his case.** (D.27.1.13.1.)

An excuse could be pleaded either at the initial stage or, if it had arisen after acceptance, as a ground for abandoning the guardianship. It could not be pleaded by anyone who had made a promise to the ward's *paterfamilias* that he would act as guardian.

What were the excuses that could be pleaded? A brief outline will have to suffice amidst the morass of detail. Among the more obvious excuses were: serious ill-health, old age (70 or above), being under 25 (until Justinian made it a disqualification), and illiteracy. One who already had three guardianships was excused, as was the parent of three legitimate children (but four outside Rome, five outside Italy). Certain magistrates and office holders were exempt. So were members of a heterogeneous array of occupations, such as grammarians, philosophers, doctors, and law teachers. And 'deadly enmity' between the appointed person and the child's late father provided an excuse (D.27.1.6.17.). Excuses could be permanent or temporary, absolute or partial. One of the most interesting examples of partial excuse concerned the inhabitants of Troy:

Callistratus, *Judicial Examinations, book 4*: **The inhabitants of Troy, who, because of the celebrated fame of the city and its connection with the origins of Rome, have long since been granted the fullest immunities...have an exemption from tutelage as regards *pupilli* who are not Trojans...** (D.27.1.17.1.)

5.4.1.3 The role of the guardian

The guardian's major functions were to manage the affairs (*tutela*) of the ward and to authorize his transactions (see later). The guardian would not normally have physical control over the ward—that would be in the hands of the ward's mother or other close relative. However, the guardian did have a duty to provide a reasonable sum out of the ward's property for the latter's maintenance (compare the Babatha archive). The guardian usually followed the expressed wishes of the deceased *paterfamilias* concerning maintenance, but they could be overridden by an application to the praetor:

Ulpian, *Edict, book 34*: **The praetor is accustomed to being approached quite often to decide where children are to be fed or maintained....[1] He usually decides whether someone ought to be better maintained by reference to the individual, his situation, and the circumstances; and sometimes the praetor overrides the father's instructions.** (D.27.2.1pr.–1.)

Before a guardian started to administer the ward's estate, he normally gave security and made an inventory. Security was given in the form of a formal promise by the guardian (backed by sureties) that the ward's property would be kept safe. All guardians were required to give security except those appointed by will or by high-ranking magistrates. The making of an inventory (under the supervision of officials) became standard in the classical period except by those testamentary guardians who were exempted by the will. Failure to make an inventory could be serious:

Ulpian, *Edict, book 35*: **A tutor who does not make....an inventory, is held to have acted fraudulently, unless perhaps some necessary and lawful reason can be alleged why this was not done. Therefore, he ought to undertake nothing before an inventory is made, except something which cannot wait even for a moderate delay.** (D.26.7.7pr.)

(a) Management of affairs (*administratio*).

Marcellus, *Digest, book 21*: **A tutor's principal duty is that he should not leave the *pupillus* unprotected.** (D.26.7.30.)

It was the proprietary interests of the ward that the guardian was meant above all to protect. *Administratio* was particularly relevant when the child was *infans*, i.e. too young to utter the set words necessary to enter certain transactions (eventually fixed as being below the age of seven). Such a ward was legally incapable of doing anything. The guardian acted for him, with wide powers of management: e.g. he could buy and sell property, collect and pay debts, make investments, and represent the ward in litigation. In the Empire, some restrictions were placed on the powers of alienation: a magistrate's permission had to be sought for the sale of certain types of land unless authorized by will. Constantine extended the prohibition to sale of valuable property of any kind; and Justinian subjected *all* the property of the ward to the ban. Sales of property in breach of these rules were voidable by the ward on attaining puberty. Contracts made by the guardian during *administratio* were binding on him, not on the ward. Only the guardian could enforce such contracts—the relationship of guardian and ward was not one of agency.

A guardian was expected, certainly in classical law, to manage the affairs of the ward in a business-like manner, selling off perishables, and making appropriate purchases and investments without undue delay. For example:

Paul, *Views, book 2*: **If a tutor on his appointment does not sue those whom he discovers to be debtors and through this they become less able to pay or if he does not invest the monies belonging to the *pupillus* within the first six months, he himself can be sued for the money owing and for the interest on the money which he has not loaned out.** (D.26.7.15.)

What was the standard of care expected of the guardian in *administratio*?

Ulpian, *Edict, book 36*: **The tutor is called to account for all that he has done which should not be done and for that which he has not done, answering for fraud, negligence, and the standard of care shown in his own affairs.** (D.27.3.1pr.)

This statement requires some consideration. In early law it is likely that the guardian was liable only for *dolus* ('fraud'). Unfortunately, the concept of *dolus* did not have a fixed meaning: originally, the term most probably signified fraud, i.e. dishonest conduct, but later it seems that it included gross negligence. Eventually, the liability of the guardian encompassed failure to match the standard of care shown in his own affairs—as the above text states—or in some cases, failing to act as the *bonus paterfamilias* would have acted:

Callistratus, *Judicial Examinations, book 4*: **Tutors and curators of *pupilli* are required to show the same care over the administration of the pupillary property as the head of the household ought in good faith to display for his own property.** (D.26.7.33pr.)

The apparent conflict in these two texts can be resolved. The former relates to the general management of a ward's interests, whereas the latter is specifically concerned with the *property* of the ward. Although the ward's property constituted a vital part of his affairs, there were other matters comprised in *administratio*. So it seems that differing standards of care applied to different areas of management. It is quite plausible that dealings with property required stricter diligence from the guardian than other aspects of *administratio*. See MacCormack, G., 'The Liability of the Tutor in Classical Roman Law' (1970) 5 IJ, 369–90.

Where damage had been caused to the ward's property, but not through the guardian's negligence, the latter was not liable:

Hermogenian, *Epitome of Laws, book 2*: **If the property of the *pupillus* is lost through being attacked by robbers or if the banker to whom the tutor gave the money…is unable to return the whole sum, the tutor is not on this account compelled to pay anything.** (D.26.7.50.)

(b) Authorization of transactions (*auctoritatis interpositio*). Once the ward ceased to be *infans* he acquired the capacity to enter legal transactions. Some he could make without the guardian's authorization—those which were unilateral and entirely for his benefit. But the transaction had to be *entirely* for his benefit: one that carried any actual or potential disadvantages was excluded.

What if a ward entered a bilateral transaction without his guardian's authorization? The ward could not be sued. Thus, if a loan was made to the ward, the creditor could not recover it. But the ward could not enforce a bilateral transaction unless he was prepared to perform his obligations. These rules meant that entering a bilateral transaction with a ward could be a fruitless business. So it was usual to insist on the guardian's authorization, which made the transaction fully binding. When authorization was given, the transaction bound the ward, not the guardian, unlike the case where the latter contracted in his own capacity in the course of *administratio*. Still, the Roman businessman no doubt preferred to contract with the guardian directly rather than with the ward. It is likely, therefore, that the process of giving authorization occurred infrequently. When it was given, it had to be done through an oral assent by the guardian. His presence was required: prior authorization or subsequent ratification, even if in writing, were insufficient. If the proposed transaction involved the guardian's personal interests, he could not validly authorize it. Could a guardian of an *impubes* ever be compelled to give his authorization? It seems not; but he would be liable for any unreasonable refusal that caused loss to the ward.

If a ward had two or more guardians (possible especially in statutory guardianship), they had several options as to how to perform their functions. They could opt for joint administration, in which case Justinian ruled that the authorization of one of them was generally sufficient to perfect a transaction by the ward. Previously, all had to authorize except if there were testamentary co-guardians (and possibly magisterial ones), in which case the authorization of one sufficed. Another option was to entrust the guardianship to one particular guardian—the *tutor gerens* (the 'active' guardian). Or the co-guardians could divide up the *administratio* between themselves, or seek directions from the praetor.

5.4.1.4 Remedies

The legal relationship between guardian and ward gave rise to a number of possible remedies:

(a) Removal. An action could be brought to remove a 'suspected' guardian, i.e. one who was shown to be untrustworthy. Anyone could bring the action except the ward. Removal was an important remedy, the only one available against a guardian *during* the guardianship. Originally, the action probably could be brought only for dishonesty, but in later law negligence sufficed. As soon as the accusation was brought the guardian was suspended. If the accusation was upheld, the guardian was removed from office and another one was appointed in his place, where necessary. If *dolus* was proved against the guardian, *infamia* resulted; but not otherwise:

Ulpian, *Edict, book 35*: **Someone who has been removed because of dilatoriness or boorishness, idleness, simpleness, or silliness is in the position of being able to leave the tutelage with his reputation intact.** (D.26.10.3.18.)

(b) Embezzlement. Under the Twelve Tables an action was allowed to a ward against his guardian, at the end of the guardianship, for embezzlement of the ward's property. Double damages were awarded and *infamia* resulted. It seems that this action was available only against statutory guardians in early law, but was later extended to all forms of guardianship. The action lay in addition to the standard delictual actions arising from the guardian's misconduct:

Ulpian, *Edict, book 36*: **However, Papinian says that a tutor who embezzled pupillary property will be liable for theft, and, if sued for theft, his having been sued in the action on tutelage for embezzlement will not release him from the action of theft. For the obligations in relation to theft and in relation to tutelage are not the same, which is to say that several actions can arise out of the same facts and several obligations. He is liable both for tutelage and theft.** (D.27.3.1.22.)

(c) *Actio tutelae*. This action, which dates from the end of the Republic, became the standard remedy for wards against guardians at the end of the guardianship. It lay for fraudulent or negligent maladministration, and condemnation involved *infamia* (probably only for fraud). The *actio tutelae* did not originally lie for failure to act, but in the early Empire it was extended to all forms of negligence, e.g. failure to render a proper account:

Ulpian, *Edict, book 36*: **It is part of the tutor's duty to compile an account of his actions and render it to his *pupillus*; if, on the other hand, he has not done this or if he does not reveal what has been done, he will be liable for it in the action on tutelage.** (D.27.3.1.3.)

If the guardian was found liable, the ward's claim took precedence over the guardian's unsecured creditors. Constantine gave the ward a tacit hypothec (implied mortgage) over the guardian's property, thus allowing the ward priority over all creditors. If the guardian was sued under the *actio tutelae*, he could deduct payments and expenses incurred on behalf of the ward, if reasonable. Later, the praetors allowed the guardian the *actio tutelae contraria* to *recover* reasonable expenses:

Ulpian, *Edict, book 36*: **The praetor proposed the *actio contraria* of tutelage and brought it into use so that tutors might undertake an administration more readily in the knowledge that the *pupillus* was to be liable to them for matters arising out of their administration . . . tutors are encouraged the more willingly to employ their own resources to the benefit of the *pupillus* when they know that they will get back what they have spent.** (D.27.4.1pr.)

Apart from the main guardianship remedies, there were other alternatives. For example, if the guardian had given security for safe management of the ward's property, his promises and those of his sureties would be enforceable at the end of the guardianship. And in some circumstances, it was possible to sue magistrates for failure to ensure that a guardian promised sufficient security.

5.4.2 Guardianship of women

Roman women who were *sui iuris* and had reached puberty were subject to guardianship (*tutela mulierum*). The origins of the institution dated from early Roman society, and were prompted by the need to protect family property. Since women were restricted from making wills in early law (see 8.4.1.1), their agnates had the expectation of inheriting from them on intestacy. Consequently, it was considered important for the property to be protected by a guardian against any injudicious disposal by the woman. There is some evidence in juristic writing and other literature that women were considered to be rather lacking in judgement in the handling of property, and thus easily deceived. This notion 'gained some colour from the ignorance of law and business practice forced on many women by their exclusion from public life, which in turn was made to justify this exclusion' (Gardner, *Women in Roman Law*, 21–2). And yet the astute Roman businesswoman was not a rare phenomenon (see e.g. Jakab, E., 'Financial Transactions by Women in Puteoli', in *New Frontiers*, 123–50). It may be that male prejudice accounted for the survival of *tutela mulierum* until the later Empire, although this form of guardianship had lost its importance much earlier. Gaius stressed in his *Institutes* that it was difficult to find any convincing arguments for the retention of guardianship of women (Inst.Gai.1.190.). See Frier and McGinn, *Casebook*, 450–6 as well as Evans Grubbs, *Women*, 23–46.

5.4.2.1 Forms of guardianship

Tutela mulierum could arise in similar forms to *tutela impuberum*, and many of the rules were identical:

(a) Testamentary. A *paterfamilias* could appoint in his will a guardian for any female descendants that might become *sui iuris* on his death. Moreover, a husband in a *manus* marriage could appoint a guardian for his wife, to act on the husband's death. It was not uncommon for the terms of the appointment to allow the widow to choose her guardian, and even to change the guardian at her discretion. The right of choosing a guardian was sometimes publicly conferred on women as a reward for services to the State.

(b) Statutory. The forms of statutory guardianship of women were similar to those in the case of guardianship of *impuberes*. Guardianship by agnates was the most important form in the Republic. Claudius demonstrated the decreasing importance of the institution in the Empire by abolishing agnatic guardianship over all women, although Constantine restored it for those below puberty.

(c) Fiduciary. If a woman had a statutory guardian, she could enter a collusive suit, by which she was 'sold' to a 'purchaser', provided the guardian consented. This freed her from statutory guardianship—the most inconvenient form of guardianship (since she could not compel the consent of the guardian). After the sale, the purchaser became the woman's fiduciary guardian; and *his* consent was compellable.

(d) Magisterial. If a woman did not have a testamentary, statutory, or fiduciary guardian, a magistrate could appoint one for her under the procedure introduced by the *lex Atilia* (see 5.4.1.1). And a magisterial guardian could be appointed even if the woman already had a guardian (but who was absent or unavailable).

5.4.2.2 Functions of the guardian

The guardian of a woman in *tutela mulierum* had a very limited role compared to that of the guardian of a child under the age of puberty. There was no *administratio*: the woman was responsible for managing her own affairs, although in practice the guardian often gave her assistance. As there was no *administratio*, it followed that he did not have to give security, or make an inventory, or render accounts; nor could any of the remedies for maladministration apply. If the guardian caused damage to the woman or to her property, his liability was based in delict and not in his capacity as guardian.

So what did the guardian do? His role was to authorize the woman's transactions where necessary. Since an adult woman had far greater legal capacity than an *impubes*, the guardian's authorization was required relatively infrequently. Generally, the greater the potential diminution of the woman's property, the more likely it was that consent was required for the transaction. It was needed, for example, to make a will, to manumit a slave, to enter a *manus* marriage, or to promise a dowry. But consent was not required, on the other hand, to enter a free marriage or to lend money. For example, graffiti discovered in Pompeii suggest that a certain Faustilla carried on an active business as a pawnbroker (see Gardner, *Women in Roman Law*, 17 ff.). In reality, the position of the woman was one of considerable independence because, even when consent was required, the guardian could be compelled to give it on an application by her to the praetor (except in the case of a statutory guardian). The reason why an exception was made in the case of statutory guardians was to protect their rights of succeeding on the woman's intestacy.

Augustus's family legislation had a considerable impact on the guardianship of women. The *lex Papia Poppaea* AD 9 released married women (and concubines) from guardianship if they had given birth to at least three children by separate births. Four were required in the case of a freedwoman, children born before manumission not counting. This right (the *ius liberorum*) was sometimes given to women who had not satisfied Augustus' criteria but who were deemed worthy of the honour. The combination of Augustus's grant of the *ius liberorum* and Claudius' abolition of the agnatic guardianship of women proved to be major factors in the gradual demise of *tutela mulierum* in the Empire.

5.4.3 Curatorship

(Inst.Gai.1.197.–200., Inst.1.23., D.27.10., 42.7., C.5.70.)

Curatorship (*cura*) was a form of guardianship that normally arose outside the main forms of *tutela* (see Frier and McGinn, *Casebook*, 438–47). However, there were situations in which a person subject to *tutela* could have a curator. For example, a curator could be appointed to protect the interests of a ward involved in litigation with his guardian or in making contracts with him; or where the guardian was incapable of acting:

Pomponius, *Manual, book 2*: **It is even customary for a curator sometimes to be appointed to someone who has a tutor on account of the tutor's ill-health or extreme age…**(D.26.1.13pr.)

5.4.3.1 Curatorship of those with diminished mental capacity

Ulpian, *Sabinus, book 1*: **The *Law of the Twelve Tables* prevents a prodigal's dealing with his property, and this was originally introduced by custom. Today, however, praetors and governors, if they encounter persons who have set neither time limit nor boundary to their expenditure, but squandered their substance by extravagance and dissipation, are accustomed to appoint a curator for them on the analogy of a lunatic. They remain in care, the lunatic until he regains his health of mind, the other until he comes to his senses; when this happens, they automatically cease to be in their curator's power.** (D.27.10.1pr.)

(a) Curatorship of the insane (*cura furiosi*). A *sui iuris* person who was insane lacked legal capacity, except during lucid intervals, and was placed by the Twelve Tables under the guardianship of his agnates (or the *gens* if there were no agnates). Later, the praetor acquired jurisdiction over the insane: he could appoint a curator if there were no agnates or if the only agnates were unsuitable. An inquiry would normally be held:

Ulpian, *All Seats of Judgement, book 1*: **The praetor must be careful not to appoint a curator for someone rashly without the fullest investigation; for many feign madness or mental illness so as to escape their legal obligations by receiving a curator.** (D.27.10.6.)

In the later Empire, formal appointment as curator became necessary in all cases, even for the closest agnates. If the insane person recovered his sanity, he became legally capable again and the guardianship ceased; but it revived if there was a relapse into insanity. In early law, only *furiosi* (i.e. lunatics, madmen) were subject to guardianship, but in the Empire the category was extended to include persons with less severe forms of mental illness or even with physical incapacities, e.g. the deaf or dumb. Typically, the jurists regarded mental incapacity as a question of fact in each particular case and eschewed the formulation of any general tests regarding the fundamental question—when is a person to be regarded as *furiosus*? See Schulz, *Classical Roman Law* (1951), 198–9.

The prime function of the curator was to manage the affairs of the afflicted person, especially his property—a *furiosus* was incapable of any legal act. It seems, however, that *cura furiosi* was not motivated entirely by proprietary considerations:

Julian, *Digest, book 21*: **The curator's concern and care should extend over the health and wellbeing of the lunatic as well as the property.** (D.27.10.7pr.)

A curator was liable for maladministration but was entitled to recover reasonable expenses.

(b) Curatorship of prodigals (*cura prodigi*). Prodigals were *sui iuris* persons who wasted inherited property (see Zak, E., 'Historical Development of Roman Guardianship of a Spendthrift', in *Mélanges Wolodkiewicz* II, 1133–56). The importance of inherited wealth in Roman society (at least among the wealthier classes) made the prospect of the dissipation of family wealth by some reckless idiot too dangerous to go unchecked.

The Twelve Tables placed persons who wasted property that had been inherited on intestacy in the guardianship of their agnates (or the *gens* if there were no agnates). Later, when the praetors acquired jurisdiction over prodigals, they extended the regime to include inheritance by will. They could appoint persons other than agnates to be curators if they felt that the agnates were unsuitable. In the developed law, the issue of prodigality—regarded purely as a question of fact—was for the praetor to decide, following an application by any interested party. If the praetor was satisfied that the alleged prodigal was wasting property, he would issue an interdict preventing the prodigal from any dealings with his property other than those entirely for his benefit. Consequently, the prodigal could not make a will or alienate property:

Ulpian, *Edict, book 16*: **Julian wrote that those who were forbidden to deal with their goods by the praetor could not convey anything to anybody, because they have no goods since they are forbidden to alienate.** (D.27.10.10pr.)

The function of the curator of a prodigal is not altogether clear. It seems that he had the right to manage the property of the prodigal and to authorize transactions that were potentially detrimental. The curatorship lasted until the praetor withdrew the interdict. He would not do this unless satisfied that it was safe to do so, i.e. that the prodigal had ceased his extravagant ways, but this might not easily be proved. Maladministration by the curator was actionable by the prodigal. The curator could recover reasonable expenditure.

5.4.3.2 Curatorship of minors (*cura minorum*)

On attaining puberty the *sui iuris* male, freed from guardianship, had full legal capacity; the female had limited capacity, being under *tutela mulierum*. Boys of 14 (and girls of 12) are not normally models of prudence and wisdom, even in Rome. They can be easily exploited. A *lex Plaetoria c.*200 BC was necessary in order to penalize anyone who defrauded a minor, i.e. a person between puberty and 25 years of age. Condemnation in the action, which could be brought by any citizen, involved *infamia*. Further, the praetors later allowed a defence under the statute against anyone who tried to enforce a transaction disadvantageous to the minor, whether or not fraud had occurred. If the transaction had already been made, the praetor could rescind it by *restitutio in integrum* (see 3.3.4.1). The lengths to which the minor could be aided are demonstrated by the fact that transactions could be questioned, even though they had occurred during *tutela* with the guardian's consent:

Modestinus, *Replies, book 2*: **Even if it can be shown that a *pupillus* has been put to a disadvantage in a case where he had received the authority of his tutor who was also his father, his curator, subsequently appointed, is not prevented from seeking *restitutio in integrum* on his account.** (D.4.4.29pr.)

The *lex Plaetoria*, as applied by the praetors, put the minor in a very advantageous position. As a result, people were wary of entering transactions (with minors) that could be easily undone. So it became the practice to insist that a third party, trusted by the minor, should be present at the transaction and should assent to it. It would then be more difficult for the minor to allege later that his inexperience had been exploited. The third party came to be known as *curator*. Neither his presence nor his consent was required in law, but provided strong evidence of the fairness of the bargain. Hence, the wise businessman would normally insist on a curator when dealing with a minor. It seems that prior authorization was sufficient evidence of the fairness of the transaction, but subsequent ratification was not.

Curators were initially used for single transactions on an *ad hoc* basis; but in the second century AD it became usual for the same curator to look after the interests of a minor on a more permanent and regular basis. An important development occurred under Marcus Aurelius—minors could apply to a magistrate for the appointment of a curator for the duration of the minority, and this became the normal practice:

Ulpian, *Edict, book 11*: **And, therefore, today, up to this age, young men are governed by curators and under this age the administration of their own property should not be entrusted to them, even though they might be able to look after their own affairs well.** (D.4.4.1.3.)

It was not just 'young men' for whom curators could be appointed—young women could request a curator, especially if they no longer had a guardian. The comment that administration 'should not be entrusted' to minors is revealing as regards the practice that had developed by this time: the curator had no formal right to manage the affairs of the minor, but was often requested to do so. The giving of consent remained an important function but, as before, its purpose was evidentiary—it was not strictly required. Even if given, consent did not *validate* anything since a transaction by a minor was valid without it. Indeed, a minor need not have a curator at all: he could enter transactions independently if he could find anyone rash enough to do business with him—it seems that the *lex Plaetoria* and the praetorian remedies were still applicable. Curatorship of minors ended at 25, but from the late classical period it could be removed at an earlier age by imperial decree. Constantine provided that this procedure was unavailable unless the minor had attained the age of 20 (18 for females).

In the later Empire *cura minorum* was increasingly institutionalized. It came to be regarded as an extension of full guardianship: management of the minor's affairs became the chief function of the curator. Many of the rules of *tutela* became applicable, e.g. the law on disqualifications and excuses. Consent to transactions acquired more than evidentiary importance: in late law it seems that a minor could not incur any liabilities without the curator's consent. The assimilation of curatorship and guardianship in late law is evident from the leading titles in the *Digest* on guardianship (in D.26. and D.27.)—many passages therein contain the phrase 'tutors and curators' as if these terms were synonymous.

 Please consult the Online Resource Centre for revision guidance on this chapter.

FURTHER READING

On the Roman family, see Hodge, P. (1974), *Roman Family Life*, London: Longman; Dixon, S. (1992), *The Roman Family*, Baltimore: Johns Hopkins University Press, especially ch. 2.

On Roman divorce, see Corbier, M., 'Constructing Kinship in Rome: Marriage and Divorce, Filiation and Adoption', in *The Family in Italy*, 127–44. See also Corbier, M., 'Divorce and Adoption as Roman Familial Strategies', in *Marriage, Divorce and Children*, 47–78. This interesting study realigns divorce and adoption within the strategies and practices of kinship and affinity which characterized Roman society in the late Republic. Finally, Treggiari, S., 'Divorce Roman Style: How Easy and How Frequent Was It?', in *Marriage, Divorce and Children*, 31–46, explores the legal and social elements of a Roman divorce.

PART III

The Law of Property and Inheritance

6

....

Interests in property

The basic 'institutional' classification of Roman private law was into persons, things, and actions. The law of things was concerned with property, obligations, and succession (Inst.Gai.2.97.). The acquisition of proprietary interests was the chief concern of the law of property. This chapter deals primarily with the various interests that could be acquired in property, particularly ownership, rights to servitudes, and possession. In theory, the interests in property may be divided into two broad categories, namely legal interests (ownership and limited real rights) and factual interests (possession). While such a division is useful, it should not be seen as absolute, since possession, though largely a question of fact, could also have certain legal consequences. But first the Roman classification of property must be considered. See Diagram 6.1.

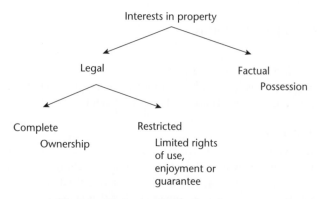

Diagram 6.1 Roman classification of property

6.1 **The classification of property**

The Institutes of Gaius, written in the mid-second century AD, contains three statements on the classification of property. The first of these, the so-called 'primary division', classifies all property as being either subject to human or to divine law. Following this statement, Gaius then proceeds to classify property falling under human law as being either corporeal/incorporeal or *res mancipi/* not *res mancipi*. The compilers of Justinian's Institutes drew on Gaius' classification of property, but introduced certain changes. First, the category of *res mancipi*/not *res mancipi* was removed to reflect the abolition of this classification in

Justinianic law. In second place, the possible types of classification of property were expanded considerably. Owing to the preservation of Gaius's Institutes, his classification of things looms large, but it must not be forgotten that certain Roman jurists classified property differently. The most important of these will be discussed here. (See Inst.2.1.)

6.1.1 Corporeal and incorporeal things

(Inst.Gai.2.12.–14., Inst.2.2.)

The word *res* is much used in Roman law: it is capable of several different meanings. Originally, its primary meaning was a 'thing', in the sense of a physical object. Later, *res* came to have a potentially much wider meaning, comprising an extended notion of property: it was any asset that had economic value. This widening of the meaning of *res* was reflected in the distinction that emerged in the later Republic between corporeal and incorporeal things (*res corporales* and *incorporales*) (cf. Inst. Gai.2.12.; 28.). This distinction was important since only corporeal things could be possessed and could be acquired in ownership through *usucapio*. A corporeal thing is something which could be touched, while an incorporeal thing, because of its immateriality, could not be touched. The chief examples of incorporeal things were an inheritance, obligations in whichever way contracted, and limited rights over property belonging to another person (*iura in re aliena*), of which the most important were servitudes—the broad equivalent of profits and easements in English law (see generally 6.3).

6.1.2 Public and private things

(Inst.Gai.2.9.–11.)

Things were classified according to whether they could be owned privately or not, a distinction of obvious practical importance (see Inst.Gai.2.1.). There were several categories of property that could not be privately owned.

6.1.2.1 *Res communes*

These were things common to all men, e.g. the air, running water, the sea. Although such things could not be owned, the law recognized a right to enjoy them: deliberate interference with enjoyment could result in a delictual remedy for insulting behaviour (see 10.4.2.1). It has been suggested that this category originally formed part of the category of *res publicae* and was only separated from it during the later classical period.

6.1.2.2 *Res publicae*

These were 'public' things, regarded as belonging to the State, e.g. public roads, harbours, ports, certain rivers, bridges, and enemy property captured in military action. Perhaps the most important 'public' property was provincial land, i.e. land in the provinces outside Italy. A distinction was drawn in the Empire between senatorial and imperial provinces. The former were regarded as belonging to the Roman people, but the latter (generally the more recently acquired territories) were classified as Imperial property. This type of ownership was not ownership according to Roman private law (i.e. quiritary ownership), but a special form of ownership governed by public law. See Schulz, *Classical Roman Law* (1951), 340–1 for a detailed discussion of this point. Although provincial land could not be owned privately, proprietary interests in it were possible (see 6.4).

Rivers were regarded as public things if they were perennial, i.e. normally flowing all the year round. Although such a river could not be owned, its beds and banks could be; but it seems that the riparian owners (i.e. the owners of the river banks) could not prevent the public from using the banks to enjoy the river. Remedies were normally available to protect the enjoyment or use of public things. Interdicts, in particular, could be used for this purpose. (On the application of this doctrine in modern Scots law, see *Will's Trustees* v *Cairngorm Canoeing and Sailing School Ltd* 1976 SC (HL) 30 at 11.2.3.5.)

6.1.2.3 *Res universitatis*

These were things that were intended for public use, owned by corporate public bodies such as municipalities and colonies. This category included, e.g., public streets and buildings, theatres, parks, racecourses, and stadia. The category is first described as such under Justinian, although it probably dates from the classical period where it is generally described as *res publicae*.

6.1.2.4 *Res nullius*

Things belonging to no one, a heterogeneous category which included wild animals, abandoned property, and 'divine' things. Such things could be subject either to human or divine law (Inst.Gai.2.3.–8.):

(a) *Res sanctae*: things considered to be protected by the gods to whom they were consecrated, crucial to the safety of Rome, e.g. city walls and gates. Anyone violating them was subject to heavy criminal sanctions (hence '*sanctae*'), including the death penalty in some cases.

(b) *Res religiosae*: tombs, sepulchres, mausoleums, cenotaphs, and land used for burial. Certain conditions had to be satisfied before burial ground was classed as 'religious'. Tomb inscriptions suggest that the Romans paid scant regard to the rule that tombs and burial land could not be owned privately—sales and gifts of such things are often mentioned. See further, Crook, *Law and Life of Rome*, 133 ff. and Toynbee, *Death and Burial in the Roman World* (1971), ch. 4.

(c) *Res sacrae*: things formally consecrated and dedicated to the gods, e.g. temples, shrines, and sacred groves (see Inst.Gai.2.3.). After the conversion to Christianity, churches were classed as *res sacrae*.

Certain *res nullius* could fall into private ownership (at which point they ceased to be *res nullius*). For example, ownership could be acquired over wild animals and abandoned property by *occupatio* (Inst.2.1.12.) (see 7.2.3).

For a survey of the ownership implications of these categories, see Schulz, *Classical Roman Law* (1951), 340–1. For a recent survey, see also Du Plessis, P. J., 'Property', in *Cambridge Companion*, 175–98.

6.1.2.5 **The seashore**

The distinction between the categories of public things was not always clear. The seashore certainly lacked a clear legal identity. One text states:

Neratius, *Parchments, book 5*:...shores are public, not in the sense that they belong to the community as such but that they are initially provided by nature and have hitherto become no one's property. (D.41.1.14pr.) (Compare Inst.2.1.3.)

Other texts describe the seashore as 'being open to all' (D.18.1.51.), or as 'common to all' (D.47.10.13.7.) or as 'belonging' to the whole people:

Celsus, *Digest, book 39*: **The shores over which the Roman people has dominion I consider to belong to the Roman people.** (D.43.8.3pr.)

More important than its theoretical status was the question of the use to which the seashore could be put. Everyone certainly had the right of access to the seashore, as in the case of riverbanks. No one could acquire any part of the seashore but shelters and similar erections could be built, if authorized, and became the property of the builder:

Pomponius, *From Plautius, book 6*: **Although what we erect on the shore or in the sea becomes ours, a decree of the praetor, nevertheless should be obtained, authorizing the erection.** (D.41.1.50.)

Whether authorization was always necessary is not clear. In D.43.8.4, we are told that building on the seashore is 'allowed' by the law of nations 'unless public use is impeded'—no hint there of the necessity for magisterial consent.

6.1.3 **Movables and immovables**

This classification of property, which was not as important in Roman law as later on in medieval law, distinguished between land (immovables) and anything else (movables) that could be owned privately. Land itself was classified as Italic land (defined eventually as land south of the River Po) or provincial land, i.e. outside Italy, the distinction having important consequences, e.g. Italic land was *res mancipi* (see 6.1.5). The classification of property into movables and immovables had some important consequences, but was less pervasive than in English law (because of the overwhelming primacy of land in English feudal society). Buckland and McNair in *Roman Law and Common Law*, refer to 'the comparative insignificance in Roman law of the distinction between land and other property' (60).

6.1.4 **Fungibles and non-fungibles**

Fungibles were things that were regarded as existing primarily in quantities (e.g. money, grain) rather than as separate entities. Fungibles are normally consumed through use. Non-fungibles were things which had a separate identity and a degree of permanence, e.g. a book, land, a chariot. The distinction between fungibles and non-fungibles was of importance particularly in the law of contract—e.g. the contract of *mutuum* (see 9.5.1) was concerned specifically with the loan of fungibles. Furthermore, sale of fungibles could only take place by way of *stipulatio*, whereas non-fungibles could be sold using *emptio venditio*. And the distinction had some significance in the law of property, e.g. in the Republic there could not be a usufruct of fungibles.

6.1.5 *Res mancipi* and *res nec mancipi*

(Inst.Gai.2.14a.–23.)

This was the most important classification of property in archaic Roman law. It dated from Rome's earliest period and survived until it was abolished by Justinian. Throughout that time, but especially in early law, the classification was of fundamental significance in the conveyance of property. Full title (*dominium*) over *res mancipi* could be transferred only through the formal modes of conveyance—*mancipatio* and *cessio* (Inst.Gai.2.18.) (see 7.1.1 and 7.1.2).

What were *res mancipi*? A satisfactory definition has proved elusive; it is easier to list the things that were recognized as *res mancipi* than to define the species. According to Gaius (Inst.2.14a.) *res mancipi* comprised the following things: slaves, beasts of draft and burden, Italic land, houses on such land, and rustic praedial servitudes (i.e. easements and profits over land). As regards the animals, there was a juristic dispute about the moment when the beasts became *res mancipi*—the Sabinians claimed that it was at birth, whereas the Proculians held that it was when the animal was broken in. Gaius lists oxen, horses, mules, and donkeys as *examples* of beasts of burden, but the list appears to have been comprehensive—no other animals seem to have been regarded as *res mancipi*. Once the category of *res mancipi* was established in early law, it did not prove susceptible to amendment. For example, camels and elephants could be regarded as beasts of burden but were encountered by the Romans after the list of *res mancipi* was established—so they did not qualify. The most probable reason for the reluctance to expand the list of *res mancipi* was that the formal modes of conveyancing necessary to transfer *dominium* in such things increasingly came to be seen as cumbersome and inconvenient.

Now that the list of *res mancipi* is known, how can the category be defined? The most accurate definition may be 'those things which had to be conveyed by *mancipatio* or *cessio* in order for *dominium* to pass', but this tells us little about the character of *res mancipi*. To describe them as the most 'valuable' things is misleading since items such as jewellery or gold caskets were not *res mancipi*. 'Important things' is a more accurate definition, but lacking in precision. Considering each constituent of Gaius's list, and the period in which it was established, *res mancipi* can best be described as things useful or essential to the household in early Roman society: 'the most important means of production of a peasant economy belonged to the *res mancipi*. Slaves, horses, oxen, asses, and mules furnished the indispensable manpower, while the land and the appertaining praedial servitudes served as a basis for the subsistence of the family' (Diósdi, *Ownership*, 57). All other things (however important, useful, or valuable) were classed as *res nec mancipi*, and did not need to be conveyed by the formal modes of conveyance; simple delivery (*traditio*) sufficed to pass full title. In later law, the distinction between *res mancipi* and *nec mancipi* lessened in importance due to the decreasing use of *mancipatio* and *cessio*, and because of the operation of bonitary ownership (see 7.2.2). By Justinian's time, the distinction had become largely an irrelevance—its abolition was long overdue (see C.7.31.1.5.).

6.2 Ownership

6.2.1 Introduction

There has been much speculation about the nature of ownership in Roman law. It seems that the Romans lacked a precise concept of ownership in early law. There was perhaps no need for one: early Roman society was structured in such a way that property disputes would be a rarity. The *paterfamilias* exercised control over the persons and things in his household. There may have been, in any case, an element of community of property in very early Rome: it seems that land was originally regarded as publicly owned, even if privately enjoyed. The concept of community of property survived to some extent in the Republic, notably in the rights of the *gens* to succeed on intestacy.

The impetus for the transition from an undifferentiated concept of ownership in early Roman law to the technical concept of *dominium* in classical law may be ascribed to a variety of factors. These include the profound social and economic changes in the later Republic coupled with the intellectualization of Roman legal science and the changes in civil procedure (see generally, Diósdi, *Ownership*). The recognition of a variety of proprietary interests necessitated the elucidation of a clearer notion of ownership, the work mainly of the jurists of the late Republic and early Empire. *Dominium* was the concept that emerged. It was the highest, the ultimate entitlement to property, specifically distinguished from lesser types of proprietary interest. In some respects, it was thus comparable to the English fee simple—you could not go beyond *dominium*. The owner was lord and master (*dominus*) of his property, entitled to a *vindicatio*—the standard proprietary remedy securing the rights of the owner (for a survey of the procedural peculiarities of this remedy, see Hausmaninger, Gamauf, and Sheets, *Casebook*, 207–22). The notion of ownership in Roman law was less flexible than in English law. For example, Roman law did not have a doctrine of tenures or estates: 'the classical jurists had an extremely concentrated notion of ownership, that is to say, although they recognized that various people could own the same thing in common at the same time, they did not attempt any division of ownership as such' (Buckland and McNair, *Roman Law and Common Law*, 81).

6.2.2 The essentials of *dominium*

Three basic conditions had to be satisfied in order for a person to have *dominium*: he or she had to have *commercium*; the property had to be capable of being privately owned; and the property must have been acquired by an appropriate method of acquisition.

6.2.2.1 *Commercium*

This requirement meant that only Roman citizens (and foreigners to whom *commercium* had been granted) could have *dominium*. Indeed, *dominium* was often described as ownership 'by the right of the *Quirites*' (an ancient name for Roman citizens). From this, it would appear that foreigners could not own things under Roman law. But that would have been absurd: Roman commerce could not have flourished if foreigners had not been allowed some legal interest in what they acquired. The law permitted such an interest—peregrine ownership. Little is known about this type of ownership, but it seems to have been protected by a modified form of *vindicatio*. Peregrine ownership could be obtained through the *ius gentium* modes of acquisition (see generally 7.1) but not through the *ius civile* modes (see 7.2). The general grant of citizenship by the Emperor Caracalla in AD 212 greatly reduced the importance of peregrine ownership. It finally disappeared under Justinian.

6.2.2.2 **Property capable of private ownership**

A person could have *dominium* only over property capable of being privately owned. We have seen already that certain types of property were outside private ownership. Provincial land was probably the most important case. Although such land strictly belonged either to the Roman people or to the Emperor, it was often, but not excusively, let out at a rent through a specific form of lease (see 6.4.1). This form of holding can be described as provincial ownership. The holders lacked *dominium* but they had an interest that was in practice close to full ownership, protected by a modified *vindicatio* and transferable by convenient *ius gentium* modes of transfer such as delivery. Provincial ownership attained considerable importance in the late Empire but became obsolete when Justinian abolished the distinction between Italic and provincial land. For a detailed survey of provincial ownership, see Schulz, *Classical Roman Law* (1951), 339–41.

6.2.2.3 **Appropriate mode of acquisition**

Dominium over *res mancipi* could not be acquired unless such property had been transferred by *mancipatio* or *cessio*. But what was the position of a transferee of *res mancipi* if *mancipatio* or *cessio* had not been used?

To begin with, it may be wondered why anyone should attempt to transfer such important property by an inappropriate mode of conveyance. *Mancipatio* and *cessio* were formal conveyances, the former requiring several witnesses and strict adherence to ceremony, while the latter necessitated the presence of a magistrate (see 7.1.1 and 7.1.2). When Rome underwent economic transformation during the Republic, these formal modes of conveyance came to be seen as cumbersome and anachronistic. Commercial life would have ground to a halt if the praetor or several witnesses had to be found every time that a slave or a horse was sold. Instead, increasing use was made of delivery (*traditio*) to transfer *res mancipi*. This would not have occurred unless the transferee's acquisition had been legally protected, i.e. recognized as a worthwhile proprietary interest, even if not strictly *dominium*. It was the praetors who were largely instrumental in protecting the transferee's interests by developing the concept of bonitary ownership.

6.2.3 **The nature of ownership**

To what extent did the owner in Roman law have unlimited freedom to do as he pleased with his property? This controversial question has prompted a wide range of views. The modern tendency is to regard Roman ownership as having been somewhat less absolute than was once thought.

6.2.3.1 **Land**

As a general rule, a landowner owned everything above and below the ground. It followed that ownership could be divided vertically but not horizontally, e.g. a farmer could divide a field by selling part of it—that is vertical division. But in a block of flats the inhabitants of the upper stories could not be owners—they were simply tenants with contractual rights, not owners. See Crook, *Law and Life of Rome*, 143 ff. However, there were exceptions to the rule that a landowner owned everything above and below ground. For example, decrees were occasionally passed in the Empire giving the State rights in precious minerals that were found underground. And if fruit fell from your neighbour's tree into your garden, he had a right under the Twelve Tables to collect it.

6.2.3.2 Restrictions on owners

There was a considerable range of restrictions to which the Roman owner was subject, mostly inspired by considerations of public policy. Most of these restrictions date from the archaic period, but additional remedies were added in classical Roman law. Under the Twelve Tables there had to be an open space of at least five feet between neighbouring properties, and owners could not plant trees within five feet of the boundary (nine feet for olive and fig trees). Rules also existed to deal with overhanging branches, fruit from the neighbour's trees falling into your yard, smoke from a neighbour's cheese factory, protrusion of walls, and boundary disputes. Such rules seem astonishingly detailed, but they were well intentioned—trying to prevent disputes between neighbours—and were an early demonstration of the Roman genius for orderliness. Further, the Twelve Tables restricted the demolition of houses, and allowed action to be taken to minimize the threat of damage from rainwater on neighbouring land, or from the defective state of the neighbour's property. The offending neighbour could be required by the praetor on application by the other party to promise security in the event of damage (*cautio damni infecti*) (D.39.2.), otherwise his neighbour would be allowed to enter the land in order to make the property safe (see D.39.2.2.; D.39.2.4.1., 4.; D.39.2.5pr.). Similarly, if the owner of a piece of land (or a usufructuary) suffered damage as a result of new building on an adjacent piece of land, the praetor could prevent the construction from continuing with an *operis novi nuntiatio* (D.39.1.). Where construction work was done forcibly or with stealth, the praetor could also grant an *interdictum quod vi aut clam* (D.43.24.) to prevent further damage (see D.43.24.1.4.–5.; D.43.24.3.7.). And a special action existed (the *actio aquae pluviae arcendae*) (D.39.3.), again under the Twelve Tables, regarding damage threatened by the construction of an aqueduct or alteration of an existing watercourse by a neighbour:

Ulpian, *Edict, book 53*: **This action is appropriate whenever water is likely to cause damage to a field as a result of a man-made construction, that is, whenever someone causes water to flow elsewhere than in its normal and natural course** ... (D.39.3.1.1.)

The neighbour whose property was threatened by these actions could sue with the *actio aquae pluviae arcendae* for removal of the structure as well as for compensation, but this action could only be brought against the neighbour who had made the alterations or altered the natural flow of water (see D.39.1.2.; D.39.3.3.). Damage threatened or caused by the alteration of the natural flow of water for the purposes of agricultural cultivation did not fall under this action (see D.39.3.1.5.).

Some of the restrictions outlined above demonstrate an admirable feature of Roman law—that an owner of property has to show respect (in the use of his property) for the interests of his neighbour. It would thus be shortsighted to view restrictions simply in negative terms. Restricting a man from using his property selfishly is to protect and enhance the ownership of his neighbour, a factor to be considered when assessing how free an owner was to do as he pleased with his property.

The need to show respect for a neighbour's enjoyment of his property can be illustrated also by the rules protecting the enjoyment of light and views. Although there is inconsistency in the texts, it seems that there was in classical law a right to light—the unreasonable blocking of light was considered unlawful. Some support for this view lies in the fact that it was possible to create a servitude allowing the building of property beyond a reasonable height. If light could have been freely obstructed, the servitude would have had little or no purpose.

If a dispute arose about the right to light, arbitrators could be appointed to adjudicate. What was considered to be a reasonable amount of light? The formulation of an appropriate rule is obviously fraught with difficulty in such a case. The Roman attempt was inevitably vague:

Marcellus, *Digest, book 4*: ... **in the case of obstructing light and thus darkening a house ... the following qualification is conceded. The light should not be blocked out entirely, but as much should remain as is sufficient for reasonable daily use of the property by the inhabitants.** (D.8.2.10.)

A right to a view is discernible in classical law, even if it was rather limited. A person could sometimes be stopped from building if this obstructed his neighbour's view. Again, some evidence for such a right is to be found in the fact that a servitude could be created allowing a view to be blocked—the servitude would hardly have been necessary if there had not been a right to a view. Not every view was protected, only those regarded as distinguished, e.g. a view of the sea or mountains, the matter being adjudicated through inspection by arbitrators. See Rodger, A., *Owners and Neighbours in Roman Law* (1972), ch. 4, also ch. 2 (right to light). The very existence of the concept of a right to a view, limited though it was, reflects great credit on Roman law, which on occasion could attain sophisticated levels of development, even by modern standards.

The law imposed all the restrictions on ownership that have been outlined so far. There were, in addition, those restrictions that were created by owners themselves (or their predecessors). This could occur, for example, through contracts, some of which were capable of creating limited proprietary interests rather than just rights *in personam*. However, it was servitudes that in practice constituted the greatest voluntary detraction from ownership. For example, the granting of a usufruct in property would substantially deprive the owner of proprietary benefits for the duration of the grant.

More than one owner, notably in cases of joint inheritance or partnership, could own property simultaneously. Co-ownership inevitably resulted in restrictions on the rights of each owner. The basic position was that each could do as he liked with his own individual share, but the disposition of the property as a whole needed unanimity.

6.3 Servitudes

(Inst.Gai.2.22.–39., Inst.2.3., D.8.1., 2., 3., 6., C.3.34.)

A servitude was a proprietary right involving the use—such as a right of way—of the property of another person. Such property can be described as 'the servient thing' because it was subject to a burden in favour of the holder of the servitude. A servitude was an incorporeal thing but could exist only over corporeal property—it was not possible to have a servitude over a servitude (e.g. a right of way over a right of way). Servitudes could be personal or praedial (see Diagram 6.2).

The latter (rights over land) approximated to easements and profits in English law, and were the only servitudes to be recognized as such in the Republic. Personal servitudes, of which usufruct was easily the most important, were possibly not recognized as servitudes until after the classical period (possibly only in Justinianic law). Their late recognition as servitudes is hardly surprising, given the uncertainty among classical jurists whether usufruct was really a form of ownership rather than a servitude. See Hausmaninger, Gamauf, and Sheets, *Casebook*, 244–5.

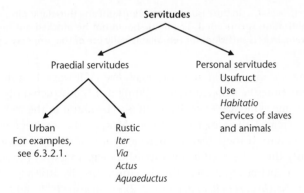

Diagram 6.2 A conceptual map of the Roman law of servitudes

6.3.1   General principles

Servitudes, whatever their type, were subject to a number of general principles.

6.3.1.1   No servitude over your own property

A servitude was a right in another person's property: a person could not be the beneficiary of a servitude over his own property. It followed that if a person who was entitled to a servitude over another's land later acquired the land, the servitude ceased:

Gaius, *Provincial Edict, book 7*: **Praedial servitudes are extinguished by merger if the same person becomes owner of both estates.** (D.8.6.1.)

If the ownership of the former properties was later divided again, the extinguished servitude did not thereby revive, as a general rule.

6.3.1.2   Servitudes could not be possessed

Since servitudes were incorporeal things, it followed that they could not be possessed. But they could be *enjoyed*, and were protected by interdicts that were mostly a modified form of the possessory ones, so that in practice servitudes were as beneficial as if they had been possessed.

6.3.1.3   Servitudes must be beneficial

Servitudes had to benefit, in a material sense, the persons entitled to them:

Pomponius, *Sabinus, book 33*: **Whenever a servitude is found not to be for the benefit of an individual or an estate, then it is of no effect in that no neighbor has any interest in it, as, for example, a servitude preventing you from walking across or occupying your own land.** (D.8.1.15pr.)

It followed that a servitude that was created purely to upset or irritate the servient owner was of no effect. Exceptionally, a servitude could be valid even if it did not benefit the person entitled, providing that it had some economic purpose.

6.3.1.4 Servitudes must be exercised reasonably

Since servitudes constituted a serious restriction of the ownership of the servient owner, the beneficiary had to exercise his right in a reasonable manner. Discussing the grant to a man of an unrestricted right of way over another's estate, Celsus says:

Celsus, *Digest, book 5*: **He may walk and drive across it without restriction, that is to say, across any part of the estate he chooses, so long as he does so in a reasonable manner**... (D.8.1.9.)

6.3.1.5 Servitudes could not impose active duties

Pomponius, *Sabinus, book 33*: **It is not in keeping with the nature of servitudes that the servient owner be required to do something, such as to remove trees to make a view more pleasant or, for the same reason, to paint something on his land. He can only be required to allow something to be done or to refrain from doing something.** (D.8.1.15.1.)

Servitudes were negative in content as far as the servient owner was concerned: he did not have to *do* anything, as a general rule, but had to refrain from doing things. For example, if A had a right of way over B's land, B had to refrain from interfering with that right. But there was an important exception to the general rule. If neighbours shared a common wall, each had a duty to support the other's wall. That meant that a neighbour had to keep his side of the wall in good repair (unless he abandoned the property):

Ulpian, *Edict, book 17*: **However…a man can claim the right to compel his opponent to repair a wall, so that it can support the load. On the other hand, Labeo writes that this servitude does not burden the individual, but the property; consequently, the owner is free to abandon the property.** (D.8.5.6.2.)

6.3.2 Praedial servitudes

Ulpian, *Institutes, book 2*: **These servitudes are called praedial because they cannot be created unless there is an estate. In fact, no one can acquire either a rustic or an urban praedial servitude, nor can anyone be bound to honor such a servitude, unless he himself has an estate.** (D.8.4.1.1.)

Praedial servitudes were the rights that a person had by virtue of ownership of land (the dominant tenement) over the land of another (the servient tenement). (See Hausmaninger, Gamauf, and Sheets, *Casebook*, 246–55). Such rights attached to the land, not to the person—they ran with the land and benefited whoever was the dominant tenement owner:

Paul, *Sabinus, book 15*: **If one estate is servient to another, the servitude passes with the land on the sale of either of the estates. If a building is servient to an estate or an estate to a building, the same rule applies.** (D.8.4.12.)

The successors in title of the servient and dominant owners were affected because praedial servitudes were regarded as perpetual, i.e. they could not be limited by time (although they could terminate in other ways). Since a praedial servitude involved the burdening of one tenement for the benefit of another, it followed that the tenements had to be close together. However, they did not have to be adjoining: e.g. a right of way could exist over land for the benefit of an adjacent estate, even though they were separated by a road running along the boundary between the estates.

Praedial servitudes were classified as either urban or rustic. The distinction was based not so much on locality as on the purpose of the servitude. If it was concerned with the use of a building, the servitude was urban; if with the use of land, it was rustic. Unfortunately, there is some inconsistency in the texts—a servitude is occasionally described as rustic by one jurist, urban by another. Did it matter very much whether a servitude was regarded as urban or rustic? Certainly—some rustic servitudes (possibly all) were *res mancipi*; urban ones were not.

6.3.2.1 Urban praedial servitudes

Gaius, *Provincial Edict, book 7*: **Urban praedial servitudes are as follows: the right to build higher and obstruct a neighbor's light or the right to prevent such building; the right to discharge eavesdrip on to a neighbor's roof or vacant ground or the right to prevent such discharge; the right to insert beams into a neighbor's wall; and, lastly, the right to have a roof or other structure projecting, as well as other similar rights.** (D.8.2.2.)

The above list was not exhaustive. 'Other similar rights' included the right of support from a common wall, the right to lay and maintain drains on a neighbour's land, or to have one's view unobstructed. The text refers to some servitudes in the alternative, e.g. the right to build higher (*altius tollendi*) 'or the right to prevent such building'. Such texts suggest that some servitudes gave rise to the possibility of 'counter-servitudes'. The term is rather misleading because these counter-servitudes were most probably a form of release (total or partial) from existing servitudes. For example, suppose A wished to construct a building that would obstruct B's general right to reasonable light. He could only legally do so if he acquired from B the servitude *altius tollendi*. The counter-servitude would then arise in this situation if A later ceded the rights that he had acquired under the original servitude.

Although most of the urban servitudes originated after the rustic ones, their importance was immense.

6.3.2.2 Rustic praedial servitudes

Ulpian, *Institutes, book 2*: **The following are rustic praedial servitudes: *iter, actus, via*, and *aquae ductus*. *Iter* is the right permitting a man to go on foot and to walk, but not to drive a beast of burden as well. *Actus* is the right to drive either a beast of burden or a vehicle. Thus, a man who has an *iter* does not have an *actus*, but a man who has an *actus* has an *iter* as well, even although the latter does not give the right to drive a beast of burden. *Via* is the right to go on foot, to drive, and to walk; in fact, *via* embraces both *iter* and *actus*. *Aquae ductus* is the right to channel water across another's land.** (D.8.3.1pr.)

Predating the Twelve Tables, these were the oldest of all servitudes. All four were *res mancipi* and were concerned with the use of land for a specific purpose. The precise content and exercise of these servitudes was regulated in remarkable detail. For example:

Gaius, *Provincial Edict, book 7*: **As regulated by the *Twelve Tables*, the width of a *via* is to be eight feet where the road is straight, and sixteen feet…where there is a bend in the road.** (D.8.3.8.)

Elsewhere, we learn that a man who is conveyed on a sedan chair or in a litter is regarded as going on foot, but not driving, and that *via* gave a man the right to drag things and also to carry a spear upright, provided that he did not thereby damage crops (D.8.3.7pr.).

The right to channel water over another's land (*aquae ductus*) was possibly the most important of the rustic servitudes. Not surprisingly, the extent of the right led to considerable legal uncertainty. For example, was the water when channelled owned by the owner of the dominant tenement? The prevailing view appears to have been that since flowing water was in the category of *res communes* (see 6.1.2.1) it could not be owned privately while it was in flow (see extensively Bannon, *Gardens and Neighbors*, ch. 4). And what powers did the dominant tenement owner have over the channel across his neighbour's land?

Pomponius, *Quintus Mucius, book 31*: ... when a man has a watercourse across another man's estate, the supply of water being used daily or in the summer or over longer intervals, he is permitted to lay in the channel a conduit of his own, be it of earthenware or any other kind of material, to obtain a wider diffusion of the water. He is also permitted to construct whatever he wishes in the channel, providing he does not make the watercourse less advantageous to the servient owner. (D.8.3.15.)

There were some later additions to the original four rustic servitudes. All, possibly, were *res mancipi*, and approximated to profits in English law—they allowed the taking of natural produce from the servient land, e.g. the right to dig for lime or sand, or to pasture or water cattle on another's land. The extent of these servitudes was the subject of much detailed regulation and juristic comment. For example, what was the position when more than the permitted number of animals was watered on the servient tenement? Could the whole herd be stopped? There was some disagreement among the jurists, as the following passage by Ulpian suggests:

Ulpian, *Edict, book 70*: Trebatius says that when a greater number of herd animals are watered than ought to be watered, the whole herd may be prevented with impunity, because the addition of herd animals to a herd that has the right to drink destroys the whole right. But Marcellus says that if anyone has the right of watering a herd and brings up more herd animals, he is not to be prevented from watering all of them, which is true, because herd animals can be separated. (D.43.20.1.18.)

6.3.3 Personal servitudes

There were four personal servitudes, of which usufruct was by far the most important. Personal servitudes attached to a person, not to land; and they were of limited duration, not perpetual. They could be created over movables as well as land. And their purpose differed markedly from that of praedial servitudes: the personal servitude was frequently created by will as a means of settling property within the testator's family. The legacy of a usufruct of property by way of a life interest to a widow or other family member (such as an unmarried daughter) was a common occurrence in Roman wills.

6.3.3.1 Usufruct

Usufruct was the right to use another's property—without impairing its substance—and to take its fruits. (See Hausmaninger, Gamauf, and Sheets, *Casebook*, 256–60.) Despite the duty to preserve the property, usufruct was considered to be a valuable right.

(a) The general position of the usufructuary. Strictly, he lacked possession but had the right to use the property and to take its fruits for the period agreed by the owner. Often, a life interest would be granted to the usufructuary; but the period could be shorter. It could not last beyond the life of the usufructuary. At the outset of the usufruct, he had to give security that he would take prudent care of the property, which had to be restored (on the termination of the usufruct) substantially unimpaired, allowing for reasonable wear and tear. This meant that if the property was destroyed or clearly altered in character, the usufruct ended even though the agreed period had not yet expired.

(b) Use of the property. The usufructuary was entitled to occupy and control the property but, because of the duty to return the property unimpaired, he had to maintain it in the state in which it was received by him (cf. D.7.1.1.). If the property consisted of buildings, they would have to be kept in good repair. The usufructuary could not use the property in an unauthorized way; nor could he alter its character, even if he thereby improved it:

Ulpian, *Sabinus, book 18*: **If the usufruct of a house is left as a legacy...the usufructuary is allowed to put in windows. He may also paint the walls and add frescoes, marble slabs, statuettes, and anything else designed to improve the appearance of the house. However, he is not permitted to alter the rooms or throw them together or divide them or to reverse the front and back entrances or to open up retreats or to alter the entrance hall or to change the layout of the pleasure gardens. In short, the usufructuary can improve what he finds, so long as he does not change the character of the house.** (D.7.1.13.7.)

The texts inevitably show inconsistencies between the jurists in their opinions as to whether work carried out by the usufructuary was an alteration rather than improvement. Indeed, some jurists seem to deny a right even to make what appear to be basic improvements—e.g. Neratius:

Neratius, *Parchments, book 3*: **The usufructuary is not entitled to replaster walls which have been left in a rough condition, because even although he would make the position of the owner better by improving the building, he still cannot do this by virtue of his rights as a usufructuary. It is one thing for him to maintain what he has received and another to make some alteration.** (D.7.1.44.)

The duty to maintain the property varied according to the circumstances and the nature of the property. If it was an agricultural estate, it had to be kept in cultivation; that required the usufructuary to sow crops, for example, or plant trees where the usufruct comprised an orchard or a timber estate. The *Digest* contains remarkably detailed rules on cutting wood and felling timber, distinguishing *inter alia* between different types of husbandry and plantation. The rule relating to cutting of timber or mining of natural resources seems to have been that a usufructuary could enjoy the benefits of these 'fruits' if they had been used as a source of income by the previous owner (cf. D.7.1.13.5.–6.). The usufructuary's exploitation of these fruits was, however, restricted since the essence of the object could not be substantially altered by it. The distinctions have survived to some extent in modern law: e.g. Article 591 of the French Civil Code allows the usufructuary to benefit from forest trees which have been subjected to *coupes réglées* (regulated cuttings). If the usufruct was over a flock or herd of animals, there was a duty to maintain numbers:

Ulpian, *Sabinus, book 17*: **But if the usufruct of a flock or herd is left as a legacy, the usufructuary will be obliged to keep up the numbers of the flock out of the young that are** subsequently born into it, that is, to allocate others to take the place of dead [Pomponius, *Sabinus, book 5*] [69]: or worthless animals, the result being that the latter, after they have been replaced, become the property of the usufructuary, so as to avoid the outcome of the operation being a gain on the part of the bare owner. (D.7.1.68.2., 69.)

The standard of care expected of the usufructuary was that of the *bonus paterfamilias*. Hence, the usufructuary had to show a high degree of care—he would be liable for any deterioration or damage to the property if caused by his negligence, however slight.

In his use of the property, the usufructuary was entitled to hire out or sell the enjoyment of the usufruct:

Ulpian, *Sabinus, book 17*: The usufructuary can either enjoy the subject matter of the usufruct himself or grant the enjoyment of it to another, or he can let for hire or sell the enjoyment; for a man who lets is making use of his right, as is one who sells. (D.7.1.12.2.)

However, although the usufructuary could transfer 'enjoyment', he could not transfer the usufruct itself since it was inalienable: he remained the usufructuary until the termination of the usufruct.

(c) Fruits. Perhaps the usufructuary's most important benefit was the right to take and own the fruits of the property subjected to the usufruct. What were fruits? They can be broadly classified as 'civil' or 'natural'. Civil fruits consisted of the income from hiring out the property comprised in the usufruct, e.g. the earnings of slaves, or rent from land. Natural fruits comprised the ordinary, natural produce of the property. Minerals were not regarded as fruits unless the land was used for quarrying or the production of minerals:

Ulpian, *Sabinus, book 17*: If the land has stone quarries on it, and the usufructuary wishes to hew stone, or if there are chalk or sand pits on it, Sabinus holds that the usufructuary may make use of all of these as a careful head of a household would do. I consider this to be the correct view. (D.7.1.9.2.)

However, juristic interpretation contributed to the emergence of the rule that *new mines* could be opened providing that the character of the land was not thereby altered. Thus, a new mine could not be opened if the usufructuary thereby appropriated a part of the land 'required for something else' or if he prejudiced 'the cultivation of the land' (D.7.1.13.5.). It seems that this rule was applied flexibly in the Empire, if not before, in order that Rome's mineral wealth should be fully exploited.

Difficulties regarding the ownership of fruits arose in usufruct over slaves and animals. For example:

Ulpian, *Sabinus, book 68*: The question was raised in times gone by whether the offspring of a female slave belonged to the usufructuary. However, the opinion of Brutus, that the rules of usufruct are not applicable to this case, has prevailed; the fact is that one human being cannot be treated as being among the fruits of another. (D.7.1.68pr.)

This justification by Brutus—a statesman and jurist of the second century BC—has been much debated. It adopts the 'noble' view that the human personality of the slave distinguishes him from other types of property; but it is arguable that the exception simply reflects the economic realities, namely that the slave-child was far too valuable an asset to belong to the usufructuary rather than the owner. Birks, P., 'An Unacceptable Face of Human Property', in *New Perspectives*, 61 ff., takes an intermediate position: 'The concession to humanity went no further than this, that the law would not countenance a rule which implied that slaves might be farmed...Offspring are not *fructus* because, differently from livestock, the fertility of slaves is not callously managed in the interests of productivity' (69).

What if a slave acquired property during the course of the usufruct—to whom did it belong? In the absence of an express provision agreed on the creation of the usufruct, the basic position was that the property belonged to the owner unless it was acquired on behalf of the usufructuary. For example, the usufructuary kept any payment for the hiring of the slave's services (see earlier). As regards *inter vivos* gifts (or legacies) made to the slave during the usufruct, the rule was:

Ulpian, *Sabinus, book 18*: ...if something is left or given to the slave out of consideration for the usufructuary, the slave will acquire for him; if it was out of consideration for the bare owner, the slave will acquire for him; if it was out of consideration for the slave himself, he will acquire for his owner... (D.7.1.22.)

The young of animals (in a herd or flock held under a usufruct) posed problems for the jurists. Some thought that the rule should be the same as for children of slave women, applying the concept that fruits could not have the same form as the 'producer' of the fruit. But the early Sabinians regarded the young of animals as belonging to the usufructuary, and that view eventually prevailed. Nevertheless, a question arose as to the extent of the usufructuary's rights since he had a duty to maintain the numbers of a flock or herd. If a lamb was born in a flock that was below strength, to whom did it belong? The view prevailed that ownership of the young was in suspense until the relevant replacements had been made (see Watson, A., 'The Acquisition of Young in the Usufructus Gregis' (1961) 12 IVRA, 210–21):

Ulpian, *Sabinus, book 17*: ...until the young are allocated and the dead animals replaced, to whom do these young belong? Julian...says that the ownership of them is in suspense, with the result that if they are allocated as replacements, they belong to the bare owner, while if they are not so allocated, they belong to the usufructuary. (D.7.1.70.1.)

In order to become the owner of natural fruits, the usufructuary had to gather or collect them (see 7.2.6). Suppose A is the usufructuary of a fruit orchard belonging to B. When A picks the fruit from the trees or gathers it from the ground he becomes owner, but not before. The young of animals may have been an exception: the texts do not expressly require an act of gathering of the newly born, perhaps because of the practical difficulties involved. As for civil fruits, they were acquired on delivery, i.e. on their receipt.

(d) Quasi-usufruct. Over what property could a usufruct be created? It had to be a corporeal thing and something that could not be consumed through use (because of the duty to restore the property substantially unimpaired). Hence, it was not possible to have a usufruct in perishables, e.g. money. The inconvenience of this rule prompted a *senatus consultum* in the early Empire whereby a quasi-usufruct was allowed in such things, the donee becoming in effect the owner of the property, with a duty to restore the equivalent value on the termination of the usufruct. This reform (which applied only to usufructs made by will) enabled a more flexible settlement to be made on family members—an innovation of considerable practical importance, and one that was consistent with the overall purposes of usufruct: 'The chief function of the classical usufruct was to provide maintenance for an individual person' (Schulz, *Classical Roman Law* (1951), 386).

(e) A 'fraction' of ownership. The legal position of the usufructuary was paradoxical. He did not have possession, but often he would seem to the entire world as if he were the owner, having limited interdictal protection for his enjoyment of the property and a right to own the fruits. The illusion of ownership would be all the stronger if the usufruct was held for life, since the duty to return the property would then rest on the usufructuary's heirs. This close affinity of usufruct to ownership was reflected in some classical texts (though the possibility of interpolation cannot be discounted). For example, Paul states:

Paul, *Edict, book 2*: **In many respects, usufruct is a fraction of ownership** ... (D.7.1.4.)

Such an attitude (not untypical of classical jurists) probably contributed to the delay in the recognition of usufruct as a servitude.

6.3.3.2 *Usus*

Ulpian, *Sabinus, book 17*: **A man to whom a right of use is left is entitled to use but not to take the fruits.** (D.7.8.2pr.)

Usus grew out of usufruct in the late Republic. It was a lesser right, giving the usuary the right to use property, but not to keep its fruits. (See Hausmaninger, Gamauf, and Sheets, *Casebook*, 261–5). The rule concerning fruits was eventually relaxed: it seems that the usuary became entitled to keep as much produce as was required to maintain his household. Unlike the usufructuary, the usuary could not sell or let out the enjoyment of the property, or allow anyone else to occupy it in his place. But a usuary could take in paying guests and lodgers, and keep the proceeds. A woman was restricted in her choice of guests:

Pomponius, *Sabinus, book 5*: **However, a woman cannot receive a man as a guest unless he is one who can, with propriety, live in the same house as she who has the right of use.** (D.7.8.7.)

If the *usus* comprised the use of a house, the usuary's family was entitled to reside there. The usuary had to give security in respect of his use of the property, and was generally in a similar position to that of the usufructuary, apart from the differences mentioned.

6.3.3.3 *Habitatio*

This was the right to occupy a *house* for life, an interest that could be created only by will. Unlike the usuary, the person entitled to *habitatio* could let out the house. There was some doubt in the classical period whether *habitatio* was an interest independent of usufruct and *usus*, but in the late Empire it came to be recognized as a separate servitude.

6.3.3.4 **Services of slaves and animals**

This was a special form of *usus*, confined to the use of slaves or animals. As in the case of *habitatio*, this right could be created only by will and was not recognized as an independent servitude until the late Empire.

6.3.4 **Creation, protection, and termination of servitudes**

6.3.4.1 **Creation**

Praedial servitudes could be created in a variety of ways.

(a) Mancipatio (see 7.1.1). This was important, in early law at least, in the creation of rustic praedial servitudes since they were *res mancipi*.

(b) Cessio (see 7.1.2). This could be used to create all praedial servitudes, including those that were *res mancipi*.

(c) Deductio. This occurred if, on the conveyance of land by *mancipatio* or *cessio*, the transferor reserved for himself a servitude over the transferred land in favour of the land that he retained:

Gaius, *Provincial Edict, book 7*: **If the owner of two estates conveys one of them to you on the terms that the estate which is conveyed is to be bound by a servitude in favor of the estate which he retains or vice versa, a servitude is held to be legally created.** (D.8.4.3.)

(d) Will. A testator could leave his land by will subject to a servitude in favour of an adjacent owner. Creation of praedial servitudes by legacy became quite common.

(e) Adiudicatio. This could result in the creation of a praedial servitude if a judge, in deciding on the division of common property, held that a servitude should run in favour of part of the land.

(f) Pact and stipulation. This method was originally used only in relation to provincial land, since servitudes in such land could not be created by the usual methods. The pact consisted of an agreement between the parties, breach of which resulted in the payment of a penalty fixed by the stipulation. *Prima facie*, such an agreement could create only contractual, not proprietary rights. But the praetors were prepared to treat such arrangements as creating rights *in rem*, and this led to the eventual recognition of pact and stipulation as a method for creating servitudes. In late law, when *mancipatio* and *cessio* fell into disuse and Justinian abolished the distinction between Italic and provincial land, pact and stipulation became the most important *inter vivos* method for creating servitudes.

(g) Long enjoyment. *Usucapio* was a possible means of acquiring a praedial servitude in early law until the method was prohibited in the late Republic by a *Lex Scribonia* of the first century BC, possibly to secure freedom of ownership. However, in the late classical period, the uninterrupted exercise of a 'right' for 10 years (*longi temporis praescriptio*) came to be regarded as evidence of the acquisition of that right:

Ulpian, *Edict, book 53*: **If a man has obtained a right to channel water by long use and, as it were, by long possession, he is not required to lead evidence to establish the legal title on which his right to the water is founded, for example, to show that it rests on a legacy or some other ground.** (D.8.5.10pr.)

The servitude could be acquired in this way provided the right had been exercised *nec vi, nec clam, nec precario* (not through force, stealth, or by permission) as against the servient tenement owner (C.7.22., 33., 39.). In Justinianic law, proof of use for 20 years was required if the parties did not reside in the same province.

As regards personal servitudes, grant through legacy was the most frequent method of creation. Indeed, it was the only method for *habitatio* and for the use of services of slaves and animals. However, usufruct and *usus* could also be created by any of the methods applicable to praedial servitudes. In addition, usufruct could arise through imposition by law, as we have seen, for example the usufruct given in late law to a *paterfamilias* over property held by family members (see 5.1.2.2).

6.3.4.2 **Protection**

The chief remedy for a person asserting entitlement to a servitude, whether praedial or personal, was the *actio confessoria*, a modified form of *vindicatio*. As for the servient tenement owner, he could bring the *actio negatoria* if he specifically wished to disprove the existence of a servitude. The latter action was unusual in that it required the plaintiff to prove a negative, i.e. that the servitude did not exist. In both actions, recovery was possible for financial loss. Moreover, praetorian interdicts were available in appropriate cases. For example, the praetors protected the exercise of rustic servitudes by granting specific interdicts for each servitude—recognition perhaps of their special status. Praetorian interdicts did not, of course, settle matters of title but simply protected the person who was exercising the servitude. A servient tenement owner, if prejudiced by the grant of such an interdict, could seek to disprove the right to the servitude through an *actio negatoria*. (See Hausmaninger, Gamauf, and Sheets, *Casebook*, 232–5).

6.3.4.3 **Termination**

(a) Praedial servitudes could end in a variety of ways:

(i) Destruction. This occurred if either the dominant or servient tenement was destroyed, or the latter underwent fundamental change, or the subject matter of the servitude ceased to exist. For example, if a stream dried up permanently, the right of draining water from it would end, although it could be restored if the stream started to flow again.

(ii) Non-use. A praedial servitude was lost if it was not exercised for two years. In the case of rustic servitudes, mere non-use sufficed; as regards urban servitudes, the period ran only from the time when the owner of the servient tenement acted as if he disregarded the existence of the servitude. If the dominant tenement owner then failed to object for two years, the servitude was extinguished. The reason for the distinction was that the non-use of rustic servitudes would be obvious since they were 'positive' in nature, e.g. pasturing cattle on someone's land, whereas urban servitudes were generally negative—how do you demonstrate non-use of the right not to have light obstructed? Consequently, proof of non-use in such circumstances initially required evidence of a positive act by the servient tenement owner:

Gaius, *Provincial Edict, book 7*: **Again, suppose your house is subject to a servitude allowing a beam to be inserted, and I remove the beam. I only lose my right if you stop up the hole from which the beam was taken, and keep things in this condition for the prescribed period. On the other hand, if you have made no alterations, the servitude remains unimpaired.** (D.8.2.6.)

Justinian extended the period to 10 years if both parties resided in the same province, 20 years if they did not.

(iii) Merger. This occurred when the dominant and servient tenements were acquired by the same owner.

(iv) Cessio. The right to a servitude was lost if it was formally ceded by the dominant tenement owner. In addition, rustic servitudes could be renounced by a formal reconveyance. In late law, when these methods had become obsolete, prae-dial servitudes could be renounced either expressly or impliedly, e.g. by toleration of an act inconsistent with the servitude. The renunciation would bar the domi-nant tenement owner from later asserting the existence of the servitude. Under Justinian, renunciation sufficed to *terminate* the servitude rather than just to pro-vide a bar to its assertion.

(v) Abandonment. The abandonment of the dominant tenement did not in itself terminate a servitude in its favour, although it could constitute non-use. What if the servient tenement owner abandoned his property? In principle, nothing changed: the property remained burdened even though there was no one against whom the servitude could be enforced. As regards the duty to support a com-mon wall, the dominant tenement owner could carry out the repairs himself by entering the servient tenement. If he then became owner of the servient tenement through occupation of the abandoned property, the servitude would be extin-guished by merger.

(b) Personal servitudes could terminate in various ways, some of which were inapplicable to praedial servitudes:

(i) Death. Since a personal servitude attached to a *person* and not to property, it followed that it was ended by the death of the holder:

Ulpian, *Sabinus, book 17*: **That a usufruct is also lost by death does not admit of any doubt, since the right of enjoyment is extinguished by death, just like any other right which attaches to the person.** (D.7.4.3.3.)

(ii) Expiry of term. Apart from *habitatio*, personal servitudes could be granted for a period less than the life of the holder. The expiry of the period ended the servitude.

(iii) Loss of status. As a general rule, loss of status (whatever the degree) ended all personal servitudes, except that *habitatio* and the services of slaves and animals were not ended by *capitis deminutio minima* (see generally 4.2).

In addition, personal servitudes could be ended in ways similar to praedial ser-vitudes, e.g. merger occurred if a usufructuary obtained ownership of the property subject to the usufruct. *Cessio* could be used to cede a personal servitude to the owner (under Justinian, an act of renunciation sufficed). Destruction or funda-mental change in the property ended a personal servitude, subject to the possibil-ity of restoration, as illustrated by Javolenus:

Javolenus, *From the Posthumous Works of Labeo, book 3*: **I had the usufruct of a garden; a river covered the garden and then receded. It is the opinion of Labeo that the right of usufruct is restored, as the legal position of the ground itself remained the same throughout. I think that this is only true if the river covered the garden as the result of a flood; if the river changed its course and began to flow in that quarter, my opinion is that the usufruct is lost, as the ground occupied by the riverbed becomes public property and cannot be restored to its original condition.** (D.7.4.24pr.)

Usufruct and *usus*, but not *habitatio* or the services of slaves and animals, could be lost through non-use—two years for land, one year for movables. Justinian altered the periods to three years for movables, 10 or 20 years for land, depending on whether the parties resided in the same province. Hiring out the property consti-tuted use, not non-use.

6.4 **Contractual proprietary interests**

As a general principle, a contract could give rise only to contractual obligations, i.e. rights *in personam*, and not to proprietary interests (rights *in rem*). There were some exceptional instances, however, where a contractual agreement was regarded as creating interests in property, without the need for any other legal formality. In certain contemporary civil law systems, these are referred to as 'dismemberments' of ownership.

6.4.1 *Emphyteusis*

(C.4.66)

Emphyteusis originated as a perpetual or long lease of land (belonging to the State or to a city) to a private individual in return for a ground rent. In the Empire, grants to private persons of provincial land became common; often the grant would be followed by a sublease by the grantee. Thus, the transfer of such land came to have important consequences for private law in the later Empire. The tenant was eventually given protection by proprietary remedies, providing that he did not default in payment of the rent:

Paul, *Edict, book 21*: **It is accepted law that those who take a lease of land from a municipality, to be enjoyed in perpetuity, although they do not become owners, yet have an action *in rem* against anyone who has taken possession and even against the municipality itself;** Ulpian, *Sabinus, book 17* [2]: **so long, that is, as they pay the rent-charge.** (D.6.3.1.1., 2.)

The tenant could sell the land but the owner had the right of first refusal. If the latter chose not to buy, he was entitled (under Justinian) to 2 per cent of the purchase price. The tenant generally could deal freely with the land (e.g. he could mortgage the property), create servitudes, leave it to his heirs; and he was entitled to fruits. Clearly, the position of the tenant in *emphyteusis* in late law approximated to that of a *dominus*; he was even given a modified *vindicatio* to protect his interest. However, the tenant had to ensure that the property was returned substantially unimpaired in the event of the termination of the interest (e.g. the expiry of the term). In late law, *emphyteusis* could be created by will or contract; and it ended through expiry of the term, forfeiture, destruction of the land, or death of the tenant without heirs.

Although *emphyteusis* originally created only contractual obligations, its later development was clearly that of a proprietary interest—in some respects akin to ownership, in other respects similar to a servitude.

6.4.2 *Superficies*

(D.43.18.)

Superficies originated in grants by the State or municipalities of land for *building* purposes. The institution grew in importance when private subleasing became popular in the later Empire. When the tenant constructed buildings on the land, he did not become their owner since they attached to the land:

Ulpian, *Edict, book 70*: **We mean by superficiary buildings those that are sited on leased land. By both civil and natural law their ownership belongs to the owner of the land.** (D.43.18.2.)

In order to encourage building on such land, tenants were given the protection of a special interdict by the praetor. In late law, *superficies* came to be regarded as a full proprietary right *in rem*, the tenant being in a position similar to that in *emphyteusis*. Although the affinity of *superficies* to ownership and servitudes is clear, it was not classed as belonging to either category.

6.4.3 Real security

Through the contracts of pledge and hypothec (see 9.5.4), a creditor could acquire a limited real right (possession protected by interdicts—see 6.5.5.1) over property belonging to a debtor. For a more expansive discussion of this, see Nicholas, *Introduction*, 149–53.

6.5 Possession

(D.41.2., 43.17.)

6.5.1 Introduction

Ulpian, *Edict, book 70*: **Ownership has nothing in common with possession . . .** (D.41.2.12.1.)

Ulpian's pithy statement will serve as an introduction to an aspect of property law that held considerable interest for the jurists. He was right in stressing the distinction between ownership and possession. Although the two concepts overlapped at times, a phenomenon discernible particularly in English law, the distinction was generally maintained in the developed law of Rome. Possession was regarded essentially as physical control of the sort that was protected by possessory interdicts, whereas ownership was the ultimate entitlement to property. Often the two went hand in hand—in practice most owners have possession—but there were many instances of the separation of ownership and possession. An unusual scenario from Ulpian:

Ulpian, *Edict, book 72*: **Pomponius discusses the question whether, when stones had been sunk in the Tiber in a shipwreck and some time later salvaged, the ownership of them remained intact throughout the time that they were submerged. My view is that I remain owner of them but I do not possess them . . .** (D.41.2.13pr.)

If we were to make an absolute truth of Ulpian's statement (in D.41.2.12.1.), we would mislead ourselves and do Ulpian an injustice in stating that there is 'nothing in common' between possession and ownership. The man in possession is often the owner, and his possession is some evidence (though not conclusive) of his ownership. Imagine a society such as Republican Rome, where title deeds were used infrequently and where there was no system of land registration until Augustus (the use of title deeds did not become common until the later Empire). Proof of ownership in early law could be problematic; hence the importance of possession as a vital steppingstone to proving ownership (see D.6.1.24.). Indeed, the concept of ownership, indistinct though it may have been in early law, probably grew out of the notion of possession:

Paul, *Edict, book 54*: **The younger Nerva says that the ownership of things originated in natural possession and that a relic thereof survives in the attitude to those things which are**

taken on land, sea, or in the air; for such things forthwith become the property of those who first take possession of them. (D.41.2.1.1.)

This passage makes clear that possession was an important factor in obtaining ownership. Several of the modes of acquiring *dominium* were based on possession. For example, *occupatio*, the mode described in the passage, consisted of taking possession of certain types of property (see 7.2.3). And *usucapio* was the acquisition of ownership through possession for a prescribed period of time (see 7.2.1). Indeed, the title on possession in the *Digest* (D.41.2.) is sandwiched between those on ownership and *usucapio*, probably as a prelude to an appreciation of the latter. The fact that only a relatively short period of prescription was required in *usucapio* reinforces the close affinity between ownership and possession.

A complicating factor in the understanding of possession in Roman law is that there were three different types or degrees of possession. We are primarily concerned with interdictal (sometimes called 'legal') possession—the possession that was protected by possessory interdicts. A variant of this form was known as 'civil' or *usucapio* possession, i.e. the possession that could ripen into ownership through lapse of time. Third, there was 'natural' possession (*detentio*), which consisted of being in physical control or custody of a thing. It was strictly not possession at all. On this form of possession, see MacCormack, G., 'Naturalis Possessio' (1967) 84 ZSS (rA), 47–69, where the author discusses the scope and evolution of this concept in relation to mere *possessio* and *possessio civilis*.

6.5.2 **The acquisition of possession**

We will look in vain for a satisfactory definition of possession in the texts. It is as if the jurists deliberately refrained from defining what is, in any case, a difficult concept. The absence of a clear definition was not necessarily a bad thing. A certain flexibility in the notion of possession had jurisprudential merit, preventing over-rigidity in the categorization of the persons regarded as having possession. It is perhaps safest to describe Roman possession as such physical control over property as was protected by possessory interdicts.

Despite the jurists' reluctance to define possession, they did the next best thing—they tell us how possession was acquired. Paul states:

Paul, *Edict, book 54*: **Now we take possession physically and mentally, not mentally alone or physically alone.** (D.41.2.3.1.)

Paul's assertion that possession requires physical control (*corpus*) and mental intent (*animus*) is generally regarded as an accurate and authoritative representation of classical law, and one that has considerably influenced the jurisprudential analysis of possession in subsequent ages. To possess 'with body and soul' is an apt image in this context.

6.5.2.1 *Corpus*

As a basic rule, a person could not possess without taking effective physical control of the property. It followed that possession could only be acquired over corporeal things. It was impossible, therefore, to possess a servitude, e.g. a right of way. Whether effective physical control was taken of a thing depended on the circumstances. For example, the possession of land could be acquired if the boundaries were indicated to the intending possessor—no actual physical holding (or contact) was required. Or possession could be acquired of a thing if it was placed, at the intending possessor's request, where he could see it. Juristic literature is typically bereft of guiding principles on the issue of *corpus* and is suspected in part of interpolation. See Hausmaninger, Gamauf, and Sheets, *Casebook*, 3–28.

6.5.2.2 *Animus*

No clear picture emerges of the meaning of *animus* from the classical texts, although it was not seriously doubted that some form of mental element was required in possession. Possibly it meant the intention to hold the property as one's own. If so, that could explain why certain holders were regarded as having or not having possession in Roman law. Or *animus* might have signified the consciousness of being in physical control of the thing. One could not acquire possession if one lacked or was incapable of the required awareness. For example, an insane person or one who was asleep could not acquire possession. The requirement of *animus* meant that you did not necessarily possess everything that was in your physical control; there had to be an awareness of what it was that you controlled:

Paul, *Sabinus, book 15*: **A person possessing a building as a whole is not deemed to possess the individual things in the building. The same applies to a ship and to a cupboard.** (D.41.2.30pr.)

Of course, if a person were aware of the things contained (or likely to be) in the building, ship, or cupboard, then he would have possession.

Could one acquire possession by *animus* alone? In principle, it would seem not but textual authority on the issue is unclear, see MacCormack, G., 'The Role of Animus in the Classical Law of Possession' (1969) 86 ZSS (rA), 105–45, where the author explains the Roman jurists' conception of this term. It was possible—in late law at least—to transfer possession by mere agreement in some circumstances. But it is arguable that the words used in such cases constituted both the *corpus* and the *animus*.

6.5.2.3 **Acquiring possession for another**

Possession could be acquired by one person on behalf of another, e.g. a slave for the master, a child for the *paterfamilias*. In such cases the general rule was that the initial acquirer had to take the property with *corpus* and *animus*, while the ultimate possessor had to have *animus*. The ambiguity of the slave's legal status is evident from the scenario where a slave acquired for his master. Strictly, it was arguable that the slave could not have *animus*, i.e. the required consciousness, but since a rigid application of this view would have produced inconvenience, the possibility that slaves could have *animus* was recognized. As regards the ultimate possessor, his *animus* could consist, for example, of prior authorization of the acquisition or subsequent knowledge of it. There were exceptional cases in which possession could be acquired even if the ultimate possessor did not have *animus*, e.g. where the master was insane, or where the slave had acquired property as part of his *peculium*. Papinian discusses the latter case:

Papinian, *Questions, book 23*: **The question was asked why possession is acquired for those who know nothing of it through a slave in respect of his *peculium*. I said that for reasons of**

convenience, the rule was adopted as an exception so that owners would not be obliged to find out at any given time the forms and titles of *peculia*. (D.41.2.44.1.)

On this matter, see Watson, A., 'Acquisition of Possession per Extraneam Personam' (1958) 29 TR, 22–42, where the author argues that the ability to acquire possession through third parties was an invention of classical Roman law that was extended, first to tutors and curators, and before the end of the classical period to any *extranea persona*; Watson, A., 'Acquisition of Possession and Usucapion per Servos et Filios' (1962) 78 LQR, 205–27, for a discussion of whether the owner/master's knowledge of the acquisition of possession was indispensable; Barton, J. L., 'Animus and Possessio Nomine Alieno', in *New Perspectives*, 43–60, a difficult text, where the author presents an interesting argument concerning the mental prerequisites for *possessio nomine alieno*. See also Hausmaninger, Gamauf, and Sheets, *Casebook*, 46–69.

6.5.3 Who had possession?

Anyone who was entitled to a possessory interdict to protect his holding was regarded as having possession. Primarily, this included persons who were in physical control of property as owners, or as potential owners (e.g. those who were in the course of *usucapio*), or those acting as if they were owners. It did not matter whether the possessor was acting in good or bad faith: thus a thief could have possession (but could not become an owner).

In addition, there was a category of derivative possessors, i.e. those whose holding was derived from the *dominus*. For example, if two parties were disputing the ownership of property, it could be deposited with a stakeholder, who had possession of it until the dispute was solved. If a loan was secured under the contract of *pignus* (see 9.5.4), the creditor obtained possession of the security and could retain it until the debt was paid. Another example was the bailee of property under the contract of *precarium* (see 9.7.5). The owner could revoke such a bailment at any time—it was a bailment at will—but during its continuance the bailee was regarded as having possession. And tenants with long leases of land owned by the State were regarded as having possession.

There were a number of derivative holders who were not regarded as having interdictal possession—they had mere custody (*detentio*) of the property. Why they were denied possession in law is not always obvious. Among the most important examples were borrowers, hirers, and depositees, all having contractual rights in the property, but not possession. The difficult case is that of the usufructuary: despite having the right to use and enjoy property, and to own its fruits, he was not regarded as having possession. When it is borne in mind that usufructuaries sometimes held their interests for life, it seems all the more curious that they were not regarded as having possession. But in theory a usufruct was regarded as an incorporeal thing and therefore could not, strictly, be possessed.

The range of persons regarded as having possession in Roman law was clearly narrower than in most modern systems, common law and civilian. In English law, for example, bailees are normally regarded as having possession, including the type of derivative holder to whom it was denied in Roman law. See Buckland and McNair, *Roman Law and Common Law*, 70 ff.

6.5.4 **The loss of possession**

The rules on the acquisition of possession (i.e. the necessity for *corpus* and *animus*) were tolerably clear. The same cannot be said for the rules on the loss of possession. Consider, for example, the following conflicting texts, both attributed to Paul:

Paul, *Edict, book 54*: **If I deliver a thing to someone else, I lose possession of it. For it is settled that we remain in possession until either we voluntarily abandon it or we are ejected by force.** (D.41.2.3.9.)

Paul, *Edict, Book 65*: **Just as no possession can be acquired except physically and with intent, so none is lost unless both elements are departed from.** (D.41.2.8.)

D.41.2.3.9. is unobjectionable in suggesting that possession ceases if either *animus* or *corpus* is lost: if both elements are required for the acquisition of possession, the loss of one of them should result in its termination. But D.41.2.8. seems to imply that possession could be retained even though the possessor had lost *animus* or *corpus*. There were perhaps some exceptional situations where it was recognized that possession could be retained despite the loss of one of the elements, e.g. if a possessor was asleep (hardly an exception—the loss of *animus* is inevitable and temporary). But D.42.1.8. cannot be supported as stating a general principle: there were many situations in which the loss of either *animus* or *corpus* was fatal to the retention of possession. For example, possession ended if property was stolen, or seized by force, or simply lost:

Pomponius, *Quintus Mucius, book 23*: **If we possess something and lose it in such circumstances that we do not know where it is, we lose possession of it.** (D.41.2.25pr.)

And where *corpus* was retained, but *animus* lost, the general rule was that possession ceased:

Ulpian, *Edict, book 76*: **There is this difference between ownership and possession: that a man remains owner even when he does not wish to be, but possession departs once one decides not to possess.** (D.41.2.17.1.)

Such texts provide evidence that late classical law regarded *animus* as probably the major constituent of possession. However, as with the acquisition of possession, the rules relating to its loss depended more on pragmatic development and *ad hoc* decisions by jurists than on general principle. For example, escaped slaves (and possession of slaves generally) caused the jurists particular difficulty. Clearly, the master has lost physical control—but has he lost possession? No text can be safely selected as an authoritative answer, but the most plausible view is that the master retained possession through *animus* alone—an exceptional occurrence. Schulz observes that 'the classical lawyers required for the acquisition of possession a fuller physical control than for its continuance' (*Classical Roman Law* (1951), 435). See also Hausmaninger, Gamauf, and Sheets, *Casebook*, 70–110.

Possession ended on the death of the possessor; it did not automatically pass to his heir. But if the latter took physical control of the property, his possession related back to that of his predecessor and was regarded as one continuous period for the purposes of prescription under *usucapio*.

6.5.5 **The protection of possession**

Ulpian, *All Seats of Judgement, book 5*: **The outcome of a dispute over possession is simply this: that the judge makes an interim finding that one of the parties possesses; the result will be that the party defeated on the issue of possession will take on the role of plaintiff when the question of ownership is contested.** (D.41.2.35.)

Since possession was a form of presumptive ownership, effective remedies were needed to protect it. But, as the above passage makes clear, a dispute about possession was frequently a preliminary step to the resolution of the issue of ownership. Whoever was held entitled to possession would be in a strong position in any subsequent contest over ownership. The possessor would be the defendant, the presumptive owner. The non-possessor would be the plaintiff, having to bring a *vindicatio* and prove that he was *dominus*. However, a dispute over possession was not always followed by a *vindicatio*. Sometimes the adjudication of the question of possession could end the whole matter, e.g. if a person who had been wrongfully dispossessed succeeded in recovering possession from the wrongdoer. See Hausmaninger, Gamauf, and Sheets, *Casebook*, 95–102.

6.5.5.1 **Possessory interdicts**

The standard remedies in disputes about possession were the possessory interdicts issued by the praetors. Process under possessory interdicts was generally much speedier and less cumbersome than in a *vindicatio*. It may be that interdicts originally had a limited application—protecting the holders of public land—but in time they came to be used extensively to protect the possession of private property. Some of the interdicts were introduced for the specific purpose of recovering possession of property that had been taken by force, e.g. the interdict *unde vi*. Others, such as those for retaining possession, demonstrated the desire of the praetors to prevent disorder: such interdicts prohibited the use of force against the person in possession.

Possessory interdicts were classified according to their purpose:

(a) Acquiring possession. The claimant sought possession of property that he had not previously possessed. The main example was the interdict *quorum bonorum*, which lay in favour of a person who was allowed possession of an estate, or part of it, under the praetorian rules on inheritance. (D.43.3., C.8.2.)

(b) Retaining possession. The possessor sought an interdict to protect his possession (cf. Inst.Gai.4.148.; Inst.4.15.4.). The appropriate interdict for land was *uti possidetis* (D.43.17., C.8.6.); for movables, *utrubi* (D.43.31.). In each case the possessor succeeded providing that his possession had not been acquired from the other by force, stealth, or permission, i.e. *nec vi, nec clam, nec precario* (see 9.7.5). The interdictal proceedings were concerned with the position of the possessor as against his opponent. It was irrelevant if such possession was flawed as against someone else. Paul, commenting on *uti possidetis*, states:

Paul, *Edict, book 65*: **It makes no difference in this interdict whether the possession against others is just or unjust. For every kind of possessor has by virtue of being a possessor more right than the nonpossessor.** (D.43.17.2.)

In proceedings for *uti possidetis* possession was normally awarded to the actual possessor; but in *utrubi* it was given to the party that had been in possession for the longer time in the previous year.

(c) Recovering possession. Where force had been used to obtain possession, the appropriate remedies were *utrubi* for movables, and the interdicts *unde vi* (C.8.4.), and *de vi armata* (D.43.16.) for immovables. (These interdicts are at the centre of Cicero's *Pro Caecina*. The technicalities of this case are thoroughly discussed in Frier, *Roman Jurists*.) The interdict *unde vi* ordered the restoration of land to one who had been evicted by force, providing that his possession had not been acquired from the other party by force, stealth, or permission. The interdict had to be sought within a year. The person evicted was entitled to be restored to the position before eviction:

Ulpian, *Edict, book 69*: **Whoever has been forcibly ejected must recover whatever damage he has sustained on account of his ejection; for he must be replaced in the original state in which he would have been if he had not been ejected.** (D.43.16.1.31.) (cf. Inst. 4.15.6.)

De vi armata differed in that it allowed recovery of possession without the limitation of a year, and even if the evicted person had previously held the land by force, stealth, or permission as against the evictor. The interdict applied only if *armed* force had been used, whether by an individual or by a gang, although it was for the latter case that the remedy was primarily designed. What constituted armed force?

Ulpian, *Edict, book 69*: **Arms are all weapons, that is, not only swords, spears, and lances, but also sticks and stones. [3] Plainly if one or another held a stick or a sword, the possessor is considered to have been ejected by arms. [4] One must go further and say that even if they came unarmed, but got to the point of taking up sticks and stones, it will be armed force. [5] Those who came armed but did not use arms for the ejection, yet did eject, are held to have done so with armed force. For terrorizing by arms is enough to be held as ejection by arms.** (D.43.16.3.2.–5.)

A decree of AD 389 (C.8.4.7.) attempted to stop the use of force in the pursuance of property claims. It provided that an owner who forcibly seized property should forfeit both ownership and possession; a non-owner had to restore the property and pay its value as a penalty. This decree reduced the importance of the interdicts: *unde vi* became infrequently used, while *de vi armata* disappeared altogether.

 online resource centre Please consult the Online Resource Centre for revision guidance on this chapter.

FURTHER READING

Those with a keen interest in specific aspects of this topic may also wish to consult Daube, D., 'Fashions and Idiosyncrasies in the Exposition of the Roman Law of Property', in *Theories of Property*, 35–50; Stein, P. G., 'Equitable Remedies for the Protection of Property', in *New Perspectives*, 185–94; Westbrook, R., 'Restrictions on Alienation of Property in Early Roman Law', in *New Perspectives*, 207–13.

7

....

Acquiring ownership

The acquisition of ownership in Roman law took various forms. These form the body of D.41.1. At the outset a distinction has to be drawn between acquiring ownership *inter vivos* and through succession, i.e. inheritance on death. Inheritance will be the subject of Chapter 8.

The methods of acquiring ownership *inter vivos* can be classified in a number of ways. For example, some methods can be described as 'original'—where the acquisition of ownership did not depend on there being a prior owner—whereas others were derivative, i.e. where ownership was derived from a prior owner (see Metzger, *Companion*, 49–65). Or some methods were formal, others causal: in the former case ownership passed because of the use of particular form and ceremony, whereas in the latter case ownership depended on the ground or 'cause' of the acquisition. In Roman law, however, Gaius described the primary classification as follows:

Gaius, *Common Matters or Golden Things*, book 2: **Of some things we acquire ownership under the law of nations which is observed, by natural reason, among all men generally, of others under the civil law which is peculiar to our city. And since the law of nations is the older, being the product of human nature itself, it is necessary to treat of it first.** (D.41.1.1pr.)

Justinian followed this basic distinction between *ius civile* and *ius gentium* modes of acquisition. The importance of the distinction lay in the fact that the *ius civile* modes were confined to those with *commercium*, i.e. mainly Roman citizens, whereas the *ius gentium* methods applied to acquisition of property by citizens and non-citizens alike (cf. Inst.2.1.1.; Inst.Gai.2.65.). The *ius civile* modes were *mancipatio, cessio in iure, usucapio,* and *adiudicatio*. The *ius gentium* modes were *occupatio, accessio, specificatio,* the acquisition of ownership of fruits, treasure-trove, and *traditio*.

The classification of the modes of acquisition of ownership into original and derivative is based on a modern interpretation of Roman law texts and it is the preferred classification in modern civilian systems. Note that the modern classification (original and derivative) cuts across the Roman categories. Let us follow this example by starting with the derivative modes of acquisition.

7.1 Derivative modes of acquiring ownership

7.1.1 *Mancipatio*

(Inst.Gai.2.22.–7.)

Mancipatio was of great importance in the history of Roman law. Originating before the Twelve Tables, it was regarded as the primary *ius civile* mode of transferring *res mancipi* until the later Empire. Moreover, it was adapted for use in creating and terminating relationships in the law of persons, as we have seen, e.g. the ceremonies in adoption and emancipation. However, as a method of conveying ownership pursuant to some *causa, mancipatio* lost its importance long before Justinian. Hence, information on *mancipatio* is to be found mainly in Gaius—in his time it had not yet become obsolete.

7.1.1.1 Formal requirements

The procedure in *mancipatio* was highly formal, as one would expect for the conveyance of important property in the early stages of development of an ancient legal system. Gaius refers to *mancipatio* as an imaginary sale (Inst.Gai.1.119.), a description that gives some insight into the required procedure. A sale being the most common (but by no means only) *causa* for the conveyance. However, this statement is perhaps misleading since in practice *mancipatio* was frequently indistinguishable from an *actual* sale, especially in early law. According to Gaius, the conveyance required the presence of the transferor and transferee, the property to be transferred, at least five witnesses, and a *libripens*, i.e. a person holding scales (see Prichard, A. M., 'Terminology in Mancipatio' (1960) 76 LQR, 412–28, for a linguistic perspective on the terminology of *mancipatio*). The witnesses and the *libripens* had to be Roman citizens of age with *commercium*. The transferee grasped the property, asserted his ownership with set words, and struck the scales with a piece of bronze which he then handed to the transferor. It may be that in early Rome, such acts were believed to have the 'magic' power of actualizing the transaction—the passing of ownership—rather than being regarded *merely* as legal formalities: but see MacCormack, G., 'Hägerstöm's Magical Interpretation of Roman Law' (1969) 4 IJ, 153–67. On the completion of this procedure, the transferee became *dominus* outright.

In the case of movables, it seems that only as much could be conveyed by one *mancipatio* as could be grasped. However, as regards a flock or herd of animals, one representative animal sufficed. As for land, a symbolic sod of earth or piece of turf was grasped: it need not have been from the actual land being mancipated (cf. Inst.Gai.1.121.). Thus, 'absent' land could be mancipated—the ceremony did not have to take place on the land or in its vicinity. This gave *mancipatio* at least one practical advantage over *traditio longa manu* (see 7.1.3.1), which partly accounts for the lengthy survival of *mancipatio*. The set words consisted of an assertion of title to the property—the same as that used in a *vindicatio*—followed by a declaration of the purchase of the thing. The piece of bronze often constituted the actual price before the use of coinage became widespread (cf. Inst.Gai.1.122.). The scales were used to weigh the bronze. Later, it became usual for the transferee to state the actual price at the end of the set words.

7.1.1.2 Legal effects

The basic rule was that a *mancipatio* of *res mancipi* transferred ownership (*dominium*) to the transferee. It is not clear whether a *mancipatio* of *res nec mancipi* had the same effect; but the transferee would almost certainly become owner in any case through *traditio*—the mancipation ceremony provided ample proof of intention and would invariably constitute a sufficient delivery. In the mancipation of *res mancipi*, ownership was transferred *unconditionally* (except that the transferor could reserve a servitude over the property) and *immediately*—it could not be postponed to take effect at some future time. If the *mancipatio* consisted of an actual sale, however, ownership normally passed only when the price was paid, a requirement that in early law was satisfied by the provision of the bronze. Provided that the *mancipatio* was correctly performed, the conveyance could not be impugned on grounds such as fraud or duress—it passed ownership irrespective of such considerations. What if the transferor lacked title? The transferee could not acquire what the transferor did not have—*nemo dat quod non habet* ('no one can give what he does not have'). However, the transferee might become owner in such a case through *usucapio* for the required length of time (see 7.2.1). If he was evicted before the expiry of the period, he was entitled to double the price under an action allowed by the Twelve Tables, the *actio auctoritatis* ('the action concerning legal title'). If the size of mancipated land was overstated, an action (the *actio de modo agri*) lay against the transferor for double the amount by which the price was excessive. These two actions may have been limited to cases where the *causa* for the conveyance was a sale.

It became increasingly frequent in the Empire to record in a written document that a *mancipatio* had taken place. Eventually, the written memorandum came to be relied on as conclusive evidence of mancipation, even if the ceremony had not actually taken place—the mere record of it sufficed. This development may have contributed at first to the survival of *mancipatio* by obviating the necessity for carrying out the formal ceremony. In due course, however, *mancipatio* came to be seen as an empty relic of a distant age. It was abolished by Justinian (see C.7.31.1.5.).

7.1.2 *Cessio in iure*

(cf. Inst.Gai.2.24.–7.)

Cessio had some similarities to *mancipatio*. It was a highly formal and cumbersome conveyance, originating before the Twelve Tables and fading in importance long before Justinian. Again, our knowledge of *cessio* is derived mainly from Gaius, who tells us (Inst.Gai.2.24.) that *cessio* was performed before a magistrate, such as the praetor (or governor), with the transferor and transferee present, together with the property to be transferred (or a symbolic sod of earth in the case of land). The transferee grasped the property and uttered the same set words as in *mancipatio*. The praetor asked the transferor whether he claimed the thing. Assuming that the latter stayed silent, or made no claim, he was taken as having ceded his rights, whereupon the praetor awarded the property to the transferee.

Cessio could be used to transfer *res mancipi* and *nec mancipi*, although *traditio* would usually be much more convenient for the latter. As regards transferring *res mancipi*, *cessio* was even more cumbersome than mancipation because of the necessity for a praetor. As Gaius said (Inst.Gai.2.25.), there was no point in doing something before a praetor that could be done 'before friends'. The chief uses of *cessio* were in relation to incorporeal things, e.g. creating servitudes, transferring inheritances. In addition, *cessio* was used in a procedural role in the law of persons, especially in adoption, emancipation, and manumission. *Cessio* passed ownership at once and unconditionally, subject to the possibility that a servitude could be reserved for the transferor (as in the case of *mancipatio*). Form was all important: as long as the *cessio* was correctly carried out, it seems that factors such as fraud and duress were irrelevant—the conveyance could not be impugned. It is not clear which remedy, if any, was available to a transferee if the transferor lacked title—the *actio auctoritatis* (see 7.1.1.2) does not seem to have applied to *cessio*. In any case, there was less scope for such problems to arise in *cessio* than in *mancipatio*, given the more limited uses to which the former was put.

7.1.3 **Delivery (*traditio*)**

(Inst.Gai.2.66.–9.)

Traditio was the transfer of ownership of a thing through delivery pursuant to a *causa*. It was by far the most widely applicable of the *ius gentium* modes of acquisition—the standard way of conveying *res nec mancipi*—and thus was of great practical importance. (See Hausmaninger, Gamauf, and Sheets, *Casebook*, 111–23.) For example, *traditio* was the mode by which the purchaser in the contract of sale normally acquired ownership (cf. Inst.Gai.2.18.–19.). It was used to transfer movables or land, although the *traditio* of *res mancipi* did not give *dominium* to the transferee, only bonitary ownership (see 7.2.2). However, since bonitary ownership was protected and would convert to *dominium* after the required period of prescription, it is not surprising that delivery of *res mancipi* became very common. When Justinian abolished the distinction between *res mancipi* and *nec mancipi*, *traditio* was recognized as conferring *dominium* over all property (see Hausmaninger, Gamauf, and Sheets, *Casebook*, 31–5).

There were two basic essentials of *traditio*: there had to be a delivery and the appropriate intent.

7.1.3.1 **Delivery**

The essence of delivery was that the transferee should be put in possession of the property. This often took the form of an actual physical transfer, but the transferee did not have to be personally involved, e.g. delivery could be made to his slave or representative; and there was no need for a handing over or physical contact in all cases. Several forms of delivery were possible, apart from an actual physical transfer:

(a) *Traditio longa manu*. This occurred when the property was indicated or pointed at, providing that it was within sight of the parties and capable of being taken at once into the transferee's control. This type of delivery was of obvious relevance in cases where the thing to be delivered could not easily be handled, e.g. land or heavy movables:

Paul, *Edict, book 54*:…there is no need for actual physical contact in order that possession may be taken; but that it can be done by sight and intent is demonstrated in the case of those things which, because of their great weight, cannot be moved, columns, for instance; for they are regarded as delivered, if the parties agree on their transfer in the presence of the thing…(D.41.2.1.21.)

(b) *Traditio brevi manu*. This was the authorization by the transferor that the transferee could keep as his own a thing over which the transferee already had control. The delivery in this situation consisted of the words of authorization; and they provided evidence of the required intention:

Gaius, *Common Matters or Golden Things, book 2*: Sometimes, indeed, the bare intent of the owner, without actual delivery, is sufficient to transfer a thing, as when I sell you something that I have already lent or let to you or deposited with you; for although I did not place the thing with you for that reason, now the fact that I allow it to remain with you on the ground of sale makes it yours. (D.41.1.9.5.)

This passage (by Gaius) is perhaps somewhat misleading in suggesting that *traditio* could be effected by 'bare intent' alone. It would be more accurate to regard delivery as essential in *all* cases of *traditio*, even if it consisted of words alone. The effect of those words was to put the transferee in possession of the property.

(c) *Constitutum possessorium.* This occurred if the transferor agreed to pass ownership of the thing to the transferee, but the former retained temporary control. The agreement to pass ownership constituted the delivery since it was regarded as vesting possession and effective control of the thing in the transferee (he could terminate the transferor's temporary rights, for example). *Constitutum possessorium* was used particularly to facilitate leaseback arrangements whereby the vendor became a tenant of the property with *detentio*. It avoided the need for an actual delivery of the property between the parties. The concept of *constitutum possessorium* remains an important element in modern law: e.g. section 930 BGB (*Bürgerliches Gesetzbuch*—the German Civil Code) provides that if an owner possesses a thing, a purchaser may obtain indirect possession from him through an agreed legal relationship instead of delivery (See Hausmaninger, Gamauf, and Sheets, *Casebook*, 39–45).

(d) Symbolic delivery. In the late Empire recognition was given to a type of delivery that can best be described as 'symbolic' (the term is medieval, not Roman). The chief examples were when a document was drawn up recording a transfer of property, or when keys to a building were handed over (the parties not being present at the site).

7.1.3.2 Intention and *iusta causa*

Both parties had to intend that ownership (and not merely possession) should be transferred by the delivery. Evidence of the required intention was provided by *iusta causa* ('a lawful cause'), i.e. a legal ground that was the reason for the delivery of the thing, and by which ownership normally passes, e.g. a sale, gift, or exchange, but there is great controversy as to whether *iusta causa* (as a separate requirement from the intention to transfer ownership by way of *traditio*) was always required in classical Roman law (see Pugsley, D., 'Was Justa Causa Necessary for Traditio in Roman Law?' (1974) THRHR, 13–17; Gordon, W. M., 'The Importance of the Iusta Causa of Traditio', in *New Perspectives*, 123–35, for a discussion of the *iusta causa* requirement in Roman and Scots law). The sources suggest that a *iusta causa* was probably necessary in every valid *traditio*:

Paul, *Edict, book 31*: **Bare delivery of itself never transfers ownership, but only when there is a prior sale or other ground on account of which the delivery follows.** (D.41.1.31pr.)

The precise role of *iusta causa* has provoked much controversy. It has been questioned whether *iusta causa* was essential in all cases, and, if it was, whether it consisted of a transaction or the parties' agreement concerning the transaction. See, e.g., Evans-Jones, R. and MacCormack, G., 'Iusta Causa Traditionis', in *New Perspectives*, 99, who affirm the dominant view: 'In classical law *traditio* was a "causal" transaction in the sense that, for ownership to pass through delivery, a valid antecedent *causa* was required. Such a *causa* consisted in a transaction or legal act that the law held to be sufficient for the passing of ownership. There is no firm evidence that any classical jurist identified *causa* either with the mere common intention to transfer and receive ownership or with the agreement of the parties as to the purpose of the transaction' (109).

What if the parties were mistaken as to *iusta causa*? For example, the transferor may have intended a sale, whereas the transferee thought that he was receiving a gift. Such mistakes were examples of putative (i.e. mistaken) *iusta causa*. The general rule was that mistakes were not fatal to a valid *traditio* provided that each party had the required intention—to pass and receive ownership.

An illustration by Julian:

Julian, *Digest, book 13*: **When we indeed agree on the thing delivered but differ over the grounds of delivery, I see no reason why the delivery should not be effective; an example would be that I think myself bound under a will to transfer land to you and you think that it is due under a stipulation. Again, if I give you coined money as a gift and you receive it as a loan, it is settled law that the fact that we disagree on the grounds of delivery and acceptance is no barrier to the transfer of ownership to you.** (D.41.1.36.)

The 'coined money' example may seem perplexing at first since the transferee received the money believing it to be 'a loan'. However, in such a situation, the transferee normally receives ownership of the money: if you borrow money from a friend, you are not expected to give back the very coins or notes that you receive, but only an equivalent. The actual money transferred becomes yours. Hence, in Julian's example, the transferee was regarded as having the intention to receive ownership, even though he thought that he was receiving a 'loan'. It would have been different if the transferred property had been a chariot: the transferee would not have acquired ownership, as he would not have intended to receive ownership. Julian's view appears inconsistent with that of Ulpian (D.12.1.18pr.) but was the one that ultimately prevailed. Both texts have been suspected of interpolation. W. M. Gordon (cited earlier) suggests that, notwithstanding the debate engendered, *iusta causa* may not have been as important an issue *in practice* as has been assumed. See *New Perspectives*, 123.

Mistakes could occur not only in relation to *iusta causa* but also, e.g., as to the identity of the property or of the transferee. Such mistakes, if material, could prevent a valid *traditio*. As to property, the crucial issue was whether there was an intention that ownership should pass of the thing actually delivered—if there was, the *traditio* was valid; but not otherwise. As for mistaken identity, it appears that a *traditio* was invalid if the transferee was not the person to whom the transferor intended to pass ownership. Such mistakes usually arose because of the dishonesty of the transferee: indeed, the illustrative texts on mistaken identity are mainly concerned with theft. Moreover, they suggest that a fraudulently induced mistake as to the *attributes* of the transferee could be fatal to a valid *traditio*:

Ulpian, *Edict, book 37*: **I wish to lend money to a respectable Titius and you present to me a penniless Titius, as if he were opulent, and then share the money with him; you will be liable for theft since theft is committed through your advice and assistance; Titius will also be liable for theft.** (D.47.2.52.21.)

However, a *traditio* could be valid even though the transferor did not have any particular transferee in mind (*traditio incertae personae*), e.g. a politician throwing coins into the crowd:

Gaius, *Common Matters or Golden Things, book 2*:…**the will of the owner may confer ownership on an unidentified person; this is so when he showers largesse on a mob; he does not know who will pick up what, but because he wishes anyone who picks something up to keep it, he makes him owner thereof forthwith.** (D.41.1.9.7.)

Cessio and *mancipatio*, together with *traditio*, comprise the Roman modes of conveying property *inter vivos*. In each case the conveyance was subject to the *nemo dat* principle but it is not clear when this principle was established: it may have been post-classical (see Schulz, *Classical Roman Law* (1951), 351–2). English law has broadly followed the *nemo dat* principle, but in modern continental systems there has been a greater readiness to accept that a possessor can give good title to a bona fide purchaser for value.

7.2 Original modes of acquiring ownership

This category is commonly divided into original *ius civile* and original *ius gentium* modes. This is yet another indication of the way in which the modern classification (original/derivative) bisects the Roman categories. The civil law modes will be dealt with first.

7.2.1 *Usucapio*

(Inst.Gai.2.40.–61., Inst.2.6., D.41.3., 4.–10., C.7.22.–31.)

Modestinus, *Encyclopaedia, book 5*: **Usucapion is the acquisition of ownership by continued possession for the period prescribed by law.** (D.41.3.3.)

Usucapio was prescriptive acquisition—a person became owner of property by holding it for the prescribed period of time (See Hausmaninger, Gamauf, and Sheets, *Casebook*, 124–49 as well as *R (Lewis) v Redcar and Cleveland Borough Council & Anor* [2010] UKSC 11). It was of great importance in practice since it allowed persons who possessed property to convert their interest into full *dominium*. The consequence was to reduce the problems caused by uncertainty over ownership:

Gaius, *Provincial Edict, book 21*: **Usucapion was introduced for the public weal, to wit, that the ownership of certain things should not be for a long period, possibly permanently, uncertain, granted that the period of time prescribed should suffice for owners to inquire after their property.** (D.41.3.1.)

The persons who benefited from *usucapio* were primarily those who had acquired property innocently, but who lacked *dominium* over it through some flaw in their ownership. This situation primarily arose, for example, through an unintentional and undetected breach of the requirements of the *mancipatio* act (cf. Inst.Gai.2.41., 43.). *Usucapio* gave the holder ownership, thus helping to reduce potential litigation. The origins of *usucapio* can be traced to at least the Twelve Tables, which laid down that land could be acquired by two years' use, one year sufficing for other things. The principles of *usucapio* were developed gradually, undergoing considerable change; but in its developed form it comprised the following essentials: possession, lapse of time, continuity, good faith, *iusta causa*, and property capable of being usucapted.

7.2.1.1 Possession

The holder had to have legal possession, i.e. the possession that was protected by interdict (see generally 6.5). Possession was the fundamental requirement of *usucapio*, as the very name signifies—'the taking by use'. It was insufficient for the holder to have mere custody (*detentio*) of the thing: he had to have possession.

7.2.1.2 Lapse of time

The requirement was for there to be two years' continuous possession of land, one year for other things. The periods seem to have been rather short, but are understandable when it is remembered that Rome was relatively small in size and population at the time of the Twelve Tables (cf. Inst.Gai.2.42.; 44.). In such a community, where property was closely guarded, and where the phenomenon of the absentee landlord was probably an infrequent occurrence, the prescribed periods appear to have provided ample time for the true owner to interrupt the possession of the holder (see Prichard, A. M., 'Early Usucapio' (1974) 90 LQR 234–45). Later, when Rome expanded, there was certainly an arguable case for lengthening the required periods. But they were not altered until Justinian's reign, some 1,000 years after their original enactment. Justinian extended the periods to three years for movables and 10 years for land (20 if the parties did not reside in the same province).

7.2.1.3 Continuity

There had to be continuous, uninterrupted possession for the required period. If the holder's possession was interrupted, he had to start again—he could not add the earlier period to the later one (see Gordon, W. M., 'Interruption of Usucapio' (1962) 9 RIDA 3, 325–33, for a discussion of the case where a possessor *alio nomine* decides to possess *suo nomine*). What constituted an interruption? It seems that it could be 'natural' or 'civil', both being fatal to a valid usucapion. There was a natural interruption if the possessor lost or parted with possession, for whatever reason. For example:

Gaius, *Provincial Edict, book 21*: **Possession is broken in fact when someone is forcibly evicted from possession or the thing is seized from him. And, in such a case, the possession is broken not only against the person who seizes the thing but against everyone.** (D.41.3.5.)

Civil interruption occurred when a legal claim was made to the property. In early law it seems that the very claim itself amounted to an interruption, but in classical law it was held that there was no interruption until judgment was given against the possessor. However, if the required period of possession elapsed between joinder of issue and judgment, the plaintiff was entitled to recover the property (if he proved his case) from the possessor since the judge had to make his decision based on the facts as they were at joinder. Although the classical rule concerning civil interruptions was clearly an improvement on that in early law, it was open to potential abuse: a possessor could try to delay proceedings against him so that time would run in his favour. It is possible that Justinian restored the original rule that interruption occurred when proceedings were commenced.

In late classical law an exception was allowed to the rule that an interruption necessitated the start of a fresh period of possession. If the possessor sold the property, the buyer could add the seller's period of possession to his own, providing that both had been in good faith at the commencement of their respective periods of possession:

Paul, *Plautius, book 13*: **The period that the vendor possessed before the sale runs for the purchaser.** (D.41.3.14pr.)

What if the possessor died before the lapse of the required period—could his heir add his predecessor's period of possession to his own?

Javolenus, *Letters, book 4*: **The testator's possession runs for his heir, provided that there is no intervening possession by another.** (D.41.3.20.)

The heir stepped into the shoes of the deceased: the period of possession of the deceased and his heir was regarded as one continuous period—death did not constitute an interruption. It was thus irrelevant if the heir was not in good faith, providing that the deceased had begun his possession in good faith.

7.2.1.4 Good faith (*bona fides*)

It seems that the requirement that the possessor must be in good faith was not recognized as an essential of *usucapio* until the later Republic. What was meant by good faith in this context? The basic test was whether the possessor believed that his possession was held honestly (cf. Inst.Gai.2.43.). For example, he would be in good faith, despite knowing that he was not the owner, if he held possession as the result of a praetorian interdict in his favour, or because he was a bonitary owner. Moreover, the possessor was in good faith if he mistakenly believed (as the bona fide possessor did) that he was the owner, providing that the mistake was one of fact, and reasonable in the circumstances:

Neratius, *Parchments, book 5*: **But a man may usucapt a thing which he believes to be his, although his belief is unfounded. This, however, is to be understood in the sense that a reasonable and plausible error will not prevent the usucapion of a possessor** ... (D.41.10.5.1.)

Although the possessor had to have good faith, he did not have to prove it: good faith was presumed until the contrary was proved. As a general rule, good faith had to be present when the possession began, but did not have to continue throughout the required period: supervening bad faith was not fatal to *usucapio*. In the case of sale, the purchaser must have been in good faith both at the time of agreement and of delivery:

Paul, *Edict, book 54*: ...**in the case of sale, we look also to the time of contracting so that a person must both have purchased in good faith and taken delivery in good faith.** (D.41.4.2pr.)

Exceptionally, in the case of a gift, the donee must have had good faith throughout the required period of possession, but Justinian eventually brought gifts within the general rule. Where possession was acquired on behalf of the possessor, the general rule was that both parties had to be in good faith—the acquirer when he acquired, and the possessor when he knew of the acquisition. However, if a master was in good faith, it is unlikely that the slave's bad faith was fatal:

Paul, *Edict, book 54*: **Again, Pomponius says that in cases where slaves possess something in their master's name, it is the mind of the master rather than that of the slave to which we must look** ... (D.41.4.2.12.)

There were some exceptional situations where good faith was not required by the possessor. The most important case was that of the vacant inheritance (*usucapio pro herede*). In some circumstances, heirs were not obliged to accept an inheritance (see 8.5.1.3). If an heir did not accept, or delayed in doing so, the inheritance was vacant and thus a *res nullius* open to the first taker—he would become its owner (despite the lack of good faith) after holding it for a year. This rule had some intelligible purpose: it was aimed at persuading heirs to decide speedily whether to accept inheritances, so that family rites could be performed, debts paid, and so that property should not lie vacant without an effective owner. *Usucapio* of vacant inheritances faded in importance following a reform by Hadrian that enabled the heir to recover the property even after the lapse of one year. And a special procedure was introduced for cases where a vacant inheritance was pillaged. This proved necessary because in theory theft could not be committed in such circumstances—the property was ownerless.

7.2.1.5 *Iusta causa*

The taking of possession had to be the result of some transaction or cause which was normally a basis for lawful acquisition, e.g. sale, gift, inheritance, exchange. It seems that this requirement was not recognized as essential until the later Republic. In *usucapio* (unlike *traditio*), the most commonly accepted rule was that mistaken *iusta causa* was insufficient. Ulpian, quoting Celsus, states:

Ulpian, *Sabinus, book 31*:…those people are mistaken who hold that if a man takes possession of a thing in good faith, he can usucapt it as his own, and it is irrelevant whether he did or did not buy it, whether or not it was given to him, provided that he thinks he bought it or received it as a gift, because there is no effective usucapion unless there be, in truth, a legacy, a gift, or a dowry, although the recipient believes so. (D.41.3.27.)

As the passage makes clear, there was juristic disagreement on this issue. Some jurists took the view that mistaken *iusta causa* was sufficient. For example, Pomponius states:

Pomponius, *Sabinus, book 22*: You delivered to me a slave whom, erroneously, you thought that you owed me on a stipulation; if I know that nothing is due to me, I will not usucapt him; but if I do not know, the more correct view is that I do usucapt him, because the very delivery, on a ground which I believe to be true, suffices to bring about a result that I possess for myself what is delivered to me. This was the recorded view of Neratius and I think it to be correct. (D.41.10.3.)

This view has the attraction of being consistent with the rule on putative *iusta causa* in *traditio* (see 7.1.3). Indeed, any distinction between *usucapio* and *traditio* in this respect is difficult to justify. However, the opposite view prevailed in the late classical period, and was accepted by Justinian—mistaken *iusta causa* was held insufficient in usucapion, as a general rule.

7.2.1.6 **Property capable of usucapion**

The basic rule was that *usucapio* applied only to property capable of being owned privately. Moreover, various things were excluded from usucapion on policy grounds, e.g. dotal immovables, and land belonging to a ward in guardianship. But the most important exclusion in practice was stolen property. Under the Twelve Tables, and a *lex Atinia* of the second century BC, stolen property could not be acquired through *usucapio* (see Inst.Gai.2.45.) (see, on this point, Pugsley, D., 'The Misinterpretation of the Lex Atinia' (1970) 17 RIDA 3, 259–72. See also, recently, Belovsky, P., 'Usucapio of Stolen Things and Slave Children' (2002) 49 RIDA 3, 57–99.) A similar rule was enacted in the late Republic in the case of property seized by force. The exclusion of stolen property had serious consequences for innocent acquirers of such property, e.g. bona fide purchasers for value. They could not become owners, however long their possession. The operation of this rule can be seen as an over-protection of the position of the *dominus*, and as contributing to insecurity of title for innocent acquirers. There seems an imbalance here between protecting the position of the rightful owner and that of the innocent acquirer. See Pugsley, *Property and Obligations*, 48 ff. However, the apparent imbalance was partially remedied by the qualification (probably introduced by the *lex Atinia*) that stolen property could be the subject of usucapion (according to some) if the owner failed to claim it, having discovered its whereabouts.

There are some difficult questions concerning the usucapion of stolen property. The precise relationship of the *lex Atinia* to the Twelve Tables is problematic. It is unlikely that the *lex Atinia* was simply a repetition of the Twelve Tables rule that prohibited usucapion of stolen property. Most probably the original rule was seen as too protective of the position of the *dominus*, and so the *lex Atinia* allowed some exceptions. However, it is possible that the Twelve Tables rule applied originally to usucapion by thieves, and that it was the *lex Atinia* which prevented the usucapion of stolen property by *anyone*. But that view is inconsistent with a text by Gaius (Inst.Gai.2.49.) that suggests that the original rule in the Twelve Tables was aimed at preventing *usucapio* by a third party rather than by the thief, as the latter could not usucapt in any case because of his lack of good faith. However, since the requirement of good faith is thought to have been a development of the later Republic, Gaius' clear implication that it was required at the time of the Twelve Tables is puzzling.

7.2.1.7 *Longi temporis praescriptio*

(C.7.33., 39.)

Usucapion of provincial land was not possible since such property was not capable of private ownership. This factor eventually led to the development of *longi temporis praescriptio*—'lengthy prescription'—which emerged in the provinces during the Empire (possibly at the end of the second century AD) as a form of prescriptive interest in provincial land. It initially started off merely as a defence against the owner's *vindicatio*, but eventually, imperial enactments—commencing with a rescript in AD 199—recognized provincial practice and gave full legal protection to long possession of provincial land (see Nörr, D., 'Time and the Acquisition of Ownership in the Law of the Roman Empire' (1968) 3 IJ, 352–62, for a discussion of the reasons for the introduction of *longi temporis praescriptio*).

The required period of possession was 10 years if the parties resided in the same province; otherwise 20 years. Most of the rules of *usucapio* were applied. For example, the possessor had to have good faith and there had to be *iusta causa*. The main difference, apart from the length of the period required, was that a possessor could add his predecessor's period of possession to his own. 'Lengthy prescription' did not originally confer ownership on the possessor but protected him against the owner, whose right of action was barred. However, the possessor's position was considered to be so strong that in the late Empire he came to be regarded as acquiring ownership, by which time the rules of usucapion and 'lengthy prescription' were virtually indistinguishable. The two systems were blended together under Justinian with the ending of the distinction between Italic and provincial land. *Usucapio* was confined to movables; land, wherever situated, was made subject to the rules of *longi temporis praescriptio*.

In the fourth century AD, an imperial decree (possibly of Constantine) provided that possession by a non-owner for 40 years extinguished the owner's right to a *vindicatio* in whatever circumstances the possession had originated (even if in bad faith). This law, *longissimi temporis praescriptio* ('very lengthy prescription'), was later amended by a reduction of the period to 30 years under Theodosius II in the fifth century AD (see C.Th.4.14.1.). Justinian ruled that if the possession had begun in good faith, the possessor acquired full title on the lapse of the period, even if the possession was otherwise defective, e.g. for lack of *iusta causa*.

7.2.2 **Protecting those en route to acquiring ownership through** *usucapio*

(D.6.2.)

Two categories of possessor could acquire ownership through *usucapio*, namely the bonitary owner and the possessor in good faith (see Hausmaninger, Gamauf, and Sheets, *Casebook*, 223–31). The bonitary owner lacked *dominium* since the parties had employed (possibly inadvertently) an inappropriate mode of conveyance while attempting to transfer ownership of an object (e.g. delivery of a *res mancipi*), while the possessor in good faith lacked *dominium* because the person who transferred ownership to him using an appropriate mode of conveyance did not have ownership himself. In both instances, *dominium* did not pass and the transferee merely acquired interdictal possession which could ripen into *dominium* through *usucapio*. The interval between conveyance and the acquisition of *dominium* was the period when the transferee was described either as a bonitary owner or a possessor in good faith depending on the nature of the defect (see Inst.Gai.2.40.). During that time, the position of both the bonitary owner and the possessor in good faith was rather precarious under the *ius civile*: they could defend their possession using interdicts, but only against immediate dispossessors and they could not prevent the rightful *dominus* from recovering it through *vindicatio*. The praetors were concerned with the potential unfairness inherent in the *ius civile* position. So they protected the bonitary owner and possessor in good faith by remedies that enabled them to assert their title and defeat claims. The level of protection depended on the position of the transferee. If the transferee was a bonitary owner, these remedies protected him from claims by any third party, even the *dominus*. If the transferee was the possessor in good faith, on the other hand, these remedies protected him only from claims by any third party with a weaker right than his own, in other words, against anyone *except* the *dominus*.

The operation of the rules depended on whether the bonitary owner or possessor in good faith was a defendant or a plaintiff. If the bonitary owner was a defendant, i.e. in possession of the disputed property, his interest would be protected against the *dominus* (the only party who could legitimately institute the *vindicatio* against him) by the praetor, who would allow a defence (*exceptio*) in the relevant *formula*. The *exceptio* would state the reason why the defendant had an interest in the property, e.g. because it had been sold to him (the usual case). If the defence was proved on the facts, the *dominus* was defeated—the bonitary owner retained possession and could be awarded ownership. If the plaintiff was not the *dominus*, but a third party, the bonitary owner could rely on possessory interdicts (see 6.5.5.1) to protect his interest. If the possessor in good faith was a defendant, i.e. in possession of the disputed property, he could protect his possession against third parties who had a weaker claim than him to the property using the possessory interdicts. As the *dominus* had a stronger right to the property than the possessor in good faith, he could successfully bring a *vindicatio*.

What if the bonitary owner or possessor in good faith was the plaintiff, i.e. seeking recovery of the property? Possessory interdicts might be available, but their applicability was somewhat limited when they were sought for the *recovery* of possession; they normally failed against the *dominus*. In 67 BC, the praetors introduced the *actio Publiciana*, which gave the bonitary owner an effective remedy as plaintiff against the *dominus* (and any third party) (see D.6.2.1pr.). The bonitary owner could allege in his *formula* a fiction—that the appropriate period of *usucapio* had elapsed. Providing that he could satisfy the other conditions of *usucapio* (e.g. that he had acquired possession in good faith), the bonitary owner's claim to the property would succeed (see Inst. Gai.4.36.). If the *dominus* relied on the defence that he was the rightful owner, the bonitary owner could raise a counter-defence based on the transfer (e.g. through sale) of the property to him by the *dominus*. The *actio Publiciana* was also available to the possessor in good faith, but the level of protection was more limited. Where the possessor in good faith was the plaintiff and the *dominus* the defendant in possession, he could not succeed with the *actio Publiciana*. Where the defendant was a third party (not the *dominus*), both the bonitary owner and possessor in good faith would succeed with their claims. See Nicholas, *Introduction*, 125–8.

Controversy surrounds the *actio Publiciana*. It does not appear to have been mentioned in juristic literature until the end of the first century AD—long after its apparent introduction. It may be that the date of the edict that introduced the action was considerably later than 67 BC—a Publicius was known to have been praetor in AD 93. But the later date was surely too late for a major praetorian reform, whereas 67 BC falls very much within the period of the most rapid development of the *ius honorarium*.

There is uncertainty, too, about the scope of the *actio Publiciana*. Whether it was originally intended to apply to bonitary owners is not clear. It may be that the action was introduced primarily as a remedy for bona fide possessors (compare 6.5.5.1) but came to be applied for the benefit of bonitary owners as well. If this supposition is correct, the *actio Publiciana* may not have been as major a reform as has been traditionally thought. That would perhaps explain why, if it had been introduced in 67 BC, there was a lack of juristic comment on it for so long. An alternative view is that the *actio Publiciana* was originally introduced for bonitary owners, and later adapted for bona fide possessors. For the controversies about the *actio Publiciana* see, e.g., Diósdi, *Ownership*, 154 ff. and Pugsley, *Property and Obligations*, 51 ff.

Bonitary ownership eventually was regarded as being as beneficial as *dominium*. Of course, once the bonitary owner had held the property for the required length of time, he became the actual *dominus*.

Let us now consider the other modes. The following are commonly classified as original *ius gentium* modes.

7.2.3 *Occupatio*

(Inst.Gai.2.66.–9.)

Occupatio is the law of 'first-taking': the first taker of ownerless property (*res nullius*) becomes its owner (see Ruddy, F. S., 'Res Nullius and Occupation in Roman and

International Law' (1968) 36 University of Missouri LR, 274–87). Property could be ownerless because it had never been owned before, or because the previous owner had intentionally ceased to be the owner (see Hausmaninger, Gamauf, and Sheets, *Casebook*, 150–62). The principle may seem, *prima facie*, somewhat crude and unsubtle, but in practice it constitutes a sensible and relatively uncomplicated method of resolving disputed ownership of such property. Indeed, 'the first in time prevails' is a principle that is well-known to modern lawyers. It reflects that basic human response—'I got there first'. The most important application of *occupatio* was in relation to things that had never had owners, enemy property, and abandoned things.

7.2.3.1 Things which had never had owners

This category included a variety of objects, which had not previously been owned and were therefore classified as *res nullius*. In Roman law, the capture of wild animals attracted juristic attention since it was an important application of the rules of *occupatio*, but this category of ownerless things also included, e.g., islands arising in the sea and gems found on the seashore. 'Wild animals' included birds, bees, and fish:

Gaius, *Common Matters or Golden Things, book 2*: **So all animals taken on land, sea, or in the air, that is wild beasts, birds, and fish, become the property of those who take them,** … (D.41.1.1.1.)

Animals were classed as wild or tame by nature (*ferae* or *mansuetae naturae*), the test being whether the animal belonged to a *species* designated as wild or tame, not whether it was wild or tame in its habits:

Gaius, *Common Matters or Golden Things, book 2*: …**there are those who have tame deer which go into and come back from the woods but whose wild nature has never been denied.** (D.41.1.5.5.)

The apparent simplicity of this classification of animals was deceptive. There was some difficulty in assigning animals to one class or another, mainly because of the existence of wild varieties of some domestic animals, or of hybrid, semi-wild species. See McLeod, G., 'Wild and Tame Animals and Birds in Roman Law', in *New Perspectives*, 169–76. Nevertheless, the classification was not without merit, as is evidenced by its continued survival in modern legal systems.

Did it matter whether animals were classed as wild or tame? Certainly—the rules as to ownership differed, animals tame by nature being regarded as ordinary movables. But to acquire ownership of a wild animal it was necessary to take effective control of it—wounding an animal, without capturing it, was probably insufficient. It was irrelevant to the question of ownership that the capture occurred on someone else's land, although intentional trespassing could constitute insulting behaviour (see generally 10.4). Ownership was retained for as long as the taker remained in *effective control* of the animal:

Gaius, *Common Matters or Golden Things, book 2*: **Any of these things which we take, however, are regarded as ours for so long as they are governed by our control. But when they escape from our custody and return to their natural state of freedom, they cease to be ours and are again open to the first taker,** [Florentinus, Institutes, book 6] **[4]: other than those tamed creatures which are in the habit of going and returning.** (D.41.1.3.2., 4.)

Animals with the 'habit of returning' (*animus revertendi*) ceased to be owned only when they abandoned the habit, i.e. lost their instinct to return. Animals without the habit of returning ceased to be owned when they escaped from custody:

Gaius, *Common Matters or Golden Things, book 2*: **An animal is deemed to regain its natural state of liberty when it escapes our sight or, though still visible, is difficult of pursuit.** (D.41.1.5pr.)

Since the owner of a wild animal ceased to be the owner when it escaped from his control, it followed that he was not responsible for any damage caused thereafter. This unsatisfactory position was remedied to some extent by an edict of the aediles that imposed strict liability (on those who kept wild animals near a highway) for damage caused by an escaped beast (see 10.6.2).

Bees were singled out for separate attention by the jurists, although the rules applicable were similar to those stated above. To obtain effective control of bees it was necessary to hive them:

Gaius, *Common Matters or Golden Things, book 2*: **Bees, again, are wild by nature and so those which swarm in our tree are, until housed by us in our hives, no more regarded as ours than birds which make a nest in our tree. Hence, if another should house or hive them, he will be their owner....[4] A swarm which flies away from our hive is deemed still to be ours so long as we have it in sight and its recovery is not difficult; otherwise it is open to the first taker.** (D.41.1.5.2., 4.)

The rules on bees, as practical as any in Roman law, have found a modern application, e.g. *Kearry v Pattinson* [1939] 1 KB 471.

7.2.3.2 Enemy property

Celsus, *Digest, book 2*: **And property of the enemy, which is on our territory, becomes not public property, but that of the first taker.** (D.41.1.51.1.)

This rule applied to enemy property captured within Roman territory in time of war, and probably to things belonging to nationals of States with which Rome did not have a treaty of friendship. However, booty captured in military action did not fall within the rule; it was usually sold or given away by the victorious general (although in theory it belonged to the State).

7.2.3.3 Abandoned property

The first taker of abandoned property became its owner providing that he had the intention of acquiring it. What was the test of abandonment? It seems that the owner must have *intended* to be rid of the property, no longer caring about its destination before it became *res nullius*:

Gaius, *Common Matters or Golden Things, book 2*: **It is another matter with those things which are jettisoned in stress of seas to lighten the vessel; they remain the property of their owners; for they are not cast overboard because the owner no longer wants them, but that the ship may have a better chance of riding the storm. Consequently, if anyone finds such things washed up by the waves or, for that matter, in the sea itself and appropriates them with a view to gain, he is guilty of theft.** (D.41.1.9.8.)

The Sabinians and Proculians disputed the question whether the previous owner lost ownership at the moment of abandonment, as the Sabinians argued, or when another person took possession of the abandoned property (the Proculian view).

The Proculians were unhappy at the possibility that important property could be ownerless for any length of time. However, the Sabinian view, more convenient in practice, seems to have prevailed.

Occupatio of abandoned *res mancipi* received surprisingly little attention from the jurists in view of the potential problems involved. For example, could the first taker of abandoned *res mancipi* acquire *dominium* over the property through *occupatio*? Certainly, if the property was then held for the relevant period of time required for prescription under *usucapio*. But whether *dominium* could arise before the lapse of the relevant period is unclear. The view that *dominium* over *res mancipi* could be acquired only through *ius civile* modes of acquisition (and therefore not through *occupatio*) is problematic since, if that were the case, abandoned *res mancipi* might not fall into ownership again—a possibility which was not likely to have been encouraged in early law. In any case, there *were* ways in which *dominium* over *res mancipi* could be acquired by *ius gentium* modes of acquisition, e.g. *avulsio* (see 7.2.4.1). The most plausible view is that *occupatio* of abandoned *res mancipi* sufficed to give *dominium immediately* without the need for a period of prescription.

7.2.4 *Accessio*

(Inst.Gai.2.73.–8.)

Accessio was the inseparable attachment of things belonging to different owners, one thing being incorporated in the other. The incorporated property was the accessory thing: it acceded to the principal thing. The general rule was that the owner of the principal thing became owner of the whole thing. Thus, if A built a house on B's land, the house acceded to the land since the latter was considered to be the principal thing. B owned the house (cf. D.41.1.26pr.).

Accessio has to be distinguished from *commixtio* and *confusio* (see Hausmaninger, Gamauf, and Sheets, *Casebook*, 194–8). A *commixtio* occurred when things belonging to different owners were mixed, but were readily separable. If this was done by agreement, the resulting mix became common property; if done without agreement, the things could be separated and returned to their respective owners—there was no change of ownership. In the latter case, the appropriate remedies were the *actio ad exhibendum* ('the action to display') for the production of the thing with a view to separation, and a *vindicatio*, where necessary. *Confusio* occurred if the things that were mixed were not readily separable and it was not possible to tell which was the principal thing, which the accessory, e.g. when A mixes his wine with B's wine. The resulting mix was owned in common in proportion to the value of the parties' respective shares, unless the parties had agreed otherwise. The rules of *confusio* were applied in *Indian Oil Corporation Ltd v Greenstone Shipping SA (Panama)* [1988] QB 345 (see 11.3.3).

As regards *accessio*, the owner of the principal thing became the owner of the whole thing, irrespective of the bona fides of the parties or the identity of the person who did the mixing or attaching. *Accessio* applied only to things that were not readily separable. The issue of separability was partly a question of law—buildings, for example, were considered to be legally inseparable from the land—and partly a question of fact. Things were considered not to be readily separable if undue effort, skill, or cost was required to separate them, or if the separation would damage the property. The operation of the rules of *accessio* is best considered by distinguishing between land and movables.

7.2.4.1 *Accessio* affecting land

The basic rule was that anything that was attached to land became part of it, since land was regarded as the principal thing (see Hausmaninger, Gamauf, and Sheets, *Casebook*, 176–85). The application of the rule occurred mainly in the following cases:

(a) Buildings. They were regarded as inseparable from the land on which they stood—hence, the landowner owned anything built on his land (the principle *superficies solo cedit* is expressed in Inst.Gai.2.73.). However, he did not necessarily own the materials comprised in the building: the law recognized a distinction between ownership of a building and ownership of the materials:

Gaius, *Common Matters or Golden Things, book 2*: **When someone builds on his own site with another's materials, he is deemed to be owner of the building because all that is built on it becomes part of the soil. However, the owner of the materials does not thereby lose his ownership of them; but he meanwhile cannot bring a** *vindicatio* **for them or an action for their production by reason of the** *Law of the Twelve Tables* **which provides that no one is required to give up materials of another built into his premises but that he must pay double their value....Hence, if the house should collapse for some reason, the owner of the materials can have a** *vindicatio* **for them and have an action for their production.** (D.41.1.7.10.)

In the situation discussed in the above text, i.e. where B builds on his land with A's materials, the legal position depended on whether there had been theft of A's materials. In the absence of theft, it seems (the texts are unclear) that A had no remedy apart from claiming the materials when the building came down. This was a dormant right. If B had stolen the materials he was liable for theft under the Twelve Tables for double their value. It would appear that the reference to 'double value' in the above text assumes that the builder had stolen the materials. This action was barred, however, if A chose to sue B for theft under the *actio furti* (see 10.3.2.2). Whichever action A chose, he retained his right to reclaim the materials when the building came down. If the materials had been stolen, but not by B, A could sue the thief and retained the right of eventual reclaim of the materials.

What if a person built with his own materials on another's land? The position depended on whether the builder had acted in good faith or not. If he had not, i.e. he realized that the land belonged to someone else, he was deemed to have made a gift of the materials to the landowner:

Gaius, *Common Matters or Golden Things, book 2*:...**if a person were to build with his own materials on someone else's site, he would make the building the property of the owner of the site, and if he knew that the site belonged to another, he would be treated as voluntarily parting with his materials so that even if the house should collapse, he would have no** *vindicatio* **for them....** (D.41.1.7.12.)

If the builder had acted in good faith, the position depended on whether the landowner had later gained possession of the building; if so, then the builder normally had no remedy, apart from eventual reclaim of the materials. If the builder was still in possession, he was entitled to recover his expenditure. However, under Justinian the *ius tollendi* ('the right to remove') was allowed to the builder in possession, irrespective it seems of good or bad faith on his part. This enabled the builder, when vacating the premises, to remove as much of his materials as he could without damaging the structure of the building. Some uncertainty surrounds the *ius tollendi*. It seems that it was known in classical law, but was available at that time only to the builder who had acted in good faith. The right probably did not apply where the owner was prepared to compensate the builder for not removing materials:

Celsus, *Digest, book 3*: **Our decision is that if the owner is prepared to pay the possessor as much as he would have if he took the materials away, he should have the power to do so. There must be no indulgence to malice. If, say, you want to scrape off plaster which you have put on walls, and deface pictures, that will serve no purpose but to annoy.…** (D.6.1.38.)

(b) Planting and sowing. The general rule was that if anything belonging to A was planted or sown in B's land, the latter became the owner when the thing took root:

Gaius, *Common Matters or Golden Things, book 2*: **If I plant someone else's cutting in my land, it will be mine; conversely, if I plant my own cutting in someone else's land, it will be his, provided, in each case, that it roots itself. For until it takes root, it remains the property of its former owner.** (D.41.1.7.13.)

Regarding compensation, if A sowed (in his own land) seeds belonging to B, A was liable for theft if he had acted in bad faith; if in good faith, A was probably liable to compensate B for the value that the seeds or plants had when they were appropriated. Where A sowed his own seeds in B's land, he was deemed to have made a gift of them if he had acted in bad faith. If he had acted in good faith, and was in possession of the land, A was entitled to the value of the seeds; if out of possession, it is doubtful whether he had a remedy.

(c) Avulsio. This occurred where an identifiable piece of land was carried by the force of a river current and was deposited against the land of another:

Gaius, *Common Matters or Golden Things, book 2*: **But if the force of the river should detach part of your land and bring it down to mine, it obviously remains yours. Of course, if it adheres to my land, over a period of time, and trees on it thrust their roots into my land, it is deemed from that time to have become part of my land.** (D.41.1.7.2.)

(d) Alluvio. This was the imperceptible accretion or deposit of soil on a person's land through the action of a river. Such deposits enlarged the land by acceding to it:

Gaius, *Common Matters or Golden Things, book 2*: **Furthermore, what the river adds to our land by alluvion becomes ours by the law of nations. Addition by alluvion is that which is gradually added so that we cannot, at any given time, discern what is added.** (D.41.1.7.1.)

It seems that *alluvio* was confined in Roman law to the action of rivers. The principles of *alluvio* have been adopted by modern systems, sometimes in modified form, e.g. in English law *alluvio* applies to ponds, lakes, and the action of the sea. See Jackson, P., 'Alluvio and the Common Law' (1983) 99 LQR, 412–31. The French Civil Code, on the other hand, restricts *alluvio* along Roman lines (Articles 556–8). Although *alluvio* has traditionally been thought to be concerned essentially with silting, it has been argued that its scope was wider than that: see Lewis, A. D. E., 'Alluvio: The Meaning of Institutes II.1.20', in *Studies J. A. C. Thomas*, 87–95.

(e) Rivers. Rivers are capricious things—they flood, they dry up, they change course. Their action can pose a variety of legal problems apart from *avulsio* and *alluvio*. For example, who owns an island arising in a river? The rule was that the island was owned by the riparian owners up to the middle line of the river unless it lay wholly to one side of a riverbank, in which case it acceded to that bank:

Gaius, *Common Matters or Golden Things, book 2*: **An island arising in a river (a frequent occurrence), if indeed it appears in the midstream of the river, is the common property of those who have holdings on either bank of the river to the extent that those holdings follow the bank; but if it lies to one side of the river rather than the other, it belongs only to those who have holdings on that bank.** (D.41.1.7.3.)

If a river changed course or dried up, the old riverbed was shared by the riparian owners up to the middle line of the bed. If part of a riparian owner's land became an island because the river divided itself, there was no change of ownership. What if the river flooded land? If the flood abated, there was no change of ownership; but if the waters did not recede, it seems that the ground covered by the river was partly lost to its previous owner—in effect it became a river bed, the rule of the imaginary middle line applying to the new situation. There was no question of compensation since such changes of ownership were the result of natural phenomena, not human acts. The same was true of *avulsio* and *alluvio*.

7.2.4.2 *Accessio* affecting movables

Here we are concerned with the case where movables (principal and accessory) were inseparably attached or mixed together without the consent of the owners. Roman law acknowledged a number of examples of *accessio* affecting movables (see Hausmaninger, Gamauf, and Sheets, *Casebook*, 186–93). As a starting point, *confusio* (blending of liquids such as wine, honey, or molten metals belonging to different owners) and *commixtio* (blending of solids such as grain or coins belonging to different owners) were excluded (see 7.2.4), but specific cases such as *textura* (inseparable weaving of costly thread owned by one party into the garment belonging to another), *ferruminatio et plumbatura* (welding or soldering an object belonging to one party to a principal object belonging to another), *scriptura* (writing on or decorating parchment belonging to another with one's own materials), and *pictura* (painting with one's paint on the canvas belonging to another) were identified. See Watkin, T. G., 'Tabula Picta: Images and Icons' (1984) 50 SDHI, 383–99, on the later history of this rule and its application in the Eastern Empire following the advent of Christianity. The resulting property generally belonged to the owner of the principal thing. The major issues in *accessio* of movables were (a) the test for deciding which thing was the principal and which the accessory, and (b) whether compensation was payable to the owner of the accessory thing.

(a) Principal or accessory? In cases involving land there was little problem in identifying the principal thing—things acceded to the land. However, as regards the *accessio* of movables to movables, there could be difficulties in deciding which the principal thing was. For example, what was the position where I painted on my canvas with your paints, or wrote a poem on your parchment? Not surprisingly, the jurists did not achieve consistency about what the appropriate test should be in such cases. For example, the following passage suggests alternative tests, based on relative size or value:

Pomponius, *Sabinus, book 30*: **If it be asked which cedes to the other, when elements belonging to each of two owners are welded together, Cassius says that an assessment is to be made of the respective portions of the final product or of the value of each element.** (D.41.1.27.2.)

These tests find a place in the French Civil Code, which regards the thing 'largest in value' as the principal thing, or the thing that is largest in 'volume' if the values are about equal (Article 569). Another test, proposed in some cases, was that of independence—that thing was the principal thing that could have an existence independently of the other thing:

Paul, *Edict, book 21*: **Whatever is written on my paper or painted on my board at once becomes mine. Although in the case of a painting some writers have held the opposite, on account of a painting's value, yet where one thing cannot exist without the other, it necessarily accedes to that other.** (D.6.1.23.3.)

But the test which was perhaps applied most widely focused on the physical *identity* of the constituent elements: that thing was principal which most retained its identity, i.e. which gave the resulting mix or attachment its essence, name, or overall character:

Paul, *Sabinus, book 14*:…**we have to look at the overall character, so that if something be added, it becomes part of the whole. Thus, if a foot or a hand be added to a statue, a base or handle to a goblet, a post to a couch, a plank to a vessel, stone to a building, the whole belongs to the erstwhile owner of the statue, and so forth.** (D.41.1.26pr.)

Consistency in deciding which thing was principal and which accessory is not to be found in the texts. Cases tended to be decided on a casuistic basis rather than by the widespread application of any one test. Paintings were an instructive case: in classical law, if A painted a picture on B's tablet, the predominant view (despite Paul's assertion in D.6.1.23.3.) was that the tablet acceded to the painting, i.e. A, the painter, owned the painting:

Gaius, *Common Matters or Golden Things, book 2*: **Pictures do not accede to the tablets on which they are painted.…On the contrary, the view established itself that the tablet accedes to the picture.** (D.41.1.9.2.)

Such a solution could be justified by the application of the identity test—it is the picture which gives the essence or overall character to the resulting thing, not the tablet or canvas. Justinian adopted the predominant classical view, but for a different reason—that of relative value. This test works well (and fairly) if there is a clear difference in the relative value of the two things, as there would be if Rembrandt had painted a portrait on your canvas. But what if *you* had painted on *his* canvas?

As regards writing, it was held to accede to parchment even if the former was more valuable, e.g. if it was done in gold leaf:

Gaius, *Common Matters or Golden Things, book 2*: **Letters, even in gold, accede to the paper or parchment just as things built or sown become part of the land. Thus, if I wrote verse or a story or a speech on your paper or parchment, not I but you would be held to own the finished work.** (D.41.1.9.1.)

The distinction made between paintings and written script is problematic. The identity test comes closest to providing a satisfactory justification for the distinction but, even with that test, there are problems—would not the overall character of parchment that contained illuminated script be determined more by the script than by the parchment? On the other hand, in the case of 'ordinary' writing on parchment, the identity test makes sense. The words, unlike a painting, are unlikely to dominate in a *visual* sense: they are meant to be read rather than viewed.

(b) Compensation. Was the owner of the accessory thing entitled to compensation once the inseparable attachment had occurred? The general position depended on whether the attachment had been effected by the owner of the principal thing or by the owner of the accessory thing. If the former had attached the things and had acted in bad faith, he was liable for theft but was nevertheless the owner. If he had acted in good faith (e.g. thinking the accessory thing belonged to him) and was in possession of the property, it seems that he was not liable to compensate the other party, until the later Empire when an action was allowed for the value of the accessory thing. If the owner of the principal thing was not in possession, he could obtain the property by *vindicatio* on paying for the value of the accessory thing. If he refused to pay, his *vindicatio* would be defeated by the other party's *exceptio doli* ('the defence of fraud') on the ground that it would be 'fraudulent' for the former to obtain the property without paying compensation.

If the owner of the accessory thing was responsible for the attachment and had acted with full knowledge of the facts, he was deemed to have made a gift of the thing. Where he had acted in good faith, he had no remedy if he was out of possession; if in possession, he was entitled to compensation.

These rules were of *general* application. It is possible that the question of ownership and compensation was decided differently in the case of *paintings*. A dubious text (in D.41.1.9.2.) suggests that the owner of the tablet was entitled to the painting if he paid 'the cost of the painting'.

7.2.5 *Specificatio*

(Inst.Gai.2.79.)

Specificatio was a method of acquiring ownership by the creation of a new thing out of someone else's materials (see Hausmaninger, Gamauf, and Sheets, *Casebook*, 201–4). For example, if A made wine out of B's grapes, A owned the wine. It appears that the term *specificatio* was post-classical although the rules were formulated by the classical period. *Specificatio* had an obvious affinity with *accessio*, and it was not always certain which was the appropriate mode of acquisition in a given situation. (On *specificatio*, see Cohen, B., 'Specificatio in Jewish and Roman Law' (1958) 5 RIDA 3, 225–90 for a comparative perspective and Plescia, J., 'The Case of Specification in Roman Law' (1973) 24 IVRA, 214–21, for a thorough overview of the basic legal rules relating to *specificatio*. Stoop, B. C., 'Non Solet Locatio Dominium Mutare: Some Remarks on Specificatio in Classical Roman Law' (1998) 66 TR, 3–24 attempts to establish at which point in classical Roman law artisans, craftsmen, and other workers were excluded from the scope of *specificatio*.) See most recently Plisecka, A., '*Accessio* and *Specificatio* Reconsidered' (2006) 74 TR, 45–60.

7.2.5.1 The Proculian–Sabinian dispute

There was a celebrated dispute between the schools about *specificatio*:

Gaius, *Common Matters or Golden Things, book 2*: **When someone makes something for himself out of another's materials, Nerva and Proculus are of opinion that the maker owns that thing because what has just been made previously belonged to no one. Sabinus and Cassius, on the other hand, take the view that natural reason requires that the owner of the materials should be owner of what is made from them, since a thing cannot exist without that of which it is made....** (D.41.1.7.7.)

The Proculian view in effect treated *specificatio* as a special form of *occupatio*: at the moment of creation the new thing was regarded as a *res nullius*, i.e. owned by no one, and thus open to the first 'occupier'—the creator. The analogy with *occupatio* was rather strained, however: the created thing can hardly be said to have been a *res nullius* if it was owned as soon as it was created. There were other views on the question of ownership of newly created things:

Gaius, *Common Matters or Golden Things, book 2*: **There is, however, the intermediate view of those who correctly hold that if the thing can be returned to its original components, the better view is that propounded by Sabinus and Cassius but that if it cannot be so reconstituted, Nerva and Proculus are sounder. Thus, a finished vase can be again reduced to a simple mass of gold, silver or copper; but wine, oil or flour cannot again become grapes, olives or ears of corn** ... (D.41.1.7.7.)

The 'intermediate' view, that the new thing belonged to the creator if it was not reducible to its original form, was the solution adopted by Justinian. Where the thing was reducible, the owner of the original materials owned the new thing; but it was not necessary that it should actually be reduced—what gave him ownership was that the thing was potentially reducible. What was the test of reducibility? The outcome depended on how feasible it was for the thing to be reduced: it would not be feasibly reducible if undue effort or skill were required, or if the substance of the thing was substantially impaired, e.g. if the process of reduction left little or nothing of the original material. If the material was owned partly by the creator, there was broad agreement that the creator owned the new thing—reducibility was irrelevant. If, however, the materials were owned by two or more persons, but not the creator, and the new thing was reducible, the owners of the materials owned the new thing, on the view adopted by Justinian, the principles of *confusio* and *commixtio* applying to determine their respective rights (see 7.2.4).

7.2.5.2 *Nova species*
The application of *specificatio* depended on whether a new thing (*nova species*) had been created. What was the test of *nova species*? The texts are inconclusive, but it seems that the new thing had to have an identity, a name of its own: it could not be simply an altered or improved thing.

Gaius states:

Gaius, *Common Matters or Golden Things, book 2*: **In my view, however, there are those who rightly say that corn threshed from someone's ears of corn remains the property of the owner of the ears; for since the corn already has its perfect form while in the ears, the thresher does not make something new, but merely uncovers what already exists.** (D.41.1.7.7.)

Thus, one who crushed grapes did not create a new thing: he simply brought about crushed grapes. But making wine from grapes, or a ship from planks of timber would be regarded as creating a new thing. It seems that some element of skill and effort had to be involved in the creation of a *nova species*. (See Van der Merwe, C. G., 'Nova Species' (2004) 6 Roman Legal Tradition, 96–115, on the history and contemporary application of this rule in Scots law.)

7.2.5.3 **Compensation**
Ownership could be acquired by the creator even if he had not acted in good faith. The existence of bad faith was relevant only to the question of compensation, the rules being similar to those in *accessio*. If the creator acquired ownership, having acted in good faith, and was in possession of the new thing (the likely scenario), it seems that the owner of the materials had no remedy. If the creator was not in

possession, he was entitled to the property, but only if he paid the other party for the value of the materials. If the creator had acted in bad faith, he could be sued for theft but was entitled to the new thing.

Where the creator did not become the owner through *specificatio*, but had acted in good faith and was in possession, he was probably entitled to compensation for his work when the owner brought a *vindicatio*. If he was out of possession, it is unlikely that he had any remedy. If the creator had acted in bad faith, he was deemed to have made a gift of his work.

The French Civil Code (Articles 570–1) has adopted the Roman rules on *specificatio*, but with some important differences. The owner of the materials can claim the new thing if he reimburses the price of labour, unless the value of the labour far surpasses the value of the materials used. In the latter case, the creator retains the thing but must reimburse the other party for the cost of the materials. The labour and the materials are valued as at the date of reimbursement.

7.2.6 **Acquisition of the ownership of fruits**

Fruits were classed as either natural or civil (see Hausmaninger, Gamauf, and Sheets, *Casebook*, 171–5). The ownership of natural fruits could be acquired as a result of *separatio*, i.e. their severance from the fruit-bearing property, or through *perceptio*—the collection or gathering of the fruits. The ownership of civil fruits (e.g. rent) was transferred by delivery. The owner of property normally owned all its natural fruits, no severance or collection being necessary. But there were situations where a person was entitled to fruits from property that he did not own, e.g. the usufructuary. These cases are best considered according to whether ownership was gained by severance or gathering.

7.2.6.1 **Severance**

All that was required was for the fruits to be severed or separated from the fruit-bearing property. A change of ownership of the fruits resulted as soon as severance occurred, whatever the manner. Thus, if apples fell from a tree, they were considered as severed. It was not necessary for control to be taken of the severed fruits—there was no need for any gathering. The chief cases where ownership of fruits could be acquired through severance were bona fide possession (see 6.5) and *emphyteusis* (see 6.4.1).

(a) Bona fide possession. The entitlement of the bona fide possessor was based on the fact that he usually appeared to the outside world as though he were the owner, and because he would often have produced the fruits through his own labour:

Paul, *Plautius, book 7*: **A purchaser in good faith undoubtedly acquires ownership for the time being by gathering fruits, even those of someone else's property, not only the fruits which are produced by his care and toil but all fruits, because, in the matter of fruits, he is virtually in the position of an owner. Indeed, even before he gathers them, the fruits belong to the purchaser in good faith as soon as they are severed from the soil.** (D.41.1.48pr.)

It seems that if the bona fide possessor discovered that he was not the owner of the property, he was no longer entitled to the fruits; but this rule could create difficulties in practice, and was not unanimously held by the jurists. Problems could arise from a rule, introduced probably in the late Empire, that the bona fide possessor had to account for any unconsumed fruits when the *dominus* legally recovered the fruit-bearing property. In such a case the ownership of the bona fide possessor was complete only when the fruits no longer existed, i.e. had been consumed—a bizarre rule. It seems that the purpose of the rule was to compensate the *dominus* as much as possible for the fact that he had been out of possession of his property. But this was potentially rough justice—the bona fide possessor could well have expended much effort in cultivating and gathering fruits, only to lose them if unconsumed.

(b) *Emphyteusis*. Since the tenant held land by way of a long or perpetual lease it is not surprising that he was entitled to the fruits of the land on their severance.

7.2.6.2 Gathering

To acquire ownership of fruits by gathering, the acquirer had to physically collect or gather them—e.g. pick apples from a tree or collect them after they had fallen. It was not necessary for the acquirer to have acted personally: the gathering was effective if done on his behalf, e.g. by his slave. It is not clear what was required by way of gathering when offspring were born to animals. If assistance was given to the animal in labour, such an act could be regarded as gathering; but it seems that, even in the absence of any such act, offspring passed to the acquirer as soon as they were born. The chief cases of acquisition of fruits through gathering were the *colonus* and the usufructuary:

(a) *Colonus*. He was an agricultural tenant, holding land from the owner under a contract of hire. In such contracts the tenant was often allowed to keep the fruits that he gathered; the gathering passed ownership provided that it occurred while the consent of the owner was operative. If the tenant appropriated the fruits without the relevant consent, he risked committing theft. What if the owner changed his mind contrary to the agreement? Any fruits already gathered remained in the ownership of the tenant—revocation of consent did not operate retrospectively. But fruits that had not yet been gathered when the revocation occurred did not go to him; his only remedy was to sue for damages for breach of the contract of hire.

(b) Usufructuary. His position as regards fruits has already been considered (see 7.2.6). Unlike the *colonus*, the usufructuary had a right to fruits that was not dependent on the continued assent of the owner. Why did the usufructuary have to gather fruits to become their owner? Why should severance have not been sufficient? The justification for the rule was that the usufructuary (and the *colonus*) lacked possession of the property that they held. Some act of appropriation of the fruits was thus necessary, whereas this was not the case with the bona fide possessor, e.g., since he had possession. The distinction is hardly convincing: a rule which holds that when apples fall off a tree they become at that moment owned by a bona fide possessor, but not by a usufructuary, is not easy to justify.

7.2.7 Finding treasure

If treasure is found, ownership of it could conceivably be claimed by a number of candidates—the original owner, the finder, the owner of the land in which it was found; possibly even the State. The Romans developed principles in this field which are still applied, in modified form, in some modern systems (see Carey Miller, D. L., 'Treasure Trove in Scots Law', in *Summa Eloquentia*, 75–90). For a survey of the most important controversies, see Hausmaninger, Gamauf, and Sheets, *Casebook*, 163–70.

7.2.7.1 **What was treasure?**

Paul, *Edict, book 31*: **Treasure is an ancient deposit of money, memory of which no longer survives, so that it is without an owner...** (D.41.1.31.1.)

This was one of the less convincing Roman attempts at definition. 'Money' was interpreted in a wide sense, since it is clear that treasure included jewellery and other valuables, e.g. gold caskets. There must have been a 'deposit'—it seems that the treasure must have been secreted in land. Things that were dropped or accidentally lost did not constitute treasure; nor did things that had been abandoned. The owner must not be traceable; if he was traceable, the property was not treasure, and belonged to the owner unless he had abandoned it. The reference to 'ancient' probably adds little, apart from embellishing the requirement of untraceability: an owner is more likely to be untraceable the longer ago that the treasure was deposited.

7.2.7.2 **Who owned treasure?**

There is uncertainty about the position in the Republic but it seems that the finder had no rights unless he was the landowner. Treasure belonged to the landowner on the principle of *accessio*, i.e. things in the land accede to it. It appears to have been irrelevant that the landowner did not know of the existence of the treasure until it was found. In the early Empire, treasure seems to have been regarded for a while as belonging to the imperial treasury rather than to the owner of the land; the finder still had no rights.

The Emperor Hadrian (mid-second century AD) eventually laid down rules which did reward the finder: he was entitled to all of the property if he found the treasure on his own land, or by chance on sacred or religious land. If the treasure was found by chance on another's land, it was shared between the finder and the landowner, even if the latter was the Emperor (Inst.2.1.39.). The finder's share was justified on the analogy of *occupatio*: the finder was the first 'occupier' of property that in reality was hardly distinguishable from *res nullius*, i.e. ownerless property. If, however, the treasure was found as the result of a deliberate search, the finder took nothing: the treasure belonged to the landowner. Although this rule discouraged trespassing, it could be said to have penalized the use of initiative on the part of the finder—if less treasure was found as a result, who gained from that?

There were further changes in the later Empire, some of them influenced by the conversion to Christianity. For example, a decree of AD 480 deprived a finder of treasure on his own land if he had used pagan rites to aid his search. Justinian preserved Hadrian's basic scheme.

Apart from the original civil law and natural law modes of acquisition of ownership described here, various statutory and other modes existed in Roman law. For a survey of these, see Lee, *Elements*, 122. One of the most important original modes was *adiudicatio*.

7.2.8 *Adiudicatio*

In certain proceedings, described as 'partition' or 'divisory' actions, a judge had to make an *adiudicatio*, whereby he awarded ownership of property to a person who either had not owned the property before, or who had owned the property in common. The object of these actions was to make a division or an adjustment of property:

Julian, *Digest, book 51*: **The actions for dividing common property, for dividing an inherit-ance, and for regulating boundaries are such that in them the individual participants have the double legal status of plaintiff and defendant.** (D.10.1.10.)

The *adiudicatio* of the judge constituted a mode of acquiring ownership: it gave the parties rights that they had not had before. For example, the action for dividing common property allowed a co-owner to own part of it separately. Such actions were not uncommon in cases, e.g., of partnership (see 9.3.4.3). The judge was directed to divide as fairly as he could in the circumstances. Thus, he could order payments to be made by the gainers to the losers if his *adiudicatio* resulted in una-voidable inequality.

The action for dividing an inheritance between joint heirs applied where they failed to agree among themselves as to its distribution. The action dated from at least the Twelve Tables and was available whether the deceased had died testate or intestate. Again, a judge could order equalizing payments to be made if his division was unavoidably unequal in the circumstances.

The action for regulating boundaries often resulted in an *adiudicatio* that had the effect of altering boundaries between neighbours. The judge could order com-pensation for the neighbour who lost land as a result, similar to the equalizing payments mentioned above.

7.3 Gifts

(Inst.2.7., D.39.5., C.5.3.)

Strictly, a gift (*donatio*) was not a mode but a ground of acquisition of ownership, i.e. it constituted *iusta causa* (as we have seen) in *traditio* and *usucapio*. Confusingly, Justinian treats gifts as methods of acquiring ownership (in Inst.2.7pr.). It will there-fore be treated here, though it must be noted that the legal rules on gifts featured primarily in the law of marriage and of inheritance. This section should therefore be read in light of these areas of Roman law. Although there were some minor exceptions when a gift sufficed to pass ownership without the need for a delivery, as a general rule it was the delivery that transferred ownership of the property comprised in a gift.

7.3.1 *Donatio inter vivos*

Such gifts, fully operative in the donor's lifetime, were subject to considerably detailed rules, of which only a brief summary will be attempted.

As regards form, a formal agreement to make a gift, e.g. by *stipulatio* (see gener-ally 9.4.3) was enforceable, but not an informal arrangement, at least in early law. In the Empire the position was gradually relaxed; under Justinian, informal agree-ments became generally enforceable. There were some important restrictions on who could be the parties to a gift. For example, gifts between husbands and wives were banned, as we have seen, with the exception of dowry and *donatio propter nuptias* (see 5.2.5.5). Gifts between a *paterfamilias* and those in his power were gen-erally invalid, but not if the child was out of *potestas*.

Restrictions were placed on the maximum amount of a gift. The *lex Cincia c.*200 BC provided that gifts above a certain limit (unknown) were unenforceable except in favour of relatives. However, if the gift was actually transferred, the donee could retain it. The motivation behind the *lex Cincia* appears to have been the distaste felt in some quarters for ostentation and luxury. The law was intended as a *guide* to sensible behaviour—it seems that there was no effective sanction against its breach. In the later Empire a system of registration of gifts was introduced. Under Justinian, all gifts over 500 *solidi* had to be registered; if unregistered, they were void to the extent of the excess, except for gifts to the Church, to the Emperor, or to charity.

Could the donor change his mind? The general rule was that once a gift was made, it could not be revoked. But if the gift was made subject to a specific limitation or for some stated purpose that was not satisfied, the donor could revoke. A patron could revoke a gift to his freedman for ingratitude. In the late Empire ingratitude by *any* donee became a ground for revocation; and it was provided that a gift to a freedman by his patron was revoked on the birth of a child to the patron if the gift had been made when the patron was childless.

7.3.2 *Donatio mortis causa*

(D.39.6., C.8.56.)

A gift *mortis causa* was a gift made in contemplation of death. Such contemplation could be general, or it could be the result of the fear of some impending danger or specific event:

Paul, *Sabinus, book 7*: **It is permissible to make a gift *mortis causa* not only on grounds of weak health, but also on grounds of impending danger of death due to enemies or robbers or the cruelty or hatred of a powerful man or when about to undertake a sea voyage,** [Gaius, *Common Matters or Golden Words, book* 1][4]: **or to travel through dangerous places,** [Ulpian, *Institutes, book* 2][5]: **or when one is worn out by old age,** [Paul, *Sabinus, book* 7][6]: **since all these circumstances represent impending danger.** (D.39.6.3.–6.)

Such gifts were hybrid in character: they were made *inter vivos*, but did not take full effect until the contemplated death of the donor occurred. Ownership in the property usually passed to the donee on the making of the gift, but the gift was revocable before death. Automatic revocation occurred if the donee predeceased the donor, or if the latter became bankrupt.

The donor of a gift in contemplation of death differed in his motivation from the donor of an *inter vivos* gift, as the following passage explains:

Paul, *Lex Julia et Papia, book 6*: **But a gift *mortis causa* differs considerably from the true and absolute sort of gift which proceeds in such a way that it can in no circumstances be revoked. In that sort of case, of course, the donor wishes the recipient rather than himself to have the property. But the person who makes a gift *mortis causa* is thinking of himself and, loving life, prefers to receive rather than to give. This is why it is commonly said: 'He wishes himself rather than the recipient to have the property, but, that said, wishes the recipient rather than the heir to have it'.** (D.39.6.35.2.)

The special nature of gifts in contemplation of death was evident from the fact that they were not subject to the *lex Cincia* (see 7.3.1); nor did the restrictions on gifts between spouses, or between parents and children, apply. However, as regards form, gifts *mortis causa* could generally be made in the same way as *inter vivos* gifts, and were subject to the registration requirements introduced in the later Empire. Justinian provided an additional method: such gifts could be made in the presence of five witnesses, in which case the effect was similar to that of a testamentary legacy—possession of the property was not transferred until the donor's death.

A gift *mortis causa* obviously bore some resemblance to a testamentary gift. The essential difference was that the former was valid without the need for a will: the gift operated outside (and irrespective of) any will that the donor might have made. Moreover, it seems that in classical law at least the donor could not revoke the gift. Nevertheless, there was a distinct tendency during the Empire to assimilate such gifts with legacies by applying common rules to both.

The concept of gifts *mortis causa* has proved to be an enduring one. Such gifts continue to be made, and the rules applicable in English law are not far different from those of classical Rome (see 11.3.3: *Sen v Headley* [1991] Ch 425). This is not an arcane area of law, irrelevant to modern conditions, but constitutes one of the most practical legacies of Roman law.

 online resource centre Please consult the Online Resource Centre for revision guidance on this chapter.

FURTHER READING

On usufruct, see Daube, D., 'Usufruct and Servitudes' (1955) 71 LQR, 342–5, for a discussion of the relationship between the two institutions. Those with a keen interest in specific aspects of this topic may wish to consult Stein, P. G., 'Generations, Life-spans and Usufructs' (1962) 9 RIDA 3, 335–56; Gordon, W. M., D.33.2.31—'Usufruct and Common Property', in *Studi Grosso* IV, 305–13; Thomas, J. A. C., 'Locare Usumfructum' (1971) IJ, 367–71; Tellegen, J. W. and Tellegen-Couperus, O. E., 'Joint Usufruct in Cicero's Pro Caecina', in *New Perspectives*, 195–205.

On *traditio*, see Gordon, W. J. (1970). *Studies in the Transfer of Property by Traditio*, Aberdeen: Aberdeen University Press, for a discussion of *traditio* (in its various forms) from classical Roman law and throughout the historical development of the European *ius commune* into modern Scots law.

8

....

Inheritance

8.1 Introduction

The importance of inheritance as a means by which property can be acquired is obvious. A Roman citizen might easily pass through life untouched by the rules, say, of usucapion or *accessio*, but he could not escape the operation of the law of inheritance (or at least his estate could not when he died). And he would often have inherited property himself on the death of family members or friends. Moreover, inheritance, unlike most other forms of acquisition of property, involved the transfer of the *whole* of a person's property.

But inheritance was not just a means of transferring property from the deceased to the beneficiaries. Indeed, there could be little or no property to be acquired, only debts and crippling obligations—the *damnosa hereditas* ('the ruinous inheritance'). The main purpose of the will was to appoint an heir to step into the shoes of the deceased and to succeed him for all legal purposes. This was known as the principle of universal succession. In appointing an heir, a Roman testator was particularly concerned (at least until the later Empire) with choosing a suitable person to carry out the family's religious duties—the *sacra*. The deceased's chosen representative was normally someone who was part of the family or very close to it. As heir, he or she was expected to carry out the deceased's wishes, to perform the *sacra*, pay off the debts, distribute the legacies, and generally to act as the deceased's successor in all things. And the heir was frequently the chief beneficiary as well as the administrator of the estate. For a good survey, see Johnston, D., 'Succession', in *Cambridge Companion*, 199–212.

8.2 Better to make a will?

Property was normally inherited either under a will or as the result of an intestacy. The latter occurred where the deceased had died without making a will, or where he had made a will that was not operative.

The frequency of will-making in Roman society has been much debated. There were important reasons why a Roman citizen would wish to make a will—to choose an heir, to provide for his spouse, children, and other family members, and to reward friends, and those who had performed services for him. The making of a will showed a proper sense of responsibility; putting one's affairs in good order was expected of a *paterfamilias*, at least among Rome's wealthier and aristocratic classes.

Moreover, wills offered testators a means of ingratiating themselves and their families with the powerful. Gifts to important citizens, politicians, and generals were frequent; and some Emperors did rather well, judging by the legacies showered on Augustus. Rich men without families were the particular object of legacy hunters. Public interest would be aroused by the death of a rich bachelor, his friends anxious to know how he had distributed his fortune, if they did not know already. Furthermore, the will offered a testator an opportunity to cast judgment—'the last judgment'—on his friends, family, enemies, the Emperor even. Augustus took a particular interest in the wills of leading citizens since such wills were regarded as evidence of what the deceased really believed, however much he had hitherto flattered the Emperor. Moreover, a will could be used to list one's achievements (Augustus took full advantage) or as a means of controlling the testator's family; e.g. unruly children could be threatened with disherison, i.e. exclusion from the will. For a vivid account of the motivation of Roman testators and the process of will-making, see Champlin, E., *Final Judgments: Duty and Emotion in Roman Wills, 200 B.C.–A.D. 250* (1991) as well as Zimmermann, R., '"Unworthiness" in the Roman Law of Succession', in *Judge and Jurist*, 325–44.

There were, in addition, technical reasons why a Roman citizen might prefer to die testate rather than intestate. The application of the law of intestacy could lead to such curious results that a desire to avoid intestacy was perfectly understandable. It has even been suggested that there was a 'horror' of intestacy in Roman society, but that view is an exaggeration. Indeed, some citizens would find the prospect of making a will somewhat uninviting owing to the complexity of the undertaking and the formalities that had to be satisfied.

Despite the variety of reasons for testation, it cannot be maintained that will-making was the norm in the Roman world. Before the extension of citizenship in the Empire, many inhabitants of the Roman world lacked *testamenti factio* (the right to make a will under Roman law) since the population consisted of large numbers of non-citizens, though it has to be assumed that these non-citizens could still make wills according to their own laws. Even among citizens it is doubtful whether will-making was extensive (see Daube, D., 'The Preponderance of Intestacy in Rome' (1964–5) 39 Tulane LR, 253–62; Cherry, D., 'Intestacy and the Roman Poor' (1996) 64 TR, 155–72). It is true that juristic discussion in the *Digest* of problems arising from wills overwhelmingly exceeds that devoted to intestacy, but this is hardly conclusive: the law relating to wills was far more extensive and complex than the law of intestacy. Furthermore, some citizens were restricted from making wills, while others would have little or nothing to leave. The latter constituted the bulk of the population, such were the economic realities: 'Why or how would the poor chaps who slept under the bridges of the Tiber make a will? They had nothing to make a will about, nor the wherewithal to engage the cheapest lawyer to draw it up' (Daube, *Roman Law*, 71 ff.). If the have-nots had made wills, Daube suggests that the provisions would have run as follows: 'Let my three sons Titius, Maevius and Sempronius be my heirs. I leave them my entire possessions, consisting of the shirt and the sandals I am wearing, in equal parts, with a usufruct for my widow for life' (75). Now this is all very entertaining but it assumes that the sole purpose of making a will was to *leave* something, and yet it is clear that wills were made for a variety of reasons, as outlined earlier. Would not those eligible to make wills be concerned, for example, about the performance of the *sacra* after their death, whatever their means (apart from those sleeping rough by the Tiber)?

Roman writers occasionally give the impression of Rome as a will-obsessed society in which the witnessing of wills was one of the tasks of daily life. But most citizens of Rome would not have found the witnessing of wills to be one of life's daily concerns. No doubt, will-making was the norm for the Roman propertied classes. No doubt, some poor citizens made wills. But the majority of citizens probably died intestate. It seems, however, that there was a keen interest taken in the operation of the law of inheritance. Disputes about wills were a staple diet of civil litigation and aroused considerable public comment. Justinian's compilers devoted a great deal of space to the law of inheritance—about one-quarter of the *Digest* and the *Institutes*—although this cannot be taken as conclusive evidence of the prevalence of inheritance cases in practice.

8.3 Intestacy

The comparative simplicity of the law of intestacy serves well as an introduction to the more complex law relating to wills: the latter can be better appreciated if intestacy has been dealt with first. The law of intestacy applied when there was no operative will, which occurred if a person failed to make a will or made one which lacked legal effect (e.g. for want of proper form or heirs). The law probably emerged at a very early date and was then enacted in the Twelve Tables. It was subjected to praetorian intervention in the later Republic, legislative modification in the classical period, and all embracing reform by Justinian. As such, it is a textbook case of the rise and decline of certain sources of law and the way in which these sources affected the original *ius civile* rules. For a survey of the most important texts, see Frier and McGinn, *Casebook*, 323–38.

8.3.1 Intestacy under the Twelve Tables

(Inst.Gai.3.1.–76., Inst.3.1., D.38.16.)

The *order* of succession under the Twelve Tables to the estates of freeborn persons was (a) *sui heredes*, (b) the nearest agnate, (c) the *gens*.

8.3.1.1 *Sui heredes*

These were the persons who became *sui iuris* on the death of the deceased, i.e. all those who had been in his power, comprising children, remoter issue through the male line (e.g. grandchildren), and a wife in a *manus* marriage (who was regarded for this purpose as his daughter). This statement requires qualification. The sons became *sui iuris* (where the deceased father had been *paterfamilias*). The children of the sons (i.e. the grandchildren of the deceased *paterfamilias*) came under the *potestas* of their father. The widow, since she had severed all ties of *potestas* through marriage, became *sui iuris*, but was subjected to lifelong guardianship (*tutela mulierum*). Neither an emancipated child nor a wife in a free marriage (infrequent in the early Republic) had a claim within the class of *sui heredes*; nor were they within the subsequent classes—they had no claim at all. The description *sui heredes* ('heirs to themselves') emphasizes that the members of this category were regarded as succeeding to what was rightfully theirs by virtue of their relationship with the deceased:

Paul, *Sabinus, book 2*: **In the case of *sui heredes*, it is more clearly evident that the continuation of ownership leads to this, that no inheritance is regarded as having taken place, as if they were already owners, being thought of as in some sense owners even in the lifetime of the father.** (D.28.2.11.)

Children adopted by the deceased were *sui heredes*; so were issue who had been conceived (but not born) at the time of the deceased's death, providing that they would have been in his *potestas* had he survived. Stirpital representation applied (each of the deceased persons' children and their families formed a separate stem (stirps) for the purposes of inheritance): grandchildren (or remoter issue) took the share that their deceased parent would have taken, i.e. they 'represented' the parent. For example, suppose that A died intestate survived by two sons, B and C, and a grandson, D, the child of E, a deceased son of A. D would take the share that his father would have taken. The inheritance would thus be shared equally between B, C, and D. The position would be the same even if B and C had children of their own. Such children would be A's grandchildren but, unlike D, they would not have become *sui iuris* on his death, and therefore were not *sui heredes*. The succession of *sui heredes* on an intestacy was automatic. Acceptance was not required on their part since they could not refuse the inheritance.

8.3.1.2 **The nearest agnate**

If there were no *sui heredes*, the inheritance passed to the nearest agnate. In practice, this would often be a brother or sister of the intestate. If there were two or more nearest agnates, i.e. of the same class (e.g. two brothers), they took equally *per capita*—there was no stirpital representation in this case. Women could take within this class until the later Republic when they were barred, possibly on reasons analogous to the *lex Voconia* 169 BC (see Van der Meer, T., 'The Voconian Law: Nova or Phoenix?' (1999) 67 TR, 115–23). The exception was that sisters of the intestate were not excluded from taking. The nearest agnate could refuse to accept the inheritance, in which case it passed to the *gens* (see below), not to the next nearest agnate. When was it determined who was the nearest agnate? Gaius states (Inst. Gai.3.11.) that the relevant time was when it was established that an intestacy had occurred. That would usually be when the intestate died, but not necessarily: he may have left a will which was not shown to be invalid until some time after his death. In that case the intestacy was not established until that later time.

8.3.1.3 **The *gens***

If there were no *sui heredes*, and no nearest agnate prepared to accept, the estate passed to the *gens*, i.e. the deceased's clan. Succession by the *gens* lends some support to the view that the concept of community of property was known to early Rome; but it is not clear how the rule operated in practice. Succession by the *gens* declined as an institution during the Republic and became obsolete in the classical period.

8.3.2 **Praetorian intervention**

Commenting on the intestacy law of the Twelve Tables, Gaius describes it as 'strictum', i.e. narrow, tight (Inst.Gai.3.18.). The main drawbacks stemmed from the constraints of agnatic relationship. Among the persons excluded from claiming were emancipated children and descendants traced through the female line.

Spouses could not succeed each other, except a widow in the case of a *manus* marriage. Mothers and children could not succeed each other, again except in the case of a *manus* marriage.

Some of these flaws, but not all, were remedied by praetorian intervention. The praetor could not declare anyone to be heir other than the person entitled under the *ius civile*. But the praetor was prepared to remedy perceived unfairness by allowing a deserving claimant to have *bonorum possessio* ('possession of property') of the whole or part of the estate, thereby reducing or even negating the entitlement of the *ius civile* heir. A claim for *bonorum possessio* had to be made within a year in the case of ascendants or descendants, otherwise within 100 days, the period running from the time when the claimant became aware of his rights (or should have done so) and was able to make the claim. Awareness of the right to claim was judged by the test of the *bonus paterfamilias*:

Ulpian, *Edict, book 49*: **The knowledge required, Pomponius says, is not that which is expected of those skilled in the law, but that which everyone was capable of acquiring either independently or through others, that is to say, by consulting those wiser than himself in the way in which it is right and proper for a careful head of a household to take advice.** (D.38.15.2.5.)

The result of praetorian intervention was that an alternative law of intestacy emerged alongside the *ius civile* rules under the Twelve Tables. Praetorian intervention mitigated some of the worst anomalies in the *ius civile* rules.

8.3.2.1 The praetorian order of succession

The thrust of the praetorian scheme was the greater recognition of the *blood tie*, i.e. the rights of cognates:

Ulpian, *Edict, book 44*: **But he divided succession on intestacy into several parts; for he made different degrees, the first of children, the second of heirs at law, the third of cognate relations, and then of husband and wife.** (D.38.6.1.1.)

This order of succession operated, as in the case of the Twelve Tables scheme, as an *order*—if there was a member of a prior class, those in subsequent classes were excluded.

(a) Children (*liberi*). The important difference from the *ius civile* rules was that the *emancipated children* of the intestate were entitled. The class included children who had been given in adoption by the intestate and then emancipated by their adoptive father before the intestate's death. If two or more children were entitled to *bonorum possessio*, they took equally. Stirpital representation applied, enabling the issue of a deceased child of the intestate to take the share that their parent would otherwise have taken.

The inclusion of emancipated children could pose problems. A son from a wealthy home might be given substantial property on emancipation, and would probably acquire more thereafter. A daughter would sometimes be emancipated on her marriage and be given a dowry. Was it not unfair to allow such children to share the intestate estate equally with the unemancipated children? The praetor certainly thought so—he required a *collatio bonorum* ('a bringing together of property') whereby the emancipated child had to bring into account whatever had been acquired on emancipation and thereafter, subject to a few exceptions, e.g. property acquired in military or State service.

Another complication that arose from the admission of an emancipated child to an intestate estate occurred if that child had children of his own. If, on his emancipation, they remained in the power of their *paterfamilias*, i.e. the grandfather, their rights as *sui heredes* (to the grandfather's intestate estate) would be threatened by their father's application for *bonorum possessio*. If the application succeeded, the grandchildren might be excluded since they were remoter to the deceased than their father. However, the praetorian edict was eventually amended so that the emancipated child and his children took one single share between them—half to the father, half to the children—subject to his having to make a *collatio bonorum*.

(b) Heirs-at-law (*legitimi*). This class comprised those who had a claim under the Twelve Tables, other than children claiming as *liberi*. The person most likely to be entitled in this class was the nearest agnate. If that agnate did not claim *bonorum possessio*, remoter agnates were excluded.

(c) Cognates. If there was no successful claimant within the first two classes, the nearest cognates took. This was a potentially large class, consisting of blood relations within the sixth (Roman) degree of relationship. If there were two or more nearest cognates, they took equally. There was no stirpital representation. Since this class comprised cognates, relations traced through females were eligible. Children could thus succeed their mothers, and vice versa. The class included children given in adoption, and adoptive relatives (despite the lack of blood tie) providing that there was an agnatic tie between them:

Ulpian, *Edict, book 46*:...It comes about, therefore, that a person given in adoption retains the rights of cognate relationship in the family of his natural father, as much as he acquires them in his adoptive family, but he only acquires such relationship in his adoptive family with those to whom he becomes an agnate, but in his natural family, he will retain his relationship with all members. (D.38.8.1.4.)

(d) Husband and wife. If there were no claimants within the previous classes, the surviving spouse of the intestate was entitled to *bonorum possessio*. This rule was not applicable to a widow in a *manus* marriage since she was in the class of *sui heredes* under the Twelve Tables, and thus qualified as an heir-at-law in the praetorian scheme.

This order of intestate succession was clearly an improvement on the arcane rules of the Twelve Tables. The greater emphasis on the blood tie no doubt reflected the realities of family relationships more closely than the *ius civile* rules. It should not be assumed, however, that *bonorum possessio* was exclusively a weapon against the *ius civile* heir. Quite often such an heir would himself apply for *bonorum possessio* in order to obtain more convenient remedies to enforce his rights than those already afforded him under the *ius civile*.

8.3.2.2 Operation of the *bonorum possessio* system

(Inst.Gai.2.147.–50., Inst.3.9., and various titles in D.37. and C.6.)

Claims for *bonorum possessio* were made before the praetor. If a *prima facie* case was made out, the praetor would make the appropriate grant, entitling the claimant to seek possession of the estate. But this was no more than a preliminary *ex parte* hearing. The grant did not vest actual possession in the claimant; it simply entitled him to seek the appropriate remedies (normally the interdict *quorum bonorum*) to obtain possession. It was only when those remedies were actually sought that the issue whether the claimant was entitled to actual possession of the estate would be fully explored. Even the grant of a remedy was not necessarily the final resolution of the matter, since the *ius civile* heir might attempt to protect his position by his chief remedy, the *hereditatis petitio* ('the seeking of the inheritance').

Whether the successful grantee of *bonorum possessio* eventually prevailed depended on the type of grant. If the grant was *cum re* (i.e. where there was no civil heir or the praetor had intervened to change the existing inequitable ruling) the position of the grantee was in effect indefeasible: the *hereditatis petitio* of the heir could be successfully resisted by an *exceptio doli* ('the defence of fraud') in favour of the grantee. If the grant was *sine re* (i.e. where *bonorum possessio* was merely granted provisionally, subject to the appearance of a civil heir), the grantee was not entitled to plead a defence; the heir prevailed if he proved his entitlement.

What was the benefit, if any, of a grant of *bonorum possessio sine re*? Superficially, the grantee's position appears weak—it seems that the heir needs only to appear and prove his entitlement in order to prevail. However, the onus is on the heir— he must appear, and within a year, otherwise the grantee will become *dominus* through usucapion. Who knows what misfortune may befall the heir en route to court? And even if he appears, he will still have to prove his entitlement—possibly a difficult task in some circumstances. It was definitely worth having a grant *sine re*.

What determined whether a grant was made *cum re* or *sine re*? No clear principle can be asserted. Much could depend on the circumstances and on the identity of the claimant. For example, if an heir or *liberi* obtained *bonorum possessio*, it was normally *cum re*. If there were two (or more) applicants, it was possible for one to be made a grant *cum re*, the other a grant *sine re* (in appropriate circumstances). The general rule during the Republic was that grants were made *sine re*; but in the classical period the tendency was increasingly for grants to be made *cum re*. By the late Empire, grants *sine re* had become rare.

8.3.3 Classical legislation

A number of enactments were made in the classical period affecting succession on intestacy. The most important were the *S. C. Tertullianum c.* AD 130 and the *S. C. Orphitianum* AD 178. See Frier and McGinn, *Casebook*, 339–41.

8.3.3.1 *S. C. Tertullianum*

(Inst.3.3., D.38.17., C.6.56.)

This was probably the first resolution of the Senate to be formally recognized as having direct, binding legal force (see 2.3.2.2). The purpose was to improve the position of mothers as regards the *intestate estates* of their children. Under the Twelve Tables, a mother had no rights of intestate succession to her children, as we have seen, except if she was a wife in a *manus* marriage. The *S. C. Tertullianum* applied to mothers with the *ius liberorum*, i.e. those who had given birth to three children or more (four if a freedwoman). This statute was partly a throwback to the Augustan policy of encouraging an increase in the birth rate. On the death intestate of the mother's child, the order of succession was as follows: *liberi* (of the intestate); father; brothers of the whole blood; sisters of the whole blood and the mother—the sisters and the mother formed one class. Thus, the mother took if the intestate child died without issue and a father and a brother of the whole blood.

If any sisters survived the intestate, the mother took half, the other half going to the sister(s). In the later Empire the Tertullian order was applied to mothers even if they failed to satisfy the requirements of the *ius liberorum*.

As a general rule, the *S. C. Tertullianum* was not intended to alter the order of succession under the previous law, but to provide a different scheme in the particular scenario specified. Indeed, it was an important principle under the enactment that it was not to give a person, apart from the mother, any greater rights than under the previous law.

8.3.3.2 *S. C. Orphitianum*

(Inst.3.4.)

This enactment dealt with the converse case—the rights of children to succeed on their mother's intestacy. It represented a major departure from the old principle of agnatic succession because it gave children, whether legitimate or illegitimate, the primary right to succeed to their mother's estate. Previously, under the *ius civile*, the nearest agnate would have taken.

These two *senatus consulta* constituted a radical change in some respects—the first recognition of the blood tie in the *ius civile* law of intestacy. But the reform was rather narrow in scope: 'What puzzles us concerning these two enactments is not that succession is granted to blood-relations, but that this was done so reluctantly and incompletely' (Schulz, F., *Classical Roman Law* (1951), 226–7).

8.3.4 **Justinian's reforms**

In the later Empire, further modifications were made to the law of intestacy, mostly aimed at diminishing the relevance of agnatic succession. Justinian introduced a new scheme of intestate succession (in *Novellae* enacted in AD 543 and 548) whereby the old rules and concepts were replaced by a system that emphasized the cognatic relationship. However, Justinian's scheme preserved the familiar rule that membership of a prior class excluded subsequent classes. The order was as follows:

(a) Descendants. This class comprised children and remoter issue, the nearer excluding the more remote. Descendants were determined purely by blood, except that adopted children were included. The principle of stirpital representation applied, so that remoter issue took the share that their parents would have taken had the latter not predeceased the intestate.

(b) Ascendants and full brothers and sisters. This was a single category—if the intestate was survived by ascendants *and* brothers and sisters of the whole blood, then they all shared equally. Stirpital representation applied to deceased brothers and sisters. Thus, if Balbus died intestate, survived by his father, brother, and a nephew (the child of a deceased sister), they each took one third of the estate. However, the representation rule applied only if there was a surviving brother or sister. Therefore, if only his father and a nephew had survived Balbus, the father took the whole inheritance. If no ascendant survived, the property went exclusively to any brothers and sisters of the whole blood, stirpital representation applying. Where the intestate was survived by two or more ascendants, the nearer excluded the more remote, e.g. a father of the intestate would exclude the grandfather.

(c) Brothers and sisters of the half-blood. Stirpital representation applied: children of deceased members of this category took the share that would have gone to their parent.

(d) Nearest other collaterals. They shared equally if they were of equal degree; if not, the nearer degree excluded the more remote. There was no stirpital representation.

(e) Surviving spouse. The surviving spouse appears rather low in the order compared to modern systems of intestacy (under which the spouse often takes the bulk of the estate). However, the rules on the destination of the dowry on the death of a spouse were of considerable benefit to the survivor. Rights in the dowry, if unsatisfied from the dotal property, were a first charge on the deceased's estate under Justinian (see 5.2.5.4).

If there were no claimants in the above categories, the estate passed to the imperial treasury as *bona vacantia*, i.e. unclaimed property. The concept of *bona vacantia* has survived to the present day, as has much of Justinian's intestacy regime. Apart from the relatively low position (within the order) of the surviving spouse, the rules would not seem out of place in modern law. For example, in both French and German law children are regarded as the primary heirs to the exclusion of other relatives. This is subject to the right of the surviving spouse to a quarter of the estate absolutely (German law) or to a usufruct in a quarter (French law). See Stein, *Legal Institutions*, 178–9. (This rule only applies, however, where there are children and a surviving spouse. If one or all of the children have predeceased, the spouse will receive more than a quarter of the estate.)

8.4 Making a will

(Inst.Gai.2.100.–50., D.28.1.)

Modestinus, *Encyclopaedia, book 2*: **A will is a lawful expression of our wishes concerning what someone wishes to be done after his death.** (D.28.1.1.)

A Roman testator's main wish would be to appoint an heir. A will without an effective appointment of an heir was invalid. In addition, the typical Roman will contained legacies for the testator's family, friends, and other beneficiaries, and might manumit slaves and appoint guardians. Apart from the appointment of an heir, the other essentials of a valid will were that the testator should have the required capacity, and that the proper form should be followed. Gaius states:

Gaius, *Institutes, book 2*: **If we are inquiring whether a will is valid, we ought first of all to consider whether the person who made the will had *testamenti factio*, and then, if he did have it, we may investigate whether he made a will in accordance with the rules of the civil law.** (D.28.1.4.)

Let us follow Gaius' advice.

8.4.1 Capacity

Capacity in relation to wills (*testamenti factio*) comprised three discrete aspects: the testator had to have capacity to make the will; a witness required capacity to perform his function; and an heir or legatee needed capacity to take under a will.

8.4.1.1 **Capacity to make a will**

Labeo, *Posthumous Works, Epitomized by Javolenus, book 1*: **In the case of someone who is making his will, at the time when he makes the will, soundness of mind is required, not health of body.** (D.28.1.2.)

As Labeo makes clear, the testator had to have capacity at the time he made the will. Moreover, the capacity had to continue, as a general rule, until the testator's death. If he lost capacity, the will failed, even if capacity was restored before death. That at least was the strict *ius civile* position. The praetor, however, would often grant *bonorum possessio* in such a case to the heirs under the failed will.

The basic requirements for capacity to make a will were that the testator should be a citizen of full age, i.e. the age of puberty, and *sui iuris*:

Gaius, *Provincial Edict, book 17*: **A person in parental power has not the right to make a will, and this is so much the case that even if his father gives him permission, he still cannot thereby lawfully make a will.** (D.28.1.6pr.)

This text certainly represents the general rule, but there were exceptions. For example, a son-in-power could make a will of his *peculium castrense* (see 5.1.2.2) while on military service and, after Hadrian, even after leaving service. And there were exceptions to the rule that non-citizens could not make wills. For example, *servi publici* (public slaves) could leave half their *peculium* by will.

An insane person obviously lacked capacity, but could make a will during a lucid interval. If a will had been made before the onset of insanity, it remained valid—an exception to the general rule on loss of capacity. Persons declared to be *intestabiles* (see 4.4.2.6) lacked capacity to make a will; so did prodigals while subject to the interdict restraining them from acting independently. However, any will made before the interdict was valid:

Ulpian, *Sabinus, book 1*: **A person interdicted by statute from managing his property cannot make a will, and if he has done so, it is invalid by operation of law; but any will which he may have antedating the interdiction will be valid....** (D.28.1.18pr.)

The position as regards women was more complicated. Originally, women lacked capacity since they could not take part in the procedure necessary for a comitial will, the earliest type of will known to Rome (see 8.4.2.1). Later, when the mancipatory will (see 8.4.2.3) became standard, the general rule emerged that freeborn women could make wills if their guardian consented (but he had no control over the will's provisions). Since consent was compellable, except in the case of a statutory guardian, many women obtained an unrestricted right of testation. As for freedwomen, the basic rule was that they could make wills only with their patron's consent.

8.4.1.2 **Capacity to witness a will**

Most of the persons who lacked capacity to make wills were also incapable of witnessing them, e.g. interdicted prodigals, *intestabiles*, and the insane (except in a lucid interval). But some could witness a will even if they could not make one, and vice versa. It is not possible to state a general principle other than that a witness normally had to be a male citizen above puberty. Consequently, women could not witness wills (although they could make them). Late classical texts state that Latins, including Junian, could be witnesses; but this conflicts with Gaius, at least as regards the mancipatory will (Inst.Gai.2.104.). Slaves were excluded:

Ulpian, *Sabinus, book 1*: **It is also right that a slave cannot be used in solemn acts as he is totally excluded from participation in the civil law, and even in the praetor's edict.** (D.28.1.20.7.)

However, where a person acted as witness, and was believed to be entitled to do so, the attestation was valid even though it later transpired that the witness had been a slave. Persons who belonged to the family of the testator were excluded from acting as witnesses. But heirs, if unrelated to the testator, could act as witnesses to the will under which they were appointed. Gaius advised against this practice (Inst.Gai.2.108.) and Justinian went a step further by barring heirs. Legatees, on the other hand, were never barred from witnessing the will that benefited them. The same is true of modern English law but the English legatee, unlike the Roman one, cannot take the gift. The potential conflict of interests that arises when the same person is both beneficiary and witness did not appear to worry the Romans sufficiently to lead them to change their rule. Horace had the following advice for the witness asked to peruse a will: 'Say no, and put the tablets aside; but get a quick glance at page one line two—whether you are sole heir or co-heir with a multitude' (*Satires* II, V, 51 ff., quoted in Crook, *Law and Life of Rome*, 128). The witness had to have capacity at the time of witnessing the will, i.e. when he affixed his seal to the will:

Ulpian, *Edict, book 39*: **We ought to examine the condition of witnesses at the time when they sealed the will not at the time of death; if, therefore, they were suitable persons to be used when they sealed, it does not matter what may have happened to them afterward.** (D.28.1.22.1.)

The witness had to understand that he was witnessing a will (unlike English law where it suffices for the *signature* of the testator to be witnessed). However, the witness did not have to know or understand the contents of the will.

8.4.1.3 Capacity to take under a will

In order to take under a will, a person had to have *testamenti factio* (which in this context was described as 'passive' and meant the right to be appointed an heir or be made a legatee) and the *ius capiendi*—the right actually to take under the will. A person with *testamenti factio* would normally have the *ius capiendi*, but not necessarily, as we shall see later.

Basically, anyone with *commercium* had passive *testamenti factio*; but no general principle can be formulated to account for all the persons who were regarded as lacking capacity—it is necessary to deal with specific cases. Foreigners, *dediticii*, and *intestabiles* were excluded, as were miscreants such as heretics (under Justinian) and widows who remarried within the customary period of mourning. Some cases, however, require special consideration:

(a) Slaves. They could be appointed heirs and made legatees, but could only take when manumitted. It was normal for a master to free his slave in the will when conferring such benefits. If a slave was made heir in someone else's will, he could not accept the inheritance without his master's permission.

(b) Women. Under the *lex Voconia* 169 BC, a woman could not be appointed as an heir by a testator who was listed in the wealthiest class of citizens in the census.

The purpose of this law has been much debated. See Gardner, *Women in Roman Law*, 170–8. Traditionally, it has been seen as an attempt to prevent the concentration of a large amount of wealth in women's hands, which otherwise might result in the dissipation of important family assets through women's supposed (by men) extravagance or lack of financial judgement. But Cicero commented that the law was passed 'for the advantage of men' (*De republica*, 3.17.) by which he probably meant that the assets of wealthy families were needed by sons who aspired to make their mark in public life: 'Voconius' law may have been meant to ensure that at least a sizeable portion of large patrimonies would always pass directly into male hands and be available for the purposes of male public life' (Gardner, *Women in Roman Law*, 176). Apart from this legislation, and the exclusion from benefiting under the comitial will (see 8.4.2.1), women were not restricted in their capacity to take. And the *lex Voconia* did not prove to be a permanent irritant—it became obsolete in the early Empire.

(c) Religious beneficiaries. In pagan times gifts to the gods became public property. After the conversion to Christianity, the Church was regarded as having capacity to take, the gift being administered by the bishop of the locality of the testator.

(d) Incertae personae. 'Unascertained persons' were those who were described in such a general way that many people could qualify within the description—e.g. 'whoever comes to my funeral'; 'the first persons to become consuls after my death' (Inst.Gai.2.238.). Their precise identity was unknown to the testator. However, such persons could take if they were within a defined class, e.g. 'whichever of my relatives now living is the first to arrive at my funeral'.

The most important category of unascertained persons consisted of *postumi*—those born after the making of the testator's will. The general rule in early law was that persons could not take under a will made before their birth. This rule caused such serious problems that it was gradually whittled away, thus enabling *postumi* to benefit in classical law (see 8.7.1.1). However, *postumi* other than the issue of the testator could not take until Justinian, subject to a possible *bonorum possessio* from the praetor.

A beneficiary had to have capacity when the will was made (another reason for the original exclusion of *postumi*) and when the will became operative, i.e. on the testator's death. Intervening lack of capacity was discounted, however:

Ulpian, *Sabinus, book 4*: **We are accustomed to say that intervening periods are not prejudicial…such as when, say, a Roman citizen who has been appointed heir became a peregrine in the lifetime of the testator and then attained Roman citizenship; the periods in between do not prejudice him.** (D.28.5.6.2.)

8.4.1.4 Ius capiendi ('The right to take')

Certain persons had *testamenti factio* but not *ius capiendi*. That meant that they could not take under a will without satisfying certain conditions. For example, Junian Latins could not take unless they became citizens before the expiry of the time allowed for the acceptance of an inheritance. This rule was part of the Augustan policy aimed at encouraging marriage and increasing the birth rate. So were the provisions of the *leges caducariae*, i.e. the *lex Julia de maritandis ordinibus* 18 BC and the *lex Papia Poppaea* AD 9, which penalized the unmarried and the childless: unmarried men aged between 25 and 60, and unmarried women between

20 and 50 could take nothing under a will, while married persons without children could take only a half (but only one-tenth under a will of their spouse). These penalties could be avoided if the requirements of the legislation were satisfied before it was too late to claim under the will. There were important exceptions to the *leges caducariae*: they did not apply, for example, to ascendants and descendants of the testator to the third degree, or to cognates to the sixth degree. Such relations had the *ius capiendi* even if they were unmarried or childless.

What happened to the gifts that were wholly or partially forfeited by the operation of the *leges caducariae*? The general rule was that they passed to the other heirs under the will providing that they had children. In the absence of such heirs the gifts went to legatees with children, failing whom the Treasury took. If there were ascendants or descendants to the third degree among the heirs or legatees, they took their share of the forfeited gifts, even if they had no children. These provisions of the *leges caducariae*, like so much of Augustus's social engineering legislation, proved somewhat unpopular; but they appear to have survived until the conversion to Christianity, when the state's interest in increasing the birth rate ceased.

8.4.2 **Formalities**

Various types of will were known in the history of Roman law, each with its own specific formal requirements. Gaius tells us (Inst.Gai.2.101.) that originally there were two kinds of will: the comitial will and the will *in procinctu* ('prepared for battle'). There later followed the mancipatory will, the praetorian will, the tripartite will, and other forms of will-making.

8.4.2.1 **Comitial will**

The earliest Roman will was very much a public affair, made before the *comitia curiata*. The will, having received prior pontifical approval, was declared to the assembly. It is not clear whether the assembly's function was to vote for the will or simply to witness it. The public element in this form of will was probably prompted by the need to supervise any potential departure from the intestacy rights of *sui heredes*. Not surprisingly, the life of the comitial will did not prove enduring: it became obsolete during the Republic.

8.4.2.2 **Will** *in procinctu*

This was the wartime counterpart of the comitial will. It consisted of a declaration by a soldier of his wishes before his comrades (those who fought beside him) *in proelium*, i.e. before battle (Inst.Gai.2.101.). It became obsolete by the late Republic.

8.4.2.3 **The mancipatory will**

This form of will became the standard *ius civile* will from the early Republic to the later Empire. It originally consisted of a *mancipatio* (with witnesses and a scale holder) of the testator's estate to a *familiae emptor*—a 'buyer of the estate'. He was given oral instructions by the testator as to how the estate was to be distributed. Gaius describes the *familiae emptor* as originally being in the position of an heir (Inst.Gai.2.103.); but in reality he probably acted more like a trustee. Whatever the case, he had to carry out the testator's expressed wishes.

By the late Republic the form had changed radically. A *mancipatio* was still necessary, but the *familiae emptor* was present in a purely formal capacity—to validate the transaction. And it became the practice to write down the testator's instructions on wax tablets; the written record in the tablets became the actual will. Once the record became the essence of the mancipatory will, important consequences followed. The will was now secret, if the testator so desired, revocable and operated only on death (the early mancipatory will had been similar to an *inter vivos* transaction).

There was never a need for the will to be signed by the testator, although he was apparently required to grasp it during the *mancipatio*. The will did not have to be written by the testator—an amanuensis could do it. One of the most remarkable passages in the *Digest* suggests some uncertainty (and a distinct lack of politeness) among the jurists over the question whether an amanuensis could be regarded as a witness:

Celsus, *Digest, book 15*: **Domitius Labeo to Celsus, his friend, greetings. I ask you whether a person, who, when he had been asked to write a will, also sealed the will when he had written it, is to be regarded as one of the witnesses. Juventius Celsus to Labeo, his friend, greetings. I do not understand what it is that you have consulted me about, or else your consultation is really stupid; for it is more than ridiculous to doubt whether someone has been lawfully used as a witness, when he also wrote the will.** (D.28.1.27.)

The witnesses to the *mancipatio*, together with the scale holder and the *familiae emptor*, had to write their names in the will and had to seal it (usually done with a ring). The various formalities had to be carried out as essentially one transaction; an interruption could invalidate the will:

Ulpian, *Sabinus, book 2*: **A will ought to be made in one continuous act. By 'one continuous act' is meant that no act unconnected with the will should intervene; but if he [the testator] does something relevant to the will, the will is not vitiated.** (D.28.1.21.3.)

In English law, the position is different: the necessary formalities for executing a will need not be carried out in one operation. However, it has been held that where a testator signs a will before writing out its provisions, the will is invalid unless these things were done as 'all one operation': *Wood v Smith* [1992] 3 All ER 556, CA.

In the classical period, although the theoretical necessity for a *mancipatio* continued, it seems that the ceremony was increasingly omitted in practice. It sufficed if the will stated that a *mancipatio* had been performed.

8.4.2.4 The praetorian will

Although the mancipatory will was far more convenient than the comitial will, it was nevertheless an unwieldy creature, certainly as long as an actual mancipation was required. So the praetors were prepared to grant *bonorum possessio* to an heir appointed in a will that was sealed by seven witnesses, even though no *mancipatio* had been performed. At first, the grant was normally made *sine re*, which meant that the heir under the praetorian will would be defeated by those entitled as the *ius civile* heirs on intestacy, if they proved their entitlement. But in the classical period the praetorian heir was normally successful since grants were increasingly made *cum re* (depending on the circumstances).

Although the praetorian will became effective in practice to pass the inheritance to the appointed heir, there is no clear evidence that it was efficacious in other respects. It seems, for example, that it could not be used to manumit slaves formally or to appoint guardians. Nevertheless, the result of praetorian intervention was to add a considerable measure of flexibility to will-making in Rome for several centuries, even if some confusion and uncertainty may have been caused thereby.

8.4.2.5 Wills in the late Empire

A number of changes occurred in the late Empire concerning formalities for making wills. By far the most important innovation was the tripartite will. It became the standard form of will following its introduction by Theodosius II in AD 439. It was named *tripartitum* because its formal requirements were drawn from three sources—the *ius civile*, praetorian law, and imperial innovation. The will had to be made before seven witnesses, who had to seal it; and it had to contain a *subscriptio* by the testator and witnesses—an acknowledgment, usually in the form of a signature (with appropriate words) of the document.

Moreover, it was possible in late law to make public, nuncupative, and holograph wills. Public wills were those entered on the records of a court or deposited in State archives. They did not need witnesses other than the appropriate officials. The nuncupative will was an oral declaration of the testator's wishes before seven witnesses. Holograph wills, i.e. those written entirely in the testator's hand, were accepted under Constantine as operative, even if not witnessed, for the purpose of benefiting *descendants*. They were later regarded as valid for all purposes, but Justinian confined them, if unwitnessed, to benefiting descendants only.

8.4.2.6 Soldiers' wills

The formal requirements of a mancipatory will were ill-suited to soldiers on active military service, although such wills were occasionally made by soldiers. See Crook, *Law and Life of Rome*, 131–2 for the text of the will of a Roman trooper made in Alexandria in AD 142. It seems that soldiers were first allowed to make wills informally under Julius Caesar, long after the will in *procinctu* had become obsolete. Eventually, Trajan (end of the first century AD) regularized the position by mandate:

Ulpian, *Edict, book 45*:…following the openness of my heart toward those excellent and most faithful fellow soldiers, I thought that provision should be made for their inexperience [in legal matters], so that whatever the way in which they made their wills, their wishes should be confirmed. Therefore, let them make their wills in any way they wish, let them make them in any way they can, and let the bare wishes of the testator suffice to settle the distribution of their property. (D.29.1.1pr.)

As the mandate confirms, the will could take virtually any form but there had to be some evidence of the testator's wishes. Oral wills were acceptable as long as a beneficiary was not the sole witness. The will remained valid during the period of service and for a year after discharge. The privilege extended to the substantive content of the will in that some of the rules and restrictions that were generally applicable to testators had no application to soldiers' wills, e.g. foreigners and Junian Latins could be made heirs; the *lex Falcidia* did not apply (see 8.6.3); nor did the *querela* procedure (see 8.7.2). The privilege of making an informal will was not restricted solely to soldiers:

Ulpian, *Edict, book 45*: Likewise, there is no doubt that ships' masters and captains of the triremes of the fleets can make a will according to military law. In the fleets, all the rowers and sailors count as soldiers. Likewise, watchmen are soldiers, and there is no doubt that they can make a will in accordance with military law. (D.37.13.1.1.)

English law retains a concept of privileged wills for soldiers and seamen that owes something to Roman law. It is said that the draftsman of the Statute of Frauds 1677—which first allowed English soldiers to make privileged wills—was versed in Roman law. And in *Drummond v Parish* (1843) 3 Curt 522, 163 ER 812, Fust J traced the privilege granted to soldiers back to Julius Caesar and suggested that Roman law should be used as an aid to interpreting the English legislation. However, there are important differences, e.g. the English soldier's will remains valid until revoked, i.e. it does not lapse after a year following discharge.

8.4.3 Appointment of heirs

(Inst.Gai.2.152.–73., Inst.2.14., D.28.5., C.6.24.)

A will was invalid unless it contained the appointment of an heir (*institutio heredis*). Gaius described the appointment of an heir as 'the source and foundation of the whole will' (Inst.Gai.2.229.). Indeed, a will did not have to contain any other provision:

Ulpian, *Sabinus, book 1*: **Someone who does not propose to leave legacies and does not propose to disinherit anyone can make his will in five words, as by saying 'Lucius Titius be my heir'; however, what is written here relates to someone who is not making his will in writing. And he will be able to make his will even in three words, as by saying 'Lucius be heir'; for both 'my' and 'Titius' are superfluous.** (D.28.5.1.3.)

Surprisingly, the English will can match the Roman for economy of words: in *Thorn v Dickens* [1906] WN 54, 'All for mother' was held to constitute a valid will (in favour of the testator's wife). It is hard to envisage a will—in English or Roman law—consisting of less than three words.

8.4.3.1 Form of appointment

Ulpian, *Sabinus, book 1*: **A person who is making a will should generally start the will with the institution of the heir. It is also permissible to begin with a disherison which he makes by name; for the deified Trajan said in a rescript that it is possible to disinherit a son by name even before the institution of the heir.** (D.28.5.1pr.)

Anything written before the appointment was invalid if it lessened the rights of the heir, e.g. gifts to other beneficiaries, manumission of slaves. However, disherison of others was valid, even if written before the appointment of the heir, since the heir's interests were not thereby lessened. The appointment of a guardian before that of an heir was probably valid, although the Sabinians took the contrary view. Justinian ruled that the order of provisions was irrelevant as long as an heir was appointed. The appointment had to be made in a formal manner, using an imperative form of words, e.g. 'Let Titius be my heir'. Consequently, 'I appoint Titius to be my heir' or 'I wish Titius to be my heir' were considered insufficient. The need for such fine distinctions was obviated in the fourth century AD, when it was decreed that any form of words was acceptable provided that the intention to appoint an heir was clearly expressed. At all times, however, it was essential that the heir should be named or sufficiently identified.

Since an heir stepped into the shoes of the deceased, the appointment could not specify on which day it was to take effect, e.g. 'Let Balbus be my heir on the tenth day after my death.' Such a qualification was simply ignored—the appointment operated from the testator's death. A similar rule applied to an appointment that limited the duration of the heir's office: the limitation was ignored as it conflicted with the basic rule 'once an heir, always an heir'.

8.4.3.2 Plurality of heirs

As many heirs could be appointed as the testator wished. They shared the inheritance equally unless the testator specified a different division. Estates were sometimes divided into twelfths (a convenient number for the purposes of division) when there was a plurality of heirs. For example, a testator with three sons could appoint one as heir to, say, five-twelfths, another to four-twelfths, the remaining son to three-twelfths.

It was a basic principle that a man could not die partially testate, partially intestate: the whole inheritance normally had to be governed either by the provisions of the will or by the law of intestacy. Thus, if the testator failed to apportion the whole of the inheritance, but had shown his intent to divide it into shares, the undisposed part accrued to the heirs (in proportion to their respective declared shares) and did not pass as intestate estate.

8.4.3.3 Conditional appointment

In the later Republic it came to be accepted that heirs could be appointed subject to a suspensive condition—a condition precedent, i.e. one that had to be satisfied before the heir entered on the inheritance, e.g. 'Let Balbus be my heir if he swims across the Tiber.' However, as suspensive conditions were potentially a serious hurdle for the designated heir to clear, they were subject to close scrutiny. What were considered illegal, immoral, and impossible conditions were struck out, the appointment taking effect unconditionally. Some jurists (mainly Proculians) argued that such conditions vitiated the whole will but their view did not prevail:

Ulpian, *Sabinus, book 5*: **It is settled that an institution made under an impossible condition or with some other blunder is not vitiated.** (D.28.7.1.)

What was the test of impossibility? It was objective: the condition had to be impossible in the nature of things—it was not impossible if it could conceivably happen, even if the designated heir found it *personally* impossible or very difficult to achieve. For the condition to be struck out, the impossibility had to exist when the testator died; supervening impossibility caused the heir to fail to take, although he might have a claim for compensation in appropriate circumstances:

Ulpian, *Edict, book 18*: ...**if I should be instituted heir on the condition of freeing the slave Stichus and Stichus is killed after the testator's death, I can sue for the value of the inheritance in the assessment of my damages; for the condition failed because of the killing.** (D.9.2.23.2.)

In the above scenario I can sue under the *lex Aquilia* (see generally 10.2) for the consequential loss resulting from the killing of the slave, i.e. the loss of the inheritance. Had Stichus been killed before the testator's death, I would have taken as heir since the condition would have lapsed on account of *initial* impossibility.

The rules on impossibility were subject to a special rule concerning sons-in-power: if a testator appointed a son as heir subject to a condition which, though not impossible, was not reasonably within the son's power to satisfy, the whole will failed since the son was deemed to have been disinherited.

Apart from illegality, immorality, and impossibility, a condition could be ignored if it was made by a testator of unsound mind (although the whole will would then be at risk):

Modestinus, *Replies, book 8*: A certain man appointed an heir in his will under a condition such as, 'if he throws my remains into the sea'; the question was asked, when the instituted heir had not met the condition, whether he should be expelled from the inheritance. Modestinus replied: the heir is to be praised rather than accused for not throwing the testator's remains into the sea according to his wishes but delivering them for burial, as a reminder of the condition of men. But this point must first be investigated, whether a man who imposed such a condition was even not of sound mind. (D.28.7.27pr.)

What was the position if someone with an interest in its non-satisfaction frustrated the fulfilment of the condition? The rule was that the condition was treated as if it had been satisfied. And the position was similar if a party refused to cooperate in the performance of the condition, where such cooperation was essential:

Pomponius, *Sabinus, book 8*: A legacy provides: 'Let Titius be heir, if he sets up statues in the town'; [Titius] is ready to erect them but the townsmen do not grant him a site; Sabinus and Proculus say that he will be heir and that the law is the same in the matter of legacies. (D.35.1.14.)

If a condition was resolutive (i.e. one which attempted to divest the heir of his position), it was normally ignored since it conflicted with the rule 'once an heir, always an heir'. A condition must not deprive an heir of the inheritance once it was vested in him.

8.4.3.4 Substitution

(Inst.Gai.2.174.–84., Inst.2.15.–16., D.28.6., C.6.26.)

A Roman testator, if anxious to avoid intestacy, would worry about the possibility of the will being invalidated on account of the failure of the appointed heirs to take the inheritance. Such failure could arise if the heirs predeceased the testator, or because of their incapacity to take, or their unwillingness to do so (in some cases). Thus, it was common for substitute heirs to be appointed (*substitutio vulgaris*—'common substitution'). The list of substitutes often included someone who could not refuse to accept, e.g. a slave, thereby ensuring that the will would be operative. See Frier and McGinn, *Casebook*, 347–8.

The appointment of substitutes was subject to the same rules as applied to heirs; e.g., an imperative form of words had to be used. The testator could appoint as many substitutes as he wished for each heir. The substitute was a conditional heir, taking only if the heir for whom he was the substitute failed to take. The substitute stepped into the position that the heir would have taken. He was thus entitled to the same share and was liable to the same burdens as the failed heir, subject to any contrary provision by the testator. A substitute could be both heir and substitute at the same time, e.g. Balbus could be heir to a part of the inheritance, and a substitute to an heir as regards another part. Indeed, the two heirs could be reciprocal substitutes, i.e. each a substitute to the other in respect of the other's share of the inheritance. This was frequently done in the case of co-heirs. An heir who had accepted a share in the inheritance was deemed to accept any additional share vesting in him as a substitute—he could not accept one and refuse the other:

Ulpian, *Sabinus, book 9*: If a person instituted heir for a share and then substituted to Titius has acted as heir before the inheritance is offered to him under the substitution, he will

be heir under the substitution also, because the share accrues to him even if he does not want it. (D.29.2.35pr.)

A chain of representation operated. Suppose that A is a substitute to B, while C is a substitute to A. C is regarded as a potential substitute to B as well, and will take B's share if A fails to do so.

When a *paterfamilias* appointed a child below the age of puberty as heir, it was customary to appoint a substitute in case the child, having succeeded as heir, died before attaining puberty. If no substitute had been appointed, and the child died, intestacy would result since a child below puberty could not make a will. This form of substitution was described as pupillary. It was usual to add a 'common substitution' (see earlier) in case the child failed to become heir in the first place. Often the same person was appointed—it was a 'double' substitution, but using the same substitute. Double substitutions became so standard in the classical period that Marcus Aurelius (latter half of the second century AD) decreed that one kind of substitution implied the other:

Modestinus, *Advice on Drafting, sole book*:...**we now apply the rule that when a father has substituted an heir to his *impubes* son in one of the two eventualities, he is regarded as having made a substitution for both eventualities, [namely] whether his son has not become heir or has become heir and has died *impubes*.** (D.28.6.4pr.)

The appointment of young children as heirs was potentially fraught with difficulty, not least because of the possibility that a pupillary substitute might be tempted to ensure that the child did not attain puberty. To forestall such temptation, it was customary to appoint the pupillary substitute in a separate sealed document annexed to the will, and to direct that the document was not to be opened before the child's death. Of course, once the child attained puberty the pupillary substitution lapsed.

(On pupillary substitution, see Gardner and Wiedemann, *Roman Household*, 119–21, for a selection of literary texts on the subject.)

8.5 **Heirs**

Pomponius, *Sabinus, book 5*: **An heir succeeds to the whole legal position of the deceased and not only to the ownership of individual things, because the assets which take the form of debts due also pass to the heir.** (D.29.2.37.)

The principle of universal succession meant that the heir stepped into the shoes of the testator for all legal purposes, taking the inheritance subject to the provisions of the will. The heir was the administrator of the estate and often the chief beneficiary. He was responsible for the payment of the testator's debts and legacies. Moreover, he had to pay the inheritance tax (at 5 per cent) that Augustus introduced in order to pay for his armies. It was later raised to 10 per cent by Caracalla but was abolished by Justinian. However, the heir could deduct the tax proportionately from the legacies in the will, unless directed otherwise by the testator.

8.5.1 **Types of heir**

The legal position of the appointed heir depended partly on the category of heir to which he belonged. There were three types of heir: *sui et necessarii heredes, necessarii heredes*, and *extranei heredes*. See Frier and McGinn, *Casebook*, 353–66.

8.5.1.1 *Sui et necessarii heredes*

(Inst.Gai.2.152., D.38.16.)

This category comprised *sui heredes*, i.e. all those who became *sui iuris* on the testator's death (including children born after his death). They were termed *necessarii* because they could not refuse the inheritance if they were appointed—they *necessarily* became heirs on the death of the testator:

Gaius, *Lex Julia et Papia, book 13*: **In the case of *sui heredes*, formal acceptance is not a requisite because they immediately fall to be heirs by operation of law.** (D.38.16.14.)

What if the estate was insolvent? The *ius civile* position was that *sui* (their shortened name) had to pay the debts out of their own pockets, if necessary. They bore the stigma (as it was perceived) and the financial cost of the insolvency of their *paterfamilias*. But the praetor came to the rescue by giving *sui* the right to 'abstain' from the inheritance (*ius abstinendi*) although strictly they remained the *ius civile* heirs. The creditors would then sell off the estate in the name of the deceased. They could not proceed against *sui* in respect of any shortfall. However, the *ius abstinendi* could be claimed only if *sui* did not meddle with the estate and showed that they did not intend to act as heirs. They could change their minds at any time before the creditors sold off the estate. Vacillating *sui* could be forced to choose, but could request that a period of time be fixed to enable them to reach a decision:

Ulpian, *Edict, book 61*: **If a person who is *suus heres*, after having refrained from [dealing with the inheritance], then asks for time for consideration, let us see whether he ought to succeed with his request; and the preferable view is that he ought to succeed in his request on cause shown, where the property has not yet been sold.** (D.28.8.8.)

Justinian fixed a maximum period of three years for *sui* to make up their minds (if the estate had not been realized by the creditors before then). If the *ius abstinendi* was exercised, and the creditors sold off the estate, *sui* were entitled to any surplus, i.e. the balance after all debts and legacies had been paid. The provisions of the will were upheld as far as possible—manumissions were valid providing that they were not intended to defraud creditors.

8.5.1.2 *Necessarii heredes*

(C.6.27.)

These were slaves who had been voluntarily manumitted by will and appointed as heirs. The appointment was considered to be ineffective unless the slave was expressly freed, but Justinian eventually provided that manumission could be implied from the appointment. The normal purpose of appointing a slave as heir was to saddle him with the stigma of a possible insolvency, since the slave could not refuse the inheritance—he was a *necessarius*. If a testator had two or more slaves, only one could be appointed as heir; if more than one was named, only the first-named was heir.

A *necessarius* was given some protection by the praetor as regards an insolvent estate. He was entitled to retain as his separate property anything personally acquired by him after the testator's death (other than as heir) and things owed to him by the deceased. His remedy was to petition for separation of property (*separatio bonorum*) providing that he had not meddled with the estate:

Ulpian, *Edict, book 64*: **It should further be known that a slave, granted his freedom and made *necessarius heres* to an inheritance, since he cannot refuse it, can petition for separation,** doubtless because, if he has no dealings with his patron's estate, he is in such a case that any subsequent acquisitions that he makes are to be appropriated to himself. So also if the testator owe him anything. (D.42.6.1.18.)

Consequently, the creditors were entitled only to the assets of the estate and anything acquired after the testator's death by the *necessarius* in his capacity as heir.

8.5.1.3 *Extranei*

(Inst.Gai.2.161.–73.)

All testamentary heirs other than *sui* and *necessarii* were *extranei*—they were 'extraneous' in the sense that usually they were not members of the testator's household. The position of *extranei* was fundamentally different from that of the other types of heir because *extranei* could refuse to accept—there was no automatic vesting of the inheritance. An acceptance was valid only if the heir took the whole of his interest in the inheritance:

Paul, *Sabinus, book 2*: **A person who can take up a whole inheritance cannot, by splitting it up, accept it only in part.** [Ulpian, *Sabinus, book 4*][**2**]: **But even if someone has been instituted in respect of several shares in the inheritance of the same person, he cannot reject certain shares and accept certain shares.** (D.29.2.1.–2.)

Acceptance was effected in the Republic by a formal declaration (*cretio*) usually made before witnesses. The testator often stated the period (commonly 100 days) within which the *cretio* was to be made. Failure to make the declaration within the required period could result in the heir losing the inheritance, if the testator had so directed. Time normally ran from the moment when the heir was in a position to accept the inheritance, but the testator could provide otherwise, e.g. time to run from his death or from the opening of the will. The praetor could intervene if he considered the period to be inadequate or excessive; or he might fix a period himself where the testator had failed to do so. In the Empire the practice of making a *cretio* waned. It ceased to be necessary unless specifically required by the testator. Moreover, the testator's direction was considered ineffective if he failed to provide a substitute in the event of the heir failing to make a *cretio*. Justinian decreed that nine months was the maximum period that could be allowed to an heir to make up his mind.

In the absence of the requirement of a *cretio*, the inheritance could be accepted informally by any act that showed acceptance, e.g. behaving as an heir by administering or meddling with the estate. But acting out of a sense of duty, piety, or a desire simply to protect the inheritance did not necessarily constitute acceptance:

Ulpian, *Edict, book 61*: **A person is regarded as acting as heir when he does some act as if he were heir…but acting as heir is not so much a matter of action as of mind; for he ought to have in mind that he wishes to be heir. But if he has done something as a matter of piety, if he has done something as a matter of protection, if he has acted not as heir, but as owner under some other title, it is clear that he is not regarded as having acted as heir.** (D.29.2.20pr.)

The *extraneus* would naturally shirk at accepting a *damnosa hereditas*—a ruinous inheritance—although he might accept it out of a feeling of respect or gratitude to the testator for past services. Such considerations apart, if the *extraneus* was unsure whether an inheritance was solvent or not, he would have difficulty in making up his mind whether to accept. And attempting to evaluate the inheritance could be construed as meddling, i.e. as an acceptance.

What was the position regarding the inheritance before the *extraneus* decided whether to accept? Assuming there were no *sui* or *necessarii*, the inheritance was vacant and could thus be acquired by a stranger through *usucapio* (see 7.2.1). A vacant inheritance could acquire rights and duties through contracts made by slaves belonging to the inheritance, or because of delicts committed by or against them. Such obligations attached to the person who eventually became heir. To that extent a vacant inheritance arguably had a measure of legal personality, although the jurists preferred to think of the inheritance rather as 'sustaining' the personality of the deceased:

Ulpian, *Disputations, book 4*: **Whenever the slave of an inheritance takes a stipulation or receives something by delivery, his act is effective by virtue of the personality of the deceased, as Julian maintains; his view has prevailed that the person to whom to look is the testator.** [Ulpian, *Census, book* 4][34]: **For the inheritance sustains the personality of the deceased, not that of the heir** ... (D.41.1.33.2., 34.)

Although this view was the predominant one in the classical period, some jurists thought that an inheritance represented the personality of the prospective heir. There was, in any case, general agreement that once the *extraneus* accepted, his position as heir operated retrospectively to the testator's death—he was subject to all the rights and duties that arose in respect of the inheritance between the testator's death and his own acceptance:

Florentinus, *Institutes, book 8*: **Whatever the time at which an heir accepts an inheritance, he is understood to have succeeded to the deceased as from the time of death.** (D.29.2.54.)

How was an interest in an intestate estate accepted by those who had a right to refuse, (e.g. the nearest agnate)? It seems that the same rules applied as to wills. If a beneficiary did not wish to take—whether under a will or intestacy—any evidence of an intention not to accept sufficed: no formal act of repudiation was required.

Once the heir accepted (or refused) the inheritance, the decision was normally irrevocable. Minors, however, could change their minds and seek *restitutio in integrum*, as could those whose decision had not been freely made, e.g. through duress.

8.5.2 Debts

An heir was responsible for the payment of the deceased's debts. If there were two or more heirs, they had to pay the debts in proportion to their respective shares in the inheritance unless the testator directed otherwise. The payment of debts could create some difficulties in practice. Consequently, certain devices were made available to help creditors and heirs, particularly *separatio bonorum* and *beneficium inventarii*.

8.5.2.1 *Separatio bonorum* for creditors

Because of the principle of universal succession, the heir's personal estate was regarded as merging with that of the deceased. That could disadvantage the creditors (including legatees) of the deceased if the heir was personally insolvent. The praetor therefore allowed them to apply for *separatio bonorum*, which ensured that the two estates were kept separate until the debts had been paid out of the inheritance— the creditors of the deceased were entitled to payment in full from the inheritance in priority to the heir's creditors. There was a time limit of five years within which claims under *separatio* had to be settled, although it is not clear whether the limitation period operated before Justinian. *Separatio* was not possible if the heir had already sold the inheritance in good faith.

8.5.2.2 *Beneficium inventarii*

Justinian greatly improved the position of all heirs by introducing the *beneficium inventarii* ('the benefit of an inventory'). An heir's liability for the deceased's debts was confined to the assets of the inheritance, provided that he made an inventory of the deceased's estate. Strict time limits were imposed: the inventory had to be begun within a month and finished within three months of a person discovering that he was heir. The inventory had to be drawn up formally before witnesses. The *beneficium inventarii* affected the position of the *extraneus*, in particular, since he was now much more likely to accept a suspect inheritance. It is surprising that the device had not been introduced much earlier. A possible reason for the delay was the development of the practice whereby *extranei* agreed to accept inheritances on condition that they paid only a proportion of what was due to the creditors.

8.5.3 **Benefits**

The principle of universal succession meant that the heir inherited the rights and benefits of the deceased, not just the debts and obligations. The heir would thus be able to enforce any contractual and delictual obligations owed to the deceased that had not been extinguished by death.

The chief *ius civile* remedy for the heir against anyone wrongfully in possession of the whole or part of an inheritance was the *hereditas petitio*. It was an action *in rem* for the recovery of the relevant property. And the defendant would have to account for his dealings with the property and any resulting profits or losses:

Ulpian, *Edict, book 15*: **Furthermore, he who is in possession of payments made for things belonging to the inheritance and likewise he who has exacted money from a debtor of the inheritance are also liable to a claim for the inheritance.** (D.5.3.16.1.)

The rule that the defendant was liable for all losses caused by his acts was confined, after Hadrian, to those who had possessed in bad faith. Bona fide possessors were liable only to the extent of their actual enrichment at the time of joinder of issue. Apart from the *ius civile* remedies, an heir could seek praetorian help through *bonorum possessio* (see generally 8.3.2).

Universal succession is a familiar concept in modern systems. In continental codes the position is generally very similar to the Roman—the inheritance passes automatically to the heirs on the deceased's death. But in England the estate passes to the deceased's personal representatives, who must administer it and distribute the residue (after payment of debts and liabilities) to those entitled under his will or intestacy.

8.6 **Legacies**

(Chiefly Inst.Gai.2.91.–2.245., Inst.2.20., D.30., 31., 32., C.6.37.)

Although the appointment of an heir was the most important function of a Roman will, the heart of the will lay in the legacies granted by the testator. It was one of the heir's principal duties to pay the legacies. The legatees took nothing unless the will was valid and there was an heir to distribute the legacies. See Frier and McGinn, *Casebook*, 387–403.

Legacies were governed by extremely detailed rules, as evidenced by their lengthy treatment in the *Digest*, which contains separate titles on legacies of furniture, dowries, stores, provisions, valuables, and sections on gifts of perfumes, clothes, statues, wine, and oil, *inter alia*. There is little purpose in struggling through the morass of detail involved—only the barest of outlines will be attempted. It must be emphasized at the outset how wide the potential scope of legacies was. It was not just corporeal things that could be gifted to legatees, but also a host of rights, interests, and privileges, e.g. servitudes, maintenance, release from debts; even entitlement to the distribution of free corn—in D.31.87pr., we find Paul discussing a legacy of a ticket 'for the corn dole'.

8.6.1 Forms of legacy

Legacies could take several forms, the most important of which were legacies *per vindicationem* and those *per damnationem*.

8.6.1.1 Legacies *per vindicationem*

Such legacies took their name from the right of the legatee to bring a *vindicatio*, if necessary, to obtain the property from the person in possession. The legatee's right arose as soon as the heir entered on the inheritance and it seems that ownership of the legacy passed directly from the testator to the legatee without vesting in the heir. However, if the legacy was conditional, the legatee could not bring a *vindicatio* until the condition was satisfied. To whom did the property belong in the meantime? The Proculians thought it was ownerless, but the Sabinian view prevailed that the property was owned by the heir (who could therefore keep any fruits):

Ulpian, *Edict, book 19*: **Anything left as a conditional legacy belongs to the heirs in the interim....** (D.10.2.12.2.)

In order to create a legacy *per vindicationem*, the testator originally had to use the words *'do, lego'* ('I give and bequeath') but Gaius tells us (Inst.Gai.2.193.) that *either* word was acceptable and that other similar expressions sufficed, at least by his time. The legacy was void unless the testator was the owner of the property both at the time of making the will and at his death—this was a major limitation. However, in the case of fungibles (see 6.1.4) it was sufficient if the testator had been their owner when he died.

8.6.1.2 Legacies *per damnationem*

These legacies took their name from the instruction by the testator to the heir to give the legacy to the legatee—the heir was charged (usually by the words *damnas esto*) with making the gift. It was a less direct form of legacy in that the testator obliged the heir to give to the legatee, whereas in the case of a legacy *per vindicationem* the testator did the giving himself. Set words had to be used originally, but the form was relaxed by the classical period. The legatee obtained a right *in personam* against the heir, enforceable by the *actio ex testamento* (double damages if the heir denied liability unsuccessfully).

Legacies *per damnationem* were of very wide scope since the testator could bequeath virtually anything, including property he did not own, e.g. property belonging to the heir or to some other person. However, as the legatee did not have a right *in rem*, the heir was not obliged to give the specified thing; the equivalent in value sufficed. Because of their potentially wide scope, legacies *per damnationem* were the most common form of legacy.

8.6.1.3 Other forms of legacy

(a) Legacy *per praeceptionem*. Such a legacy could be created if the testator used the word *praecipito* ('let him take before'). This allowed the legatee to take the gift before the inheritance was distributed. The Sabinians regarded such a legacy as possible only if made in favour of a joint heir; but the Proculians denied the restriction, and their view prevailed. The right was enforceable by a *vindicatio*. The testator did not have to be the owner; and property acquired after the making of the will could be bequeathed in this manner.

(b) Legacy *sinendi modo* ('in the permissive manner'). In this form of legacy the heir was charged with the duty to permit the legatee to take the thing for himself, e.g. 'Let my heir be charged to allow Lucius Titius to take the slave Stichus and have him as his own' (Inst.Gai.2.209.). Such legacies could be made of anything that belonged to the testator or his heir at the time of the testator's death. The legatee had a right *in personam*, enforceable through an *actio ex testamento*. This form of legacy eventually faded from use, as did the legacy *per praeceptionem*.

8.6.1.4 Incorrect form

What if a legacy was made in the incorrect form? In early law the position was strict—the legacy failed. Thus, if A gave B a legacy in the form *'do, lego'* of property belonging to C, the gift failed. The position was considerably relaxed by the *S. C. Neronianum* AD 64 as the result of a case where a testator had attempted to leave a legacy *per vindicationem* of property which he did not own. The *senatus consultum* provided that the legacy should be construed in the most favourable form to make it effective, namely as a legacy *per damnationem*. See Schulz, F., *Classical Roman Law* (1951), 318–19. In the later Empire it was decreed that the intention of the testator was paramount, the form of words used being unimportant. Justinian confirmed the trend by ruling that legacies were of one nature, enforceable by any of three remedies at the option of the legatee: *vindicatio, actio ex testamento,* and *actio hypothecaria*. The last of these was provided because Justinian subjected inheritances to a mortgage for the payment of legacies.

8.6.2 Time of enforcement

When could the legatee enforce his claim? A distinction was drawn between the time when the legatee acquired his right to the legacy, and thus to any accretions, and the time when he could actually enforce his claim through legal action. The right to a legacy normally arose on the testator's death. Augustus, however, provided that the right arose only when the will was opened; but Justinian reverted to the previous position. As regards the enforcement of the right, the general rule was that the legatee had to wait until the heir accepted:

Ulpian, *Sabinus, book 20*: **Though a legacy cannot be demanded until the heir has accepted, its vesting is not postponed.** (D.36.2.7pr.)

It followed that when heirs took automatically, i.e. as *sui* or *necessarii*, the time when the right to a legacy arose, and when it became enforceable, coincided.

8.6.3 **The** *lex Falcidia*

(D.35.2., C.6.50.)

An *extraneus* was more likely to accept the inheritance if he stood to benefit from it substantially. Hence, if the testator was too generous in his legacies to others, he ran the risk that the *extraneus* might refuse the inheritance, and that intestacy would thus result. Republican legislation was occasionally passed aimed at restricting the size of legacies. The most effective and important measure was the *lex Falcidia* 40 BC:

Paul, *Lex Falcidia, sole book*: **Any Roman citizen who … makes his will shall have the right and power, under the general law, to give and bequeath money to any Roman citizen so long as the legacy [or legacies] be such that the heirs take not less than a quarter of the estate under the will … (D.35.2.1pr.)**

The *lex Falcidia* did not guarantee that the heir would benefit from the inheritance—he would take nothing, e.g., if the estate was insolvent. But the statute entitled the heir to at least a quarter of the *net* estate, i.e. that remaining after the payment of funeral expenses and debts (see Stein, P. G., 'Lex Falcidia' (1987) 75 Athenaeum, 454–7; Gardner and Wiedemann, *Roman Household*, 125–6). In calculating the net estate, the value of slaves manumitted by the will had to be deducted. Legacies were reduced proportionately if they exceeded three-quarters of the net estate, which was valued as at the time of the testator's death.

If there were two or more heirs, their entitlement was to at least a quarter of the net estate *between* them—not to a quarter each. But the testator could direct that certain legacies should be charged on particular heirs; or he might exempt certain legacies from reduction, in which case the unexempted legacies would have to bear a greater share of the necessary reduction. Whatever the testator did, each heir was entitled to at least his share of one-quarter of the net estate. What if a legacy (that had to be reduced) had been given in an indivisible form? The legatee could retain the legacy but had to refund a proportionate share:

Gaius, *Praetor's Edict, Legacies, book 3*: **Legacies, then, which do not admit of division, belong exclusively to the legatee. The heir, though, can invoke the relief that having valued the legacy, he may give notice to the legatee that the latter bear his share of the valuation … (D.35.2.80.1.)**

An accurate valuation of the net estate might not have been possible for some time after the testator's death, in which case it would have been uncertain whether a Falcidian reduction was necessary. Rather than delaying a legatee from benefiting, it became the practice to allow him to take the whole gift on his undertaking to repay whatever proved to be excessive:

Ulpian, *Edict, book 79*: **If someone receive a legacy beyond the legal maximum and there be valid ground for doubt whether or not the *lex Falcidia* should come into account, the praetor affords the heir the relief that the legatee is to give him an undertaking that should it become apparent that he has taken by way of legacy more than is permitted to him by the *lex Falcidia*, he will give him the money value of the excess … (D.35.3.1pr.)**

Although there were a few exceptional cases where the *lex Falcidia* did not apply, notably soldiers' wills, its provisions remained virtually unchanged until the late Empire. Justinian made important changes: the heir could claim his quarter providing that he made an inventory of the estate and the testator had not prohibited him from taking. Previously, the testator could not prevent the heir from taking a quarter.

8.6.4 Special cases

Certain categories of legacy merit attention because of the special rules applying to them. The most important were as follows.

8.6.4.1 Conditional legacies

The general rule was that the legatee had to satisfy the condition before taking the legacy. However, as in the case of the appointment of heirs, illegal, immoral, impossible, and resolutive conditions were ignored, the legatee taking free of them. But if the condition was 'not to do something', e.g. 'if Milo does not manumit Stichus', a special rule was applied. For such cases, the *cautio Muciana* was devised by the jurist Quintus Mucius Scaevola (see 2.2.3.2), a procedure whereby the legatee took the gift on his undertaking to repay the legacy should he break the condition. The procedure was applied in the late Empire to gifts of the inheritance, not just to legacies.

8.6.4.2 Legacy of an option (*legatum optionis*)

This was a legacy whereby the legatee was expressly given the right to choose from two or more things. The legatee had an unrestricted choice within the option—he could choose the best thing available. What if the legatee died before making his selection? The legacy failed since it was considered to be conditional on a choice being made. Justinian, however, held that the right to choose passed to the legatee's heirs.

8.6.4.3 Legacy of a thing of a kind (*legatum generis*)

This was a legacy of a thing of a kind, something not specifically identified, e.g. 'I give Balbus a horse.' The legatee did not have an unrestricted choice; indeed, he might not have a choice at all—if the legacy was *per damnationem*, the choice was with the heir. But the exercise of the choice was subject to the following rules: if the heir had the choice, he could not choose the worst; if the legatee chose, he could not choose the best. Thus, if there were only two things from which the choice had to be made, it was more beneficial not to have the choice. If the legatee failed to make a choice, the right passed to his heirs.

8.6.4.4 Legacy of part of the inheritance (*legatum partitionis*)

This occurred if a legatee was given a share of the inheritance, e.g. 'Let my heir, Balbus, share the inheritance with Milo.' The legatee could not become heir in this way since he had not been appointed as heir. It was normal for the heir and legatee to enter into an agreement specifying their respective rights and liabilities. The jurists disputed whether the legatee was entitled to an actual share of the inheritance or simply the value of the share:

Pomponius, *Sabinus, book 5*: When part of an estate has been bequeathed and it is doubtful whether a share of the things or the value is due, Sabinus and Cassius held that the value has been left, Proculus and Nerva a share of the things. But it is necessary to come to the relief of the heir, so that he himself may choose whether he prefers to give a share of things or the value. However, an heir is permitted to give a part of such things as may be divided

without loss. If they are by nature undivided or cannot be divided without loss, the value must be paid by the heir in all cases. (D.30.26.2.)

8.6.4.5 Legacy of a debt (*legatum debiti*)

If the testator gave a legacy to his creditor, consisting of the debt that the testator owed, the legacy was a nullity since the creditor had received nothing of value. But it was different if the creditor received some extra benefit, e.g. earlier payment of the debt than was required. Such a legacy, the *legatum debiti*, was valid according to Julian:

Julian, *Digest, book 36*: **I have given it as my opinion that whenever a debtor made a legacy to his creditor, it was thus ineffective, unless the creditor derived some new cause of action on the will as opposed to the former obligation.** (D.34.3.11.)

8.7 Testamentary freedom

Although a testator could do largely as he pleased in his will, he was subject nevertheless to some restrictions, as we have seen. For example, he could not validly leave property to those who lacked capacity to take; nor could he validly impose a condition that was regarded as illegal, immoral, or impossible. The most important restrictions, however, were the rules relating to *exheredatio* and the *querela*.

8.7.1 *Exheredatio*

(Inst.2.13., D.28.2., C.6.28.)

Gaius, *Provincial Edict, book 17*: **Among all the other things which it is essential to look for in drawing up wills the main legal provisions are those concerning the institution of children as heirs or their disherison, so that the will is not broken because they have been passed over; for if a son who is in power has been passed over, the will is invalid.** (D.28.2.30.)

The rules on disherison (*exheredatio*) were among the most complicated in Roman law. It is necessary at the outset to distinguish between the *ius civile* rules and the praetorian system.

8.7.1.1 The *ius civile* position

The rules of disherison originated in early law to protect *sui heredes*. *Sui* could not be excluded from benefiting under a will except by express provision to that effect. So the testator could disinherit *sui*, but only if he followed the correct form. The rule was established that *sui* had to be either expressly appointed as heirs or expressly disinherited: ignoring or passing them over could result in the will's invalidity. This at least is the traditional view, but Schulz doubts whether the rules *bound* the testator to appoint or disinherit: 'The republican lawyers had the very natural desire to save the inheritance for the *sui*, but did not venture to impugn openly the father's will and for that reason did not interfere when he had instituted or disinherited them. But if the will was silent with regard to them, they then dared to help the *sui*' (*Classical Roman Law* (1951), 269). The disherison clause often preceded the appointment of the heirs. Disherison was common but did not necessarily imply that there were bad relations between the testator and the disinherited person. Disinherited *sui* usually received legacies. A typical Roman will might appoint the testator's sons as his heirs, disinherit his daughters, but leave his wife and daughters appropriate legacies.

The operation of the *ius civile* rules depended on the type of *sui heredes* that were being disinherited. Sons-in-power had to be disinherited by name, as a general rule; other *sui* could be disinherited by name or by a general clause, e.g. 'Let my daughters be disinherited.' However, it seems that a general clause could validly disinherit a son-in-power if he was the only son of the testator:

> Paul, *Replies, book 12*: **Titius instituted an heir in his will, and, having a son, he put in a disherison clause as follows: 'Let all the others, sons and my daughters, be disinherited.' Paul replied that the son was to be regarded as correctly disinherited.** (D.28.2.25pr.)

What if the testator failed to appoint or disinherit *sui heredes* in the correct manner? If this occurred in the case of a son-in-power, the will was void and an intestacy resulted; otherwise, the will stood but the omitted *sui* (i.e. those not properly appointed or disinherited) were allowed to share the inheritance.

A complicating factor was the position of *sui heredes* who were born after the making of the will. As they were *postumi*, they were considered to be 'unascertained persons' and thus incapable of being appointed as heirs (see 8.4.1.3). On the other hand, as they were *sui heredes* of the testator when he died, they should have been either appointed or disinherited in the will according to the rules of disherison. The interaction of these rules with those on capacity thus created a potential legal impasse for the Roman testator. Since a will was void if the rules on disherison were breached in the case of a son-in-power, testators were forced in the Republic into one of two courses of action: either to delay making a will until the possibility of further *sui* being born had faded, or to make a fresh will on the birth of any *sui*. Both courses had obvious drawbacks.

This unsatisfactory position for testators was gradually improved from the late Republic. The trend of the complex reforms was to allow testators to anticipate the birth of *sui heredes* after the making of the will, by appointing or disinheriting them in clauses such as 'whatever children may be born to my wife.' For example, the *lex Junia Velleia c.* AD 28 validated wills which had appointed or disinherited *postumi* born between the making of the will and the death of the testator. However, these reforms generally did not apply to *postumi* through adoption, i.e. those who were adopted by the testator after the making of the will.

The *ius civile* rules on disherison may appear to have been rather artificial and overladen with traps for the unwary testator. They were. But the rules did at least help to focus the testator's attention on the importance of what he was doing, i.e. appointing or disinheriting very close family members.

8.7.1.2 Praetorian *exheredatio*

The praetors introduced their own rules, mainly in an attempt to achieve consistency with their scheme of intestacy. All male *sui* had to be appointed or disinherited by name, as a rule, but a general clause sufficed for other *sui*. If the will did not satisfy these requirements, the omitted *sui* could seek *bonorum possessio contra tabulas* ('possession of the estate contrary to the tablets', i.e. the will) from the praetor. Certain persons who were not protected by the *ius civile* rules were included in the praetorian scheme, notably emancipated children (who strictly had ceased to be *sui* on emancipation). However, emancipated children who obtained *bonorum possessio* had to account (as against any *sui* appointed as heirs) for property obtained as a result of the emancipation, i.e. there had to be a *collatio bonorum*.

The praetors altered the position concerning the case of omitted *postumi* who had predeceased the testator. The strict *ius civile* position was that the will failed, but the praetors allowed the heir to take:

Ulpian, *Disputations, book 4*: **A *postumus*, who had been passed over, having been born in the lifetime of the testator, died; although by the strictness and undue nicety of the law the will is regarded as broken, still, if the will has been sealed, the heir appointed can claim *bonorum possessio*...**(D.28.3.12pr.)

8.7.1.3 Justinian's reforms

Justinian typically swept away much of the old law, substituting for it a greatly simplified scheme. The basic position on disherison was that descendants, whether male or female, had to be expressly disinherited by name. Failure to do this was generally fatal for the will.

8.7.2 *Querela*

(D.5.2.)

In early law a testator could disinherit his family members provided that he satisfied the requirements of *exheredatio*. They had no remedy, assuming the will was validly made. But a testator who acted capriciously, disinheriting members of his family for no good reason, could easily incur social opprobrium. Causeless failure to provide for one's family in a will was regarded as a breach of moral duty. In due course moral duty was translated into legal remedy: a procedure was developed in the late Republic by which a will could be challenged on the ground that the testator had failed in his duty. The procedure was known as the *querela inofficiosi testamenti*—'the complaint concerning the undutiful will'. The complaint was normally heard by the court of the *centumviri*, such cases often attracting considerable public interest. See Frier and McGinn, *Casebook*, 377–85.

The original justification for allowing such challenges was that the testator must have been insane to make an undutiful will; but this was pretence as it is clear that insanity was not really the issue:

Marcian, *Institutes, book 4*: **The supposition on which an action for undutiful will is brought is that the testators were of unsound mind for making a will. And by this is meant not that the testator was really a lunatic or out of his mind but that the will was correctly made but without a due regard for natural claims; for if he were really a lunatic or out of his mind, the will is void.** (D.5.2.2.)

Three main issues need consideration in examining the operation of the *querela* procedure. In what circumstances could the *querela* be brought? Who could bring it? And what were the consequences of a successful complaint?

8.7.2.1 When could the *querela* be brought?

The essence of the complaint was that the testator had acted undutifully, i.e. had unjustly failed to provide for the complainant. Until Justinian the question whether exclusion was unjust was largely a matter for the discretion of the court. It is probable that a consistent practice was developed by the *centumviri* in the matter. A misunderstanding by the testator often amounted to an unjust exclusion:

Marcellus, *Digest, book 3*: **To say a will is undutiful is to argue one should not have been disinherited or passed over. This generally happens when parents disinherit or pass over their children through a misunderstanding.** (D.5.2.3.)

The deliberate exclusion by a testator of his children by a previous wife in favour of a subsequent wife, a scenario not unknown in the modern world, could sometimes lead to a successful *querela*, as in the case of Attia Viriola, the wife of an ex-praetor. She was successful in her complaint against her father's will in which she had been disinherited in favour of her stepmother—'the bride he had wooed, won, wed and widowed in the space of a week or two' (Gardner, *Women in Roman Law*, 185). In this respect, the timeless and universal relevance of Roman law is vividly demonstrated by the following text:

Gaius, *Lex Glitia, sole book*: **For parents should not be allowed to treat their children unjustly in their wills. They generally do this, passing an adverse judgment on their own flesh and blood, when they have been led astray by the blandishments or incitements of stepmothers.** (D.5.2.4.)

In the classical period the scope of the *querela* was considerably widened. It became possible to bring the action on the grounds of inadequate provision as well as total exclusion: the complainant could bring the *querela* even though he had received *something* under the will. What was the test of whether provision was adequate? The rule came to be accepted, probably under the influence of the *lex Falcidia* (see 8.6.3), that provision was adequate if it amounted to at least one-quarter of what would have been received under intestacy. This entitlement to the minimum of a quarter was known as the *legitima portio* ('the lawful share').

An important restriction on the bringing of a *querela* was that the procedure could only be used as a last resort, not if there were other remedies. Thus, if persons omitted from the will had a claim under the rules of *exheredatio*, they could not bring the *querela*. The *querela* had to be brought within five years (originally two) from the entry of the heir on the inheritance.

8.7.2.2 Who could bring *querela*?

Ulpian, *Edict, book 14*: **It should be noted that complaints against the undutiful are common; for it is possible for everyone to argue want of duty, parents as well as children. For one's cognates beyond the degree of brother would do better not to trouble themselves with useless expense since they are not in a position to succeed.** (D.5.2.1.)

The *querela* could only be brought by those who would have succeeded to the deceased's estate (under the *ius civile* or praetorian law) had he died *intestate*. The class was confined to the following: descendants, ascendants, brothers, and sisters. In the later Empire collaterals were barred from the action unless a 'base' person had been appointed heir, e.g. anyone pursuing a disreputable profession. The members of the class constituted an *order* (as set out earlier). Thus, if there were no descendants, or none that challenged the will successfully, the right to bring the *querela* passed to ascendants. The *querela* was generally not available to anyone who had 'accepted' the will by agreeing to receive benefits under it.

What if the complainant died before the *querela* was resolved? The action passed to his heir if the complainant had commenced with it before his death, although in the later Empire it sufficed if there was evidence of intention on his part to bring the claim prior to his death.

8.7.2.3 What were the consequences of the *querela*?

Bringing a *querela* was something of a gamble since, if it failed, the complainant might forfeit any benefits under the will:

Ulpian, *Edict, book 14*: **One should bear in mind that a person who has without justification brought a complaint of undutiful will and has been unsuccessful loses what he received under the will, and this is claimed for the imperial treasury on the ground that he did not deserve it. But only the person who has continued with an unjustified suit right up to the judges' verdict has what he was given under the will taken from him. But if he has left off or died before the verdict, what he was given is not taken from him....** (D.5.2.8.14.)

The effect of a successful *querela* depended on the circumstances. If there was only one heir, the will failed and an intestacy resulted; similarly, if there were two or more heirs and the *querela* was brought successfully against all of them. But where the *querela* was successful against one heir but not another, or where it had been brought against one but not another, a partial intestacy would result from the successful claim—an important exception to the rule that a man could not die partly testate:

Papinian, *Questions, book 14*: **A son who, after taking two heirs to court in an action for undutiful will, got differing decisions from the judges, defeating one heir and being beaten by the other, can in part sue debtors and himself be sued by creditors and also claim items and divide up the inheritance. For it is right for an action for dividing an inheritance to be available, since we believe that he has become in part a *legitimus heres*, and for this reason, part of the inheritance has remained subject to the will; and it does not seem ridiculous to be held intestate in part.** (D.5.2.15.2.)

What was the effect of a successful *querela* on the testator's *inter vivos* gifts, e.g. a gift of a dowry?

Modestinus, *Replies, book 3*: **[E]ven if a complaint of undutiful will has succeeded, gifts which the testator is alleged to have made during his lifetime are not, however, for that reason rendered void and no claim can be made for part of what has been given as dowry.** (D.5.2.11.)

However, in the late classical period a special *querela* procedure was introduced in cases where the testator was alleged to have made *inter vivos* gifts in order to frustrate claims made on his death. The gifts could be ordered to be reduced by half, the donee having to repay the relevant amount to the estate. These anti-evasion measures are comparable to provisions in English law under the Inheritance (Provision for Family and Dependants) Act 1975, whereby certain *inter vivos* dispositions, made by the deceased with a view to defeating claims for financial provision under the Act, are regarded as net estate (and thus available for the satisfaction of claims).

8.7.2.4 The *querela* under Justinian

Important changes were made to the *querela* system in the late Empire, especially by Justinian. He restored the original rule that the *querela* was confined to cases where the complainant had been excluded from the will altogether. He specified various grounds for which exclusion would be considered just, provided that they were stated in the will by the testator. And he insisted that ascendants should expressly appoint as heirs those of their descendants who would have a claim on intestacy (and vice versa). Failure to do so rendered the actual appointments invalid, although the rest of the will remained operative, the omitted person becoming heir via the *querela* procedure. It is unclear how this rule operated in practice in the light of Justinian's reforms of *exheredatio*.

Legitima portio was retained for persons who had been left something under the will, but less than their entitlement. They were given an action (originally introduced in the late Empire, before Justinian) to make up the deficiency. A successful action did not invalidate the will. Justinian changed the rules of *legitima portio* as regards the testator's children. If there were four surviving children or fewer, they were entitled to a share in a minimum of one-third of the inheritance; if five or more, they were entitled to at least a half.

The concept of the *legitima portio*, essentially a fixed right of inheritance, has had a considerable influence in European legal history. In some modern systems of inheritance the concept has a central role, e.g. *la réserve légale* in French law and the German *Pflichtteilsrecht*. Article 913 of the *Code Civil* imposes restrictions on wills depending on the number of children surviving the testator. Thus, if one child survives, the will may not dispose of more than half of the estate (but one-third if there are two children, a quarter if there are three or more). The BGB allows next-of-kin left less than a half of their statutory portion to claim the deficiency (s. 2305). See Stein, *Legal Institutions*, 179–80. Even in systems in which fixed rights of inheritance have little or no place, such as the modern English law of succession, the concept of fixed rights is seen as a potential alternative, useful in testing the efficacy of the law *in situ*.

8.8 **Failure**

We are concerned here with the failure of wills, heirs, and legacies.

8.8.1 **Failure of wills**

(D.28.3.)

Papinian, *Definitions, book 1*: **A will is said to be not lawfully made, where the legal solemnities have not been observed; or to be of no effect, when a son who was in his father's power has been passed over; or it is broken by another will under which there can be an heir or by the addition of a *suus heres* to the agnatic family; or it is rendered ineffectual by the nonacceptance of the inheritance.** (D.28.3.1.)

As Papinian's text demonstrates, wills could fail for a variety of reasons arising either at the time the will was made or subsequently. Whatever the cause of failure, an intestacy would normally result.

8.8.1.1 **Wills void *ab initio***

A will was *iniustum*, i.e. void when made, if the testator lacked the capacity to make it, or if the will was made without due form. The capacity and formalities for making wills have been considered previously.

8.8.1.2 **Ineffectual and broken wills**

Wills could fail because of events occurring after the making of the will. The jurists described such situations as ones where the will was 'ineffectual' (*irritum*) or 'broken' (*ruptum*), although little appears to have hung on the distinction. A will was ineffectual in two situations—when it failed through lack of heirs, or when the testator suffered loss of status:

Ulpian, *Sabinus, book 10*: **A will is rendered ineffectual whenever something has happened to the testator himself, let us say, if he loses citizenship through falling into slavery, for example, by being captured by the enemy or if, being more than twenty years old, he has allowed himself to be sold with a view to performing an act or sharing in the price.** (D.28.3.6.5.)

However, it will be recalled that the will of a Roman soldier who died in captivity was given effect if the will had been made before his capture (see 4.3.3.3).

A will was regarded as broken if, for example, there was a successful *querela* or if the will was revoked. As regards the latter case, the basic *ius civile* rule was that revocation of a mancipatory will was possible only by a subsequent mancipatory will. The revocation occurred even if the subsequent will failed, providing that it had been validly made. However, the praetors were prepared to recognize alternative methods of revocation, both for mancipatory and praetorian wills, e.g. destroying the whole will, erasing the names of the heirs, or tearing off the seals. Whatever the form of revocation, it would be ineffective unless the testator had a clear intention to revoke. One who had lost his reason could not revoke except in a lucid interval. In the fifth century AD, additional methods of revocation were introduced. It was decreed that a later will (even if not validly made) revoked an earlier one, providing that the following conditions were satisfied: the later will must have been witnessed by at least five witnesses; and the heirs under it must have been entitled to take on intestacy, but not those under the earlier will. It was also provided that a will should be automatically revoked by the lapse of 10 years after its making. But lapse of time did not revoke a will under Justinian unless the testator made a formal declaration of revocation.

8.8.2 **Failure of heirs**

An heir might fail to take for a variety of reasons, e.g. through change of status, or by refusing the inheritance (in the case of an *extraneus*), or by predeceasing the testator. If the only heir or all the heirs failed to take, and their substitutes did likewise, the will failed. But what if there was a partial lapse of heirs? The basic rule in the Republic was that the lapsed share of the inheritance went to the remaining heirs by *ius accrescendi*, i.e. the right of survivorship. Legacies that were charged specifically on the lapsed share of the inheritance failed. The heir who eventually took the share was not bound to pay such legacies; he could keep them:

Celsus, *Digest, book 36*: **If my son is heir and there accrues to him the share of a person on whom a legacy had been charged by name, he will not deliver the legacy, which he takes by ancient right.** (D.31.29.2.)

The rule was changed in the late classical period, the heir becoming liable to pay legacies charged on lapsed shares that passed to him.

Augustus's *leges caducariae* made important changes to the principle of *ius accrescendi* as regards the lapsed shares of an inheritance, whatever the cause of the lapse. As a general rule, the share passed to any remaining heirs *with children*; if none then to any legatees with children; if none then to the Treasury (see further 8.4.1.4). In the later Empire the caducary laws were gradually abolished, Justinian returning to the original rule—the *ius accrescendi* applied irrespective of the existence of children.

8.8.3 Failure of legacies

The various grounds on which legacies failed can usefully be classified, as in the case of wills, according to the type of failure.

8.8.3.1 Legacies void *ab initio*

A legacy would fail *ab initio* if, for example, it was given in the incorrect form (at least in early law), or to a person lacking the capacity to take it, or where the will itself was defective for lack of form or capacity. Could such a legacy be validated by events subsequent to the making of the will? It seems not, according to a rule of construction known as the *regula Catoniana*:

Celsus, *Digest, book 35*: **The Catonian Rule is as follows: 'Any legacy which would have been invalid if the testator had died at the time of the making of the will is invalid whenever he dies'.** (D.34.7.1pr.)

8.8.3.2 Failure after the making of the will

Even if a legacy was validly made, it could fail on various grounds arising after the time of testation. For example, the legatee could predecease the testator or might refuse to take the legacy. Or the will itself might fail for reasons arising after testation. Moreover, a legacy could fail through forfeiture if the legatee was considered unworthy to take it, in which case it was usually confiscated by the Treasury—a potential source of easy revenue for unscrupulous Emperors. There was considerable room for abuse since there were no clear guidelines as to what constituted unworthiness. Among the examples of unworthy legatees in the *Digest* we find those who denounced testators for illegal activities (D.34.9.1.) or who made abusive remarks in public about them (D.34.9.9.1.). A legacy would fail if the estate was insolvent; or if the subject matter of the legacy was physically destroyed. But if the destruction was the fault of the heir, the legatee was entitled to the value of the legacy.

Legacies failed through revocation, which could be either express (e.g. by use of formal words in a subsequent will) or implied. The latter form of revocation occurred, for example, in circumstances similar to ademption in the modern English law of succession, e.g. where the testator disposed of the subject matter of the legacy prior to his death. And legacies could be impliedly revoked if enmity arose between testator and legatee:

Ulpian, *Lex Julia et Papia, book 14*: **The preferable view is that if mortal hatred arises between legatee and testator and it becomes probable that the testator did not wish any legacy...to be executed in favor of the person to whom it was appointed or left, the legacy cannot be claimed by the latter.** (D.34.9.9pr.)

A legacy did not fail if there was a misdescription of the subject matter of the gift or of the legatee, providing that the description was sufficient to identify them—*falsa demonstratio non nocet* ('a wrong description does not harm')—a rule still operative in English law. Nor did a legacy fail simply because the reason for the gift was incorrectly stated:

Papinian, *Questions, book 18*: **The truer view is that an incorrect motivation is no impediment to a legacy because the reason for a bequest is no part of the bequest**...(D.35.1.72.6.)

In early law failed legacies went to the heirs equally unless a legacy had been specifically charged on one heir, in which case he alone benefited. Augustus changed the destination of lapsed legacies through his *leges caducariae*, which applied to failed legacies as well as failed heirs. Justinian restored the pre-Augustus rules. As regards the failure of joint legacies, the rules were complicated by distinctions made as to the type of joint legacy. For example, if a share failed of a joint legacy *per vindicationem*, it went to the other co-legatees; but to the heirs in the case of a legacy *per damnationem*. These rules were later subjected to Augustus's *leges caducariae*. Justinian simplified the position by decreeing that, as a general rule, failed shares of joint legacies went to co-legatees.

8.9 Codicils and trusts

8.9.1 Codicils

Originally, codicils consisted of informal attempts to dispose of property on death. They could exist quite independently of wills. It seems that codicils were first recognized as valid under Augustus. A certain Lucius Lentulus, when dying in Africa, made codicils in which he appointed Augustus as one of his heirs and asked him to perform a service by way of a trust. The Emperor consulted his leading jurists, who advised that codicils should be upheld because of the difficulties of making proper wills in the course of 'lengthy journeys'. Augustus followed the advice and performed the trust. So codicils and trusts gained legal recognition at the same time. Codicils soon came to be upheld whether or not they were made as the result of lengthy journeys. They could be made by anyone who could make a will, i.e. anyone with *testamenti factio*. No particular formalities were required until the later Empire, when Theodosius II decreed that seven witnesses were necessary (but only five under Justinian).

A distinction was drawn between codicils that were confirmed by will and those that were not. At first, codicils were not considered valid unless confirmed, whether prospectively or retrospectively. Prospective confirmation was effected by the testator stating in his will that effect was to be given to codicils made after the will. Retrospective confirmation was the ratification of a codicil made before the will. A codicil that was confirmed by will could do almost anything that a will could do, but could not appoint an heir. On the other hand, codicils that were not confirmed by will were regarded as valid only for the purpose of creating a trust; but then that was the primary purpose of codicils in any case. When Justinian fused the law of legacies with that of trusts (see 8.9.2.5), the distinction between confirmed and unconfirmed codicils lost its force.

The importance of codicils as an alternative form of disposing of property on death led to the development of an ingenious practice in the classical period: testators would insert a clause in their wills to the effect that, in the event of failure, the will should be construed as a codicil, imposing trusts on the heirs entitled on intestacy. This practice was intended as a form of extra 'insurance' against the possibility of intestacy.

8.9.2 Trusts (*fideicommissa*)

Trusts were a comparatively late development in Roman law (see Watson, A., 'The Early History of Fidei-Commissa' (1970) 1 Index, 178–83). But once their validity was recognized, they came to exercise an enormous and dynamic influence on the practical operation of the law of inheritance. See generally Johnston, D., *The Roman Law of Trusts* (1988). Indeed, it is clear that in the classical period there was not one law of inheritance, but three: the *ius civile* system, the *bonorum possessio* of the praetors, and the law of trusts. Trusts were obligations that were imposed on heirs or other beneficiaries under a will, to hold property (and usually to transfer it) for the benefit of the persons designated by the testator. Trusts could be imposed also on heirs to an intestate estate. It can be seen at once that Roman trusts differed in some important respects from the notion of a trust in English law. For example, the English trust can operate *inter vivos* as well as on death. cf. Frier and McGinn, *Casebook*, 404–12.

8.9.2.1 Origins

Roman testators sometimes entrusted the care of a particular item of property to an heir (or legatee) with a request that it should be passed on to some other person. In this practice can be detected the origins of *fideicommissa*, the heirs being entrusted with the carrying out of the testator's request. At first, the obligation had no legal force—the beneficiary under the trust depended on the good faith of the heir. However, given the concern with preserving one's good name and honour, the breaking of a trust would not be something that the Roman heir would contemplate lightly, particularly if others knew of its provisions.

Trusts acquired legal recognition, as we have seen, when Augustus followed his jurists' advice and carried out the trust requested of him in Lentulus's codicils. But trusts did not become legally enforceable overnight. What Augustus did was to create a machinery for their recognition on an *ad hoc* basis. The rule developed that a person could not take an inheritance (or a legacy) without performing any trust that may have been imposed on the gift. The consuls were given jurisdiction over the enforcement of trusts. Despite the uncertainty engendered by the discretionary nature of the jurisdiction, the popularity of trusts grew, necessitating the creation under Claudius of a new magistracy, the *praetor fideicommissarius*. His particular function was to oversee the operation of trusts as between heirs and beneficiaries. It seems that the consuls retained their jurisdiction, at least in cases involving large sums or distinguished citizens. See Johnston, D., *The Roman Law of Trusts* (1988), 222.

Although the recognition of trusts under Augustus was, in jurisprudential terms, an imaginative and progressive development, it was also something of a surprise in that it contradicted other aspects of the Emperor's legal policy, e.g. the ban on unmarried persons benefiting under a will—trusts were frequently used to evade such restrictions. There seems little to be gained in enacting such a ban if machinery is installed which makes circumvention possible.

8.9.2.2 **Purpose of trusts**

Why is it that trusts became popular? What could be done through them that was not possible through the normal channels of the law of inheritance? A great deal. We saw earlier how various categories of people could not take under wills (see 8.4.1.3). Trusts were employed to circumvent the strict *ius civile* rules on capacity to take, a development paralleled in medieval English law when the concept of the use, the forerunner of the modern trust, was employed to avoid (*inter alia*) the restrictions on disposing of realty by will. So the Roman testator, if he wished to benefit a foreigner, say, would entrust property to his heir to pass it to the intended beneficiary, thus avoiding a breach of the rules as to capacity. The foreigner took under the trust, not under the will. (See Johnston, D., 'Successive Rights and Successful Remedies: Life Interests in Roman Law', in *New Perspectives*, 153–67, for an insightful article in which the benefits and disadvantages of usufruct and *fideicommisum* from the perspective of the Roman testator are discussed. For an interesting comparison between Roman and English law on the subject, see Thomas, J. A. C., 'Perpetuities and Fideicommissary Substitutions' (1958) 5 RIDA 3, 571–90.)

Besides benefiting persons who normally could not take under a will, trusts had other uses. For example, a testator could attempt to free another's slave by subjecting his own heir to a trust under which the slave was to be bought and freed. And it was possible to die intestate without undue worry by imposing a trust on the heirs on intestacy in favour of the deceased's preferred beneficiary. Trusts were particularly important in the making of Roman family settlements since they could be created in favour of 'unascertained persons' such as future-born children (see Johnston, D., 'Prohibitions and Perpetuities: Family Settlements in Roman Law' (1985) 102 ZSS (rA), 220–90, for a discussion of this aspect in classical Roman law (latter part of the second and start of the third century AD)). Moreover, a trust could be made subject to another trust—this was known as fideicommissary substitution. The combined effect of these possibilities was that a testator could effectively preserve property in the family for generations by creating successive trusts. This was something of a departure in view of 'the great reluctance of Roman law to permit entailing . . . it is feudalism that fosters the entail, and Rome was fundamentally un-feudal' (Crook, *Law and Life of Rome*, 122).

The legal recognition of trusts in Augustus's reign inevitably led to their being closely regulated and restricted in scope. For example, trusts in favour of foreigners were eventually banned under Vespasian, and the *S. C. Pegasianum c.* AD 73 prevented childless beneficiaries from taking under trusts. Testators attempted to circumvent such restrictions by making secret trusts either outside the will or by the use of a suitably cryptic phrase within it, e.g. 'I request you to transfer the property according to the instructions given to you'. Such trusts were not legally enforceable: their performance was dependent on the good faith of the heir, as in the case of non-secret trusts before Augustus. See further Johnston, D., *The Roman Law of Trusts* (1988), ch. 3.

Potentially the most important restriction was the banning by Hadrian of trusts in favour of 'unascertained persons'. Testators who wished to preserve property within the family were forced to find a way around this ban. The solution was for the testator to impose a trust on family members not to dispose of specified property outside the family. Such directions came to be regarded as binding. Moreover, the jurists were generally prepared to give a wide interpretation to restrictions placed by testators (by way of a trust) on the disposal of family property. For example, dying intestate could be regarded as a form of disposal of property on the evidence of the following text by Cervidius Scaevola:

Scaevola, *Replies, book 3*: **A testator appointed his mother and wife as heirs and provided as follows: 'I ask you, my dearest wife, that you should not leave anything after your death to your brothers. You have sons of your sisters to whom you may leave property. You know that one of your brothers killed our son while robbing him; and another, too, has done me injury.' Question: Now that the wife has died intestate and her inheritance belongs to the brother as *legitimus heres*, can the sister's sons claim the *fideicommissum* from him? I replied that it could be argued that the *fideicommissum* is due.** (D.31.1.88.16.)

Justinian returned at first to the pre-Hadrian position, allowing trusts to be made in favour of 'unascertained persons', but he later limited the efficacy of such trusts to a maximum of four generations.

8.9.2.3 **Form**

How were trusts created? With a minimum of formality—it seems that any clear expression of intention sufficed, whether made orally or in writing, or possibly even by gesture in some cases. Johnston regards this as fundamental in the rise of the trust: 'The barest requirements had to be met to validate a trust: only a form-less expression of intention was needed; and this was paralleled by remarkable procedural flexibility' (*The Roman Law of Trusts* (1988), 288). And he considers that such factors were more important than the use of the trust for circumventing the law: 'Its significant role was not to provide a surreptitious means of passing ben-efits to the disqualified…its importance lay in its freedom, the potential it offered the jurists to expand and develop an entire system from a few modest principles' (Johnston, *The Roman Law of Trusts* (1988), 288).

Probably the most common form of trust consisted of a suitable written direc-tion by a testator in his will or codicil, beginning with words of request, whether express or implied:

Neratius, *Rules, book 10*: **A *fideicommissum* left in terms such as 'I require', 'I desire that you give', is valid, and even if worded 'I wish my inheritance to be Titius's', 'I know that you will remit my inheritance to Titius'.** (D.30.118.)

However, if the words left it to the discretion of the heir whether he passed the property to the beneficiary, the trust was not operative; similarly, where there was a commendation as opposed to a request:

Ulpian, *Fideicommissa, book 2*: **If anyone has written, 'I commend such a one to you,' the dei-fied Pius ruled in a rescript that a *fideicommissum* is not due; for it is one thing to commend a person and another to intimate to one's heirs the intention of leaving a *fideicommissum*.** (D.32.11.2.)

Trusts could apply to the whole or part of an inheritance or legacy, or to specific items of the deceased's property; and they could be imposed on anyone who ben-efited under the deceased's estate—heirs, legatees, and beneficiaries under trusts.

8.9.2.4 **Heir and beneficiary**

The legal relationship between the heir and the beneficiary under the trust was of overriding importance in the operation of *fideicommissa*. A trust depended on there being an operative will, except in those cases where trusts were specifically imposed on the *sui heredes* on intestacy. If the heir refused the inheritance, any trusts that were imposed on him would fail. An heir would be unlikely to accept an inheritance that was subject to a trust extending over the whole or a large part of the estate, because, if he did so, he would be responsible for administering the will, and paying debts, and legacies, while his own benefit might be consumed by the trust. It became the normal practice, therefore, for the heir and the beneficiary under the trust to come to an arrangement under which the latter 'bought' the inheritance by a mock *mancipatio*. The parties entered mutual stipulations whereby the heir promised to transfer all assets to the beneficiary and to allow him to bring any appropriate actions, e.g. to recover debts owed to the inheritance; whereas the beneficiary undertook to defend actions against the estate and to indemnify the heir for payments reasonably made on its behalf. Where the trust comprised less than the whole inheritance, the *mancipatio* and mutual stipulations would still be made, but in proportion to the amount of the inheritance that was subject to the trust.

Imagine yourself as an heir involved in such arrangements. Would you accept an inheritance if little or no benefit was to come your way? It is true that the mutual stipulations ensured that you would not suffer financially, but you could still be involved in considerable time and effort in carrying out your responsibilities under the agreed arrangements. And you remained the heir—the *position* could not be sold through the mock mancipation. All things considered, you would be seriously tempted to wash your hands of the inheritance, assuming that you were an *extraneus*. Further inducements were needed. They were provided by two important *senatus consulta* of the first century:

(a) *S. C. Trebellianum* AD 56. In effect this enactment implied the mutual stipulations outlined earlier. The need to make specific stipulations was ended, thus considerably reducing the administrative involvement of the heir. Once he consented to the vesting of the inheritance in the beneficiary under the trust, the latter was in the position of an heir: any actions (for or against the estate) passed to him. If the creditors sued the true heir, he could defeat them by relying on the appropriate defence under the statute. The *S. C. Trebellianum* applied also to trusts imposed on heirs on intestacy. And, as a general rule, it applied pro rata if the trust affected only a part of the inheritance.

Although this statute improved the heir's position, the reform was procedural rather than substantive. The heir was not given any greater benefit—he might still receive nothing from the estate if the trust extended over the whole inheritance. In such cases the beneficiary would be tempted to offer the heir an inducement to persuade him to accept.

(b) *S. C. Pegasianum c.* AD 73. This enactment applied the *lex Falcidia* (see 8.6.3) to trusts by allowing the heir to take at least a quarter of the net estate, provided that he had accepted the inheritance voluntarily. If he had refused, it seems that he could be compelled to accept on an application by the beneficiary, in which case the position was as under the *S. C. Trebellianum*—the heir was not entitled to a quarter.

8.9.2.5 Justinian's reforms

Justinian combined the advantages of the Trebellian and Pegasian reforms, consolidating them under one statute, a redrafted *S. C. Trebellianum*. The beneficiary under the trust was regarded as being in the position of an heir, so that the true heir could not be affected by litigation concerning the inheritance. If the trust did not apply to the whole inheritance, the position was regulated pro rata, i.e. actions passed to and against the beneficiary in proportion to his share. The heir could be compelled to accept, as before, and his right to a quarter was preserved, although Justinian decreed that the testator could direct that the quarter should not be taken. This innovation was similar to that applied by Justinian to legacies. Indeed, this development was part of his overall assimilation of legacies and trusts:

Ulpian, *Edict, book 67*: **Legacies are held to be equal to *fideicommissa* in all respects.** (D.30.1.)

It is unusual for a title in the *Digest* to begin with such a broad assertion of principle. The statement is attributed to Ulpian but it is doubtful whether he made it—no substantial assimilation of legacies and trusts occurred in the classical period. But it certainly took place under Justinian, not least because of the fusion of remedies for the enforcement of legacies and trusts: for the first time a beneficiary under a trust was allowed a *vindicatio* to secure his interest. Previously, the only remedy had been an action *in personam* against the heir.

 online resource centre Please consult the Online Resource Centre for revision guidance on this chapter.

FURTHER READING

On the Roman law of succession, see comprehensively Watson, A. (1971), *The Law of Succession in the Later Roman Republic*, Oxford: Clarendon Press; Tellegen-Couperus, O. E. (1982) *Testamentary Succession in the Constitutions of Diocletian*, Zutphen: Terra Publishing Co., an interesting work in which the law on testamentary succession in the constitutions of Diocletian is compared to the position in classical Roman law; Crook, J. A., 'Women in Roman Succession', in *Family in Ancient Rome*, 58–82, an insightful article exploring the legal rules relating to the succession of women to property in classical Roman law compared with evidence of actual practice. On this point, see also Saller, R. P., 'Roman Heirship Strategies in Principle and in Practice', in *The Family in Italy*, 26–47.

PART IV

The Law of Obligations

9

....

Obligations: general principles and obligations arising from contracts

9.1 Obligations in general

9.1.1 The nature of obligations

An obligation is a legal tie which binds us to the necessity of making some performance in accordance with the laws of our state. (Inst.3.13pr.)

The definition in the *Institutes* of Justinian of an obligation as a 'legal tie' (*vinculum iuris*) or a legal bond between creditor and debtor, though post-classical, aptly evokes images of the concept of personal liability (seizure of the debtor's body) in archaic Roman law from which the law of obligations developed. In classical and Justinianic Roman law, this branch of law is concerned with situations where a person has incurred a personal liability for which he is answerable at law:

Paul, *Institutes, book 2*: **The essence of obligations does not consist in that it makes some property or a servitude ours, but that it binds another person to give, do, or perform something for us.** (D.44.7.3pr.)

Paul's comment emphasizes that the law of obligations deals with rights and duties *in personam*, not *in rem*. However, it fails to emphasize that this area of the law is concerned with obligations arising from the acts of the parties themselves, and not from their *status*. We have already seen that in the law of persons a variety of duties arose from the fact that a person was of a certain status. Paul's statement could apply equally well to such duties, but they are not strictly part of the law of obligations, which focuses on obligations *incurred* by the parties rather than those automatically imposed on them.

How were obligations incurred? Mainly either by contracts made by the parties, or through delicts committed by one against the other. That an obligation can arise from a contract can readily be appreciated as a natural consequence of the agreement between the two parties. That a delict, essentially a unilateral act, can create an obligation is perhaps less obvious, but is understandable: a wrongful and damaging act should incur a duty to compensate the victim in a civilized legal system. There is clearly an 'obligation' in such a case. Nevertheless, there was a tendency to treat contractual liability as the principal source of obligation.

An obligation had twofold consequences: a *duty* arose on the part of the person incurring the obligation; and there was a corresponding *right* in the other person to enforce that duty by legal action (an *actio in personam*), which would normally result (in the developed law) in an award of damages. Hence, from the plaintiff's point of view, an obligation was an asset, a *res incorporalis*; it was thus part of the law of things in Gaius's tripartite classification of civil law (see 2.3.4.4):

Incorporeal things are things that are intangible, consisting of a right for example an inheritance, a usufruct, and an obligation however contracted. (Inst.Gai.2.14.)

Since obligations were regarded as creating a personal relationship between the parties, they could not generally affect third parties. In early law, the obligation lapsed when the party subject to it died. That remained the general position as regards delictual liability but, as regards contracts, there was a gradual change towards enforcing obligations against the heirs of a deceased party.

The rendition of the Institutional scheme in Diagram 9.1 demonstrates the conceptual location of the law of obligations. For an overview of the Roman 'conceptual map' of obligations, see Birks, *Obligations*, 1–23.

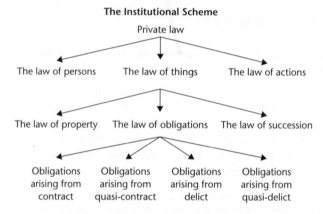

The Institutional Scheme

Private law

The law of persons   The law of things   The law of actions

The law of property   The law of obligations   The law of succession

Obligations arising from contract   Obligations arising from quasi-contract   Obligations arising from delict   Obligations arising from quasi-delict

Diagram 9.1 The Institutional Scheme

9.1.2 **The classification of obligations**

Obligations were classified in a variety of ways, the earliest of which seems to have been the distinction between obligations arising from the *ius civile* and those from the *ius honorarium*. To this twofold division was added a third category in the classical period—natural obligations (probably in the mid-second century AD). In this period, obligations were also variously classified as unilateral or bilateral, depending on whether one or both parties were bound—in the contract of sale, obligations were clearly bilateral; in delict, they were normally unilateral. Or obligations could be *stricti iuris* or *bonae fidei*, depending on whether the *formula* in the action that enforced them pointed to a strict or a discretionary application of the law to the facts (a classification of great prominence in Justinianic law). This distinction between *stricti iuris* and *bonae fidei* contracts had a profound impact on the development of this branch of law and should be taken into account when studying the 'general features' outlined later. Consequently, form was all-important in disputes concerning *stricti iuris* contracts, whereas in *bonae fidei* contracts matters such as mistake, fraud, and duress could more easily be taken into account. As a general rule, unilateral contracts were *stricti iuris*, bilateral ones were *bonae fidei*.

9.1.2.1 **Natural obligations**

These consisted mainly of agreements that were not legally enforceable but which could have legal consequences. If a slave made an agreement with his master or some other party, it could not be enforced on manumission—the obligation of the other party was 'natural' only. But if that other party initially kept to the promise, but later tried to resile, he could be prevented from using the argument that the initial agreement was void:

Tryphoninus, *Disputations, book 7*: **Suppose an owner has a debt to his slave and pays it after manumission. He cannot recover, not even if he believed the other could sue him by some action; for his payment acknowledges his natural indebtedness. For in the sense that freedom is the condition of natural law and subjection the invention of the law of the world, so for the** *condictio* **the question whether there is or is not a debt is to be taken on the natural plane.** (D.12.6.64.)

Another important type of natural obligation was that which arose from agreements made between a *paterfamilias* and members of his family. Although the agreement had no effect while the family member was in *potestas*, it could have thereafter. For example, if a father 'owed' money to his son under an agreement made before the son's emancipation, and then paid the debt after the emancipation, the payment could not be recovered. In this case, as in the previous example, the natural obligation worked to the advantage of the 'creditor'—i.e. the slave or the son. But it could work to their disadvantage:

Ulpian, *Edict, book 12*: **Those who have incurred a change of civil status remain under a natural obligation with respect to matters which have arisen prior to such a change.** (D.4.5.2.2.)

The concept of the natural obligation survives in modern law, even if in a different context. For example, the BGB recognizes the existence of nonbinding obligations, such as the promise of a fee to a marriage broker (s. 656) and obligations arising from betting and gaming (s. 762). See Zimmermann, *Obligations*, 7 ff.

9.1.2.2 **The source of the obligation**

The most important classification of obligations was according to the *causa* of the obligation, i.e. its source. This classification has prompted some controversy, partly because of the seemingly inconsistent texts. Gaius states:

Gaius, *Golden Words, book 2*: **Obligations arise either from contract or from wrongdoing or by some special right from various types of causes.** (D.44.7.1pr.)

By 'wrongdoing', Gaius is referring to delict. So his classification appears to be threefold—obligations arise from contract, delict, or 'special right'. Suspicion that this text, apparently taken from Gaius' *Golden Words*, might be an interpolation is strengthened by comparing it to a passage in Gaius' *Institutes* (Inst.Gai.3.88.) where he maintains that there are just two sources of obligation—contract and delict:

Let us now proceed to obligations. They are divided into two main species: for every obligation arises either from contract of from delict. (Inst.Gai.3.88.)

Some scholars maintain that Gaius used the term 'contract' loosely in this (earlier) text to refer to any obligation arising from lawful conduct. In classical Roman law, however, the term 'contract' acquired a narrower technical meaning. This rendered Gaius' principal division unsatisfactory and necessitated the introduction of a third category (special right form various types of causes) in D.44.7.1pr. (see Metzger, *Companion*, 127–8).

Justinian states in his *Institutes* (Inst.3.13.2.) that the sources of obligation were fourfold: contract, delict, quasi-contract, and quasi-delict. This seems, *prima facie*, at odds with the classification attributed to Gaius in the *Digest*, but it is possible to reconcile the passages by regarding quasi-contract and quasi-delict as obligations arising 'by some special right' (as per D.44.7.1pr.). Indeed, when examining the circumstances in which quasi-contract and quasi-delict applied, the picture emerges of a number of diverse cases to which Gaius' description fits well. But the difficulty with this line of argument is that Gaius regards obligations as arising exclusively from the *ius civile*, whereas quasi-delict was largely the product of praetorian intervention. It is thus difficult to maintain that Gaius was referring to quasi-delict in the phrase 'special right from various types of causes'.

The twofold classification of obligations—contract and delict—in Gaius' *Institutes* has proved seminal in Western jurisprudence, although there has inevitably been some overlap between the categories. In English law, the overlap was partly the legacy of the development of *assumpsit*—which became the standard contractual remedy—from its tortious roots.

9.1.2.3 Justinian's classification

Justinian regarded obligations as stemming from four sources: contract, quasi-contract, delict, and quasi-delict.

(a) Contract. A contract can be broadly defined as an agreement that is enforceable at law. Gaius classified contracts into four categories, and Justinian adopted his basic scheme. These categories were differentiated according to the source of the obligation:

(i) consensual contracts: the obligation arose simply from the agreement of the parties;

(ii) verbal contracts: the pronouncement of particular words in a set form created the obligation;

(iii) contracts *re*: the delivery of a *res* created the obligation, e.g. loan, deposit;

(iv) contracts *litteris* ('by written record'): originally the obligation arose from an entry written in a ledger, although by Justinian's time its source was simply a written acknowledgement of a fictitious loan.

In the consensual contracts, agreement alone sufficed, but in the other categories some extra ingredient was necessary. However, in all cases an agreement between the parties was essential:

Ulpian, *Edict, book 12*: **Moreover, so true is it that the word 'agreement' has a general significance that Pedius neatly says that there is no contract, no obligation which does not consist of agreement, whether it is achieved by the handing over of something or by the use of certain words.** (D.2.14.1.3.)

Justinian's fourfold classification of contracts is unsatisfactory, as it does not take account of other agreements that undoubtedly had a contractual effect, e.g. pacts and innominate contracts. It may be that Justinian was unwilling to disturb the superficially attractive symmetry of a fourfold classification. It is a classification that recurs regularly throughout the law of obligations, not just in relation to types of contract. However, Zimmermann considers that this method of arranging the law was not adopted for the sake of symmetry: 'like most people in the ancient world, he [Justinian] was influenced by the symbolism of numbers. The number four has always had a special significance, usually relating—in contrast to the sacred number three—to the more external or secular structure of the world', e.g. the four points of the compass, the four seasons, the four elements: Zimmermann, *Obligations*, 15. For a substantive discussion of the conceptual arrangement of the Roman law of contracts and the possible motivations behind it, see Birks, *Obligations*, 26–36. To this must be added the profound insights of Fiori, R., 'The Roman Conception of Contract', in *Obligations in Roman Law*, 40–75.

(b) Quasi-contract. This category comprised a number of situations that were not strictly contractual (but were largely analogous to contract), in which liability *in personam* arose. It is difficult to find any common principle or link among them. An important example was *negotiorum gestio*, i.e. performing services for another person without their knowledge; unjust enrichment was another.

(c) Delict:

Gaius, *Golden Words, book 3*: **Obligations arise from delict, for example, theft, damage, robbery, and insult. They are all of one nature; for they consist in what is done, that is, the wrongdoing itself.** (D.44.7.4.)

This category of obligations arose from the commission of civil wrongs, the broad equivalent of English torts. Delicts often had penal consequences, e.g. the damages awarded against the defendant could substantially exceed the actual loss caused to the plaintiff.

(d) Quasi-delict. This was another untidy category that, as in the case of quasi-contract, lacked a unifying principle.

The Roman classification of obligations has proved to be a model for modern codes. The French Civil Code, notably, follows the fourfold division. However, the problems inherent in determining the scope of the categories, especially quasi-contract and quasi-delict, and distinguishing between them, have led to other approaches. The German Civil Code, for example, simply lists 25 different 'particular' obligations without attempting to fit them into any overall classification. For the advisability of attempting to apply Roman classification to English law, see Birks, P., 'Obligations: One Tier or Two?', in *Studies J. A. C. Thomas*, 18–38. For other general aspects of obligations (such as discharge), see Buckland, *Textbook*, ch. 12.

9.2 General features of Roman contracts

The developed Roman law of contract was a law of *discrete transactions*: it lacked a fundamental unifying principle other than the necessity for an agreement. In some respects, it resembled the English medieval law of contract—a set of remedies for particular situations, each remedy containing its own distinctive rules. But, whereas the emergence of the writ of *assumpsit* ('he undertook') eventually helped to give the English law of contract a considerable degree of cohesion, in Roman law the development was, if anything, the opposite. In early Rome, the law revolved largely around a single contract—the *stipulatio* (see 9.4.3)—but later became a law of *contracts* rather than a law of contract. The comparison needs to be made cautiously, however, for it is clear that, despite its unitary appearance, English law comprises a number of discrete transactions: 'Now of course the lawyer in practice knows that it really does matter what the transaction is, because different rules do apply to different transactions' (Weir, T., 'Contracts in Rome and England' (1992) 66 Tulane LR, 1615–48 at 1642). Diagram 9.2 provides a rendition of the conceptual map of the Roman law of contracts.

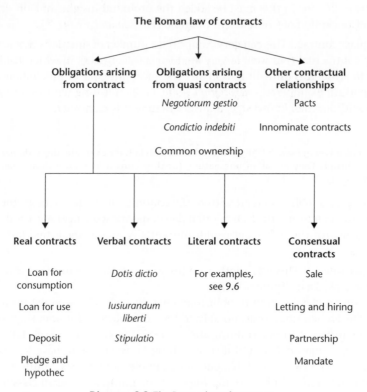

The Roman law of contracts

Obligations arising from contract	**Obligations arising from quasi contracts**	**Other contractual relationships**
	Negotiorum gestio	Pacts
	Condictio indebiti	Innominate contracts
	Common ownership	

Real contracts	**Verbal contracts**	**Literal contracts**	**Consensual contracts**
Loan for consumption	*Dotis dictio*	For examples, see 9.6	Sale
Loan for use	*Iusiurandum liberti*		Letting and hiring
Deposit	*Stipulatio*		Partnership
Pledge and hypothec			Mandate

Diagram 9.2 The Roman law of contracts

All contracts in Roman law were either *bonae fidei* or *stricti iuris*, depending on whether the *formula* of the action empowered the *iudex* to apply his equitable discretion to the facts of the case (see 9.1.2). *Stricti iuris* contracts (the older category) arose from the *ius civile*, while *bonae fidei* contracts were introduced through the *ius honorarium*. The legality of *stricti iuris* contracts (e.g. *stipulatio*), unlike *bonae fidei* contracts, was dictated by strict observance of the outward formalities of the act. Most *stricti iuris* contracts imposed a unilateral obligation to perform on one party, whereas *bonae fidei* contracts generated bilateral obligations for both parties to the contract (e.g. sale). For a good recent overview, see Aubert, J. J., 'Commerce', in *Cambridge Companion*, 213–45.

The Roman law of contracts possessed a number of general features. What follows should not be taken to imply that the Romans ever developed 'a general principle of contract' as is found in modern civilian systems. The general principle of contract is an invention of the early modern period. Rather, the following section sets out some of the main features (consent etc.) shared by most of the individual contracts in Roman law.

9.2.1 **Consensus**

Agreement between the parties was essential to the making of a contract. There had to be a genuine meeting of minds, a *consensus ad idem* ('agreement about the same thing') at the moment when the contract was made. If there was an unresolved ambiguity in the language used by the parties, the contract would be void; but a judge would strive to resolve the ambiguity by considering the conduct of the parties and the custom of the region where the contract was made. Ambiguities were interpreted so as to make the transaction as efficacious as possible. As a last resort, a judge could fall back on the rule that ambiguities were construed against the party who could be regarded as having the principal role in the formulation of the particular term in question.

For example:

Paul, *Sabinus, book 5*: **Labeo writes that where a term of the contract is obscure, it should be construed against the vendor who stated it rather than against the purchaser, because the vendor could have declared his will more explicitly before the contract was entered into.** (D.18.1.21.)

Even if the agreement was unambiguous, genuine consensus might be lacking because of factors such as mistake, duress, and fraud. See also Procchi, F., 'Roman Contracts and the Construction of Fault in their Formation', in *Obligations in Roman Law*, 76–101.

9.2.1.1 **Mistake**

What type of mistake vitiated a contract? The texts present an unclear picture, but generally the Roman judge was less reluctant than his English counterpart to nullify contracts made by mistake (see *Futter & Anor v Revenue and Customs* [2013] UKSC 26). The common law doctrine of mistake is of rather narrow application (although it has a partner in the rules on misrepresentation). But in Roman law, the requirement of a strict *consensus ad idem* resulted in a wider role for rules on mistake. The following types of mistake were regarded as fatal to a contract:

(a) Mistaken transaction (*error in negotio*): where one or both parties were mistaken about the type of transaction intended, e.g. where A intended a sale, but B thought it was a loan.

(b) Mistaken subject matter (*error in corpore*): where one or both parties were mistaken over the identity of the thing that was the central object of the contract:

Ulpian, *Sabinus, book 28*: ... **if I thought that I was buying the Cornelian farm and you that you were selling the Sempronian, the sale is void because we were not agreed upon the thing sold. The same is true if I intended to sell Stichus and you thought that I was selling you Pamphilus, the slave himself not being there** ... (D.18.1.9pr.)

If the mistake was about the identity of some accessory thing, not central to the contract, the mistake was not operative—the contract was valid.

(c) Mistaken identity (*error in persona*): where one or both parties were mistaken about the identity of the other party. But the mistake was only operative in such a case if the identity of the other party was relevant, as in the contract of partnership, for example.

A fourth type of mistake appears to have been recognized, but possibly not until the post-classical period—mistake about the quality of the subject matter of the contract (*error in substantia*). Such a mistake is far less drastic than those considered previously; one can thus understand the reluctance to invalidate contracts on that ground. The position appears to have been that such mistakes were irrelevant as regards *stricti iuris* contracts, but *could* invalidate *bonae fidei* contracts if the mistake was fundamental—e.g. if something that was sold was in a different category from what the buyer supposed:

Ulpian, *Sabinus, book 28*: **If, however, I think that I am buying a virgin when she is, in fact, a woman, the sale is valid, there being no mistake over her sex. But if I sell you a woman and you think that you are buying a male slave, the error over sex makes the sale void.** (D.18.1.11.1.)

The texts on mistakes about quality are far from clear, and may have been the object of some interpolation. They reveal some disagreement among the jurists, as the following passage (attributed to Ulpian) suggests:

Ulpian, *Sabinus, book 28*: **The next question is whether there is a good sale when there is no mistake over the identity of the thing but there is over its substance: Suppose that vinegar is sold as wine, copper as gold or lead, or something else similar to silver as silver. Marcellus, . . . writes that there is a sale because there is agreement on the thing despite the mistake over its substance. I would agree in the case of the wine, because the essence is much the same, that is, if the wine has gone sour; if it be not sour wine, however, but was vinegar from the beginning such as brewed vinegar, then it emerges that one thing has been sold as another. But in the other cases, I think that there is no sale by reason of the error over the material.** (D.18.1.9.2.)

In this text, Ulpian understandably treats 'the other cases' as *error in corpore*; but his apparent agreement with Marcellus concerning wine turned sour is puzzling since it denies a role for *error in substantia* in this case, and is thus arguably inconsistent with D.18.1.11.1. (also attributed to Ulpian). Such textual problems render it difficult to maintain categorical assertions about the role of *error in substantia*.

The effect of an operative mistake, whatever the type, was to render a contract void, but that did not prevent legal action being taken in respect of the contract: e.g. a buyer would have an action for recovery of the price paid, while the seller could recover the thing delivered.

The Roman doctrine of *error*—particularly *error in substantia*—has provided a rich vein of law for analysis, adaptation, and application in modern systems. Article 1110 of the French Civil Code provides that error nullifies a transaction if it affects *'la substance même'*—the very substance of the thing; this has been interpreted, under the influence of Pothier's *Traité des obligations*, to include error about quality. The BGB no longer follows the Roman classification although there is some recognition of *error in substantia*: rescission is possible for an error as to those characteristics of a person or thing regarded as essential in business (s. 119). The rules on mistake in English law clearly bear considerable similarity to the Roman doctrine of *error*, even if the process by which it was achieved was different. See particularly, Lawson, F. H., 'Error in Substantia' (1936) 52 LQR, 79–105, and Zimmermann, *Obligations*, 609 ff.

9.2.1.2 **Duress**

A contract was regarded as made under duress if a party (or members of his family) had been threatened with 'serious evil' unless he consented to the contract (see further 10.5.2). One might have expected duress to invalidate all contracts, and one can find texts that appear to support that view:

Ulpian, *Edict, book 11*: **Nothing is so contrary to consent, which sustains cases of good faith, as force or duress; it is contrary to good behavior to approve of either of them.** (D.50.17.116.)

But the position was not quite so simple: the effect of duress varied according to the type of contract. If a party made a *stricti iuris* contract under duress, the contract was formally valid in early law. However, the aggrieved party would hope that the praetor might prevent the enforcement of such an agreement or that he would grant *restitutio*. In the late Republic, the *exceptio metus* ('the defence of duress') was allowed against a party trying to enforce an agreement made under duress. Moreover, an *actio metus* was allowed to an aggrieved party who had suffered loss as the result of duress (see 10.5.2). As regards *bonae fidei* contracts, the most plausible view is that duress did not necessarily invalidate them, but that it was certainly a factor to be taken into account by the judge.

What if actual physical force was used to compel someone to enter a contract? It seems that there was no *consensus* at all in such cases—a contract made through force was invalid.

9.2.1.3 Fraud

What constituted fraud?

Ulpian, *Edict, book 11*: ... **every kind of cunning, trickery or contrivance practiced in order to cheat, trick or deceive another.** (D.4.3.1.2.)

Fraud was similar in legal effect to duress. A party induced by fraud to enter a *stricti iuris* contract had no defence or remedy as of right until the introduction of the *exceptio doli* and *actio doli* in the late Republic (see 10.5.3). Thereafter, the *exceptio doli* provided a defence if specifically pleaded in the *formula*. The introduction of this defence brought about a considerable extension of the judge's equitable discretion, even in *stricti iuris* actions. It did not have to be pleaded in actions arising out of *bonae fidei* contracts since the *formula* would contain the appropriate good faith clause: thus the judge would be automatically directed in such cases to take good faith into account. Generally, if fraud induced a mistake of the sort that invalidated a contract, the ground of failure was regarded as mistake rather than fraud.

9.2.2 *Causa*

Not all agreements amounted to contracts, only those that were actionable at law. What made an agreement actionable? It was the existence of some ground, reason or 'cause' (*causa*) for enforcing the agreement:

Ulpian, *Edict, book 4*: **But, when no ground exists, it is settled that no obligation arises from the agreement....** (D.2.14.7.4.)

If *causa* was the reason why an agreement was actionable, what determined whether it was present in certain types of agreement, i.e. contracts, but not in others? In some contracts, the answer was obvious—it was the form of the agreement that constituted the *causa*, e.g. the written entry in the contract *litteris* (see 9.6.1). In the contracts *re*, (e.g. loan, deposit) the *causa* consisted of the delivery of the thing. But what of the consensual contracts, such as sale, where mere agreement sufficed to create the contract? Where was the *causa* there? It seems that the answer has to be sought outside the contract itself—in the socio-economic conditions of Rome. The period when the consensual contracts became fully established was the third century BC, the time when Rome was beginning to develop into a formidable economic power. These contracts developed partly because of the needs of commerce. So it seems that the *causa* in these contracts lay in the commercial necessity for recognizing such agreements as actionable. However, it is difficult to generalize about *causa* because its meaning was not fixed but differed according to the context. For example, *causa* could also mean the motive for a transaction, or could signify the interdependence of promises. Indeed, it is possible that *causa* (in whatever form) was not essential to every Roman contract, and that medieval scholars exaggerated its importance. Zimmermann holds that the origins of the doctrine of *causa* lay in medieval law, influenced by the scholastic doctrine of causation whereby every effect was regarded as resulting from its cause. He considers that texts such as D.2.14.7.4. do not purport to be of general application: *Obligations*, 549 ff.

Causa is regarded as an essential element of contracts in some modern continental systems. For example, Article 1131 of the French Civil Code provides that an obligation '*sans cause*' cannot have any effect (however, the *cause* need not be expressed: Article 1132). In German law, on the other hand, *causa* is not required. In those systems where *causa* is regarded as essential, it occupies a place similar to that of the requirement of consideration in English law—a unifying factor in the law of contract. Indeed, Zimmermann identifies *causa* with consideration: 'the requirement of *causa* became part and parcel of the English common law and survives, to this day, in the form of the doctrine of consideration' (*Obligations*, 554). While this can be justified as a broad generalization, the total identification of *causa* with consideration should be resisted. The traditional requirement of a reciprocal exchange of benefit and detriment in consideration marks it out as different from *causa* in at least that important respect.

9.2.3 Capacity

A contract was not valid unless the parties had capacity to make it. The rules on capacity have already been considered in relation to the law of persons (see chs. 4 and 5).

9.2.4 Illegality and immorality

Ulpian, *Sabinus*, book 42: **We generally recognize that immoral stipulations have no validity,** [Pomponius, *Sabinus*, book 22] **[27pr.]: for instance, if a man promises to commit murder or sacrilege. Indeed, it is part of the praetor's duty to refuse an action on obligations of this kind.** (D.45.1.26–27pr.)

As a general rule—at least in the Empire—an agreement to perform an illegal or immoral act was a nullity. The question of illegality could easily be tested by reference to the enactment alleged to have been breached. In the Republic, legislation was regularly passed which did not necessarily invalidate transactions made in breach of the statutory provisions, e.g. the *lex Cincia* on gifts (see 7.3.1). But in the early Empire, it became the invariable practice for statutes to impose the sanction of invalidity.

Whether transactions were immoral (*contra bonos mores*) would be determined by reference to contemporary standards of morality, as determined by censors, praetors, and, later, Emperors. It is debatable whether religious or philosophical doctrines ever influenced this concept of good morals. In general, the Romans had a clear sense of right and wrong throughout their history, and one that in some respects changed little (on immorality and illegality generally, see Zimmermann, *Obligations*, 697 ff.).

9.2.5 **Impossibility**

Celsus, *Digest, book 8*: **There is no obligation to do anything which is impossible.** (D.50.17.185.)

So runs one of the very last excerpts in the *Digest*. It is deceptively simple. A distinction has to be drawn at the outset between initial and supervening impossibility.

9.2.5.1 **Initial impossibility**

This occurred if the agreement was already impossible to perform at the time when it was made. Such an agreement was regarded as void. The test of impossibility was objective, as in the case of testamentary conditions (see 8.4.3.3)—was the performance of the agreement impossible in the nature of things for *anyone*, not just for the party involved? Impossibility did not have to be physical—legal impossibility, e.g. agreements to convey things that could not be legally conveyed, sufficed to invalidate contracts:

Modestinus, *Encyclopaedia, book 5*: **A freeman cannot be the subject of a stipulation, because it cannot be alleged that he should be conveyed, nor can his value be paid over, any more than if one were to stipulate for a dead man or for enemy land.** (D.45.1.103.)

9.2.5.2 **Supervening impossibility**

This arose when the performance of a contract became impossible on account of events occurring after it was made. The general rule in Roman law was that the contract was valid but that it could not be enforced against a party, provided that he was not to blame for the occurrence of the frustrating event, and that he was not *in mora* ('in delay'). *Mora* signified a party's failure to satisfy his obligations properly under the contract, e.g. unjustifiable delay by the buyer in accepting delivery of purchased goods. Similar rules are commonly found in modern systems. For example, s. 275 BGB provides that a party is relieved from his obligation to perform if performance becomes impossible because of circumstances—for which he is not responsible—occurring after the creation of the obligation. The development of the common law doctrine of frustration was partly influenced by the Roman rules.

9.2.6 **Privity**

To what extent could a contract confer benefits or impose duties on someone who was not a party to the contract?

Paul, *Edict, book 72*: **A contract is made between stipulator and promisor. So one promising for something to be given or done on behalf of another does not bind him; for each must promise for himself.** (D.45.1.83pr.)

The Roman rule was clear: a contract could be enforced by or against the parties to a contract, and not by or against third parties. This was primarily due to the form of the *stipulatio*, probably the most widely used contract in early law. It consisted of a unilateral promise made by one party in response to a question put by the other in each other's presence: 'Privity is built into the form' (Weir (1992) 66 Tulane LR, 1615 cited earlier, at 1620). The rule was strictly applied, much more so than in modern English law (in which the number of exceptions has all but eroded the rule). There may have been some exceptions in later Roman law but the texts are inconclusive. It seems, for example, that a promise to benefit or bind the heirs of the parties was enforceable by or against those heirs, a rule introduced by Justinian. Given the Roman concept of universal succession, Justinian's rule scarcely amounted to an exception. The strict Roman rule on privity is generally not followed in modern continental systems.

Were promises that benefited or bound third parties enforceable between the contracting parties themselves? If A promised B that C would do something for B, we know from the general rule of privity that C was not bound by A's promise. But was A liable if C failed to perform? He was not, it seems, unless he had agreed to pay a penalty in the event of C's non-performance. What if A made a promise to B to do something for C? Could B enforce the promise? Again, no, unless B had an 'interest' in its performance, e.g. where A had promised B to pay C a debt owed by B to C.

9.2.7 Modalities

One final general feature of the Roman law of contract is the so-called modalities in a contract, especially *dies* and *condiciones*. These were ways in which a performance could be delayed (suspensive condition) or undone (resolutive condition) by making it subject to the occurrence of an uncertain future event. Initially, Roman law only knew the suspensive condition, but other types developed in classical and Justinianic Roman law, see Buckland, *Textbook*, 422–6.

9.3 Consensual contracts

(Inst.Gai.3. 135.–8., Inst.3.22.)

The consensual contracts were bilateral and *bonae fidei* (see Birks, *Obligations*, 65). Their origins are uncertain but they were certainly not the earliest contracts to have emerged in Roman law. Their development was prompted largely by the needs of the expanding Roman economy in the middle Republic. All four consensual contracts—sale, hire, partnership, mandate—had a distinct commercial character. As the influx of foreigners into Rome was one of the signal factors in her economic transformation, the development of the consensual contracts probably owed much to the work of the peregrine praetor. Despite their comparatively late origins, the consensual contracts came to have an immense importance. They merit prime consideration.

Obligations contracted by mere consent are exemplified by sale, hire, partnership and agency, which are called consensual contracts because no writing, nor the presence of the

parties, nor any delivery is required to make the obligation actionable, but the consent of the parties is sufficient. (Inst.3.22pr.–1.)

9.3.1 Sale (*emptio venditio*)

(Inst.Gai.3.139.–41., Inst.3.23., D.19.1., C.4.38., 49.)

Sale was in practice the most important of all Roman contracts. In early law, sales were effected either by *mancipatio* (as a real sale) or by *stipulatio*. Both required a certain amount of form—understandable in early Rome, but something of an inconvenience when Rome's economic activity started to grow quickly. The need to recognize the validity of agreements that were made without the necessary form contributed to the development of a separate contract of sale: 'From the beginning of the second century BC the pulse of trade began to beat too fast for the leisurely methods which had suited the cautious Roman peasant well enough. The kinds of things dealt in multiplied indefinitely and the dealers were often *peregrini*, men outside the native cautelary tradition. It became necessary to give effect, not merely to what the parties had had the foresight to incorporate in a formal contract, but also the general implications of good faith' (de Zulueta, F., *The Roman Law of Sale* (1945), 5. cf. Watson, A., 'The Origin of Consensual Sale: a Hypothesis', (1964) 32 TR, 245–54; and Metzger, *Companion*, 151–9 as well as Birks, *Obligations*, 66–96).

How was the contract of sale formed? The essential requirements were that there should be an agreement about the thing sold and the price.

9.3.1.1 Agreement

An agreement of wills (*consensus*) orally, in writing, or even by messenger was required. This could be proved in several ways. The conduct of the parties often constituted such proof, e.g. shaking hands or exchanging rings. There was no need, however, to prove that the parties had made the agreement in each other's presence (potentially an advantage over *mancipatio* and *stipulatio*):

Paul, *Edict, book 33*: **Sale is a contract of the law of nations and so is concluded by simple agreement; it can thus be contracted by parties not present together, through messengers, or by correspondence.** (D.18.1.1.2.)

Ulpian, *Sabinus, book 28*: **It is obvious that in contracts of sale there must be consent; the sale is invalid if there is disagreement either as to the fact of sale or the price or any other matter.** (D.18.1.9pr.)

The practice of giving *arra* ('earnest money') made proof of agreement relatively straightforward. *Arra* was a token of good faith and seriousness of purpose, given by the buyer to the seller to cement the bargain. The idea was not a specifically Roman one—there were Greek and Egyptian models for the practice. The *arra* could consist of money (in which case it amounted in effect to a deposit) or of some other item of value, e.g. a ring. It did not have to be of particular commercial value, although the seller occasionally demanded something valuable as a penalty should the buyer default—if the buyer did so, he forfeited the *arra*. But if the buyer performed his obligations, he could redeem the *arra* unless it was a deposit, in which case it would be credited to him against the price. What if the seller defaulted? The Greek practice was that the seller would have to return the *arra* twice over, i.e. the *arra* itself plus an equivalent amount. It is possible that the Romans adopted a similar rule, but the texts are inconclusive (cf. Inst.3.23pr.; C.4.21.17.2.).

At no stage of Roman law was *arra* regarded as necessary for the validity of a contract of sale. Its function was to provide proof of serious intent:

A contract of sale is concluded ... even if no *arra* has been given. For what is given by way of *arra* is [merely] evidence of a contract of sale having been concluded. (Inst.Gai.3.139.)

Gaius, *Provincial Edict, book 10*: **The common practice of giving earnest in respect of a purchase does not suggest that without the earnest there would be no contract but facilitates proof of the fact of agreement on the price.** (D.18.1.35pr.)

The practice of giving *arra* was considered in *Workers Trust and Merchant Bank Ltd v Dojap Investments Ltd* [1993] AC 573 (see 11.3.3).

Another form of proof, increasingly common during the Empire in the case of important contracts of sale, was the use of writing. But that practice brought with it a complication—if the parties agreed to put their contract into writing, when did it become binding? Was it when the parties agreed on the essentials, i.e. price and subject matter, or when the contract was put into writing? Justinian decreed that such a contract was not binding until put into writing. Until that time, either party could withdraw; but if *arra* had been given, it would be forfeited by the party refusing to abide by the contract. (cf. Lee, *Elements*, 302.)

9.3.1.2 **The thing sold**

Paul, *Edict, book 33*: **There can be a valid sale of anything which one may have, possess, or sue for; but there can be no sale of anything which is excluded from *commercium* by natural law, the law of nations, or the observances of the state.** (D.18.1.34.1.)

The general rule was that anything (both corporeal and incorporeal) could be sold unless it was excluded from *commercium*. But there were some exceptional categories of things that need comment:

(a) Prohibited things. A number of 'observances of the state' forbade the sale of things in certain circumstances. For example, a ban was introduced in the early Empire on the selling of houses with a view to their demolition for profit. And there were restrictions on the sale of dotal immovables (see 5.2.5.3–4) and on the sale of property belonging to wards (see 5.4.1.3).

(b) Things excluded from private ownership. Such things could not be the subject of a valid contract of sale if the purchaser knew the facts:

A buyer who knows he is buying a sacred or religious place, or a public one ... achieves nothing at all. However, if he is misled by the seller and buys them as private or secular, he can bring an action on purchase against the seller, on the ground that he has not been allowed to remain in possession. The action will allow him to recover his interest in not being misled. (Inst.3.23.5.)

Pomponius, *Sabinus, book 9*: **... you cannot wittingly buy a freeman or anything, the alienation of which you know to be forbidden; for instance, sacred or religious land or land excluded from private dealings, such as those public lands which are not in private possession but are for public use, such as the Field of Mars.** (D.18.1.6pr.)

What if the purchaser did not know that he was buying such things? It seems that a sale in such circumstances could have legal effect:

Pomponius, *Sabinus, book 9*: **The purchase of a freeman or of sacred or religious land who or which cannot be held as property is considered valid, so long as the purchaser does not**

know, [Paul, *Sabinus, book 5*] **[5]: because it can be difficult to distinguish a freeman from a slave.** (D.18.1.4–5.)

The contract was valid only to the extent of allowing the purchaser to recover the value of his bargain, but not for other purposes—a freeman bought mistakenly as a slave could not be considered 'sold', once the truth was discovered, because there was no sale. However, if the freeman had acted fraudulently, he could be enslaved (see 4.3.3.2). On the sale of things excluded from private ownership, see MacCormack, G. and Evans-Jones, R., 'The Sale of Res Extra Commercium in Roman Law' (1995) 112 ZSS (rA), 330–51.

(c) Things belonging to the purchaser. A sale of property to a man who already owned it was a nullity—the seller has nothing to sell in such a situation. Indeed, if the seller had acted dishonestly, he would probably be liable for theft. If the buyer bought property in which he had a proprietary interest, but not an absolute one, the sale was valid to the extent to which the buyer's title had been incomplete, e.g. where he was a co-owner:

Pomponius, *Sabinus, book 9*: **Again, if a thing which he owns in common with someone else should be sold to the purchaser, it must be said that, the price being apportioned, the purchase is valid in part, in part invalid.** (D.18.1.18pr.)

(d) Non-existent things:

Pomponius, *Sabinus, book 9*: **There can be no sale without a thing to be sold.** (D.18.1.8pr.)

A distinction has to be drawn between things which have ceased to exist before the contract was made, (i.e. 'perished things'), and those which come into existence after its making, (i.e. 'future things'):

(i) Perished things. A sale of property that had perished or had lost its identity before the contract was made was void:

Paul, *Sabinus, book 5*: **Even though there is agreement on the thing, if the thing ceases to exist before the sale, the contract is void.** (D.18.1.15pr.)

The rule could apply even where only a part of the subject matter had perished:

Marcian, *Rules, book 3*: **Should a man buy together, for one price, two slaves, one of whom is dead at the time of the sale, there is no purchase of the other one, either.** (D.18.1.44.)

However, consider the following text concerning the sale of a house that had been partially burned down at the time of the making of the contract (the parties not knowing this):

Paul, *Plautius, book 5*: ...**the issue is largely dependent on how much of the house remains; if the greater part of it has been destroyed, the purchaser will not be obliged to perform the contract and can recover anything which he may have paid; if, however, half or less has been consumed by fire, then the purchaser will be required to honor the contract, an estimate being made, on the standard of an honorable man, to relieve him of payment of the amount by which the fire has reduced the value of the house.** (D.18.1.57pr.)

It is the later scenario which appears to conflict with the case of the two slaves in D.18.1.44. In both situations part of the subject matter has perished, and yet there is a valid contract in one case, but not in the other. It is arguable, however, that the two situations are distinguishable. In the case of the two slaves, the subject matter of the contract (i.e. two slaves) did not exist at the time of the making of the contract because only one slave was alive: whereas, in the case of the burned house, a house did exist at the relevant time (or at least half a house) even though it was a damaged house. But this attempt to reconcile the texts is fraught with difficulty—what is 'half' a house? Is half a house worth having? Is it a house?

In the above discussion, it was assumed that neither of the parties knew about the state of the house when making the contract. Would knowledge of the facts have made a difference? If both knew that the house had been burned, the contract was void. If the buyer knew, but the seller did not, the sale was valid. And if the seller knew, but the buyer did not, then:

Paul, *Plautius, book 5*: …**no sale exists, if the whole house was destroyed before the contract was made; but if any part of the building remains, the contract stands, and the vendor must make good his damages to the purchaser.** (D.18.1.57.1.)

(ii) Future things. A contract to sell things with a potential existence was normally valid, an exception to the general rule that there could not be a sale if there was no thing to be sold. The selling of potential agricultural produce, e.g. 'next year's crop of wheat', was a common practice that necessitated legal recognition, an interesting example of how the law was shaped by economic realities. The position was the same as regards the sale of unborn children of slave-girls.

A distinction was made between the sale of an 'expected thing' (*emptio rei spera-tae*) and the sale of a 'chance' (*emptio spei*). Both were valid contracts, but the former was a conditional sale, whereas the latter was an absolute one. If a buyer agreed to buy an expected thing, the operation of the contract was conditional on the thing materializing in the future—if nothing materialized, there was no obligation. But if the buyer bought a chance he took the risk that the thing might never materialize, and had to pay the agreed price whatever happened:

Pomponius, *Sabinus, book 9*: **Sometimes, indeed, there is held to be a sale even without a thing, as where what is bought is, as it were, a chance. This is the case with the purchase of a catch of birds or fish**…(D.18.1.8.1.)

The distinction could be difficult to draw in practice. Much depended on the intentions of the buyer—did he intend to pay only if something materialized? If so, then he bought an expected thing; otherwise, he bought a chance. Some things naturally fitted one category more than another. For example, 'next year's fruit crop' could be regarded as an expected thing—there was bound to be some sort of crop, even if it was a disappointing one. But 'the next catch in the fisherman's net' was likely to be regarded as the purchase of a chance—there could easily be no catch whatsoever. However, what if the sale was of 'the next haul of the trawler's nets'? Neither category springs obviously to mind.

Could an inheritance be sold? Strictly, an heir could not sell his *position* as heir. Subject to that, an existing inheritance (i.e. where the testator or intestate has died) could be sold, as could rights in it, but not a future inheritance:

Pomponius, *Sabinus, book 9*: **The sale of the inheritance of a living or non-existent person is a nullity because the thing sold is not in existence.** (D.18.4.1.)

The rule was necessary to dissuade unseemly dealings and speculation about the chances of succeeding to the estates of living persons.

(e) *Res aliena* ('another's property'). Things belonging to a third party could be validly sold if the seller and buyer were unaware of the third party's rights. In such a case, the purchaser had to return the property to the owner and could sue for breach of the seller's duties to guarantee against eviction. What if either the seller or the buyer, or both, knew of the third party's title? In such a scenario, the property would most probably consist of stolen goods:

Paul, *Edict, book 33*: **Again, if both parties to a sale know that the object sold is stolen, no obligation is created on either side; if the purchaser alone knows, the vendor will incur no obligation, though he can obtain nothing under the contract unless he voluntarily performs what he agreed to do; but if the vendor knows and the purchaser does not, both parties are bound by the contract....** (D.18.1.34.3.)

That was the contractual position, but there could also be delictual liability for theft for dishonest handling of property belonging to another.

(f) Generic things. Could there be a valid contract of sale in respect of things described generically—non-specific goods of a defined class, e.g. '100 bottles of olive oil'? The texts are inconclusive but it seems that if the source of the goods was sufficiently identified, there would be a valid contract; e.g. a sale of '100 bottles of olive oil from my store', or a sale of wine from a particular vat, would be valid (cf. D.18.1.35.7.). Otherwise, the general rule was that it was not possible to have a sale of generic goods, because sale in practice was a market transaction where goods would most probably be described specifically when purchased. See Zimmermann, *Obligations*, 236 ff.

9.3.1.3 The price

Ulpian, *Sabinus, book 1*: **There is no sale without a price.** (D.18.1.2.1.)

Agreement on the price was an essential of the contract of sale. In the course of time, a number of rules emerged clarifying this requirement:

(a) The price had to consist of money: this rule was certainly controversial, and possibly not established till the late classical period. Paul provides an interesting historical perspective:

Paul, *Edict, book 33*: **All buying and selling has its origin in exchange or barter. For there was once a time when no such thing as money existed and no such terms as 'merchandise' and 'price' were known; rather did every man barter what was useless to him for that which was useful, according to the exigencies of his current needs; for it often happens that what one man has in plenty another lacks. But since it did not always and easily happen that when you had something which I wanted, I, for my part, had something that you were willing to accept, a material was selected which, being given a stable value by the state, avoided the problems of barter by providing a constant medium of exchange. That material, struck in due form by the mint, demonstrates its utility and title not by its substance as such but by its quantity, so that no longer are the things exchanged both called wares but one of them is termed the price.** (D.18.1.1pr.)

Here we come across one of the celebrated disputes between the Proculians and the Sabinians. The latter argued that the price in sale need not consist of money—that exchanging things constituted a sale, e.g. my cow for your ox (cf. Inst.Gai.3.141.; Inst.3.23.2.). The Proculians took the view that sale and exchange were dissimilar, the distinguishing factor being that sale consisted of the exchange not of two things, but of money for a thing. However, is money not a *thing*?

It was the Proculian view that eventually prevailed. Because the seller and buyer had different duties in the contract of sale, and their respective remedies were different, it was essential to determine which party was the buyer, which the seller, a very difficult task if the price did not have to consist of money:

Paul, *Edict, book 33*: **Still the view of Nerva and Proculus is the sounder one; for it is one thing to sell, another to buy; one person again is vendor and the other, purchaser; and, in the same way, the price is one thing, the object of sale, another; but, in exchange, one cannot discern which party is vendor and which, purchaser.** (D.18.1.1.1.)

Did the price have to consist exclusively of money? The texts suggest that the price could consist of money plus the performance of a service:

Pomponius, *Sabinus, book 9*: **If I sold you a building in exchange for a fixed sum of money plus your promise to repair another building of mine, I may sue on the purchase to force this repair; but if our agreement was only that you repair it, a contract of sale is not construed as having been made....** (D.19.1.6.1.)

There is a paucity of texts dealing with the question of whether the price could consist of money plus a *thing*, e.g. 'my cow and 1,000 *sesterces* for your horse'. The most plausible view is that this was a sale—the Sabinians would think so, and so probably would the Proculians as it is quite feasible to describe me as the buyer, you as the seller in the above example.

(b) The price had to be genuine (*verum*): the price must not be a sham—it must be *intended* by the parties to be paid. If the price was derisory or a sham, there was a gift, not a sale. What if the price was low though not derisory? The adequacy of the price was generally irrelevant, as in the case of consideration in English contract law. An exception to the general rule was made in the case of husband and wife—a sale at a low price could be deemed to be a gift, and thus a nullity:

Ulpian, *Disputations, book 7*: **If someone, intending a gift, sells something below its worth, the sale is valid. For we say that a sale is wholly void only when it is made entirely as a gift; but when the sale is made at a cheap price for reasons of liberality, there is no doubt that the sale is good. At least, in general, as between spouses, a sale made at a low price by way of gift is of no effect.** (D.18.1.38.)

In the later Empire, a rule was introduced (cf. C.4.44.2.; C.4.44.8.) whereby, if the price paid for land was less than half its market value at the time of the sale, the seller could rescind the contract unless the buyer made up the difference. This rule, known as *laesio enormis* ('huge loss'), was likely prompted by the desire to protect small landowners against powerful neighbours and speculators. It has traditionally been thought that the rule was decreed by Diocletian, but Zimmermann believes that it was enacted by Justinian consequent on his taxation reforms (which had precipitated the sale of smallholdings by peasant farmers): 'Christian teaching, as well as stoic moral philosophy, demanded an infusion of ethics and of *humanitas* into the law and it was in this spirit that the Emperor was supposed to render aid to the weak and poor and to relax the rigours of the law' (*Obligations*, 261). It is unclear whether the application of this rule was subsequently extended to movable property.

Laesio enormis was subjected to much analysis in the medieval period and applied well beyond its original limits. Its more recent history has been erratic. It is to be found in the French Civil Code: Article 1674 retains the original restriction to sales of land but applies only if the seller has suffered a loss of more than seven-twelfths of the market price. The rule was excluded from the BGB, but Zimmermann considers that modern concepts of consumer protection and equality of exchange have led to 'a renaissance' of *laesio enormis* (*Obligations*, 268 ff.). For the later history of *laesio enormis* in the European *ius commune*, see Dias, R., 'Laesio Enormis: The Roman–Dutch Story', in *Studies in the Roman Law of Sale*, 46–63.

(c) The price had to be certain or at least ascertainable: there had to be certainty of price as well as of subject matter. The parties had to agree on the price, otherwise the contract was void. The common law rule that a reasonable price can be implied (if none had been agreed) was unknown in Roman law. But if the price, though not fixed, was ascertainable by reference to verifiable facts, the contract was valid through the operation of the maxim *certum est quod certum reddi potest*—'that is certain which is capable of being made certain':

Ulpian, *Sabinus, book 28*: **A purchase 'for what you paid for it' or 'for what I have in my cash box' is valid; there is no uncertainty of price in so obvious a sale: The case is one of ignorance of its amount rather than of the real existence of the price.** (D.18.1.7.1.)

What if the parties agreed to allow a third party to fix the price in the future? Strictly, there was no sale—the price had not been fixed; nor could it be said to be ascertainable by reference to existing facts. Some jurists, however, argued that the contract was valid (cf. Inst.Gai.3.140.). Justinian settled the controversy by ruling that the sale was conditional on a third party, named by the seller and buyer, fixing the price.

Once the parties had agreed on the subject matter and the price, the contract was 'perfect', i.e. fully made. Important legal consequences followed from the making of the contract: both parties acquired certain duties, and the risk of damage to the property sold was transferred to the buyer.

9.3.1.4 Transfer of risk and accretions

Paul, *Edict, book 33*: **It is essential to know when a sale is perfect because we then know who bears the risk in the thing; for once the sale is perfect, risk is on the purchaser.** (D.18.6.8pr.)

The doctrine of risk deals with an important and difficult question—who is to bear the loss if the property sold is damaged, lost, or destroyed before delivery if neither party is at fault? It seems that the loss must fall on one of two innocent parties unless it is apportioned between them (see Gordon, W. M., 'Risk in Sale in Roman Law', in *Collatio Iuris Romani* I, 123–30, and Gordon, W. M., 'Risk in Sale—From Roman Law to Scots Law', in *Studies Litewski*, 115–24, where Roman-law foundations of this aspect of Scots law are discussed). The parties could vary the default risk rule by mutual consent. Before the contract became 'perfect', the risk of the loss lay with the seller (*res perit domino*). A contract of sale was deemed to have become 'perfect' when the parties had agreed on the object of sale and the price. When the contract became 'perfect', the risk of the loss passed to the buyer even though he did not become owner of the property until delivery had occurred:

Where a contract of sale is made, which as we have said happens as soon as the price is agreed if the contract is not in writing, the risk passes immediately to the buyer. This is so even if the thing has not yet been delivered....In such cases the buyer must bear the loss and he must pay the price despite not having obtained the thing. (Inst.3.23.3.)

This seems a harsh and illogical rule, at least from the buyer's perspective. He was not even the owner of the property until delivery, since the making of the contract of sale did not effect a transfer of ownership. Yet, even though the damage occurred while the property was in the seller's possession, the rule was that the buyer bore the loss. An economic justification for the rule could be offered—placing the risk of loss on the seller would probably discourage commercial activity. But might not such activity be affected by imposing the loss on buyers?

However, on closer examination, the buyer's position seems more tolerable. The seller had to assign to the buyer any actions that were available against third parties in respect of damage (actual or prospective) to the property. Further, if the seller was in *mora*, e.g. because of late delivery, then he bore the risk of any damage caused to the property between the agreed and the actual date of delivery. And the buyer could attempt to avoid being saddled with the risk of loss by making a suitable agreement with the seller. In any case, the buyer was entitled to any accretions or fruits (of the purchased property) that arose after the sale was completed. So, if A bought B's flock of sheep, and lambs were born after the agreement was made but before delivery, A was entitled to the lambs as well as to the sheep:

Pomponius, *Quintus Mucius, book 39*: **When we convey a thing, we transfer ownership of it together with all that would pertain to it, if it had remained ours.** (D.18.1.67.)

Although the position of the buyer as regards risk was not as disadvantageous as appears at first sight, nevertheless the separation of risk and ownership in the contract of sale was one of the more questionable doctrines of Roman civil law. The rule was probably conditioned by the early nature of sale—essentially, a cash transaction where the agreement and the transfer of ownership were virtually simultaneous: 'Where every sale is executed immediately, both risk and ownership are bound to pass at one and the same time, namely when the contract is concluded. It was only with the rise of the fully executory contract that a divergence became possible' (Zimmermann, *Obligations*, 290). Modern systems have generally eschewed the Roman rule and tend to regard risk as passing to the purchaser when he becomes owner (as in English and French law). In German law, risk passes when the property is delivered.

9.3.1.5 Duties of the seller

The seller had four principal duties: to care for the property before delivery, to deliver it with vacant possession, to warrant against eviction, and to warrant against defects.

(a) Care of property before delivery. Since the risk of loss passed to the buyer only when the contract became 'perfect', the seller had the duty to care for the property until delivery. It seems odd that there should have been a duty to care for one's own property (which belonged to the seller until delivery) but that was one of the consequences of the separation of risk and ownership in Roman law. In Justinianic law, the standard of care expected of the seller was that of the *bonus paterfamilias*; hence, he was liable for even slight acts of negligence. So, the rule that the risk of loss passed to the buyer was really quite narrow in application— the buyer bore the loss only if the seller was blameless (such as through accident). It is possible that in the classical period the seller was liable for *custodia*, which can be defined as strict liability for the safety of the property apart from loss caused by circumstances beyond the seller's control, e.g. natural events or *vis maior* ('overwhelming force'). Thus, the seller would not be in breach of *custodia* if a slave died, before delivery to the buyer, from natural causes or by being struck by lightning. *Vis maior* included disasters such as floods, storms, earthquakes; also violent theft (i.e. robbery):

Neratius, *Parchments, book 3*: **If I should be held responsible for a thing because of a sale and it is taken away from me by force, then although I should guard it, still it is better that there be no further consequence than my having to provide the buyer with the actions for recovering it; for safekeeping is of slight avail against force.** (D.19.1.31pr.)

Vis maior is often described as 'act of God' but, in view of the inclusion of robbery, 'overwhelming force' would be a more accurate and theologically less objectionable translation.

(b) Delivery with vacant possession. This duty required the seller to deliver the purchased property with vacant possession. As regards delivery, it had to be made at the agreed place and time, providing that the buyer had either paid the price or was able and willing to do so. In the absence of agreement about the time of delivery, the seller's duty was to deliver at once, allowing a reasonable time for ensuring (where necessary) that the property was in a deliverable state. If the place of delivery had not been agreed, it was assumed to be the place where the thing was situated when the contract was made. But the parties usually agreed on the place and time of delivery.

The seller had to deliver not only the purchased property but also any fruits or accretions coming into existence after the making of the contract. Moreover, any accessories had to be delivered, i.e. things expressly or implicitly sold in conjunction with the 'main' property. Accessories included, for example, any clothes that were worn by a slave when he was sold; similarly, the trappings of a beast of burden were comprised in its sale. The sale of land carried with it all fixtures on the land.

The seller's duty was to deliver the property with vacant possession, i.e. legally protected possession—the seller had to put the property under the buyer's exclusive and effective control. It followed that the property had to be free of charges or encumbrances other than those agreed on. It was not, however, part of the seller's duty to transfer ownership, i.e. to make the buyer the owner:

Ulpian, *Edict, book 32*: **And in the first place, the seller must provide the object itself, that is, deliver it. If the seller was its owner, his act [of delivery] makes the buyer the owner also; if he was not, his act obligates the seller only for an eviction, provided that the price was paid or security was given for it.** (D.19.1.11.2.)

The phrase 'obligates the seller only for an eviction' emphasizes that the seller was not in breach of his duty to deliver vacant possession simply because he failed to transfer ownership. The rule that the seller did not have to make the buyer the owner of the purchased property appears rather questionable, *prima facie*, but at least it had the merit of commercial convenience as it obviated the need for the seller to prove ownership.

(c) Guarantee against eviction. Although the seller did not have to make the buyer the owner, a guarantee was implied in classical law that the buyer would not be evicted. The guarantee could not prevent an eviction—the rightful owner was entitled to recover his property by legal process—but it entitled the buyer to sue for damages when evicted.

The evolution of this duty of the seller demonstrates a gradual improvement in the buyer's position. In early law, an evicted buyer had no remedy unless the property had been transferred to him through a *mancipatio*, in which case the Twelve Tables allowed him to recover double the price by the *actio auctoritatis*. So it became the practice to insist that the seller should make a stipulation to compensate the buyer in case of eviction—usually for double the price as regards valuable things (*stipulatio duplae*) (cf. *Sententiae Pauli*, 2.17.1.–4.). By the classical period, it was regarded as a breach of good faith for the seller to refuse to make the necessary stipulation—he could be sued for his failure to do so:

Paul, *Sabinus, book 5*: **If the vendor does not give the undertaking for double the price and is sued on that ground, he must be condemned, as a defendant, for double the price.** (D.21.2.2.)

The next stage in the evolution of this duty occurred during the classical period. The guarantee against eviction came to be implied in all contracts of sale, the *actio empti* ('the action on the purchase') being allowed for the recovery of a simple indemnity, i.e. single damages. But buyers still insisted on a stipulation for double the price (or more) in appropriate cases. However, in certain circumstances, the *actio empti* was preferable—it allowed unliquidated damages to be recovered rather than a fixed sum.

   (d) Guarantee against defects. At the outset a distinction has to be made between patent and latent defects in the property sold. Patent defects were those of which the buyer was aware, or which were so obvious that he should have been aware of them. The general rule was *caveat emptor*—'let the buyer beware'. Hence, the seller was not liable for such defects, even if he had given an express undertaking as to soundness:

Florentinus, *Institutes, book 8*: **There are, further, even some undertakings which do not bind the vendor, the case being such that the purchaser cannot be unaware of the facts; an instance is that of one buying a slave who has lost his eyes and stipulating for his soundness in which case, the stipulation is taken to refer to the rest of his body rather than to that in respect of which the purchaser has deceived himself.** (D.18.1.43.1.)

As regards latent defects, i.e. those other than patent, the position was more complicated. In early law the seller was generally not liable for latent defects. However, if he gave an express undertaking as to the fitness of the goods, he would be liable for its breach. In the middle Republic, dishonesty by the seller made him liable under the *actio empti*, since fraudulent behaviour came to be regarded as inconsistent with the requirement of good faith in the contract of sale. Accordingly, the seller became liable for failure to disclose defects known to him, but not known to the buyer:

Ulpian, *Sabinus, book 28*: **If the seller concealed a servitude which he knew was owed, he will not escape an action on the purchase unless the buyer was also aware of this fact; anything done contrary to good faith comes under the action on purchase.** (D.19.1.1.1.)

Florentinus, *Institutes, book 8*: **A seller must warrant the absence of fraud on his part, and it is fraud not merely If one uses obscure language, but also if one is guilty of artful concealment.** (D.18.1.43.2.)

In the late Republic the sharp practices of slave and cattle dealers prompted the issuing of edicts by the aediles, which had a major effect on the evolution of the contract of sale (cf. D.21.1.1.2. and Metzger, *Companion*, 158–9). The edict that dealt with slaves ran as follows:

Ulpian, *Curule Aediles' Edict, book 1*: **Those who sell slaves are to apprise purchasers of any disease or defect in their wares and whether a given slave is a runaway, a loiterer on errands, or still subject to noxal liability; all these matters they must proclaim in due manner when the slaves are sold. If a slave be sold without compliance with this regulation or contrary to what has been said or promised in respect of him at the time of his sale…we will grant to** the purchaser and to all other interested parties an action for rescission in respect of the slave. (D.21.1.1.1.)

The edict applied to physical and character defects in slaves who were sold in the open market. It demanded that the seller should declare the slave's known defects and undertake that the slave was free from undeclared defects:

In the part of the edict of the curule aediles regulating the sale of slaves the following words appear: 'Care must be taken that the descriptive notice of each slave be so written that it can be clearly understood what disease or defect each has, and which of them is a runaway or a vagrant or not free from noxal liability.' (Aulus Gellius, *Attic Nights*, 4.2.1.)

What if the seller refused to give the undertaking? The buyer might well desist from the transaction in such a case but, even if he went ahead, he was given remedies:

Gaius, *Curule Aediles' Edict, book 1*: Should the vendor not give an undertaking on the matters contained in their edict, the curule aediles promise against him an action for rescission within two months and an action for diminution within six. (D.21.1.28.)

The action for rescission (*actio redhibitoria*) entitled the buyer to recover the full purchase price, with interest, on returning the slave to the seller. But this action was available only if serious defects were discovered, i.e. those that undermined the usefulness of the thing sold. For less serious defects, the appropriate action was the 'action for diminution' (*actio quanti minoris*), which did not rescind the sale but allowed the buyer to recover part of the purchase price, i.e. the difference between the slave's actual value at the time of the sale and the price paid.

What was the position if the seller gave the necessary undertakings but the slave proved defective? Then the buyer could bring the *actio redhibitoria* for rescission, within six months of the sale, or the *actio quanti minoris* for diminution of the price (time-limit of one year). In effect the edict introduced an implied guarantee of quality that applied even where the seller was unaware of the defects:

Ulpian, *Curule Aediles' Edict, book 1*: This edict was promulgated to check the wiles of vendors and to give relief to purchasers circumvented by their vendors. It must, though, be recognized that the vendor is still liable, even though he be unaware of the defects which the aediles require to be declared. There is nothing inequitable about this; the vendor could have made himself conversant with these matters; and in any case, it is no concern of the purchaser whether his deception derives from the ignorance or the sharp practice of his vendor. (D.21.1.1.2.)

The last few words of this text emphasize the conceptual progress achieved in this edict. The buyer is indeed not interested why his purchase is defective. What he requires is an effective remedy irrespective of the culpability of the seller. The edict gave the buyer just such a remedy, thereby increasing what modern economists sometimes refer to as 'consumer confidence'. Liability for latent defects of which the seller is unaware is taken for granted in modern society, but it is a legally sophisticated concept, and one that represents a major achievement of Roman law. The aediles introduced similar provisions for the sale of certain beasts of burden (later extended to other cattle):

Ulpian, *Curule Aediles' Edict, book 2*: Those who sell beasts of burden must declare with all due publicity any disease or defect which the beasts have. (D.21.1.38pr.)

Under these edicts, liability was also imposed for 'what has been said or promised' by the seller. Such statements (*dicta promissave*)—often made in order to assert some particular quality of the thing sold—extended liability beyond the *implied* guarantee.

These provisions, restricted in scope at first to the sale of slaves and cattle in the market, nevertheless proved to be seminal. They were extended to sales of slaves and cattle outside the market, and then to sales of anything, anywhere (cf. D.21.1.1pr.). It is not clear when these extensions occurred but Ulpian says:

Ulpian, *Curule Aediles' Edict, book 1*: **It must be realized that this edict applies to all sales, not only those of slaves but also those of anything else.** (D.21.1.63.)

This text has been suspected of interpolation: it is arguable that the extension of the edict to all sales probably did not occur until Justinian. But Ulpian was writing some 200 years after the introduction of the edicts. It is very probable that by that time, the extension had occurred. After all, these edicts dealt with the sale of *res mancipi* in very public places. Everybody would have known of the aediles' provisions. It is scarcely conceivable that the new practice would have been confined to the sale of just slaves and cattle for over 500 years, even allowing for the innate conservatism of the Romans. See further Honoré, A. M., in *Studies in the Roman Law of Sale*, 132. This collection of essays contains a number of excellent contributions on the issue of latent defects (see, e.g., the contributions of Nicholas, Rogerson, and Stein). See also Pugsley, D., 'The Aedilician Edict', in *Daube Noster*, 253–64.

The Roman rules concerning latent defects have had an enormous influence on modern systems. For example, they have been substantially incorporated in French, German, and Roman-Dutch law. Article 1641 of the French Civil Code implies a guarantee by the seller against latent defects that render the thing sold unsuitable for the use for which it was intended; s. 459 BGB is similar. In South Africa, the *actio redhibitoria* and *actio quanti minoris* continue to provide remedies for sale of defective goods, albeit with some modifications (see Evans-Jones, R., 'The Actio Quanti Minoris in Mixed Legal Systems', in *Studies Litewski*, 79–92). In English law, the fundamental common law principle has been *caveat emptor*, and it was not until the Sale of Goods Act 1893 that guarantees about the fitness of goods were implied in every sale. That Act, and the developments preceding it, were unquestionably influenced by the Roman rules.

9.3.1.6 The *actio empti*

This action was the main remedy for the buyer in the contract of sale for breach of the seller's duties. As regards defective goods, it is not clear what the relationship was between the *actio empti* and the actions introduced by the aediles. The remedies clearly overlapped although there were important differences. Damages could be recovered under the *actio empti* (and not just a reduction of the price) and the action was not subject to the short limitation periods of the aedilitian remedies. On the other hand, the *actio empti* could be brought in respect of defective goods only if the seller knew of the defects. In late law, it appears that the remedies were assimilated (with the shorter limitation periods normally applicable). See Zimmermann, *Obligations*, 322 ff.

What was the measure of damages under the *actio empti*? The general rule was that the measure was based on the buyer's interest in the thing sold. That allowed the buyer to recover for consequential loss. As regards defective goods, consequential loss could normally be recovered only if the seller knew of the defect. Attempts were made to limit the type of consequential loss that was generally recoverable under the *actio empti*:

Paul, *Edict, book 33*: **When the seller is responsible for nondelivery of an object, every benefit to the buyer is taken into account provided that it stands in close connection with this matter. If he could have completed a deal and made a profit from wine, this should not be reckoned in, no more than if he buys wheat and his household suffers from starvation because it was not delivered; he receives the price of the grain, not the price of slaves killed by starvation.** (D.19.1.21.3.)

Inconsistency in the texts makes it difficult to state the rule on remoteness of damage with any precision. If the seller had behaved fraudulently, it seems probable that he was liable for *all* resulting damage, however remote. Justinian ensured a degree of certainty by ruling that the buyer could not recover more than double the price of the property that he had bought.

9.3.1.7 The duties of the buyer

The buyer had to pay the price and any interest that was payable in the case of late payment; he had to accept delivery of the property; and he had to reimburse the seller for expenses.

(a) Paying the price:

Ulpian, *Edict, book 32*: **The seller has the action on sale to obtain whatever the buyer ought to provide to him. [20] The following matters are included in this action: First of all, the price for which the object was sold; next, after the day of delivery, interest on the price, since it is entirely equitable that the buyer pay interest on the price after he enjoys the object.** (D.19.1.13.19.–20.)

The buyer had to pay the price at the agreed time or, if no time had been agreed, then at the time of delivery. Until the buyer paid the price, he was not entitled to sue under the *actio empti*. But he did not have to pay the price if the seller had failed to deliver, or was unable to do so, or was in breach of any of his other duties. If the buyer delayed payment without good cause, the seller was entitled to any interest agreed between the parties, providing that it did not exceed the legal maximum (6 per cent under Justinian). In the absence of any agreement on interest, a judge could award an amount up to the legal maximum.

(b) Accepting delivery. The buyer had to accept delivery at the agreed time and place but could delay acceptance if the seller was in breach of his duties. What if the seller was not in breach? Then the buyer would be liable for not accepting delivery, and the seller's duty to safeguard the property would no longer apply unless the seller acted in bad faith:

Pomponius, *Quintus Mucius, book 31*: **It should be known that once the purchaser is in delay, the vendor is no longer liable for negligence, but only for bad faith....** (D.18.6.18.)

(c) Reimbursing expenses. The cost of safeguarding the property between the making of the contract and the delivery was borne by the buyer. Hence, the seller was entitled to recover expenses that had been properly incurred:

Ulpian, *Edict, book 32*: **By an action for sale, he also recovers his expenditures on the object of sale, for example, any outlay on buildings that were sold....likewise, if before delivery money was spent for care of a sick slave or if something [was spent] for training which it was probable the buyer wished to be spent. Labeo states further that if something was spent** for the funeral of a dead slave, it too can be recovered by a suit on sale, provided that he did not die due to the seller's fault. (D.19.1.13.22.)

The seller's remedy was the *actio venditi*, under which the measure of damages was assessed on the basis of the seller's interest in the sale taking place.

9.3.1.8 Variation by pacta

The legal effects of the contract of sale could be varied by a broad range of *pacta*—special terms or clauses agreed by the parties (see 9.8). If the terms were agreed at the time of the contract, they were fully enforceable; but pacts made thereafter generally had effect only as a defence. For example, if the seller agreed to reduce the original price, he would be bound by that pact—the buyer could rely on it if the seller sued for the original price. But if a buyer consented to pay more than the original agreed price, the seller could not enforce such a pact. Among the most common pacts were the following:

(a) Seller's right to withdraw. This was a clause reserving to the seller the right to call off the sale (and thus recover the property sold) if the price was not fully paid by a certain date (cf. D.41.4.2.3.). It was in effect a forfeiture clause, of particular relevance where the buyer received the goods first and was meant to pay later. Of course, a seller could sue a buyer for the price under the *actio venditi*, but a forfeiture clause gave the seller the choice whether to sue for the price or to withdraw from the sale:

Ulpian, *Edict, book 32*:...once the forfeiture clause becomes operative, the vendor must decide whether he wishes to exercise its provision or to hold out for the price and, once having opted for forfeiture, he cannot later change his mind. (D.18.3.4.2.)

This text makes clear that the seller could not sue for the price once he had opted to withdraw from the contract. There were circumstances, however, where the seller could bring the *actio venditi* for compensation in addition to relying on the forfeiture clause, e.g. if the buyer had damaged the property.

(b) Seller's right to accept a better offer. This was a clause allowing the seller to call off the sale if he received a better offer within a certain date (cf. D.18.2.1.). The original buyer had the right to be informed of the later offer so that he could try to match it. Who decided whether the offer was better or not? It was primarily a matter for the seller, but his decision required a certain element of objectivity: it was not the case that an offer was better simply because the seller said so. For example, the offer had to be genuine, not a sham. It is clear that factors in addition to the price were relevant in deciding which offer was the better one:

Ulpian, *Sabinus, book 28*: A better offer can be seen in an increased price. But even without addition to the price, there is a better offer if easier or earlier payment be proposed, as also if a more convenient place of payment be suggested....an offer is also deemed better, if made by a more reliable person. (D.18.2.4.6.)

(c) Seller's right of first refusal. This clause allowed the seller to buy the property back if the buyer should decide to sell it in the future. If, in the event of the buyer reselling, offers were received from other parties, the original seller had to match the offers to secure the purchase (cf. D.19.5.12.).

(d) Buyer's right to reject. This was a clause enabling the buyer to reject the goods if they were found to be unsatisfactory after a period of trial, i.e. sale on approval (cf. D.18.1.3.). Such a clause would often be used in cases where an extended trial might be necessary, e.g. sale of a slave or a beast of burden. In the sale of certain consumables such as wine, sale on approval was the usual practice:

Ulpian, *Sabinus, book 28*: **If a quantity of wine be sold for a lump sum, the vendor is liable only for its safekeeping. It will be apparent from this that if the wine be not sold with a provision for tasting, the vendor has no liability for acidity or mustiness and that all risk is on the purchaser. At the same time, it is hard to believe that anyone would buy wine without a proviso that it is to be tasted. Hence, if a period for tasting be fixed, the purchaser may taste when he can and, until he does taste, the risk of sourness and mustiness is on the vendor** ... (D.18.6.4.1.)

In such cases, an extended trial was obviously inappropriate. The seller normally specified that the tasting should be carried out within a few days. If the buyer did not taste within the specified period, he was deemed to have approved the purchase. If the property that was held on approval was damaged or destroyed without the buyer's fault, the seller bore the loss.

9.3.2 Letting and hiring (*locatio conductio*)

(Inst.Gai.3.142.–7., Inst.3.24., D.19.2., C.4.65.)

Hire was a bilateral *bonae fidei* contract whereby a person (the *locator*) let out a thing, or his services, or the completion of a piece of work to another person (the *conductor*) (see Metzger, *Companion*, 159–62 as well as Birks, *Obligations*, 97–128). The contract of hire had certain similarities with sale—it was formed under similar rules:

Gaius, *Common Matters, book 2*: **Lease and hire is close to sale and purchase, and it is formed by the same rules of law. Sale and purchase is contracted if the price is agreed upon; similarly, lease and hire is considered to be contracted once the rent is agreed upon.** (D.19.2.2pr.) (cf. Inst.3.24pr.)

So close was the similarity, that there could be some uncertainty as to whether the parties had agreed a sale or hire (see Prichard, A. M., 'Sale and Hire', in *Studies in the Roman Law of Sale*, 1–8):

Gaius, *Common Matters, book 2*: **...in some cases the question frequently arises whether the contract is sale and purchase or lease and hire. For example, if a goldsmith and I agree that he make for me, from his own gold, rings of a fixed weight and form, and if he receives, for example, three hundred [in payment], is this sale and purchase or lease and hire? The general view is that there is a single transaction which is predominantly sale and purchase. But if I give my gold and a fee is set for labor, this is undoubtedly lease and hire.** (D.19.2.2.1.)

For the sake of exposition, three different types of hire can be distinguished—hire of a thing, hire of services, and hire of a piece of work. This distinction was unknown to Roman law and the Romans regarded the types of lease as different *transactions* within a single uniform *contract*. The foundation of the contract of letting and hiring, in its various forms, was the notion of a performance (the contractually agreed use and enjoyment of a thing, services or the completion of a piece of work) for an agreed period of time in return for the payment of an amount of rent.

9.3.2.1 Hire of a thing (*locatio conductio rei*)

This occurred where the *conductor* was allowed the use and enjoyment of a thing by the *locator* in return for payment of rent. The contract was made when the parties agreed on the subject matter of the hire and on the amount of payment. As in sale, certainty was required but the contract was valid if the payment was readily ascertainable. Payment normally had to consist of money, although there was an important exception in the case of agricultural land—part of the produce of the land was frequently used as payment (see Thomas, J. A. C., 'The Nature of Merces' (1958) AJ, 191–9). The thing that was hired would normally be a corporeal thing, and something not consumable through use. In certain respects, a greater range of things could be hired than could be sold, since some of the restrictions on selling things did not apply to hire, e.g. a husband could hire out dotal immovables.

It was usual to agree a period of duration for the hire, failing which either party could renounce at any time. If they did specify the duration, the hire would normally terminate on the expiry of the relevant period. But in the case of agricultural land, an implied reletting was possible on a year-to-year basis. In practice, this meant that the *conductor* would continue as tenant unless he was given notice to quit before the expiry of the original period. However, the implied extension was regarded as a new lease rather than a continuation of the old. Also, hire could end through the destruction or termination of the subject matter, or through the misconduct of either party. Thus, if the *locator* substantially prevented the *conductor* from enjoying the property, the latter could terminate the contract and sue for damages:

Paul, *Edict, book 34*: **A tenant farmer, if he is not permitted to enjoy, may rightly sue forthwith for the entire five-year period even if the farm's owner should permit enjoyment during the remaining years; the owner is not discharged from his obligation because he will permit enjoyment of the farm in the second or third year....** (D.19.2.24.4.)

What if the *locator* sold the property to a third party? The sale did not *automatically* terminate the contract of hire, but it could amount to a substantial interference with the rights of the *conductor* if the third party exercised his rights as owner. The *conductor* could sue the *locator* for damages but could not insist on the continuation of the hire—he could be evicted. To that extent, 'sale broke hire', to use a maxim employed by medieval lawyers. Misconduct by the *conductor*, justifying termination of the contract, occurred primarily where he grossly abused the property or failed to pay the rent. The death of either party did not terminate the contract, unless the parties had agreed the contrary.

What were the duties of the parties?

(a) Duties of the *locator*. He had to deliver the property to the *conductor*, who received custody (*detentio*) of it, but not possession. Any accessories that were normally required for the use of the property had to be handed over. For example, in the case of the lease of a farm, it seems that the tenant was to be provided, *inter alia*, with storage jars, a press and grinder, and cauldrons in which olives could be washed with hot water (D.19.2.19.2.). See Frier, B. W. 'Law, Technology and Social Change: The Equipping of Italian Farm Tenancies' (1979) 96 ZSS (rA), 204–28. Since the *locator* had to ensure that the *conductor* was able to enjoy the property for the period agreed, it was customary—where the property was sold before the expiry of the hire—for the buyer's agreement to be secured not to interfere with the enjoyment of the *conductor*. The *locator* had to maintain the hired thing in good repair throughout the period of hire (unless damage had been caused by the negligence of the *conductor*). Thus, if the *conductor* incurred reasonable expenses in the maintenance of the property, he was normally entitled to recover them. Consider the following text that would not be out of place in a modern tenancy agreement:

Papinian, *Care of Cities*: **Each person is to keep the public street outside his own house in repair and clean out the open gutters and ensure that no vehicle is prevented from access. Occupiers of rented accommodation must carry out these repairs themselves if the owner fails to do so and deduct their expenses from the rent.** (D.43.10.1.3.)

What if the hired property was defective? It had to be fit for the use normally expected of it; consequently, the *locator* was liable for damage caused by undisclosed defects of which he was aware or should have been aware. The standard of care expected of the *locator* was that of the *bonus paterfamilias*.

(b) Duties of the *conductor*. He had to accept delivery of the hired property, and normally had to pay for the hire either by a lump sum or by instalments (i.e. rent), the latter being more usual in cases of hire for long periods. Security for the payment of the rent could be expressly agreed (see 9.5.4), and was *implied* in the hire of land, e.g. the produce of agricultural land was regarded as the security, the *locator* having a lien (*hypotheca*) on the crops:

Pomponius, *Readings, book 13*: **As regards rural land the crops are impliedly taken to be hypothecated to the owner of the land, even if not agreed in so many words.** (D.20.2.7pr.)

The essential character of the property had to be preserved; and it could not be used by the *conductor* in an unauthorized way. He had to exercise the care of a *bonus paterfamilias* in his dealing with the property. At the end of the period of hire, the property had to be returned substantially in its original state, subject to normal wear and tear. Allowing the property to decrease in value could amount to a breach of this duty:

Ulpian, *Edict, book 32*: **Likewise, the lessee should take care in no way to lower in value the thing's legal or physical condition, nor to allow it to become lower.** (D.19.2.11.2.)

What happened if the property was destroyed or damaged during the period of hire without the *conductor*'s fault? The risk of accidental or unpreventable loss was normally on the *locator*. For example:

Ulpian, *Edict, book 32*: …**if an earthquake so completely destroys the land that it no longer exists, the owner bears the loss: for he must present the land to the lessee for his enjoyment.** (D.19.2.15.2.)

What if the loss was only partial, e.g. if the damage resulted in a bad harvest rather than a ruined harvest? The position was that the tenant was entitled to a rebate or remission of the rent if the damage was caused by exceptionally abnormal conditions, but not otherwise. See De Neeve, P. W., 'Remissio Mercedis' (1983) 100 ZSS (rA), 296–339 and Frier, B. W., 'Law, Economics and Disasters Down on the Farm: "Remissio Mercedis" Revisited' (1989–90) BIDR (31–2), 237–70. The rule, the legal foundation of which remains controversial, has been adopted (with variations) by modern systems, e.g., French and German law. See Zimmermann, *Obligations*, 371 ff.

The duties of both parties could be varied by agreement, the rules being similar to those in sale. The remedies available to the parties for the enforcement of their respective duties were the *actio locati* for the *locator* and the *actio conducti* for the *conductor.* The measure of damages was the plaintiff's 'interest' in the performance of the contract.

As we have seen before, tenants generally did not have proprietary interests in Roman law: the law of landlord and tenant was essentially contractual, determined largely by the rules of *locatio conductio rei.* In the cities, tenants tended to live in *insulae*—large blocks of flats—where the activities of careless neighbours and the dangers of fire and structural collapse were constant worries, providing a fecund source of juristic activity. Bruce Frier emphasizes that those consulting the jurists tended to be rich, so that the jurists created a law of 'upper-class' leasehold: 'Wherever we can assess the content of the real or hypothetical cases discussed by the jurists, these cases reflect the upper classes—either upper class tenants or the entrepreneurial middlemen who rented and then subleased *insulae*' (*Landlords and Tenants in Imperial Rome* (1980), 52, and generally). A similar attitude may be detected in juristic discussion of agricultural tenancy (Kehoe, D. P., *Investment, Profit and Tenancy* (1997), 237–40 and generally).

9.3.2.2 Hire of services (*locatio conductio operarum*)

In this type of hire, the *locator* placed his services at the disposal of the *conductor* in return for payment. The rules were largely similar to those applicable to the hire of a thing. For example, both parties were subject to the *bonus paterfamilias* standard of care. The *locator* thus had to perform his services with due diligence—if he professed some particular expertise, he had to prove competent for the work he undertook (see further 10.2.4.2). The *conductor* could incur liability through failure, for example, to provide safe premises or a safe system of work.

What was the effect of death on this type of hire? The basic rule was that the death of the *locator* terminated the contract, but not necessarily the death of the *conductor.* If the service had not been a purely personal one, the death of the *conductor* did not end the contract—his heirs were bound. In any case, the *locator* was entitled to payment for the duration of the hire:

Paul, *Rules, sole book*: **A man who leases out his labor should receive wages for the entire term if he is not responsible for his labor not being rendered.** (D.19.2.38pr.)

The above principle was perhaps too widely stated as it seems that if the *locator* found alternative employment, he might not be able to sue for all the wages that he was prevented from earning by the death of the *conductor*:

Ulpian, *Edict, book 32*: **When a scribe leased out his own labor and his employer then died, the Emperor Antonius together with the deified Severus replied by rescript to the scribe's petition in these words: 'Since you allege that you are not responsible for your not providing the labor…it is fair that the promise [of wages] in the contract be fulfilled if during the year in question you received no wages from anyone else'.** (D.19.2.19.9.)

Which services could be hired? Only those that were typically performed by slaves (*operae illiberales*) (see Thomas, J. A. C., 'Locatio and Operae' (1961) 64 BIDR, 231–47 for a comprehensive discussion of this aspect). Slaves often performed menial tasks but we have seen that their services could be used in an extensive range of activities. *Operae illiberales* thus came to have a wide meaning, so that the services that were excluded from the contract of hire were confined to 'liberal' pursuits. The rationale behind this development was that those engaged in such pursuits would not wish to perform their services in return for anything as sordid as money. For example, Ulpian tells us that philosophers could not be hired as they should avoid 'mercenary activity' (D.50.13.1.4.). Other services that could not be hired included those of jurists, advocates, physicians, surveyors, and teachers in higher education. How did all these worthies make a living? The practice was to grant them an honorarium, enforceable through the contract of mandate (see generally 9.3.3).

The distinction between *operae illiberales* and other services can seem confusing. For example, the Romans did not generally regard engagement in the creative arts as a liberal pursuit. The position as regards teachers provides some insight into how the distinction was made. Those in higher education could not be hired, but other teachers could be. It thus seems that the distinction between liberal pursuits and other services depended to some extent on the status of the person performing the service, and not solely on the nature of the service.

9.3.2.3 Hire of a piece of work (*locatio conductio operis*)

This type of hire was a hybrid form of the two types already considered, occurring where the *locator* placed a thing with the *conductor* in order for the latter to do some work in relation to it, e.g. X gives Y some bronze with which to make a statue. The principles relevant to the hire of a thing (see earlier) were largely applicable to *locatio conductio operis*; but, whereas in the other types of hire it was the *conductor* who paid, in the hire of a piece of work it was the *locator*. The *conductor* could subcontract the work unless he had promised to do it personally.

If the materials belonged to the person who was working on them, the agreement was normally regarded as sale rather than hire, e.g. where Y made a bronze statue for X out of Y's materials. But building contracts under which the builder supplied the materials were regarded, exceptionally, as hire. It was common to agree in building contracts that payment should be made in instalments, subject to satisfactory progress. See Martin, S. D., 'A Reconsideration of Probatio Operis' (1986) 103 ZSS (rA), 321–37. The approval of the *locator* was tested objectively—he could not disapprove of the work without reasonable grounds. The standard of the *bonus vir*, the 'upright' man, applied:

Paul, *Edict, book 34*: **If it is provided in a lease clause [of a job] that the owner is to judge the work acceptable, this is construed to mean that what they had called for was the judgment of an upright man, and the same rule holds had they provided for judgment by some third party....**(D.19.2.24pr.)

This test was applied generally in the hire of a piece of work, not just to building contracts. The work had to be completed within the time specified or, if no time had been agreed, within a reasonable time (taking into account the nature of the task). Both parties were required to show the standard of care of a *bonus paterfamilias*, the *locator* in relation to the materials supplied, the *conductor* as regards his work. See Martin, S. D., 'The Case of the Collapsing Watercourse: Builders' Responsibility for Damage in Classical Roman Law' (1986) 4 LHR, 423–37. Inexperience was not a defence—an important principle in practice (and one adopted by modern systems):

Ulpian, *Edict, book 32*: ...**inexperience should also be counted as fault; if someone contracts to pasture calves or to repair or to adorn something, he should be held responsible for fault, and it is fault when he errs due to inexperience, since, as Celsus says, it was obviously as a craftsman that he took the job.** (D.19.2.9.5.)

If the materials were damaged or destroyed while the *conductor* was working with them, the risk initially lay with him:

Ulpian, *Edict, book 32*: **If a fuller takes in clothes for cleaning and mice then gnaw at them, he is liable on the lease [of a job] because he should have guarded against this.** (D.19.2.13.6.)

But if destruction was through *vis maior*, the risk lay with the *locator*—he would have to make payment even though he received nothing in return. Similarly, it seems, if the loss occurred after the *locator* had accepted the work, a rule incorporated by s. 644 BGB. See Zimmermann, *Obligations*, 401 ff. As regards death, the general rule was that the contract was not terminated by the death of either party; their respective heirs were bound.

If A placed cargo for carriage in B's ship, the agreement could amount to the hire of a piece of work. Special rules were introduced for such contracts, among them a rule adopted from the maritime code of Rhodes:

Paul, *Sentences, book 2*: **The Rhodian law provides that if cargo has been jettisoned in order to lighten a ship, the sacrifice for the common good must be made good by common contribution. [Paul, *Edict, book 34*] [2]: ... the owners who have lost the cargo for whose carriage they contracted may sue the captain on their contracts. Then, the captain may bring an action on his contracts of carriage against the others whose goods have been saved, so as to distribute the loss proportionately.** (D.14.2.1.–2pr.)

The rule ensured that all concerned shared the loss proportionately, the amount of the contribution depending on the respective values of the property that had been saved and lost. It is probable that in practice the captain retained the cargo until each party had made the appropriate contribution, thus avoiding the cumbersome litigation mentioned in the text. If the jettisoned property was eventually saved, the Rhodian law no longer applied—any contributions that had been made could be recovered. Jettisoned goods remained the property of their owners—they were not treated as abandoned (see 7.2.3.3).

The Rhodian–Roman rules were adopted by maritime powers in the medieval period throughout Western Europe, and survive in modern law—e.g. in the German Commercial Code. The Court of Admiralty, staffed largely by civilians, adopted the rules into English law. And the principle of shared contribution in situations of common danger was applied by medieval lawyers beyond the maritime sphere, e.g. in the case of fire. See Zimmermann, *Obligations*, 409 ff. See most recently, Aubert, J.-J. 'Dealing with the Abyss: The Nature and Purpose of the Rhodian Sea-law on Jettison', in *Beyond Dogmatics*, 157–72.

9.3.3 **Mandate (*mandatum*)**

(Inst.Gai.3.155.–62., Inst.3.26., D.17.1., C.4.35.)

Mandate was a *bonae fidei* contract made when a promisor gratuitously agreed to perform a service requested by another, the *mandator* (cf. Inst.Gai.3.162.). The origins of the contract are unclear but probably lay in requests between friends to perform a particular service in legal proceedings, e.g. to act as a guarantor, or as a representative in legal proceedings. (See generally Watson, A., *Contract of Mandate in Roman Law* (1961) and Metzger, *Companion*, 165–8). The use of mandate later widened considerably—the contract acquired great commercial significance. For example, it was used to appoint general business managers and agents. Mandates as contracts should not be confused with *mandata* as a form of imperial decree (see 2.3.2.6).

9.3.3.1 The essentials of mandate

The promise had to be made gratuitously, otherwise the agreement would amount to hire:

Paul, *Edict, book 32*: **There is no mandate unless it is gratuitous. The reason is that it derives its origins from duty and friendship, and the fact is that payment for services rendered is incompatible with this duty. For if money is involved, the matter rather pertains to hire.** (D.17.1.1.4.) (cf. Inst. 3.26.13.)

However, if an honorarium was agreed, it could be enforced from the early Empire under the *cognitio extraordinaria* procedure. In this way, the theory that mandate was gratuitous was preserved, since payment could not be recovered by a 'normal' action before a judge, yet the promisor was allowed a reward for his services—a triumph of Roman pragmatism, if not strict logic.

Only services that were moral, legal, and possible could be enforced (cf. Inst. 3.26.7.). Moreover, some texts suggest that the mandator had to have an 'interest' in the service in the sense that it had to concern him. Ulpian states:

Ulpian, *Edict, book 31*: **The action on mandate is competent when the person who gave the mandate first has an interest; but if he ceases to have an interest, the action on mandate does not lie; what is more, the action only lies to the extent of his interest.** (D.17.1.8.6.) (cf. Inst. 3.26pr.)

It did not matter if the mandate was in the interest of the promisor as well, or of some third party, as long as the *mandator* retained some interest himself. However, another text by Ulpian seems to deny the need for the *mandator* to have an interest:

Ulpian, *Edict, book 31*: **Should I give you a mandate that is not in my interests, for example, that you should stand surety for Seius or lend to Titius, I will have the action on mandate against you....** (D.17.1.6.4.)

The texts could be reconciled if 'interests' in the latter passage was interpreted as *apparent* interests. An interest might not be apparent on the face of the transaction, but nevertheless still exist. Suppose that Seius, in the above example, was my debtor—then it would certainly be in my interest that you should act as his surety, even if this interest was not apparent from the actual terms of the mandate. Regardless of such attempts to reconcile the texts, it is not obvious why in principle an interest should have been required of the *mandator*.

9.3.3.2 The duties of the parties

Their duties did not arise simultaneously—the contract can thus be described as imperfectly bilateral. The promisor's duties commenced as soon as he promised to carry out the request; but the duties of the *mandator* were mostly contingent on the performance of the service.

(a) Duties of the promisor. His primary duty was to perform the mandate, subject to the right of renunciation. In carrying out the task the promisor could do whatever was reasonably necessary to achieve it, but he could not exceed his powers—he could not act *ultra vires* (cf. Inst.3.26.8.). The strict application of the *ultra vires* rule could cause unfortunate results. Suppose that A gave B a mandate to buy a chariot for A for 1,000 *sesterces*, and B bought it for double that amount. What amount can

B recover from A—2,000 *sesterces*, 1,000, or nothing? The Sabinians took the strict line that B should recover nothing as he had not complied with the mandate. The Proculians felt that the Sabinian view was rather harsh—in effect, A had acquired a chariot for nothing while B had lost 2,000 *sesterces*. The Proculian view was that the promisor should be able to recover up to the limit of his authority, (i.e. 1,000 *sesterces* in the above example):

Paul, *Edict, book 32*:…if I specified a price and you bought at a figure in excess of this, some [authorities] have held that you do not have the action on mandate, even though you may have been prepared to let the excess go [Gaius, *Common Matters (or Golden Sayings), book 2*]:… But Proculus is of the opinion, and rightly, that [the buyer] will have an action up to the limit of the price specified. This is certainly the more liberal view. (D.17.1.3.2., 4.)

The promisor could not profit from the mandate; he had to render a proper account and had to transfer any proceeds or rights acquired through his performance:

Paul, *Sabinus, book 11*: Nothing obtained as a result of a mandate ought to be left in the hands of the person who undertook the mandate…(D.17.1.20pr.)

Which standard of care applied to the performance of the request by the promisor? Before the classical period, the promisor was liable only for *dolus*, but it seems that the *bonus paterfamilias* standard had become the rule by the end of the era. The imposition of the more exacting standard was probably a reflection of the growing practice of paying the promisor an honorarium—as the promisor was no longer acting gratuitously, in reality, there was a case for expecting a higher standard of care from him. (See Gordon, W. M., 'The Liability of the Mandatary', in *Synteleia Arangio-Ruiz* I, 202–5, who argues that the liability of the mandatary varied between *dolus* and *culpa* according to circumstances; similarly, MacCormack, G., 'The Liability of the Mandatary' (1972) 18 Labeo, 156–72 and Nörr, D., 'Reflections on Faith, Friendship, Mandate' (1990–2) IJ, 302–10.)

(b) Duties of the *mandator*. His chief duty was to accept the performance of the promisor, including any liabilities and expenses that had been properly incurred in carrying out the request. The *mandator* was subject to the *bonus paterfamilias* standard of care as regards the task requested of the promisor, e.g. if the mandate consisted of the renovation of a villa, the *mandator* had to provide a safe system of work.

The remedies available to the parties were the *actio mandati directa* for the *mandator*, and the *actio mandati contraria* for the promisor. If the promisor was found liable, *infamia* resulted. This seemingly harsh rule had its origins in early law when the condemnation of the promisor was possible only if he had acted fraudulently, i.e. with *dolus*.

9.3.3.3 Termination of mandate

Several factors could bring about the termination of mandate. For example, a mandate could end by mutual consent, or if the promise became impossible (in the nature of things) to perform, or on the completion of the task. However, the causes of termination that require particular comment were renunciation and death.

(a) Renunciation. The basic rule was that the contract could be renounced, without liability, by either party before the promisor had commenced performance. But, if the promisor's renunciation prevented the *mandator* from obtaining a similar service from another person, the promisor would be liable to that extent. What if the renunciation took place after the promisor had commenced performance? It would be effective in that it ended the mandate, but the party renouncing would be liable for any damage or expense caused to the other party. A *mandator* who renounced had to give notice to any third parties dealing with the promisor, since they were entitled to treat the mandate as continuing until otherwise informed.

(b) Death. The death of either party ended the mandate. However, if it was the *mandator* who died, his heirs had to give notice to the promisor and had to reimburse him for expenses incurred up to that time. What if the mandate consisted of a promise to do something after the death of one of the parties? If it was to be performed after the promisor's death, the mandate was void because of the rule of classical law that an obligation could not begin with an heir. If the mandate was to be performed after the *mandator's* death, it seems that it could be upheld in some circumstances:

Ulpian, *Edict, book 31*: **Marcellus also tells us that if a man has given a mandate for the erection of a monument to him after his death, his heir can bring an action on mandate.** (D.17.1.12.17.)

This text is hard to reconcile with passages attributed to some other jurists, but it is more consistent with the position under Justinian, who was generally prepared to enforce mandates that were to be performed after the *mandator's* death.

9.3.3.4 The contract of mandate and Roman approaches to agency

Mandate could be put to many uses, especially in the field of commercial relations. It could be used, for example, to effect an assignment of obligations, or to guarantee loans, or to appoint business managers and representatives (see Aubert, J-J., *Business Managers in Ancient Rome* (1994), ch. 2). The most important function was the use of mandate to create a form of agency. In modern legal systems, the agent creates contractual relations directly between his principal and the third party, but generally acquires no rights or liabilities himself through his agency. Roman law had no strict equivalent but developed a broadly similar position through the use of mandate. To appreciate the complexity of this development, an example will be used. A *mandator* entered into a contract of mandate with the promisor in terms of which the promisor agreed to achieve a certain result (e.g. buy a racehorse at auction) as set out in the contract. The promisor's acts could not, *prima facie*, create contractual relations between the *mandator* and a third party, owing to the existence in Roman law of the principle of privity of contract (see 9.2.6). But, since the promisor had to transfer to the *mandator* any rights or obligations (using *cessio in iure*) resulting from the performance of the promise under the terms of the contract of mandate, the promisor was acting in effect as an agent (albeit indirect). It was not true agency, in the modern sense, because the *mandator* could not sue on the contract made by the promisor with the third party—only the promisor could sue or be sued. He had to avail himself of the contractual remedies of the contract of mandate against the promisor.

  This unsatisfactory state of affairs whereby a third party did not have any legal recourse directly against the *mandator* had undergone various stages of development until, in Justinianic law, a third party had certain legal remedies directly against the *mandator*. The earliest developments in this regard occurred within the Roman *familia*, the final stage outside it. First, legal remedies were developed to address the use of slaves and sons-in-power as commercial agents. It is not clear whether the legal remedies were first created for slaves and extended to sons-in-power or vice versa. Finally, these remedies were extended through juristic interpretation to all forms of agency, even where the promisor was an independent person who was *sui iuris*.

The use of persons with no contractual capacity such as slaves as agents deserves closer attention. Slaves had no contractual capacity and any transactions that they entered into were either void or could not be directly enforced against them. These restrictions proved inconvenient in the rapidly expanding world of Roman commerce that necessitated the use of slaves as agents. The praetors therefore made a crucial intervention in the late Republic by allowing actions directly against the *paterfamilias* (who normally would also be the owner of the slave) in certain circumstances. These actions, collectively known as *actiones adiecticiae qualitatis* (medieval terminology), enabled parties, who had contracted with slaves acting as business agents, to sue the latter directly. These actions were not based on the notion of mandate (as there could be no legally binding contract of mandate between *paterfamilias* and slave), but created an 'exceptional' liability for the *paterfamilias*, hence the terminology *actiones adiecticiae qualitatis*. The actions were all founded on a 'debt' incurred by the slave acting as a business agent on behalf of the *paterfamilias*. In the formulary procedure, the actions were usually worded by inserting the name of the business agent as the person who had incurred the debt, but citing the *paterfamilias* as the person who would be subject to the *condemnatio*.

(a) *Actio de peculio*. (D.15.1., 2.) Where slaves demonstrated particular economic skill, owners gave them a fund of assets (*peculium*) with which to engage in commerce. The fund, though technically the property of the owner, was administered *de facto* by the slave on the basis that he had been granted free administration of it. If creditors were to sue on account of debts incurred by the slave when trading using his *peculium*, the slave could not be sued directly as he did not have legal standing in a court of law. Creditors instead had to use an action which was based on the existence of the fund (*peculium*) given to the slave (see Inst.4.7.4.). The *paterfamilias* (as owner of the slave) had to be sued, but his liability was limited to the extent of the value of the *peculium at the time of judgment* after an assessment of the value of the *peculium* would be made. Such an assessment took into account all the assets, but also allowed the *paterfamilias* and other members of the *familia* to deduct any money owed to them as preferred creditors. Because of the notion of 'free administration' of the *peculium*, the action was used where the *paterfamilias* did not know the details of the transactions from which the liability arose (see Johnston, *Roman Law in Context*, 99–105), but there were drawbacks in suing on the basis of the *peculium* (see Johnston, D., 'Peculiar Questions', in *Thinking Like a Lawyer*, 5–13). The creditors could bring this action against the *paterfamilias* as long as the value of the *peculium* could support such claims. Since its value was not assessed until the time of judgment, an element of faith (or commercial caution) on the part of the creditors must have been required. The effect of the action was primarily to limit the liability of the *paterfamilias* to the value of the *peculium*, based on the assumption that the value of the *peculium* would always be smaller than the owner's entire estate. See Kirschenbaum, *Sons, Slaves and Freedmen* (1987), 47–71 for a comprehensive assessment of the *actio de peculio*.

(b) *Actio de in rem verso*. (D.15.3) This action, often employed in conjunction with the *actio de peculio*, was used where a slave used the benefits obtained from commercial transactions to enrich the estate of the *paterfamilias*. This occurred, for example, where a slave borrowed money to pay the debts of the *paterfamilias*:

Ulpian, *Edict, book 29*: **The *actio de in rem verso* is not a useless provision: it is not as if the *actio de peculio* were enough. For as Labeo quite rightly says, it may be that the property has been turned over [to the master] and the *actio de peculio* is not available. What if the master has taken away the *peculium* without *dolus malus*? What if the *peculium* has ceased to operate because of the slave's death and the year for the action has ended?** (D.15.3.1.1.)

What constituted a benefit? It seems that the rule was directed at the necessities, not the luxuries of life:

Ulpian, *Edict, book 29*: **Labeo says that a slave who spends money to feed or clothe himself is treated as conferring a benefit on the master if he does so in accordance with the master's usual practice, that is, within the limits of the provision which the master normally made. [4] But he will not be treated as conferring a benefit if he uses borrowed money to adorn his master's house with stucco or other useless luxuries...** (D.15.3.3.3.–4.)

The *paterfamilias'* liability was limited to the extent of his enrichment at the time of condemnation. On this action, see MacCormack, G., 'The Later History of the "Actio de in rem verso" (Proculus—Ulpian)', (1982) 48 SDHI, 318–67. See also extensively, Kirschenbaum, *Sons, Slaves and Freedmen* (1978), 72–88.

(c) *Actio tributoria*. (D.14.4) This action had limited application. When a slave used his *peculium* in trade with the knowledge of the *paterfamilias* and incurred debts which exceeded the value of the *peculium*, the praetor could force the *paterfamilias* to liquidate the assets comprising the *peculium* and to divide the proceeds amongst the creditors. Liability was limited to the *part* of the *peculium* actually used in trading (rather than the whole of it). The *paterfamilias* could not deduct anything that was owed to him before awarding each creditor his share. Creditors who suspected that the *paterfamilias* had acted unfairly in the division of the *peculium* among the creditors could sue him with this action to force a fairer division of the assets among creditors (cf. Inst.Gai.4.72.; Inst.4.7.3.).

(d) *Actio quod iussu*. (D.15.4.) The *paterfamilias* was fully liable (without limitation) under this action for a commercial transaction that he had expressly authorized (*iussum*) a third party to enter into with his slave (cf. Inst.Gai.4.70.; Inst.4.7.1.). Authorization could take various forms:

Ulpian, *Edict, book 29*: **Authorization in this connection may be given by will or by letter or orally or through an intermediary and either specifically for a single transaction or generally. So a person who states publicly, 'do any business you like with my slave Stichus; it will be at my risk', is taken to have authorized all kinds of transactions unless there is a specific exclusionary clause.** (D.15.4.1.1.)

It is possible that the *paterfamilias'* express authority had to be communicated to the other party in some way, but the texts are ambiguous.

Gaius mentions that these actions were available to third parties dealing with servile agents as well as with agents who were sons-in-power. (For the position of daughters-in-power and other members of the *familia*, see Buckland, *Textbook*, 535.)

Apart from the four actions just mentioned, the category of *actiones adiecticiae qualitatis* traditionally also includes two further actions dealing with aspects of agency. Juristic commentary on these two actions demonstrate that they were used both where agents were slaves or sons-in-power and where they were individuals who were *sui iuris*.

(e) *Actio institoria.* (D14.3., C.4.25.) This action lay against someone to enforce contracts made by another (whether slave, son-in-power or *sui iuris* employee) who had been appointed to manage his business. Some scholars suggest that the master or employer's liability was in this case founded on the terms of the appointment as business manager and therefore extended also to employees, who were not in power. The master or employer was fully liable for such transactions, provided that they were within the scope (express or implied) of the business agent's authority:

Ulpian, *Edict, book* 28: **Not all transactions with a manager bind the person who appointed him, but only contracts relating to the matter which he was appointed to manage, that is, only those within the scope of the appointment.** (D.14.3.5.11.)

(f) *Actio exercitoria.* (C.4.25.) A shipowner was fully liable under this action for commercial debts made by his or another's slave or worker employed as captain of a merchant ship, provided the transaction was within the scope of the captain's authority (cf. Inst.Gai.4.71.; Inst. 4.7.2.).

On these two actions, see Kirschenbaum, *Sons, Slaves and Freedmen* (1987), 90–121.

9.3.4 Partnership (*societas*)

(Inst.Gai.3.148.–154b., Inst.3.25., D.17.2., C.4.37.)

Societas was a *bonae fidei* contract whereby two or more persons agreed to associate in a common venture for their mutual benefit. Partnerships were often formed with a view to making a financial profit (see Földi, A., 'Remarks on the Legal Structure of Enterprises in Roman Law' (1996) 43 RIDA 3, 179–211; Andreau, J., *Banking and Business in the Roman World* (1999) and in general, Metzger, *Companion*, 162–5), but this was not an essential requirement of the contract—the mutual benefit did not have to be pecuniary.

9.3.4.1 The essentials of partnership

The common venture had to be physically possible, lawful, and not immoral or incompatible with good faith, see Watson, A., 'The Notion of Equivalence of Contractual Obligation and Classical Roman Partnership' (1981) 97 LQR, 275–86. Each partner had to contribute to the common venture: it might be capital, labour or some skill, or expertise. But the contributions did not have to be of equal value, and frequently were not. Each partner had to be allowed a share in the benefits resulting from the partnership; the respective shares would normally be agreed between the partners. What if there was no agreement?

Ulpian, *Sabinus, book 30*: **If shares in a partnership have been left unspecified, it is agreed that they are to be equal….** (D.17.2.29pr.)

This rule applied to losses as well—they were shared equally unless the partners agreed the contrary. However, the contribution of some individuals might be so prized that it would be worth securing their involvement by an arrangement under which they did not share in any losses:

Ulpian, *Sabinus, book 30*: **It is Cassius's opinion that a partnership can be formed on the terms that one partner is to suffer no part of any loss whereas profits are to be shared. An agreement of this kind will indeed be valid, in the view of Sabinus, if services are rendered** commensurate with the loss incurred. Very often a partner works so hard for the partnership that his contribution is worth more to it than money, for example, if he were to be the only partner to travel by sea or go abroad at all or expose himself to such dangers. (D.17.2.29.1.)

It was essential that there should be an intention to form a partnership; and, given that it was essentially a cooperative venture based on trust, there had to be agreement about its membership—no partner could introduce a new partner without the consent of the others, as Ulpian emphasized in one of his more succinct moods:

Ulpian, *Edict, book 31*: ... my partner's partner is not my partner. (D.17.2.20.)

9.3.4.2 Position of the partners

Partners had to make the agreed contribution and had to share in the administration of the common venture, subject to any contrary agreement. In the case of a business it was common to appoint a manager, but he did not have to be one of the partners. Each partner had to account for his activities in pursuance of the common venture. If a partner made a contract in relation to partnership business, he alone could sue or be sued on it; but the duty to account for his actions meant that the other partners would be affected by the contract. Thus, if property was acquired for the partnership, each partner would have a right *in personam* to secure his respective share.

Which standard of care was expected of a partner? In early law the only requirement was that a partner should act in good faith, i.e. avoid *dolus*. Later, probably in the classical period, he became liable for negligence, the standard applied being that expected of a man in his own affairs:

Gaius, *Common Matters, book 2*: A partner is responsible to his co-partner even on the score of negligence, that is, laziness and carelessness. But negligence should not be assessed on the basis of a comparison with the most stringent standards of diligence. It is enough that a partner show diligence in the affairs of the partnership commensurate with that which he is accustomed to exhibit in his own affairs. (D.17.2.72.)

Any loss to the partnership that resulted from a partner's negligence (or *dolus*) had to be borne entirely by that partner: the agreement between partners about the sharing of losses applied only to those for which no partner was to blame. If a partner caused loss through his fault, he could not set it off against any profits that he might have formerly produced for the partnership:

Paul, *Sabinus, book 6*: Where the partnership has been ruined by the negligence of a partner, the risk that he bears is not reduced by the fact that in many other operations the partnership has prospered as a result of his hard work. (D.17.2.25.)

Partners were entitled to be reimbursed for expenses that were properly incurred. This area of Roman law certainly has modern parallels—we have strayed here into the world of business partners and expense accounts, even if some of the expenses would not normally be incurred by the businessman of today:

Ulpian, *Edict, book 31*: Where a partner has set out on a journey on partnership business, for example, to purchase goods, he can charge to the partnership only those expenses incurred to that end. Therefore, he is entitled to charge it with traveling expenses in connection with his own accommodation and the stabling of his horse, and the hire of pack animals and carts to carry himself, his luggage, and his goods. (D.17.2.52.15.)

Which expenses were recoverable? The jurists were not unanimous. Some took the view that the expenses must have been incurred strictly *in pursuance* of the common venture, and not simply *in consequence* of it:

Pomponius, *Sabinus, book 13*: **A partner was wounded in trying to prevent slaves kept by the partnership for sale from breaking out and escaping. Labeo says he cannot get back through a partnership action the expenses he incurred in having himself treated, for the reason that the expenditure, though a consequence of partnership, was not made for partnership purposes…** (D.17.2.60.1.)

Labeo's somewhat harsh view seems wrong and it was not accepted by some later jurists (Julian and Ulpian, for example), who would have allowed recovery of medical expenses in these circumstances.

9.3.4.3 Remedies

The main remedy in the contract of partnership was the *actio pro socio* ('the action for a partner'). It could be brought as a friendly suit to make minor adjustments in the position of the partners, or as a hostile action for breach of a partner's duties. In the latter case, the action had two important consequences: condemnation resulted in *infamia*, and the partnership was terminated. Other actions were possible; e.g. the *actio communi dividundo* ('the action for dividing things held in common') was necessary for the distribution of partnership property at the end of the partnership. Moreover, delictual actions might be available in appropriate circumstances, e.g. where a partner stole partnership property:

Ulpian, *Sabinus, book 30*: **A partner may be sued for theft in respect of common property, if he took something away by fraud or deceit, or if he handles common property with intent to conceal it. But he is also liable to an action on partnership, and the one action does not exclude the other.** (D.17.2.45.)

9.3.4.4 Types of partnership

Although the scope of the common venture that the parties might undertake was very wide, partnerships were broadly of four types:

(a) Partnership for a single transaction: where the parties came together for a single transaction or operation, e.g. to buy a particular property. The partnership in *pro Roscio*—one of Cicero's best-known cases—illustrates this category: an arrangement whereby Roscius, an actor, was to train a man's slave for the stage, profits to be shared between owner and trainer.

(b) Partnership in a particular business: where the parties agreed to operate a particular kind of business, e.g. moneylending, slave-dealing, or tax farming. The farming of taxes was a notable feature of Roman life for several centuries. The State sold the right to collect taxes to partnerships of tax farmers (*publicani*). The contract normally lasted for five years—it was linked to the census—but was renewable. For the State, this system was obviously convenient and efficient, but it inevitably led to abuses, corruption, and strained relations between taxpayers and *publicani* (they became hated figures). Their powers and influence were gradually curbed by imperial regulation. A text attributed to Gaius (D.3.4.1pr.) suggests that *publicani* had some *corporate* personality—able to own property, for example—but it is regarded as very dubious.

More typical were the partnerships engaged in small-scale manufacturing, such as the production of pots for imported foodstuffs for which ample evidence has been found from the Monte Testaccio—an artificial hill in Rome composed of the remains of pots discarded from the Tiber warehouses. It appears that it was quite common for such enterprises to be operated by family partnerships consisting of fathers, sons, and freedmen. See Crook, *Law and Life of Rome*, 229 ff.

(c) Partnership in general business: where the parties associated for the purpose of all business transactions. If it was not clear which type of partnership the partners intended, the presumption was that they intended a general business partnership:

Ulpian, *Sabinus, book 30*: **It is also permissible to form a partnership without specific terms; and if no terms have been specified, the partnership is held to be formed in all that comes in the way of profit, that is, in whatever return comes from purchase and sale, letting and hiring.** (D.17.2.7.)

(d) Partnership in all assets: where all the property of the parties formed a common fund of assets. On the creation of such a partnership, all property held by the partners was pooled, as was property acquired thereafter. This was the oldest form of partnership, originating in the practice whereby family co-heirs sometimes agreed not to distribute an inheritance but to preserve it intact for common enjoyment.

9.3.4.5 Termination of partnership

Modestinus, *Rules, book 3*: **It is dissolved through renunciation, death, change of civil status, and poverty.** (D.17.2.4.1.)

(a) Renunciation. If any partner renounced, i.e. wished to withdraw, the partnership ended (even if the partners had specifically agreed the contrary). But a partner who renounced would have to compensate the others if his withdrawal unreasonably prejudiced their interests:

Paul, *Edict, book 32*: **Suppose, for example, we form a partnership and buy slaves, and then you renounce at a time which is disadvantageous for selling slaves, you are liable to an action on partnership, because in this case you are altering my prospects for the worse.** (D.17.2.65.5.)

Moreover, if a partner acted fraudulently in renouncing, he would have to share with the others any profit that accrued to him through the renunciation. Paul considers what would happen if a man renounced a partnership in all assets, having discovered that he was coming into an inheritance:

Paul, *Edict, book 32*: **In such a case, if the inheritance brings him loss, this will be borne by the man who renounced, whereas he may be compelled by an action on partnership to share any profit.** (D.17.2.65.3.)

A renunciation would normally be made expressly but could also be implied, e.g. where a partner sold property in breach of the partnership agreement. Although renunciation terminated a partnership, the remaining partners could continue in business by forming a new partnership.

(b) Death. A partnership ended on the death of any partner, as a general rule, even if the original partnership agreement had provided that his heir could succeed a deceased partner. This was because *societas* was a common venture based on trust—the heir might be unknown to the other partners. The heir might indeed become a partner, but only in a new partnership (if the surviving partners wished to carry on). The general rule did not apply to tax farming partnerships—they survived the death of a partner.

What was the position of an heir of a deceased partner? Whether he became a partner or not, the principle of universal succession meant that he took over all the rights and liabilities of the deceased; and he had to complete unfinished partnership business:

Pomponius, *Sabinus, book 17*: **Although the heir of a partner is not a partner, he ought to complete such business as was begun by the dead man.** (D.17.2.40.)

(c) Loss of civil status. Originally, if a partner suffered *capitis deminutio*, whatever its form, the partnership was terminated, although the remaining partners could form a new one. In later law only the more serious forms of *capitis deminutio* had a terminating effect, not if it was *minima* (see 4.2).

(d) Poverty. A partnership ended when a partner was made bankrupt or had his property confiscated by the State. It seems that a generally impoverished condition was insufficient—there had to be proof of some 'event' (such as the examples mentioned earlier) that caused the poverty.

There were other grounds for the termination of a partnership. A hostile *actio pro socio* ended a partnership, as we have seen. Moreover, a partnership ended if its subject matter was exhausted, lost, or destroyed:

Ulpian, *Edict, book 31*: **You had three horses and I one, and we formed a partnership on the terms that you would take my horse, sell the horses as a team of four, and give me a quarter of the proceeds. Then my horse dies before the sale. Celsus says that in his opinion the partnership no longer exists, and I am owed no part of the price received from the sale of your horses; for the partnership was made not to form but to sell a team of four.** (D.17.2.58pr.)

Further, a partnership ended if its purpose was accomplished or (conversely) became impossible to achieve; where the partnership was for a fixed duration and the relevant period elapsed; where the continuation of a partnership was made subject to a condition that was not satisfied; and by mutual consent.

English law has been substantially influenced by the rules of *societas*, especially in the emphasis on the personal (as opposed to corporate) character of partnership. The same is true of South African and German law, although the latter regards partnership property as common property separate from the private assets of individual partners (s. 718 BGB). See Zimmermann, *Obligations*, 471 ff.

9.4 **Verbal contracts**

The obligations that were created in verbal contracts resulted from the uttering of particular words in a specified manner. There were three verbal contracts mentioned in Gaius' *Institutes* (Inst.Gai.3.92.–109.), *stipulatio* being by far the most important. All three were unilateral and *stricti iuris*. See Birks, *Obligations*, 52–64.

9.4.1 *Dotis dictio*

Dotis dictio ('the pronouncing of the dowry') was a solemn declaration of the composition of a dowry, usually made before marriage. It could be made by the bride, if *sui iuris*, or by her *paterfamilias*, or by her debtor (if authorized by her). The promisee, normally the bridegroom, had to be present. *Dotis dictio* became obsolete in the late Empire when informal promises to create a dowry were given full validity (see Katzoff, R., 'Oral Establishment of Dowry in Jewish and Roman law: D'Varim Haniknim ba'Amira and Dotis Dictio', in *Critical Studies*, 157–71 for a comparative perspective).

9.4.2 *Iusiurandum liberti*

Iusiurandum liberti ('the oath of the freedman') was made when a freedman took a solemn oath in his patron's presence, immediately after manumission, to render services for the patron (see generally Duff, A. M., *Freedmen in the Early Roman Empire* (1958) and Treggiari, S., *Roman Freedmen during the Late Republic* (1969)). This oath would normally have been preceded by another taken before manumission. The earlier oath could not be legally binding but it provided evidence of ingratitude should the freedman refuse to take the second oath on being freed. *Iusiurandum liberti* became infrequent in the Empire, apparently because of the increased use of *stipulatio* to achieve the same end.

9.4.3 *Stipulatio*

(Inst.Gai.3.92.–109., Inst.3.15., 18., 19., D.45.1., C.8.37.)

Stipulatio was a unilateral and *stricti iuris* contract consisting of a formal promise made in answer to a formal question:

Pomponius, *Sabinus, book 26*: **A stipulation is a verbal expression in which the man who is asked replies that he will give or do what he has been asked.** (D.45.1.5.1.) (cf. Inst.Gai.3.92.)

9.4.3.1 **Introduction**

Stipulatio was of enormous importance in the Roman law of contract. Its origins are unclear but appear to predate the Twelve Tables (Metzger, *Companion*, 134). It seems that *stipulatio* developed out of *sponsio*, a formal guarantee to pay the debt of another. It is possible that *sponsio* originally required the making of an oath to the gods, and that *stipulatio* was the secular contract that emerged when the religious associations faded. (See Nicholas, B., 'The Form of the Stipulation in Roman Law' (1953) 69 LQR, 63–79; Thomas, J. A. C., 'Words are Tools, not Masters', in *Studi Biscardi* I, 23–32 and MacCormack, G., 'The Oral and Written Stipulation in the Institutes', in *Studies J. A. C. Thomas*, 96–108, on the continued existence of the oral *stipulatio* in Justinianic law.)

Stipulatio probably had a limited use at first, confined mainly to formal undertakings made by litigants in the course of litigation. Soon, the use of stipulations was greatly extended—virtually any legal agreement could be effected by them. For example, a sale could be effected through the making of the appropriate stipulations by the parties. The potential universality of *stipulatio* suggests that in early Rome there was a law of contract rather than contracts. However, the development of *stipulatio* remains a puzzling question. Why did other contracts emerge and flourish long after the establishment of *stipulatio* as a contract of wide scope? It appears to have been gradually sidelined by the emergence of less formal contracts. The drawbacks of *stipulatio*—especially the emphasis on formality, and the need for the actual presence of the parties—undoubtedly contributed to the development of the consensual contracts. But that ignores developments in the Empire when it is clear that *stipulatio* was being increasingly used in certain transactions.

In *The Evolution of Law* (1985), Alan Watson takes the view that in early law the Romans did have a general theory of contract because of the all-embracing nature of *stipulatio*. He describes later developments thus: 'in most cases an individual type of Roman contract arose subsequently to *stipulatio* when, for whatever reason, a *stipulatio* was inappropriate or inefficient for that type of situation and when there was a societal need. Thus, almost every subsequent contractual type is a derogation from *stipulatio*' (7). For example, he considers that the contact of mandate developed because the formality of *stipulatio* was ill-suited to gratuitous promises usually made between friends.

David Pugsley has argued that *stipulatio* was probably confined originally to the future conveyance of *res mancipi* and that it did not become an all-purpose contract until the classical period, much later than generally thought. He doubts whether *stipulatio* could have had widespread application so early in Roman legal history when the rest of the law was rudimentary. He considers that the classical law of contract was 'a complicated and heterogeneous collection of legal rules which seems to have developed piecemeal to satisfy the needs of commerce. The whole of this elaborate structure would have been superfluous if any transaction could be summed up in a *stipulatio* and so given legal force' (*Property and Obligations* (1972), 65 ff.).

9.4.3.2 **Formal requirements**

A formal question was required from the promisee, followed by a formal answer by the promisor. The question contained the subject matter of the stipulation, e.g. 'Do you promise to give me 1,000 *sesterces*?' The promisor answered, 'I do promise.' The parties had to use the words *spondesne*? ('Do you promise?') and *spondeo* ('I do promise'). Tony Weir likens the form to the exchange of questions and answers in the marriage service, and he describes the following passage from *The Owl and the Pussy Cat* (Edward Lear) as 'the most perfect *stipulatio* in English literature': '"Dear Pig, are you willing to sell for one shilling Your ring?" Said the Piggy, "I will"' (quoted in (1992) 66 Tulane LR, 1615 cited earlier, at 1620). The promisor had to make a verbal answer—it was insufficient simply to nod the head in assent. The question and answer had to form one continuous transaction—a substantial interval between them could invalidate the contract:

Venuleius, *Stipulations, book 1:* **The acts of stipulator and promisor must be continuous, though a moment or two may naturally intervene. The reply must be made when the stipulator is at hand. If, after the question, something else is begun, the proceeding is invalid, even if the reply is given on the same day.** (D.45.1.137pr.)

The terms of a stipulation had to be clear—any ambiguity was construed against the promisee. Moreover, there had to be congruence between the question and the answer: the answer could not introduce fresh terms or be made conditionally in response to an unconditional question. However, there may have been some exceptions to the requirement of congruence. Consider the following, for example:

Ulpian, *Sabinus, book 48*: If, when I stipulate, 'ten,' you reply, 'twenty,' it is clear that an obligation has been made only for ten. Conversely, also, if I ask for 'twenty' and you reply, 'ten,' an obligation will only have been made for ten. For granted that the sum ought to be consistent, yet it is absolutely obvious that ten is part of twenty. (D.45.1.1.4.)

The approach in this passage is to regard the promise as good for the lesser sum common to both the question and answer—a sensible and practical solution. However, the passage is inconsistent with Gaius (Inst.Gai.3.102.) and may be an interpolation.

The strict insistence on the use of *spondesne? spondeo* was relaxed during the Republic, other words being allowed, e.g. *promittisne? promitto* ('Do you promise?' 'I do promise'); *dabisne? dabo* ('Will you give?' 'I will give'). A further relaxation occurred in the classical period when languages other than Latin came to be regarded as sufficient (see Metzger, *Companion*, 135):

Ulpian, *Sabinus, book 48*: It makes no difference whether the reply is made in the same language or in another. For instance, if a man asks in Latin but receives a reply in Greek, as long as the reply is consistent, the obligation is settled. Whether we extend this rule to the Greek language only or even to another, such as Punic or Assyrian or some other tongue, is a matter of doubt. The writings of Sabinus, however, allow it to be true that all tongues can produce a verbal obligation, provided that both parties understand each other's language, either of their own accord or by means of a truthful interpreter. (D.45.1.1.6.)

The view that there was a gradual relaxation of the form of *stipulatio* during the Republic and early Empire has been questioned—possibly all the relaxations were of the late classical period, or later still. See Nicholas, B., 'The Form of the Stipulation in Roman Law' (1953) 69 LQR, 63 (part II), at 233–52 (cf. Inst.3.15.1. and C.8.37.10.). But is it plausible that the strict requirements of *stipulatio* would have remained unchanged for so long, unaffected by factors such as Rome's commercial expansion and increasingly cosmopolitan population?

Although a *stipulatio* required (at least in theory) a verbal exchange between two parties, important stipulations are unlikely to have been made in practice without witnesses or some written record (*cautio*) of the transaction. The making of a *cautio* became usual from the late Republic, its function being to record that the question-and-answer form had been followed. However, following a rescript in the late classical period, it was *presumed* that a question had preceded the answer if a *cautio* alleged that a promise had been made. Consequently, evidence of the question was no longer necessary. Further changes occurred in the late Empire. A rescript of AD 472 (Emperor Leo) provided that a stipulation should be valid, whatever the form of words used, as long as the intention of the parties was clear. The need for an actual question and answer appears to have been formally abandoned by this ruling, a recognition of the prevalent practice (but Nicholas, cited earlier, argues that the rescript only removed the need to use formal words). And Justinian was responsible for an important erosion of the requirement of simultaneous presence: it could be presumed that the parties were present if the stipulation was evidenced by a *cautio* which alleged their presence (cf. C.8.37.1., Inst.3.19.12.). Such a presumption was rebuttable, however, by proof that one of the parties was absent when the *cautio* was made. Although the use of a *cautio* became widespread in the Empire, the purely oral *stipulatio* remained perfectly valid. It was never a requirement of *stipulatio* that it should be evidenced in writing.

9.4.3.3 Remedies

If a *stipulatio* was made for the payment of a specific sum of money or some specific thing, the appropriate remedy was a *condictio* (see 3.2.2.1); otherwise, the promisee had the *actio ex stipulatu* (cf. Inst.3.15pr.). The latter remedy was less convenient for the plaintiff than a *condictio*, which did not have to state the basis of liability in the *formula* of the action (see generally Liebs, D., 'The History of the Roman Condictio up to Justinian', in *The Legal Mind*, 163–83). Consequently, whether property was sufficiently specified (to enable the plaintiff to use a *condictio*) was a matter of procedural importance. Some illustrations of stipulations for which a *condictio* would be appropriate:

Gaius, *Provincial Edict, book 8*: **Some stipulations are certain, some uncertain. That is certain wherein it appears from the terms what, of what quality, and how much is due, as, for example, ten gold coins, the Tusculan estate, the slave Stichus, a hundred measures of best African corn, a hundred jars of best Campanian wine.** (D.45.1.74.)

As the contract was unilateral, only one party (the promisee) could have a remedy. But in practice contracts would often consist of several stipulations by both parties—essentially a bilateral transaction, even if each stipulation was regarded in theory as a separate contract.

9.4.3.4 Classification of stipulatio

(Inst.3.18., D.46.5.)

The primary classification of stipulations was based on the source of the obligation:

Pomponius, *Sabinus, book 26*: **Some stipulations are judicial, some praetorian, some conventional.... Judicial stipulations are only those which originate from the true office of a judge.... Praetorian stipulations are those which originate from the true office of the praetor.... Conventional stipulations are those which come about as a result of an agreement between the parties** ... (D.45.1.5pr.)

Judicial and praetorian stipulations were not really contracts at all, but promises made under legal compulsion to do or abstain from doing something. The *cautio de dolo* ('the promise regarding fraud') was a prime example of a judicial stipulation—a promise by a party in the course of legal proceedings to restore property without any fraud on his part. The *cautio damni infecti*, whereby an occupier of dangerous property was compelled by the praetor to promise to indemnify his neighbours for any damage caused, was an important example of a praetorian stipulation. Also, there were some stipulations (termed 'common') that could be ordered either by a judge or a magistrate, e.g. a promise from a guardian to keep his ward's property safe.

Another important classification was into simple, *ex die* or conditional stipulations. A simple stipulation, the most usual type, was one where the obligation arose at once and unconditionally. An *ex die* stipulation was one where the obligation arose at once, but which could not be enforced until a specified day or the occurrence of some specified event that was certain to happen, e.g. a promise to do something 'when Titus dies'. Although the performance of an *ex die* stipulation could not be demanded until the relevant day or event had occurred, the promisor could choose to perform at an earlier date:

Celsus, *Digest, book 26*: **What is promised for a certain day may indeed be given at once; for the whole intervening period is regarded as open to the debtor for paying.** (D.46.3.70.)

If I made a stipulation to do something 'when I die', it was valid: the duty to perform was regarded as vesting at the last moment of life, and was thus inherited by my heir. However, a promise to perform 'after my death' was a nullity—an obligation could not *begin* with an heir as that would have breached the general rule that a contract could not impose a duty on a third party. This distinction between 'when I die' and 'after my death' appears artificial and unconvincing. The rules on *ex die* obligations were not confined to *stipulatio* but were applicable to several contracts in which the operation of the rules was appropriate. For example, the contract of sale could be made *ex die*.

A conditional stipulation differed from *ex die* ones in that the obligation to perform might never arise in the former, but was inevitable in the latter. If Balbus made a stipulation whereby he promised to give Titus a gold ring 'if Titus left Rome', a conditional stipulation resulted—Balbus' duty to pay the money was dependent on the satisfaction of the condition. Hence, such conditions were suspensive and precedent: the satisfaction of the condition *preceded* the performance of the obligation, which was *suspended* until that time. It followed that an agreement dependent on the existence of some fact, past or present, was not a true conditional contract:

Papinian, *Definitions, book 1*: **When a condition relates to the present time, a stipulation is not suspended, and if the condition is true, the stipulation binds, even though the contracting parties do not know its result. An example is: 'Do you promise to give one hundred if the king of the Parthians is alive?' The same considerations apply when a condition relates to time past.** (D.12.1.37.)

What was the position of the promisor prior to the satisfaction of the condition? Although he was not obliged to perform until the condition was satisfied, he was bound in other respects. For example, he could not revoke his promise; nor could he do anything to prevent the fulfilment of the condition:

Paul, *Edict, book 75*: **Whoever, while obliged conditionally, took steps to see that the condition would not be fulfilled is nonetheless bound.** (D.45.1.85.7.)

A stipulation could be made subject to a resolutive condition, i.e. a term defining the termination of the obligation, e.g. a promise to pay 1,000 *sesterces* a month 'until Titus becomes consul'. Such a stipulation was treated in theory as an unqualified promise, although it seems that the promisor was allowed a defence against a promisee who claimed any further payment after the satisfaction of the condition.

9.4.3.5 *Stipulatio* and finance

The potential scope of *stipulatio* can be illustrated by its important role in the world of Roman commerce and finance (see Johnston, *Roman Law in Context*, 84–95). For example, a loan of money (see 9.5.1) would normally be accompanied by a stipulation as to the rate of interest that the debtor agreed to pay. Three particularly important uses of *stipulatio* were the novation of debts, the creation of surety, and the imposition of penalties.

(a) Novation. This was the process whereby an obligation was terminated and replaced by a new one created by *stipulatio*. The new obligation had to arise from the extinguished one, but it could not be identical—there had to be some change, at least in classical law:

Pomponius, *Sabinus, book 10*: **If a man promises the same thing twice, he is not automatically more liable than if he promises it once.** (D.45.1.18.)

Why bother novating a debt? Why not simply rely on the original promise? Because the promisee improved his position through novation—the new obligation was obviously more recent, more easily provable, and enforceable by the effective remedies available for breach of a stipulation.

(b) Surety. There were two forms of surety that could be created by stipulation— *adstipulatio* and *adpromissio*.

(i) Adstipulatio. In this form of surety a debt that was already owed to one creditor was promised to another creditor, e.g. A is promised money by B who then promises the same amount to C—the second promise is the *adstipulatio*. Why this rigmarole? Because C will be acting on the understanding that if A cannot ensure the performance of B's obligation, C will enforce it and will account for the proceeds. Hence, C is acting as a form of surety for A (although it is arguably more a type of trusteeship than a true form of surety). As far as the debtor was concerned, he could choose whom he paid—he owed only one debt. But if he paid C, the latter had to make over whatever he obtained to the principal creditor. If the accessory creditor defrauded the principal, he was liable to compensate the latter under ch. 2 of the *lex Aquilia* 287 BC. *Adstipulatio* was eventually superseded by the contract of mandate and became obsolete by the late Empire (see Inst.Gai.3.215.–16.).

(ii) Adpromissio. This form of surety consisted of a stipulation to pay the debt of the principal debtor if he failed to pay (Metzger, *Companion*, 145–6). There were three forms of *adpromissio*. The earliest, *sponsio* (see 9.4.3.1), was confined to citizens; but the second to emerge, *fidepromissio*, was open to foreigners as well. There was a variation in the formal words used but, apart from these differences, the two contracts were similar. They were subject to a number of restrictions that eventually made them unattractive to creditors. For example, these contracts could only be used to guarantee obligations that had been created by *stipulatio* and they did not bind the heirs of the guarantor. Legislation passed to protect guarantors made these early contracts of surety even more unpopular with creditors. For example, the *lex Furia* c.200 BC provided that guarantees lapsed after two years (from the time when the debt became due) and that if there was a plurality of guarantors, each was liable only for his proportionate part of the debt—the debt was divided between the number of guarantors living at the time when the debt became due. Thus, if a guarantor became insolvent after the debt became enforceable, the creditor was disadvantaged.

The latest of these three surety contracts, *fideiussio*, emerged in the late Republic and eventually became the most frequently used, superseding the other two. *Fideiussio* was not subject to a limitation period; it did bind the heirs of the guarantor; and it could be used to guarantee any debt. Moreover, if there were two or more guarantors, the creditor could enforce payment against any of them (the others being released thereby). However, Hadrian allowed a guarantor to claim *beneficium divisionis* ('the privilege of sharing') whereby he was liable only for his proportionate share of the debt. This was calculated by dividing the debt between the number of guarantors who were solvent when the debt became due. Under Justinian, if the creditor sued one of several persons liable for the same debt, the others were no longer automatically released. However, the creditor could be compelled by a surety to proceed against the principal debtor first.

The *S. C. Velleianum c.* AD 46 prohibited women from interceding 'on behalf of others': thus they could not thereafter act as sureties for anyone. The most likely reason for this enactment was that women were not regarded as suited to be sureties because of their alleged weakness of judgement.

The rules on *adpromissio* have been substantially incorporated into modern law, civilian, and common law. Zimmermann considers that the Roman contracts of surety are 'a model for all times' (114) and that they have had 'a profound influence' (142) on modern systems. See *Obligations*, 114 ff.

The obligations that could arise in *adpromissio* and other forms of plurality of parties are sometimes described, somewhat unhelpfully, as solidary or correal. An obligation was solidary if it benefited or bound persons jointly, and those persons could sue or be sued individually for the whole of what was due under the obligation. If the bringing of an action by or against one party did not exclude or discharge the others, the case was one of simple solidarity; if it did, the obligation was correal. Javolenus describes correal obligations thus:

Javolenus, *From Plautius, book 3*: **When two persons have either promised or stipulated for the same sum of money, they are by operation of law bound or entitled severally for the full amount; and so the whole obligation is extinguished by a legal claim by, or a formal release of, one of them.** (D.45.2.2.)

The classification of obligations as solidary or correal applied not only in the case of *stipulatio*, but generally throughout the Roman law of contract and delict.

(c) Penalties. The imposition of penalties by *stipulatio* was common in Roman law. A penalty clause (*stipulatio poenae*) could be used to secure, for example, obligations arising under various contracts. It is probable that their predominant use was in commerce, but they were also frequently used in other areas of law, e.g. property and the law of actions. Equitable rules came to be applied as to the forfeiture of such clauses, but the fact that the penalty might be considered excessive was not generally recognized as a ground for its non-application.

Modern systems have generally eschewed the rather inflexible Roman position on excessive penalties. For example, s. 343 BGB allows a court to reduce a penalty which is disproportionately high. Article 1152 of the *Code Civil* (as amended in 1975) enables a judge to alter a penalty if it is manifestly excessive (or too low). In English law, however, penalty clauses are unenforceable; but a clause that attempts a genuine assessment of the likely loss consequential on a breach of contractual obligation may be upheld. See Zimmermann, *Obligations*, 95 ff.

9.5 Contracts *re*

This category comprised four contracts: *mutuum, commodatum, depositum*, and *pignus*. The common denominator was that the obligations in these contracts arose from the delivery of a corporeal thing—hence the name 'contract *re*', i.e. 'by a thing' (delivered) (see Metzger, *Companion*, 128–9 as well as Birks, *Obligations*, 129–30).

9.5.1 *Mutuum*

(Inst.Gai.3.90.–1., Inst.3.14., D.12.1.)

Mutuum was a unilateral and *stricti iuris* contract, consisting of an essentially gratuitous 'loan' for consumption of things that could be measured and that were consumable through use, i.e. fungibles (often an amount of money):

Paul, *Edict, book 28*: **This kind of lending happens in relation to those things which are dealt in by weight, number or measure.** (D.12.1.2.1.)

The description 'lending' is somewhat misleading. There was strictly no loan since *ownership* of the thing was transferred (using a *traditio*) to the borrower:

Paul, *Edict, book 28*: **The word for loan for consumption, *mutuum*, is formed from *meum* and *tuum*, because what is mine becomes yours.** (D.12.1.2.2.)

9.5.1.1 Development

Mutuum was the oldest of the contracts *re*. Its origins are obscure, but what is undeniable is that it grew in importance after the *lex Poetelia* 326 BC (see Kelly, J. M., 'A Hypothesis on the Origin of Mutuum', (1970) 5 IJ, 156–63). Before that time, obligations were often incurred through *nexum*, a formal ceremony similar to *mancipatio*. *Nexum* was a form of bond: a debtor bound himself by pledging his body as security for the payment of a debt. A defaulting debtor was liable to seizure (*manus iniectio*) by the creditor, and thereafter to possible enslavement or even execution (see 3.2.3.1). The *lex Poetelia* greatly improved the debtor's position by insisting on legal judgment before seizure, and by removing the threat of death and sale into slavery. *Nexum* thereafter declined in importance (it ceased to exist by the time of the late Republic) and was superseded by *mutuum* that had probably been confined to informal loans up to that time. *Mutuum* (unlike *nexum*) could be contracted by persons without *commercium*—an important factor in the development of *mutuum*. See Birks, *Obligations*, 131–5.

The most frequent use of *mutuum* was in relation to money—it became the standard moneylending contract of the Republic. It was common to attach subsidiary terms by stipulations, e.g. as to the interest payable or the date of repayment, since *mutuum* was essentially gratuitous and bare agreements to pay interest were unenforceable (Metzger, *Companion*, 129). Rates of interest were regulated throughout Roman legal history, and harsh penalties were exacted on lenders who tried to exceed the limit. Although *professional* moneylenders were regarded with great distaste, it appears that the practice of lending money at interest was widespread, at least among the wealthy: 'Here we are with a civil war on, with Pompey under siege by a Roman army; and yet there is the City the same as usual, the courts in session, the games in preparation, and, as usual, the great and the good are clocking up their interest' (Cicero, *ad Atticum*, IX, 12, 3 quoted by Crook, *Law and Life of Rome*, 211) (see also Andreau, J., *Banking and Business* (1999), 9–29). The maximum rate during the classical period was generally 12 per cent, Justinian reducing it to 6 per cent for commercial loans, 4 per cent for private ones (cf. C.4.32.26.). Compound interest was not allowed. In later law, the whole agreement was often made through *stipulatio*, and thus *mutuum* lost its importance.

9.5.1.2 **The duty to restore**

The borrower had to restore not the thing itself—it would be consumed by use—but the equivalent (see MacCormack, G., 'Gift, Debt, Obligation and the Real Contracts' (1985) 31 Labeo, 131–54). This duty was precisely interpreted: the thing that was returned had to be equivalent in size, number, and quality to the borrowed thing:

Pomponius, *Sabinus, book 27*: **Even if there is no provision in a loan for consumption that the thing returned should be of the same quality, the debtor is not allowed to give back some thing which, though of the same kind, is of inferior quality, for example, new wine for old. The reason is that when a contract is made, the nature of the transaction is given effect just as though expressly provided for; and the nature of this one is taken to be that the thing paid back must be of the same kind and quality as the thing given.** (D.12.1.3.)

The fact that the object had been lost or stolen did not relieve the borrower from his duty to restore it, since the contract was *stricti iuris* (Metzger, *Companion*, 129). However, if a loan was made to finance the voyage of a cargo ship (bottomry), the loan was repayable only if the ship completed the journey safely. The lenders took the risks, so they were allowed to charge unlimited rates of interest, at least until Justinian fixed the maximum at 12 per cent for such loans (cf. D.22.2.3., C.4.32.26.1.). The position was similar in the case of loans made to professional athletes for their maintenance and expenses (D.22.2.5pr.). The loan was returnable, together with interest, only if victory was gained. See Zimmermann, *Obligations*, 181 ff.

The duties of the borrower could be enforced by *condictio*. The lender in *mutuum* did not have contractual duties (since the contract was unilateral). If he lent something for consumption that was defective, he might be liable for delict if he was at fault and damage resulted; but there was no contractual liability.

9.5.1.3 *S. C. Macedonianum* (Second half of the 1st century AD)

(D.14.6., C.4.28.)

Moneylending inevitably leads to problems—abuses, corruption, and exploitation. Roman society was no exception:

Ulpian, *Edict, book 29*: **Whereas Macedo's borrowings gave him an added incentive to commit a crime to which he was naturally predisposed and whereas those who lend money on terms which are dubious, to say the least, often provide evil men with the means of wrongdoing, it has been decided, in order to teach pernicious moneylenders that a son's debt cannot be made good by waiting for his father's death, that a person who has lent money to a son-in-power is to have no claim or action even after the death of the person in whose power he was.** (D.14.6.1pr.)

This enactment of the early Empire was concerned with loans of money, not of other property. It applied to loans made to children and remoter issue under *potestas*. The reform protected not only the borrower but also his *paterfamilias* and any guarantor. The blanket exclusion of such loans from lawful recovery, although well-intentioned, could have had unfortunate economic repercussions. Accordingly, the provision was subjected to generally restrictive interpretation. For example, the rule was excluded if the *paterfamilias* had consented to the loan, or if the lender had honestly believed that the borrower was not in power, or if the borrower had

peculium castrense or *quasi castrense* (see 5.1.2.2), or if the borrower had acknowledged the loan on becoming *sui iuris*.

9.5.2 *Commodatum*

(Inst.Gai.3.90.–1., Inst.3.14.2., D.13.6., C.4.23.)

Commodatum consisted of a gratuitous loan of a corporeal thing (mostly movables, rarely immovables) for use, the thing to be returned at the end of the loan
(see Birks, *Obligations*, 135–42). Unlike *mutuum*, ownership of the object remained
with the lender. It was a bilateral and *bonae fidei* contract, the development of
which owed much to praetorian intervention. The loan had to be gratuitous: if
it was for money, the contract would be *locatio conductio*, not *commodatum*. The
loan was usually made for a specified purpose and duration, but if the duration
was not fixed, the borrower could keep the thing for a reasonable time (taking
into account the purpose of the loan). Land could be the subject of *commodatum*
(although this was doubted before the classical period) but perishables could not
be, subject to minor exceptions, e.g. where things were let for display purposes
(D.13.6.3.6.). The borrower did not receive ownership, unlike the case in *mutuum*.
Nor did he acquire possession of the thing—he received only physical control.
It followed that there could be a valid *commodatum* even though the lender was
not the owner. Indeed, a thief could properly be the lender, with a right to sue
on the contract:

Paul, *Edict, book 29*: **It is possible to lend for use property which belongs to another but
which is in our possession, even where we know it is another person's property we possess.**
[Marcellus, *Digest, book* 5] **[16]: This is carried to the extent of enabling even a thief or robber
who lends to have the action on loan for use.** (D.13.6.15.–16.)

9.5.2.1 **Duties of the borrower**

He had to use the property for the purposes agreed, otherwise he was liable for
theft unless he honestly believed that the lender would have consented. Even if
the borrower did have that belief, he would normally be liable for any damage
caused to the property during unauthorized use, irrespective of fault (even damage
through *vis maior*). Moreover, the borrower was liable for any damage, howsoever
caused, if he was in *mora*, e.g. if he had delayed in returning the property.

Which standard of care was expected of the borrower? In the absence of any
agreement to the contrary, the following standard applied:

Gaius, *Provincial Edict, book 9*: **The standard of care to be adhered to in relation to things
lent for use is that which any very careful head of a family keeps to in relation to his own
affairs to the extent that the borrower is only not liable for those events which cannot be
prevented, such as deaths of slaves occurring without fault on his part, attacks of robbers
and enemies, surprises by pirates, shipwreck, fire, and escape of slaves not usually confined.**
(D.13.6.18pr.)

The reference to the 'very careful head of a family' (*diligentissimus paterfamilias*)
suggests that the standard of care was beyond that of the *bonus paterfamilias* (see
Metzger, *Companion*, 131). Most probably, the borrower was subject to liability
for *custodia*, i.e. any loss other than that caused by *vis maior*. As theft (without
violence) was regarded as preventable, it followed that the borrower was liable for
failure to restore the property to the lender if a third party had stolen it. However,

the borrower had the *actio furti* (the action for theft) for damages against the thief; the lender did not, since his contractual rights protected him against the borrower. But if the borrower was insolvent, and thus unable to compensate the lender, the latter could bring the action for theft. Justinian gave the lender a choice (irrespective of the borrower's solvency) of suing the borrower or the thief. If the lender sued the thief, the borrower could not do so but no longer had to compensate the lender.

At the end of the loan, the borrower had to return the property, together with any accretions, in substantially the same condition as when he received it:

Ulpian, *Edict, book 28*: **If the thing lent is indeed returned but returned in worse condition, it is understood not to have been returned at all, unless the lender's interest is made good.** (D.13.6.3.1.)

9.5.2.2 Duties of the lender

He had to allow the borrower the use of the thing for the agreed period; but if the borrower misused the property the lender could recover it immediately. The lender had to reimburse the borrower for any abnormal expenses incurred in using the thing and the borrower could lawfully retain the object until such expenses had been paid. It seems that the lender was not liable for negligence, only for *dolus*. Hence, he was liable for damage caused by the thing if he knew of the defects and failed to disclose them:

Gaius, *Provincial Edict, book 9*: **Again, someone who knowingly lends defective containers must, if wine or oil poured in is spoiled or spilled, be condemned on that account.** (D.13.6.18.3.)

9.5.2.3 Joint benefit

What if the loan benefited both parties? Then it seems that the borrower was subject to the standard of care expected of him in his own affairs (*diligentia quam suis rebus*). If the loan was for the benefit of the lender alone, the borrower was liable for *dolus* only:

Ulpian, *Edict, book 28*: **There are clearly cases in which the borrower will be liable only for willful harm, for example, when that is what is agreed, or where the loan is only in the interest of the lender, as by a man to his fiancée or wife to enable her to dress with greater dignity for her presentation to him or by a praetor putting on games to actors or indeed by someone only too glad to lend to the praetor.** (D.13.6.5.10.)

As for the lender, if he benefited from the loan, he was liable for any damage caused by defects of which he *ought* to have known. The shifting standard of care in these scenarios reflects the principle of utility applied by the jurists; namely, that the liability of the parties is conditioned by the balance of their interests in the performance of the contract. See Zimmermann, *Obligations*, 198–9.

9.5.2.4 Remedies

The lender had the *actio commodati* ('the action on the loan') to enforce the borrower's duties. The latter could retain the borrowed thing as a set-off against whatever might be owed to him by the lender. In addition, the borrower had the *actio commodati contraria*—useful, for example, if the borrower's expenses exceeded the value of the property that had been loaned.

9.5.3 **Depositum**

(Inst.3.14., D.16.3., C.4.34.)

Deposit was a *bonae fidei*, imperfectly bilateral contract whereby a movable thing was handed over to another person (the depositee) for safekeeping (see Birks, *Obligations*, 142–6). There could not be a deposit of land. The deposit had to be gratuitous, otherwise the transaction would constitute hire:

Ulpian, *Edict, book 30*: **If clothes given to the keeper of a bath for safekeeping are lost and if the keeper has received no fee for the safekeeping, I think that he is liable in an action on deposit and that he ought to be responsible only for his fraud; but where he has received a fee, he is liable on the action on hire.** (D.16.3.1.8.) (cf. Inst. 3.14.3.)

As in *commodatum*, the depositee did not receive ownership or possession. Consequently, the depositor need not be the owner—he could even be a thief. Unlike *commodatum*, however, the contract of deposit was entirely for the benefit of the depositor: if the depositee benefited, the contract would be treated as *commodatum* (but as hire if he was remunerated).

9.5.3.1 **Duties of the depositee**

The obligations in *depositum* were primarily on the depositee. He had to keep the thing safe but was liable only for *dolus*, as we have seen in D.16.3.1.8. (above). However, *dolus* was sometimes equated with gross negligence, and could consist of the failure to do what a man would do in his own affairs, according to the following passage attributed to Celsus:

Celsus, *Digest, book 11*: **The statement made by Nerva that gross fault is equivalent to fraud was not accepted by Proculus but seems to me to be very true. For even if a person is not careful in the degree required by the nature of man, still, unless he shows in the deposit the care customary with him, he is not free from fraud; for good faith is not maintained if he shows less care than in relation to his own affairs.** (D.16.3.32.)

It is doubtful whether this controversial text was generally equating *dolus* with failure to behave as one normally would in one's own affairs: it is more likely that it was concerned with the particular case of deposit. See Zimmermann, *Obligations*, 208 ff.

Of course, the parties could agree, as in other contracts, to vary the depositee's duty of care by imposing on him the *bonus paterfamilias* standard (see Litewski, W., 'Depository's Liability in Roman Law' (1976) 190 AG, 3–78). But they could not validly agree to absolve him from *dolus*. The depositee could not use the deposited thing—if he did so in bad faith, he would be liable for theft of use (cf. Inst. Gai.3.196.). Generally, he had to return the thing on demand, and in substantially the same condition as when it was received, subject to reasonable wear and tear. Any accretions that arose during the deposit had to be handed over as well.

9.5.3.2 **Duties of the depositor**

He was liable, if negligent, for damage caused by the deposited thing, the *bonus paterfamilias* standard applying. He had to reimburse the depositee for expenses incurred in looking after the property and in returning it at the venue chosen by the depositor:

Pomponius, *Sabinus, book 22*: **If a deposit is made in Asia to be returned at Rome, it is seen to have been intended that this occur, not at the expense of him with whom the deposit was made, but at the expense of him who deposited.** (D.16.3.12pr.)

9.5.3.3 **Remedies**

The depositor had the *actio depositi* for the depositee's breach of duty (see Metzger, *Companion*, 132). If the depositee was found liable, *infamia* resulted—a seemingly harsh rule but justifiable, at least to the Roman mind, on the grounds that *dolus* by the depositee represented a breach of trust on his part. Also, the depositee would have to pay damages. They were doubled if the deposit had been made in an emergency, e.g. during a riot or fire, since in such circumstances the depositor had less opportunity to choose his man:

Ulpian, *Edict, book 30*:…when someone has chosen to rely on the trustworthiness of another and the deposit is not returned, he ought to be content with simple damages. However, when he deposits through necessity, the crime of perfidy increases and the public welfare demands retribution for the sake of protecting the common interest; for it is harmful to betray trust in cases of this kind. (D.16.3.1.4.)

The depositee had the *actio depositi contraria* against the depositor for the recovery of expenses. And probably the depositee had a right to retain the thing as a set-off against unpaid expenses, but Justinian appears to have terminated the right.

9.5.3.4 **Special deposits**

There were some special cases of deposit, with different rules from those already outlined. *Depositum irregulare* was a transfer of fungible things (usually money) to a depositee (usually a banker) with the intention that he should become the *owner* of the property, with a duty to restore the equivalent on demand (see Andreau, *Banking and Business* (1999), ch. 3). This looks very much like *mutuum*, but the difference was that *depositum irregulare* was not primarily intended to benefit the transferee—he was more a custodian than a borrower.

Sequestratio was a deposit of property by two or more persons in dispute about their rights in the thing. The purpose of the deposit was that the depositee should hold the property until the dispute was settled. He received legal possession of the property, thus preventing time running (for the purposes of *usucapio*) in favour of any of the disputants. When the dispute was settled, the property had to be returned to the successful party. It seems that both land and movables could be the subject of a *sequestratio*.

9.5.4 *Pignus*

(Inst.Gai.3.115.–27., Inst.3.14., D.13.7., C.4.24.)

Pignus ('a pledge') was a *bonae fidei* and bilateral contract, consisting of the transfer of property as security by a borrower to a lender by way of mortgage (see Birks, *Obligations*, 146–55). The lender received legal possession of the property (which could be land or movables). The effect of this contract was to create a strong, limited real right over property. Thus, any discussions of the contract of pledge should be read in conjunction with the discussion of real security in the law of property. The proprietary aspects of pledge and hypothec are discussed in D.20.1 and C.8.13. For a comprehensive survey of the main texts, see Hausmaninger, Gamauf, and Sheets, *Casebook*, 266–320. This section should also be read in conjunction with ch. 6, 'Interests in Property'.

9.5.4.1 **Development**

Pignus developed from the original form of real security, *fiducia*, under which the borrower transferred the ownership of property that was pledged as security to the lender (see Metzger, *Companion*, 133). The transfer in *fiducia* had to be effected by formal conveyance, i.e. *mancipatio* or *cessio in iure*. The lender undertook to reconvey the property once the debt was fully paid. However, being owner, the lender could sell the property if the borrower defaulted. Apart from being cumbersome, *fiducia* had the disadvantage of depriving the borrower of ownership of the thing that had been pledged.

Pignus was free of these disadvantages since the transfer could be effected by *traditio*, and the borrower retained ownership, parting only with possession. However, *fiducia* did not disappear until the late Empire, when the formal modes of conveyance became obsolete. Its lengthy survival was due to its relative popularity with lenders—they had greater rights over the property than was the case in *pignus*. So, *fiducia* and *pignus* co-existed side by side for several centuries, although it was the latter that became the most usual form of real security.

9.5.4.2 **Position of the parties**

The borrower in *pignus* was liable for damage caused by defects in the property transferred as security, the standard of care being that of the *bonus paterfamilias* (cf. Inst.3.14.4.). The lender received possession of the thing, although in practice the borrower was sometimes allowed to keep physical control. If the lender had actual control (the usual case), he had to safeguard the property, the *bonus paterfamilias* standard of care applying. If the lender mistreated the property, the contract was terminated:

Ulpian, *Edict, book 30*: **It is something to be taken into account under the action on *pignus* if the creditor mistreats pledged property....If, therefore, he puts a slave-girl to prostitution or compels her to some other disreputable conduct, the *pignus* of her is discharged on the spot.** (D.13.7.24.3.)

The lender was entitled to recover expenses that were properly incurred in looking after the property. Any profit that he made out of the property was regarded as a set-off against the debt. If the debt was repaid, the lender had to return the thing, together with any accretions (e.g. where a racehorse produced offspring).

9.5.4.3 **Remedies**

The lender's duties could be enforced only if the borrower paid the debt (with the *actio pigneraticia*), or was ready to tender payment, or gave 'satisfaction' for it:

Ulpian, *Edict, book 28*: **The pledgor's action on *pignus* only arises when all the money is paid or satisfaction is given for it. By satisfaction we mean anything that suits the lender in the absence of actual payment....It is right to say quite generally that whenever the creditor chooses to give up the pledge he is understood to have been satisfied, so long as whatever he wants is assured to him, even though he be let down in relation to it.** (D.13.7.9.3.)

What if the borrower failed to pay the debt? The basic position was that the lender could retain possession of the security until the debt was paid; but he could not become its owner, nor could he sell or otherwise dispose of it. In short, his position was not very favourable. Therefore, it was customary for the parties to agree that the lender should have a right of sale if the debt was not paid. If the lender sold the property for more than the amount of the debt, he had to account for any excess after deducting the debt, the interest, and his expenses in arranging the sale. The practice of allowing the lender a right of sale became so widespread that it came to be implied in the classical period in all contracts of *pignus* unless expressly excluded.

Another arrangement, often made in practice, was to agree that the lender should acquire ownership of the property if the debt was not paid on the specified date, i.e. automatic foreclosure. But such agreements were eventually banned under Constantine. However, a delayed form of foreclosure was possible under a procedure dating from the middle Empire, whereby the lender could apply to a court to have ownership vested in him (after the lapse of the appropriate period of *usucapio*) unless the borrower paid the debt in the intervening period.

9.5.4.4 Hypothec

Although *pignus* was more advantageous to the borrower than *fiducia*, it, nevertheless, required the transfer of the possession of the security to the lender. The borrower would lose the benefit of the property, and he could use it to secure only one loan at a time. In response to the need for a more flexible form of mortgage contract, there emerged in the later Republic a modified form of *pignus*—the hypothec—under which the lender was promised rights in the borrower's property in the event of the debt being unpaid, the borrower meanwhile retaining ownership and possession. Hypothec probably developed from the practice whereby tenants agreed that the landlord could distrain on goods or crops if rent was unpaid. Hypothec came to be used mainly in mortgages of land, although it could be applied to movables as well.

Under a hypothec, the borrower could secure more than one loan on the same piece of property. Such a possibility necessitated the development of rules concerning priority of charges. The basic rule was that priority was determined by the order of creation of the charges, i.e. the first in time prevailed:

Gaius, *Action on Mortgage, sole book*: **The mortgagee who first lent money and took a mortgage is preferred, although the debtor had previously agreed to mortgage the property to another if he gave him a loan (even if the loan was later made).** (D.20.4.11pr.)

Since priority depended on the time of creation of the charge, the borrower was under a duty to give notice (to a potential lender) of any existing charges. It became a criminal offence to fail to disclose a prior charge. In the late Empire, the priority rules were significantly amended. Priority was given to charges that were formally registered or witnessed, in preference to informal charges. And certain charges were given automatic priority, e.g. the wife's implied mortgage (over her husband's property) as security for her rights in the dowry.

Apart from real security formed by contract, Roman law also knew real security implied by law. On this, see Zimmermann, *Obligations*, 203 ff.

9.5.5 Modern use

The Roman contracts *re* have had a substantial influence on modern law. For example, the distinctions between the different types of loan are maintained—as in ss. 598–610 BGB and Articles 1874–1914 of the *Code Civil*—as are (with some variations) the rules on standards of care. Thus, in a gratuitous loan for use, s. 599 BGB provides that the lender is liable only for wilful conduct and gross negligence; while Article 1880 of the *Code Civil* applies the *bon père de famille* test to the duty of the borrower to care for the property. English law too has been clearly affected by the Roman contracts, especially *commodatum, depositum*, and *pignus*. The fundamental analysis of bailment by Holt CJKB in *Coggs v Bernard* (1703) 2 Ld Rayn 909, 92 ER 107, was largely inspired by the Roman rules. See Zimmermann, *Obligations*, 203 ff.

9.6 Contracts *litteris*

(Inst.Gai.3.128.–34., Inst.3.21.)

9.6.1 Early development

It was the practice for the responsible *paterfamilias* to record financial transactions; they would first be noted in a daybook and then transferred to a ledger (Metzger, *Companion*, 148–50). There were two sorts of entries—those that were *evidence* of a debt, and those that created a debt. In the former case, the entry did not create a contractual obligation but acted as confirmation of it, e.g. A records that he lent B 1,000 *sesterces* that day (cf. Inst.Gai.3.131.). But what if A had not lent B any money that day, but had nevertheless recorded that B owed him 1,000 *sesterces*? Then the written entry created a monetary obligation—the contract *litteris* ('by written record') (cf. Inst.Gai.3.128.). The debtor had to consent to the entry but it is not clear how such consent was evidenced. Indeed, there is much that is unclear about the contract *litteris*. The main account (that of Gaius) was written at a time when the contract was beginning to fade in importance. As it had become obsolete long before Justinian, the contract *litteris* (in its original form) was not discussed in the *Digest*. It is clear, however, that the presence of both parties was not necessary for the making of the entry—an important advantage compared to *stipulatio*, for example. For a discussion of the importance of this type of contract, see Birks, *Obligations*, 37–51.

It seems that only Roman citizens could be parties to the contract; at least this was the Proculian view, based partly on the suggestion that this form of bookkeeping was peculiarly Roman. The Sabinians, however, argued that a foreigner could be a party, but only as a debtor. The contract was unilateral and *stricti iuris*, which made it attractive to the creditor in certain circumstances. Suppose that A owes B money under the contract of sale—B can novate the obligation by entering it in his ledger. The effect will be to replace the original obligation and to create a new one, which might be more easily provable (through production of the ledger) and which will afford the debtor fewer opportunities for disputing the debt, given that the contract is *stricti iuris*. Novation of existing obligations became the chief purpose of the contract *litteris*.

9.6.2 Later development

The practice of keeping private ledgers started to decline in the Empire owing to the growth of banking. So, the contract *litteris* became obsolete by the late Empire.

Nevertheless, Justinian included a contract *litteris* as part of his fourfold classification of contracts. What then was the contract *litteris* of Justinian's time? It consisted of the written acknowledgment of a fictitious loan of money, i.e. a loan that had not been made at all, or one where the amount loaned was less than that recorded. Such an acknowledgment bound the debtor: the creditor could sue on it, using it as evidence of the alleged debt. The burden of proof, originally on the debtor if he wished to deny the debt, was eventually imposed on the creditor, i.e. he had to show that he had made the alleged loan. Under Justinian, the debtor had two years in which to deny the debt. If he failed to do that, he was bound by the original acknowledgment—it acquired contractual force even though it was primarily evidentiary in function.

Justinian's inclusion of the contract *litteris* of his time within his fourfold classification does seem rather artificial. His classification essentially focused on the *source* of contractual obligations, and thus did not readily encompass transactions that were evidential rather than creative in function.

9.7 Innominate contracts

This group of contracts consisted of certain agreements for mutual services, enforceable because one party had performed his part of the bargain, i.e. there was part performance. The artificiality of the fourfold classification of contracts is nowhere better demonstrated than in the case of the so-called innominate contracts (see Metzger, *Companion*, 168–9). They did not readily fit into any of Justinian's four categories but constituted a separate, fifth category. As such, this category should have been properly recognized and named, and probably would have been had it not been for the perverse reluctance to disturb the symmetry of a fourfold division. So, this category of contracts remained unnamed, other than as 'innominate contracts'—a misleading description since the most important innominate contracts did have specific names. It was not the contracts themselves that were innominate, but their category (see on this point MacCormack, G., 'Contractual Theory and the Innominate Contracts' (1985) 51 SDHI, 131–52).

9.7.1 Development

The evolution of these contracts was not uniform. Some dated from Rome's earliest days, others were of comparatively late development. However, it was not until the late classical period, or even thereafter, that these agreements were thought of as comprising a separate category of contracts. Their development owes much to the fact that the number of contracts in Roman law was quite limited throughout much of Rome's legal history. The need was eventually felt to give certain agreements contractual force, even though they did not constitute any of the recognized contracts, as in the case of barter (*permutatio*), for example. Previously, the remedy of the plaintiff had been to bring a *condictio* to recover anything that had passed under such agreements to the defaulting party, or to bring an action for fraud. Such remedies restored the pre-contractual *status quo* but did not enforce the bargain. When the innominate contracts started to be given full recognition, actions were allowed that did enforce the bargain, putting the parties into the position in which they would have been if both parties had carried out their obligations. It was the practice in such actions to state the particular facts of each case at the beginning of the *formula*. This practice explains the name of the general action that was established for these cases—the *actio praescriptis verbis* ('the action of the introductory words'). The use of this *general* action may further explain why these contracts were regarded as innominate.

It appears then that during the Empire, a general principle was gradually established that agreements for mutual services would be given contractual force providing there had been performance by one side. The *Digest* gives numerous illustrations of the circumstances in which the *actio praescriptis verbis* would be appropriate, most of the cases being analogous to standard contracts such as sale, hire, or mandate. For example:

Gaius, *Provincial Edict, book 10*: **I give you clothes for cleaning or mending. If you undertake this work for free, the obligation is in mandate; but if a fee was paid or agreed upon, then the transaction is lease and hire. But if you do not undertake this work for free and no fee was given or agreed upon, but the transaction is instead undertaken with the intention that whatever amount we would have agreed on be paid afterward as a fee, the accepted view is that an *actio in factum*, that is, *praescriptis verbis*, be accorded on the theory that a new kind of transaction is involved.** (D.19.5.22.)

(Actio in factum: 'action on the facts'.)

Within the category of innominate contracts, four particularly stand out because of their practical importance: *transactio, aestimatum, permutatio,* and *precarium.*

9.7.2 *Transactio*

(D.2.15., C.2.4.)

Transactio was the compromise (informal settlement) of a legal action, i.e. the abandoning of a claim or a defence in legal proceedings in return for some benefit given or promised by the other party (cf. C.2.4.6.1.). A formal compromise could be effected by *stipulatio*, often with a penalty attached for breach of the agreement. In such a case the appropriate action would be to sue on the stipulation. Where the compromise was agreed informally, however, there was no remedy available to enforce the agreement, in the absence of fraud, until the *actio praescriptis verbis* was allowed to the party who had performed his part of the agreement. The compromise would normally be agreed before judgment, but there were other possibilities:

Ulpian, *Disputations, book 7*: **A transactio after judgment is valid either if there has been an appeal or if an appeal is possible.** (D.2.15.7pr.)

Even in the absence of an appeal, a post-judgment compromise could be made, e.g. if doubt existed about the validity of the judgment. The important requirement was that there should be some element of doubt or uncertainty about the final outcome when the compromise was made:

Ulpian, *Edict, book 50*: **A person who makes a compromise does so on the basis that a matter is doubtful and the outcome of a lawsuit uncertain or not yet determined.** (D.2.15.1.)

9.7.3 *Aestimatum*

(D.19.3.)

This was a type of conditional sale in which the owner of a thing entrusted it to a transferee on a sale-or-return basis. The parties would specify a period within which the transferee was to return the property or an agreed price for it. The transferee usually intended to sell the property to a third party at a profit, the owner retaining ownership until such time as the possibility of return had passed, i.e. when the property was sold to a third party, or when the time limit had expired. Although the transferee did not obtain ownership through the transfer, he nevertheless passed ownership of the property when he sold it—an exception to the principle *nemo dat quod non habet* (see 7.2.1). If the transferee failed to find a buyer, and did not return the thing within the agreed time limit, he became its owner and had to pay the agreed price.

On whom was the risk of damage or loss while the property was in the transferee's hands? There is some inconsistency in the texts on this important issue, but the most plausible view is that, in the absence of agreement, risk lay with the transferor unless the transferee had initiated the transaction. Where the risk lay with the transferor, it was in respect of accidental loss, i.e. the *transferee* would be liable for loss or damage caused through his own fault.

It seems that *aestimatum* was an arrangement that did not fall clearly within the ambit of any one of the recognized contracts. However, it contained elements of several, which most probably explains its recognition as an enforceable contract. See Zimmermann, *Obligations*, 535 ff.

9.7.4 *Permutatio*

(D.19.4., C.4.64.)

This was the contract of exchange or barter. It will be remembered that the Proculian view prevailed that an exchange of goods could not amount to a sale (see 9.3.1.3). Justinian followed that view, regarding barter as an innominate contract. However, many of the rules of sale applied to barter, e.g. the rules on compensation for defective goods:

Paul, *Plautius, book 5*: **Aristo says that since barter is akin to purchase, there should be a warranty that a slave given for this reason is healthy, free of thefts and delicts, and not a runaway.** (D.19.4.2.)

The major difference between sale and barter, apart from the necessity for money to constitute at least part of the price in sale, was that there was a duty to pass ownership in barter. It followed that a transferee could sue for any defect in title *before* he was evicted by the rightful owner, unlike the case with sale. Another difference was that the obligations in barter arose only when one party had performed, and not on mere agreement (as was the case in sale). As to risk, the rule was that once A had transferred his thing to B, the risk of accidental loss or damage to the property that had not yet been transferred (i.e. B's thing) lay with A, but B was liable if the thing was damaged through his fault. If one party transferred his thing, but the other did not, the transferor could reclaim the thing by bringing a *condictio*, and could sue for damages for the other party's failure to transfer. However, if A had delivered his thing, but without ownership, and B had not delivered, A could not sue for damages since there was no valid contract of barter; but A could recover the property through a *condictio*. On the late recognition of barter as an enforceable contract see Watson, *The Evolution of Law* (1985), 23 ff.

9.7.5 *Precarium*

(D.43.26., C.8.9.)

Ulpian, *Institutes, book 1*: **Precarium is what is conceded to one who asks for it for his use for as long as the person who made the concession suffers it. [2]...And it differs from a gift in that someone who makes a gift does it on terms of not getting it back, whereas someone who makes a concession by *precarium* gives it expecting to get it back when he chooses to dissolve the *precarium*.** (D.43.26.1pr., 2.)

This contract consisted of the gratuitous grant of the enjoyment of land or movables. *Precarium* was commonly used in relation to land, and was in this respect similar to the tenancy-at-will in English law. It differed from *commodatum* in that the grant was not of fixed duration, the grantor being able to terminate the arrangement at any time; and that in *precarium* the grantee had general enjoyment of the property, and a right to its fruits—he was not restricted to any particular use. Moreover, the grantee normally received possession, unlike the case in *commodatum*, and was liable for *dolus* (but not negligence) in his occupancy of the property. The grantor's remedy for recovery of the property was the interdict *de precario*; but Justinian allowed him the *actio praescriptis verbis*, converting *precarium* into an innominate contract. Previously, *precarium* had not exhibited the features normally associated with such contracts. (Note the requirements for the possessory interdicts: *nec vi, nec clam, nec precario*.)

9.8 **Pacts**

(Mainly D.2.14., C.2.3.)

There were some agreements which fell outside the scope of the standard and the innominate contracts, but which were nevertheless given a degree of legal recognition. They constituted informal bargains (or 'naked' agreements) known as pacts. A pact could not originally be used as a ground of action, but it could provide a defence according to this famous text by Ulpian:

Ulpian, *Edict, book 4*:...**a naked agreement gives rise not to an obligation but to a defence.** (D.2.14.7.4.)

Already in the Twelve Tables we find the rule that an agreement not to sue for personal injury was effective to bar proceedings. The praetor extended the rule significantly—a pact not to sue became a defence to any action. Eventually, certain pacts known as *pacta vestita* ('clothed') came to be regarded as providing a ground of action, i.e. they became enforceable by plaintiffs. Three categories of such pacts emerged—subsidiary, praetorian, and statutory.

9.8.1 **Subsidiary pacts**

These were subsidiary agreements or terms that were added to the main contract, e.g. a clause giving the seller the right of first refusal if the buyer should wish to resell (see 9.3.1.8). But a distinction was drawn between pacts that were made contemporaneously with the main contract and those made subsequently:

Ulpian, *Edict, book 4*: **For we generally say that agreements by way of pact are incorporated in good faith actions. But this is understood to mean that only if the pacts have followed immediately upon [the main contract] are they incorporated in the plaintiff's action; if concluded after an interval, they are not incorporated, nor will they avail the plaintiff, should he sue, since an action cannot arise from a pact,** ... (D.2.14.7.5.)

Pacts made after an interval could not 'avail the plaintiff', but they were not without force—they could be used as a defence. However, if the later pact radically altered the original contract, it could take effect as a substantially new agreement, enforceable by either party:

Ulpian, *Edict, book 4*: ... **by a pact, one can withdraw in part from a sale, the effect being as though the sale as to part has been made afresh.** (D.2.14.7.6.)

9.8.2 **Praetorian pacts**

These were independent informal agreements (not attached to any contract) that were fully enforceable through an *actio in factum* granted by praetorian edict. An *actio in factum* was an action in which the plaintiff did not allege a *ius civile* right but a set of facts which he hoped that the praetor would regard as justifying a remedy. There were two important examples of praetorian pacts—*constitutum* and *receptum*.

9.8.2.1 *Constitutum debiti*

This was an informal undertaking to pay a debt or to discharge an existing liability at an agreed time or on an agreed date. The enforcement of this type of informal arrangement was justified as follows:

Ulpian, *Edict, book 27*: **With this edict, the praetor promotes natural equity in that he protects a *constitutum* made by agreement on the ground that it is a serious matter to go back on one's word.** (D.13.5.1pr.)

Constitutum debiti was the reinforcement of a debt; but it was not novation—the original debt remained. If the debtor paid, the *constitutum* would normally be discharged along with the principal debt. An undertaking to pay or to do something different from the original debt or obligation was valid if accepted by the creditor. *Constitutum* was sometimes used as a form of surety agreement, the promisor agreeing to pay someone else's debt. Cervidius Scaevola writes:

Scaevola, *Replies, book 1*: **A man wrote on these lines to a creditor: 'Sir, you may look to me, interest apart, for the ten lent from your cashbox to Lucius Titius'. My advice was that on the facts as given he had incurred liability to the action on a money *constitutum*.** (D.13.5.26.)

The use of *constitutum* as a form of surety declined in the late Empire because of the popularity of *fideiussio* (see 9.4.3.5) with which Justinian largely assimilated it.

9.8.2.2 *Receptum*

This was the name given to a miscellaneous category of informal agreements enforced by the praetors where one party assumed a guarantee for a specific effect or result. *Receptum arbitri* ('the undertaking of the arbitrator') was important enough to warrant a title in the *Digest*. It was an informal agreement to act as an arbitrator in a legal dispute. Once the agreement was made, the praetor could force the arbitrator to act unless there was a valid excuse:

Ulpian, *Edict, book 13*: Moreover, although the praetor states without reservation in the edict that he will compel an *arbiter* to make his award, yet he ought at times to take account of his position and entertain an excuse on cause being shown, as, for example, where his reputation has been attacked by the parties or if a mortal enmity arises between him and the parties or one of them or if age or subsequent illness releases him from his duty or concern with his own affairs or an urgent journey or some service on behalf of the state, ... (D.4.8.15.)

Another form of *receptum* was that arising from informal guarantees given by inn-keepers, stablekeepers, or ships' masters concerning the safety of property left in their care. This form of *receptum* gave the customer an alternative remedy to suing under quasi-delict (see 10.7.3). Under the latter head of liability the defendant was responsible for damage caused by his employees, whereas liability in *receptum* extended to damage or loss howsoever caused, apart from overwhelming force. *Receptum argentarii* ('the undertaking of the banker') was an agreement by a banker to honour his client's debt to a third party. It was fused with *constitutum debiti* and *fideiussio* (see 9.4.3.5) under Justinian.

9.8.3 Statutory pacts

During the late Empire a number of informal agreements came to be recognized (through imperial decree) as enforceable, e.g. *pactum dotis*—a promise to give dowry; *pactum donationis*—a promise to make a gift; and *compromissum*—an agreement by two parties to submit to arbitration.

9.9 Quasi-contract

Quasi-contract is one of the four categories of obligation in Justinian's classification. The artificiality of the classification is again evident when we consider the content of the quasi-contractual category—a group of obligations which have little in common apart from some characteristics analogous to those of contract. The main cases were *negotiorum gestio, condictio indebiti,* and common ownership (cf. Inst.3.27pr.; see also Metzger, *Companion*, 169–70 and Birks, *Obligations*, 248–63 for a discussion of the nature of the category and its content).

9.9.1 *Negotiorum gestio*

(D.3.5., C.2.18.)

Negotiorum gestio was the 'conducting of another person's affairs' without their authorization. Clearly, there is no contract in such a case as there is no actual agreement between the parties. But the law treats the situation as if (*quasi*) there were a contract between them. Suppose, for example, that you are serving abroad in the legions and that fences around your property are destroyed by storms in your absence. Your neighbour repairs the fences, thereby incurring expense. Had you known the facts, would you not have approved what was done for your benefit, and would you not be willing to reimburse your altruistic neighbour for his expenses? Of course you would—at least that is what was assumed in law: 'It is a prime example of the sober sense of realism with which the Roman lawyers were able to attune law and social ethics to each other and, more specifically, to balance the individualistic interest in not having one's own affairs interfered with and the interests of society in encouraging ethically desirable activities on behalf of others' (Zimmermann, *Obligations*, 436).

If *negotiorum gestio* had been confined to absentee landlords, its scope would have been narrow; but in practice it could apply to a multitude of situations— whenever someone performed an unrequested service for another.

9.9.1.1 Position of the parties

The duties of the person performing the service, the *gestor*, were to complete what he had started, and to account for any proceeds or loss. He was liable for negligence in the performance of the service, the *bonus paterfamilias* standard applying. However, if the *gestor* had acted in an emergency, he was liable only for *dolus*. But if loss had resulted from doing something that the principal would not have done, the *gestor* was strictly liable, although he could set off losses against the benefits that accrued from the unauthorized acts:

Pomponius, *Quintus Mucius, book 21*: **If you act as the agent of a person who is absent and in ignorance, you have to answer for both negligence and fraud. But Proculus says that sometimes you have to answer for accident as well, for example, if in the name of your absentee principal you transact business he did not usually do....For if any loss comes from this, it will come to you, but a profit to the absent principal. However, if there has been a profit in some transactions and a loss in others, the absent principal has to set off the profit against the loss.** (D.3.5.10.)

The duties of the principal were to accept the performance and to reimburse the *gestor* for expenses that had been properly incurred.

9.9.1.2 Conditions for reimbursement

In order to be reimbursed, the *gestor* had to satisfy a number of conditions:

(a) The *gestor* must have acted reasonably; thus, not only must the service have been a reasonable act in itself, but also it must have been reasonable in the circumstances for the *gestor* to act rather than leave the matter to the principal or to someone else. If the principal had expressly forbidden the act to be done, the *gestor* could not be said to have acted reasonably.

(b) The act must have been beneficial when done; thus, it was irrelevant that the act did not *prove* useful, provided that it was useful when done. As Ulpian puts it:

Ulpian, *Edict, book 10*: **A person who brings an action for unauthorized administration will have the use of that action not only if he was successful in the business he transacted, but it is enough that he acted beneficially, even if what he did was unsuccessful. For this reason, if he shored up a tenement or took care of a sick slave, even if the tenement was burned down or the slave died, he will bring an action for unauthorized administration,...** (D.3.5.9.1.)

However, it was insufficient for the *gestor* to show that he *thought* he was acting beneficially if in fact his acts were not useful. But he was entitled to reimbursement, despite the act not being beneficial when done, if the principal accepted or ratified the act.

(c) The act must have been done in the principal's interest; the *gestor* had to show that he had acted in the affairs of another, not in his own affairs. But it did not matter if the *gestor* made a mistake as to the *identity* of the principal, providing that he was acting in the latter's interest. Where the act was in the interest of both the principal and the *gestor*, the latter had no remedy unless he could demonstrate that he could have protected his own interests without protecting those of the principal: only in such circumstances could the *gestor* be said to be truly acting in the principal's interest.

(d) It seems that the act must have been done with the expectation of reimbursement in mind; if the act was done simply by way of gift, or as the result of duty or feelings of friendship, the *gestor* could not recover expenses (cf. C.2.18.11., 15.). The remedy was the *actio negotiorum gestorum*. The direct action, available to the principal, was aimed at recovering the object and its fruits as well as compensation for any damages caused by the carelessness of the gestor. The *contraria* action, available to the gestor, was primarily aimed at the reimbursement of expenses incurred in looking after the object in the principal's absence.

The common law does not have a doctrine generally comparable to *negotiorum gestio*: the predominant attitude has been one of 'mind your own business' rather than recompensing the Good Samaritan. But in some situations compensation is recoverable for unrequested services, e.g. rescue and salvage at sea; and the doctrine of 'agency of necessity' is, as regards emergency situations, very close to the Roman doctrine. *Negotiorum gestio* has not been an automatic choice in modern civilian codes, although both French and German law has incorporated it. Articles 1372–5 of the *Code Civil* enact the basic Roman rules, applying the standard of the *bon père de famille* to the *gestor* (Article 1374). In the BGB *negotiorum gestio* is regarded virtually as an adjunct of mandate (ss. 677–87). The duty of the *gestor* is to manage the affair in the interest of the principal, having regard to the latter's actual or presumptive wishes (s. 677). Issues such as whether the *gestor* is entitled to damages—and not just expenses—have proved controversial in German law. For example, the courts have allowed 'reasonable compensation', but not full damages, to a motorist who steered into a tree in order to avoid colliding with a child who had run into the street. See Zimmermann, *Obligations*, 433 ff. For an interesting recent comparative perspective, see Kortmann, J., *Altruism in Private Law* (2005).

9.9.1.3 *Actio funeraria*

This was a special action, analogous to the action for unauthorized administration, available to anyone who had incurred funeral expenses with the intention of being reimbursed for them. It lay against the person who was legally responsible for burying the deceased (normally the heir) for failure to do so. The person who actually buried the deceased could recover such expenses as were reasonable in the circumstances:

Ulpian, *Edict, book 25*: **Funeral expenses are assessed according to the wealth or rank of the deceased.** (D.11.7.12.5.)

However, the *actio funeraria* would not lie if the expenses that had been incurred were so low as to be insulting. The priority was to bury the corpse; hence, expenses could be recovered even where the heir had expressly prohibited the burial:

Ulpian, *Edict, book 25*: **Labeo also says that if you bury a testator even though the heir forbids it, an action for funeral expenses is available to you if good reason is shown**.... (D.11.7.14.13.)

9.9.2 *Condictio indebiti*

(D.12.6., C.4.5.)

Ulpian, *Edict, book 26*: **If someone mistakenly pays what is not due he can recover by this condictio....** (D.12.6.1.1.)

We are concerned here with unjustified enrichment—a familiar concept in modern systems, thanks to our Roman forebears. This was the work particularly of Labeo, who appears to have been the first jurist to establish the doctrine. If a person mistakenly paid money or transferred a thing to another, both wrongly believing that the debt or transfer was owed, the transferor had the *condictio indebiti* ('the recovery of a thing not owed') for its recovery. The rationale behind the remedy was readily understandable—the concept of fairness: in D.12.6.66., we are told that the *condictio* was 'grounded in the idea of what is good and fair'. The Institutes of Justinian (3.27.6) lists the *condictio indebiti* as one of the quasi-contracts. It should be borne in mind, however, that this was not the only enrichment action known to Roman law (see 9.9.2.2). Various other enrichment actions existed which were classified according to the cause of the enrichment.

9.9.2.1 Position of the parties

The plaintiff had to show that he had made a payment or a transfer, and that the debt or obligation was not owed. But the action was not available if the transferee had acted in bad faith, because such behaviour would have amounted to theft (for which there were discrete remedies). Nor was the action available if both parties had acted illegally or immorally: the rule applied that if the conduct of both was reprehensible, the position of the possessor was stronger (D.12.5.8.). But exceptions were allowed—e.g. where the conduct of the plaintiff was clearly less blameworthy than that of the recipient.

What was it that the plaintiff could recover under the *condictio*? Was it the thing transferred, or the extent of the defendant's enrichment? The texts are inconclusive but the most plausible view is that the action was concerned with enrichment. The defendant thus had to return the thing transferred, or its equivalent, together with any resulting profits and accretions, but allowing for expenses:

Paul, *Plautius, book 17*: **The plaintiff in the case of a supposed debt ought also to obtain restitution in respect of fruits and offspring, a deduction being made for expenses.** (D.12.6.65.5.)

9.9.2.2 Analogous cases

Other forms of *condictio* were allowed in analogous cases of unjust (or unjustified) enrichment, e.g. where property was given as dowry in expectation of a marriage which did not take place, or as an inducement not to commit a crime or to do something which the recipient was already bound to do. Of special significance was the *condictio sine causa* ('recovery on no specific ground'), a residuary action intended for any case of unjust enrichment that did not fall within the standard forms of *condictio*. An illustration from Ulpian:

Ulpian, *Edict, book 32*: **A cleaner takes a laundry contract, and then when the clothes have gone missing, he is sued by the owner in an action on hire and pays up their price. Then the owner finds the clothes. By what action should the cleaner recover the price he paid? And Cassius holds that he can not only sue by action on hire but can also maintain a *condictio* against** the owner. I think he can definitely bring the action on hire. It has, however, been doubted whether he can also have the *condictio,* in that what he gave was not something not owed. Yet maybe we can hold him able to have the *condictio* as for something given without any basis. For once the clothes are found, it does seem as though the giving had no basis. (D.12.7.2.)

The very existence of the *condictio sine causa,* and the other forms of *condictio,* points to the emergence of an important general principle—that persons who are unjustly enriched may not be able to benefit from their enrichment, even though they acted entirely in good faith. The development of this principle, one of the most impressive achievements of Roman law, was further aided by the availability of the action for unauthorized administration to the *gestor* against an 'enriched' principal (*ante*), and the *actio de peculio* against a master or *paterfamilias* enriched by contracts made by those in their power. Nevertheless, Roman law never did achieve an *all-embracing* principle of unjust enrichment—more a case of providing specific remedies which *in toto* approximated to such a principle.

9.9.2.3 Unjustified enrichment today

Modern systems espouse unjust enrichment in various degrees. See generally Zimmermann, *Obligations,* 834 ff. Although the *Code Civil* does not provide a general enrichment action, the courts have succeeded in doing so, at least for enrichment *sans cause.* On the other hand, the BGB does allow a general action; the principle is that if a person acquires—through transfer or in any other manner—something at the expense of another without any legal ground, he must return it to him: s. 812. The very generality of the principle has caused difficult problems of interpretation, and a distinction has had to be drawn between enrichment through transfer and otherwise. Roman–Dutch law has not applied the enrichment principle *generally* despite its advocacy by Grotius (who saw it as emanating from natural justice). However, enrichment claims are allowed in specific cases. Recent developments in South Africa suggest an increasingly extensive application of enrichment remedies.

English law too has eschewed the *general* application of the enrichment principle. However, the underlying basis of the law of restitution is clearly the principle of unjust enrichment. That law has long been an untidy mixture of elements of common law and equity, seemingly not fitted into any unitary scheme. But recently the trend has been—certainly in legal writing—towards the recognition of unjust enrichment as a principle of general application, or at least as an organizing concept for rationalization of the law. The analytical scheme proposed attempts to give the law of restitution some much-needed structure: the proposed basis of a restitution claim depends, first, on whether the defendant was enriched; second, on whether the enrichment was at the plaintiff's expense; third, on whether it would be unjust for the benefit to be retained by the defendant; and, fourth, on whether there is an appropriate defence. Moreover, cases such as *Lipkin Gorman v Karpnale Ltd* [1991] 2 AC 548, HL—where the Playboy Club was held to have been unjustly enriched by a partner of a solicitor's firm who used the firm's money to gamble there—have helped to fuel the current dynamic state of the law of restitution.

9.9.3 Common ownership

(D10.3., C.3.37.)

Common ownership often resulted from agreement, in which case the contract of partnership applied. But it could also arise in the absence of agreement, e.g.

as the result of a gift or inheritance, in which case the owners were in a quasi-contractual position, the law implying certain rights and duties between them. Their position could be regulated by the *actio communi dividundo*, the action for dividing common property—the same remedy that was allowed to the members of a partnership. There was a special action for the division of an inheritance between co-heirs, but for other cases of common ownership the *actio communi dividundo* was the appropriate action.

As a general rule, the position of common owners was similar whether they were partners in a *societas* or co-owners in the quasi-contractual sense. The latter were liable, e.g., for losses caused through their negligence, the standard of care required being that expected of them in their own affairs. They had to account for profits but were entitled to expenses that had been reasonably incurred. However, unlike the case in most partnerships, the death of a co-owner did not end the common ownership.

9.9.4 A common link?

Despite the earlier assertion that the chief instances of quasi-contract appear to lack a unifying principle, it can be argued that they all amount to attempts to prevent unjust enrichment. This is clearly the case in *condictio indebiti*; but is it so in the other cases? In *negotiorum gestio* the *gestor* is allowed to recover expenses otherwise the principal would be unjustly enriched by the beneficial service that was rendered to him. Similarly, the heir would be unjustly enriched by another's payment for the deceased's funeral if the *actio funeraria* was not available against the heir. And with regard to common ownership, the *actio communi dividundo* can be regarded as preventing the unjust enrichment of any of the co-owners. The argument can also be applied to other instances of quasi-contractual liability—e.g. that of the heir in respect of his duty to pay legacies. It could be objected to this line of reasoning that the quasi-contractual remedies are essentially concerned with preventing unjust *loss* to one party rather than the unjust *enrichment* of the other, but these are arguably two sides of the same coin. There may be some justification, then, in regarding the prevention of unjust enrichment (or loss) as the link between the quasi-contractual remedies. On the other hand, is this alleged link a specific enough explanation for the individual cases of quasi-contract? Is it not the fundamental object of the civil law to prevent the unjust enrichment (in a broad sense) of one party at the expense of another?

 Please consult the Online Resource Centre for revision guidance on this chapter.

FURTHER READING

On the classification of obligations, see Biscardi, A., 'Some Critical Remarks on the Roman Law of Obligations' (1978) 4 Scripta Classica Israelica, 106–21.

On the standards of contractual liability in Roman law, see MacCormack, G., 'Juristic Use of the Term Dolus: Contract' (1983) 100 ZSS (rA), 520–32 and by the same author, 'Dolus, Culpa, Custodia and Diligentia—Criteria of Liability or Content of Obligation', in *Omaggio Peter Stein*, 189–209.

On the issue of the transfer of risk in sale, see Honoré, A. M., 'Sale and the Transfer of Ownership: The Compilers' Point of View', in *Studies J. A. C. Thomas*, 56–72.

The contract of lease (*locatio conductio*) has generated a vast body of research in recent years. See, e.g., Frier, B. W. (1980), *Landlords and tenants in Imperial Rome*, Princeton: Princeton University Press (on urban leasehold); De Neeve, P. W. (1984), *Colonus: Private Farm-Tenancy in Roman Italy during the Republic and the Early Principate*, Amsterdam: J.C. Gieben (on agricultural leasehold); Martin, S. D. (1989), *The Roman Jurists and the Organisation of Private Building in the Late Republic and Early Empire*, Brussels: Latomus (on *locatio conductio operis*); and Kehoe, D. P. (1997), *Investment, Profit and Tenancy—The Jurists and the Roman Agrarian Economy*, Ann Arbor: University of Michigan Press. See most recently Kehoe, D.P. (2007), *Law and the Rural Economy in the Roman Empire*, Ann Arbor: University of Michigan Press.

On the contract of mandate, see Klami, H. T., 'Mandatum and Labour in Roman Law' (1989) 106 ZSS (rA), 575–86 and Watson, A., 'Mandate and the Boundaries of Roman Contract' (1991–2) 33–4 BIDR, 41–8. An impressive recent study on a related topic is that of Aubert, J.-J. (1994), *Business Managers in Ancient Rome—A Social and Economic Study of Institores 200 B.C.–A.D. 250*, Leiden: Brill. See, furthermore, the abbreviated English translation of Andreau, J. (1999), *Banking and Business in the Roman World*, Cambridge: Cambridge University Press.

On the contract of deposit, see Evans-Jones, R., 'The Actio Depositi in Factum as a Noxal Action' (1980) 83 BIDR, 191–206; by the same author, 'The Penal Characteristics of the Actio Depositi in Factum' (1986) 52 SDHI, 105–60, and 'The Action of the XII Tables ex Causa Depositi' (1988) 34 Labeo, 188–208.

10

Obligations arising from delict

10.1 Introduction

A delict, as one of the main sources of an obligation, can be defined in broad terms as a wrongful act which causes damage to someone's personality, his family, or his property, and for which the victim or his heirs is entitled to compensation. There is an obvious parallel between the Roman delict and the common law tort; but the analogy should not be pursued too far since the Roman law of delict had a strong penal element—the law penalized the conduct of the wrongdoer, as well as ensuring that the victim was adequately compensated. In theft, for example, the victim was normally entitled not only to the recovery of the stolen property, or its equivalent, but also to damages (representing a multiple of the victim's interest); and the thief was subject to *infamia*. For a good recent overview, see Sirks, A. J. B. 'Delicts', in *Cambridge Companion*, 246–71.

Why was the law of delicts penal? The traditional explanation is that in early Roman law, as in other legal systems, there was no clear distinction between crimes and civil wrongs (delicts). In modern legal systems the distinction is reasonably clear: crimes are usually prosecuted by the State whereas civil wrongs result in private redress, normally damages. But even then, some confusion may arise from the fact that certain wrongful acts may be both crimes and civil wrongs, e.g. physical assault. In early Rome there were certainly some wrongs that attracted a purely criminal sanction imposed by the State. But the criminal law was generally less developed than the civil law: it lacked specific content, largely because crimes tended to be dealt with by individual magistrates in the exercise of their power to punish for matters falling within their jurisdiction. So the law of delict partly fulfilled the role of a penal law until the late Republic, when criminal jurisdiction was given a more specific content through the introduction of *quaestiones perpetuae*, i.e. standing jury courts, each trying a particular crime or category of crimes. This development may partly account for the relative infrequency of litigation concerning delict (see Cascione, C., ' Roman Delicts and Criminal Law', in *Obligations in Roman law*, 267–95). Kelly has suggested that delict was one of the least litigated areas of Roman Law: *Civil Judicature*, ch. 3. See also Lintott, A., 'Crime and Punishment', in *Cambridge Companion*, 301–31.

Originally, it seems that the remedy for the commission of wrongs was largely a matter of custom. Private revenge could be exacted on the wrongdoer, a primitive custom which in time needed to be regulated. Rules were introduced allowing some wrongdoers to avoid retaliation by agreeing to pay compensation. That in turn led to the development of a civil procedure under which the seeking of monetary compensation in the courts became the normal (and, finally, the only permissible) mode of redress. But the law of delict never entirely threw off its early penal flavour.

Liability in delict generally depended on fault (originally *dolus* only, later also *culpa*), a principle that was hardly surprising in view of the penal character of delict (see Ankum, J. A., 'Actions By Which We Claim a Thing (res) and a Penalty (Poena) in Classical Roman Law' (1982) 24 BIDR, 15–39). In some delicts, e.g. theft or insulting behaviour, proof of fault necessitated showing that the defendant had acted intentionally; in others, e.g. wrongful damage to property, negligence sufficed (see Cursi, F., 'Roman Delicts and the Construction of Fault', in *Obligations in Roman Law*, 296–319).

The actions available to the victim in each of the delicts discussed in this chapter have been classified collectively as 'penal actions' as they exhibit a number of common features. Unlike the case with contracts, liability in delict was strictly personal. The death of the wrongdoer ended his liability; it could not be imposed on his heir except to the extent that the heir had benefited from the wrongdoing:

Pomponius, *Sabinus, book 29*: **Just as the heir of a dead person cannot be bound to pay the penalty arising from a delict, so he cannot benefit from it either if anything came to him as a result of the affair in question.** (D.50.17.38.)

On the other hand, the death of the victim did not end the wrongdoer's liability: as a general rule, the victim's heir could maintain a delictual action against the wrongdoer. The principle that liability was personal (and penal) is illustrated by the rule that if a delict was committed jointly, each wrongdoer was personally liable in full, i.e. as if he alone were responsible:

Ulpian, *Edict, book 18*: **But if several people do a slave to death, let us see whether they are all liable as for killing. If it is clear from whose blow he perished, that person is liable for killing; but if it is not clear, Julian says that all the assailants are liable as if they had all killed; and if the action is brought against only one of them, the others are not released from liability; for under the** *lex Aquilia* **what one pays does not lessen what is due from another, as it is a penal law.** (D.9.2.11.2.)

There was an absence in the Roman law of delicts, even in its most developed state, of fundamental principles of general application. Nor did any one delict come to dominate litigation. To that extent it was a law of delicts rather than delict—a number of discrete actions, each with its own specific rules (cf. Inst.Gai.3.182. and Inst.4.1pr.). One could liken the position to the English law of torts prior to the emergence of negligence as the dominant tort in practice.

There were four major 'Institutional' delicts: wrongful damage to property, theft, robbery, and insulting behaviour (see Diagram 10.1).

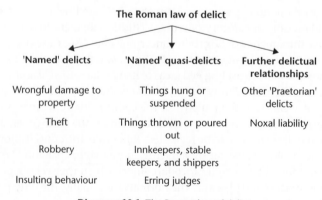

The Roman law of delict

'Named' delicts	'Named' quasi-delicts	Further delictual relationships
Wrongful damage to property	Things hung or suspended	Other 'Praetorian' delicts
Theft	Things thrown or poured out	Noxal liability
Robbery	Innkeepers, stable keepers, and shippers	
Insulting behaviour	Erring judges	

Diagram 10.1 The Roman law of delict

10.2 **Wrongful damage to property**

(Inst.Gai.3.210.–15., Inst.4.3., D.9.2., C.3.35.)

10.2.1 **Evolution**

The history of the delict of wrongful damage to property (*damnum iniuria datum*) followed an interesting path: fragmented beginnings, succeeded by legislative reform that was eventually extended well beyond its original framework by praetorian intervention and juristic interpretation. See Birks, *Obligations*, 192–220.

A number of actions concerned with damage to property are known to have existed in early law. The Twelve Tables mention, for example, an *actio de pastu*, allowed where a person's cattle wrongfully grazed on another's land; and an *actio de arboribus succisis* for wrongfully cutting down another's trees. But the decisive development occurred in the middle Republic with the enactment of the *lex Aquilia* by the *concilium plebis*. The most significant drawback of the earlier remedies was their fixed monetary penalties that did not take account of fluctuations in the value of the currency. There is no general agreement as to when the *lex Aquilia* was enacted, but 287 BC is the most plausible (and generally held) date (see Zimmermann, *Obligations*, 953–61; *Roman Statutes* II, 724–6 and most recently Ibbetson, D., 'The Dating of the Lex Aquilia', in *Judge and Jurist*, 167–77). It was then that the plebeian assembly acquired (through the *lex Hortensia)* the right to bind the whole people without the need for patrician ratification. A radical and substantial reform of the law relating to damage to property would seem a natural outcome, given the civil disturbances preceding the legislation. It is possible that a major purpose of the enactment was to redress plebeian grievances against the patricians. On the other hand, arguing for a later date, one can question whether a substantive reform such as the *lex Aquilia* was likely to have been enacted at a generally conservative period in the development of Roman civil law. But this argument is undermined if one takes the view that the *lex Aquilia* was a reform of rather narrow scope, as is suggested by the fact that several important extensions of it were later found necessary. Another factor pointing to *c.*287 BC rather than a later date is that the *lex Aquilia* was originally confined to Roman citizens. Had it been passed, say, *c.*200 BC, it is unlikely to have excluded foreigners, given their considerable presence in Rome by that time. Honoré, A. M., 'Linguistic and Social Context of the Lex Aquilia' (1972) 7 IJ, 138–50, has argued for the latter date on economic grounds—the second Punic War resulted in a period of high inflation when it might be expected that new remedies would be substituted for the now inadequate fixed penalties under the Twelve Tables.

What happened to the old actions? Ulpian explains:

Ulpian, *Edict, book 18*: **The *lex Aquilia* took away the force of all earlier laws which dealt with unlawful damage, the *Twelve Tables* and others alike, and it is no longer necessary to refer to them.** (D.9.2.1pr.)

'Took away the force' is best interpreted as 'rendered unimportant' rather than 'nullified', as it seems that the old actions did survive for some time after the enactment of the *lex Aquilia*. See Lawson, F. H., *Negligence in the Civil Law* (1950), 4 ff. and generally on this *lex*. See also Frier, *Casebook on Delict*, 4–6.

10.2.2 **First chapter**

The *lex Aquilia* was divided into sections known as 'chapters'. Wrongful damage to property was dealt with in the first and third chapters. The second chapter dealt with the contract of *adstipulatio* (see 9.4.3.5), imposing liability on a secondary creditor who wrongfully released the debtor as against the principal creditor. This contract seems to have become obsolete by the second century AD, see Inst.Gai.3.216., D.9.2.27.4. (on the origin and purpose of the second chapter, see Birks, P., 'Wrongful Loss by Co-Promisees' (1994) 22 Index, 181–8, and the interesting, yet controversial theory of Westbrook, R., 'The Coherence of the Lex Aquilia' (1995) 42 RIDA 3, 437–71. See most recently also Pugsley, D., 'A Potted History of Chapter 1 of the Lex Aquilia', in *Liber Amicorum Guido Tsuno*, 335–40). This apparently illogical sequence gives added support (but not much) to the view that the *lex Aquilia* was rushed through at speed during the civil unrest *c*.287 BC.

The first chapter stated:

Gaius, *Provincial Edict, book 7*: **If anyone kills unlawfully a slave or servant-girl belonging to someone else or a four-footed beast of the class of cattle, let him be condemned to pay the owner the highest value that the property had attained in the preceding year.** (D.9.2.2pr.) (See *Roman Statutes* II, 724.)

The first chapter seems, *prima facie*, to be a rather narrow provision, dealing only with the killing (*occidere*), through the direct application of bodily force, of slaves and beasts of pasture. But such property (being *res mancipi*) was of the highest importance in that era: it is thus not surprising that slaves and beasts were singled out by the first chapter (on the significance of these animals in the context of the *Lex Aquilia*, see McLeod, G., 'Pigs, Boars and Livestock under the Lex Aquilia', in *Critical Studies*, 83–92). The owner could recover the highest value that the property had been worth in the preceding year, i.e. the year preceding the killing. But suppose that the death of the slave or animal had occurred a considerable time after the killing—from when was the year reckoned back? Juristic interpretation settled that 'the preceding year' in such circumstances meant the year before *the act* that caused the later death.

It was the 'highest' value that the owner could recover, not just the value at the time of death:

Ulpian, *Edict, book 18*: **Julian also writes that the valuation of the dead slave is made as at that time in the preceding year when he was worth most; and accordingly, if the thumb of a most valuable painter had been cut off beforehand and within a year of its loss he is killed, the Aquilian action lies and he must be valued at his price before he lost his skill together with his thumb.** (D.9.2.23.3.) (cf. Inst.Gai.3.214.)

This rule vividly illustrates what some scholars refer to as the penal character of the delict. The owner clearly did rather well in cases where the property's value had diminished by the time of the killing—he recovered more than his actual loss. This may seem hard to justify, but the rule expressed society's indignation at the wrongdoing, and was intended to have a deterrent effect.

Beasts of pasture included sheep, goats, mules, cattle, and (after some doubt) pigs. Dogs were not within the class; nor were wild animals, as a general rule, although by the classical period camels and elephants were specifically included.

10.2.3 **Third chapter**

Ulpian, *Edict, book 18*: 'In the case of all other things apart from slaves or cattle that have been killed, if anyone does damage to another by wrongfully burning, breaking, or spoiling his property, let him be condemned to pay to the owner whatever the damage shall prove to be worth in the next thirty days.' *('Ceterarum rerum praeter hominem et pecudem occisos, si quis alteri damnum faxit, quod usserit fregerit ruperit iniuria, quanti ea res erit in diebus triginta proximis, tantum aes domino dare damnas esto'*: D.9.2.27.5.)

10.2.3.1 **The content of the third chapter**

The passage quoted above is attributed to Ulpian, who was writing some 500 years after the enactment of the *lex Aquilia*. Its accuracy cannot be guaranteed: 'great difficulty and controversy attends any attempt to reconstruct the actual wording, and every such attempt is the concomitant of some hypothesis as to the original scope and meaning of the statute. The problem is exacerbated by the volume of juristic interpretation this statute underwent' (see *Roman Statutes* II, 723). There has been much disagreement whether the original enactment contained the phrases *ceterarum rerum* (of other things') or *praeter...occisos* ('apart from...killed'); whether *ea res* means 'that thing' or 'that damage'; whether it was actually *fuit* ('has been') or *fuerit* ('will have been') rather than *erit* ('will be'); and whether *proximis* means 'next', 'nearest', or 'preceding'. The English rendering quoted above will serve as our basis, but no one can be sure what the third chapter originally stated.

10.2.3.2 **Scope of the third chapter**

To what sort of damage was the third chapter applicable? It appears to have applied, at first sight, to all wrongful damage other than that covered by the first chapter. But the damage must have occurred through *urere, frangere, or rumpere*—'burning, breaking or tearing asunder' (for the significance of these 'harm-verbs' in constituting liability under the statute see Birks, P., 'Doing and Causing to be Done', in *Roman Law Tradition*, 31–53.). The use of such words suggests that the third chapter covered only serious damage, and this is consistent with the probability that the *lex Aquilia* was enacted after a period of civil unrest. Jolowicz, H. F., 'The Original Scope of the Lex Aquilia and the Question of Damages' (1922) 38 LQR, 220–30, went further and maintained that the third chapter originally dealt only with total destruction of inanimate objects, thus complementing the first chapter. The view gains support from the likelihood that *urere, frangere*, and *rumpere* signified total destruction in early Roman usage. But would the drafters of the *lex Aquilia* have been so shortsighted as not to include less serious damage? Possibly, if the statute was an emergency measure aimed at deterring violent damage to property. The most plausible view is that the third chapter was aimed expressly at serious damage, but that it was later interpreted as covering lesser damage; *rumpere* (in the third chapter) originally meant 'tearing apart', but this meaning was soon found to be too restrictive. It seems that the early jurists probably came to interpret *rumpere* first as *quasi-rumpere* and later as *corrumpere*, i.e. 'spoiling', thus making the third chapter much broader in scope (cf. D.9.2.27.13.; 15.; 16.; Inst.4.3.13.).

10.2.3.3 **Measure of damages**

The third chapter seems to makes sense—the owner could recover the loss that he had sustained, i.e. the difference between the value of the property when it was damaged and its worth at the end of the following 30 days. But other interpreta-tions are possible in view of the ambiguity of part of the third chapter, namely the phrase '*quanti ea res erit in diebus triginta proximis*'. It can be taken to mean that the owner was entitled to the value—interpreted as highest value—which the damaged thing had had in the 30 days preceding the wrongful act. This appears to be a startling rule—the owner seemingly could recover the full worth of the property, even though it had been only partially damaged. So if I dented your chariot in a collision, I was liable to pay the highest value that the chariot had been worth in the previous 30 days. This seems absurd. I may as well chop the chariot to pieces—my liability will be the same. However, such a rule appears less absurd when account is taken of the penal character of delict and the likelihood that the third chapter originally applied to serious damage. Being required to pay the full value of property that one has seriously damaged or totally destroyed is not an irrational rule.

Various opinions have been offered as to the measure of damages under the third chapter. See particularly MacCormack, G., 'On the Third Chapter of the Lex Aquilia' (1970) 5 IJ, 164–78. The dominant continental view has been that the owner could always recover the highest value the property had in the 30 days preceding the act which damaged it. MacCormack broadly agrees but thinks that originally liability was confined to 'serious wounds to slaves and animals and seri-ous injuries to inanimate objects' (165). Jolowicz (cited earlier) naturally adopts the highest value approach given his belief that the third chapter was originally concerned only with the total destruction of inanimate objects. Daube, on the other hand, argues that the third chapter originally dealt only with the wound-ing of slaves and animals, and allowed recovery for loss rather than value, namely compensation for such damage as appeared within 30 days after the wrongful act: (Daube, D., 'On the Third Chapter of the Lex Aquilia' (1936) 52 LQR, 253–68). Zimmermann agrees that the chapter was concerned with the diminution in value of the damaged property, and that the time rule has to be read forwards rather than backwards. But he considers that the chapter applied to inanimate as well as animate property and that the 30-day period is a reference to the procedural rule under the Twelve Tables whereby that length of time had to elapse before the judge could be asked to assess damage. See *Obligations*, 962 ff. Pugsley has suggested the possibility that the measure of damages was based neither on diminution of value, nor on the value of the property at a certain time, but on value in a cer-tain period—the nearest 30 days—e.g. the cost of replacing an injured slave for a month. See *Americans are Aliens*, 43.

10.2.4 Liability under the *lex Aquilia*

To succeed under the first or third chapters of the *lex Aquilia*, the owner would have to prove that the defendant wrongfully caused loss.

10.2.4.1 Loss

Whatever the defendant's conduct, the owner could not succeed under the *lex Aquilia* unless he could prove that he had suffered loss in the sense of a deprecia-tion in *the value of the object*, and that the loss was ascertainable. (See Daube, D., 'On the Use of the Term Damnum', in *Studi Solazzi*, 93–156. See also Frier, *Casebook on Delict*, 55–71. Most recently, see Rodger, A., 'What did Damnum Iniuria Actually

Mean?', in *Mapping the Law*, 421–38 as well as Cursi, F., 'What did Occidere Iniuria in the lex Aquilia Actually Mean?' (2011) 7 Roman Legal Tradition, 16–29.) Hence, sentimental damages could not be recovered. For example, the owner of an injured slave could not recover greater damages simply because he was particularly fond of the slave. Nor could speculative damages be recovered—if a fisherman's nets were damaged while he was fishing, he could recover for the damage to the nets, but not for the loss of the fish that may have been caught:

Ulpian, *Edict, book 18*: **But where action is brought for wrongful damage to the nets no account is to be taken of the fish which were not caught because of the damage, as it is so uncertain whether they would have been caught. The same is true in the cases of the prospective catches of both hunters and bird-catchers.** (D.9.2.29.3.)

Consequential damages could be recovered by the classical period, if not earlier. The concept of suing for the highest value proved broad enough to include consequential damages, so that the principle emerged that the plaintiff could recover his *interesse*, i.e. his interest—whatever the thing was worth to him. Thus, a loss of profit (*lucrum cessans*) could be recovered if it was ascertainable:

Ulpian, *Edict, book 18*: ...**if a slave who has been instituted as heir is killed, the value of the inheritance comes into the reckoning.** (D.9.2.23pr.)

Another type of consequential damage was *damnum emergens* ('damage that comes to light'). So if your slave had been wrongfully killed, you could recover not only for the actual loss of the slave but also for any indirect loss caused, e.g. medical expenses incurred in trying to save him (and see now Sirks, A. J. B., 'An Inheritance Lost and a Fraudulent Slave', in *Judge and Jurist*, 265–76). If the slave's death resulted in the depreciation of your other slaves, that also was *damnum emergens*:

Paul, *Edict, book 22*: **Furthermore, other heads of damage necessarily connected are taken into account, if, for example, someone kills one of a troupe of actors or musicians or one of twins or of a chariot team or one of a (matched) pair of mules: for not only must a valuation be made of the object destroyed but it must also be borne in mind how much the value of the others has been lessened.** (D.9.2.22.1.)

10.2.4.2 **Fault**

The defendant must have caused loss wrongfully, i.e. through an *iniuria*. It is not clear whether *iniuria* originally signified fault on the defendant's part or simply the absence of legal justification for his act. But in the classical period the term was identified with the requirement to prove fault, namely intentional or culpable conduct (see MacCormack, G., 'Aquilian Culpa', in *Daube Noster*, 201–24; Frier, *Casebook on Delict*, 40–54 as well as Scott, H., 'Pits and Pruners: Culpa and Social Practice in D.9.2', in *Judge and Jurist*, 251–64). As regards the latter, the standard of care was that of the *bonus paterfamilias*:

Ulpian, *Sabinus, book 42*: **Under the *lex Aquilia* even the slightest degree of fault counts.** (D.9.2.44pr.)

However, another text appears to lay down a different test:

Paul, *Sabinus, book 10*: ...**there is fault when what could have been foreseen by a diligent man was not foreseen**... (D.9.2.31.)

It is arguable that the 'diligent man' test required perhaps a lower standard of care, but in fact there was no real contradiction since the diligent man should be equated with the *bonus paterfamilias*. See Tellegen-Couperus, O. E., 'The Limits of Culpa Levissima' (2008) 76 (1–2) The Legal History Review, 19–25.

The degree of care that was expected from the defendant depended partly on the skills and expertise that he purported to have, especially if he was a professional. He would be expected to display the appropriate level of skill—*imperitia culpae adnumeratur* ('inexperience is counted as fault'):

Gaius, *Provincial Edict, book 7*: **Furthermore, if a mule driver cannot control his mules because he is inexperienced and as a result they run down somebody's slave, he is generally said to be liable on grounds of negligence. It is the same if it is because of weakness that he cannot hold back his mules—and it does not seem unreasonable that weakness should be deemed negligence; for no one should undertake a task in which he knows or ought to know that his weakness may be a danger to others. (D.9.2.8.1.)**

The principle that those who purport to have skills should be judged by the level of expertise expected of such persons is a familiar one in modern legal systems.

Even if the defendant was shown to have acted intentionally or carelessly, such conduct was not necessarily wrongful if a defence could be pleaded successfully (see Zimmermann, *Obligations*, 998–1013; Frier, *Casebook on Delict*, 88–108). For example, it was possible for the defendant to exclude liability for carelessness by an exclusion clause in a contract—this sometimes occurred in the case of a professional performing services for his client. In such cases, the client in effect consented to run the risk of damage. The principle of consent was also applicable in cases where the damage was inflicted in public sporting contests, e.g. boxing or wrestling matches—both parties were regarded as having consented to the risk of injury. Moreover, the contributory negligence of the plaintiff was a defence, providing that the defendant had acted carelessly:

Ulpian, *Edict, book 18*:…**if when other people were already throwing javelins in a field a slave walked across the same field, the Aquilian action fails, because he should not make his way at an inopportune time across a field where javelin throwing is practiced. However, anyone who deliberately aims at him is liable under the *lex Aquilia*. (D.9.2.9.4.)**

Contributory negligence was a complete defence—there was no attempt to award damages in proportion to the respective blame of the parties, as is done in modern English law (cf. Buckland, *Textbook*, 587). Moreover, the jurists did not generally isolate the plaintiff's conduct as a separate issue in their assessment of fault—it was simply one of the factors to be considered: 'they determined liability using a flexible, casuistic inquiry that considered the case as a whole' (Travis Laster, J., 'The Role of the Victim's Conduct in Assessing Fault under the Lex Aquilia: Insights into the Analytical Methods of Roman Jurists' (1996) 25 Anglo-Am LR, 188–220, at 220). To that extent, it may be misleading to talk of a Roman rule of 'contributory negligence'. The matter was viewed as essentially one of causation: the negligence of the slave in walking across the field is what caused the accident rather than the negligence of the thrower. The point is further illustrated by the following scenario in which the victim can be said to have inflicted the injury on himself:

Ulpian, *Edict, book 18*: **Further, Mela writes that, when some people were playing with a ball, one of them hit it hard and it knocked the hands of a barber with the result that the throat of a slave whom the barber was shaving was cut by the jerking of the razor. In which of the parties does the fault lie? For it is he who is liable under the *lex Aquilia*. Proculus says the blame is the barber's, and surely, if he was doing shaving in a place where people customarily played games or where there was much going to and fro, the blame will be imputed to** him; but it is no bad point in reply that if someone entrusts himself to a barber who has his chair in a dangerous place he has only himself to blame for his own misfortune. (D.9.2.11pr.)

Despite appearances, this famous text by Ulpian does not necessarily posit any wide-ranging principle of contributory negligence: 'Ulpian seems merely to be giving another example to show the variability of the fault inquiry. . . . The multi-factor case-by-case analysis explains the barber scenario' (Laster (cited earlier), 213–14). There are, of course, other issues which one might have expected to be dealt with in this text, particularly the potential liability of the people playing ball.

Self-defence was accepted as a complete defence; and so was necessity. There is hardly any textual analysis of necessity but it is clear that the concept was recognized. For example, we are told that damage is not done wrongfully:

Ulpian, *Disputations, book 9*: . . . **where it is done under compulsion of overwhelming necessity, as Celsus writes about the man who pulled down his neighbor's house to keep a fire off his own.** (D.9.2.49.1.)

The subsequent discussion in the text implies that the defence applied only if the defendant had acted in reasonable fear that the fire would spread to his own house.

10.2.4.3 Loss caused by the defendant

Causation is a problematic area of law even in the most sophisticated and developed of legal systems. It is hardly surprising that no clear test or general principles of causation emerged in Roman law, although some of the illustrations in the *Digest* are consistent with tests familiar to modern lawyers, e.g. was the defendant's act the substantive and operative cause of the damage? The Roman approach to causation was typically casuistic, attempting to provide solutions to each individual problem without sustained resort to overriding principle (cf. Frier, *Casebook on Delict*, 77–87). Particular problems arose concerning intervening acts:

Ulpian, *Edict, book 18*: **Celsus writes that if one attacker inflicts a mortal wound on a slave and another person later finishes him off, he who struck the earlier blow will not be liable for a killing, but for wounding, because he actually perished as the result of another wound,** . . . (D.9.2.11.3.)

This makes good sense and is consistent with D.9.2.15.1. in which a person is held liable for wounding a slave (but not for killing him) where he mortally wounded the slave, whose death was accelerated subsequently by the collapse of a house. On the other hand, consider:

Julian, *Digest, book 86*: . . . **if someone wounds a slave mortally and then after a while someone else inflicts a further injury, as a result of which he dies sooner than would otherwise have been the case, it is clear that both assailants are liable for killing.** (D.9.2.51pr.)

'It is clear'? Hardly—the passages are difficult to reconcile. One attempt to do so is to regard the original act in D.9.2.51pr. as closer, more proximate to the slave's death than in the earlier passages, but this is hardly convincing.

If the defendant's conduct caused damage that may not have occurred in other property of the same type, the defendant was nevertheless liable. He had to take his victim as he found him—a principle known as the 'thin skull' rule in common law:

Ulpian, *Edict, book 18*: **But if someone gives a light blow to a sickly slave and he dies from it, Labeo rightly says that he is liable under the *lex Aquilia*; for different things are lethal for different people.** (D.9.2.7.5.)

Did the plaintiff have to prove that the damage was caused by an *act*? Could the defendant be liable for not acting, i.e. for omissions? The general rule which emerged was that the failure to act constituted wrongful conduct if there was a *duty to act*. The duty could arise through imposition by law, or it might be self-imposed, e.g. where someone voluntarily undertook responsibility to act. In such cases the failure to act was not regarded as an omission but as negligent conduct. So if you failed to warn your neighbour that there was a fire in his garden, you were not liable for the resulting damage; but you would be liable if, having started a bonfire in your own garden, you failed to supervise it properly, and it damaged your neighbour's property (see McCusker, D., 'Liability for Omission under the Lex Aquilia' (1999) 50(3) Northern Ireland LQ, 380–402).

Under the *lex Aquilia* the damage had to be *directly* caused by the defendant's conduct—it had to be inflicted *corpore corpori*, i.e. 'by the body, to the body (object)'. For example, if your slave was struck and killed by a chariot that was being driven negligently, the driver would be liable since the damage had been caused *corpore corpori*. But there would be no liability if someone scared your horse, which then jumped to its death over a cliff. This rule came to be regarded as unduly restrictive; by the classical period indirect forms of causing damage became actionable (see 10.2.5.2).

The onus of proof was on the plaintiff. If his property was damaged, but it could not be proved that the defendant was responsible, the plaintiff could not succeed:

Paul, *Sabinus, book 10*: **When two slaves were jumping over some burning straw, they jumped into each other, fell, and one was burned to death. No action can be brought on that account if it is not known which was knocked over by which.** (D.9.2.45.3.)

10.2.4.4 **The Aquilian action**

The *actio legis Aquiliae* lay for the recovery of the financial value of the loss caused: the defendant had to pay double if he denied liability but was held liable (cf. Buckland, *Textbook*, 586). This seemingly peculiar rule can be regarded as a penal feature of this delict; but a more plausible explanation is that the rule was intended to encourage settlements between the parties. This would have been an important aim at the time when the *lex Aquilia* was probably passed, in view of the level of civil unrest at that time.

As in other delicts, if the wrongdoer died, the action could not be brought against the heirs unless they had been enriched by the wrongful act. But the action did survive against the wrongdoer for the heirs of the victim. (cf. Frier, *Casebook on Delict*, 24–8.)

10.2.5 **Extensions to the *lex Aquilia***

The *lex Aquilia* was originally quite narrow in its verbal formulation but its scope was greatly widened by a combination of juristic interpretation and praetorian intervention. The latter took the form of supplementing the *lex Aquilia* by granting actions additional to the original *actio legis Aquiliae* (cf. Frier, *Casebook on Delict*, 7–23). These supplementary actions consisted either of an *actio utilis* or an *actio in factum*. The difference between them is not clear. It is possible that the *actio utilis* was granted in situations more analogous to the original *lex Aquilia* than was the case with an *actio in factum*; but the *Digest* generally refers to the two actions as if they were interchangeable (see Zimmermann, *Obligations*, 993–6). It is probable that the double damages rule of the *actio legis Aquiliae* did not apply to the supplementary actions (see Stein, P., 'School Attitudes in the Law of Delicts', in *Studi Biscardi* II, 281–93). It was thus advantageous for the plaintiff to sue under the *lex Aquilia* if possible.

10.2.5.1 Miscellaneous extensions

Some of the extensions (through juristic interpretation) have already been noted in passing, e.g. the interpretation of 'highest value' to include consequential damage, the interpretation of 'four-footed beast of the class of cattle' to include camels and elephants, and the interpretation of *rumpere* to include any form of 'spoiling'. Apart from these, there were several others, which came about through praetorian intervention (cf. Lee, *Elements*, 388):

(a) Non-owners The *lex Aquilia* initially allowed only an owner to sue—everyone else was excluded. Eventually, the praetors allowed certain non-owners to sue under the supplementary actions, e.g. usufructuaries and bona fide possessors (for exceptions, see Lee, *Elements*, 388 and Buckland, *Textbook*, 588).

(b) Foreigners. They could not sue as the *lex Aquilia* originally applied to Roman citizens only. Later, foreigners were allowed an action on the fiction that they were citizens (Inst.Gai.4.37.).

(c) Persons in *potestas*. The *lex Aquilia* applied to property (originally perhaps only movable property, but later also immovables), not to human beings (compare the position of slaves). Consequently, a *paterfamilias* could not sue for injuries inflicted on his children and others in his *potestas*. There would in any case be an obvious problem as to how to assess damages in such cases under the particular provisions of the *lex Aquilia*. However, an action (*utilis*) was eventually allowed for recovery of consequential damages such as medical expenses or loss of a son's earning capacity (D.9.2.5.3.). But it is not clear when this extension occurred and whether its source was praetorian or juristic (see Buckland, *Textbook*, 589).

(d) Personal injuries. The general rule was that a freeman could not recover for personal injury, but an exception was granted in the case of a freeman who was injured whilst acting as a slave (mistakenly thinking that he was a slave). The probable reason for the general rule was that the *lex Aquilia* protected rights in *property*, but Weir has argued that it had to do with the fact that most of the work in Rome was done by slaves—personal injuries tended to occur in employment (with which the freeman was generally not concerned): (Weir, T., 'Contracts in Rome and England' (1992) 66 Tulane LR, 1615–48, at 1637). The general exclusion of personal injuries partially explains why delict litigation was allegedly low. Later, an action was allowed for personal injuries:

Ulpian, *Edict, book 18*: **For an injury to himself a freeman has on his own account an *actio utilis* after the manner of the Aquilian action. He cannot have the direct action under the *lex* because no one is deemed to be the owner of his own limbs.** (D.9.2.13pr.)

This appears to be a major departure from the original scope of the *lex Aquilia*, and yet it receives little mention in the *Digest*. The attribution of the passage to Ulpian is rather dubious—the extension was most probably a post-classical development, possibly as late as Justinian.

10.2.5.2 **Damage caused indirectly**

It will be recalled that liability under the 'harm-verbs' of the *lex Aquilia* was originally confined to direct physical acts. The interpretation of such words was strict. For example, N. H. Andrews considers that *occidere* (to kill) in the first chapter had a core literal meaning, when the statute was enacted, which the jurists felt generally compelled to follow, even in the classical period (see Andrews, N. H., '"Occidere" and the Lex Aquilia' (1987) 46 Cambridge LJ, 315–29). The rule that damage must be *corpore corpori* was gradually eroded through the grant of supplementary actions for various forms of indirect killing or damage. It would appear that both the jurists and the praetors assisted this development. For indirect killing, Roman jurists used the term *mortis causam praebere* (furnishing a cause of death) (see Nörr, D., 'Causam Mortis Praebere', in *The Legal Mind*, 203–17). This was arguably the most significant extension of all. How this came about is a matter of some speculation. The *Digest* title on the *lex Aquilia* is replete with juristic discussion whether particular misconduct is *corpore corpori*, and thus actionable under the *lex Aquilia*, or whether a supplementary action is required. It seems that the first development was that the praetors allowed an action if the damage was *corpore* but not *corpori*, i.e. by the body but not to the body:

Ulpian, *Edict, book 18*: **If a man knocks coins out of my hand, Sabinus thinks that there is an action for wrongful damage if they roll away and thus do not come into someone else's hands if, for example, they fall into a river or the sea or into a drain,** ... (D.9.2.27.21.)

Under the original *lex Aquilia* there was no liability in the above situation since there was no damage to the coin, i.e. to its *body*. Later, an action was allowed where the damage was *corpori* but not *corpore*. An illustration (probably hypothetical) from Ulpian concerning the death of a woman in labour:

Ulpian, *Edict, book 18*: **Labeo makes this distinction if a midwife gives a drug from which the woman dies: if she administers it with her own hands it would appear that she killed; but if she gave it to the woman for her to take it herself an *actio in factum* must be granted. This opinion is correct; for she provided a cause of death rather than killed.** (D.9.2.9pr.)

The final development was to allow an action even where the damage was neither *corpore* nor *corpori*, provided that there was a causal link between the wrongdoer's acts and the damage sustained:

Ulpian, *Edict, book 18*: **If when my slave is out riding you scare his horse so that he is thrown into a river and dies as a result, Ofilius writes that an *actio in factum* must be given in just the same way as when my slave is lured into an ambush by one man and killed by another.** (D.9.2.9.3.)

For procedural aspects of the *lex Aquilia*, see the texts collected by Frier, *Casebook on Delict*, 109–36.

10.2.6 **Modern developments**

It is obvious that liability under the *lex Aquilia* was transformed between the mid-Republic and the time of Justinian. The medieval lawyers tinkered with it further: e.g. they abandoned the penal elements and the method of assessing damage by reference to the time limits of one year or 30 days. The core of the Aquilian action remained intact, however, namely liability for loss caused through fault: 'There is little doubt that the older civilians regarded their law of negligent damage as a modernised version of the Roman' (Lawson, F. H., *Negligence in the Civil Law* (1950), 27).

The Roman concept that delictual liability is firmly based on fault is one that has been largely entrenched in modern systems (even if increasingly questioned of late). For example, Article 1382 of the *Code Civil* commences the French law of delict with the wide-ranging principle that any act which causes damage to another obliges the person at fault to make reparation. The all-embracing nature of this provision has inevitably led to difficulties in interpretation for the courts. German law is perhaps closer to the spirit of the original Roman law by enumerating the various protected interests: s. 823 BGB imposes the duty to compensate on a person who causes unlawful damage, wilfully or negligently, to the life, body, health, freedom, property, or other right of another.

English law, though it borrowed some elements of the Roman law, generally lacked an organizing concept as the foundation of liability until comparatively recently (some would say not until *Donoghue v Stevenson* [1932] AC 562, HL). The notion of the duty of care has provided such an organizing concept, but its extent has caused considerable problems (e.g. the issue of liability for pure economic loss). The *notion* of a duty of care as a legal principle did not emerge in Roman law, although the overall picture presented by the casuistic Roman texts resembles that notion (especially in the Roman law of contracts). See generally Lawson, F. H., *Negligence in the Civil Law* (1950), 27 ff. and Zimmermann, *Obligations*, 1017 ff.; cf. Frier, *Casebook on Delict*, 30–9.

10.3 **Theft and robbery**

(Inst.Gai.3.183.–208., Inst.4.1., D.47.2. and C.6.2.)

We are concerned here with theft as a delict rather than as a crime. Thieves were often not worth suing, particularly if they had disposed of the property that they had stolen. Consequently, it may be that thieves were dealt with predominantly through criminal sanctions, at least from the late Republic onwards (see 10.3.2.3). Nevertheless, the delict retained some importance throughout the history of Roman law, not least because of the legal issues which could arise concerning stolen property. And not all thieves were necessarily men of straw—some might have been worth suing by civil action. See Frier, *Casebook on Delict*, 150–76 as well as Birks, *Obligations*, 158–87.

10.3.1 **The essentials of theft (*furtum*)**

Paul, *Edict, book 39*: **Theft is a fraudulent interference with a thing with a view to gain, whether by the thing itself or by the use or possession of it.** (D.47.2.1.3.) (cf. the definition in Inst.4.1.1.)

Theft consisted of several constituent elements, as emphasized in Paul's definition. Each needs consideration. It should be noted, however, that this definition of theft (and the related one in Inst.4.1.1.) are post-classical and it is a matter of contention whether all the elements were necessary requirements from the start.

(See Watson, A., 'The Definition of Furtum and the Trichotomy' (1958) 28 TR, 197–210 on the evolution of the concept of theft in Roman law and Ibbetson, D., 'The Danger of Definition: Contractatio and Appropriation', in *The Roman Law Tradition*, 54–72).

10.3.1.1 'Interference'

There had to be—at least in classical law—a *contrectatio* by the thief, i.e. some physical interference with (or handling of) the property. A thief normally takes away the property that he is stealing, and it seems that an act of removal was necessary in early law. But the requirement proved too restrictive in that it potentially excluded a wide range of conduct that in practice was theftuous, e.g. attempting to steal. So the concept of removal gave way to that of interference, most probably well before the classical period, although Pugsley has argued that *contrectatio* was not a general requirement of theft until Justinian (Pugsley, D., 'Contrectatio', (1980) 15 IJ, 341–55). A parallel can be found in English law: the Theft Act 1968 introduced the concept of appropriation in place of the previous requirement of asportation. Unfortunately, *contrectatio* never received a clear definition. Perhaps the jurists felt it best to avoid precision, and therefore rigidity, in this particular instance. *Contrectatio* could equally well mean handling, meddling, or interfering; but did it require actual physical contact, i.e. touching the property? Although theft normally involved physical contact between the thief and the stolen property, there could be exceptional situations in which theft was committed despite the absence of physical contact:

Pomponius, *Sabinus, book 19*: **If, when my tame peacock escaped from my house, you chased it so that it disappeared, I could have the action for theft against you if someone else should take it.** (D.47.2.37.)

There was no physical contact in this scenario, and yet it was theft because you were 'interfering' with my property.

What if a man took part of the whole, e.g. a shovelful from a heap of corn—had he interfered with the part only, or with the whole? The problem did not arise in early law: you stole only what you took (since removal was necessary). But once handling became the *actus reus* of theft it was arguable that a man stole whatever he interfered with, even if he removed only a part of it. Paul states:

Paul, *Sabinus, book 40*:…**Ofilius thinks that he steals the whole heap; for similarly, Trebatius says that one who touches the ear of a person touches the whole person. And in the same way, one who opens a wine jar and abstracts a small quantity of wine therefrom is deemed a thief not only of what he takes but of the whole contents. But the truth is that these people are liable in the action on theft only for what they took.** (D.47.2.21pr.)

It is not clear whether Paul is agreeing in this passage with Ofilius and Trebatius. The analogy with touching an ear is unconvincing: the ear is inseparable from the body whereas a heap of corn consists of separate grains. The most plausible explanation of this passage is that strictly there is theft of the whole heap, but that the thief is liable only for what he takes. The confusion is made worse by the application of different tests in other passages:

Paul, *Sabinus, book 9*: **If a chest be broken into so that, say, pearls may be removed and they are handled with theftuous intent, it is only of them that theft may be held to be committed…The remaining things, set aside to get at the pearls, are not tampered with for the purpose of their theft.** (D.47.2.22.1.)

This approach to the problem, linking the act of interference with the intent to steal, makes good sense; however, there is no clear indication in the texts which of the tests discussed was thought to be correct. Indeed, it seems that the test varied according to the circumstances and the nature of the thing stolen. For example, it would appear that a thing could not be stolen if it was too heavy to be moved:

Paul, *Sabinus, book 40*: **If, again, a person open or break into something of too great weight to be removed, an action for theft will lie against him, not for the whole contents but only for what he removes, because he could not remove the whole thing....** (D.47.2.21.8.)

This passage suggests that asportation was still required in some cases of theft in the classical period, even if it was no longer necessary in all cases. The problems discussed in D.47.2.21. need to be seen in the context of the tension caused by the shift from removal to handling. See Ibbetson cited above in *Roman Law Tradition*, 54, for an analysis of the main texts.

10.3.1.2 'Fraudulent'

The interference must have been fraudulent—there could be no liability unless the defendant acted dishonestly (cf. D.47.2.52.20.). So he had to be capable of dishonest intent. It followed that the insane could not commit theft, except during a lucid interval; nor could children unless they were old enough to be capable of dishonest intent (cf. Inst.Gai.3.208.). The test of dishonesty was purely subjective—what mattered was the defendant's genuine belief. If he genuinely thought that he was entitled to take the property, he could not be liable, however inconceivable or unlikely his belief. This, at least, was the rule that prevailed in the classical period. The view of Sabinus that the defendant's belief must be founded on reasonable grounds was not generally accepted. Of course, the more unreasonable the belief, the more unlikely it would be that the judge would accept the defendant's story.

The interference had to be without the consent of the owner: if he consented, there could be no theft, however dishonestly the defendant had acted. But setting a trap for the thief, e.g. by leaving goods lying around invitingly, did not constitute consent. If the owner did not consent to the taking but the defendant genuinely thought otherwise, there was no theft. What of the converse case, i.e. where the owner consented but the defendant did not know this? This could not be theft: the defendant has been dishonest but he has interfered with the property with the consent of the owner. Pomponius thought differently but his view did not prevail. In proving fraudulent interference it was not necessary to show, unlike the case with theft under the Theft Act 1968, that the defendant intended to deprive the owner permanently of the property. Even very temporary unauthorized use could amount to theft.

What if the defendant showed repentance after committing theft? Apparently, it made no difference:

Ulpian, *Curule Aediles' Edict, book 1*: **One who appropriates another's thing with a view to his own gain is a thief, even if, changing his mind, he later returns it to the owner; no one ceases to be guilty by his own repentance over such a wrong.** (D.47.2.66.)

This may be so, but it is unlikely that a repentant thief would have been sued in such a case (i.e. where he restored the property), unless the owner had suffered some particular loss through being deprived of the property.

10.3.1.3 'A thing'

Things could not be stolen unless they were capable of being privately owned. Hence, there could not be theft of things such as city gates or walls, for example. But woe betide you if you did 'interfere' with such things—a criminal sanction would almost certainly be imposed. To be stolen the thing had to be owned, or at least there had to be someone with rights in the property sufficient to sustain an action for theft. Thus, if the property had been abandoned, there could be no theft, however dishonest the defendant might have been:

Ulpian, *Sabinus, book 41*: **If its owner has abandoned something, I will not commit theft of it, even though I take it with theftuous intent; for there can be no theft without an owner of the object**...(D.47.2.43.5.)

What if the thing had not been abandoned, but the defendant had taken it believing that it was abandoned? This could not be theft since the taking was not fraudulent, providing that the belief had been genuinely held.

Could land be stolen? After some controversy amongst the jurists (Sabinus, for example) the rule emerged in the classical period that land could not be stolen, but that things forming part of the land could be, e.g. fixtures, crops, minerals. Severing and removing such things could amount to theft, or handling them after their severance by someone else; but not simply interfering with unsevered things:

Alfenus, *Digest, Epitomized by Paul, book 4*: **If someone dig a hole to remove lime and he does remove it, he is a thief, not for digging but for taking.** (D.47.2.58.)

Could human beings be stolen? Slaves could be, of course. The kidnapping of slaves was not uncommon: if the slave consented, he would be regarded as an accomplice. A slave who escaped from his master was regarded (with somewhat harsh logic) as having stolen himself, and as constituting stolen property. This had the important consequence of preventing the slave from being acquired by a third party through *usucapio*. Free persons too could be stolen, e.g. a child in *potestas*, or a wife in a *manus* marriage, the action for theft being available to the *paterfamilias* or husband respectively. (Consider the crime of kidnapping (*plagium*) in Roman criminal law, see Robinson, O. F., *Criminal Law of Ancient Rome* (1995), 32–5.)

10.3.1.4 'With a view to gain' (*animus lucrandi*)

The purpose of this requirement was to distinguish between theft and acts of wanton destruction (which could result in liability under the *lex Aquilia*). It was important to make the distinction because the delicts had different remedies:

Ulpian, *Edict, book 37*: **If a man wave a red flag and cattle rush off to fall into the hands of thieves, assuming that he has a malicious intent, he is liable to the action for theft. But even if he did not act with theftuous design, he should not go unpunished for such pernicious conduct; hence, Labeo writes that an *actio in factum* should be given against him.** (D.47.2.50.4.)

There is little guidance in the texts on the meaning of 'gain', but it seems that it was widely construed and was not restricted to economic gain. For example, taking A's property to give it to B, thereby gaining favour with B, amounted to theft. However, merely obtaining a sense of satisfaction, or acting purely out of spite, would be insufficient to constitute gain.

A further problem with *animus lucrandi* is that it was not stated to be an essential requirement of theft in the definitions contained in the *Institutes* of Gaius and Justinian. It is arguable that the requirement of an intention to gain was not part of classical law, but that it was added in the time of Justinian to differentiate between theft and wrongful damage under the *lex Aquilia*. According to this argument, the passages in the *Digest* concerning intention to gain must be interpolated. But was not the need to distinguish between the two delicts just as acute in the classical period as in the late Empire? The requirement of *animus lucrandi* makes good sense—the most plausible view is that it was certainly part of late classical law. Why it was omitted from Justinian's *Institutes* remains unclear.

10.3.1.5 Theft of 'use' (*furtum usus*)

Theft could be committed not only by taking a thing dishonestly but also by unauthorized use of a thing belonging to someone else. In the latter case, the normal scenario was that the wrongdoer acquired the use of the thing lawfully (through a contract) but then stole the use by misusing the property. So if you lent a chariot to enable me to drive myself to the market to purchase groceries, and I used it instead to race in the arena, I committed theft if my conduct amounted to unauthorized use (however temporary) of the chariot. But unauthorized use could not amount to theft unless there was dishonest intent:

Pomponius, *Quintus Mucius, book 38*: **One who uses a thing which he has borrowed or which was deposited with him otherwise than on the terms on which he accepts it, will not be liable for theft, if he believe that he is not acting contrary to the owner's will.** ...(D.47.2.77pr.)

On theft of use, see Watson, A., 'D.47.2.52.20: the Jackass, the Mares and "Furtum" ' in *Studi Volterra* II, 445–9.

10.3.1.6 Theft of 'possession' (*furtum possessionis*)

If an owner of property dishonestly interfered with someone else's rights in that property, he committed theft—he had stolen the 'possession' of the property. The concept that a person could simultaneously be both the owner and the thief of the same property seems, *prima facie*, somewhat strange, but is one that can be readily justified in appropriate circumstances. For example, if A sold a thing to B which A had pledged to C as security, A committed theft. Theft of possession could occur only if the victim had a right *in rem* in the property. (See Thomas, J. A. C., 'Furtum Pignoris: A Commentary on Commentaries', in *Studi Sanfilippo* I, 585–600 and Van den Bergh, G. C. J. J., 'Custodia and Furtum Pignoris', in *Studi Sanfilippo* I, 601–14.)

10.3.2 Remedies

There were two types of civil remedy for theft: recovery of the stolen property, and the obtaining of damages. These remedies were cumulative, not mutually exclusive—a thief, if found liable, would have to return the property (or its equivalent) *and* pay damages, as a general rule (cf. Inst.Gai.4.4.).

10.3.2.1 Recovery of property

The standard proprietary remedies, i.e. *vindicatio*, the possessory interdicts, and in classical Roman law the *actio ad exhibendum* ('the action to display') were available against the thief or his heirs; or against anyone shown to be in possession of the stolen property, even if their possession had been acquired honestly, e.g. innocent third-party purchasers. The chief disadvantage of the *vindicatio* and the possessory interdicts was that they were not available if the stolen property could not be traced, or if it had lost its identity or had been destroyed. In such a case the *condictio furtiva* ('the action for stolen property') was allowed to the owner against the thief or his heir for recovery of the equivalent value. The *condictio* eventually became the most frequently used of these actions (assuming that the thief had been found) as it was not essential to prove the whereabouts of the property (compare D.13.1. and C.4.8. where this remedy is discussed in detail).

10.3.2.2 Damages

The action for damages was called the *actio furti* ('the action for theft'). It was a penal action in that the plaintiff could recover double or fourfold damages from the defendant, depending on the type of theft that had been committed, i.e. whether it was manifest theft or not. Additionally, the thief was subject to *infamia*. The potential sanctions were certainly onerous in the civil law, but the thief had first to be caught—that might not happen very frequently in a big city without an adequate police force. And, even if caught, the thief might not be worth suing.

(a) Manifest and non-manifest theft. The plaintiff could recover fourfold damages for manifest theft (*furtum manifestum*), twofold for non-manifest theft. Manifest theft was originally punished harshly under the Twelve Tables—a slave could be executed, a freeman could be enslaved by his victim. The praetors eventually replaced the original sanctions with the action for fourfold damages.

What was manifest theft? In early law it seems that the test was whether the thief had been caught in the act of stealing—if he had been, the theft would have been obvious, i.e. manifest. This may explain why manifest theft led to more severe sanctions than non-manifest theft: the former was considered more outrageous. If you catch someone burgling your home, your shock and sense of outrage will probably be much higher than if you discover the burglary after the bird has flown. Pugsley has controversially suggested that originally *furtum manifestum* consisted of the theft of *res mancipi*: the theft of such important property would be obvious in very early Rome (*Property and Obligations*, 28 ff.). In the classical period a wider test of manifest theft came to be applied:

Ulpian, *Sabinus, book 41*: **But is a thief manifest only if he be caught in the act or also if he be apprehended elsewhere? The better view is that which appears in the writings of Julian, that is to say, that although he be not taken at the scene of the offense, he will still be a manifest thief if he be taken with the stolen thing, before he has taken it to its intended destination.** (D.47.2.3.2.)

From this passage it seems that the timing of the arrest was crucial. If the thief was arrested after he had taken the property to his intended destination, the theft was no longer manifest, even if the thief was caught in possession. But an actual arrest was not always necessary—an attempted arrest might suffice in some circumstances:

Ulpian, *Sabinus, book 41*: **Celsus, though, on the issue of apprehension, adds that if, when you saw the thief in the act and ran to arrest him, he made his escape by discarding his loot, he would be a manifest thief.** (D.47.2.7.2.)

Moreover, it was manifest theft if stolen property was found in a man's premises following a ritual search. The ritual required that the searcher (presumably a male) should wear only a loincloth, and that he should carry a platter. The former requirement lessened the possibility of planting property on the premises, while the platter was possibly intended to carry an offering to the gods, at least in early times, or to provide a receptacle for the goods when found. This procedure, sanctioned by the Twelve Tables, became obsolete during the Republic. Gaius referred to it as an ancient practice, and as something of a joke—*'lex tota ridicula est'* (Inst. Gai.3.193a.).

(b) Measure of damages. What was it that was doubled or quadrupled under the *actio furti*? There is some inconsistency in the texts. Ulpian appears to take the view that it was the value of the property stolen:

Ulpian, *Edict, book 37*: **In the action for theft, it is not the plaintiff's interest which is quadrupled or doubled but the true value of the thing.** (D.47.2.50pr.)

However, this text is contradicted by other jurists, and even by Ulpian himself in the following passage:

Ulpian, *Edict, book 37*: **If a slave be stolen who has been named as heir in a will, the plaintiff, in the action for theft, will recover also the value of the inheritance, if the slave be dead before he could accept the estate at his master's direction....** (D.47.2.52.28.)

One can argue that there is no real conflict in these passages in that 'true value' surely encompasses 'the plaintiff's interest', but that is not what Ulpian appears to be saying in D.47.2.50pr. (see earlier). Moreover, the *formula* used in the *actio furti* suggests that what the plaintiff was seeking was double or quadruple the amount that the theft 'cost' him. Thus, the most probable view is that the measure of damages was the plaintiff's 'interest' in the stolen property, and not the property's value. Certainly, consequential loss resulting from the theft could be recovered if the measure of damages was based on the plaintiff's interest. For example:

Celsus, *Digest, book 12*: **If something be stolen from you which you had promised under penalty to deliver by a certain date with the result that you have to pay the penalty, that can be taken into the assessment in the action for theft.** (D.47.2.68.1.)

The plaintiff was entitled to the highest value that his interest had been worth between the theft and the trial. Thus, if the interest had depreciated after the theft, its value at the time of theft was taken into account, not its depreciated value. If the property appreciated in value, then it was the higher value to which the plaintiff was entitled.

(c) The plaintiff. Who could sue under the *actio furti*?

Ulpian, *Sabinus, book 29*: **A person who has an interest in the thing not being stolen will have the action for theft.** (D.47.2.10.) (cf. Inst.Gai.3.203.)

Behind this deceptively simple rule lie some difficulties. There were some persons who could not sue even though they could be reasonably said to have had 'an interest in the thing not being stolen'. For example, a creditor could not sue for theft of a thing from his debtor, unless it was pledged under the contract of *pignus* (see 9.5.4) (cf. Thomas, J. A. C., 'Furtum Pignoris' (1970) 38 TR, 135–62), even if there was no other effective security for the debt.

Who *did* have 'an interest in the thing not being stolen'? The jurists' approach was casuistic—they were content to list instances when someone could or could not bring the action, but they eschewed the formulation of general principles. However, it is possible to classify those entitled to sue as having either a positive or negative interest. A positive interest connotes that the plaintiff was owner, or in certain respects in the position of an owner, such as a bona fide possessor, or a usufructuary. The position of the usufructuary depended on which part of the usufruct was stolen. If the theft was of the fruits, then the usufructuary alone had the action (as long as he had gathered the fruits). But if the thief stole the actual property that was held on usufruct, the action was divided:

Ulpian, *Sabinus, book 42*: **If a fructuary slave be stolen, both the fructuary and the owner have the action for theft. The action is thus divided between fructuary and owner; the fructuary sues for twofold the value of the fruits or for his interest in the slave's not being stolen; the owner for his interest in his property not being stolen.** (D.47.2.46.1.)

A holder was said to have a negative interest, sufficient to enable him to bring the *actio furti*, if he had a contractual duty to compensate the owner for failure to return the property (such as the borrower, the *conductor operis*, and the mandatary). The owner was protected well: he had the proprietary remedies against the thief and was entitled to compensation from the holder for failure to return the property. However, if the holder sued the thief under the *actio furti*, the owner could not do so—the negative interest barred the positive interest. This appears to have given the holder of the negative interest an advantage if the theft was manifest: he could recover fourfold, whereas the owner recovered double, i.e. the thing (or its equivalent value) and the contractual compensation. But the holder had to find the thief.

What if the holder was insolvent? This made an important difference because in such a case the owner was unlikely to receive compensation from the holder. So the owner was given the *actio furti*:

Ulpian, *Sabinus, book 29*: **And so a fuller who accepts garments for cleaning and attention will always have the action because he is liable for their safekeeping. But if he should be insolvent, the action reverts to the owner; for nothing is at the risk of one who has nothing to lose.** (D.47.2.12pr.)

However, in the case of *commodatum* (see 9.5.2) Justinian altered the position. Whether the borrower was solvent or not, the lender was given the choice of suing the borrower under the contract of loan, or the thief under the *actio furti*. In the latter case, the borrower no longer had a negative interest (since he could not be sued under the contract) and thus could not proceed against the thief.

The position of a buyer before delivery of the goods was unusual in that he was strictly neither a positive nor a negative interest holder. Until delivery the seller remained owner, the buyer having only a contractual right—he did not have a positive interest. Nor did he satisfy the criteria necessary to be a negative interest holder, i.e. contractual liability for failure to return property. Thus, if the goods were stolen before the seller had delivered them, the right to sue remained in theory with the seller; but it seems that the buyer could insist on that right being assigned to him. And if the seller himself sued the thief, the buyer was entitled to the fruits of the action, i.e. whatever the seller recovered. For other exceptional cases, see Buckland, *Textbook*, 580.

The interest of the plaintiff, whether positive or negative, must have been acquired without fraud: it had to be 'honest'.

(d) The defendant. Who could be sued under the *actio furti*? The action lay against the thief but not against his heirs. Accomplices were fully liable; payment by one did not absolve the others. The basic rule was that an accomplice was someone who helped the thief by giving advice or physical assistance:

Ulpian, *Edict, book 37*: **A person is deemed to be an accomplice, as adviser, who persuades, directs, and, by instruction, gets the theft committed; a man gives assistance, who provides aid or assistance at the actual taking of the goods.** (D.47.2.50.3.)

It seems that originally both elements—physical assistance (*ops*) and advice (*consilium*)—had to be proved against the defendant accomplice, but in the classical period he became liable on either ground (see MacCormack, G., 'Ope Consilio Furtum Factum' (1983) 51 TR, 271–93 for a discussion on the origin of the distinction between theft and complicity as well as the criteria used to establish the latter). Moreover, the accomplice must have been shown to have acted dishonestly.

The *actio furti* could not be brought against family members for domestic thefts as domestic authority sufficed. Consequently, husband and wife could not sue one another for theft committed during marriage; but the praetors introduced a special action, the *actio rerum amotarum* ('the action for things taken away'), available after divorce for the recovery of compensation. It is possible that the action was confined to things that had been taken in contemplation of the divorce. Fathers and children-in-power could not sue each other for theft, except in respect of a son's acquisitions on military service. Nor could the *actio furti* be brought against other members of the household, e.g. slaves, or freedmen. However, in all these cases a theft had been committed; so, although no action was possible against the principal, an accomplice who was not part of the household could be sued.

10.3.2.3 Other remedies

A number of special actions, pre-classical in origin, were available in certain unusual circumstances (cf. Buckland, *Textbook*, 588 and Lee, *Elements*, 373–5). An act amounting to theft could constitute another delict, e.g. wrongful damage to property or insulting behaviour. In such cases the plaintiff would have to choose the most favourable action—he could not recover twice over (or more) in different actions. In the Empire, criminal prosecutions for theft became increasingly frequent under the *cognitio extraordinaria* procedure (see generally 3.4):

Ulpian, *Edict, book 38*: **It must be remembered that now criminal proceedings for theft are common and the complainant lays an allegation. It is not a kind of public prosecution in the normal sense, but it seemed proper that the temerity of those who do such wrongs should be punishable on extraordinary scrutiny. Still, if that be the party's wish, he can bring civil proceedings for theft.** (D.47.2.93.)

It seems that judgment in such proceedings barred the *actio furti*, and vice versa.

10.3.3 Robbery (*rapina*)

(Inst.Gai.3.209, Inst.4.2, D.47.8)

Damages under the *actio furti* were not affected by proof that the theft had been committed violently. However, a praetorian edict in 77 BC introduced a special action for violent theft (robbery)—the *actio vi bonorum raptorum* ('the action for goods violently taken'). It was a response to the mob violence of the disturbed conditions of the time, and was aimed particularly at the activities of armed gangs. In due course this action came to be treated as a separate delict, although in reality it was little more than an adjunct of theft. See Birks, *Obligations*, 188–91.

10.3.3.1 Essentials

Robbery shared many of the substantive principles of theft:

Ulpian, *Edict, book 56*: **And generally, it is to be said that wherever I could have the action for theft for something done by stealth, I will have the present action.** (D.47.8.2.23.)

There had to be a dishonest and forcible taking of property; if the taker acted in good faith, he was not liable. This rule appears to have exonerated those who violently enforced genuinely held claims. Not surprisingly, Marcus Aurelius decreed that bona fide claims should be forfeited if enforced in a violent manner. In the late Empire an unfounded bona fide claim, if pursued violently, would necessitate not only return of the property seized but also its equivalent value (cf. Buckland, *Textbook*, 584).

What degree of violence was required? The texts do not provide a clear answer. The most plausible view is that even a small amount of violence sufficed, whether committed by an armed mob or an unarmed man.

10.3.3.2 Remedies

Fourfold damages were recoverable, providing that the action was brought within a year. The value of the property that had been seized was included in the damages— the action was part compensatory (recovery of simple value), part penal (threefold penalty). If the plaintiff obtained fourfold damages, he was barred from bringing a proprietary remedy for recovery of the property seized. However, if he preferred, he could seek to recover the property and sue for threefold damages. If the action was brought after a year, only the simple value could be recovered. The measure of damages was based on the value of the property, not on the plaintiff's interest in it (unlike the case with theft). The action was available to the heir of the victim but not against the heir of the defendant.

Who could bring the *actio vi bonorum raptorum*?

Ulpian, *Edict, book 56*: ... **Hence, whether it be lent, let, or pledged to me, or deposited with me, so that I have an interest in its not being removed, or if I possess it in good faith or have a usufruct or other right in it, such that I have an interest in its not being forcibly taken, it must be said that I have the action under discussion** ... (D.47.8.2.22.)

The rule was thus identical to that in theft (see Inst.4.2.).

Robbery was tried by *recuperatores*, a body of lay jurors (see 3.2.2.3); condemnation involved *infamia*. Criminal proceedings were possible as an alternative, it seems, to the civil action. As regards civil proceedings, the plaintiff had a choice between the action for robbery and the *actio furti*. If the robbery amounted to a manifest theft, the *actio furti* would be more attractive since it was not limited to a year and gave fourfold damages plus recovery of the property or its value. Only if the violent theft had not been manifest would the action for robbery be generally preferable. If the plaintiff brought that action, it barred him from suing under the *actio furti*. But the converse did not necessarily apply:

Paul, *Edict, book 22*: **If the action for taking by force be brought first, the action for theft will be refused; but if the action for theft be brought first, the other will lie to recover the balance available.** (D.47.8.1.)

Thus, if the plaintiff brought the *actio furti* for a non-manifest violent theft, he could later bring the action for robbery to recover the balance to which he was entitled.

10.4 **Insulting behaviour**

(Inst.Gai.3.220.–5., Inst.4.3.2–3., 4.4pr., D.47.10., C.9.35.)

This delict consisted of an *iniuria*, which in this context meant any act that deliberately affronted the dignity of another person (cf. Frier, *Casebook on Delict*, 177–200 as well as Birks, *Obligations*, 221–46). In its developed form *iniuria* was of enormous scope, applicable to a wide range of human misconduct. But the essence was the hurting of another person by insulting behaviour (contumely), whether by acts or words:

Ulpian, *Edict, book 56*: **Labeo says that contumely can be perpetrated by act or by words: by act, when an assault is made; by words, there is insult whenever there is no physical attack. [2] Every contumely is inflicted on the person or relates to one's dignity or involves disgrace: It is to the person when someone is struck; it pertains to dignity when a lady's companion is led astray; and to disgrace when an attempt is made upon a person's chastity.** (D.47.10.1.1–2.)

10.4.1 **Historical development**

Iniuria was initially very narrow in scope (see Birks, P., 'The Early History of Iniuria' (1969) 37 TR, 163–208). The Twelve Tables laid down somewhat primitive penalties for various types of physical assault (see Du Plessis, P.J., 'An Infringement of the Corpus as a Form of Iniuria: Roman and Medieval Reflections', in *Iniuria and the Common Law*, 141–53). For a maimed limb, retaliation was allowed if the parties could not settle. For less serious assaults, a tariff system operated: 300 *asses* for the broken bone of a freeman; 150 for that of a slave; 25 for the least serious assaults (the *as* was a unit of currency) (see Watson, A., 'Personal Injuries in the XII Tables' (1975) 43 TR, 213–22; Halpin, A. K. W., 'The Usage of Iniuria in the Twelve Tables' (1976) 11 IJ, 344–54). The monetary penalties in the Twelve Tables remained unaltered and it seems likely that they eventually became worthless because of the falling value of money. Reform became a necessity. It appears to have been precipitated in the mid-Republic by a certain Lucius Veratius who highlighted the inadequacy of the law by a novel form of amusement—slapping people on the face, his slave immediately giving the victim 25 *asses* as compensation (see Aulus Gellius, *Noctes Atticae*, 20.1.10–13). The praetors issued a series of edicts that in effect superseded the Twelve Tables tariffs. They allowed the plaintiff an *actio in factum* in which he specified the precise nature of the defendant's misconduct, and claimed damages. The first of these edicts was possibly intended to apply only to the physical assaults comprised in the Twelve Tables (physical injuries to the body of a free man); but its terms were sufficiently wide to be extended to a much greater range of misconduct. It came to be known as the *edictum generale*, to distinguish it from later edicts that tended to deal with specific types of behaviour. The codified version of the edict produced during the reign of the Emperor Hadrian lists four cases in which an *actio iniuriarum* would be available. These included (a) assembling at another's house and raising an insulting and abusive clamour; (b) removing the companion or attendant from a married woman or youth and accosting such a person, thus making them vulnerable to attack; (c) any kind of defamation, not only libel; and (d) assaulting the slave of another without the permission of the owner. This widening of the scope of *iniuria*, and the introduction of the new action, constituted one of the most significant praetorian contributions to Roman law.

10.4.2 The essentials of *iniuria*

Iniuria occurred when a person intentionally upset the feelings of another by unjustifiable and insulting behaviour (see Plescia, J., 'The Development of "Iniuria" ', (1977) 23 Labeo, 271–89 as well as Ibbetson, D., 'Iniuria, Roman and English', in *Iniuria and the Common Law*, 33–45).

10.4.2.1 The insulting act

The plaintiff had to prove insulting behaviour on the part of the defendant. Illustrations from the *Digest* demonstrate the wide range of behaviour that was considered to be an affront to the dignity of the victim:

Ulpian, *Praetor's Edict, book 1*: **If a freeman be seized as being a runaway slave, the action for insult lies.** (D.47.10.22.)

Ulpian, *Edict, book 57*: **If, to annoy me, someone interrupt me in an insulting manner when speaking before some court, I can bring the action for insult.** (D.47.10.13.3.)

Ulpian, *Edict, book 57*: **If someone prevent me from fishing in the sea or from lowering my net . . . can I have the action for insult against him? There are those who think that I can. And Pomponius and the majority are of opinion that the complainant's case is similar to that of one who is not allowed to use the public baths or to sit in a theater seat or to conduct business, sit or converse in some other such place, or to use his own property; for in these cases too, an action for insult is apposite. . . . (D.47.10.13.7.)**

Ulpian, *Edict, book 77*: **The question is also raised by Labeo whether, if a person derange another's mind by a drug or some other means, the action for insult lies against him; and he says that it does.** (D.47.10.15pr.)

Among other forms of insulting behaviour described in the *Digest* we find: raising a tumult against a person; wrongfully appropriating another's assets; and falsely publicizing a debtor's inability to pay his debts (cf. Inst.Gai.3.220.). It could be *iniuria* to wear filthy clothes in some circumstances or to let the beard grow unkempt (see below). Sexual harassment of various forms constituted *iniuria*, e.g. making obscene advances, or following people about if done 'contrary to good morals': D.47.10.15.22–3. As a general rule, anything that lowered a person's reputation was *iniuria*:

Ulpian, *Edict, book 77*: **The praetor bans generally anything which would be to another's disrepute. And so whatever one do or say to bring another into disrepute gives rise to the action for insult. Here are instances of conduct to another's disrepute: to lower another's reputation, one wears mourning or filthy garments or lets one's beard grow or lets one's hair down or writes a lampoon or issues or sings something detrimental to another's honor.** (D.47.10.15.27.)

Defamation was actionable; indeed, it was the subject of a specific praetorian edict. That such an edict was required in the late Republic suggests that defamatory abuse had possibly become a problem in Roman society: the abuse of men in public life was common. But there is little evidence that the lampooning of public figures resulted in much litigation. If you were in the public eye, it would not be good form to sue everyone who was defaming you—a certain amount of abuse was to be expected and tolerated in public life, then as now. It was not essential to prove that the defamatory words had been published to a third party. The insult was enough: the delict was concerned primarily with hurt feelings rather than damaged reputations.

10.4.2.2 Insult must be unjustifiable

An insulting act was not actionable if it was considered justifiable. Consequently, an assault in the course of self-defence did not constitute *iniuria*; nor did defamatory words if they were true (but see Descheemaeker, E., '"Veritas non est defamatio?" Truth as a Defence in the Law of Defamation' (2011) 31 Legal Studies, 1–20); nor raising a tumult against a person in legal disgrace; nor indecent proposals to a prostitute or to a woman dressed as one. And acting in the execution of legal powers was not actionable (e.g. *manus iniectio*):

Ulpian, *Edict, book 57*: **A person who does something under the public law will not be treated as having done it with a view to affront; there is no wrong in the administration of the law.** (D.47.10.13.1.)

10.4.2.3 Intention

Iniuria required an intentional act: it could not be committed negligently. Further, the defendant must have intended to insult the plaintiff (presumably established from the facts of the case). In some cases, however, a plaintiff could sue for insulting behaviour that had not been directed at him personally.

(a) Children. An insult to a child-in-power enabled the *paterfamilias* to sue for the 'indirect' insult to himself as well as for the insult to the child. The child could have the action in certain circumstances, e.g. where the *paterfamilias* was unable or unwilling to bring the action:

Ulpian, *Edict, book 57*: **But we believe that the action for insult should sometimes be granted to the son even though the father waive the affront, for instance, if the father be vile and abject, while the son is a decent man; for a grossly debased father should not evaluate the insult to his son by the standards of his own turpitude.** (D.47.10.17.13.)

(b) Wives. A husband could sue for an insult to his wife; she too could sue, and so could her *paterfamilias*—insulting someone's wife was really best avoided as it could be a very costly business:

Ulpian, *Edict, book 56*: **. . . sometimes the action for insult will lie to three people in respect of the one affront, and the right of action of none will be consumed by reason of proceedings by one. Suppose that my wife who is a daughter-in-power be affronted; the action for insult forthwith becomes available to me, to her, and to her father.** (D.47.10.1.9.)

What of the converse case—could wives sue for insults to their husbands?

Paul, *Edict, book 50*: **But if a husband suffer affront, the wife does not have an action: for it is right that wives should be defended by their husbands but not husbands by their wives.** (D.47.10.2.)

Such reasoning might no longer find universal acclamation. Similar rules applied to the betrothed: fiancés could sue for insults to their fiancées, but not vice versa.

(c) Slaves. Could you insult a slave? Not really—how can a thing be insulted? However, as an exception (as mentioned in the codified version of the edict), the slave's master could bring an action for *iniuria* if, for example, the slave had been tortured or severely beaten, whether or not there had been any intent to insult the master (see 10.4.1). Moreover, the master could sue for less serious acts if they were intended to insult him. Ulpian summarizes the general rule as follows:

Ulpian, *Edict, book 77*: **If someone so inflict outrage upon a slave that it be done to his master, in my view the master can bring the action for insult in his own right; but if the beating was not directed to the master, the outrage perpetrated upon the slave as such should not be left unavenged by the praetor, especially if it occurred through a thrashing or through torture: for it is obvious that the slave himself feels such things.** (D.47.10.15.35.)

(d) Heirs. Improper behaviour at a funeral could amount to *iniuria*, as could showing disrespect for the dead, e.g. desecrating the deceased's grave. Such behaviour was regarded as insulting either to the heirs or to the inheritance, depending on the circumstances:

Ulpian, *Edict, book 56*: **Now whenever there be any affront at the testator's funeral or to his corpse, if it occur after the inheritance has been accepted, it must be said that in a sense, the insult is to the heir (for it is always the heir's obligation to vindicate the reputation of the deceased); but if it be before acceptance, the insult is rather to the inheritance itself and it is thus through the inheritance that the heir will acquire the action....** (D.47.10.1.6.)

10.4.2.4 Hurt feelings

The plaintiff had to prove that his feelings had been hurt, i.e. that he had actually been upset by the insult. If he had not been upset, he could not sue even though the defendant had intended to insult him. There had to be some evidence of hurt feelings:

Ulpian, *Edict, book 57*: **The action for insult is one based on what is good and equitable and will not lie in the event of dissimulation by the victim. For if someone ignore the affront, that is, as soon as he suffers it, he does not direct his mind to it, he cannot, on second thoughts, revive the affront which he let pass.** (D.47.10.11.1.)

Thus, if you wanted to sue, you must not have stifled your emotions, or adopted a 'stiff upper lip' attitude, or tried to negotiate a settlement with the wrongdoer when the insult occurred. In some exceptional situations, however, *iniuria* could occur even though the plaintiff was absent when the insulting behaviour took place, e.g. where a mob raised a tumult against someone who happened to be absent at the time. In such cases the plaintiff had to prove that he was upset when he learned of the offending behaviour. On this, see the fascinating chapter by Mitchell, P., 'Dissimulatio', in *Iniuria and the Common Law*, 97–117.

10.4.3 Remedies

10.4.3.1 The action for *iniuria*

The action (the *actio iniuriarum*) had to be brought within one year. This was hardly surprising—if the plaintiff took any longer, it could be argued that he was not particularly upset by the offending behaviour. A defendant who was found liable was subject to *infamia*. The action did not pass to or against the heirs of the parties

(D.47.10.13pr.). If two or more participants committed the insult, whether as principals or accomplices, the usual rule applied—each was fully liable:

Gaius, *Provincial Edict, book 13*: **If several slaves together beat someone or shout abuse at them, each commits his own offence and, the more of them there are, the greater is the affront. Indeed, there are as many insults as there are participants.** (D.47.10.34.)

The action had to be very specific in its allegations because of the subjective nature of the claim, (i.e. hurt feelings) and because of the gravity of the consequences for the defendant:

Ulpian, *Edict, book 57*: **In his edict, the praetor said: 'He who brings the action for insult must particularize what has been done that is affronting'; for one who brings an action which entails infamy should not be vague, at the peril of another's reputation, but should specify and set out in detail the affront that he claims to have suffered.** (D.47.10.7pr.)

How were damages assessed? How do you compensate someone for hurt feelings? Under the formulary procedure, the plaintiff would state in his *formula* the amount that he claimed. The praetor would normally indicate the maximum damages which could be allowed by the judge (or *recuperatores*), taking into account factors such as the gravity of the insult and the standing of the respective parties (see Inst. Gai.3.224.–5.). The court would make an appropriate reduction of the plaintiff's claim if it was considered excessive. In cases of aggravated insult (*atrox iniuria*) the praetor normally assessed the damages himself. An insult could be considered *atrox* if the person who was insulted was of important status (or one deserving respect); or if the nature of the insult was extreme; or if the place where the insult occurred was public or prestigious. The following passage suggests that *time* could be a factor that made an insult aggravated, but it is likely that it was the *concurrence* of time and place which was crucial:

Ulpian, *Edict, book 57*: **Labeo says that an affront may be aggravated by virtue of the person, the time, and its very nature. It is aggravated by virtue of the person, when inflicted on, say, a magistrate, one's parent, or patron; by reason of time, if inflicted at the games or in full view; for Labeo says that it is of great importance whether the affront be perpetrated in the view of the people or in private, the former being aggravated. Labeo says that it is aggravated by its very nature if, say, a wound be inflicted or someone receive a blow in the face.** (D.47.10.7.8.)

10.4.3.2 The *lex Cornelia*

The violence and unrest of the late Republic led to the passing of the *lex Cornelia de iniuriis* 81 BC, which provided a criminal process for certain types of insulting behaviour:

Ulpian, *Edict, book 56*: **The *lex Cornelia* on contumelies applies to one who wishes to bring the action for insult on the ground that he declares himself to have been beaten or thrashed or his house to have been entered by force.** (D.47.10.5pr.)

What was the relationship of the *lex Cornelia* to the action for insult? It is probable that the victim always had a choice whether to pursue the civil or the criminal remedy (they were mutually exclusive). It is not clear what the sanction was under the *lex Cornelia*, although Justinian refers to it as an 'extraordinary penalty' (possibly very severe) (Inst.4.4.10.). Since the prosecutor (i.e. the victim) kept the penalty, the most plausible view is that it consisted of a penal pecuniary award, exceeding the damages that would be awarded under the action for insult. This may explain why process under the *lex Cornelia* seems to have been the more popular option.

Moreover, the statute appears to have been extended in the classical period to include all insulting behaviour of a physical nature.

The 'named' delicts discussed thus far are all mentioned in the *Institutes* of Justinian, but they do not represent the full spectrum of delictual liability known to Roman law. Apart from these, other delictual relationships also existed in Roman law, though these seemingly did not fit neatly into the Institutional scheme. Some of these were remnants of early law found in the Twelve Tables (e.g. unlawfully cutting down another's trees), others were Praetorian or statutory inventions. Of these, the most important were Praetorian delicts and noxal liability for damage caused by animals.

10.5 Praetorian delicts

The praetorian delicts (not a Roman term) consisted of a variety of remedies of a delictual nature, introduced by the praetor to supplement the *ius civile*. Their description as 'praetorian' refers to remedies *created* by the praetors rather than merely extended by them (see Nicholas, *Introduction*, 222–3). The absence of the praetorian delicts from Justinian's basic classification of delicts is not a true reflection of their importance—more an indication of the perversity of the classification. The most important examples were the corruption of slaves, duress, and fraud. For others, see Buckland, *Textbook*, 597–8.

10.5.1 Corruption of slaves (*servi corruptio*)

(D.11.3., C.6.2.)

The praetor allowed an action for double damages against anyone who deliberately and fraudulently caused the deterioration of a slave, whether mental, physical, or moral (see Frier, *Casebook on Delict*, 222–6). This action potentially overlapped with the remedies under the *lex Aquilia*, see Buckland, *Textbook*, 595 as well as Du Plessis, P. J., 'Damaging a Slave', in *Judge and Jurist*, 157–65. Where the plaintiff had a choice (he could not bring both), he would probably prefer to sue under the action for corrupting slaves since damages were always double, even if the wrongdoer had admitted liability, unlike the case with the *lex Aquilia*.

What type of conduct 'corrupted' a slave? Broadly, anything which made the slave less valuable to his master:

Ulpian, *Edict, book 23*: One also makes a slave worse if one persuades him to commit an injury or theft, to run away, to incite another man's slave, to mismanage his *peculium*, to become a lover, to play truant, to practice evil arts, to spend too much time at public entertainments, or to become seditious; or if, by argument or bribe, one persuades a slave-agent to tamper with or falsify his master's accounts, or to confuse accounts entrusted to him; [Ulpian, *Edict, book 19*] [2]: or if one makes a slave extravagant or defiant; or persuades him to be debauched. (D.11.3.1.5.–D.11.3.2.)

What if the slave was 'bad' to start with, i.e. already corrupt? The action still lay, provided that the slave could be said to have been made worse by the defendant's conduct:

Ulpian, *Edict, book 23*: So whether one makes a good slave bad or a bad slave more so, one is held to have made him worse. (D.11.3.1.4.)

The defendant must have acted fraudulently, not just intentionally. It seems that in this delict 'fraudulently' meant acting with malice. The plaintiff could recover for the actual depreciation in the slave and for consequential loss. For example, if the slave stole as the result of being corrupted, his master (being liable for the theft) was entitled to take the theft into account when suing the corrupter:

Paul, *Edict, book 19*: **Accordingly, it is agreed that if you persuade my slave to steal from Titius, you are not only liable for the amount of harm done to the slave but also for what I have to give to Titius.** (D.11.3.14.6.)

The action for corrupting a slave lay in favour of the heirs of the plaintiff, but not against the heirs of the defendant. There was no time limit on the action, and it seems that the action survived the death of the slave, or his sale or manumission.

10.5.2 **Duress (*metus*)**

(D.4.2., D.44.4.)

Where someone incurred loss (or potential loss) by being forced to enter a transaction or to commit some disadvantageous act, several remedies were available (see Frier, *Casebook on Delict*, 213–21). The victim could plead the duress as a defence (*exceptio metus*) against the enforcement of the transaction; or, if the transaction had been completed or the damaging act had occurred, he could seek *restitutio* to restore him to the position before the duress. That would normally entitle him to recover any property that had been transferred involuntarily, together with fruits.

Moreover, the praetors allowed the victim a delictual action, the *actio metus*, for damages if the defendant failed to make restitution. Fourfold damages were awarded if the action was brought within a year; simple damages otherwise. It was not possible to bring the action after a year unless the plaintiff could show that he had no other remedy. The damages were assessed as a multiple of what should have been restored, including any consequential loss (see Bauman, R. A., 'The Rape of Lucretia, "Quod Metus Causa" and the Criminal Law' (1993) 52 Latomus, 550–66). However, the plaintiff had to show that he had acted to his detriment. If there had been no loss, there could be no action:

Ulpian, *Edict, book 11*: **Julian says that a person who brings force to bear on his debtor in order to make the latter pay him is not liable under this edict on account of the nature of the action which requires loss on the ground of duress**...(D.4.2.12.2.)

In the above case the debtor cannot bring the *actio metus* because he has not suffered any loss—he paid what he had to pay. However, creditors who exercised duress on their debtors could forfeit their claims under legislation introduced in the late Republic. As a *general* rule, however, no remedy was allowed for duress if it was justifiably exercised, e.g. where a magistrate threatened punishment in the proper execution of his duties.

What kind of threats amounted to duress?

Ulpian, *Edict, book 11*: **Labeo says that duress is to be understood not as any alarm whatever but as fear of a serious evil.** [Gaius, *Provincial Edict, book 4*] **[6]: Moreover, we say that the duress relevant to this edict is not that experienced by a weak-minded man but that which reasonably has an effect upon a man of the most resolute character.** (D.4.2.5–6.)

The test was objective—that of the man of 'most resolute character' (*vir constan-tissimus*). 'Fear of serious evil' comprised threats of death or serious physical harm, enslavement, exposure to a capital charge, and of sexual assault. The threat need not necessarily be directed at the complainant: it was sufficient if it was directed against his children:

Paul, *Edict, book 11*:...it makes no difference whether someone fears for himself or for his children, since their affections make parents prone to terror more with regard to their children than themselves. (D.4.2.8.3.)

Threats to other close members of the family probably sufficed, although textual evidence for this is inconclusive. The threat of harm had to be imminent. Thus, if you abandoned your house on hearing armed men approaching, that was probably not duress; but it would be if you left after they had forced an entry—a 'most resolute' man would not flee at least until that moment.

An unusual feature of the action for duress was that it could be brought in some circumstances against an innocent party:

Ulpian, *Edict, book 11*: In this action, no inquiry is made as to whether it was the defendant who used duress or someone else. For it suffices that the plaintiff shows that duress or force was brought to bear on him and that the person sued on account of the affair has made a gain although he has committed no offense....(D.4.2.14.3.)

In such cases the defendant was liable to the extent of his enrichment. He could, of course, escape the fourfold penalty by returning the profit before the proceedings. In accordance with the usual rule, the heirs of the plaintiff could sue but the heirs of the defendant could not be sued, except to the extent of any enrichment. And where there were joint wrongdoers, each was liable in full; however, if one of them satisfied the plaintiff's claims, the others were released—a departure from the normal rule.

Modern codes retain elements of the Roman rules of *metus* but with substantial variations. For example, in French and German law duress is a ground for rescinding a contract but not for fourfold damages. Under the *Code Civil* the test of duress is whether a *'personne raisonnable'*—and not the *vir constantissimus*—would fear his person or property being exposed to considerable harm (the age, sex, and condition of the person are taken into account): Article 1112. The BGB eschews any test about the resoluteness of the victim of the duress, and simply provides the remedy of rescission for anyone who has been subjected to unlawful threats: s. 123. Both these provisions have been interpreted as encompassing economic duress. See Zimmermann, *Obligations*, 658 ff.

10.5.3 Fraud (*dolus*)

(D.4.3., C.2.20.)

Let Ulpian introduce this delict for us:

Ulpian, *Edict, book 11*: By this edict the praetor affords relief against shifty and deceitful persons who by a certain cunning have harmed others, so as to prevent either their wickedness benefiting the former or their simplicity harming the latter. (D.4.3.1pr.)

This delict had an enormous potential range, as the *Digest* illustrates. For example, it included fraud perpetrated in business and commerce; falsely supporting someone's claim to freedom; destroying a will after the death of the testator; and the following unacceptable behaviour:

Ulpian, *Sabinus, book 42*: **Where you have allowed me to take stone from your land or dig for clay or sand and I have incurred expense on this account and then you do not allow me to remove anything, no action other than that for fraud will lie.** (D.4.3.34.)

The remedies for fraud were similar to those for duress. The victim of fraud could plead an *exceptio doli* as a defence against a plaintiff seeking to enforce a fraudulent transaction. As plaintiff, the victim could seek *restitutio*, failing which he could bring the *actio doli*. The action lay for simple damages, and had to be brought within a year. If found liable, the defendant was subject to *infamia*. (See MacCormack, G., 'Roman Jurisprudence and Interpretation: on Dolus as Ground of the Classical Actio de Dolo', in *Ricerche Gallo*, 539–60. cf. Frier, *Casebook on Delict*, 202–12.)

The gravity of the charge of fraud, and its consequences, restricted the use of the *actio doli*. It was not allowed except in the case of serious and manifest deceit; and the plaintiff had to show that he had no other remedy. To that extent the potentially wide range of *dolus* was illusory—the action was brought only as a last resort. For example, it would not be available for fraud arising out of a contract if a contractual remedy existed, as was often the case. What if another remedy existed, but was barred by lapse of time? The *actio doli* did not lie (as the plaintiff had himself to blame) unless the lapse of time had itself been brought about by fraudulent conduct.

Because of the gravity of the allegation, certain categories of individuals could not be sued under the *actio doli*:

Ulpian, *Edict, book 11*: **Moreover, it will not be given to certain persons, for example children or freedmen against parents or patrons, since it involves *infamia*. Nor ought it to be given to a man of low rank against someone of higher rank, for example, to a plebeian against a man of consular rank possessing acknowledged authority or to a man of licentious or spendthrift or other worthless habits against a man of more correct behavior....** (D.4.3.11.1.)

Here we have a vivid reminder of the type of paternalism sometimes found in Roman society. The 'worthy' man is being protected: his 'inferior' cannot sue him for fraud, because it is a rather nasty action. However, the plaintiff was not necessarily without a remedy in such a case. An *actio in factum* for damages might be given to him by the praetor, under which the defendant's reputation would survive largely intact since the *formula* of the action omitted any reference to fraud. *Infamia* did not result in such a case—a satisfactory result all round in Roman eyes.

The action for fraud could only be brought against the wrongdoer, not against his heirs or any third parties; but the action survived for the benefit of the heirs of the plaintiff. Although joint wrongdoers were each fully liable, restitution or payment by one was deemed to release the others.

Certain types of fraud were the subject of special actions outside the scope of the *actio doli* (see Buckland, *Textbook*, 596–7). For example, if a debtor deliberately diminished his assets in order to disadvantage his creditors, an action was given to the creditors to nullify the debtor's acts. It could be brought against the debtor or anyone who had acquired from him with knowledge of the fraud, or even innocently (if the acquisition had been gratuitous). If a freedman disposed of his assets with the intention of reducing his patron's rights of inheritance, an action was allowed to the patron. It could only be brought after the freedman's death, and was available against any donee, however innocent:

Ulpian, *Edict, book 44*: **But every transaction carried out with a view to defrauding a patron is voidable.** (D.38.5.1.3.)

Medieval lawyers drew a distinction between fundamental and incidental fraud, based on a controversial text (D.4.3.7pr.). The former was fraud which had induced a party to enter a transaction (which was thus invalidated). Incidental fraud, on the other hand, related to a specific element or term of the transaction. It did not invalidate the transaction, but the innocent party would be entitled to some form of compensation. The distinction was incorporated into the French Civil Code (Articles 1116–17) and survives in South African law, but not in the BGB. See Zimmermann, *Obligations*, 670 ff.

The term 'noxal liability' referred to the liability which attached itself to the *paterfamilias* for delicts committed by sons-in-power. It also extended to delicts committed by slaves. The *paterfamilias* or owner of the slave either had to pay compensation or surrender the perpetrator into debt bondage (see Inst.4.8). cf. Thomas, *Textbook*, 381–2. This form of liability seemingly also extended to damage caused by animals. See Nicholas, *Introduction*, 224.

10.6 Liability for damage caused by animals

We are concerned here with damage caused *by* animals, rather than *to* animals. And it is not just domestic animals and cattle that are in issue: from the late Republic large numbers of exotic animals were imported to Rome, partly to satisfy the Roman passion for spectacle and games. While many of these animals were slaughtered for the amusement of the public, some would find a home with a private owner—from which they sometimes escaped.

Liability for the acts of animals could arise in various ways. If the defendant was at fault he might incur liability under the standard delicts, e.g. insulting behaviour or wrongful damage to property. Encouraging a dog to perform its natural functions on another's property could well amount to insulting behaviour if the required intention was present. And if, for example, a mule driver failed to control his mules, with the result that they trampled over someone, the driver would be liable under the *lex Aquilia* (see 10.2.4.2). The defendant could be anyone who was at fault, not necessarily the owner. Moreover, liability for wrongful grazing on another's land lay under the *actio de pastu*, a Twelve Tables remedy that appears to have survived the *lex Aquilia*.

What if no one was at fault? Depending on the circumstances, a choice of two actions might be available to the victim. Though liability was strict in both these actions, they were largely delictual in character and in consequences, and can be conveniently dealt with here (cf. Buckland, *Textbook*, 599–603).

10.6.1 *Actio de pauperie*

(Inst.4.9., D.9.1.)

Ulpian, *Edict, book 18*: **In cases where a four-footed animal is alleged to have committed** *pauperies,* **a right of action is derived from the** *Twelve Tables,* **which statute provides that that which has caused the offense (that is, the animal which caused harm) should be**

handed over or that pecuniary damages should be offered for the amount of the harm done. (D.9.1.1pr.)

Pauperies meant damage that was caused by an animal in circumstances where no one was at fault (cf. Frier, *Casebook on Delict*, 138–45). The action was based on the notion of noxal liability. The owner had to compensate for the loss caused, or had to surrender the animal. It seems that surrender could be demanded in early law, but later damages came to be regarded as the more appropriate remedy (as in the case of noxal liability in the law of persons). There appears to have been a require-ment that the animal must have acted contrary to its nature:

Ulpian, *Edict, book 18:* . . . **if a horse kicks out because it is upset by pain, this action will not lie. . . . But if the horse kicked someone who was stroking it or someone who was patting it, this action will be available.** (D.9.1.1.7.)

From this it appears that the action was not available in respect of animals wild by nature—unpredictable behaviour by them could hardly be classed as contrary to nature. But consider the following passage (also by Ulpian) concerning the action:

Ulpian, *Edict, book 18*: **But it does not lie in the case of beasts which are wild by nature: there-fore, if a bear breaks loose and so causes harm, its former owner cannot be sued because he ceased to be owner as soon as the wild animal escaped. . . .** (D.9.1.1.10.)

The implication of the phrase 'because he ceased to be the owner' is that there could be liability, in some circumstances, if the animal did not escape, i.e. that there was liability for damage caused by wild animals during their captivity. Such apparent inconsistencies raise a suspicion of interpolation. The most plausible view is that the 'contrary to nature' requirement was a post-classical development, and that the action was previously available in respect of animals both tame and wild by nature. The action was not available where animals had been provoked or had acted out of self-defence.

The action lay for simple damages only, yet it was considered to be penal. Consequently, it did not lie against the heirs of the owner but did survive in favour of the heirs of the victim.

For an in-depth analysis of this action and its place in Roman law, see the excel-lent recent work by Polojac, M., *Actio de Pauperie and Liability for Damage Caused by Animals in Roman Law* (2003).

10.6.2 **Edict of the aediles**

(D.21.1.)

Ulpian, *Curule Aediles' Edict, book 2:* . . . **'No one is to have a dog, any wild boar, wolf, bear, panther, lion,** [Paul, *Curule Aediles' Edict, book 2*] **[41]: and generally any dangerous animal, whether at large or so bound or chained that it did not inflict harm** [Ulpian, *Curule Aediles' Edict, book 2*] **[42], where there is frequent traffic and it might injure someone or cause dam-age. The penalty for any contravention of this provision is, if a freeman's death result from it, two hundred *solidi*; if a freeman be said to have been injured, what a judge regards as right and proper; in all other cases, double the value of the damage done.'** (D.21.1.40–2.)

This provision is mentioned in the *Digest* as a brief aside from the detailed consid-eration of the aediles' edict on the sale of animals. Liability was imposed where the animal was kept on or near a public highway (cf. Frier, *Casebook on Delict*, 146–8). The keeper of the animal that caused the damage was liable, irrespective of fault.

Public policy lay behind this provision: if you chose to keep a dangerous animal near a highway, you did so at your peril.

The Roman rules, especially those on *pauperies*, have influenced modern law in various degrees (although noxality has been largely abandoned). For example, s. 833 BGB imposes strict liability (with some exceptions) on the keeper of an animal that kills or injures a person, or damages property. In South Africa, the aedilitian edict has been applied in the case of an ostrich bitten to death by a dog, and the *actio de pastu* and *actio de pauperie* are still applied in their uncodified form. The 'contrary to nature' principle has provoked much controversy as to whether a subjective or an objective test is appropriate. Some cases have held that for liability to be incurred the animal must have acted differently from what was expected of a well-behaved animal of the same kind: 'What this boils down to, effectively, is the judicial creation of the "reasonable cow" or the "reasonable duck" as a criterion to determine the owner's liability' (Zimmermann, *Obligations*, 1116 and generally 1108 ff.).

10.7 Quasi-delict

(Inst.4.5.)

This designation comprised a group of actions of no obvious similarity, yet classified by Justinian as analogous to delictual obligations. For an interesting hypothesis regarding the internal coherence of this category, see Descheemaeker, *Division*, chs. 3–4. There were four such cases.

10.7.1 Things hung or suspended

(D.9.3.)

Ulpian, *Edict, book 23*: **The praetor says: 'No one shall place anything on an eave or projecting roof over a spot where the public pass or congregate which would injure anyone if it fell. If anyone is in breach of this regulation, I will grant an** *actio in factum* **against him for ten** *solidi*'. (D.9.3.5.6.)

In this situation, an action could be brought by anyone against the occupier of the building, even if he was totally blameless, the purpose being to *prevent* harm—the action lay even though no damage had occurred. The occupier, if found liable, had to pay a fixed fine. If the suspended thing actually fell and caused damage, there could be liability under the *lex Aquilia* if the person who had placed or suspended the thing had acted negligently. The action for *res suspensae* did not lie against the heirs of the defendant. For a summary of the relevant texts, see Frier, *Casebook on Delict*, 228–32.

10.7.2 Things poured or thrown

(D.9.3.)

Ulpian, *Edict, book 23*: **If anything should be thrown out or poured out from a building onto a place where people commonly pass and repass or stand about, I will grant an action to be brought against whoever lives there for double the damage caused or done as a result. If** it is alleged that a freeman was killed by whatever fell, I will grant an action for fifty *aurei*. If he is alleged to be injured, but survives, I will grant an action for whatever it seems right to the judge that the defendant should be condemned to pay. (D.9.3.1pr.) (cf. Inst.4.5.1.)

A praetorian edict introduced this action, imposing strict liability on the occupier of premises (for twice the value of the loss caused), even if he was absent when the wrongful act occurred. An occupier could seek to recover the damages that he had paid from the actual wrongdoer. If it could be proved who did the throwing or pouring, the person responsible might incur liability under the *lex Aquilia*. If a freeman was killed, there could be a number of potential plaintiffs as the action in such a case was *popularis*, i.e. open to informers. Preference would be given, however, to the victim's relatives or to those with a special interest in the matter. (See Stein, P. G., 'The Actio de Effusis vel Dejectis and the Concept of Quasi-Delict in Scots Law' (1955) 4 ICLQ, 356–75.) See also Frier, *Casebook on Delict*, 228–32.

10.7.3 Shippers, innkeepers, stablekeepers

(D.4.9., compare D.47.5.)

Ulpian, *Edict, book 14*: **The praetor says: 'I will give an action against seamen, innkeepers and stablekeepers in respect of what they have received and undertaken to keep safe, unless they restore it.' [1] This edict is of the greatest benefit, because it is necessary generally to trust these persons and deliver property into their custody.** (D.4.9.1pr.–1.)

Liability under this edict lay in respect of theft or damage committed by the employees of shippers, innkeepers, and stable keepers. In addition, innkeepers were liable for the acts of permanent residents, but not casual guests or travellers. The distinction was justified, according to Ulpian, in that the innkeeper was regarded as choosing his permanent residents, but not passing travellers (D.47.5.1.6.). We are concerned here with vicarious rather than strict liability: the defendant cannot be regarded as without fault if he has employed persons who steal or damage property that has been entrusted to him. The action lay for double the loss that was caused. It survived for the benefit of heirs but not against them. The plaintiff might have alternative actions available to him (e.g. for theft or wrongful damage to property) if the actual wrongdoer could be identified. Or there might be a contractual remedy under *receptum* (see 9.8.2.2). Mackintosh, J., '*Nautae caupones stabularii*: Special Liabilities of Shipmaster, Innkeepers, and Stablers' (1935) 47 JR, 54 ff.; Bogen, D. S., 'Ignoring History: The Liability of Ships' Masters, Innkeepers and Stablekeepers under Roman Law' (1992) 36 AJLH, 326 ff. See also Frier, *Casebook on Delict*, 233–6.

10.7.4 Erring judges

(D.44.7.)

A judge could be sued *si litem suam fecerit*—'if he made the case his own', i.e. if he acted in a partial manner, and not as a judge. The development of this rule in early law owed much to the absence of a general system of appeals. It allowed some recourse against a judge who had reached a perverse verdict: he was liable for the loss he had caused thereby. The judge's liability was not founded on supposed errors in reasoning, since the nature of the Roman trial did not require the judge to reveal any more than his (oral) decision. Instead, his liability was based on his visible handling of the trial. (See MacCormack, G., 'The Liability of the Judge in the Republic and Principate' (1982) 14 ANRW II, 3–28; Birks, P., 'A New Argument for a Narrow View of Litem Suam Facere' (1984) 52 TR, 373–87; Robinson, O. F., 'The Iudex Qui Litem Suam Fecit Explained' (1999) 116 ZSS (rA), 195–9; Robinson, O. F., 'Justinian and the Compiler's View on the Iudex Qui Litem Suam Fecit', in *Status Familiae* 389–96.) The judge might also be subject to a criminal sanction, e.g. taking bribes was a capital offence under the Twelve Tables.

The erring judge had to pay whatever the plaintiff had lost through the perverse judgment. What degree of blame was required of the judge? In early law, it seems that the judge was liable only for giving a deliberately wrong judgment; but later, negligence sufficed. It is possible even that strict liability was imposed in the classical period: the judge was liable for *any* wrong judgment. But the texts are inconclusive. Gaius suggests that at least some degree of blame was required:

Gaius, *Golden Words, book 3*: **If a judge has made a cause his own, he does not, properly speaking, seem to be liable in delict, but because he was not found in contract either, yet surely is considered to have done wrong in some way, albeit through imprudence, he is regarded as liable in quasi-delict.** (D.44.7.5.4.)

The operation of this quasi-delict in practice remains a matter of some speculation. For example, it is not clear which criteria were applied in deciding whether a judgment was perverse or wrong, especially in the absence of a proper appeal system until the later Empire. See Frier, *Casebook on Delict*, 237–8.

10.7.5 A common link?

It is difficult to find a satisfactory explanation why Justinian classified these cases as a separate group. Strict liability has been suggested as the common link; so has vicarious liability. But neither suggestion is convincing. Perhaps a more satisfactory approach is to view these quasi-delicts as situations where the defendant has been *entrusted* with the 'safety' of a thing (cf. Descheemaeker, *Division*, 99). The judge is entrusted with the safety of the case he is trying; the innkeeper with the safety of the property of guests at the inn; the occupier with the safety of his home. Admittedly, in the last case the concept of entrusting has to be stretched somewhat; nevertheless, it can be viewed as a form of public duty that occupiers should ensure the safety of their premises—the occupiers are 'entrusted' with making them safe.

The notion of responsibility for the safety of things as a basis for delictual or quasi-delictual liability can be found in Article 1384 of the *Code Civil*: a person is liable not only for damage caused by his own acts but also for that caused by the acts of persons for whom he is responsible, or by things in his keeping. This provision has been interpreted as encompassing strict liability, apart from damage caused by overwhelming force. See Zimmermann, *Obligations*, 1141–2, and generally on quasi-delict in modern law, 1126 ff.

 online resource centre   Please consult the Online Resource Centre for revision guidance on this chapter.

FURTHER READING

See Bauman, R. A., 'The Interface of Greek and Roman Law: Contract, Delict and Crime' (1996) 43 RIDA 3, 39–62 for an interesting discussion on delict and crime.

On the *Lex Aquilia*, see the comprehensive bibliography in *Roman Statutes* II, 723. See also Lawson, F. H. and Markesinis, B. S. (1982), *Tortious Liability for Unintentional Harm in the Common Law and the Civil Law*, Cambridge: Cambridge University Press.

On the early history of theft, see Daube, D., 'Furtum Proprium and Furtum Improprium' (1938) 6 Cambridge LJ, 217–34; Watson, A., 'Si Adorat Furto', (1975) 21 Labeo, 193–6; and Pugsley, D., 'Furtum in the XII Tables' (1969) 4 IJ, 139–52.

On the *contrectatio* requirement in theft, see, for a comparative perspective, Cohen, B., 'Contrectatio in Jewish and Roman Law', in *Mélanges de Visscher*, 133–56; Watson, A., 'Contrectatio as an Essential of Furtum' (1961) 77 LQR, 526–32; Thomas, J. A. C., 'Contrectatio, Complicity and Furtum' (1962) 13 IVRA, 70–88; by the same author, 'Contrectatio—My Last Word' (1963) 14 IVRA, 180–5; Nicholas, B., 'Theophilus and Contrectatio', in *Studies J. A. C. Thomas*, 118–24.

On the *animus furandi*, see Thomas, J. A. C., 'Animus Furandi' (1968) 19 IVRA, 1–32; Birks, P., 'The Case of the Filched Pedigree: D.47.2.52.20', in *Sodalitas* II, 731–48 and Pugsley, D., 'Animus Furandi', in *Sodalitas* V, 341–55.

PART V

Roman Law and
the Modern World

11

Roman law and the European
ius commune

The influence of Roman law in the modern world has been immense: it constitutes the historical and conceptual basis of many legal systems throughout the world. Its impact has not been confined to those countries in Western Europe that historically formed part of the Roman Empire. Wherever Europeans settled, they normally took their law (usually based to some extent on the principles of Roman law) with them. And some countries, although not witnesses to European settlement, adopted legal codes that were largely based on Roman-law principles. As for those countries with systems derived from the English common law, they too have not been untouched by the influence of Roman law. For a good recent overview, see Zimmermann, R., 'Roman Law in the Modern World', in *Cambridge Companion*, 452–80.

Given the importance of law as a fundamental element of an enlightened community, the contribution of Roman law to modern civilization is all embracing. It is not just in the concepts, substantive rules, and doctrines of law that the influence of Roman law has been felt, but also in civil procedure and technique, particularly as regards the classification of law and the science of casuistic analysis. The lawyer with a grasp of the fundamentals of Roman law has a passport to the understanding of the law and legal systems of many countries. For Roman law has twice in the past fulfilled the function of a *ius commune*—the communal law of a large part of the world. The first time, at the height of the Roman Empire when 'all the world was Rome' and Roman law was used (at least in theory) in all the provinces of the Empire extending over the greater part of Western Europe and North Africa. Although this Empire was destined to disintegrate over time, Roman law would prove to be one of its most enduring legacies. The second life of Roman law as a *ius commune* began at the end of the eleventh century. With the scientific rediscovery of Roman law in Italy and its transformation and adaptation by Italian and French jurists during the next two centuries, medieval learned law (a combination of Roman and canon law interspersed with local custom) rose to become the *ius commune* of late-medieval Europe. See Coing, H., 'The Roman Law as Ius Commune on the Continent' (1973) 89 LQR, 505–17 as well as Mayali, L., 'The Legacy of Roman Law', in *Cambridge Companion*, 374–95. This does not mean that there was a single homogenous body of law extending across Western Europe during this period. Nothing could be further from the truth. The term European *ius commune* (in its historical sense) merely signifies that, from the fourteenth to the start of the sixteenth centuries, most of Europe shared a common legal tradition. Many local and regional variations on the law existed, but the terminology, concepts and structure provided by elements of Roman law provided a common framework.

Numerous instances of the continuing application and influence of the principles of Roman law in modern legal systems have already been mentioned. It is the aim of this final chapter to trace how it was that Justinian's codification came to influence the modern world.

11.1 The legacy of Justinian's codification in the Dark Ages

11.1.1 The Eastern Empire

The administrative separation of the Roman Empire began during the reign of Diocletian (AD 284–305) and was formalized in AD 395. During the course of the fourth and fifth centuries, two distinct empires emerged which steadily drifted apart in constitutional, administrative, and theological matters. With the fall of the Western Empire in AD 476, the centre of power, which had long since ceased to be Rome, shifted to Constantinople (later called Byzantium) on the Bosphorus, by then the capital of the Eastern Empire. Although the inhabitants of this Empire continued to regard themselves as Romans, the *lingua franca* was Greek and strong cultural influences from Greece and the Near East steadily transformed it into the Byzantine Empire. And on this, see Stolte, B., 'The Law of New Rome: Byzantine Law', in *Cambridge Companion*, 355–73.

The history of Byzantine law is generally divided into three periods: the sixth century to the start of the ninth century; the ninth century to the start of the thirteenth century; and from then until the fall of Byzantium in 1453. Although later Byzantine law (apart from the *Corpus Iuris Civilis*) as such did not have a direct influence on the emergence of the *ius commune* in Western Europe, its literature, which became available in Western Europe only after the fall of Byzantium in the mid-fifteenth century, had a profound impact on the study of Roman law, especially in the works of the French legal humanists of the sixteenth century (see 11.2.3.1).

In the sixth century, Byzantine legal science rose to prominence as a result of Justinian's legislative endeavours. The foundation of law schools throughout the Eastern Empire, in which parts of this new codification were actively taught and studied, contributed to the emergence of a sophisticated legal culture. Although Justinian had prohibited commentaries on his codification, translations, and brief summaries were allowed. His instructions were not sufficiently clear, however, to prevent attempts to make the codification more accessible to the predominantly Greek-speaking citizens of the Byzantine Empire. These commentaries, such as the Greek paraphrase of Justinian's *Institutes* by Theophilus, were mainly prepared by academic jurists from the law schools of the East. The *Digest*, regarded as a difficult text even in Justinian's reign, faded from use in its original form soon after his death, if not before; but it proved ripe for both private and official abridgements.

Following the death of Justinian in the mid-sixth century, the standard of Byzantine legal science inevitably declined. Large parts of the reconquered West (including Italy) were again lost to the 'barbarians' and the boundaries of the Byzantine Empire receded. Many of the law schools set up during the sixth century closed down and the teaching of law came to be handled largely by advocates whose interests lay in legal practice rather than legal science. This process of decline continued until the mid-seventh century. By this time, the existence of numerous abridgements and translations of Justinian's codification, combined with a legal culture dominated by legal practice, had caused uncertainty about the state of the law. In an attempt to provide clarity, efforts were made to restate the law. These culminated in the enactment in *c.* AD 741 of the *Ecloga Legum* ('Select Passages') during the reign of the Emperor Leo III. This work was a summary of the major parts of Justinian's codification, but containing some amendments of the law, e.g. mothers were allowed to exercise *potestas* over children in certain circumstances. It was intended mainly for use by practitioners, who generally could not cope with the complexity of the original codification. Apart from the *Ecloga legum*, attempts were made to restate other areas of the law and various unofficial codes such as the Military Code, the Farmers' Code, and the Rhodian Maritime Code were produced during the eighth century.

The ninth century witnessed a renewed interest in the codification of Justinian as the foundation of Byzantine law. This was partly fuelled by successive Byzantine rulers' reinforcement of the popular notion that the Byzantine Empire was a continuation of the Roman Empire. Thus, attempts were made through compilations such as the *Eisagoge* (also known as the *Epanagoge*) (*c.* AD 885) and its revised form, the *Procheiros Nomos* (compiled during the tenth century) to adapt Justinianic law to the circumstances of the period and to eliminate obsolete elements. However, by far the most important work emanating from this period was the *Basilica* ('Imperial Books'), started by the Emperor Basil I but completed in *c.* AD 890 by his son, Leo the Wise. This was a Greek paraphrase of Justinian's codification, issued as one work in 60 books. It represented a significant achievement in a period that witnessed a revival of intellectual standards in the Byzantine Empire and an attempt to emulate some of the achievements of the past. The aim was to make Justinian's codification more serviceable by arranging the material in a more orderly manner, by excising obsolete laws, and by giving the work a greater sense of unity and harmony. Leo claimed that the *Basilica* contained no contradictions or obsolete material—a familiar claim—but he was wrong. Nevertheless, the work was an impressive achievement, making Justinian's codification more accessible to the practitioner. The *Basilica* was intended as an aid in interpreting Justinian but became so popular that it acquired great authority in its own right. In due course it came to be regarded as too unwieldy and difficult for everyday use. Epitomes were regularly made of it, themselves the object of further epitomes such as the *Hexabiblos* ('Six Books') of 1345. Through such works a form of Roman law (inevitably distorted) survived the collapse of the Eastern Empire in 1453 and remained as the law of the Greek-speaking areas until this century. See Lawson, F. H., 'The Basilica' (1930) 46 LQR, 486–501 and continued in (1931) 47 LQR, 536–56.

The final period of Byzantine legal history, from the thirteenth to the mid-fifteenth century is again characterized by a decline in Byzantine legal standards brought about largely by the unsettled political climate of the period. The borders of the Byzantine Empire were gradually retreating under pressure from various neighbouring forces (both Christian and Muslim) and the sacking of Byzantium in 1204 during the fourth crusade signalled the beginning of the end. The reasons for this invasion were largely political. The Venetian Republic, formally still a vassal of Byzantium, but seeking its independence and access to Byzantine trade routes, financed the fourth crusade in the hope that it would lead to the destruction of the Byzantine Empire. The Church of the West happily obliged since it: 'hardly even saw [the Byzantine Empire] as a part of Christendom, given a century and a half of schisms between the Churches' (Roberts, *History*, 183). When the seat of government was temporarily restored in 1261, Byzantine rulers attempted to reverse the decline in legal standards by reforming the court system. Apart from procedural reforms, however, no attempts were made to systematize the law and it remained in chaos. From *c.*1400, it was clear that the end of the Byzantine Empire was drawing closer. The Ottoman Turks had begun to surround Byzantium from all sides and the kingdoms of the West seemed unwilling to render assistance. Attempts were even made in 1439 to breach the schism between the Churches of the East and the West when the Byzantine Emperor John VIII attended the ecumenical council in Florence and accepted the primacy of the Pope and a union with Rome. However, all these efforts to ward off the advancing Ottoman Empire eventually proved futile and in 1453 the Byzantine Empire disintegrated. This event would prove instrumental to the spread of the knowledge of Justinian's codification in Western Europe. With the fall of Byzantium, books and manuscripts from antiquity, which had thus far been thought lost, once again became freely available, first in northern Italy and thereafter in Western Europe. These (predominantly Greek) works provided the impetus for the French legal humanists of the sixteenth century to develop the historical context of Roman legal texts (see 11.2.3.1). (On the history of Byzantine law and its influence on the development of the European *ius commune*, see Robinson et al., *ELH*, s. 1.2; Stein, *Roman Law*, 32–6; Tamm, *Roman Law*, 196–7.)

11.1.2 **The West**

Although Justinian's codification was enacted as law in Italy in AD 554 after the defeat of the Goths, it had little opportunity to make a lasting impact in the West because of the tenuous and short-lived nature of Justinian's reconquest of the area. By the time of his death the Germanic tribes were again gaining control of the areas liberated by his generals. If anything, it was the Theodosian Code—longer established—which provided the backbone of Roman law in the West.

   In the following centuries (from the sixth to the end of the tenth century), the so-called Dark Ages (or early medieval period), the picture is rather confused. The Germanic tribes' struggle for territorial supremacy in the immediate aftermath of the collapse of the Western Empire caused widespread destruction. The countryside became practically deserted and the inhabitants retreated behind the walls of a few fortified cities. The already fragmented legal system of the former Western Empire crumbled. Widespread illiteracy led to a decline in knowledge of the law and communities came to rely increasingly on localized (largely oral) custom. The 'professional jurist' skilled in law—a key feature of classical Roman law—disappeared to be replaced by councils of laymen who had knowledge of local custom. By the end of the sixth century, most Germanic migrations had come to an end and the borders of the medieval kingdoms had been defined. A form of legal pluralism prevailed in most of these kingdoms. The Roman subjects of the areas that had previously constituted the heart of the Western Empire continued to live under a mixture of laws—the Theodosian Code, parts of Justinian's codification, and the laws of the Germanic kings, while the Germanic subjects continued to use their own customary laws (the personality principle, see Tamm, *Legal History*, 193 ff.). The interaction between Roman and Germanic subjects within these kingdoms and the application of the personality principle in legal disputes necessitated the compilation of the laws in force in these kingdoms. These codes show varying degrees of borrowing from Roman law, but their impact must have been slight, since illiteracy was rife and the codes were in effect: 'like an archipelago of tiny islands in the vast sea of custom' (Bellomo, *Common Legal Past*, 42). It is hardly surprising that the tenuous survival of Roman law in this period has been likened to 'a ghost story' (Vinogradoff, P., *Roman Law in Medieval Europe* (1929), 13).

The Goths—especially the Visigoths and Ostrogoths—were most influenced by Roman law. Despite the fact that their relationship with Rome had run a decidedly erratic course, the Goths had settled among the Roman population and become largely assimilated into the Roman way of life before the fall of the Western Empire: 'their leaders became Roman magistrates, their legislation, originally derived from that of the Empire, was drafted by Roman literati and clerics, and the local Roman administration generally remained in place. These people found nothing at odds with their own thinking and feeling in the venerable and brilliant culture they met' (Wieacker, *History*, 20). By far the most important Germanic code in the West throughout the Dark Ages—and well into the medieval period—was the *lex Romana Visigothorum* promulgated in AD 506 (see 2.4.3.3). It was intended principally for use by the Roman populations of Gaul (the kingdom of the Ostrogoths) and Spain (the kingdom of the Visigoths). The code represents a considerable achievement, although any attempt to produce a workable code at that confused time, and with relatively meagre resources, was bound to be problematic. For example, particular use was made of Gaius' *Institutes* and Paul's *Sententiae*, but the desire to produce a simple code resulted in a somewhat bowdlerized version of the former at least. The Gothic kings continued to enact codes strictly for their own non-Roman subjects, and these showed considerable borrowing from Roman law, although based on Germanic custom.

Another Germanic people, the Lombards, invaded Italy in AD 568 and established control for some 200 years over most of the northern and central part of the mainland. They too borrowed from Roman law, but to a lesser degree than the Goths. Their codes—principally that of King Liutprand (AD 712–44)—are essentially enactments of Lombard custom interspersed with rules clearly Roman in origin. However, Lombard government—based at the royal court at Pavia—tended to be more centralized and better administered than was the case in other Germanic kingdoms. In the long term, these factors, combined with greater adherence to the written word and royal authority, made Lombard law resemble Roman law in some important characteristics. Moreover, the growth of economic activity in northern Italy led to sporadic recourse to the Roman law of obligations in particular.

The Franks proved to be the most militarily successful of the Germanic peoples in the long term. Under Charlemagne (reigned AD 768–814) they captured Pavia and subjugated the Lombards. The Franks established such a hegemony over much of Western and central Europe that a new empire—the Holy Roman Empire—was created, with Charlemagne crowned as Emperor by the Pope in AD 800: 'the idea of universal empire, which was to prepare the way for the rebirth of Roman law in the High Middle Ages, was already discernible' (Wieacker, *History*, 22). The Frankish codes primarily enacted Frankish custom with only occasional Roman influence (mostly the law of obligations). Where parts of Roman law were incorporated, it was in a somewhat debased form, as in the case of the *lex Romana Curiensis c.* AD 800. This code—applied in northern Italy and the Alpine region beyond—was a mixture of Frankish and Lombard custom incorporated with a distorted summary of the *lex Romana Visigothorum*, and containing references to 'Scifola' and 'Gagius' (instead of Scaevola and Gaius). See generally Vinogradoff, *Roman Law in Medieval Europe* (1929), ch. 1 and Robinson et al., *ELH*, ch. 1.

But even codes such as these at least served the purpose of preserving some elements of Roman law, and a degree of continuity of legal tradition, however thin. On the other hand, in northwest Europe and other outlying regions of the former Western Empire, Roman law virtually disappeared. Fortunately, in the remaining regions, the survival of Roman law during the Dark Ages was greatly aided by the rise of the (Catholic) Church in the West (see Robinson et al., *ELH*, ss. 1.4.2–1.4.3). Once the borders of the medieval kingdoms had solidified during the sixth century, the Church became an important political agent within these kingdoms while at the same time developing its own legal system (based on Roman law) to deal with matters falling within its jurisdiction. The interaction between the ecclesiastical jurisdiction of the Church and the secular jurisdiction of the ruler was defined shortly after the collapse of the Western Empire in a comment made by Pope Gelasius I in a letter to the Eastern Emperor Anastasius in AD 494. According to the Gelasian principle (as it came to be called) the Church would only issue decrees with general application concerning matters falling within its ecclesiastical jurisdiction (*sacerdotium*), while the secular ruler would have the right to issue decrees over all other civic matters falling within his secular jurisdiction (*imperium*). This division of ecclesiastical and secular jurisdiction did not cause conflict in the early centuries of the Dark Ages, but as the Church became more powerful and Popes continued to interfere with secular matters it eventually culminated in the Investiture Contest during the tenth and eleventh centuries (see 11.2.2.1). (See Robinson et al., *ELH*, ss. 1.5.1–1.13.4; Bellomo, *Common Legal Past*, 34–54; Stein, *Roman Law*, 29–32, 38–43; Lesaffer, *ELH*, ch. 3.)

11.2 The second life of Roman law

11.2.1 The term 'Reception' and its phases

The Reception of Roman law can be broadly described as the trend (predominantly in Western Europe) towards the increasing Romanization of law and legal institutions during the late medieval period. It was the process whereby Roman law, in danger of oblivion during the Dark Ages, was revived to such an extent that it became the *ius commune* of much of Western Europe, supplementing and sometimes replacing the feudal, customary law then prevalent: 'the essential feature of the Reception was that it signalled the change from acting out of unconsidered habit to acting on the basis of theory: it was a process of intellectual and technical rationalization consonant with the nature of the modern state, particularly its monopoly of making and administering law' (Wieacker, *History*, 191). Though an important part of the general history of Europe, only an outline of this process can be attempted here. At the outset, it must be appreciated that the Reception took as many different forms as there were countries or areas affected by it: no two countries experienced an identical development. As a broad generalization, it can be said that the Reception tended to be gradual in those areas where Roman law had never died out, i.e. the heart of the former Western Empire, but delayed and comparatively sudden elsewhere.

Universal agreement is lacking as to meaning of 'the Reception' and therefore as to its time span. Some would argue that the Reception is strictly a sixteenth-century phenomenon sparked mainly by developments in the legal systems of the Holy Roman Empire, but this is a blinkered view. Alan Watson has suggested that an early Reception occurred some 1,000 years earlier when the codes of the Germanic tribes extensively borrowed from Roman law (although he considers that *the* Reception started in the eleventh century): *The Evolution of Law* (1985), ch. 3. At the other extreme, it is arguable that a late phase of the Reception commenced with the era of modern codification, in which case the Reception has lasted the best part of 1,000 years and may have life in it still. There is even speculation at present about the potential role of Roman law should a 'new' European private law emerge. See Zimmermann, R., 'Savigny's Legacy: Legal History, Comparative Law and the Emergence of a European Legal Science' (1996) 112 LQR, 576–605; Legrand, P., 'European Legal Systems are not Converging' (1996) 45 ICLQ, 52–81; Johnston, D., 'The Renewal of the Old' (1997) 58 Cambridge LJ, 80–95.

The reception of Roman law in Western Europe may be divided into three phases which are linked to the rise of certain legal–philosophical currents. The first phase, from the scientific rediscovery of Roman law in Italy at the end of the eleventh century to the start of the sixteenth century, is generally regarded as the formative period of the European *ius commune*. It was during this period that the principles, terminology, and structure of Roman law were moulded into a medieval learned law to become the backbone of a common European legal culture in which the existing customary law could develop into national legal systems. It must always be remembered that: '[w]hat was received was not classical Roman law in its original form, which was indeed unknown at that time. Nor the law of Justinian as such. Rather, it was the *ius commune* of Europe, produced out of Justinian's *Corpus Iuris* by the Glossators, and to an even greater extent, by the Commentators, who incorporated current statutes, customs, trade practices, especially those of northern Italy' (Wieacker, *History*, 98).

The second stage of reception, from the start of the sixteenth century to the mid-eighteenth century, is linked to the rise of the nation state and the development of national legal systems based on the principles of the European *ius commune*. The influence of the principles of Roman law on legal development during this period was somewhat different. As Stein (*Roman Law*, 75) has noted: 'By the end of the fifteenth century the *ius commune* developed by the Bartolists was becoming more and more influential throughout Europe, as new universities were founded and more jurists were trained in the traditional learning. At the same time, however, the more it was adapted to find solutions to contemporary problems, the further the *ius commune* moved away from the law of Justinian, from which its authority derived.' It was also during this second phase of reception that the universal applicability of Roman law as the basis of the European *ius commune* came to be called into question, first by the legal humanists of the sixteenth century and thereafter by the supporters of the secularized natural-law doctrine during the seventeenth century.

The third and final phase of reception, from the mid-eighteenth century to the end of the nineteenth century, witnessed the emergence of various national codifications of law in Western Europe. As will be shown later, the principles and structure of Roman law also fulfilled an important function during this period. The adoption of codes such as the French, German, and Swiss by other countries also resulted in a late Reception of Roman law outside Western Europe. In virtually every legal system in the world, other than those that adhere to an English common law tradition or Marxist ethos, the influence of Roman law continues to be strongly felt. The United States is generally regarded as a common law system, but for some half a century following independence there was a real prospect that civil law would prove supreme (it actually did in Louisiana, which promulgated an influential Romanist code in 1825 based on French and Spanish law). Some of the outstanding statesmen of the period, such as John Adams and Thomas Jefferson, were not only great admirers of ancient Rome but erudite in her law. See Sellers, M. N. S., *American Republicanism* (1994). Not surprisingly, following the Revolution there was a certain hostility towards the common law, and a receptiveness to French influences. Civil and natural law were important elements of legal education, American jurists read Pothier, and legal literature of the period was decidedly enthusiastic about civil law. However, the legal profession did not share the enthusiasm, and this was perhaps the major factor why Roman law gradually faded as a potentially dominant influence. See Stein, *Character and Influence*, 411 ff.

11.2.2 **The birth of the European *ius commune***

11.2.2.1 **The Glossators**

The Reception was made possible by a revival of the study of Roman law in the eleventh century, particular interest being shown in Justinian's *Digest* (which had long been forgotten in Western Europe, see Tamm, *Roman Law*, 201–2). This revival was part of the wide-ranging intellectual and artistic movement affecting all aspects of society during the eleventh and twelfth centuries. Central to this 'renaissance' were various factors, including the gradual relaxation of feudal structures, the rise of towns and urban civilization in Italy as well as an increase in trade and commerce between Italian city states and other regions in Western Europe. The crucial elements, as far as the study of law was concerned, were the rise of the professional jurist and the work of the law schools in the universities of northern Italy, especially Ravenna, Pavia, Verona, and above all, Bologna where law (and more specifically Roman law), for the first time since the fall of the Western Empire, came to be studied as an autonomous discipline. The extent to which Roman law was studied before this period is uncertain. The legal education offered at monastery and cathedral schools during the Dark Ages probably comprised some study of Roman law—largely from the Germanic codes—as well as canon law. The position was the same in the law schools at Ravenna and Pavia. The latter was particularly active in the study of Lombardic customary law, using the technique of exposition through glossing the text (see below) which the Bologna school was to perfect.

The revival of interest in the *Digest* was stimulated, amongst other things, by the Investiture Contest, a dispute between Pope and Holy Roman Emperor over the right to appoint bishops and lesser clergy and to invest them with the symbols of their office. This dispute formed part of a larger debate concerning the relationship between the ecclesiastical jurisdiction of the Church and the secular jurisdiction of the ruler (see 11.2.1). It arose during the papacy of Gregory VII (1073–85) and was not settled until 1122 with the Concordat of Worms. During the course of this dispute, both sides searched the ancient authorities for supporting arguments, and it is at this time that the *Digest* was 'rediscovered', perhaps in Ravenna (see *Roman Law Tradition*, 3). However, it was at Bologna that the outstanding figure of the period, Irnerius (*c.*1055–1130), led the way in the textual analysis of the *Digest*. His work, and particularly that of his outstanding successors, Bulgarus and Martinus Gosia was instrumental in the scientific revival of the study of Roman law. A typical analytical device used by the Glossators was the adding of brief comments (or 'glosses') in the margins of the text in order to expound it more easily by explaining difficult points, making distinctions where necessary, and by adding copious cross-references to related texts. In this way the Glossators reintroduced scientific method into the study of Roman law in a manner similar to—if not identical with—that of the classical jurists. They sought a harmonious order in the texts, believing that the *Digest* in particular was the ultimate authority for most legal problems. Their work was clearly influenced by Scholasticism, the philosophy which propounded that the universe was determined by a harmonious, logical, and divine order: 'the whole attitude of the Glossators corresponded to the aims of Scholasticism—to harmonize and systemize, to use reason to explain and justify an authority which was at the centre of their studies as a guide to the harmonious order which they sought to discover... For the civilians the central authority was the *Corpus Iuris Civilis*, as the Bible and the Fathers of the Church were for the theologians, and Aristotle for the philosophers' (Robinson et al., *ELH*, s. 3.3.3).

Apart from annotating the texts, the Glossators wrote a great deal, especially summaries and commentaries on their glossing of the *Digest*, culminating with the monumental *Glossa Ordinaria* ('Standard Gloss'), the work of another Bologna scholar, Accursius (*c.*1184–1263). This work, containing some 97,000 entries, became accepted as the standard commentary on Justinian's codification. It took the form known as *apparatus*—a comprehensive compilation of glosses. Large-scale commentaries on sections of the *Corpus Iuris Civilis* were called *summae*, the most celebrated of which was the *Summa Codicis* of Azo (*c.*1150–1230). This work became an indispensable textbook for practitioners—'Do not go to court without Azo', ran the saying. Other literary forms included *tractatus*—general treatises on parts of the law not specifically related to Justinian's arrangement; *notabilia*—noteworthy points, mainly for use in solving real and hypothetical cases; and *quaestiones*—controversial points arising from conflicting passages. *Quaestiones* were sometimes compiled following disputations on points arising in lectures. Indeed, much of the Glossators' literature was the result of their work as teachers: see Robinson et al., *ELH*, s. 3.4.

The Bologna doctors regularly lectured on their work—with attendant disputations—attracting students from all over Europe (see Stein, *Roman Law*, 52–4). Roman law became the focus of law as a university subject, to be studied for a period of five years, with oral examinations necessary for the award of a degree: Robinson et al. consider that the concept of a university law school began at Bologna (*ELH*, s. 3.8.1; Bellomo, *Common Legal Past*, 112–25). Exposition of the *Corpus Iuris Civilis* became part of the intellectual mainstream of early medieval Europe. This sparked an interest in the study of Roman law in other centres of learning. For example, evidence suggests that the subject was being taught in the universities of Paris and Oxford in the second half of the twelfth century. But the most important centres, apart from northern Italy, were in southern France, particularly in Provence. The law schools at Montpellier, Arles, and Toulouse achieved a high reputation in the study of Justinian's codification under scholars such as

Rogerius and Placentinus, both of whom had studied at Bologna (see 11.2.2.3). Two important works date from this period: the *Exceptiones Petri*, a compilation of rules extracted from Justinian, and meant for practical use in the administration of the law; and *Lo Codi*, a manual written in *Provençal* dialect (possibly by Rogerius) intended for use by judges which draws on Roman rules for the solution of cases. See Vinogradoff, *Roman Law in Medieval Europe* (1929), ch. 2.

The Bologna doctors sometimes took part in important affairs of State. Bulgarus, for example, was an adviser to both the Pope and the Holy Roman Emperor, and he and others became embroiled in the difficult relations between Church and State at that time. In England, Glossators are thought to have appeared against King John in disputes over ecclesiastical appointments. Thus, their work at times had a vital practical application, even if its main thrust was the exposition of Justinian's law.

Although it cannot be denied that the Glossators were instrumental in the rediscovery of Roman law and that they provided the initial impetus for the reception of Roman law across Western Europe, their methodology was not without its critics. Owing to the lack of available sources, most Glossators did not have a clear grasp of the history of the Roman Empire or the technicalities of classical legal Latin and many of their observations on the texts were wildly speculative and historically unsound. Furthermore, many of the Glossators did not read Greek and thus excluded large parts of the Code and the Novels from their glosses or commentaries. More significantly, though, the Glossators' reverence for the text precluded them from rearranging the order of the fragments, which in the eleventh and twelfth centuries was still somewhat speculative. Nonetheless, without the groundbreaking work of the Glossators, the scientific rebirth of Roman law and the resulting transformation of the principles of Roman law into the *ius commune* of Western Europe would not have occurred. (On the Glossators and their significance, see Robinson et al., *ELH*, ss. 3.1–3.8.6; Stein, *Roman Law*, 43–9; Bellomo, *Common Legal Past*, 55–77; Tamm, *Roman Law*, 203–6; Lesaffer, *ELH*, ch. 4.)

11.2.2.2 **Canon law**

Canon law consisted of the canons of the Church—ecclesiastical decrees concerned mainly with the administration of the Church, doctrinal issues, and jurisdiction over matters such as marriage and wills. In some respects, it had close affinity with Roman law, was influenced by it, and in turn influenced its revival. During the early centuries of the Dark Ages, the Church had taken advantage of the disintegration of civil authority in the west to extend its jurisdiction and to develop its own legal system based on Roman law for use in its ecclesiastical courts. During the next few centuries, canon law became an important force in medieval society. Its prominence is reflected in a number of unofficial compilations of canon law that appeared during the course of the sixth to the eleventh centuries (see Mousourakis, *Historical and Institutional Context*, 430–1; Lesaffer, *ELH*, ch. 4). And on this see now, Helmholz, R., 'Canon Law and Roman Law', in *Cambridge Companion*, 396–422.

The transformation of canon law into a science in the late medieval period, which occurred roughly at the same time as the scientific rediscovery of Roman law, was largely the work of Gratian, a monk working at Bologna. In *c*.1140, he produced a systematic compilation of the canons of the Church that, though unofficial and never promulgated as law, was soon considered authoritative. This compilation—the *Decretum Gratiani*—provided a rich source for the study of canon law. A school of Decretists emerged, using methods similar to those of the Glossators—glossing the texts, with the attendant literary output.

Canon law had two distinct advantages over Roman law (or civil law as it came to be called) in the late medieval period. First, it had direct application in ecclesiastical courts, while civil law only had subsidiary application where local customary law proved ineffective. Second, and more importantly, Gratian's *Decretum* was not a closed compilation, unlike Justinian's codification. Popes and ecumenical councils were frequently producing more material that supplemented and developed existing canon law into a more efficient legal system. During the course of the thirteenth and fourteenth centuries, for example, three new compilations appeared which were designed to supplement Gratian's work. These were the *Liber Extra* of Pope Gregory IX produced in 1234; the *Liber Sextus* of Pope Boniface VIII in 1298; and the *Clementinae* of Pope Clement V in 1317. These compilations gave rise to a second group of canonist scholars, the Decretalists, who wrote commentaries on the *Liber Sextus* and the *Liber Extra*.

It was said that canon law could not be understood without studying Roman law, and vice versa, because of their close relationship. For example, both systems were founded on written law; Bologna was the leading centre for a while of both canon law and Roman law scholarship, similar methods (glossing the texts) being used in both; the clerics of the Church often studied both—some of the leading canonists were pupils of Glossators; canon law procedure was based largely on the *cognitio* process of the later Roman Empire (hence described as 'Romano-canonical' procedure); and even the unofficial name given to the classical body of canon law—*Corpus Iuris Canonici* (a collection of the above-mentioned compilations together with the *Extravagantes* first produced in 1580)—resembled the title of Justinian's codification, the *Corpus Iuris Civilis*. See Wieacker, *History*, 47 ff. He emphasizes the 'interchange of legal rules' which in his view was facilitated by 'a mutual principle of subsidiarity: spiritual courts used to apply Roman law in the absence of law of their own, and secular courts likewise applied the general principles of canon law' (54).

The fact that many leading clerics—often among the leading statesmen of the secular State in the medieval period—were versed in Roman law contributed to the revival of Roman law. So did the prevalent use of *cognitio* procedure in the ecclesiastical courts, especially in matters of 'secular' interest such as marriage and wills (see Robinson et al., *ELH*, s. 5.7 for a detailed discussion of the local application of canon law). Moreover, the universality of canon law acted as an example for the secular law: 'This universality of legal thinking and practice must have been an important factor in the creation of the *ius commune*, and in bringing such outlying areas of medieval Europe as Scotland within the framework of European legal civilisation' (Robinson et al., *ELH*, s. 5.1.3, and generally ch. 5). (On medieval canon law, see Robinson et al., *ELH*, ss. 5.1–5.9; Stein, *Roman Law*, 49–52; Bellomo, *Common Legal Past*, 65–77; Tamm, *Roman Law*, 211–15; Helmholz, *Spirit*, ch. 5.)

11.2.2.3 The school of Orléans (*Ultramontani*)

From the mid- to the late thirteenth century, the University of Orléans became an important centre for the scientific study of Roman law. While the glossatorial methodology was still being followed at many Italian universities, it had lost much of its appeal following the publication of Accursius' *Glossa Ordinaria* and the time had come for the development of a new approach to the study of Roman law.

This approach came from a country to the North of Italy 'across the mountains' (*Ultramontani*, meaning 'those beyond the mountains', was an Italian description). Although the teaching of Roman law had earlier (in 1219) been forbidden in Paris by Pope Honorius III, his successor Gregory IX had declared in 1235 that this prohibition did not apply to Orléans, thereby paving the way for the scientific study of Roman law at this university. The appointment of legal scholars from Italy such as Guido de Cumis also contributed to the rise of this university as an important centre for the scientific study of Roman law. Two jurists commonly associated with the School of Orléans are Jacques de Revigny and Pierre de Belleperche. Although the methodological approach of these jurists largely followed that of their predecessors, their liberal approach to the texts was to have a lasting impact on a later group of Italian jurists, the 'Commentators'. The school at Orléans concentrated on teaching Roman law to clerics destined for high office, but took a less reverential approach than the Glossators to the Roman texts. Those who attained high office, especially in the service of the royal court, became adept at balancing the claims of custom against the rules of Roman law in dealing with the practical issues of the day. (See Robinson et al., *ELH*, ss. 4.2.1–4.3.3; Stein, *Roman Law*, 67–8.)

11.2.2.4 **The commentators**

From the late thirteenth century onwards, an important shift of emphasis occurred in the study of Roman law. The law of the time, largely a mixture of feudal custom and remnants from the codes of vulgar law of the Dark Ages, was inevitably influenced by the academic revival of Roman law in the universities. This process was enhanced by the fact that the scholars who flocked from all over Europe to Bologna and the other law schools occasionally attained high office in their countries. The scholars of the later medieval period, known as the 'Commentators', aimed principally at adapting Roman law for contemporary use. In contrast to the Glossators, they were not interested in the exegesis of Roman legal texts in isolation, but attempted to construct a system of law suitable to the needs of fourteenth-century Italy by adapting the texts to the circumstances of their time and by distilling legal principles from these texts.

Not only had Justinian's codification achieved a revered status through the work of the Bologna doctors, but it came to be regarded (the *Digest* in particular) as a repository of solutions to virtually all legal problems. The conflicts, inconsistencies, and varying opinions found in the *Digest*, Justinian's best efforts notwithstanding, offered a rich store of possibilities: 'the Commentators were able to transform the law of Justinian into *ius commune*, a common law for the whole of Europe, and to apply to the rich variety of the non-Roman laws in Europe their ways of thinking about law' (Wieacker, *History*, 57). Their work was clearly influenced by the *Ultramontani*.

The Commentators, principally Italian jurists of the fourteenth century, became influential mainly through their teaching and literary output. Teaching methods were similar to those of the Glossators. Bologna was no longer the preeminent school: several other Italian universities were closely associated with the Commentators, including Padua, Perugia, and Naples. Their literary output took two main forms: extensive commentaries or monographs on Justinian's codification (as glossed by the Glossators) and collections of opinions on specific legal problems. In both types of work, the writers took particular account of local statute and custom, and as a consequence were prepared to interpret the Roman texts much more freely than the Glossators, thus making them more directly relevant to the conditions of the time: '*This* literature was the major catalyst in the Reception of Roman law in Germany after the fifteenth century, for whenever learned decision-making took the place of unsophisticated judicature this literature was used' (Wieacker, *History*, 60).

The two most outstanding Commentators were Bartolus de Saxoferrato (1314–57) and his pupil Baldus de Ubaldis (1327–1400). Bartolus wrote the most important commentary of the period, a work that became the standard text for subsequent ages, and led to the quip 'no one is a jurist unless he is a Bartolist'. The task of adapting Roman law for practical use in systems that were based partly on customary law led Bartolus to anticipate the problems that could arise through the conflict of laws in different regions of Europe. A fundamental problem was the potential conflict between local law and the *Corpus Iuris Civilis*. Bartolus rejected the notion that the latter must automatically prevail. Instead he took the view that the problem was essentially one of interpretation of the scope of the local law. To that extent he can be legitimately viewed as the 'father' of the conflict of laws as a specific legal discipline. See Stein, *Character and Influence*, 83 ff., who thinks that the importance of Bartolus lies: 'not so much for his specific doctrines but rather because for the first time he offered a systematic survey of the various categories of problem that were likely to occur in practice' (90).

Baldus, a scholar of wide-ranging interests, was responsible for the richest collection of opinions in his era. His work and that of Bartolus inspired succeeding generations of scholars, so that by the middle of the fifteenth century the Commentators were active in academic centres throughout much of Europe. The result was the growth of a European legal tradition, a common legal language deriving its core from Roman law, just as some of the languages of Europe possessed common roots in Latin. 'The influence of these Italians is one of the best examples in history of the constant cultural interchange between the peoples in Europe' (Wieacker, *History*, 61). Moreover, the supremacy of Roman law, when compared to the vagaries of the feudal law that permeated much of Europe in the medieval period, was much touted by academic and practising lawyers. Public disputations on the merits of Roman law were not uncommon, especially in the universities of Germany; and the teaching of Roman law in universities throughout much of Europe was one of the intellectual achievements of the age. (Robinson et al., *ELH*, ss. 4.4.1–4.6.8; Stein, *Roman Law*, 71–4; Bellomo, *Common Legal Past*, 147–8; Tamm, *Roman Law*, 206–8.)

11.2.3 Towards a European *ius commune* and beyond

By the end of the fourteenth century, Roman law had been transformed into the European *ius commune*. This process had occurred in three phases. During the twelfth century, Justinian's codification had been meticulously cross-referenced by Glossators and had lent much of its vocabulary and doctrine to the emerging canon law. During the thirteenth century, the liberal interpretation of the School of Orléans had provided a new slant on the interpretation of these texts, while the 'Commentators' of the fourteenth century had blended Roman law together with local custom and statute into a legal system suited to their particular needs. Through the endeavours of these jurists, a Romanization of the law had begun that was not dissimilar to the transformation that had occurred in the life of the territories settled by the Romans in the heyday of the Roman Empire. This process, which continued until the start of the sixteenth century, did not always lead to a substantial change in the *content* of the law; the transformation was often more evident in the structure and procedure of legal systems, and in the methods of thinking and the techniques adopted by academic and practising lawyers.

The Romanization of the law also owed much to political and economic factors. The growth of the idea of statehood, a characteristic trait of the fifteenth and sixteenth centuries, made Roman law attractive to some of the rulers of the developing states of Europe, since it was regarded as imperialistic, authoritarian, centralized, and secular in character. And the growing merchant classes in European states often found in Roman law (particularly its law of contracts) a surer legal basis for mercantile endeavour than the outdated, fragmented customary laws then prevalent. The mere fact that Roman law was *written* law (with clearly identifiable sources) gave it certainty and authority, and therefore a pronounced advantage compared to largely unwritten custom. And see now Ryan, M., 'Political Thought', in *Cambridge Companion*, 423–51.

The Romanization of the law in Italy was influenced by an unusual factor—the operation of the *podestà* constitution. Italian cities in the medieval period sometimes became ungovernable, primarily because of strife between warring factions and families. The expedient was occasionally tried of inviting an unbiased outsider—the *podestà*—to act in a judicial and administrative capacity as governor to restore good order. He might find that the problem lay partly in the operation of the local law, in which case it could make sense to resort to a 'neutral' law—namely, Roman law—in adjudicating difficult cases. The *podestà* would normally be trained in Roman law—indeed, some Glossators and Commentators were known to accept the invitation.

With hindsight, the many and disparate factors contributing to the revival of Roman law in the medieval period can be seen to lead to the Reception with a certain inevitability. To this extent it is surprising to read in Vinogradoff: 'Within the whole range of history there is no more momentous and puzzling problem than that connected with the fate of Roman law after the downfall of the Roman State. How is it that a system shaped to meet certain historical conditions not only survived those conditions, but has retained its vitality even to the present day, when political and social surroundings are entirely altered?' (*Roman Law in Medieval Europe* (1929), 11). Watson, on the other hand, takes the view that massive, voluntary legal borrowing from Roman law was to be expected in societies with a primarily customary system of law, even though very different conditions—whether political, social, economic, or religious—prevailed there. Thus: 'it is a non-Reception which would have constituted the most puzzling problem of history. The first (and most) important step in understanding the Reception is to know that we should explain its cause by not explaining its causes' (*The Evolution of Law* (1985) 97, and generally ch. 3). The notion that the search for *causes* is somehow misconceived—if that is what Watson argues—is difficult to maintain, although the thesis that legal borrowing between societies is probable, or even inevitable, is readily understandable. As Wieacker puts it: 'The adoption by one people of cultural elements fashioned by another is simply one instance among many of the constant changes on which all human civilization ultimately depends. The very idea of Reception illustrates our sense of the continuity of human history as a whole, or at any rate the continuity of great civilizations' (*History*, 91).

Romanization of the law took diverse forms and proceeded at a disparate pace in different countries (Lesaffer, *ELH*, ch. 5). Generalizations are particularly fallible when made in relation to the Reception, but it can be safely asserted that nowhere was there a sudden, overnight metamorphosis from feudal custom to Roman law. There occurred, however, certain events (such as the reform of existing courts or the introduction of new appellate courts using learned law) that undoubtedly hastened the progress of the Reception. Individual rulers tended to staff their highest courts with jurists trained in Roman law. That led to a greater reliance on skilled advocates, themselves trained in Roman law at the universities. The staffing of appellate courts by judges trained in Roman law proved to be an important factor in the course of the Reception in several countries apart from Germany, especially in the Netherlands and Scotland.

In the countries of the western Mediterranean—Spain, France, and Italy—the Reception generally took a slower, more gradual course. There was an absence of momentous events in the later stages of the Reception in these countries, largely due to the fact that Roman law had retained a foothold in parts of this area throughout the Dark Ages. In Spain, for example, it was present in Visigothic law and survived the Moorish invasions. In the thirteenth century, a succession of Castilian kings extended royal authority at the expense of local custom by imposing the *Fuero Juzgo* ('the custom of the judges')—Visigothic law applied normally in appellate tribunals. The revival of Roman law in Spain was typically aided by those in royal service who had studied in Italy or at the University of Salamanca. In the reign of Alfonso X (1252–84) there was promulgated a comprehensive statement of law, *Las Siete Partidas* (The Seven Parts of Law). Based on Roman law, it gradually achieved general recognition during the period of reconquest of Spanish cities from the Moors, and came to be regarded as the foundation of Spanish law (and thus the law of the New World (South America) when Spain started to acquire its vast overseas empire). See Robinson et al., *ELH*, s. 7.6.

Scarcely a country in Europe was unaffected by the Reception of Roman law, although in some areas—especially Scandinavia and parts of Eastern Europe, such as Poland—the influence was minor, at least until the sixteenth century, despite the teaching of canon law and some Roman law at the universities. Russia was largely outside the European mainstream until even later.

11.2.3.1 France

As already seen, French scholars were at the forefront of the scientific revival of Roman law in the late medieval period—notably Glossators such as Rogerius in Provence and the *Ultramontani* of Orléans (see 11.2.2.3 and generally Tamm, *Roman Law*, 220). However, the influence of Roman law during the medieval period was confined to the southern regions of France. Broadly, there was a north–south divide in terms of legal development. The south was the *pays de droit écrit* ('the land of written law') because there Roman law gradually became a dominant influence— the general law which was applied unless local custom dictated otherwise. The reasons for the more comprehensive Reception of Roman law in the south of France are diverse. The region's geographical proximity to Italy ensured that a strong Latin tradition remained throughout the Dark Ages. The 'barbarian' codes containing elements of Roman law also remained in force in the south of France throughout this period and later medieval compilations of customary law from the southern regions of France show the extent to which Roman law had been received (see Stein, *Roman Law*, 54–6). Finally, the foundation of universities at Montpellier and Toulouse during the twelfth century and the academic migrations of Italian scholars to these universities contributed to a strong Roman-law influence in the south of France.

The north was the *pays de droit coutumier* ('the land of customary law') where mainly Frankish custom was followed. The strength of the customary laws of the north—particularly in Normandy, Brittany, and the Île-de-France (Paris and environs)—delayed substantial Romanization of the law. The prominence of customary law in the northern regions of France was aided, amongst other things, by the decree of Pope Honorius III in 1219. By the end of the thirteenth century, customary law had become the local law in force in the northern regions of France (see Robinson *et al.*, *ELH*, s. 7.5). However, even in the north it is clear that parts of the customary law, especially procedure, property, and contract, were influenced by Roman notions, e.g. the *Coutumes de Beauvaisis c.*1280. See Vinogradoff, *Roman Law in Medieval Europe* (1929) 80 ff. The influence of the framework and terminology of Roman law are also visible in the numerous compilations of customary law that had arisen by the fifteenth century. The compilation of French customary law had been an ongoing project of the French Crown since the fifteenth century (initiated by the Ordinance of Montils-lès-Tours in 1454). By *c.*1600, a series of separate codes for each region existed—e.g. the Custom of Paris was issued in 1510. Nevertheless, the application of the customary law by the *parlements* (superior royal courts) in the provinces, the eventual codification of these laws, and the suspicion of some French kings that Roman law constituted a threat to their privileges, prevented a full-scale Reception in the north. (See Robinson et al., *ELH*, ss. 7.5.1–7.5.14 on French courts and their use of customary law; Bellomo, *Common Legal Past*, 101–6; Tamm, *Roman Law*, 219–22.)

There was, however, a notable development in France of academic interest in the study of Roman law—the 'humanist' revival of the sixteenth and early seventeenth centuries. See Stein, P. G., 'Legal Humanism and Legal Science', in Stein, *Character and Influence*, 91–100 (also in (1986) 54 TR, 297–306). It formed part of a cultural and intellectual re-evaluation of the classical cultures of Greece and Rome that had started in northern Italy during the latter part of the fifteenth century. This methodology eventually came to dominate all aspects of society in Western Europe during the sixteenth century. 'Legal humanism' was essentially a reaction against the aims and methods of the Commentators, which French jurists (as well as certain of their Italian and German contemporaries) considered to be somewhat crude and conducive to the distortion of Roman law. The humanists therefore focused on the original Latin and Greek texts (with their motto *petere fontes*), largely discarding the glosses, and attempted to rediscover classical Roman law in its original context. This task was of course aided by a great number of classical texts that had once again become available in the West after the fall of Byzantium (see 11.1.1). Their editions of Justinian's codification bear witness to a greater clarity and refinement in style and method ('elegant jurisprudence') than that displayed by the Commentators. But then the latter were aiming at different and arguably more important things. The humanist soon found sympathizers in other countries, particularly in Germany in the early sixteenth century and later in the Netherlands. However, it was France that was to prove to be the most important home of the humanist revival, especially the law school at the University of Bourges. The pioneering work of stripping the texts of all the glosses and commentaries which had engulfed it since the twelfth century was done by the Frenchman Guillaume Budé (Budaeus) (1467–1540) and the Italian, Andrea Alciato (Alciatus) (1492–1550) who taught law at various French universities. It was carried on by illustrious French jurists such as François Baudouin (Balduinus) (1520–73), Jacques Cujas (Cujacius) (1522–90), Hugues Doneau (Donellus) (1527–91), François Hotman (Hotomannus) (1524–90), and Antoine Favre (Faber) (1557–1624). For much of the sixteenth century Bourges was: 'the most exciting institution for legal study not only in France but in all Europe' (Robinson et al., *ELH*, s. 10.2). Some of the French humanists had Protestant leanings, and thus had to leave France when the persecution of the Huguenots became intolerable in the 1570s. Some settled in Germany, but it was chiefly in the Netherlands that they carried on their work, helping to foster there a humanist tradition in Roman legal studies (see 11.2.3.3).

The work of the humanists took various forms, emanating from the central aim of returning to the original texts, which could only be properly understood— argued the humanists—within their historical context. That required a student of the texts to view them in the light of knowledge about the history, language, customs, and traditions of the time, as well as disciplines such as philosophy and medicine: total immersion in classical antiquity was *de rigueur*. The connection between law and its historical context had a significant impact on the widely held view concerning the universal applicability of Roman law. By equating law with history, the legal humanists showed how different the historical context of Roman law was from the circumstances of the sixteenth century and thereby challenged the way in which Roman law should be studied. This was the first serious challenge to the universal applicability of Roman law and by implication also to the idea of a European *ius commune*.

By stripping the texts of all the glosses and commentaries and exploring its historical context, legal humanists also became involved in the search for interpolations as they realized that the texts preserved in Justinian's codification contained layers of law from different periods (see 2.5.3.2). Moreover, some humanists were concerned to provide a more systematic ordering of the material and looked towards the division of Justinian's *Institutes* into persons, actions, and things as an alternative arrangement. The efforts of predecessors such as the Glossators were likened (rather unfairly) to 'quack medicine' and the difference was described in the phrases *mos italicus*—'the Italian way', namely the work of the Glossators and Commentators—and *mos gallicus*, 'the French way', the humanist approach. (On legal humanism in France, see Robinson et al., *ELH*, ss. 10.2–10.5.8; Stein, *Roman Law*, 75–82; Bellomo, *Common Legal Past*, 203–10; Tamm, *Roman Law*, 222–4.)

The influence of French legal humanism on legal practice was minimal and the courts in France (and elsewhere) continued in the Bartolist tradition. These courts (especially in the North) applied local customary laws that, by the fifteenth century, were available in many compilations. Although compilations of regional customary law made it more accessible, legal uncertainty still prevailed on account of the limited applicability of local customary law and its inability to deal effectively with many aspects of commerce. Though there were calls for reform of customary law throughout the sixteenth century and attempts were made to blend customs of entire provinces into a more standardized system, uniformity of custom was never achieved. Many commentaries on these customary compilations were produced during the sixteenth and seventeenth centuries. These commentaries proved influential to the development of French national law (see Robinson et al., *ELH*, ss. 12.1–12.5.5). Arguably the most influential jurist on French national law during the sixteenth century was Charles Dumoulin (Molinaeus) (1500–66) whose Commentary on Customs of Paris was an attempt to find a general custom suitable for France. The most influential proponent of French national law during the seventeenth century was Jean Domat (1625–96) who wrote an extensive commentary on the Reception of Roman law in France entitled *Les lois civiles dans leur ordre naturel* (1694). This work was strongly influenced by the secularized natural law doctrine of the seventeenth century (see 11.2.3.3), but it also supported the methodology of the *usus modernus Pandectarum* (see 11.2.3.2) in Germany. During the eighteenth century, French national law was dominated by Robert Pothier (1699–1772) who, though 'not a particular original thinker[,] had an immense knowledge and tremendous organizing ability' (Robinson et al., *ELH*, s. 15.7.2). His well-known work *The Pandects of Justinian in New Order* (1748) attempted to reorder the text of the *Digest* within their specific titles in order to illustrate principles of law. He also wrote on the Customs of Orléans and produced treatises on various areas of the law of property and obligations which proved very influential, not only in the development of French private law, but also in the development of other legal systems, such as the Netherlands.

Although the codification of French law had in a certain sense already begun during the sixteenth century when attempts were made to compile regional customary law (see Robinson et al., *ELH*, s. 15.7.1), the true stimulus for codification came from the unsettled political climate of eighteenth-century France. The eighteenth century was the age of the Enlightenment—a shared view of the world based on a profound scepticism towards traditional systems of authority. In the second part of the eighteenth century, this scepticism would fuel the French Revolution and would lead, albeit indirectly, to the eventual codification of French law. As Stein (*Roman Law*, 114) observes: 'They [the sons and daughters of the Revolution] sought to sweep away the legal structure that propped up the *ancien régime*, and replace it with a short, simple code, that would express the aspirations of liberty, equality and fraternity.'

Various attempts at codification were made between 1793 and 1799, but it was only when Napoleon Bonaparte came to power in 1799 that the codification of French law became a reality. A commission of four jurists, all of whom had been trained in Roman law, drafted the French Civil Code of 1804. Napoleon Bonaparte took a keen interest in the project and appears to have personally drafted some of the provisions. The Code was based mainly on the *Corpus Iuris Civilis*, especially Justinian's *Institutes*, in the light of custom and natural law. Napoleon's commission was greatly aided by the organization and exposition of French law by eighteenth-century jurists, notably Robert Pothier and Jean Domat. Since its promulgation the *Code Civil* has generally been regarded as a model of rational principles, clearly and simply expressed. No code has been more widely admired and copied all over the world than the *Code Civil*. It was Napoleon's finest achievement and represents one of France's most enduring contributions to world civilization. Its stirring emphasis on human rights and liberties has given it universal appeal. (On the codification of French law, see Robinson et al., *ELH*, ss. 15.7.1–15.7.11; Stein, *Roman Law*, 114–15; Bellomo, *Common Legal Past*, 6–11; Tamm, *Roman Law*, 245–52.)

11.2.3.2 **Germany**

The Reception in Germany was relatively sudden and late (from the fifteenth century onwards) compared to that of the Mediterranean countries. Scholars have therefore remarked that: 'Germany had no real part in the creation of the *ius commune*. When the learned law was received there, it had already been modified' (Robinson et al., *ELH*, s. 7.4.3). Large parts of Germany—predominantly in the north and east—had experienced little or no contact with Roman civilization in antiquity, and by the late Middle Ages had acquired an effective customary law which was enforced by local courts (called *schöffen* courts) using a largely oral procedure. This was particularly true of the ports and cities of the Hanseatic League—which operated under an efficient customary commercial code—and Saxony with its relatively enlightened compilation of customary and feudal law, the *Sachsenspiegel*, produced during the first half of the thirteenth century. Romanization of the law during this period was far less pronounced than in the Mediterranean countries and authors such as Bellomo have likened the situation in Germany prior to the fifteenth century to that of the *pays de droit coutumier* in France (*Common Legal Past*, 109). Nevertheless, in Wieacker's view there was a clearly discernible 'Pre-Reception' prior to the fifteenth century (*History*, 84 ff.). Signs of this 'pre-Reception' are visible in, for example, trading links with the cities of northern Italy that encouraged adoption of Roman practices. German graduates from Bologna often entered imperial administration, or the service of city councils or the various territorial powers within the Holy Roman Empire. A major factor was the influence of canon law. Most German universities were founded (from the mid-fourteenth century onwards) with the primary aim to teach canon law that, in pre-reformation Germany, exerted a wide sphere of influence over many areas of the law through its application in ecclesiastical courts. Notaries, who had the important function of drafting public legal documents, were trained in canon law. Moreover, an embryonic legal literature emerged, largely the work of canonists and civilians.

The pronounced political and legal fragmentation of the Holy Roman Empire made her particularly susceptible to the Reception of Roman law. The breakdown of imperial hegemony resulted in a profusion of States and territories with a large degree of autonomy in the late medieval period. The lack of centralized political authority was mirrored in the diverse and localized legal systems throughout the Empire, lacking an effective judicial hierarchy. Moreover, law differed not only from territory to territory (*Landrecht*) but also according to status: e.g. feudal relations between lord and tenant were encompassed by the *Lehnrecht*, but there were also a manorial law, a municipal law, a trade guild law, and so forth. It can thus be seen how significant the developments of the fifteenth century were when the supremacy of customary law in Germany was challenged. The challenge presented itself on two fronts. First, the *schöffen* courts began to allow litigants to use the Romano-canonical procedure used by ecclesiastical courts in the Holy Roman Empire since the thirteenth century. Soon thereafter, the complexity of this procedure combined with the increased use of Roman-law elements as the foundation for more intricate legal claims forced these courts to enlist the aid of scholars trained in learned law. By the end of the fifteenth century, the practice of *Aktenversendung* had developed whereby local courts requested legal opinions from academic scholars in faculties of law. Since both canon and Roman law had been actively studied at these faculties since the foundation of German universities, this practice contributed to the infiltration of additional elements of the *ius commune* into legal procedure and substantive law applied in courts.

A second and more important factor in the Reception of Roman law in Germany was the foundation of the *Reichskammergericht* (the supreme court of the Holy Roman Empire) at the end of the fifteenth century (1495). The motives for the foundation of this court were undoubtedly political and it was a conscious attempt to introduce a new legal order based on the *ius commune* for the Holy Roman Empire. Not only was a written procedure used in this court from its inception (which soon developed into the Romano-canonical procedure), but the requirement that at least half of the judges presiding over this court had to be trained in learned law had a definite impact on the Reception of Roman law. The judges of this court were specifically instructed to judge cases according to the 'law of the Empire', which was in effect an instruction to judge cases according to the principles of the *ius commune*. Thus, by the end of the fifteenth century, Roman law had become the most viable candidate to fulfil the function of a *ius commune* for the Holy Roman Empire. It was now taught extensively at the universities, which in time came to be regarded as authoritative interpreters of the law (not unlike the classical Roman jurists). See Robinson et al., *ELH*, s. 11.2., and generally Part V of this book. The circulation of legal literature concerned with Roman law became widespread following the invention of printing with movable type in Germany, and German legal scholars, notably Ulrich Zasius, were among the foremost humanists of the era. Although the Reception was delayed in the north and east, the superiority of Roman law over indigenous and diverse German custom came to be generally recognized among those holding power: 'The real forces behind the actual Reception were city councils, local rulers, and the territorial estates who saw that if professional lawyers were allowed to extend to judicature their existing monopoly of administration, law could become rational, uniform, and unprejudiced' (Wieacker, *History*, 109, and generally chs. 6–11). These various factors led to the widespread application of Justinian's law to 'modern' conditions (*usus modernus Pandectarum*) as the communal law of Germany. (See Robinson et al., *ELH*, ss. 7.4.1–7.4.3; 11.1–11.5; Stein, *Roman Law*, 88–94; Bellomo, *Common Legal Past*, 106–11; 217–20; Wieacker, *History*, 71–112; Tamm, *Roman Law*, 208–10.)

The *usus modernus Pandectarum* dominated German legal scholarship of the seventeenth and early eighteenth centuries. It was not a 'movement' of jurists with similar views, as such, but rather a shared methodological approach to the use of Roman law texts. Unlike the French legal humanists of the previous century who had focused on the historical context of Roman law, the *usus modernus* used Roman law texts as practical solutions to real legal problems. In doing so, they contributed greatly to the development of new doctrines in private law based on existing Roman-law elements. According to Wieacker (*History*, 167): '[i]t is to the legal science of this age—a legal science based on German decision-making, set out in books both learned and practical, broadened because the discipline of the *ius commune* was now applied to the whole of the law—that we owe the particular kinds of law teaching and writing with which we are still familiar today.' The *usus modernus* was an important phase in the development of German national law and contributed to the rise of a national legal consciousness in academic works such as those of Benedikt Carpzov (1595–1666) and Samuel Stryk (1640–1710), while reforms in legal education gave rise to a new German legal science. The *usus modernus*, while predominantly centred in Germany, also had influential supporters in France, the Netherlands, and elsewhere in Western Europe (see Tamm, *Roman Law*, 225).

The seventeenth century saw Western Europe struggling to recover from the Protestant reformation that had fragmented the power of the Church. The rejection of papal authority also had widespread intellectual consequences. It became the age of scientific revolution where authority was rejected in favour of empirical exploration. Furthermore, the seventeenth century saw the rise of a new approach to natural law that rejected the existence of a higher order and proposed that the principles of natural law could be discovered through rational thought (see generally Tamm, *Roman Law*, 231–8). One of the most influential proponents of this view was the Dutch scholar Hugo Grotius whose views on natural law also found favour in Germany in the works of Pufendorf, Wolff, and Thomasius. These scholars, who represent the 'German school of natural lawyers', continued to develop Grotius' notion that natural law should be freed from all authority and suppositions and moulded into a system that could be deduced logically through rational thought. The most famous exponent of this view was Samuel Pufendorf (1632–94). By the start of the eighteenth century, the German concept of natural law had reached new levels of abstraction in the works of Christian Wolff (1679–1754) and Christian Thomasius (1655–1728).

From the middle of the eighteenth century there was evident another form of Reception—this time through the medium of codification. States began to issue national codes that were based in varying degrees on Roman law, which thus ceased to be a direct source of law in these countries but survived as the foundation of their codified law. The trend towards codification was a signal part of the Enlightenment, the intellectual movement—bedded in part in natural law—driven by a philosophy characterized by a reliance on rationalist thought. Reformers invariably desired clarification and rationalization of the law, with the emphasis on organizing it into a simple and manageable system. See Robinson et al., *ELH*, chs. 15–16. Supporters of codification often had opposing views on the purpose of a codification. Some wanted radical and sweeping reform designed to abolish all previous systems of authority (as in France), while others: 'wanted to consolidate a society divided into "orders," "estates" or "levels" and to assure the stability to each of these groups, to guarantee its existence and guide it, in exchange for obedience to a sole and single law (the "code") willed and imposed by a recognized and incontestable sovereign authority' (Bellomo, *Common Legal Past*, 4). Bavaria and Prussia were the forerunners of this latter type of codification, inspired by natural law and brought about by enlightened rulers and their ministers. For example, the Bavarian Civil Code 1756—heavily based on Roman law—was largely the creation of the Elector Max Joseph III and his Chancellor, von Kreittmayr. Efforts to codify Prussian law actually preceded those in Bavaria but did not fully materialize until the code of 1794. The Prussian code—the work primarily of von Carmer and Suarez, encouraged by Frederick William I and II—was extremely detailed and (unlike the Bavarian code) superseded all previous laws (see Tamm, *Roman Law*, 238–9).

The process of codification in Germany was delayed by diverse factors, most notably the academic debate which arose during the early nineteenth century between supporters of the 'Historical School' in Germany. This debate was sparked by A. F. J. Thibaut (1772–1840), a professor from Heidelberg, who published a pamphlet calling for the enactment of a code for Germany. This view was opposed by

Friederich Carl von Savigny (1779–1861), Germany's leading jurist of the early nineteenth century and a staunch supporter of Roman law, who was strongly opposed to codification (and natural law for that matter) on the grounds that Germany was not then ready for it. Indeed, it is difficult to see how a general codification could have been achieved before German unification (which did not occur until 1871). There was, moreover, considerable disagreement as to what codification should entail between the Germanists within the 'Historical School', who emphasized the importance of native tradition, and the Romanists, who advocated Roman law as the foundation of German law. Even within these broad divisions there were sub-currents. For example, the 'Pandectists'—an offshoot of the 'Historical School' headed by Georg Puchta (1798–1846) that dominated German legal scholarship during the second half of the nineteenth century—favoured classical Roman law rather than later models.

The codification process, started soon after the unification of Germany, lasted virtually a quarter of a century and culminated in the enactment of the German Civil Code (*Bürgerliches Gesetzbuch* = BGB) in 1900. Pandectist influence in the codification commissions was substantial, but the final product was a blend of Roman law and Germanic practice. As in the case of the *Code Civil*, the Roman influence was especially pronounced in the law of obligations. Compared to the French code, the BGB is more detailed, but at the same time more abstract and less related to life. 'The Code betrays in both its form and its content the intellectual and social conditions prevailing at the time of its creation. It is general and abstract private law, a system geared not to the conditions of life in society…but to the conceptual apparatus of law' (Wieacker, *History*, 376). In some respects, then, the BGB can be compared to the work of the Roman classical jurists, particularly in their legal isolationism and high degree of conceptualisation (as emphasized by Watson). This characteristic helps to explain the appeal of the German code: '[I]ts scholarly and technical merits outweighed the fact that it had little emotional appeal, political colour, or concern for current social problems. On the contrary, the very abstraction of the BGB apparently made it easier for alien cultures and social orders to assimilate it' (Wieacker, *History*, 384). Among the 'alien cultures' to adopt the BGB were Japan and Brazil. (On the significance of the 'Historical School' in Germany, see Bellomo, *Common Legal Past*, 14–18; Stein, *Roman Law*, 115–18; Robinson et al., *ELH*, ss. 16.2.1–16.2.11; Tamm, *Roman Law*, 252–8. On the 'Pandectists' and their influence on the BGB, see Stein, *Roman Law*, 119–23; Robinson et al., *ELH*, ss. 16.3.1–16.3.8. On the structure of the BGB, see Robinson et al., *ELH*, ss. 16.4.1–16.4.9.)

11.2.3.3 The Netherlands

To understand the way in which the principles of the *ius commune* contributed to the formation of Dutch national law, a brief historical synopsis of what is today known as the Netherlands and Belgium is required. During the late medieval period, the Netherlands (including Belgium) came to be ruled by the powerful and expansionist Dukes of Burgundy, mainly the result of a series of dynastic marriages that incorporated Flanders into the Duchy of Burgundy (thus creating an area as flourishing artistically and economically as any in Europe). The Dukes of Burgundy nominally owed allegiance to the French Crown but in practice were independent. In the sixteenth century, the Netherlands came under the control of the Spanish Crown through a chain of events too tortuous to relate. The Spanish rule of the Netherlands was unpopular with the local population from the start. The rise of Protestantism in the northern regions of the Netherlands and the desire for self-determination fuelled a revolt in the 1560s against the rule of Philip II of Spain. In 1579, the seven northern provinces of the Netherlands seceded from Spain under the Union of Utrecht. The provinces were organized into a confederation (the United Provinces), each retaining a large measure of autonomy through its own laws and courts, but with the province of Holland, because of its wealth and prominence, as its leader. This marked the start of nearly a century of intermittent wars (the so-called 80-year war) through which the Dutch eventually obtained their independence under the Treaty of Münster in 1648. Ironically, despite (or perhaps as a result of) the turbulent political events prevailing in the Netherlands during the sixteenth and seventeenth centuries, it was also one of the most creative periods in Dutch legal history in which the *ius commune* had its most pronounced influence on the formation of Dutch national law.

It is, of course, worth noting that learned law was already prevalent in the Netherlands by the thirteenth century. Flemish and Dutch students attended universities in Italy (and later in France) and the presence of the Church ensured that canon law and the Romano-canonical procedure used in ecclesiastical courts were familiar to the regions of the Netherlands. For much of the fourteenth and fifteenth centuries, however, localized customary law still prevailed. It was only in the latter part of the fifteenth century that the influence of the *ius commune* in the Netherlands became more pronounced. The reasons for this are many and varied, but the following factors deserve mention. The prevalence of localized customary law and the absence of a unified legal system contributed to the Reception of learned law. Two courts with appellate jurisdiction were founded during the fifteenth century in which jurists trained in learned law were employed. In the north, the Court of Holland, Zeeland, and West Friesland (founded in 1428) functioned as the provincial court of appeal for these regions, while the Great Council of Malines (re-established in 1504, based on an earlier model) fulfilled the same function in the south. During the struggle against the Spanish, the Netherlands—predominantly Protestant in the north—became a haven for French humanists escaping the Wars of Religion. This development not only helped to preserve the humanist movement but also fostered a rich tradition of Dutch contribution to jurisprudence, especially in the seventeenth century.

It was also during this century that most Dutch universities were founded (Leyden in 1575, Franeker in 1585). Apart from the infusion of learned law through legal practice, the contributions of academic jurists to the foundation of a legal system for the Netherlands cannot be denied. The term 'Roman–Dutch law', first used by the Dutch jurist Simon de Leeuwen in the seventeenth century, is an indication of the prominence of Roman law in the development of a national legal identity for the United Provinces. In the words of Stein (*Roman Law*, 97–8):

The law of the United Provinces was largely created by Dutch Professors, particularly those of Leyden, and by the judges of the High Courts of the provinces, particularly the *Hooge Raad* of Holland. Through their synthesis of legal science and legal practice, the Netherlands led the rest of Europe in the seventeenth century in the way that France had set the pace in the sixteenth.

Dutch legal science reached its formative peak during the seventeenth century. It was the period in which Roman–Dutch law developed into a fully fledged legal system suited to the needs of an enlightened and wealthy Protestant Dutch Republic with trading interests spreading as far as India and Africa. The outstanding figure of this period was Hugo Grotius (Huig de Groot 1583–1645) whose diverse talents and profound achievements mark him out to be as great a jurist as any in history, ancient or modern. His monumental work *De Iure Belli ac Pacis* ('On the Law of War and Peace') was published in 1625. In it he formulates a system of international law based on his vision of natural law: rational principles—derived from practice, experience, and tradition—which could be regarded as binding on any State. Grotius' vision of natural law represented a significant reinterpretation of the medieval view of natural law (in which divine reason was the source of all law) and was destined to become an important and influential legal–philosophical current in the seventeenth century. It was undoubtedly influenced by the Protestant reformation of the previous century, which had shattered the authority of the Church in Europe, as well as the scientific revolution of the seventeenth century whereby the authority of God as the source of all wisdom was rejected in favour of empirical research and exploration (see Kelly, *Short History*, 222–7). It is through this work that Grotius is widely recognized as the father of international law and modern natural law, as well as influencing major jurists in other jurisdictions such as Pufendorf and the 'German School of Natural Lawyers' in Germany (see 11.2.3.2) and Stair in Scotland (see 11.2.3.4).

Another outstanding work by Grotius was the *Introduction to the Jurisprudence of Holland* (1631) in which he achieved a synthesis of Roman law, custom, and natural law in outlining a *national* legal system. This work is regarded as the literary foundation of Roman–Dutch law. Remarkably, it was mainly written while Grotius was imprisoned for his religious beliefs.

The French humanist influence on the formative period of Roman–Dutch law set the trend for the development of a unique approach to legal scholarship known as 'elegant jurisprudence'. This approach developed principally at the universities of Leyden and Utrecht by a number of distinguished jurists was based on the idea that legal education should consist of a synthesis of theory and practice. Although students of law were primarily trained to become practitioners of law, a course in the basic principles of law (i.e. Roman law) was fundamental to legal education.

Apart from Hugo Grotius whose religious affiliations forced him to spend much of his life away from the Netherlands, other Dutch jurists greatly contributed to the development of Roman–Dutch law as a legal system. While Grotius is often regarded as having laid the literary foundations of this new system in his *Introduction to the Jurisprudence of Holland*, his contemporary Arnold Vinnius (1588–1657), professor of law at Leyden, demonstrated the practical side of Roman–Dutch law in his extensive commentary on the *Institutes* in which he synthesized not only the opinions of German and French writers of the period, but also demonstrated how the rules of law applied to legal practice. Another influential jurist was Johannes Voet (1636–94), also professor at Leyden and a supporter of the *usus modernus Pandectarum*, who produced a majestic commentary on the *Digest* in which Roman law was synthesized with modern custom and legislation.

In the 1650s, the Dutch started to settle at the Cape of Good Hope to try to establish a supply base for the East Indies trade. The settlers brought their own law with them. Thus, Roman–Dutch law became the law of what is now South Africa, as well as throughout the Dutch Empire: 'It is, of course, in itself somewhat ironic that the southern tip of Africa should have become one of the last strongholds in the modern world of European jurisprudence in its original uncodified form' (see Zimmermann, R., in *Civil Law Tradition*, 41 and 44). Roman–Dutch law is still regarded as a formal source of law. However, although Roman–Dutch law has traditionally been the common law of South Africa, it is clear that the influence of English law has been so pronounced that the South African system is best described as a mixed legal system. See Zimmermann, R., *Roman Law in a Mixed Legal System: The South African Experience in Civil Law Tradition*, 41–80 and Fagan, E., 'Roman–Dutch Law in its South African Historical Context', in *Southern Cross*, 33–64.

The history of the codification of Dutch law in the first half of the nineteenth century is closely linked to expansion of the French Empire under Napoleon. In 1795, the Dutch Republic collapsed and was briefly replaced by the Batavian Republic (1795–1806). From 1806 to 1810, Louis Napoleon, brother of the French Emperor, ruled as king over the Netherlands and its existing system of Roman–Dutch law was heavily influenced by French law. During this period the first steps toward the codification of Dutch law were also taken. In 1807, Louis Napoleon instructed Johannes van der Linden, one of the most prominent Roman–Dutch jurists of the nineteenth century to draft a proposed code. The code was largely based on Roman–Dutch law, but it was never enacted. In 1808, under pressure from Napoleon, the French Civil Code was adapted for the Netherlands and enacted in the following year as the *Wetboek Napoleon ingerigt voor het Koninkrijk Holland* (the Code of Napoleon adapted for the Kingdom of Holland). In 1810, the Netherlands was annexed as part of the expanding French Empire and the French Civil Code remained in force until 1815 when French control of the Netherlands ceased. In this year, the sovereign Kingdom of the Netherlands was proclaimed. The next 15 years witnessed two draft codes and the secession of Belgium, but in 1830 the Dutch Civil Code (*Burgerlijk Wetboek* = BW) was enacted. (See Stein, *Roman Law*, 97–11 and Robinson et al., *ELH*, ss. 13.4.1–13.4.7 on Dutch elegant jurisprudence. Bellomo, *Common Legal Past*, 232–4 provides a readable account of the significance of Hugo Grotius and the secularized natural law doctrine of the seventeenth century.)

11.2.3.4 Scotland—a mixed experience

The Roman occupation of Scotland was relatively short-lived, and limited to the south. The Antonine wall—extending roughly between the Clyde and Forth estuaries—marked the northernmost extent of serious Roman expansion in Britain. It is unclear how far Roman legal institutions penetrated to Scotland during the occupation, but following the withdrawal of the Roman armies it is highly improbable that much survived. Little is known about the law in Scotland prior to the eleventh century. It is generally believed that unwritten customary law, which had some affinity to Celtic law, prevailed during this period (see Robinson et al., *ELH*, s. 9.1 and Sellar, W. D. H., 'A Historical Perspective', in Meston, M.C. et al. (1991), *The Scottish Legal Tradition*, Edinburgh: Saltire Society and Stair Society).

The period from the introduction of Anglo-Norman law in Scotland in the twelfth century during the reign of David I until the mid-fifteenth century witnessed some Romanization of local law, but it can hardly be said that a 'Reception' occurred at such an early stage. The law consisted predominantly of custom applied by the local sheriff courts which had limited civil and criminal jurisdiction. Itinerant royal officials known as 'justiciars' also dispensed civil and criminal justice. The King and his Council had a theoretical supervisory jurisdiction over them, but in practice this did not result in any substantial degree of centralization. Local courts (both Sheriff and Franchise) applied the customary law relevant to its jurisdiction: there was thus a very high degree of legal fragmentation. For example, certain towns were granted burgh status, which entitled them to various privileges, including exemption of trade from feudal restrictions. The burgh court would apply the particular customs pertaining to that town. However, although the ground for Romanization was promising, a full-scale Reception never materialized in Scotland. Roman law became an important subsidiary source of law, but it was regarded as at best persuasive rather than binding, and not as the sole or general law of the land. Customary law was never buried by the increasing influence of Roman law; indeed, the burgh laws in particular retained their vitality for a long time.

As elsewhere in late medieval Europe, the canon law of the church courts proved important in the gradual infiltration of Roman notions, especially through the use of Romano-canonical procedure in litigation—its use soon spread to the secular courts. See Robertson, J. J., 'The Canon Law Vehicle of Civilian Influence with particular reference to Scotland' in *Civilian Tradition*, 117–34. This process of infiltration was aided by the existence of ecclesiastical courts alongside sheriff courts (until the reformation during the sixteenth century) to deal with all matters falling within the jurisdiction of the Church. Crucial also was the migration abroad of Scottish students to study Roman and canon law, since there were no universities in Scotland prior to the fifteenth century.

The students at first studied mainly at the Northern Italian universities, then France (especially Paris and Orléans) and later still, Cologne and Louvain. Some of the returning scholars attained high office and contributed vitally to the Romanization of the law. For example, William Elphinstone—who had studied Roman law at Orléans—became Bishop of Aberdeen and Chancellor of Scotland. He appears to have inspired the enactment of the Education Act 1496 which imposed a duty on substantial freeholders to ensure that their sons learned Latin and attended schools of law so as to understand better the laws which they might one day administer. He was also the founder of the University of Aberdeen. The universities of St Andrews and Glasgow had been founded earlier in the fifteenth century through the efforts of bishops who had studied Roman law abroad. A major reason for the foundation of the Scottish universities was to satisfy the obvious need for instruction in canon and Roman law. W. M. Gordon sees this as significant: 'One of the important indications of the value of Roman and Canon law in legal practice is the foundation of universities which had as one of their specific aims the provision of legal education' (*Civil Law Tradition*, 19).

The extent of the use of Roman law in medieval Scotland is difficult to gauge, but there is documentary evidence of Romanist arguments being employed in two celebrated cases *c*.1380: one concerned the issue whether the Abbey of Lindores held lands of the Crown or the Earl of Douglas; the other tested the validity of a decision by the Bishop of Aberdeen that lands had not been validly granted by a former bishop to a certain John Crab. The same was true in the dispute about the succession to the Scottish Crown between John Balliol and Robert Bruce in 1291–92—the Great Cause. See Stein, *Character and Influence*, 294 ff. Moreover, there is evidence of some Roman law influence in early Scottish literature from the thirteenth century onwards, particularly *Regiam Majestatem*, a commentary on legal procedure in royal courts in civil and criminal cases dating probably from the early fourteenth century and *Quoniam Attachiamenta*, a treatise on procedure in baronial courts. And medieval charters point to the level of expertise then current in Roman law: they contain 'renunciations'—clauses expressly excluding specific civilian remedies. The widespread use of renunciations is some evidence—though not conclusive—of the extent to which Roman law was applicable in practice.

The pace and extent of Romanization of the law increased from the late fifteenth century, probably due to increasing reliance by professional advocates (eventually the Faculty of Advocates) on arguments derived from Roman law, and their acceptance by the judges. Indeed, in the seventeenth century, competence in Roman law became an examined element in the general requirements for entry to the Faculty. The Roman law that was received was of course not necessarily that of Justinian, it was that of the *ius commune*—the law as glossed by the Glossators and adapted by the Commentators. In 1532, a supreme appellate court was established—the Court of Session—staffed by a professional judiciary consisting partly of judges trained in Roman and canon law, and operating a Romano-canonical procedure for the most part. The evidence suggests that the judges of Session were prepared to resort to Roman law whenever the indigenous law could not resolve an issue. This more systematic resort to Roman law influenced the local courts, similar to the effect of the restructuring of the *Reichskammergericht*. Moreover, it is possible that political ties with France—the 'Auld Alliance'—strengthened by dynastic intermarriage, contributed to the increased pace of Reception. Scotsmen continued to study in France, especially Bourges, but later the universities of the Netherlands became more popular, Leyden in particular.

The extent of the Reception in Scotland can best be gauged by the literature of the institutional writers, authors whose works are regarded as an authoritative source of Scots law. The work of the institutional writers should be seen in the context of the rise of a national legal identity in Scotland during the sixteenth and seventeenth centuries. See Cairns, J. W. 'Institutional Writings in Scotland Reconsidered' (1983) 4 JLH, 76–117. The sixteenth century was intellectually dominated by the works of the French legal humanists and Scotland's contact with both France and the Netherlands ensured that their views had a lasting impact on the formation of Scots law. See Cairns, J. W., Fergus J. D., and MacQueen, H. L., 'Legal Humanism in Renaissance Scotland' (1990) 11 JLH, 40–69. At the same time, the rise of a national legal identity necessitated the writing of a work similar to Grotius' *Introduction to the Jurisprudence of Holland*, in which Scots law was systematically set out as a legal system based on a combination of learned and customary law. See Luig, K., 'The Institutes of National Law in the Seventeenth and Eighteenth Centuries' (1972) Juridical Review, 193–226. This work was Viscount Stair's *Institutions of the Law of Scotland*, published in 1681. Stair, who became Lord President of the Court of Session, achieved a comprehensive exposition of Scots law, consistent with the rational principles of modern natural law, in which Roman law is acknowledged as a persuasive (if not binding) source of law in the absence of native custom. Other institutional writers of importance included Craig, Mackenzie, Erskine, and Bell. See Robinson et al., *ELH*, s. 14.2.

Union with England in 1707 led to some Anglicization of the law in the long term, and to a corresponding decline in the influence of Roman law. However, the Scottish legal system remains markedly different from its English counterpart in many respects, much of the difference being attributable to the legacy of the

Romanist tradition in Scotland. See Stein, *Character and Influence*, 336 ff. where he concludes: 'the Roman notions which were introduced into Scots law during its formative period were embedded so firmly in its structure that many parts still bear an unmistakably Roman stamp; they cannot be fully comprehended without a knowledge of the Roman institutions from which they derive' (358–9). Robin Evans-Jones suggests that Scotland, essentially a mixed legal system, needs to maintain at least 'two distinct legal cultures of high quality' and that it should occupy 'a challenging position at the interface of the Civil and Common law where it will be well placed, when appropriate, to select what is best from each' (*The Civil Law Tradition in Scotland* (1995), 11). See also Evans-Jones, R., 'Receptions of Law, Mixed Legal Systems and the Myth of the Genius of Scots Private Law' (1998) 114 LQR, 228–49 and Sellar, W. D. H., 'Scots Law: Mixed from the Very Beginning? A Tale of Two Receptions' (2000) 4(1) Edinburgh LR, 3–18. (On the reception of Roman law in Scotland, see Robinson et al., *ELH*, s. 14.1–14.5.8; Stein, *Roman Law*, 87; and comprehensively, Cairns, J. W., 'Historical Introduction', in Reid, K. G. C. and Zimmermann, R. (eds.) (2000), *A History of Private Law in Scotland*, vol. 1.)

11.2.3.5 Roman law in modern Scots law

The reception of Roman law (in its *ius commune* guise) in modern Scots law is a continuing process. The uncodified nature of the legal system and its compatibility with other mixed jurisdictions in areas of property and obligations enables Scottish courts and jurists to make ample use of the civilian heritage of Scots law. See Rodger, A., 'The Use of Civil Law in Scottish Courts', in *Civilian Tradition*, 225–37. The following cases are but a few examples of Scottish courts' use of Roman law in recent decisions.

Sloans Dairies Ltd v Glasgow Corporation 1977 SC 223; 1979 SLT 17
This case dealt with the risk of accidental destruction in a contract of sale (see 9.3.1.4). SD had entered into negotiations with GC to purchase certain buildings. The missives stated that the parties would agree at some point in the future on the date of entry. Before the parties could agree on a date of entry, the buildings were gutted by fire and had to be demolished. GC refused to implement the contract and SD brought an action to enforce it. In the court of the first instance, the Lord Ordinary held:

The rule that the risk of accidental damage to the property passes to the purchaser on the conclusion of the contract stems from the Roman Law of Sale as set out in the Institutes of Justinian ... With the possible exception of Stair (I.14.6) where the position of the purchaser of goods which has perished without fault of the seller is treated as an undecided question, the importation of the rule into Scots law is supported by a long line of authority (Erskine, *Institutes* 337; Bankton I.19.35; Bell's *Commentaries* 2321; Bell's *Principles* (10th edn.) para. 87; ... [at 226–7.]

The court decided that the missives had created a valid contract of sale even though a precise date of entry had not been agreed. Furthermore, it was the opinion of the court that once the missives had been concluded, the risk of accidental destruction passed to the purchaser. GC reclaimed upon the latter point, but the reclaiming motion was refused (see 1979 SLT 17).

Will's Trustees v Cairngorm Canoeing and Sailing School Ltd 1976 SC (HL) 30
This case concerned the status of the river Spey as either a private navigable water-course in which the owners of the riverbanks had exclusive rights of navigation

or a public navigable watercourse to which members of the public had legitimate access (see 6.1.2.2). WT as owners of large stretches of both banks of the river brought an action against CCSS who used said river for recreational purposes. The Lord Ordinary found in favour of CCSS. WT reclaimed, but the decision was upheld. It was decided that, even though the river Spey was not technically a public navigable watercourse, CCSS had established a restricted public right in favour of recreational use of the river. WT appeal to the House of Lords. In the latter decision, the Roman-law position and the writings of the institutional writers in light of an earlier decision (*Grant v Gordon M. 12820*) were extensively examined. The court found in favour of CCSS.

Cantiere San Rocco v Clyde Shipbuilding & Engineering Co. 1923 SC (HL) 105
This case dealt with unjustified enrichment (see 9.9.2). In 1914, Clyde SE contracted with CSR to build and supply a set of maritime engines. The terms of their contract stated that CSR would pay half the purchase price when the contract was signed, while the remaining monies would be paid at specific stages of the construction process. After the first instalment had been paid, but before construction could commence, war broke out. After the war, CSR brought a action in the Court of Session (1922 S.C. 723) stating that the contract had been dissolved by the intervention of war and reclaiming the deposit already paid. The court concurred, but granted Clyde SE leave to reclaim. In the second instance, the earlier decision was overturned in favour of Clyde SE. CSR appealed to the House of Lords. The House of Lords reversed the decision of the first division of the Court of Session and found in favour of CSR. The court reasoned that the instalment had been paid as part of the price for the engines and, since the delivery of the engines had been rendered impossible by the outbreak of war, Clyde SE was responsible for the return of the deposit (subject to any counterclaim that they may have) on the basis of the *condictio causa data causa non secuta*. In its decision, the court examined both Roman law and the views of the institutional writers on the subject.

Morgan Guaranty Trust Co. of New York v Lothian Regional Council 1995 SLT 299
This case dealt with unjustified enrichment (see 9.9.2). In 1987, a local authority (LRC) had entered into an interest rate and currency exchange agreement with a merchant bank (MGT). The agreement would continue until 1992. In 1989, however, a decision in a divisional court in England (*Hazell v Hammersmith and Fulham London Borough Council* (1992) 2 AC 1) found such agreements to be *ultra vires* for local authorities and unlawful. The merchant bank (MGT) reclaimed the amounts paid to LRC. The Lord Ordinary concurred with the decision of the English divisional court on the matter, but found that he was bound by a Scottish case law in which it had been decided that an error of law in the interpretation of a public general statute concerning the contractual capacity of a local authority excluded the use of the *condictio indebiti*. MGT reclaimed and the decision of the Lord Ordinary was reversed. It was decided, after an extensive review of the institutional writers on the point (see 1995 SLT 311) that the *condictio indebiti* did indeed cover this situation and was the appropriate remedy.

McDyer v The Celtic Football and Athletic Co. Ltd. 2000 SC 379
This case concerned the application of the *actio de positis vel suspensis* (see 10.7.1). McDyer was injured when a piece of wood fell from the stadium canopy while he waited for the opening of the European Summer Special Olympic Games. He

sued Celtic FAC (first defenders) as the occupiers of the stadium in terms of s. 2 of the Occupiers' Liability (Scotland) Act 1960 and the organizers of the Special Olympics (second defenders), but did not include the cause of the wood falling or the fault of the defenders in his initial claim. Instead, he relied on the principle of *res ipsa loquitur*. The Lord Ordinary dismissed the claim. McDyer reclaimed to the first division of the Court of Session and was allowed to amend his claim to reflect, *inter alia*, that the defenders incurred strict liability at common law for the incident based on the Roman-law rule of said action which was adopted and modified in Scots law (see 383E–F). The court examined the Roman-law position and the comments of the institutional writers on this point (see 387H–390E). It concurred with the pursuer, following a reading of Bankton, that the Roman-law rule had been received into Scots law, but noted that there was some uncertainty in the works of other institutional writers and later court decisions concerning the basis of the liability. In the end, however, it was the place where the injury had occurred which persuaded the judges *not* to resort to liability on the basis of the *actio de positis vel suspensis*:

> We find it unnecessary in the present case to explore any more fully the questions which counsel for the reclaimer and second respondents raised about the nature of the liability under the old Roman law or about the passages in Bankton and Hume. It is noteworthy that both the Roman law provisions and the Scottish authorities upon which counsel for the reclaimer sought to rely were really concerned with the liability of occupiers and owners of buildings for injury and damage caused to those outside the premises, whether in the streets or in open spaces or on neighbouring properties. In this case, by contrast, we are concerned with the liability of Celtic and European to the pursuer who was actually in some part of the stadium when the piece of wood fell from the canopy area of the stadium. Indeed in each of the alternative cases, the pursuer recognises this and avers that Celtic and European are liable under the Occupiers' Liability (Scotland) Act 1960. In these circumstances it appears to us that the law relating to the liability of the defenders to the pursuers is to be found in terms of the 1960 Act. [at 390G–H]

11.3 Roman law in England

When the Romans colonized Britain, Roman law became the law of the province. But it is not clear to what extent Roman law applied to non-citizens before the general grant of citizenship in AD 212. It is known that Papinian, Paul, and Ulpian were in Britain in AD 208, presumably hearing cases rather than just sightseeing. It is unlikely that Roman law survived for long after the withdrawal of the Roman armies in the early fifth century. Some parallels have been drawn between the codes promulgated by the Anglo-Saxon Kings and the Twelve Tables, but this is not persuasive evidence for the continuity of Roman law in Britain. In all probability Roman law was swept away in the course of the Anglo-Saxon invasions. However, the establishment of the Christian Church in Anglo-Saxon England was largely the work of ecclesiastics from abroad who would have studied canon law and possibly Roman law. Churchmen normally sat in the 'courts' of the time, so it is likely that some of their learning influenced the proceedings.

11.3.1 The medieval period

England was not unaffected by the early stages of the Reception of Roman law. English scholars studied in the law schools abroad; Glossators from Bologna lectured in England; and Roman law became one of the earliest disciplines taught at the universities. Lanfranc, Archbishop of Canterbury and chief counsellor under William the Conqueror, was a notable scholar from Pavia where he studied canon law, Roman law, and Lombard law, before distinguishing himself as a teacher (he was possibly a predecessor of Irnerius at Bologna). He adjudicated on legal issues, but the extent to which he applied his Romanist learning is unclear. Another foreign scholar, Vacarius, a teacher from Bologna, was invited by Archbishop Theobald *c.*1143 to help him administer Canterbury. Vacarius produced the *Liber Pauperum* ('The Book of the Poor'), a compilation of extracts from Justinian's codification for students who could not afford the full texts. The book became heavily used in Roman law studies during the second half of the twelfth century. By 1200 Roman law teaching was flourishing at Oxford but whether Vacarius ever taught there is doubtful. See de Zulueta, F. and Stein, P. G., *The Teaching of Roman Law in England Around 1200* (1990).

The most important works on English law in the early medieval period, commentaries on the 'law and customs' of England by Glanvill and Bracton, demonstrate appreciation of Roman law and some borrowing, mostly of organizational concepts rather than substantial rules. For example, the work attributed to Glanvill—dating from the 1180s when he was Henry II's chief justiciar—makes use of Justinian's *Institutes* in the classification of contractual obligations. Bracton's work (he was probably not the sole author) was written some 50 years later and shows an even more substantial Roman influence. Indeed, Bracton quotes extensively from Justinian, and his treatise demonstrates that Roman law and the work of the Glossators considerably influenced his thinking as a lawyer and judge. Bracton found valuable precedents in Roman law that gave him the tools for presenting English law as a coherent body of law. The royal judges of the time, often trained in Roman canon and civil law, used their learning to fill the gaps in the nascent common law. Some important remedies were possibly inspired by Roman precedents, notably the assize of novel disseisin, which bore resemblance to the praetorian possessory interdicts.

The influence of Roman law in the medieval period can also be seen in the operation of the courts. See Siepp, D. J., 'The Reception of Canon Law and Civil Law in the Common Law Courts before 1600' (1993) 13 Oxford Journal LS, 388–420; Tamm, *Roman Law*, 226–8. Medieval chancellors tended to be trained in Roman canon and civil law. So it is not really surprising that Chancery employed an inquisitorial process conducted by a magistrate (the Lord Chancellor) without the use of a jury, namely Romano-canonical procedure. Star Chamber was similar. The ecclesiastical courts, which had an important jurisdiction in matters such as marriage and wills, applied the canon law of the Roman Catholic Church. The Court of Admiralty was both Romanist in its procedure and in much of the law that it applied (based partly on the maritime code of Rhodes which had been adopted by the Romans). The personnel staffing these courts were largely trained in Roman law. Moreover, civilians were sometimes asked to adjudicate upon issues of State, as on the continent. For example, civilians were included in the commission that determined Richard II's fate when he was deposed.

However, there were developments in medieval England which were not paralleled elsewhere, and which were to prove the decisive obstacle to a full Reception of Roman law in England. A centralized legal system was developed—based on the royal courts at Westminster—and a common law was established throughout the country, thus reducing the importance of local law and custom. Notable among the medieval kings who helped to achieve this transformation were Henry II and Edward I. Moreover, an enduring common law tradition was fostered through the growth of an active legal profession and the evolution of the Inns of Court. The influence of the universities on the operation of the legal system waned sharply. Consequently, the mixture of factors which were conducive to the Reception elsewhere in Europe in the fifteenth and sixteenth centuries—the existence of customary law, fragmented political units, and a university-trained legal profession erudite in Roman law—was absent in England. Nor did the common law courts use Romano-canonical procedure.

11.3.2 **The Tudor period and beyond**

Not all was well with the common law at the time of the crucial stage of the Reception in Europe. By 1500, the common law system was creaking through a combination of rigid formalism, arcane procedures, and a complacent conservatism in Common Pleas, the senior court of the land. There is some evidence (though not conclusive) that the business of the common law courts was declining in the first two or three decades of the sixteenth century. Traditional areas of common law jurisdiction were certainly under threat from the activities of Chancery and Star Chamber, particularly under Wolsey (Lord Chancellor 1515–29). He was deeply hostile to the common law and was accused of trying to subvert it. Nevertheless, hardly anyone (the odd crank apart) seriously called for the replacement of the common law by Roman law. Even had there been a vociferous demand in that direction, it is difficult to see how such a legal transformation could have been achieved: 'A revolutionary Reception was practically impossible because the principles of the common law were part and parcel of the English constitution. To supersede the common law by Roman rules it would have been necessary to sweep away, or at least to modify profoundly, the existing machinery of government; and this...was wholly contrary to the methods, and, indeed, beyond the powers of the Tudor kings' (Holdsworth, W. S., 'The Reception of Roman Law in the Sixteenth Century' (1912) 28 LQR, 236–54, at 247).

Following Wolsey's fall and the break with Rome, the possibility of the common law being replaced by Roman law became even more remote. However, Henry VIII was prepared to create a Regius Professorship of Civil Law at Cambridge in 1540. The first holder—Sir Thomas Smith—acquired a reputation as a civilian in the French humanist tradition. See Stein, *Character and Influence*, 186 ff. On the other hand, when Wriothesley LC allegedly tried to introduce further Roman practices in Chancery in 1546, he was dismissed. The pulses of Romanists may have quickened for a while in the early seventeenth century when James I, who as James VI of Scotland had ruled for some years in a country experiencing a partial reception, found himself much at odds with the common law of England. The eventual defeat of the royalist cause in the reign of Charles I certainly ended any lingering possibility of a delayed Reception in England. Nevertheless, Roman law continued to exercise an influence on English law. For example, that outstanding seventeenth-century judge and common lawyer, Sir Matthew Hale, applied his admiration for Roman law in advocating the need for greater method and organization in English law. And his humanist leanings enabled him to view the evolution of English law in comparative terms, and thus in a more intellectually satisfying manner than had been previously achieved.

Later, outstanding judges such as Holt CJKB and Lord Mansfield made use
of their erudition in Roman law in the development of the commercial law of
England. Moreover, English jurisprudence came to be influenced by Roman law.
For example, the views of Austin, one of the founders of English positivism, were
coloured by his studies in Bonn of the work of early nineteenth-century German
jurists such as Savigny. Austin's study of Roman law clearly influenced his theories
about the nature of law, particularly his view of law as the command of a sovereign
(see Tamm, *Roman Law*, 240–1).

11.3.3 Roman law and modern English law

Although Roman law never became a dominant influence in England, it has
made a significant contribution to English legal culture. Part of the stock-in-
trade of the modern English lawyer consists of the language of Rome and her
law—*animus, consensus ad idem, restitutio in integrum, sui iuris, inter vivos, ultra
vires, eiusdem generis*, and so forth. But it is more than just a question of vocabulary: the grammar of English law has been influenced, especially as regards the
basic distinctions and the classification of the law, e.g. the distinction between
actions *in rem* and *in personam*, or between gifts *inter vivos* and *mortis causa*. And
well-known maxims such as *id certum est quod certum reddi potest* and concepts
such as *nec vi, nec clam, nec precario*, in the operation of easements (see *Newnham
v Willison* later in the chapter) testify that the substantive content of modern
English law has some Roman borrowings. The law of easements and of bailment
have been particularly influenced. Indeed, there continues a regular flow of cases
in which the principles and institutions of Roman law are found to have relevance
(often in providing the historical background to a particular rule applied by the
court). Among such cases in recent years are the following:

Workers Trust and Merchant Bank Ltd v Dojap Investments Ltd [1993] AC 573
The issue in this case was whether a deposit that had been paid under a contract of
sale of land was forfeited to the vendor on the failure by the purchaser to complete
on the due date. The Bank had sold premises to Dojap under a contract requiring a
deposit of 25 per cent, the deposit to be forfeited if the purchaser failed to complete
in time (time being of the essence). Dojap failed to complete in time. In the course
of the judgment of the Privy Council, Lord Browne-Wilkinson stated (578–9):

In general, a contractual provision which requires one party in the event of his breach of
the contract to pay or forfeit a sum of money to the other party is unlawful as being a penalty, unless such provision can be justified as being a payment of liquidated damages being
a genuine pre-estimate of the loss which the innocent party will incur by reason of the
breach. One exception to this general rule is the provision for the payment of a deposit by
the purchaser on a contract for the sale of land. Ancient law has established that the forfeiture of such a deposit (customarily 10 per cent of the contract price) does not fall within the
general rule and can be validly forfeited even though the amount of the deposit bears no
reference to the anticipated loss to the vendor flowing from the breach of contract...The
special treatment afforded to such a deposit derives from the ancient custom of providing
an earnest for the performance of a contract in the form of giving either some physical
token of earnest (such as a ring) or earnest money. The history of the law of deposits can be
traced to the Roman law of *arra*, and possibly further back still: see Howe v. Smith (1884)
27 ChD 89 per Fry LJ at pp. 101–2. Ever since the decision in Howe v. Smith, the nature of
such a deposit has been settled in English law. Even in the absence of express contractual
provision, it is an earnest for the performance of the contract: in the event of completion of

the contract the deposit is applicable towards payment of the purchase price; in the event of the purchaser's failure to complete in accordance with the terms of the contract, the deposit is forfeit, equity having no power to relieve against such forfeiture.

However, the special treatment afforded to deposits is plainly capable of being abused if the parties to a contract, by attaching the label 'deposit' to any penalty, could escape the general rule which renders penalties unenforceable.

The Privy Council's view was that the deposit in this case was not a true deposit by way of earnest; that the forfeiture provision was a penalty; and that the deposit should be returned, subject to the retention of a fund by the Bank for any damage that it might have suffered by reason of the failure to complete on time.

Sen v Headley [1991] Ch 425

The issue was whether there could be a valid *donatio mortis causa* (see 7.3.2) of realty. Shortly before his death from terminal cancer, the donor told the donee that he was giving her his house. The deeds were kept in a steel box, the key to which had been given to the donee by the donor. The Court of Appeal held that a valid *donatio mortis causa* had been made. The decision was controversial because there had previously been considerable doubt whether land could be the subject of such a gift. And property lawyers were understandably concerned that valuable realty could be legally transferred by little more than the utterance of a few words. Nevertheless, the result was consistent with the position in Roman law, although the court did not specifically rely on Roman principles in reaching its decision. But the court did recognize the Roman ancestry of the rules that the gift must be made in contemplation of death and that the gift was to be regarded as absolute only when the donor died.

Newnham v Willison (1987) 56 P & CR 8

This was a dispute between neighbours concerning the plaintiff's use of tracks over the defendant's land. The plaintiff had a right of way over the tracks and contended that the junction between them was a curve rather than a corner. However, he failed to establish the requisite 20 years' use (of the junction as a curve) immediately prior to the proceedings because for over a year prior to the action the defendant had objected to the particular way in which the plaintiff was using the tracks, and had occasionally tried to obstruct him. The plaintiff thus failed to show that his use was not by force, secrecy, or permission, i.e. *nec vi, nec clam, nec precario*. An extract from the judgment of Kerr LJ in the Court of Appeal (17):

In Megarry and Wade [Law of Real Property, 5th edn. at p. 870] the following passage in my view presents a correct summary of the position on the authorities. The heading is 'User as of right': 'The claimant must show that he has used the right as if he were entitled to it, for otherwise there is no ground for presuming that he enjoys it under a grant. From early times English authorities have followed the definition of Roman law: the user which will support a prescriptive claim must be user *nec vi, nec clam, nec precario* (without force, without secrecy, without permission). The essence of this rule is that the claimant must prove not only his own user but also circumstances which show that the servient owner acquiesced in it as in an established right. Since the necessary conditions are negative, it is usually the servient owner who alleges that the user was either forcible, secret or permissive; but the burden of proof on these matters nevertheless rests on the claimant'.

Newnham v Willison is one of a stream of cases down the years in which the *nec vi, nec clam, nec precario* principle has been at issue. Scarcely any other rule of Roman law has had (and continues to have) such widespread application in English law. A more recent example is:

Mills v Silver [1991] 1 All ER 449
The case concerned the acquisition of a prescriptive right of way. The defendants alleged that they were entitled to drive vehicles over a rough track leading from their upland farm in the Black Mountains (one of the highest points of agricultural land in England) across the plaintiffs' land to a public road. Although the plaintiffs made it clear that they did not accept that the defendants had any right to cross the land with vehicles, the latter continued to use the track for that purpose. Indeed, they employed contractors to lay some 700 tons of stone to make the track passable in all weathers. The plaintiffs sought a declaration that the defendants were not entitled to use the track with vehicles, an injunction restraining them from doing so, and damages for trespass. The plaintiffs were successful at first instance, but the Court of Appeal ruled that the defendants had a right of way with vehicles. A crucial issue was whether such user had been *nec precario*. Micklem J held at first instance that the tolerance of such user by previous owners of the plaintiffs' land constituted implied permission. The user was thus by permission (*precario*) and hence prevented a prescriptive right of way from arising. But on appeal it was held that the user was *nec precario*: the user could not be regarded as being by permission simply because the previous landowner had tolerated it. The award of damages for trespass stood, however, because the improvements made to the track went beyond the defendant's right to make repairs.

Waverley Borough Council v Fletcher [1995] 4 All ER 756
The defendant found a valuable medieval gold brooch whilst scanning ground in a public park with his metal detector (he had to dig some nine inches for it). The plaintiffs—the owners of the park—claimed the brooch after a coroner's inquisition had decided that the brooch was not treasure trove. At first instance it was held that the defendant was entitled to it; but the Court of Appeal held in favour of the local authority, applying the principle that an owner of land owned all that was in or attached to it. This was a superior right to that of the finder. In Roman law, the owner would have been absolutely entitled—assuming the brooch was not treasure—without the issue of 'superior right' obtruding. Auld LJ commented that 'the English law of ownership and possession, unlike that of Roman law, is not a system of identifying absolute entitlement but of priority of entitlement' (764).

Indian Oil Corporation Ltd v Greenstone Shipping SA (Panama) [1988] QB 345
This case illustrates how even the most arcane rules of Roman law may have a vital application in modern law. The owners of an oil tanker, chartered to transport a quantity of Russian crude oil belonging to Indian Oil Corporation, wrongfully mixed the Russian oil with their own crude on board the ship. The mixture of oils could not be separated—a classic case of *confusio* (see 7.2.4). Having received short delivery, Indian Oil Corporation claimed damages, and that it was entitled to the residue of oil on board the tanker. The court, upholding the arbitrators' decision, allowed damages but held that the claim to all the oil on board the ship must fail. Where a party wrongfully mixed his own goods with those of another, and they could not practicably be separated, the resulting mixture was held in common, the innocent party being entitled to a quantity equal to that of his goods in the mixture.

The judgment in this case was in effect an application of the Roman principles on *confusio*. Oil, international trade, tankers…and *confusio*—oil drives the modern world and yet its ownership depends in some circumstances on principles formulated in ancient Rome.

 online resource centre   Please consult the Online Resource Centre for revision guidance on this chapter.

FURTHER READING

Backman, C. R. (2003), *The Worlds of Medieval Europe*, Oxford: Oxford University Press, contains a particularly readable account of the history of Byzantine law and society. For an overview of later Byzantine law, see Laiou, A. E. and Simon, D. (1994), *Law and Society in Byzantium: Ninth–Twelfth Centuries*, Washington, D.C.: Dumbarton Oaks Research Library and Collection.

On medieval learned law, see Van Caenegem, R. C. (1991), *Legal History: A European Perspective*, London: Hambledon; and Drew, K. F. (1988), *Law and Society in Early Medieval Europe*, London: Variorum, for an informative overview of the period. Those with a keen interest in specific aspects of this period may also wish to consult one of the following works, Ullmann, W. (1975), *Law and Politics in the Middle Ages*, Cambridge: Cambridge University Press; Ullmann, W. (1980), *Jurisprudence in the Middle Ages*, London: Variorum; Ullmann, W. (1988), *Law and Jurisdiction in the Middle Ages*, London: Variorum.

On medieval canon law, see specifically Brundage, J. A. (1995), *Medieval Canon Law*, London: Longman, and Evans, G. R. (2002), *Law and Theology in the Middle Ages*, London: Routledge. Those with a specialized interest may also wish to consult Ullmann, W. (1975), *The Church and the Law in the Earlier Middle Ages*, London: Variorum; Kuttner, S. (1983), *Gratian and the Schools of Law 1140–1234*, London: Variorum; Winroth, A. (2000), *The Making of Gratian's Decretum*, Cambridge: Cambridge University Press.

On the reformation and its effect on the development of the European *ius commune*, see comprehensively Berman, H. J. (2003), *Law and Revolution II: The Impact of Protestant Reformations on the Western Legal Tradition*, Cambridge, MA: Harvard University Press.

On natural law, Enlightenment and codification, see Stein, P. (1980), *Legal Evolution: The Story of an Idea*, Cambridge: Cambridge University Press; Watson, A. (1981), *The Making of the Civil Law*, Cambridge, MA: Harvard University Press.

On the reception of Roman law in Germany, see Kunkel, W., 'The Reception of Roman Law in Germany', in *Pre-Reformation Germany*, 263–81; Berman, H. J. (1983), *Law and Revolution*, Cambridge, MA: Harvard University Press; Whitman, J. Q. (1990), *The Legacy of Roman Law in the German Romantic Era*, Princeton: Princeton University Press; Stein, P. G., 'Legal Education in Mid-Nineteenth Century in Germany through English Eyes', in *Quaestiones Iuris*, 233–7; Van Caenegem, R. C. (2002), *European Law in the Past and the Future—Unity and Diversity over Two Millennia*, Cambridge: Cambridge University Press.

On the reception of Roman law in the Netherlands, see the particularly readable account of Zimmermann, R., 'Roman–Dutch Jurisprudence and its Contribution to European Private Law' (1992) 66 Tulane LR, 1685–1721. Those with a keen interest in this topic may also wish to consult Van Caenegem, R. C. (1994), *Law, History, the Low Countries and Europe*, London: Hambledon, as well as Feenstra, R. and Waal, C. J. D. (1975), *Seventeenth-Century Leyden Law Professors and their Influence on the Development of the Civil Law: A Study of Bronchorst, Vinnius and Voet*, Amsterdam: North-Holland Publishing Company.

On customary law in pre-feudal and feudal Scotland, see Stein, P. G., 'Roman Law in Medieval Scotland', in Stein, *Character and Influence*, 269 ff.; Sellar, W. D. H., 'The Common Law of Scotland and the Common Law of England', in Davies, R. R. (ed.) (1988), *The British Isles, 1100–1500*, Edinburgh: John Donald, 82–99.

On the reception of Roman law in Scotland, see Stein, P. G., 'The Influence of Roman Law on the Law of Scotland' (1963) Juridical Review, 205–45; Stein, P. G. (1968), *Roman Law in Scotland* (*Ius Romanum Medii Aevi*, pars v, 13b), Milan: Giuffrè; and Cairns, J. W., 'The Civil Law Tradition in Scottish Legal Thought', in *Civilian Tradition*, 191–224.

On English common law, see Van Caenegem, R. C., 'The English Common Law: A Divergence from the European Pattern' (1979) 47 TR, 1–7; Van Caenegem, R. C. (1988), *Birth of the English Common Law* (2nd edn.) Cambridge: Cambridge University Press; Hudson, J. (1996), *The Formation of the English Common Law: Law and Society in England from the Norman Conquest to the Magna Carta*, London: Longman.

On the debate concerning the use of Roman law as the basis of the new *ius commune* of the European Union, see Cairns, J. W., 'Comparative Law, Unification and Scholarly Creation of a New Ius Commune' (1981) 32 Northern Ireland LQ, 272–83; Schulze, R., 'European Legal History—A New Field of Research in Germany' (1992) 13 JLH, 270–95; Zimmermann, R., 'Roman Law and Comparative Law: The European Perspective' (1995) 16 JLH, 21–33; Luig, K., 'The History of Roman Private law and the Unification of European Private Law' (1997) 5 ZEP, 405–27.

BIBLIOGRAPHY

1. BOOKS CITED IN ABBREVIATED FORMAT

Bablitz, *Actors and Audience* — Bablitz, L. (2007). *Actors and Audience in the Roman Courtroom*, London/New York: Routledge.

Bannon, *Gardens and Neighbors* — Bannon, C. J. (2009). *Gardens and Neighbors: Private Water Rights in Roman Italy*, Ann Arbor, MI: University of Michigan Press.

Bauman, *Lawyers and Politics* — Bauman, R. A. (1989). *Lawyers and Politics in the Early Roman Empire*, Munich: Beck.

Bauman, *Lawyers in Roman Republican Politics* — Bauman, R. A. (1983). *Lawyers in Roman Republican Politics: A Study of the Roman Jurists in their Political Setting 316–82 BC*, Munich: Beck.

Bellomo, *Common Legal Past* — Bellomo, M. (1995). *The Common Legal Past of Europe, 1000–1800*, trans. from 2nd edn. by Lydia G. Cochrane, Washington, DC: Catholic University of America Press.

Birks, *Obligations* — Birks, P. *The Roman Law of Obligations*, edited by E. Descheemaeker, Oxford: Oxford University Press.

Brennan, *Praetorship* — Brennan, T. C. (2000). *The Praetorship in the Roman Republic*, New York: Oxford University Press.

Buckland, *Textbook* — Buckland, W. W. (1975). *A Textbook of Roman Law*, 3rd revd. edn. by P. Stein, Cambridge: Cambridge University Press.

Buckland and McNair, *Roman Law and Common Law* — Buckland W. W. and McNair, A. D. (1965). *Roman Law and Common Law: A Comparison in Outline*, 2nd revd. edn. by F. H. Lawson, Cambridge: Cambridge University Press.

Crook, *Law and Life of Rome* — Crook, J. A. (1967). *Law and Life of Rome, 90 BC–AD 212*, Ithaca, NY: Cornell University Press.

Daube, *Roman Law* — Daube, D. (1969). *Roman Law: Linguistic, Social and Philosophical Aspects*, Edinburgh: Edinburgh University Press.

Descheemaeker, *Division* — Descheemaeker, E. (2009). *The Division of Wrongs*, Oxford: Oxford University Press.

Diósdi, *Ownership* — Diósdi, G. (1970), *Ownership in Ancient and Preclassical Roman Law*, Budapest: Akadémiai Kiadó.

Evans Grubbs, *Women* — Evans Grubbs, J. (2002), *Women and the Law in the Roman Empire: a Sourcebook on Marriage, Divorce and Widowhood*, London/New York: Routledge

Frier, *Casebook on Delict* — Frier, B. W. (1989). *A Casebook on the Roman Law of Delict*, Atlanta, GA: Scholars Press.

Frier, *Roman Jurists*   Frier, B. W. (1985). *The Rise of the Roman Jurists: Studies in Cicero's Pro Caecina*, Princeton, NJ: Princeton University Press.

Frier and McGinn,   Frier, B. W. and McGinn, T. A. J. (2004). *A Casebook*
   Casebook   *on Roman Family Law*, Oxford: Oxford University Press.

Gardner, *Roman Citizen*   Gardner, J. F. (1993). *Being a Roman Citizen*, London: Routledge.

Gardner, *Women in*   Gardner, J. F. (1986). *Women in Roman Law and Society*,
   Roman Law   London: Croom Helm.

Gardner and   Gardner J. F. and Wiedemann, T. (1991). *The Roman*
   Wiedemann, *Roman*   *Household: A Sourcebook*, London: Routledge.
   Household

Gordon, *Transfer of*   Gordon, W. M. (1970). *Studies in the Transfer of*
   Property   *Property by Traditio*, Aberdeen: Aberdeen University Press.

Hausmaninger,   Hausmaninger, H. Gamauf, R., and Sheets, G. (2012).
   Gamauf, and Sheets,   *A Casebook on Roman Property Law*, Oxford: Oxford
   Casebook   University Press.

Helmholz, *Spirit*   Helmholz, R. (1996). *The Spirit of Classical Canon Law*, Athens, GA/London: University of Georgia Press.

Johnston, *Roman Law*   Johnston, D. (1999). *Roman Law in Context*,
   in Context   Cambridge: Cambridge University Press.

Jolowicz and Nicholas,   Jolowicz, H. F. (1972). *Historical Introduction to the*
   Historical Introduction   *Study of Roman Law*, 3rd edn. by B. Nicholas, London: Cambridge University Press.

Kelly, *Civil Judicature*   Kelly, J. M. (1976). *Studies in the Civil Judicature of the Roman Republic*, Oxford: Clarendon Press.

Kelly, *Roman Litigation*   Kelly, J. M. (1966). *Roman Litigation*, Oxford: Clarendon Press.

Kelly, *Short History*   Kelly, J. M. (1992). *A Short History of Western Legal Theory*, Oxford: Clarendon Press.

Lee, *Elements*   Lee, R. W. (1944). *The Elements of Roman Law*, London: Sweet & Maxwell.

Lesaffer, *ELH*   Lesaffer, R. (2009). *European Legal History*, Cambridge: Cambridge University Press.

Lintott, *Constitution*   Lintott, A. (1999). *The Constitution of the Roman Republic*, Oxford: Clarendon Press.

McGinn, *Prostitution*   McGinn, T. A. J. (2003). *Prostitution, Sexuality and the Law in Ancient Rome*, Oxford: Oxford University Press.

Metzger, *Companion*   Metzger, E. (ed.) (1998). *A Companion to Justinian's Institutes*, London: Duckworth.

Metzger, *Litigation*   Metzger, E. (2005). *Litigation in Roman Law*, Oxford: Oxford University Press.

Mousourakis, *Historical and Institutional Context*	Mousourakis, G. (2003). *The Historical and Institutional Context of Roman Law*, Aldershot: Ashgate.
Mousourakis, *Legal History*	Mousourakis, G. (2007). *A Legal History of Rome*, London/New York: Routledge.
Nicholas, *Introduction*	Nicholas, B. (2008). *An Introduction to Roman Law*, with an introductory foreword, revd. bibliography, and glossary of Latin terms by E. Metzger, Oxford: Oxford University Press.
Pugsley, *Justinian's Digest and the Compilers*	Pugsley, D. (1995). *Justinian's Digest and the Compilers* (vol. 1), Exeter: Exeter University Press. Vol. 2 (2000).
Pugsley, *Property and Obligations*	Pugsley, D. (1972). *The Roman Law of Property and Obligations: An Historical Introduction to Some of the Main Institutions*, Cape Town: Juta.
Roberts, *History*	Roberts, J. M. (1996). *A History of Europe*, Oxford: Helicon.
Robinson, *Sources*	Robinson, O. F. (1997). *The Sources of Roman Law: Problems and Methods for Ancient Historians*, London: Routledge.
Robinson et al., *ELH*	Robinson, O. F., Fergus, T. D., and Gordon, W. M. (2000). *European Legal History: Sources and Institutions*, 3rd edn., London: Butterworths.
Schulz, *Classical Roman Law*	Schulz, F. (1951). *Classical Roman Law*, Oxford: Clarendon Press.
Schulz, *History of Roman Legal Science*	Schulz, F. (1946). *History of Roman Legal Science*, Oxford: Clarendon Press.
Stein, *Character and Influence*	Stein, P. G. (1988). *The Character and Influence of Roman Law: Historical Essays*, London: Hambledon.
Stein, *Legal Institutions*	Stein, P. G. (1984). *Legal Institutions: The Development of Dispute Settlement*, London: Butterworths.
Stein, *Roman Law*	Stein, P. G. (1999). *Roman Law in European History*, Cambridge: Cambridge University Press.
Tamm, *Roman Law*	Tamm, D. (1997). *Roman Law and European Legal History*, Copenhagen: Djøf.
Tellegen-Couperus, *Short History*	Tellegen-Couperus, O. E. (1993). *A Short History of Roman Law*, London: Routledge.
Watson, *Law Making*	Watson, A. (1974). *Law Making in the Later Roman Republic*, Oxford: Clarendon Press.
Watson, *Spirit of Roman Law*	Watson, A. (1995). *The Spirit of Roman Law*, Athens, GA: University of Georgia Press.
Watson, *Twelve Tables*	Watson, A. (1975). *Rome of the XII Tables: Persons and Property*, Princeton, NJ: Princeton University Press.
Wieacker, *Festschrift*	Wieacker, F. (1978). *Festschrift für Franz Wieacker zum siebzigsten Geburtstag*, Göttingen: Vandenhoeck und Ruprecht.

Wieacker, *History*	Wieacker, F. (1995). *A History of Private Law in Europe: With Particular Reference to Germany*, trans. by Tony Weir, Oxford: Clarendon Press.
Zimmermann, *Obligations*	Zimmermann, R. (1996). *The Law of Obligations: Roman Foundations of the Civilian Tradition*, Oxford: Clarendon Press.

2. COLLECTED WORKS CITED IN ABBREVIATED FORMAT

Americans are Aliens	Pugsley, D. (ed.) (1989). *Americans are Aliens: And Other Essays on Roman Law*, Exeter: Exeter University Press.
Beyond Dogmatics	Cairns, J. W. and Du Plessis, P. J. (eds.) (2007). *Beyond Dogmatics: Law and Society in the Roman World*, Edinburgh: Edinburgh University Press.
Cambridge Companion	Johnston, D. (ed.) (2015). *The Cambridge Companion to Roman Law*, Cambridge: Cambridge University Press.
Civil Law Tradition	Evans-Jones, R. (ed.) (1995). *The Civil Law Tradition in Scotland*, Edinburgh: Stair Society.
Civilian Tradition	Carey Miller, D. L. and Zimmermann, R. (eds.) (1997). *The Civilian Tradition and Scots Law: Aberdeen Quincentenary Essays*, Berlin: Duncker & Humblot.
Collatio Iuris Romani	Feenstra, R. et al. (eds.) (1995). *Collatio Iuris Romani: Études Dédiées à Hans Ankum à l'occasion de son 65e Anniversaire*, (2 vols.), Amsterdam: J. C. Gieben.
Critical Studies	Cairns, J. W. and Robinson, O. F. (eds.) (2001). *Critical Studies in Ancient Law, Comparative Law and Legal History*, Oxford: Hart Publishing.
Daube Collected Studies	Cohen, D. and Simon, D. (eds.) (1991). *Collected Studies in Roman Law: David Daube*, Frankfurt am Main: Vittorio Klostermann.
Daube Collected Works	Carmichael, C. M. (ed.) (1992). *Collected Works of David Daube*, (2 vols.), Los Angeles, CA: UCLA Berkeley, Robbins Collection Publications.
Daube Noster	Watson, A. (ed.) (1974). *Daube Noster: Essays in Legal History for David Daube*, Edinburgh: Scottish Academic Press.
Family in Ancient Rome	Rawson, B. (ed.) (1986) (new edn. 1992). *The Family in Ancient Rome: New Perspectives*, London: Croom Helm.
Forms of Control	Yuge, T. and Doi, M. (eds.) (1988). *Forms of Control and Subordination in Antiquity*, Leiden: Brill.
Iniuria and the Common Law	Descheemaeker, E. and Scott, H. (eds.) (2013). *Iniuria and the Common Law*, Oxford: Hart Publishing.
Judge and Jurist	Burrows, A. et al. (eds.) (2013). *Judge and Jurist—Essays in Memory of Lord Rodger of Earlsferry*, Oxford: Oxford University Press.
Liber Amicorum Guido Tsuno	Sturm, F. et al. (eds.) (2013). *Liber Amicorum Guido Tsuno*, Frankfurt am Main: Vico.

Maior Viginti   Spruit, J. E. (ed.) (1979). *Maior Viginti Quinque Annis: Essays*
   Quinque Annis   *in Commemoration of the Sixth Lustrum of the Institute*
                            for Legal History of the University of Utrecht, Assen (The
                            Netherlands): Van Gorcum.

Mapping the Law   Burrows, A. and Rodger, A. (eds.) (2006). *Mapping the*
                            Law: Essays in Memory of Peter Birks, Oxford: Oxford
                            University Press.

Marriage, Divorce   Rawson, B. (ed.) (1991). *Marriage, Divorce and Children in*
   and Children   *Ancient Rome*, Oxford: Clarendon Press.

Mélanges de   Caes, L. et al. (eds.) (1949–50). *Mélanges Ferdinand de Visscher*, (4
   Visscher   vols.) Brussels: Office international de librairie.

Mélanges de   Zablocka, M. et al. (eds.) (2000). *Au-delà des Frontières:*
   Wolodkiewicz   *Mélanges de Droit Romain Offerts à Witold Wolodkiewicz*,
                            Warsaw: Liber.

New Perspectives   Birks, P. (ed.) (1989). *New Perspectives in the Roman Law of*
                            Property: Essays for Barry Nicholas, Oxford: Clarendon Press.

Obligations in   McGinn, T. A. J. (ed.) (2012). *Obligations in Roman Law: Past*
   Roman Law   *Present and Future*, Ann Arbor MI: The University of
                            Michigan Press.

Omaggio à Peter   *Omaggio à Peter Stein*, Naples: Jovene. Special Edition of
   Stein   (1994) 22 Index.

Quaestiones Iuris   Manthe, U. et al. (eds.) (2000). *Quaestiones Iuris: Festschrift*
                            für Joseph Georg Wolf zum 70. Geburtstag, Berlin: Duncker &
                            Humblot.

Ricerche Gallo   Romano, S. (ed.) (1997). *Nozione, Formazione e Interpretazione*
                            del Diritto: Dall'età Romana alle Esperienze Moderne: Ricerche
                            Dedicate al Professor Filippo Gallo, (4 vols.) Naples: Jovene.

Roman Law   Lewis, A. D. E. and Ibbetson, D. (eds.) (1994). *The Roman Law*
   Tradition   *Tradition*, Cambridge: Cambridge University Press.

Roman Statutes   Crawford, M. H. (ed.) (1996). *Roman Statutes*, (2 vols.)
                            London: University of London.

Senatus   Paananen, U. et al. (eds.) (1993). *Senatus Populusque*
   Populusque   *Romanus: Studies in Roman Republican Legislation*,
   Romanus   Helsinki: Institutum Romanum Finlandiae.

Slavery and Unfree   Archer, L. J. (ed.) (1988). *Slavery and Other Forms of Unfree*
   Labour   *Labour*, London: Routledge.

Sodalitas   Giuffrè, V. (ed.) (1984–5). *Sodalitas: Scritti in Onore di Antonio*
                            Guarino, Naples: Jovene.

Southern Cross   Zimmermann, R. and Visser, D. (eds.) (1996). *Southern Cross:*
                            Civil and Common Law in South Africa, Cape Town: Juta.

Speculum Iuris   Aubert, J-J. and Sirks, A. J. B. (eds.) (2002). *Speculum*
                            Iuris: Roman Law as a Reflection of Social and Economic Life in
                            Antiquity, Ann Arbor, MI: University of Michigan Press.

Status Familiae   Knothe, H-G. and Kohler, J. (eds.) (2001). *Status*
                            Familiae: Festschrift für Andreas Wacke zum 65. Geburtstag,
                            Munich: Beck.

Studi Albertario	Lavaggi, G. et al. (eds). (1953). *Studi in Memoria di Emilio Albertario*, Milan: Giuffrè.
Studi Biscardi	Pastori, F. et al. (eds.) (1982). *Studi in onore di Arnaldo Biscardi*, Milan: Istituto editoriale Cisalpino, La Goliardica.
Studi Grosso	(1968–74). *Studi in Onore di Guiseppe Grosso*, (4 vols.) Turin: G. Giappichelli.
Studi Sanfilippo	(1982). *Studi in Onore di Cesare Sanfilippo*, Milan: Giuffrè.
Studi Solazzi	(1948). *Studi in onore di Siro Solazzi nel Cinquantesimo Anniversario del suo Insegnamento Universitario (1899–1948)*, Naples: Jovene.
Studi Volterra	Aru, L. et al. (1971). *Studi in Onore di Edoardo Volterra*, Milan: Giuffrè.
Studies A. A. Schiller	Bagnall, R. S. and Harris, W. V. (eds.) (1986). *Studies in Roman Law in Memory of A. Arthur Schiller*, Leiden: Brill.
Studies in the Roman Law of Sale	Daube, D. (ed.) (1959). *Studies in the Roman Law of Sale Dedicated to the Memory of Francis de Zulueta*, Oxford: Clarendon Press.
Studies J. A. C. Thomas	Stein, P. G. and Lewis, A. D. E. (eds.) (1983). *Studies in Justinian's Institutes in Memory of J. A. C. Thomas*, London: Sweet & Maxwell.
Studies Litewski	Sondel, J. et al. (eds.) (2003). *Roman Law as Formative of Modern Legal Systems: Studies in Honour of Wieslaw Litewski*, Kraków: Jagiellonian University.
Studies in Roman Property	Finley, M. I. (ed.) (1976). *Studies in Roman Property*, Cambridge: Cambridge University Press.
Summa Eloquentia	Van den Bergh, H. (ed.) (2002). *Summa Eloquentia: Essays in Honour of Margaret Hewett*, Pretoria: University of South Africa.
Synteleia Arangio-Ruiz	Guarino, A. and Labruna, L. (eds.) (1964). *Synteleia Vincenzo Arangio-Ruiz*, (2 vols.) Naples: Jovene.
The Family in Italy	Kertzer, D. I. and Saller, R. P. (eds.) (1991). *The Family in Italy: From Antiquity to the Present*, New Haven: Yale University Press.
The Legal Mind	MacCormick, N. and Birks, P. (eds.) (1986). *The Legal Mind: Essays for Tony Honoré*, Oxford: Clarendon Press.
Theories of Property	Parel, A. and Flanagan, T. (eds.) (1979). *Theories of Property: Aristotle to the Present*, Waterloo, Ont.: Wilfried Laurier University Press.
Thinking Like a Lawyer	McKechnie, P. (ed.) (2002). *Thinking Like a Lawyer: Essays on Legal History and General History for John Crook on his Eightieth Birthday*, Leiden: Brill.

The amount of published material on Roman law (in English alone) is immense. The following is a small selection of works that the student will find helpful, as the authors did in preparing this book.

3. ORIGINAL TEXTS AND COMMENTARIES

The Institutes of Gaius—This work is available in many English translations. A useful recent translation with corresponding Latin text and vocabulary is, Gordon, W. M. and Robinson, O. F. (1988), *The Institutes of Gaius*, London: Duckworth. An older, yet equally useful translation is de Zulueta, F. (1946–53), *The Institutes of Gaius, Text, Translation and Commentary*, Oxford: Clarendon Press. de Zulueta's detailed commentary on individual texts in the second part of this work is a testament to the genius of this scholar and remains extremely useful, despite its age.

The Institutes of Justinian—English translations of this work include, Moyle, J. B. (various editions), *The Institutes of Justinian*, Oxford: Clarendon Press, a two-volume set consisting of the Latin text with a thorough commentary in the footnotes in volume 1 and an English translation in volume 2; Lee, R. W. (1952), *Elements of Roman Law*, London: Sweet & Maxwell; and Thomas, J. A. C. (1975), *Justinian's Institutes, text, translation and commentary*, Amsterdam: North-Holland Publishing Co. A useful recent translation with corresponding Latin text is, Birks, P. and McLeod, G. (1987), *Justinian's Institutes Translated With an Introduction*, London: Duckworth. The introduction to this translation contains many useful insights, particularly concerning the institutional scheme and its importance in European legal history. To this list should be added Metzger, E. (ed.) (1998), *A Companion to Justinian's Institutes*, London: Duckworth. This work contains a detailed commentary on individual texts of the *Institutes* by many of the foremost Scottish Romanists.

The Digest and the Code—The most recent English translation is that of Watson, A. (ed.) (1985), *Justinian's Digest*, text by T. Mommsen with the aid of P. Krueger, Philadelphia: University of Pennsylvania Press. Although this work has been criticized for its 'Americanisms', it remains an indispensable teaching tool, since the quality of the translations is overall much better than the dubious attempts in Scott, S. P. (1932), *The Civil Law*, Cincinnati: The Central Trust Company. There is an excellent modern English translation of Justinian's *Codex* to be found online at: http://www.uwyo.edu/lawlib/blume-justinian/. While an attempt was made in Scott's *Civil Law*, the translation should be approached with caution.

The Theodosian Code and the Novels—The standard English translation is Pharr, C. (ed.) (1952), *The Theodosian Code and Novels: and the Sirmondian Constitutions—A Translation with Commentary, Glossary, and Bibliography*, Princeton, NJ: Princeton University Press. The main drawback of this translation is that the corresponding Greek and Latin texts have not been included. An English translation of the Novels may be found at http://uwacadweb.uwyo.edu/blume&justinian/default.asp

It is not the purpose of this work to provide a comprehensive instruction manual for those wishing to engage in Roman-law research, but it is worth noting that many recent works on the external legal history of Roman law contain excellent accounts of the use of non-legal sources. On the nature and location of these sources, see Robinson, *Sources*, 66–73 and Mousourakis, *Historical and Institutional Context*, 6–16 (especially the footnotes). For a survey of the literary and epigraphic sources of each period in the historical evolution of Roman law, see Tellegen-Couperus, *Short History*, s. 1.1 (Archaic law), s. 4.1 (Late Republic), s. 7.1 (Principate), s. 10.1 (Dominate). Nearly all of the literary sources (Greek and Latin) are available in translation (with corresponding text) in the Loeb Classical Library Series. Translations appearing in older editions of this series should be approached with great care, since they tend to be rather florid and somewhat inaccurate. Many English translations of classical texts and epigraphic sources are also available online. For more information, follow the links on the companion website.

4. TEXTBOOKS

Buckland, W. W. (1931). *The Main Institutions of Roman Private Law*, Cambridge: Cambridge University Press.

Buckland, W. W. (1963). *A Textbook of Roman Law from Augustus to Justinian*, 3rd edn. by P. G. Stein, Cambridge: Cambridge University Press.

Kaser, M. (1968). *Roman Private Law*, 2nd edn., trans. by R. Dannenbring, London: Butterworths.

Leage, R. W. (1961). *Leage's Roman Private Law Founded on the Institutes of Gaius and Justinian*, 3rd edn., by A. M. Prichard, London: Macmillan.

Lee, R. W. (1956). *The Elements of Roman Law*, 4th edn., London: Sweet & Maxwell.

Nicholas, B. (1962). *An Introduction to Roman Law*, Oxford: Clarendon Press.

Schulz, F. (1951). *Classical Roman Law*, Oxford: Clarendon Press.

Thomas, J. A. C. (1976). *Textbook of Roman Law*, Amsterdam: North-Holland Publishing Co.

Van Warmelo, P. (1976). *An Introduction to the Principles of Roman Civil Law*, Cape Town: Juta.

5. HISTORY AND SOURCES OF ROMAN LAW

Anderson, C. (2009). *Roman Law [Law Essentials]*, Dundee: University Press.

Bauman, R. A. (1985). *Lawyers in Roman Transitional Politics: A Study of the Roman Jurists in their Political Setting in the Late Republic and Triumvirate*, Munich: Beck.

Cornell, T. (1995), The Beginnings of Rome: Italy and Rome from the Bronze Age to the Punic Wars (c. 1000–264 B.C.), London/New York: Routledge.

Grant, M. (1996). *History of Rome*, London: Weidenfeld & Nicholson.

Grant, M. (1996). *The Fall of the Roman Empire*, London: Weidenfeld & Nicholson.

Grubbs, J. E. (1995). *Law and Family in Late Antiquity—The Emperor Constantine's Marriage Legislation*, Oxford: Oxford University Press.

Honoré, A. M. (1962). *Gaius*, Oxford: Clarendon Press.

Honoré, A. M. (1978). *Tribonian*, London: Duckworth.

Honoré, A. M. (1981). *Emperors and Lawyers*, London: Duckworth.

Honoré, A. M. (1982). *Ulpian*, Oxford: Clarendon Press.

Honoré, A. M. (1994). *Emperors and Lawyers: With a Palingenesia of Third-Century Imperial Rescripts, 119–305 AD*, 2nd completely revd edn., Oxford: Clarendon Press.

Honoré, A. M. (2002). *Ulpian: Pioneer of Human Rights*, Oxford: Oxford University Press.

Kunkel, W. (1966). *An Introduction to Roman Legal and Constitutional History*, trans. by J. M. Kelly, Oxford: Clarendon Press.

Schiller, A. A. (1978). *Roman Law: Mechanisms of Development*, New York: Mouton Publishers.

Schulz, F. (1946). *History of Roman Legal Science*, Oxford: Clarendon Press.

Sellers, M. N. S. (1994). *American Republicanism: Roman Ideology in the United States Constitution*, London: Macmillan.

Syme, R. (1939). *The Roman Revolution*, Oxford: University Press.

Toynbee, J. M. C. (1971). *Death and Burial in the Roman World*, Baltimore, MD: Johns Hopkins University Press.

Vinogradoff, P. (1929). *Roman Law in Medieval Europe*, 2nd edn., Oxford: Clarendon Press.

Watson, A. (1985). *The Evolution of Law*, Oxford: Blackwell.

Zulueta, F. de and Stein, P. G. (1990). *The Teaching of Roman Law in England Around 1200*, London: Selden Society.

6. OTHER WORKS

Duff, A. M. (1958). *Freedmen in the Early Roman Empire*, Cambridge: W. Heffer.

Duff, P. W. (1938). *Personality in Roman Private Law*, Cambridge: Cambridge University Press.

Johnston, D. (1988). *The Roman Law of Trusts*, Oxford: Clarendon Press.

Jolowicz, H. F. (1957). *Roman Foundations of Modern Law*, Oxford: Clarendon Press.

Kelly, J. M. (1966). *Roman Litigation*, Oxford: Clarendon Press.

Kirschenbaum, A. (1987). *Sons, Slaves and Freedmen in Roman Commerce*, Washington, DC: Catholic University of America Press.

Kortmann, J. (2005). *Altruism in Private Law*, Oxford: Oxford University Press.

Lawson, F. H. (1950). *Negligence in the Civil Law: Introduction and Select Texts*, Oxford: Clarendon Press.

Lintott, A. (1993). *Imperium Romanum: Politics and Administration*, London: Routledge.

Polojac, M. (2003). *Actio de Pauperie and Liability for Damage Caused by Animals in Roman Law*, Belgrade: Dosije.

Robinson, O. F. (1994). *Ancient Rome: City Planning and Administration*, 2nd edn., London: Routledge.

Robinson, O.F. (1995). *The Criminal Law of Ancient Rome*, Baltimore MD: Johns Hopkins University Press.

Rodger, A. (1972). *Owners and Neighbours in Roman Law*, Oxford: Clarendon Press.

Samuel, G. (1994). *The Foundations of Legal Reasoning*, Antwerp: Maklu.

Treggiari, S. (1969). *Roman Freedmen during the Late Republic*, Oxford: Clarendon Press.

Treggiari, S. (1991). *Roman Marriage: Iusti Coniuges from the Time of Cicero to the Time of Ulpian*, Oxford: Clarendon Press.

Watson, A. (1961). *Contract of Mandate in Roman Law*, Oxford: Clarendon Press.

Watson, A. (1965). *The Law of Obligations in the Later Roman Republic*, Oxford: Oxford University Press.

Watson, A. (1967). *The Law of Persons in the Later Roman Republic*, Oxford: Clarendon Press.

Watson, A. (1968). *The Law of Property in the Later Roman Republic*, Oxford: Clarendon Press.

Watson, A. (1987). *Roman Slave Law*, Baltimore, MD: Johns Hopkins University Press.

Wiedemann, T. (1981). *Greek and Roman Slavery*, London: Routledge.

Zulueta, F. de (1945). *The Roman Law of Sale: Introduction and Select Texts*, Oxford: Clarendon Press.

A note on Handbooks, Companions, and Sourcebooks:

The proliferation of Handbooks, Companions, and Sourcebooks produced by the major publishing houses has resulted in many useful chapters being written on topics relating to Roman law. The reader will benefit greatly from the following short list of works as there is much on Roman law contained in them:

Barchiesi, A. and Scheidel, W. (eds.) (2010). *The Oxford Handbook of Roman Studies*, Oxford: Oxford University Press.

Erdkamp, P. (ed.) (2013). *The Cambridge Companion to Ancient Rome*, Cambridge: Cambridge University Press.

Flower, H. (ed.) (2004). *The Cambridge Companion to the Roman Republic*, Cambridge: Cambridge University Press.

Parkin, T. amd Pomeroy, A. (2007). *Roman Social History*, London: Routledge.

Peachin, M. (ed.) (2011) *The Oxford Handbook of Social Relations in the Roman World*, Oxford: Oxford University Press.

Scheidel, W. (ed.) (2012). *The Cambidge Companion to the Roman Economy*, Cambridge: Cambridge University Press.

Scheidel, W., Morris, I., and Saller, R.P. (eds.) (2007). *The Cambridge Economic History of the Greco-Roman World*, Cambridge: Cambridge University Press.

Shelton, J. (1998). *As the Romans Did*, 2nd edn., Oxford: Oxford University Press.

INDEX OF TEXTS

INDEX

Note: References are to page number. Bibliographic references are not included in the index. Extracts from original sources are listed separately in the Index of Texts. The method of alphabetization used is word-by-word.